The Dream

The Diner's Dictionary

To Jean

the
DINER'S
dictionary

WORD ORIGINS OF FOOD & DRINK

SECOND EDITION

JOHN AYTO

OXFORD
UNIVERSITY PRESS

OXFORD
UNIVERSITY PRESS

Great Clarendon Street, Oxford, OX2 6DP,
United Kingdom

Oxford University Press is a department of the University of Oxford.
It furthers the University's objective of excellence in research, scholarship,
and education by publishing worldwide. Oxford is a registered trade mark of
Oxford University Press in the UK and in certain other countries

© First edition Routledge 1990

© New and revised material Oxford University Press 1993, 2012

The moral rights of the author have been asserted

First Edition published in 1990 by Routledge as *The Glutton's Glossary*
Revised edition published 1993 by arrangement with Routledge as *The Diner's Dictionary*
First issued as an Oxford University Press paperback 1994 as *The Gourmet's Guide*
Second edition published 2012 by arrangement with Routledge as *The Diner's Dictionary*

Impression: 1

British Library Cataloguing in Publication Data

Data available

ISBN 978-0-19-964024-9

Printed in Great Britain by
Clays Ltd, St Ives plc

Preface

by Alan Davidson

If anything I am about to write gives the impression that this book is mainly aimed at and fit for students and professors, banish the thought. It's a rattling good read for everyone, whether in the kitchen, the study, or bed, and quite addictive. Look up one word and I'll wager that you can't resist reading the adjacent entry, and that when you've turned the page you'll be reading on and turning more pages, and again and again. That is as it should be and is the hallmark of a great reference book.

However, it must be said that there is one problem about John Ayto's book, and that is a word problem, befitting a work which is so deeply and charmingly concerned with words. The problem is that there is no word which does justice to the nature and scope of the book. 'Glossary' is too slight, too marginal (the margin, after all, was where glosses were originally put) and narrow; 'dictionary' and 'lexicon' suggest something drier and devoid of entertainment; 'encyclopaedia', on the other hand, would indicate something of grosser size and less discriminating content. So what do we call it? I propose having recourse to the eighteenth-century practice of an extended title which would look something like this: *A Companion Guide to English Food and Drink Words and Phrases, A to Z compiled on lexicographical, historical, cultural, and anecdotal principles*. I realise that no twenty-first-century publisher would even contemplate a title like that, but never mind.

Titles certainly do matter. I recall vividly how one of the book's earlier and less felicitous titles nearly caused me, on first encounter, not even to open it. The book lay, strange to relate, on a table of reduced price books in Waterstones on the King's Road in Chelsea. It bore, then, the title *The Glutton's Glossary*. I recoiled. I'm no glutton, thought I (except perhaps for hard work—I was busy writing *The Oxford Companion to Food*), and was about to pass on, when a contrary impulse took hold of me. I paused and opened the book. As I recall, it fell open at page 100 and my eyes lit on the entry for *crumpet*. Repeat my experience, reader, or glance at the entries for *custard*, *jam*, and *jelly* (some of my favourite foods as well as favourite entries), and you will understand that I lost no time in enrolling myself as a disciple of John Ayto. He was covering so brilliantly, so succinctly, and in a style at once erudite and entertaining, so much of the ground that I was striving to cover in the *Oxford Companion* that I knew instantly that I was Aladdin entering the Cave. The only difference being that he knew what he was looking for whereas I had not even dreamed of such riches. A blessed moment.

However, the invaluable help which the book has afforded me personally is but a slight matter when compared with the more general considerations which make its reissue, in 2002 [and in this 2012 edition], exceptionally timely. The context in which it reappears is significantly different from that which prevailed in 1990, the year of its first publication. What has changed is that, in the last two decades, the subject of food history has been attracting much wider interest than ever before and has come to be recognized as something important in its own right. The growing interest has been reflected in an upsurge of books and essays which deal with the historical aspects of food; likewise the setting up of many food history symposia and kindred gatherings. In all this activity, no other single line of enquiry is more illuminating than an explanation of the origin of food terms, such as Ayto provides.

Oxford was the pioneer in organizing symposia and those held at St Antony's College there continue to flourish, with counterparts as far away as Louisiana, South Australia,

Turkey, and elsewhere. In many places, such meetings mark the footholds which food history has been securing in academic institutions. It is clearly on the way to establishing itself, as it should, as a major subject for study within as well as outside academe. This is not surprising. Food is something we all need, and enjoy, and food studies possess for this reason a reality and immediacy which few other subjects can enjoy. But, precisely because food studies embrace or overlap with many other fields of study (notably biology, chemistry, nutrition, economic and political history, sociology) they have been slow to emerge with their own distinctive identity.

I am currently engaged in cinema history studies, and marvel at the huge number of university faculties and textbooks and meetings which are the infrastructure thereof. I would be the last to suggest that these are excessive. But the fact that food studies are still very far from matching this apparatus seems to me paradoxical. Many of us watch films, but all of us eat. And while films are a desirable feature of our lives, food is an essential one and has been since the year dot.

Food, even the food of one country or culture, comes close to being a subject of infinite extent. Knowing this, let us marvel at the extent and depth of John Ayto's knowledge. To adapt a verse from Goldsmith, 'And still I gazed, and still my wonder grew / That one small head could carry all he knew.'. . . and convey it to the rest of us with such grace and wit.

ALAN DAVIDSON

December 2001

Introduction to the first edition

That voracious sponge, the English language, has sucked into itself over the past millennium the riches of the world's gastronomic vocabulary. Few aspects of the English lexicon reflect so vividly as its food and drink terms, the external influences that have been brought to bear on the inhabitants of Britain, either as invaders or invaded, down the centuries. Each successive wave, from the Norman conquerors of the eleventh century to returning continental holidaymakers of the post-Second World War period, has left its mark, making our culinary terminology a microcosm of the language as a whole—a magpie's haphazard hoard of linguistic borrowings. *The Diner's Dictionary* tells the story of these words: when and how they arrived in the language; where they came from; and how in many cases their meanings have changed over the years. And at the same time it records the changing diet of the British—how particular foodstuffs have come into and gone out of fashion, and particular dishes have changed in character with the passing of time.

A few very basic food terms can be traced right back to our remotest Indo-European ancestors, between 8,000 and 6,000 years ago. These include *apple*, *dough*, and *salt*, and also *mead*, *meat*, *milk*, and *nut*. And many more had established themselves by the time Old English began to emerge as a separate language from the West Germanic dialects around the fifth century AD—among them *loaf* and *honey*, *ale* and *beer*, and *garlic* and *leek*.

The first great influx of new terminology was instigated by the events of 1066. Everyone is familiar with the fact that English is indebted to French for its 'refined' meat vocabulary—*beef*, *mutton*, *pork*, *veal*, *venison*—which made it possible to distinguish the live animal from its flesh used as food (although it would be a mistake necessarily to think of these words crossing the Channel with William the Conqueror; the earliest records we have for any of them are from the thirteenth century). But the French contribution to English food vocabulary in the Middle Ages is far wider than that. A whole rich culinary tradition was introduced to England by the Normans and their successors, and many of its terms—*blancmange* and *pudding*, *gravy* and *lard*, *claret* and *vinegar*, *onion*, *salad*, and *giblets*—still survive.

Gastronomic niceties were not such a preoccupation with the Vikings, who had infiltrated the north of Britain before their Norman cousins arrived in the south, but even they have given English a few food words, among them *cake* and *steak*.

As European explorers and merchants began to venture out over the world's oceans in the fifteenth and sixteenth centuries a new flood of exotic food terms washed back into English. The New World made a notable contribution: most famously *potato* and *tomato*, of course, but also *chocolate* and *cocoa*, *squash* and *avocado* (whose Central American ancestor meant 'testicle'), *pecan* and *cashew*, *pemmican* and *jerked beef*. And Asia and Africa were equally bountiful sources, giving us *ketchup*, *okra*, *sago*, and, from China, *tea*. But Asia's most prolific donor to English culinary vocabulary was to be India: the years of the Raj produced *chutney*, *curry*, *kedgeree*, *mulligatawny*, *punch*, and *toddy*, amongst many other terms.

The eighteenth and particularly the nineteenth centuries saw a new influx of French gastronomic terminology, reflecting the great flowering of French haute cuisine, and the success of its proselytizers in Britain—chefs such as Carême, Soyer, and Escoffier. To this period belong *aspic* and *soufflé*, *macedoine* and *vol-au-vent*, *nesselrode* and *timbale*.

The early twentieth century was a comparatively fallow period, when Britain's reputation as a country careless of food—long a standing joke in France—slowly congealed: Oskar Schmitz's characterization of England as *das Land ohne Musik* would have been countered by a French chef with *la pays sans cuisine*. But after the Second World War, two factors combined to reverse the trend. First, more and more Britons became able to take holidays in Europe. They surprised themselves by liking what they ate, and (egged on by the writings of Elizabeth David) began to hanker after it on their own tables. This is the impetus behind such new English terms as *cassoulet* and *quiche*, *hummus* and *tapas*, *aïoli* and *frisée*, *radicchio* and *bresaola*. Second, immigrants from India and the Caribbean brought their foodstuffs and dishes, and the names for these to Britain. Indian restaurants have introduced a new wave of the subcontinent's culinary terms into English, including *tandoori*, *biryani*, *tikka*, and *samosa*. West Indian influence has on the whole been seen on market stalls, and latterly in supermarkets, rather than in restaurants, replenishing the English stock of vegetables and fruit with *callaloo* and *eddoes*, *dasheen* and *soursop*. Equally forceful in its cultural impact has been the Chinese restaurant, familiarizing British eaters and English speakers with *dim sum*, *hoisin sauce*, and *wun tun* (although much Chinese food terminology has been translated rather than transliterated into English).

The menu of English food vocabulary is so long that an account of every single item would be indigestible indeed. So I have specifically excluded two particular categories. First, animals in the broadest sense. Most forms of animate life have at one time or another found their way on to British tables, from hedgehogs baked in clay to tinned kangaroo, but I have not attempted to mention every mammal, bird, fish, etc. that has figured in the British diet. I only include terms that refer specifically to animals as food. So in *The Diner's Dictionary* you will find *mutton* but not *lamb*, *venison* but not *deer*, *capon* but not *chicken*. Second, I have excluded drinks whose names are simply a reflection of the places where they originated, or with which they are closely associated, since these are usually too obvious to be of linguistic interest. So *claret* and *whisky* find a place here, but not *burgundy* or *mosel*. The only exceptions to this are cases (like *hock* and *sherry*) where the original place-name has become so altered over the centuries as to be no longer recognizable.

Although *The Diner's Dictionary* delves at times into the roots of the English language (and of other languages), I have tried to avoid the use of abstruse linguistic terminology, and the only specialized key needed to unlock the following pages is the knowledge that an asterisk in front of a word indicates that it has never actually been found in a piece of text, but has been reconstructed by linguists from the evidence of related forms. Thus (in the entry for *apple*) we know that the Indo-European word for 'apple' was (something like) **apel-*, even though it died out long before the advent of writing, because the evidence of its descendants, such as English *apple*, Lithuanian *óbuolas*, and Welsh *afal*, enables us to infer it. Cross-references in the text to words entered elsewhere in the dictionary are shown in SMALL CAPITAL letters.

I am greatly indebted to Frank Abate and Jay Wilson for their comments on the text, particularly in the area of American usage.

Introduction to the second edition

In the twenty and more years since this book first appeared, the food horizons of English-speakers have expanded with a rapidity only the boldest would have dared to predict. Not only are we more familiar and comfortable with a wide range of other cuisines—of that, more later—but food and its history and preparation have become subjects of enthusiastic study, contemplation, and participation. Straws had been in the wind since the early 1980s: the late Alan Davidson (whose characteristically generous preface precedes these introductions) founded the annual Oxford Symposia on Food and Food History in 1981, for example, and in 1982 the word *foodie* made its debut. The trickle that began then has become a flood of books, blogs, learned articles, conference papers, radio programmes, television channels, and the like exploring the farthest reaches of gastro-history and bringing food and drink as a subject to an ever-widening audience.

The ground has shifted seismically beneath this dictionary's feet, and this new edition, with over a thousand new entries and hundreds of expanded and updated ones, seeks to encompass the much-enlarged scope of the English language's gastronomic vocabulary. There are many neologisms to record—*alcopop, builder's tea, freedom fries, microgreens, rose veal, smoothie,* for instance—but also much terminology from past times that now excites new interest: the likes of *brewis* and *frumenty, calipash* and *calipee.* Furthermore, some words with a lengthy pedigree have, for various reasons, enjoyed a revival, such as *shank* (as in 'lamb shanks') and *spelt,* or been put to new metaphorical uses (*Marmite, Spam*). In some cases, recent research has cast fresh light on the derivation of a word—those with a history stretching back many centuries, such as *marzipan, pitta, pizza,* and *scampi,* and more recent coinages, such as *hot dog.*

By far the largest contribution to new English food-and-drink vocabulary in the last two decades has come from other languages. As English-speakers have continued to embrace the cuisines of other cultures, so have they assimilated the terminology of these cuisines. Sometimes it has been food we thought we knew, but found that perhaps we did not. 'Real' Italian regional cuisine, for example, as pioneered in the UK by London's River Café (opened in 1987), which has (almost) consigned the straw-covered chianti flask and the priapic peppermill to history, has given us *burrata, cavolo nero, coppa, fregola, mostarda di Cremona, orzo, panini, ribollita,* among many others. Similar developments have expanded our knowledge of the food of Spain (*jabugo, membrillo, morcilla, patatas bravas*); South Asia (*chaat, methi, phal, sambar*); China (*bang-bang chicken, char siu, monk's vegetables, mooncake*); and Japan (*bento, donburi, mizuna, Wagyu*). Even in the case of our oldest gastronomic creditor, France, the combination of a desire to explore beneath the surface gloss of haute cuisine and perhaps a greater exposure to the kitchen-French of chefs at work at the hob-face has enriched our word-larder with the likes of *bavette, jus, onglet, panaché, ratte,* and *tartiflette.*

Other cuisines, however, have only started to become truly familiar to us in the past quarter of a century, most notably those of Southeast Asia (*jungle curry, mussaman, nam pla,* and *pad thai* from Thailand, for example, and *bun cha* and *pho* from Vietnam); of Korea (*bibimbap, galbi jjin, kimchi*); of North Africa (*bastilla, merguez, ras-el-hanout*); and of Central and South America (*chimichurri, dulce de leche, huevos rancheros, mole*).

English swallows new vocabulary as greedily as ever, and the binge it has been on over the past twenty years must surely confirm food and drink as the most cosmopolitan part of its lexicon. We have the world on a plate, and we are well equipped to talk about it.

I must record my gratitude to John Simpson and his team at the *Oxford English Dictionary* (in particular Katrin Thier) for finding time to answer my queries, etymological and otherwise, on obscure corners of English gastronomic terminology, and to Jamie Crowther of Oxford University Press for his guidance past the occasional IED of computerized publishing.

JOHN AYTO
London, 2012

Abernethy biscuit A firm-textured semi-sweet Scottish biscuit characteristically flavoured with caraway seeds. It takes its name (which was first recorded in 1834) from Dr John Abernethy (1764–1831), a Scottish surgeon who made the suggestion to his local baker that he should add sugar and caraway to his plain biscuit recipe.

Abondance Abondance (also called *tomme d'Abondance*) is a firm cheese produced in Savoie, in southeastern France. It is made from milk of the Abondance breed of cattle—hence its name.

absinthe An unsweetened green liqueur whose principal and characteristic ingredient is oil of wormwood (*see* VERMOUTH). Wormwood is a small plant of the genus *Artemisia* with greyish-green silky leaves and insignificant-looking round yellow flowers, which grows on waste ground, particularly near the sea (its species name is *absinthium*, which comes ultimately from Greek *apsínthion*, a word probably of pre-Hellenic origin). Its oil is bitter, and in fact poisonous. Absinthe became extremely popular in France in the nineteenth century (it was known colloquially as *la verte* 'the green one'), and the number of people who suffered its deleterious or even fatal effects reached such a point as almost to foreshadow the drug epidemics of the late twentieth century: Manet's famous picture, the *Absinthe Drinker* (1859), shows a devotee staring gloomily at a glass, its contents the cloudy yellow characteristic of absinthe mixed, as was the usual practice, with water. In the 1870s the French writer 'Alexandre Dumas *père* . . . remarked that any regimental surgeon would agree that absinthe had killed more French soldiers in Africa than had Arab weapons', Alan Davidson, *Oxford Companion to Food* (2006). All this failed to put off the party-goers of the Jazz Age: many cocktails of the 1920s and 1930s, such as the Monkey Gland and the Rattlesnake, were based on absinthe. Nevertheless, such was official concern that in 1915, following the lead of several other countries including the US (but not Britain), the French government prohibited absinthe. Many countries lifted their ban in the early twenty-first century, and although the ban remains in force in France, the drink can now be sold there provided it is labelled as '*boisson spiritueuse aux plantes d'absinthe*'.

  Absinthe was invented in the eighteenth century by one Dr Ordinaire, a Frenchman living in Couvet, Switzerland, who in 1797 sold his recipe to Monsieur Pernod. After its prohibition, the firm of Pernod took the lead in the manufacture of the aniseed-flavoured pastis which occupies the niche vacated by absinthe.

acerola The more usual name in North America for the Barbados cherry. It was introduced into English from American Spanish around the middle of the twentieth century. It was originally a Spanish term, adopted and adapted from Arabic *az-zu'rūr*, for a similar but unrelated fruit.

acid drops These sharp-tasting sweets flavoured with tartaric acid first appeared on the scene in the early nineteenth century. At first they were called *acidulated drops* (Dickens mentions them in *Sketches by Boz* (1836): 'Ma, in the openness of her heart, offered the governess an acidulated drop'), and this term survived until the beginning of the twentieth century. The abbreviated *acid drop*, however (and the now obsolete acid tablet), arose at about the same time, and *acid drop* has lasted the course. In their earlier incarnations they seem often to have been fruit-flavoured—raspberry, for instance, and orange—but latterly they have been restricted to their plain unvarnished form. Nowadays they have largely disappeared from sweet shops, but they remain sufficiently in the memory of the language to be available as a metaphor for tartness—most notably in *Acid Drops* (1980), a compilation of sharp anecdotes by Kenneth Williams. The nearest equivalents to acid drops in the US are termed *sourballs*.

ackee Ackee, or *akee*, is the red pear-shaped fruit of a tropical African tree, related to the lychee. Inside, it has large shiny black seeds surrounded by creamy white flesh. It was supposedly brought to the West Indies by Captain Bligh of the *Bounty*, and has since become a leading feature of Caribbean cuisine. Its main role is as an accompaniment to saltfish. The name *ackee* comes from Kru, a group of West African languages.

açorda A frugal bread-based Portuguese dish, somewhere between a thick soup and a thin stew. Its main ingredient is stock-soaked bread, which is cooked with olive oil, garlic, coriander, and an egg. The Portuguese word derives from Arabic *al-thurda* 'the thurda', *thurda* or *tharida* being the name of an ancient Arabian dish of bread mixed with stewed meat.

acquacotta The original Italian name (now often used in English) of the traditional Tuscan peasant soup that is also known by its literal translation, 'cooked water'.

advocaat A thick, sweet, creamy, yellow, alcoholic drink of Dutch origin that is made from egg yolks and brandy. It does not seem to have become well known in Britain until the 1930s. Its name in Dutch is short for *advocaatenborrel* 'lawyer's drink', a compound of *advocaat* 'advocate, lawyer' and *borrel* 'drink.'

adzuki bean These small red beans (also known as *aduki beans*) are of oriental origin, and are particularly associated with Japan (*azuki* is Japanese for 'red bean'). In the West over the past couple of decades they have firmly established themselves among vegetarians' pulsy alternatives to meat, but in the East they often form the basis of sweets, either coated with sugar, dragee-like, or made into a sweet paste.

afelia A Greek Cypriot dish in which pork is stewed in red wine with coriander seeds. The term may come from modern Greek *afeleia* meaning 'simplicity, crudeness'.

affogato An Italian dessert consisting essentially of hot espresso coffee poured over vanilla ice cream. The word in Italian means literally 'drowned'.

agar-agar Agar-agar (or *agar*, as it is also simply called) is a gelatinous substance made from certain types of seaweed. In cooking and food manufacture, it is used in ice cream and jellies, and as a thickening agent (its e-number is E406). The word is Malay in origin, and means literally 'jelly' or 'gelatine'.

aguardiente Strictly speaking, a term (used in English since the early nineteenth century) for a fairly basic grade of Spanish brandy, but its usage has broadened out to cover any coarse, throat-burning spirit with Spanish or Latin American connections. The word is a compound formed from Spanish *agua* 'water' and *ardiente* 'burning', so it is first cousin to English *firewater*.

aiguillette A long thin slice of the choicest, tenderest meat taken from either side of the breastbone of a duck or other fowl (sometimes extended to apply to any thin slice of meat). The word means literally 'little needle'—*aiguille* is French for 'needle'. Its other metaphorical application is to 'tags', particularly ornamental ones used on military uniforms, and in fact in this sense the word was borrowed into English as long ago as the fifteenth century, in the form *aglet*.

aïoli Aïoli is one of the classic components of Provençal cuisine. It is essentially a garlic-flavoured mayonnaise, made with egg yolks, olive oil, and garlic. Perhaps its most typical role is to accompany the poached salt cod of Provence, but it really comes into its own during summer high days and holidays, when villages organize a *grand aïoli*, or even an *aïoli monstre*. Each member of the population ends up with a plate piled high with salt cod,  boiled meat, a generous array of vegetables, stewed squid, snails, and hard-boiled eggs, the whole lubricated with large dollops of fragrant aïoli. The word, like the dish itself, is a compound of *ail* 'garlic' and *oli*, the Provençal word for 'oil'. *See also* ALLIOLI.

aitch bone A cheap and rather bony cut of beef from the hindquarters of the animal, close to the point where its tail emerges. This cut is seldom encountered nowadays, and its name is no longer widely recognized, but the word *aitch* dates back to the Middle Ages, when English adopted Old French *nache,* meaning 'buttock'. Before long (in a process which also produced English *adder* and *umpire*) the combination *a nache* came to be misinterpreted as *an ache,* and so the *aitch bone* was born. Over the centuries it has been subject to a number of bizarre alterations, including *ash-bone, edge-bone,* and *ice-bone,* but the form that finally won out incorporates the conventionalized spelling of the letter H.

ajwain An Indian spice (the word is Hindi) consisting of the seeds of the plant *Trachyspermum ammi.* Its taste has been compared to caraway. It is sometimes called *bishop's weed,* but strictly speaking that name belongs to other related umbelliferous plants. Another alternative name is *carom seed.*

Alaska strawberries A facetious nineteenth-century American euphemism for 'dried beans', an ingredient in need of some talking up to make it palatable.

albariño An Iberian wine-grape variety, grown particularly in Galicia in northwestern Spain, and in neighbouring areas of northern Portugal (where it is called *alvarinho*). It produces white grapes, whence its name, which means literally in Spanish 'white (wine) from the Rhine'. It was probably brought to Spain in the twelfth century by Cluniac monks, and may well be a clone of the riesling grape. Its fresh, fragrant style helped considerably towards the end of the twentieth century in dispelling the negative image of Spanish white wines as heavy, over-oaked, and often oxidized.

alcopop A commercially produced drink that resembles a soft drink but contains alcohol. The cheapness and availability of such drinks, which were originally developed in the US in the 1970s, is held by many to be a major contributory factor in the surge in alcohol consumption among the young at the end of the twentieth century. The term is first recorded in 1995.

ale The standard word for an 'alcoholic drink made by fermenting malt' in Anglo-Saxon England was *ealu*, source of modern English *ale* (*bēor*, modern English *beer*, existed, but was not in common use). Then in the fifteenth century a distinction in usage arose between *beer*, which was flavoured with hops, and *ale*, which had no additional flavouring. In succeeding centuries this term gradually died out, leaving *beer* as the main word for the drink, hopped or unhopped, in most areas and *ale* as the poor relation of the pair. In modern English it survives dialectally as an all-embracing 'beer'-word—in northern England, for instance—and hence as a sort of folksy-cum-nostalgic synonym for *beer* (as in the 'Campaign for Real Ale'). It is also used for special types of beer, although as a term its application is less than precise: it can stand for a beer made from unroasted malt, giving it a pale colour (*light ale* or *pale ale*), or for a drink that is stronger and heavier than ordinary beer (little bottles labelled *old ale* generally pack quite a punch), while in American and Canadian English it denotes a drink made with hops quickly fermented at a high temperature.

The word *ale* itself, which has relatives in Swedish *öl*, Danish *øl*, and Old Russian *olu*, goes back to a prehistoric Germanic base **alu-*, which is probably connected etymologically with Greek *alúdoimos* 'bitter' and Latin *alūmen* 'alum'. (The word *bridal*, incidentally, now an adjective, was in the Old English period a noun, literally a *bride ale*, that is, a beer-drinking session to celebrate a marriage.)

alexander These days, for most people an *alexander* means a *brandy alexander*, a cocktail made from brandy with crème de cacao and cream. It originated, however (in the cocktail era, the 1920s), as a general cocktail recipe featuring crème de cacao and cream, to be mixed with any base spirit—indeed, one of the earliest records of it in print, from 1930, specifies gin. The source of the name is not known.

aligot A creamy cheesy potato dish that is a speciality of the Auvergne region of central France. Cream and grated young Cantal cheese are stirred into mashed potato to produce a smooth and slightly stringy purée. The word was adopted into French from Provençal, and may be related to *haricot* 'ragout, stew'. *See* HARICOT BEAN.

aligoté A grape variety used for producing a rather acidic white wine. Its home area is Burgundy, where it used to be planted in large quantities and smuggled into white burgundy. But nowadays, when more strictly enforced *appellation contrôllé* laws ensure that only chardonnay gets into the *grand vin*, it is relegated to the more lowly *bourgogne aligoté* wine. This is a frequent vehicle for kir. Its name probably comes from Old French *harigoter* 'to tear up'.

allioli The Catalan equivalent of Provençal *aïoli* (which is essentially a garlic mayonnaise). The Spanish version more closely reflects its name, as it often consists only of garlic (*alli*) and olive oil (*oli*), without the egg-yolk component of *aïoli*.

allspice Named from the supposed resemblance of its hot aromatic smell and taste to the combined savours of cinnamon, cloves, and nutmeg, allspice is the dried, unripened berry of a West Indian tree, *Pimenta dioica*, of the eucalyptus family (a discovery of Christopher Columbus). It was first mentioned in English by Robert Burton, in his compendious satire on the futility of human endeavour, *Anatomy of Melancholy* (1621), and it became a popular spice in succeeding centuries, easily imported from Britain's Caribbean colonies. The berries can be used either whole or ground, and it is equally at home in sweet or savoury dishes.

It has gone by other names in its time. *Jamaica pepper* dates from the mid-seventeenth century, but is no longer heard. More confusingly, it has also been called the *pimento* (in reference to its Latin name), although it has no connection at all with the red capsicum to which the term *pimento* is now generally applied.

allumette French *allumette* means 'match' (of the incendiary sort). In culinary contexts it is most commonly encountered in English in *allumette potatoes* (in French, *pommes allumettes*), denoting very finely cut chips or French fries. The equivalent vernacular term is *matchstick*.

almond The almond tree, a plant of the rose family and closely related to the plum, peach, and apricot, originated in Asia, and may have been introduced to Europe via Greece (a name used by the Romans for its edible nut was 'Greek nut'). The Greek word for 'almond', perhaps borrowed from some non-Indo-European language, was *amugdálè*, which was taken over by Latin as *amygdala* (source of English *amygdala* 'almond-shaped mass of nerve tissue in the brain', *amygdalin* 'glucoside obtained from bitter almonds', and *amygdaloid* 'type of rock with almond-shaped cavities'). In post-classical times, *amygdala* became *amandula* (whence Italian *mandola*, Portuguese *amendoa*, and German *mandel*). In its passage into Old French, this seems to have acquired the prefix *al-*, presumably on the model of the many words of Arabic origin—such as *alcohol* and *algebra*—which the Romance languages took over complete with the Arabic definite article *al*, 'the'. This would have produced **almandle*, a form never recorded but deducible from Old French *almande*—source of English *almond*. The word is standardly pronounced /ˈahmənd/, but the spelling pronunciation /ˈalmənd/ is becoming increasingly common.

There are essentially two types of almond: bitter almonds, which contain prussic acid but can be used in very sparing quantities as a flavouring, and ordinary eating almonds. Of the latter, Jordan almonds are probably the most highly regarded variety. Their long thin shape may have inspired the comparison of oriental women's eyes to almonds. They have no connection whatsoever with Jordan (they are mainly grown in Spain, in fact); their name is an alteration of Middle English *jarden* ['garden'] *almond*.

Almonds were widely used in the ancient world, and their versatility persisted into the Middle Ages, when they featured largely in savoury as well as sweet dishes, and were used as a basis for almond milk, a substitute for milk made with water and ground almonds. Marzipan, also known as *almond paste*, is a survival of this wide-ranging use, as is the popular combination of almonds with trout, but for the most part these days almonds are eaten whole (a popular version these days is salted hickory-smoked almonds) or flaked as cake or dessert decorations, or reduced to a flavouring essence.

Alphonso mango An Indian variety of mango that is commonly eaten raw, and is widely available in the West. It derives its name from Alfonso de Albuquerque (1453–1515), the Portuguese admiral who established the Portuguese empire in India. He contributed the term for the fruit not just to English, but also to various indigenous languages, including Marathi (*haapoos*) and Kannada (*aapoos*).

amaretto An almond-flavoured liqueur made in northern Italy (first devised, according to legend, in the early sixteenth century by the landlady of an inn in Saronno as a present for an artist who had painted her portrait). The name is a derivative of Italian *amaro* 'bitter', in reference to the bitter almonds which are its chief flavouring ingredient.

Amaretti are also sweet Italian almond biscuits, like small macaroons. Some well-known brands come in individual tissue-paper wrappers.

amarone An Italian red wine made in the Valpolicella area of the Veneto in northeastern Italy from air-dried grapes (its full name is *amarone della Valpolicella*). It is rich and concentrated but all the grape's sugar is fermented out, so in comparison with its first cousin recioto, it is fairly astringent. Hence its name, formed from Italian *amaro* 'bitter'

and the augmentative suffix *-one*: the 'big bitter one'. The term is a relatively recent one, not recorded in Italian before 1953. In the US it is a proprietary name.

amatriciana A dish of pasta described as *all'amatriciana* will be served with a sauce made from tomatoes, bacon (or salt pork), onions, and garlic, sprinkled with grated Pecorino cheese. The phrase means literally 'in the style of Amatrice', a small town in the Apennine mountains to the northeast of Rome. It is often misanalysed, not least in Italy, as *alla matriciana*.

américaine A lobster prepared *à l'américaine* is sautéed and then briefly cooked in white wine, brandy, and olive oil with tomatoes, shallots, and garlic.

There is a long-standing and ultimately irresolvable controversy over whether the method should really be termed *à l'Américaine*. There is an alternative school which maintains that *à l'armoricaine* 'in the style of Armorica' is the authentic appellation. *Armorica* is the ancient name for Brittany, which would be an appropriate home for a lobster recipe. But the French gastronome Curnonsky (1872–1956) claimed to have had from the horse's mouth the story of its creation, which supports the 'American' name. Apparently it was invented in the 1860s by a chef called Pierre Fraisse, when faced with a party of late guests and only lobsters and the above-mentioned accompaniments at hand. This Fraisse had previously worked for some time as a chef in Chicago, and had even anglicized his name to Peters—hence *à l'Américaine*.

Americano Short for *café Americano* (first recorded in 1964), which denotes a cup of relatively mild or weak coffee, especially espresso diluted with water. It is an English adoption of a Central American Spanish term meaning literally 'American coffee', which seems to have originated in the early 1950s, apparently as an insulting reflection of Spanish-speakers' opinion of the beverage typically available further north.

amontillado Strictly, amontillado is a fino sherry which has been aged in cask until it achieves an added depth of colour and pungency of flavour—reminiscent, for aficionados, of the fortified wine produced in Montilla, to the northeast of Jerez (hence the name: *amontillado* means 'Montilla-ed' in Spanish). The majority of amontillado sherry commercially available in Britain has been sweetened, however, so that the term has come to stand loosely for any middlebrow medium-sweet brown sherry.

amuse gueule A small choice titbit of food (as it might be a miniature soufflé, a shot-glass of some elaborate savoury confection, a canapé), served 'free' in a restaurant in addition to the items ordered and intended to show off the chef's skill and versatility. It typically appears at the beginning of a meal, to beguile the time between ordering and the appearance of the first course. The term, which in French means literally 'amuse (the) mouth', is first recorded in English in 1963. In recent years there has been a tendency to replace it with *amuse bouche*, perhaps owing to a perception that *bouche* is a more polite French word for 'mouth' than *gueule* (which verges on 'gob' territory); *amuse bouche* is comparatively rare in French, though, and it could even be that this term was originally created by English-speakers. In the argot of restaurateurs and food critics the term is often shortened to simply *amuse*: 'Flashes of old Michel Roux brilliance are still there, as in a superb amuse of deep-fried ravioli of crab, resting in a little pool of red pepper sauce', *Good Food Guide* (2008).

amydon A term used between the fourteenth and sixteenth centuries for a superfine grade of wheat flour, similar in appearance and use to modern cornflour. English adopted it from French *amidon* 'starch', which came ultimately from late Latin *amidum*, an alteration of classical Latin *amylum* 'starch'.

Anaheim chilli A long, narrow, relatively mild red or green American variety of chilli (also known as *Anaheim pepper*). It gets its name from Anaheim, now a suburb of Los Angeles, California, to where a farmer called Emilio Ortega apparently brought its seeds in the early twentieth century. An alternative term for it in America is *California chili*.

anchoïade *Anchoïade* or *anchoyade* is the Provençal name for a purée of anchovies, garlic, and olive oil. It is typically served on bread or with raw vegetables. A similar anchovy preparation is made in Italy and other parts of the Mediterranean.

andouille A large sausage of French origin, made from the stomach lining of pigs together with various assorted innards and a leavening of belly of pork, and stuffed inside the pig's intestine. It is usually smoked, and typically served cold, sliced, as an hors d'oeuvre. Both the word and the sausage were familiar in Britain from the Middle Ages up to the eighteenth century (a text of 1605 refers to a 'table of necessarie provisions for the whole yeare ... Andulees, potatoes, kidshead, colflory, etc.', and Randle Cotgrave in his *Dictionarie of the French and English Tongues* (1611) defined it as 'A big hogges gut stuffed with small guts (and other intrailes) cut into small pieces, and seasoned with pepper and salt'), but then the sausage disappeared from view, and it took the growth of interest in gastronomy in the latter part of the twentieth century to re-raise its profile. In America, though, andouille is widely used in Cajun cookery, for example as an ingredient of jambalaya. The French word itself came from late Latin *inductilia*, which was ultimately a derivative of Latin *inducere* 'to put in, insert', so the underlying idea is clearly of 'stuffing' the sausage.

andouillette A small version of the andouille, always eaten hot rather than cold. The word is a derivative, formed from *andouille* with the suffix *-ette*. The first record of it in English dates from 1611.

angel cake A type of extremely light sponge cake, which is made with stiffly beaten egg whites but no yolks or any other sort of fat. The earliest evidence of it is from the 1880s, in the US, where it more usually goes under the name *angel food cake* or *angel's food cake*: 'They distributed ... stuffed olives, potato salad, and angel's-food cake', Sinclair Lewis, *Main Street* (1920). *See also* DEVIL'S FOOD CAKE.

angel hair A very delicate type of pasta, like the thinnest imaginable spaghetti. The term is a direct translation of Italian *capelli d'angelo*.

angelica A plant of the carrot family with small pinkish-white flowers in star-burst clusters. Medieval and Renaissance herbals ascribed to it the property of warding off poisons and pestilence ('The rootes of Angelica are contrarie to all poyson', Henry Lyte, *Dodoens' Niewe Herball* (1578)); hence the name *angelica*, short for Latin *herba angelica* 'angelic herb'. Both the leaves and the roots have been used for infusions, and in the seventeenth and eighteenth centuries angelica water, or angel water, was popular for washing the face, but in recent times its main use has been in the form of its candied stalks, for providing rather luridly green decoration for cakes, trifles, etc.

   The wild form of the plant has a variety of dialectal names in Britain, including *kewsies* (Lincolnshire), *spoots* (Shetland), and *water squirt* (Somerset).

angels on horseback The angels are oysters wrapped in rashers of bacon, cooked quickly under the grill, and riding on slivers of toast. The dish is a British contribution to gastronomy, and it was popular as a hot savoury postlude to a meal in the later nineteenth century and the early part of the twentieth century. It seems first to have been mentioned in the 1888 edition of Mrs Beeton's *Book of Household Management*, which gives an alternative French name, *anges à cheval*. Now that oysters are decidedly on the luxury list, angels on horseback are often encountered in a more downmarket version as party snacks, with cocktail sausages substituting for the shellfish. *See* DEVILS ON HORSEBACK, which is often used simply as a synonym for *angels on horseback*.

Angostura A proprietary brand of bitters whose most salient ingredient is the bitter aromatic bark of either of two South American trees of the orange family, *Galipea officinalis* or *Cusparia felorifuga*. It was invented in 1824 by Dr J. G. B. Siegert as a medicine, but it is now mainly used for giving a twist of bitterness to cocktails and other mixed drinks. It was named after Angostura, a town on the river Orinoco in eastern Venezuela where it was first made (the town was renamed Ciudad Bolivar in 1849, and Angostura is now made in Trinidad).

aniseed Aniseed is, naturally enough, the seed of the anise plant, *Pimpinella anisum*. Other parts of the plant have been used by herbalists and in the kitchen, but it is for its seed that it has always been valued—so much so, indeed, that at one point a tax was levied on its importation into England. Although it can be used for flavouring bread, pies, pickles, etc., it is pre-eminently when chewed in isolation that the seeds release their full, rather liquorice-like pungency. Used as a digestive, for sweetening the breath, or simply for its pleasant flavour, aniseed was as early as the fourteenth century made into comfits—that is, encrusted in successive layers of sugar until it formed a small sweet—ancestor of the modern aniseed ball. (The first record of aniseed balls, interestingly enough, is in the mouth of that arch-consumer of anarchic small boys' food, Richmal Crompton's William Brown, in 1924.)

The other main role of aniseed is in the flavouring of alcoholic drinks: it is the basis of the French liqueur *anisette*, the most celebrated examples of which come from around Bordeaux, made by firms such as Marie Brizard; and it is the chief ingredient of French *pastis*, Greek *ouzo*, and Turkish *raki*.

Anise should not be confused with *star anise*, the product of an entirely different plant, named for its similarity in taste to the original anise.

Anna Anna potatoes, or, in its original French, *pommes Anna,* is a potato cake made by building up layers of thinly sliced potatoes in a heavy round pan and baking it with copious amounts of butter in a very hot oven. It was created by the chef Adolphe Dugléré (1805–84), and named after a 'woman of fashion' (as *Larousse Gastronomique* delicately puts it) of the time of Napoleon III. She is usually identified as Anna Deslions, but Anna Judic is another possibility.

antipasto *Antipasto* has nothing to do with antagonism towards pasta. It is an Italian term for 'hors d'oeuvres', compounded from *anti-* 'before' and *pasto* 'meal' (a descendant of Latin *pâstus* 'food', which also turns up in English *repast*). English actually took the word over in the sixteenth century, and partially naturalized it to *antepast* ('The first mess [course], or antepast as they call it, is some fine meat to urge them to have an appetite,' quoted in the *Harleian Miscellany* (1590)). Typical antipasto snacks might be olives, slices of sausage or ham, bruschette, marinated vegetables, etc.

Anya A variety of potato that is a cross between the Desirée and the pink fir apple. It was developed specifically for the Sainsbury's supermarket chain, and named in honour of Anya Linden, Lady Sainsbury. It made its commercial debut in 1996.

ANZAC biscuit An antipodean sweet biscuit whose main characteristic ingredients are rolled oats and desiccated coconut. It was a product of the First World War period (there is evidence of something along similar lines from 1917, although the fully fledged biscuit is not recorded before 1921), sent by wives and girlfriends to their menfolk serving in the Allied cause in Europe and elsewhere. Hence its name, for ANZAC is an acronym (first recorded in 1915) formed from 'Australian and New Zealand Army Corps'.

A1 sauce A brand of brown sauce. The recipe was created in 1824 by H. W. Brand, who was chef to George IV. The story goes that the king declared the sauce 'A1' (that is, excellent), and the name stuck. Commercial production of it began in 1831, and it has been around ever since, in America as well as Britain.

aperitif A general term for an alcoholic drink taken before a meal to stimulate the appetite. To perform this function most efficiently it needs to be not too sweet—a dry white wine or a dry sherry—but in practice a multitude of appetite deadeners, from cocktails and sweet sherry to neat whisky, have masqueraded under the title *aperitif*. The word, which was first used in English at the end of the nineteenth century, comes from French *apéritif*, which traces its history back to Latin *aperīre* 'to open up' (as in English *aperture*)—hence, 'opening the appetite up'. It does not do to remind sippers of preprandial fino that another English relative is *aperient* 'laxative'.

apple The apple was probably the earliest of all fruits to be cultivated by human beings. Its wild ancestor was a sharp, mouth-puckering little thing, like today's crab apple, and this *abel-*, as our Indo-European ancestors called it, no doubt needed sweetening with honey. But as it spread through northern Europe, taking its name with it (German *apfel*, Dutch *appel*, Swedish *äpple*, Gothic *apel*, Russian *jabloko*, Lithuanian *óbuolas*, Welsh *afal*, English *apple*), it grew larger, redder, and sweeter (the Romans introduced cultivated apples into Britain). The southern European languages have, by and large, not distinguished too clearly between words for 'apple' and words for 'fruit' in general, a clear sign of the apple's centrality: Greek *melon*, for instance, source of English *melon* and Latin *mālum*, signified any fruit as well as specifically 'apple', and Latin *pōmum*, source of French *pomme* 'apple', meant 'fruit'. It is no coincidence that the fruit of the tree of the knowledge of good and evil in the Garden of Eden, which Adam and Eve ate with such disastrous consequences, and which is not specifically named in Genesis, has come to be identified in popular culture as an apple.

A sure indication of the apple's antiquity is the number of metaphors it has gathered about itself. The 'apple of someone's eye' was originally the pupil, so-called because it was once thought to be spherical, but the phrase's figurative application to 'someone or something much loved' dates back at least to King Alfred's time. In Australian English, 'she's apples' means 'everything's fine' (it was originally rhyming slang—*apples and rice* 'nice'); and of course Cockney rhyming slang has *apples and pears*—or just *apples* for short—for 'stairs'. The use of 'the Big Apple' as a sobriquet of New York City goes back to 1920, when the American racing journalist John J. FitzGerald heard two stable hands in New Orleans use the phrase to refer to the racetracks of New York (perhaps with the underlying idea of an apple being a toothsome treat, as a win in New York would be for out-of-towners).

He used it in print in that sense in 1921, and by 1924 he had expanded its reference to cover the city of New York itself. It achieved some general currency after that, and was in fairly wide use by the 1940s. It was revived and popularized in the early 1970s as part of a publicity campaign for the city. 'The Big Apple' was also the name given to a type of jazz dance popular in the late 1930s: 'It was an earthquake, a trembler. California was doing the Big Apple!', Ellery Queen, *The Four of Hearts* (1938).

applejack An American English term for apple brandy, a spirit distilled from cider (the equivalent of French *calvados*); the element *jack* probably harks back to an early colloquial use of *jack* for 'chap, fellow', as in 'every man jack'.

Applejack is also a dialectal term (eastern counties of England and in North Carolina) for an 'apple turnover'.

apple-John An obsolete term for an apple that has been kept for two years and is deemed, in defiance of its wrinkled skin and shrivelled appearance, to have reached a perfect condition for consumption (in *Henry IV, Part 2* (1597), Shakespeare puns on *apple-John* and Sir *John* Falstaff: 'The Prince once set a dish of apple-johns before him [Falstaff], and told him there were five more Sir Johns, and, putting off his hat, said "I will now take my leave of these six dry, round, old, withered knights" '). It was common for the elements to be reversed, to *John apple*: 'Take two dozen of pippins or John apples and slice them into water', Hannah Glasse, *The Art of Cookery Made Plain and Easy* (1747). The *John* is said to be a reference to St John's Day, 24 June—perhaps because at around that time the apple reaches its shrivelled acme.

apple pie The apple pie is the quintessential Anglo-Saxon pudding, on both sides of the Atlantic—'as American as apple pie'—but although there is ample evidence of apples being placed in tarts and similar pastry or dough cases since the Middle Ages, the earliest record of the actual term *apple pie* (and an evocatively approving one at that) does not occur until the late sixteenth century: 'Thy breath is like the steame of apple-pyes,' Robert Greene, *Arcadia* (1589).

Neither of the common idiomatic English expressions incorporating *apple pie* (which date from the eighteenth century) appear to have any original connection with apple pies. *Apple-pie order* may be an alteration of (an admittedly unrecorded) *cap-a-pie order*, from Old French *cap a pie* 'head to foot', while the *apple-pie bed*, the disarrangement of bedclothes as a practical joke, possibly had its origins in French *nappe pliée* 'folded sheet' (Parson James Woodforde recorded in his diary for 3 February 1781 'Had but an indifferent night of Sleep, Mrs Davie and Nancy made me up an Apple Pye Bed last night').

apricot The apricot has an involved linguistic history. The Romans called it *praecocum*, literally 'the precocious one', because of its most welcome habit of ripening in early summer, before the peach or the plum. Byzantine Greek borrowed the word as *beríkokken*, and the Arabs took it over as *birqūq*. The Moorish occupation passed it to Spanish, along with the definite article *al* 'the', and Spanish *albaricoque* has since spread to other European languages. The fruit was introduced into England from Italy in 1542 by Jean Le Loup, Henry VIII's gardener, and so probably the Italian form *albercocco* is the immediate source of the earliest English version of the word, *abrecock*. Modern English *apricot* developed from this fairly quickly (although *apricock* remained current into the eighteenth century): the *-cot* ending comes from French *abricot*, while the substitution of *apri-* for *abri-* may be due to an erroneous linking of the word with Latin *apricus*, 'sunny' (put about by the lexicographer John Minsheu in his *Guide Into Tongues* (1617)).

The apricot originated in China, and spread westward only gradually. Its earliest Latin name, *Prunum armeniacum*, 'Armenian plum' (predating *praecocum*) suggests that it was introduced to Europe from Armenia. Today, the best apricots are reckoned to come from the Hunza valley in Kashmir.

In British English, incidentally, the first syllable of the word is pronounced as in the word *ape*, whereas American English tends to prefer the pronunciation found in the first syllable of *apple*.

aquavit A colourless or pale straw-coloured Scandinavian spirit distilled from potato or grain mash and flavoured with caraway seeds. The word is an Anglicization (dating from the late nineteenth century) of Danish, Norwegian, and Swedish *akvavit*, itself an adaptation of Latin *aqua vītae*; this, like French *eau de vie* and, ultimately, English *whisky*, means 'water of life'.

arabica The most widely grown type of coffee bean, from which most standard- and good-quality coffee is made. The name, first recorded in English in 1922, is a shortening of its Latin name *Coffea arabica*, literally 'Arabian coffee'. This reflects the fact that the cultivation and consumption of coffee began in Arabia. *See also* ROBUSTA.

arborio An Italian variety of short-grained rice, used especially in the making of risotto. It derives its name from the town of Arborio in the Po valley.

Arctic Roll The proprietary name of a frozen dessert popular in Britain in the 1960s, 1970s, and 1980s, consisting of a cylindrical block of vanilla ice cream surrounded with a covering of sponge cake, with a layer of jam in between. It appears to have been invented by Ernest Velden, the Czech-born owner of a British frozen-food company who sold his business to the firm of Birds Eye in 1959.

argan oil An edible oil obtained from the seeds of a Moroccan evergreen tree *Argania spinosa*. *Argan* represents a North African Arabic pronunciation of the classical Arabic name of the tree, *arjān*. The oil is used for eating (for example, as a dip or dressing) rather than for cooking, and the popularity of Moroccan cuisine in the latter part of the twentieth century made it increasingly familiar in the West.

Arnold Bennett An 'omelette Arnold Bennett' is an omelette that incorporates smoked haddock, some sort of hard cheese (typically cheddar), and cream. It was created at the Savoy Grill for the English novelist Arnold Bennett (1867–1931), and named in his honour (Bennett was a frequent post-theatre diner there in his later years, and indeed wrote a novel—*Imperial Palace* (1930)—which is set in the Savoy Hotel).

arrabbiata An Italian pasta dish that is served *all' arrabbiata* comes with a sauce containing tomatoes, pancetta, and chillis. The Italian word means literally 'angry' (it comes from the past participle of the verb *arrabbiare* 'to enrage', a derivative of *rabbia* 'rabies, rage'), and alludes to the fierce heat of the chillis.

arrack Arrack, or *arak*, is a potent alcoholic spirit distilled in the Far East, and also in the Middle East, from fermented rice and molasses, to which is often added the fermented sap of the coconut palm. Aficionados claim that Indonesia makes the best arrack. Its name came via various unspecifiable Indian languages from Arabic ‹araq 'juice'. From the seventeenth to the nineteenth centuries an abbreviated form *rack* was often used in English: 'I would take refuge in weak punch, but rack wakes me next morning with its synonym,' Byron, *Don Juan* (1821).

arrowroot The finely ground root of a tropical American plant *Maranta arundinacea*. Its fleshy tubers contain a substance once used by Amerindians to cure wounds made by poisoned arrows (hence, either as an independent coinage or as an English rationalization of Aruak *aru-aru* 'meal of meals', the name *arrowroot*). Consisting essentially of starch, arrowroot is used mainly as a thickening agent for sauces. It was introduced into European cookery at the beginning of the nineteenth century.

An insipid-sounding dish called *arrowroot*—made from arrowroot starch and water with, if you were lucky, some sort of flavouring—was popular amongst the Victorians for feeding to invalids. It was valued for its easy digestibility, and Florence Nightingale praised it as 'a grand dependence of the nurse'.

artichoke The English language recognizes two completely different and unrelated artichokes, but in truth the *Jerusalem artichoke*, grown for its knobbly edible tubers, is a seventeenth-century usurper of the name originally owned by the globe artichoke. This is a plant of the thistle family perhaps unique in gastronomy in that the parts that are eaten are the base of the flower head and its fleshy bracts. Before the flower opens these form a purplish-green scaly sphere which inspired the name *globe artichoke* (coined in the mid-nineteenth century to distinguish it from the Jerusalem artichoke). The word *artichoke* itself was borrowed in the sixteenth century from northern Italian *articiocco*. This

 was an alteration of an earlier *arcicioffo*, which came via Old Spanish *alcarchofa* from Arabic *al-kharshôf*, literally 'the artichoke'. The earliest English version was *artechock*; the ending -*choke* arose by association with *choke* (a term subsequently applied from the eighteenth century to the inedible mass of immature florets inside the artichoke head).

The artichoke first became fashionable in the courts of Europe in the sixteenth century—Catherine de Medici is recorded as giving herself severe stomach problems in 1575 by overindulging in artichokes—and its reputation as an aristocrat of the dinner table has persisted since then (perhaps, as Jane Grigson suggests in her *Vegetable Book* (1978), because it is so fiddly to eat that it cannot be bolted unthinkingly).

arugula The usual American term for the salad plant rocket. It is probably of Italian dialectal origin, related to the Lombardy dialect form *arigola* and derived ultimately from Italian *ruca* 'rocket' (source of English *rocket*). *See also* RUGOLA.

asafoetida A pungent gum resin obtained from the roots of various oriental plants related to fennel. It is used in South Asian cookery to add an oniony flavour to dishes. The Hindi name for it is *hing*, which was used in English in the sixteenth and seventeenth centuries, but it lost out in the long run to the apothecaries' medieval Latin term *asafoetida*. This incorporated a Latinized form of Persian *azā*, denoting mastic, an aromatic resin obtained from a tree of the sumach family, and Latin *foetida* 'stinking'.

asiago An Italian cows'-milk cheese with an open springy texture, produced in the form of large wheels. It gets its name from the commune of Asiago in the province of Vincenza, northeastern Italy, where it is made.

Asian pear An alternative name for the NASHI PEAR.

asparagus Ask an etymologist for an example of folk etymology (the process by which an outlandish-sounding word, perhaps borrowed from a foreign language, is reshaped using elements from one's own language, so as to seem reassuringly familiar), and the answer is likely to be *sparrowgrass*, a fanciful variation on the theme *asparagus* which held the centre of the lexical stage in the eighteenth century and survives in the greengrocer's term *grass* (now used particularly for young asparagus shoots).

In fact, this is only one twist in the contorted history of the word *asparagus*. Its ultimate origins are not known, but it first appears in ancient Greek as *aspáragos*. Latin borrowed this as *asparagus*, but in post-classical times this became abbreviated to *sparagus*, which was the basis of the Anglicized forms *sparage* and *sperage* current in the sixteenth and early seventeenth centuries: 'Some report that of rams' horns buried, or hid in the ground, is brought forth an herb, called asparagus, in English sperage,' John Bossewell, *Works of Armoury* (1572). Around 1600, the original Latin form *asparagus* began to become more familiar, and within a generation the abbreviated *sparagus* had replaced the earlier *sparage* and *sperage*. But it was evidently not felt to be a completely pukka English word, and by 1650 what no doubt started as a casual witticism, *sparrowgrass*, had become established as the normal term for the vegetable (in 1667, for instance, Samuel Pepys recorded in his diary 'Brought with me from Fenchurch Street, a hundred of Sparrowgrass'). It remained so throughout the eighteenth century, and indeed in 1791 John Walker, in his *Pronouncing Dictionary*, wrote 'The corruption of the word into *sparrowgrass* is so general that *asparagus* has an air of stiffness and pedantry'. *Asparagus* began to make its presumably definitive comeback at the beginning of the nineteenth century.

aspic The original meaning of *aspic* was 'a cold dish of meat, fish, eggs, etc. set in moulded jelly', and only gradually did the term come to be used for the jelly itself. The earliest reference to aspic in English (by Dr Johnson's friend Mrs Piozzi in 1789) is in the plural, and Thackeray in *Vanity Fair* (1848) has General Tiptoff dying 'of an aspic of plovers' eggs'.

English borrowed the word from French, but its ultimate origins are wrapped in obscurity. The various theories put forward rely on a supposed connection with other words spelled identically or similarly: with French *aspic* 'snake' (as in English *asp*), on the basis either of the resemblance of the snake's coloration to the various colours of aspics, or of an old French simile 'cold as an aspic'; with French *aspic* 'lavender' or 'spikenard', on the basis that aspic was formerly flavoured with these; and with Greek *aspís* 'shield', on the basis that the earliest aspic moulds were made in this shape.

It was the French chef Antonin Carême who began the vogue for aspic at the turn of the nineteenth century, and bizarre creations of moulded, fluted, and chopped aspic became a hallmark of the ponderous haute cuisine of the Victorian era.

Athole brose Athole brose, or *Atholl brose*, is a warming Scottish concoction of oatmeal, honey, and whisky. The first recorded reference to it is by Sir Walter Scott in *Heart of Midlothian* (1818): 'his morning draught of Athole brose'. To the Scots a *brose* is, or was, a porridge-like dish made by pouring hot water or milk over oatmeal and then adding salt or butter. The word was borrowed from Old French *broez*, which is related ultimately to English *broth*. As for the *Athole*, the story goes that in the fifteenth century the Earl of Athole captured the rebellious Earl of Ross by putting a mixture of honey and whisky into a small well in a rock from which Ross used to drink.

aubergine The aubergine has a complex etymological history. The word comes ultimately from Sanskrit *vatinganah*, reflecting the plant's tropical Asian origins. The term appears to have meant literally 'wind-go'. 'Wind' here is certainly being used in its metaphorical sense 'intestinal gas', but it is not clear whether 'go' is intended to convey 'be in progress', in which case the aubergine would be etymologically the 'vegetable that makes you fart', or 'go away, depart', in which case it would be the 'anti-fart vegetable'. Jane Grigson in her *Vegetable Book* (1978) supports the latter interpretation, although others claim that the aubergine is decidedly flatulent. (It may be in fact that the word was originally a non-Indo-European borrowing into Sanskrit, only later folk-etymologized to refer to 'wind-going'.) In Persian *vatinganah* became *badingan*, which, when it was brought into Arabic, acquired the definite article *al*, giving *al-badhinjan*. When the Arabs invaded Spain they brought the aubergine with them, and the local inhabitants, misanalysing the Arabic term as a single word, adopted it as *alberginia*. French borrowed the Catalan term and turned it into *aubergine*, the form in which English acquired it in the late eighteenth century. In British English it has gradually superseded the somewhat earlier *eggplant*, which is still the main form in American English.

The term used in India and Africa for the aubergine is *brinjal*. It comes from Portuguese *bringella* or *beringela*, a borrowing from Arabic *badhinjan*.

In Britain we are mainly familiar with the large somewhat bulbous purple aubergine (indeed the term *aubergine* has been applied since the late nineteenth century to a particular shade of purple), but the vegetable in fact occurs in a variety of other shapes and colours: long and thin, egg-shaped, pale purple, yellow, white (the term *eggplant* was originally applied to white egg-shaped aubergines). In many parts of the tropics grows, for instance, the pea aubergine, little bigger than a cherry.

auslese *Auslese* means literally 'selection', and denotes a category of German and Austrian white wine made from perfectly ripe grapes. The wines have a marked degree of sweetness, although not usually the intense lusciousness of the next category up, *beerenauslese*, where not just the bunches but the individual grapes are carefully selected. *See also* BEERENAUSLESE, SPÄTLESE, TROCKENBEERENAUSLESE.

avgolemono A Greek soup made with eggs and lemons. The word is a modern Greek compound formed from *avgon* 'egg' and *lemonion* 'lemon'.

avocado Both the avocado itself and its name first reached Britain in the seventeenth century from Central America, via the Spanish. They were rather nonplussed by the local name in the Nahuatl language, *ahuacatl* (perhaps not surprisingly, as it means 'testicle'—a reference to the shape of the fruit), so by the process known as folk etymology—substituting a similar-sounding familiar word for an unfamiliar foreign one—they changed it to *avocado*, literally 'lawyer' (perhaps prompted by the similarity of Spanish *bocado* 'titbit'). English speakers evidently found similar difficulty in coping with Spanish *avocado*, since, having modified it somewhat to *avigato*, they folk-etymologized it in the eighteenth century to *alligator pear* (the fruit's only connection with the true pears is of course its shape; its skin often has the colour and roughness of an alligator's). Avocados were a rarity in Britain for nearly 300 years after their discovery, heard of mainly in reports sent home by colonial servants overseas (hence early nicknames such as *midshipman's butter* and *subaltern's butter*); they did not achieve widespread popularity until Israel took up their production on a vast commercial scale after the Second World War.

baba An open-textured, yeast-leavened cake, sometimes including raisins, and moistened with rum and sugar syrup. The first reference to it in English is by L. E. Ude, in *French Cook* (1827). Its origins, which are Polish, have been richly embroidered. It is said to have been invented by King Stanislas Leczinski, whose favourite reading was the *Thousand and One Nights*, and who consequently named his creation after the character Ali Baba. Less apocryphal, perhaps, is the story that it was introduced into Western Europe at the beginning of the nineteenth century by the Parisian pastrycook Sthorer, who encountered it amongst members of the Polish court then visiting France. However that may be, the word itself represents Polish *baba*, literally 'old woman' (Russian has a cognate term, more familiar to us in its diminutive form *babushka*, 'grandmother').

baba ganoush A dish of puréed chargrilled aubergines mixed with sesame seeds (or tahini), olive oil, lemon, garlic, and parsley, which forms a standard element of a mezze in eastern Mediterranean countries. The name is Egyptian Arabic, based on Arabic *bābā*, literally 'father', and *ghannūj*, which may originally have been a personal name. Elsewhere in the Middle East it is known as *moutabal. Melitzanosalata* is a similar Greek dish.

babyback ribs A rack of pork ribs taken from the top of the ribcage, between the backbone above and spareribs below.

Babybel The proprietary name of an international variety of cheese introduced in 1952 by the French-based multinational cheese-marketing company Bel Group, which was founded in the Jura in 1865 by Jules Bel. It is probably best known in the form of Mini Babybels, small flat round cheeses of edam type coated in red wax. They came on the scene in 1977. The same company produces the international cheese brand *La Vache qui Rit* ('The Laughing Cow').

bacalhau The Portuguese national dish, basically dried salted cod, but the Portuguese have devised such an ingenious and all-pervasive repertoire of recipes for it that one would scarcely be surprised to see it turning up as a dessert course. The word *bacalhau*, whose primary meaning, like that of its Spanish counterpart *bacalao*, is simply 'cod', appears to have originated in the language of an indigenous people of Newfoundland: 'Cabot him selfe named those landes *Baccallaos*, bycause that in the seas ther about he found so great multitude of certayne bigge fysshes . . . which thinhabitantes caule Baccallaos,' Richard Eden, *Decades of the Newe Worlde* (1555).

Bacardi The proprietary name of a brand of white rum made originally in Cuba by the Compania Ron Bacardi, which was founded in Santiago de Cuba in 1862 by the Spanish wine merchant Facundo Bacardi and his brother José (Ron Bacardi is not a family member: *ron* is Spanish for 'rum'). The term *Bacardi* is also applied to a cocktail, similar to a daiquiri, made from white rum, lime juice, and a dash of grenadine.

bacon Etymologically, *bacon* means 'meat from the back of an animal'. The word appears to come from a prehistoric Germanic base *bak-*, which was also the source of English *back*. Germanic *bakkon* passed into Frankish *bako*, which French borrowed as *bacon*. English acquired the word in the twelfth century, and seems at first to have used it as a synonym for the native term *flitch* 'side of cured pig meat'. By the fourteenth century, however, we find it being applied to the cured meat itself (and sometimes indeed to fresh pork too, but this usage gradually died out). Nowadays, although most dictionaries continue to define *bacon* as cured meat from the 'back and sides' of the pig, in practice the term is now applied generally to salted (and often smoked) pig meat—one can have a bacon joint, for instance, and most people would include gammon, from the hind quarters and hind leg, under the category of *bacon*. On the other hand there is little doubt that the most typical manifestation of bacon, as featured in the traditional British breakfast of fried bacon and eggs, comes in *rashers* (a sixteenth-century term of unknown origin) and in *streaky*, with alternating bands of fat and lean (*streaky* is first recorded in Dickens's *Oliver Twist* (1838)). Like many other 'traditions', incidentally, the great British breakfast of bacon and eggs with all the trimmings is not as old as it seems. Up until late Victorian times, bacon had to fight for a place on the breakfast sideboard with a welter of other meats; Mrs Beeton, in her recommendations for breakfast, gives an exhaustive list, including mutton chops, rump steaks, cold chicken, veal-and-ham pies, and cold tongue. *See also* FULL ENGLISH.

Confusingly, the general French term for 'bacon' is *lard*, although the word *bacon* is used when referring to British-style rashers.

The expression 'save one's bacon', presumably an equation of a side of bacon with one's own flesh or body, dates from the mid-seventeenth century.

bagel A ring-shaped white bread roll characteristic of Jewish, and particularly New York Jewish, cuisine. The word itself comes from Yiddish *beygel*, which was a development of a diminutive form of Middle High German *boug-*, *bouc-* 'ring, bracelet'. Before being baked the rings of bagel dough (made with high-gluten flour) are poached; this gives bagels their rather tough exterior. They are halved and filled with a variety of fillings, but perhaps their quintessential partner is cream cheese and smoked salmon—forming the classic New York breakfast of lox and bagels.

In tennis slang, a *bagel* is a 6–0 result in a set (the inspiration, as with cricket's *duck*, short for *duck's egg*, is the shape of a zero). Hence a *double bagel* is a 6–0, 6–0 defeat/ victory. The usage is first recorded in 1976.

bagna cauda An Italian version of fondue. A speciality of Piedmont, it consists of olive oil thickened and flavoured with a generous amount of anchovy and garlic, which is heated up in a terracotta container. Into it are dipped strips of raw vegetable (in Piedmont, typically cardoons), pieces of marinated meat, or peperoni sausage. *Bagna cauda* means literally 'hot bath' in the Piedmontese dialect.

bags of mystery A blackly humorous term for sausages, reflecting their often dubious contents. It is first recorded in 1864.

baguette A long thin loaf of French bread of the type more commonly known in English until recently as a *French stick*, or, more vaguely still, as a *French loaf*. The term has become increasingly familiar in English since the 1960s. It means literally 'little rod', and is a diminutive form derived ultimately from Latin *baculum* 'stick, staff' (source also of English *bacillus*).

The term *baguette* has also been applied to a recently developed cheese, similar to Maroilles, made at Laon, to the north of Reims.

Bailey's In full, *Bailey's Irish Cream,* the proprietary name of a brand of liqueur based on Irish whiskey and cream. It was introduced on to the market in 1974, and soon became very popular, establishing the genre of 'Irish Cream' and spawning a number of competitors. Despite the authentic-sounding signature 'R. A. Bailey' on the bottle, no one called Bailey was involved in its development. The name is said to have been inspired by Bailey's Hotel, a well-known and historic hotel in South Kensington, London.

bake A relatively simple dish containing a mix of ingredients (vegetables, pasta, meat), often with a sauce, baked in the oven: 'a tender, flavour-packed pumpkin and tomato bake laced with fresh rosemary', *Time Out London, Eating and Drinking* (2008). The usage, a conversion of verb to noun, is first recorded in 1963. It decidedly suggests home cooking rather than fine dining.

baked Alaska A pudding consisting of a block of ice cream surrounded with meringue and then baked for a short time in a very hot oven. Credit for the original idea of cooking an ice dessert within an insulating covering has been claimed for both the American statesman, inventor, and scientist Benjamin Franklin (1706–90) and the American-born British physicist and statesman Benjamin Thompson, Count Rumford (1753–1814). A dessert of this general sort is said to have been made by a French chef called Balzac on the occasion of a visit by a Chinese delegation to Paris in 1867, and the American chef Charles Ranhofer described something similar in print, which he referred to as 'Alaska, Florida'. The name *baked Alaska* is first recorded in 1909, the allusion being to Alaska's icy cold weather.

baked beans Boston baked beans is one of the central dishes of traditional American cuisine. It is made from haricot beans, or navy beans as they are called in the US (the same type of bean used in the French cassoulet). They are baked for several hours in a rich sauce of brown sugar, spices, and often pieces of salt pork. This is the origin of today's ubiquitous baked beans. Their cousin, *pork 'n' beans*, first appeared on the scene in tins in America in 1880, but they did not take off in a big way until 1895, when H. J. Heinz of Pittsburgh, Pennsylvania entered the market with its own particular brand. The company tried to introduce them into Britain in 1905, but without much success. In the 1920s, however, it had another go (the head of its British branch, C. H. Hellen, is said to have vowed 'I'm going to manufacture baked beans in England, and they're going to like it'), and since then the baked bean has never looked back.

In British rhyming slang, *baked bean* equals 'queen': "The Baked Bean". How Cockney police protection officers refer to Her Majesty, according to Andrew Marr's forthcoming BBC1 series, *The Diamond Queen', Guardian* (2012).

Bakewell tart Bakewell tart, or *Bakewell pudding,* as it was originally called (*tart* seems to be an early twentieth-century alteration), appeared on the scene in the mid-nineteenth century. The first recorded reference to it is in *The Housekeeper's Book* (1837), an American publication, and in her *Modern Cookery* (1845) Eliza Acton wrote 'this pudding is famous not only in Derbyshire, but in several of our northern counties, where it is usually served on all holiday-occasions.' Its basic concept, however, of a layer of jam beneath a main filling, was far from new then; it is part of a long tradition of so-called 'transparent' puddings, in which a layer of jam, preserved fruit, or candied peel was overlaid with a sugar, egg, and butter mixture and baked. They were made with or without a pastry case—and indeed Eliza Acton's recipe for Bakewell pudding makes no mention of pastry (Mrs Beeton, however, in 1861, has a version of Bakewell pudding with a puff-pastry case). The characteristic feature of Bakewell puddings, as opposed to all other such puddings, was and is almonds. Originally they were introduced in the form of a few drops of almond essence in the overlaying sugar, egg, and butter mixture, but gradually it became the custom to use ground almonds, thereby radically altering the nature and consistency of the topping. The dish is, of course, named after Bakewell, a town in Derbyshire, but how this came about is not known. Legend (and probably no more than that) has it that the pudding was created by accident in the kitchens of the Rutland Arms (or alternatively the White Horse) in the centre of the town.

baklava A popular dessert of the eastern Mediterranean and the Middle East, consisting of chopped nuts—walnuts, almonds, or pistachios—sandwiched between thin layers of filo pastry, and coated in syrup. It seems first to have appeared during the time of the Ottoman empire; its name is Turkish.

balchao A Goan speciality consisting typically of small dried prawns in a garlicky vinegary pickle.

ballottine In classical French cuisine, a ballottine is a hot or cold dish consisting of boned meat or poultry that is stuffed, rolled, tied up (often inside a cloth), and braised or poached. Its name is a diminutive form of French *ballotte*, which in turn is derived from *balle* 'bale'.

Balmain bug *See* MORETON BAY BUG.

baloney *See* POLONY.

balsamic vinegar A dark sweet type of Italian vinegar, originally made in the northern Italian city of Modena. It is made by simmering grape juice for a long period, to reduce its volume by up to a third while it ferments and acidifies, and then maturing it in a series of wooden barrels as its colour deepens, its flavour gains complexity, and its volume reduces still further. The resulting highly concentrated (and expensive) liquid is used in very small quantities. It suddenly became fashionable among foodies in the 1980s, and market demand for it was met by much more quickly made vinegars that resemble but are nowhere near as complex and concentrated as the original version. Its name is a direct translation of Italian *aceto balsamico*, where *balsamico* relates the supposed health-giving properties of the vinegar to 'healing' balm or balsam.

balti The balti comes from northern Pakistan via Birmingham. As a term it covers any of a range of spiced meat, poultry, and vegetable dishes that are cooked and served in a wok-like metal vessel called a *karahi*. It is typically accompanied by extremely large naan breads. The general style of cooking is believed to have originated in Baltistan, a mountainous region on the Northwest frontier of Pakistan, from which it spread out more widely into Kashmir and the Punjab, carrying with it the abbreviated name of the region (which is also used as a synonym of *karahi*). It was the Pakistani balti houses (restaurants) of Birmingham, however, that turned it into a craze in the early 1990s. The area to the south of the city centre including parts of Sparkbrook, Sparkhill, and Balsall Heath, which contains a particularly high concentration of balti houses, became known as the 'Balti Triangle'.

bamboo shoot The tip of a newly growing bamboo stem, eaten, especially in China and Southeast Asia, as a vegetable. It has a crisp nutty flavour. The term is first recorded in English in 1889.

banana *Banana* appears to be a tropical African word, but its lexical origins represent only a single stage in the fruit's worldwide wanderings before it reached British shores. It probably first grew in Southeast Asia, and did not make a big impact elsewhere until the early Islamic period when it was brought from India to the Middle East, and thence to Africa. The odd banana had turned up in Europe before that, of course, but only as an exotic rarity: in ancient Rome, for instance, it had to make do with borrowing the name of the fig (a notion which lived on in the early French term for 'banana', *figue du paradis*). Spanish and Portuguese colonists took the banana with them across the Atlantic from Africa to the Americas, and along with it they brought its African name, *banana*, apparently a word from one of the languages of the Congo area (it has been speculated that it derives ultimately from Arabic *banana* 'finger, toe', an origin which would be echoed in the English term *hand* for a bunch of bananas, and serves as a reminder that many varieties of banana are quite small, not like the monstrous articles standardly imported into Britain). The first banana to reach Britain came from Bermuda in 1633, and was sold in the shop of the herbalist Thomas Johnson, but its name had been known to the British (often in the form *bonana* or *bonano*, which in Spanish is strictly the term for the 'banana tree') for a good forty years before that. To begin with, bananas were generally not eaten raw, but cooked in tarts and dumplings.

The colloquial use of *bananas* for 'mad, crazy' is a surprisingly recent development. There is an isolated record of it from the US in the 1930s meaning 'sexually perverted, degenerate', but the current usage seems to have originated in US college slang of the mid to late 1960s. It is not clear how it arose. Some connection has been suggested with the earlier slang term *banana oil* 'nonsense', which dates from the 1920s, but since the origins of that too are unknown, the suggestion only pushes the mystery one stage further back.

Since the end of the nineteenth century *Bananaland* has been used by Australians as a colloquial and not altogether complimentary name for Queensland, a state where the banana is a key crop. Even less complimentary is *banana republic*, a term coined in the 1930s for small volatile states of the American tropics (from their economic dependence on the export of bananas).

bananas Foster An American dessert consisting of sliced bananas briefly flambéed in a mixture of rum and brown sugar, and served with vanilla ice cream. It was created in Brennan's Restaurant in New Orleans in the 1950s, and named after one Richard Foster, a regular habitué of the restaurant and a friend of the owner, Owen Brennan.

banana split A dessert of American origin, consisting of a banana cut in half lengthwise, surmounted by three scoops of ice cream (in the classic version, chocolate, vanilla, and strawberry), the whole then enveloped in any of various sweet sauces and topped off with whipped cream. The term is first recorded in 1920.

Banbury cake A small flat cake made from puff pastry with a spicy currant filling (not dissimilar to an Eccles cake). It gets its name (which is first recorded in the late sixteenth century) from the town of Banbury in Oxfordshire, where it was originally made. The earliest known recipe for it, in Gervase Markham's *The English Housewife* (1615), describes a much larger cake than the present-day one, made with yeast-raised dough rather than pastry, but it includes the defining currants.

bang-bang chicken Pieces of shredded cold chicken enlivened with a salty sweet-and-sour sauce containing rice vinegar, soy sauce, sesame paste and oil, and sugar. It originated as a snack sold by street vendors in the Szechuan province of western China. Its name (in Chinese *bang-bang jī*) is said to mimic the pounding of the chicken with a mallet to tenderize it.

banger *See* SAUSAGE.

bannock Bannocks are the bread of the less privileged fringes of Britain. While southern England luxuriated in soft leavened wheat bread, areas like Scotland, Wales, and northern England had largely to make do in former times with round fairly flat loaves made from oatmeal or barley flour and baked on griddles and bakestones. *Bannock* was the name given to such loaves made from barley in Scotland, and in northern England it was used for a thick version of the oatcake. Scotland also has currant bannocks, containing dried fruit. The word *bannock* is probably of Celtic origin; it may be related to Breton *bannach* 'drop, bit', and Cornish *banna* 'drop' (the idea that it could be connected with Latin *pānis* 'bread' is no longer accepted).

banoffee pie A dessert consisting of bananas, cream, and condensed milk baked in a pastry case. It was invented in 1972 by Ian Dowding and Nigel Mackenzie of the Hungry Monk restaurant in Jevington, East Sussex, and soon went, as a later generation would put it, viral (many subsequent versions of it replaced the pastry case with a base of crushed biscuits and butter, of which the originators did not necessarily approve). The name is a blend of *banana* and *toffee,* the latter element reflecting the effect of baking on the cream and condensed milk.

bap Baps are soft flattish bread rolls made with white flour, lard, yeast, milk, and water, and usually dusted with flour. Particularly associated with Scotland, they are traditionally eaten at breakfast. The origins of the word, which is first recorded in a sixteenth-century Scottish text, are not known.

The term *bap-an'-thack* denoted in Scotland 'baps spread with jam' (*thack* is a Scots variant of *thatch*).

In British slang, a woman's *baps* are her breasts: 'Bravely she defied the mullahs in Tehran by exercising her human right to get her baps out for a French magazine', Rod Liddle, *Sunday Times* (2012). The usage seems to have originated in the 1980s, probably in Ulster.

bara brith A Welsh fruit bread, made typically with currants, raisins, and candied peel. *Bara,* the Welsh word for 'bread', is related to English *barley* and Latin *farīna* 'flour'. *Brith* means 'speckled'.

Barbados cherry The small round bright-red fruit of a diminutive tree of the Malpighiaceae family of tropical American flowering shrubs, which greatly resembles but is not at all related to the cherry. It is widely grown in the West Indies (hence its name, first recorded in 1858), and is extremely rich in vitamin C. It is now widely stocked in health-food shops in Britain. Another name for it is *acerola*.

barbecue sauce A highly seasoned commercially produced sauce containing vinegar, sugar, spices, and usually chillis, and characteristically used to baste barbecuing meat or as an accompaniment to the result. Many versions have smoky flavouring added. The term (often spelled *BBQ sauce*) appears to date from the 1890s. The same basic flavouring has been extended to other products, such as *barbecue dip* and *barbecue crisps*.

barberry The elongated red berry of various spiny shrubs of the genus *Berberis*. European varieties are fairly tart, and used mainly in making jellies and syrups, but some North American species are sweet enough to be eaten raw. The name, which dates from the fourteenth century, comes from Old French *berberis*, altered by association with English *berry*.

barigoule The term *à la barigoule* denotes a Provençal method of preparing globe artichokes, or rather, one of two methods. In the case of young small artichokes, they are cooked unstuffed on a bed of vegetables; older sturdier specimens are stuffed with a mixture of chopped mushrooms and fat bacon, and simmered in white wine. *Barigoule* is the Provençal name for the morel mushroom, so very likely the recipe originally specified morels.

bark An American confection consisting of white chocolate mixed with roasted almonds.

barley Barley was perhaps the earliest of cereals cultivated by human beings (in the Neolithic period). It is little used in making bread (its gluten content is too low), but it quickly found its metier as the grain from which beer could be made, usually after malting, or being made to germinate. Later came stronger stuff—as witness the personification *John Barleycorn* for 'malt spirits' (first recorded in 1620). Barley is also widely used for thickening soups, stews, etc., in the form pearl barley, its seeds ground into small round grains.

The Old English word for 'barley' was *bære* (a relative of Latin *farīna* 'flour'), and *barley* itself was originally an adjectival derivative of it, meaning 'of barley'. A close relative is the word *barn*, which etymologically means 'barley-house'.

barley grass Leaves of newly sprouted barley that are processed into a dark green liquid. In recent years it has jumped up alongside wheatgrass on the health-food bandwagon: 'You can also get freshly made smoothies with faddy ingredients such as gogi berries and barley grass', *Time Out London, Eating and Drinking* (2008).

barley sugar A clear hard amber-coloured sweet, once (but no longer) made by boiling sugar in water in which barley had been boiled. In the days of its popularity, the eighteenth and nineteenth centuries and the early part of the twentieth century, it was often made in long twisted sticks, and *barleysugar* came to be used as an architectural and design term applied to twisted columns and pillars.

barley water Originally, barley water was no more than a drink made by boiling barley (latterly pearl barley) in water—a simple idea, not far from the starting point of beer, which has no doubt been around for several millennia (the first mention of it in an English text is from around 1320). Nowadays, however, the term denotes essentially a sort of lemon- or orange-flavoured soft drink, first cousin to lemon or orange squash. It still seems to retain the reputation of being somehow 'good for you', a hangover perhaps from the nineteenth century, when barley water was recommended for its beneficial effects on the kidneys.

barley wine In current British English, *barley wine* is a commercial term for any particularly strong beer, sold typically in small bottles. The usage does not seem to be particularly ancient—it has been traced back in print no further than 1940—but the term itself goes back much further. In the nineteenth century it was used for an alcoholic drink prepared from barley by the ancient Greeks, and Eliza Smith's *Compleat Housewife* (1728) gave a recipe for another sort of 'Barley wine . . . Take Barley, boil it, mix it with white Wine, Borage water, Cluny-water, Lemons, Sugar . . . bottle it up.'

barm The yeast-induced froth on top of fermenting beer, which traditionally has been used to leaven bread and also to start fermentation in other liquors. The modern word has evolved from Old English *beorma,* which is related to Latin *fermentum* 'yeast'. (The derivative *barmy* 'mad, daft', which can be traced back to the seventeenth century, grew out of the idea of 'frothiness'.)

barmbrack Barmbrack, or *barnbrack,* is a type of soft spicy fruit loaf, originally made in Ireland. The name, first recorded in 1878, is an alteration of Irish Gaelic *bairin breac* 'speckled cake'.

barm cake A term in Northern England for a soft flattish bread roll, originally leavened with barm.

Barnsley chop A cut of lamb or mutton consisting of two conjoined chops from either side of the saddle. The history of the term is not altogether straightforward. It appears originally, in the mid-nineteenth century, to have been applied to an extra-large chop, comprising the first three ribs after the shoulder, that was served to hungry farmers on market day at the King's Head Hotel in the town of Barnsley, in the West Riding of Yorkshire. The present-day usage is said to have originated at the Brooklands Restaurant, also in Barnsley.

baron of beef A British term for a joint of beef consisting of two sirloins joined at the backbone. As Dorothy Hartley says in her *Food in England* (1954), 'Expert chefs roast this for great banquets. It is too large for any other usage'. It is not clear whether *baron*, first recorded in this sense in 1755, is the same word as the noble title.

Bartlett The American name of the Williams pear. It commemorates Enoch Bartlett, who was the first to distribute the pear in the US, in the early nineteenth century.

basil To the ancient Greeks basil (a plant of the mint family whose leaves have a penetrating fragrance) was the 'royal herb'. It was perhaps used in some ointment or medicine reserved specifically for those of royal blood, and legend has it that only the king was allowed to cut it. It was therefore named *basilikón* 'royal' (a derivative of *basileús* 'king'), and the term passed via medieval Latin *basilicum* and Old French *basile* into English (its earliest forms led to its being popularly associated with the mythical beast, the basilisk, and in fact modern French *basilic* means 'basilisk' as well as 'basil'). Basil was a popular herb in Britain in the sixteenth and seventeenth centuries, but it seems gradually to have gone out of favour (in 1861 Mrs Beeton noted that 'it is not much employed in English cookery, but is a favourite with French cooks'), and in the nineteenth century most of those who knew of it did so through Keats's poem 'Isabella, or the pot of basil' (1820), a story taken from Boccaccio in which a young woman conceals the head of her murdered lover in a pot of earth and then plants some basil in it. In the late twentieth century, however, increased awareness of the magical partnership of basil and tomatoes in Mediterranean cookery, and of the aromatic pesto sauce made with basil, led to a revival of interest in it in Britain and America. *See also* HOLY BASIL, THAI BASIL.

In British English the word is pronounced /'bazəl/, but in America /'bayzəl/ and /'baysəl/ are common alternatives.

basmati rice A high-quality variety of Indian long-grain rice, characterized by its particular fragrance when cooked (Hindi *bāsmatī* means literally 'fragrant'). It is generally considered the best rice for accompanying curries. Early references to it in English texts of the nineteenth century spell it *basmuttee*, and it is only really since the 1960s that the current form has established itself.

bastilla A bastilla, or *bestilla*, or *b'stilla*, or *pastilla*, is a Moroccan pigeon pie. Minced or sliced pigeon is mixed with egg, almonds, and spices, enclosed in an envelope of filo-like pastry called *ouarka*, sprinkled with sugar and cinnamon, and baked. The dish is the product of the Moorish occupation of Spain, and the name is of Spanish origin too (hence its pronunciation, /bə'steeə/), a derivative of *pastel* 'pie'.

batavia An alternative name for the *escarole*, a lettuce-like variety of endive. Its origins are not documented, but presumably it contains some reference to the provenance of the vegetable in the Low Countries (*Batavia* is an old name for Holland).

batch A loaf baked with several others in one large tin, so that as they cook their sides partially merge together, and the finished loaves when separated have a crustless side or sides. *Batch* originated, probably in Anglo-Saxon times, as an abstract noun derived from the verb *bake*, and to begin with it meant simply 'baking'. By the fifteenth century it had become specialized to 'quantity of bread made at one baking', and in the seventeenth century it was even used for 'bread' itself ('Those blest with the true batch of life may ever rest so satisfied,' Earl of Westmorland, *Otia Sacra* (1648)), but the term *batch bread*, the forerunner of the present-day *batch loaf*, is not recorded before the 1860s. (The extension of *batch* from 'amount of baked goods produced at one time' to 'amount of anything produced at one time' probably took place in the late seventeenth century.)

Bath bun A sweet sticky bun made from a milk-based white dough with candied peel, raisins, etc., and a topping of sugar crystals. It first appeared in the middle of the eighteenth century, when it was known as the *Bath cake*: Elizabeth Raffald, in her *Experienced English Housekeeper* (1769), gives a recipe which makes it clear that it was a teacake with a fairly light, brioche-like texture, quite distinct from its somewhat stodgy descendant. But the first reference to Bath buns as such comes, appropriately enough, in a letter of Jane Austen, remorseless recorder of the early nineteenth-century social scene in the West Country city of Bath, after which the bun was named: in January 1801 she wrote plaintively of 'disordering my Stomach with Bath bunns'. Elizabeth David speculates that the enormous rise in popularity of the Bath bun, from the status of a local delicacy in the first half of the nineteenth century to the mass-produced mediocrity of the early twentieth century, was fuelled by the 1851 Great Exhibition in London, at which during less than six months 943,691 Bath buns were eaten.

Bath chap Bath chaps are the smoked or pickled cheeks of a pig, which are usually boiled and then eaten cold. In this context, *chaps* is almost certainly the same word as *chops* (as in 'lick one's chops'), but its ultimate derivation is obscure. Nor is the dish's connection with the city of Bath altogether clear, although it does always seem to have had West Country associations. In the nineteenth century, when it was much commoner than it is today, it was often referred to as simply *chaps*: 'The feast was chaps and eggs', *Daily News* (1870). (An alternative possibility is some connection with French *bajoue* 'pig's jowls', a compound of *bas* 'lower' and *joue* 'cheek'.) Bath chaps were still to be found fairly generally in butcher's and grocer's shops up until the early 1950s, the size and shape of monster ice-cream cones with a coating of luridly yellow commercial breadcrumbs, but in the twentyfirst century they are hard indeed to track down.

Bath Oliver Bath Olivers are extremely plain, unsweetened biscuits, today usually eaten with cheese. They are round and have in their centre an impressionistic portrait of an eighteenth-century gentleman presumably intended to represent William Oliver (1695–1764), the Bath doctor credited with their invention. Originally they were called simply *Olivers*, and it is not until 1878 that we encounter the first reference to *Bath Olivers* (in the Cunard Steamship Company's *Official Guide and Album*).

bathtub gin A colloquial term, probably dating from the 1920s, for illicitly produced low-quality gin (imagined as being distilled in a bathtub), and hence for any throat-rasping gin or similar spirit.

battenberg An oblong cake made up of four square-sectioned sponges diagonally coloured pink and white or yellow, and enclosed in marzipan. It seems to have been created towards the end of the nineteenth century (the first record of it in print comes in 1903) and named in honour of the marriage of Princess Victoria of Hesse-Darmstadt, granddaughter of Queen Victoria, to Prince Louis of Battenberg in 1884. A member of the Prussian noble family of Battenberg, he took British nationality, was made First Sea Lord in 1912, and in 1917 (because of anti-German sentiment) renounced his German titles and translated his name into English as Mountbatten. The Battenberg connection was reinforced in 1885, when Queen Victoria's daughter Beatrice married Prince Henry of Battenberg. The two-toned battenberg cake was probably designed to mimic the marbled effect of many German breads and cakes.

batter A fluid mixture of flour, a liquid (such as water, milk, or beer), and usually eggs—essentially a thin, pourable version of dough. It is used for making pancakes, waffles, crumpets, and batter puddings, and for coating items of food to be fried. The origins of the term, which is first recorded in the early fifteenth century ('Of almond milk and amydon [fine flour] make batter,' *Liber cocorum* (1420)), are not known for certain, but it is probably an adaptation of the verb *batter*, with reference to the action of beating the mixture.

Batter puddings were once a common feature of English cuisine—Mrs Beeton gives four different recipes for sweet versions—but today they survive mainly in the unsweetened Yorkshire pudding, and its close relative toad-in-the-hole. The French *clafoutis* is a sort of batter pudding.

bavarois A creamy cold dessert made with an egg-custard base into which are mixed cream, beaten egg whites, a flavouring (such as chocolate or orange), and gelatine. It is then set in a mould. The *bavarois*, or *bavaroise* (the gender seems to be interchangeable: the masculine form derives from French *fromage bavarois*, the feminine from *crème bavaroise*), has been popular in Britain since the mid-nineteenth century, frequently under the Anglicized name *Bavarian cream*. The 1868 edition of *Modern Cookery for Private Families*, for instance, includes directions for making it, although it did not appear in Eliza Acton's original 1845 version. It is not known what its original connection with Bavaria was.

bavette The French name for what in English is generally termed *flanksteak* or *goose flank*. In recent years it has begun to make its presence felt on upmarket restaurant menus and butchers' lists. French *bavette* means literally 'bib' (it is a derivative of *bave* 'slime, dribble'), and its metaphorical use refers to the position of this cut of meat on the animal's carcase.

bay The bay, a tree of the laurel family, has been held in high esteem since ancient times. In Greece, it was sacred to Apollo, and its leaves were used for crowning victors in the Pythian games. Culinarily, too, the leaves were valued for their pungent, peppery flavour, and were probably introduced to Britain from the Mediterranean by the Romans. Bay has become a stock herb in European cuisine, and is a standard component of the bouquet garni. The term *bay* actually originally denoted the fruit or berry of the laurel, and comes ultimately from Latin *bāca* 'berry' (John de Trevisa, in his translation of *De Proprietatibus Rerum* (1398), noted 'the fruit of the laurel tree are called bays'). Hence the tree itself came to be known as the *bay laurel* or *bay tree* and, by the mid-sixteenth century, as simply *bay*.

bean The bean is one of the most ancient of human foods—it was a staple dietary item in many parts of the world for our hunter-gatherer ancestors over 12,000 years ago—and also one of the most versatile. Just as no part of the pig is wasted after its slaughter, so every phase of the bean's life cycle is exploited, from its earliest sprouts, through its tender young pods, to its mature seeds—which if not eaten fresh are dried for future use.

In Britain, the bean has until comparatively recently been synonymous with what we now call the broad bean. This is the vegetable the Greeks knew as *pháselos*, the Romans as *faba* (source of French *fève*), and our Anglo-Saxon ancestors as *bean*. The link between these terms is that they all seem to derive from a source which denoted 'swelling'.

The discovery of America, however, opened an Aladdin's cave of new bean varieties, eagerly seized on by the Old World: runner beans, French beans, haricot beans, butter beans, kidney beans, and many more were suddenly available in the sixteenth century to supplement the samey diet of broad beans. And subsequently the East has broadened our repertoire of beans still further, with soya beans, mung beans, adzuki beans, and the like.

The beans on the menu at the original beanfeast, incidentally, were probably haricot beans. It was the practice of employers in the nineteenth century (and probably long before that) to give their workforce an annual blowout, on the menu of which bacon and beans featured largely: 'At a late bean feast, a Gentleman Taylor, noted for his liberality, gave a rich treat to his men, at his occasional country residence. It was called a Bean Feast; but, exclusive of the beans, the table literally groaned with bacon,' *Sporting Magazine* (1805). Hence *beanfeast* came to be used for any celebratory occasion or free party. In printers' jargon the word was abbreviated to *beano*. *See also* BAKED BEANS.

bean sprouts Beans, especially mung beans and soya beans, that have been allowed to germinate and produce shoots up to 7–8 cm long before being harvested. The notion is Chinese, but it has been popularized in the West over the past century (the term is first recorded in English in 1921). Stir-frying is a widely used method of cooking the bean sprouts.

béarnaise A hot creamy sauce made from butter, egg yolks, and vinegar or lemon juice, flavoured with shallots, tarragon, chervil, thyme, bay leaves, etc. It is generally served with grilled meat or fish. It takes its name from Béarn, a region in southwestern France.

Beaufort A type of hard cheese made from the milk of cows that graze the Alpine pastures around Beaufort in Savoie, southeastern France, just to the southwest of Mont Blanc.

béchamel A basic white sauce made from milk or cream and a flour-and-butter roux. It gets its name from the Marquis de Béchamel (1630–1703), a general of Louis XIV of France, who is said to have invented it. It was evidently still fairly unfamiliar in Britain in the mid-eighteenth century, for Hannah Glasse in her *Art of Cookery* (1747) refers to it as *bishemel*, but it became thoroughly naturalized during the nineteenth century.

It should not be confused with the fairly similar velouté sauce, which is made with stock rather than milk (in fact the Marquis de Béchamel is said originally to have made béchamel sauce by adding cream to a velouté).

beef *Beef* crossed the Channel not, as is commonly supposed, with William the Conqueror, but a good deal later, towards the end of the thirteenth century. Although it provided a useful word for the meat of the ox or cow, it was by no means used exclusively for the dead animal's flesh at first. Indeed, it remains in use to this day as a technical term for a fully-grown bull or cow, particularly one fattened for food (its plural is *beeves* or, mainly in American English, *beefs*). Nor has the blunter Anglo-Saxon terminology died out entirely, especially when it comes to miscellaneous parts of the animal: *ox cheek, ox heart, ox liver, ox tongue, oxtail, cowheel*—not forgetting Desperate Dan's *cow pie*.

The word *beef* comes via Anglo-Norman *boef* or *buef* from Latin *bovem*, the accusative form of *bōs* 'ox'. This goes back ultimately to a prehistoric Indo-European **gwōus*, which also produced English *cow*, so by a roundabout route *beef* and *cow* are essentially the same word.

There are records of the flesh of cows being eaten in ancient Sumer, nearly 4,500 years ago, and the practice has persisted ever since wherever in the world cattle are kept, but it is with the British Isles that beef has always been particularly connected. Beef cattle were being exported from Britain to continental Europe even before the Roman conquest, and beef was the preferred food of the Romans when they did arrive. The Anglo-Saxons on the whole tended to prefer mutton and pork, but the Normans were distinctly keener on beef, and this, coupled with a growing preference for cow's milk over ewe's milk, saw a steady rise in the British cattle population, so that by the thirteenth century beef had established itself as the Englishman's favourite meat. It has retained that position, at least by reputation, ever since, and the 'roast beef of Old England', with its traditional

accompaniments of Yorkshire pudding and horseradish sauce, occupies a very special place in the national culinary pantheon (the cliché perhaps originated in Henry Fielding's 'Oh! The roast beef of England, and old England's roast beef,' *Grub Street Opera* (1731)).

The metaphorical application of the word to 'muscular power or effort' dates from the mid-nineteenth century, its verbal use for 'complain' (probably based on the notion of a fractious steer kicking and bucking) from the late nineteenth century. Both originated in the USA.

The term *beefeater*, as applied to the yeoman warders of the Tower of London, dates from at least the 1670s. A number of fanciful etymologies have been concocted to account for it, but in fact it simply originated as a contemptuous seventeenth-century term for a well-fed servant, who had had too much of his master's beef.

For *beefcake*, see CHEESECAKE.

beef olive Beef olives—slices of beef rolled up round a stuffing of, say, bread-crumbs, onions, and herbs, and braised—have no direct connection with olives. The term *olive* arose in the sixteenth century by folk etymology—the process of reformulating a less familiar word along the lines of a more familiar one—from an earlier *aloes*, *allowes*, or *alaunder*: 'Item, all chopped onions, boil them in clean, water before they go to any work, except in aloes,' *Goud Kokery* (a fourteenth-century cookery book). This was a borrowing from Old French *alou* 'lark' (modern French for 'lark' is *alouette*), a term applied to these small meat rolls on account of their supposed resemblance to small birds, particularly headless ones prepared for the table. The standard French word for this dish is *paupiette*, but an alternative name is *alouettes sans tête*, literally 'larks without heads'. From earliest times, mutton and veal had been used in the recipe as well as beef (Gervase Markham, in his *English Housewife* (1615), gives a recipe for 'Olives of Veal'), but gradually beef came to predominate—it is the meat specified by Elizabeth Raffald in the eighteenth century and Mrs Beeton in the nineteenth century.

beefsteak tomato A name given to a very large, dense-fleshed, bright red type of tomato. It originated in the US, and is first recorded in 1896. In British English, it appears to be ousting the similarly inspired *beef tomato*.

beef tea A thin and rather discouraging broth made from beef (or from a stock cube or stock concentrate) and associated mainly with the sick-room. In former times it was administered to invalids and those recuperating from illness, in order to build up their strength: 'She made beef tea, having begged the beef from the neighbours, she spooned it into Lucy's cracked lips, she wiped her face, she stroked her hands, she bent over and pulled back the red eyelids', A. S. Byatt, *The Children's Book* (2009). The term is first recorded in 1783.

beef Wellington A dish consisting of a fillet of beef coated in pâté and/or a duxelles of mushrooms and shallots, wrapped in pastry (traditionally puff pastry), and baked. It appears to have originated in the US in the late 1930s: Diana Ashley in her *Where to Dine in Thirty-nine* (1939), a guide to New York restaurants, refers to a 'tenderloin of beef Wellington' which is clearly the same dish. The earliest known reference to *beef Wellington, tout court,* dates from 1948. It was in the 1960s that it began to make a significant impact in Britain, the expense of its chief ingredient making it the epitome of the luxurious dinner-party main course. Since then, *Wellington* has become a generic term applied to any piece of boneless meat cooked in pastry (in 1999, for example, *Food and Wine* magazine referred to an 'ostrich Wellington', and in 2012 bison Wellington was served to guests at a White House banquet in honour of British prime minister David Cameron), and there are even meat-free versions: 'Vegetarians might opt for broccoli and pine nut Wellington', *Time Out, London's Best Restaurants* (2010).

The question of its naming remains unresolved. The obvious assumption (though it would not sit particularly well with the American origins of the dish) is of some sort of connection with Arthur Wellesley, first Duke of Wellington (1769–1855), premier British military hero of the nineteenth century. It has accordingly been asserted that a similar association of beef and pastry was the Iron Duke's favourite dish, but no evidence to that effect has ever been produced. This has left the field open to other suggestions, including a link with the capital city of New Zealand and (a rather desperate throw) a similarity between the baked pastry case and the leg of a Wellington boot.

beer In Anglo-Saxon times the usual term for an alcoholic drink made by fermenting malt was *ealu* (modern English *ale*). The word *beer* (in Old English *beor*) existed then, but from the tenth century it appears to have languished as a technical term for the sweet infusion of malt, or 'wort', before it had begun to ferment, and it did not return to common use for the finished article until the fifteenth century. The sudden increase in its frequency was due to a new role which then developed for it in distinguishing the drink flavoured with hops (*beer*)—a taste introduced from Flanders—from the plain unflavoured drink (*ale*) ('Beere is a Dutch boorish Liquor, a thing not knowne in England, till of late dayes an Alien to our Nation, till such times as Hops and Heresies came amongst us, it is a sawcy intruder in this Land,' John Taylor, *Ale Ale-vated into the Ale-titude* (1651)). Gradually, though, this distinction faded out; *beer* came to be used as a general term for all such drinks, and *ale* became ghettoized as a word for a particular type of beer, or as a folksy alternative to *beer*. *Beer* has additionally been used since Anglo-Saxon times for non-alcoholic drinks resembling true beer more in appearance than in flavour, such as *ginger beer, nettle beer*, and *root beer. See also* SMALL BEER.

The precise moment in history when the trick of making beer was discovered (no doubt by accident, when perhaps someone noted the pleasing effect on the drinker of liquid in which some bits of bread had been immersed for a day or so) is of course long lost, but it is clear that before 2000 BC the Sumerians were skilled makers and prodigious drinkers of beer (eight different types of beer made from barley are recorded from that time, and a further eight from wheat), and the ancient Egyptians also went in for it in a big way. The Greeks and Romans, however, scarcely knew of beer except as an exotic brew (the only words for it in their languages are foreign borrowings), and they considered it markedly inferior to their wine: the Greeks held, for instance, that their wine god Dionysus fled from Mesopotamia because all he could get to drink there was beer. But northern Europe, where growing grapes was more of a struggle, if not downright impossible, was ideal territory for beer, and Germany, the Low Countries, and Scandinavia have a beer culture stretching back into the Iron Age. Britain, to which the drink was introduced by its Anglo-Saxon conquerors, is no exception—indeed, as Sydney Smith remarked, 'What two ideas are more inseparable than Beer and Britannia?'

The origins of the word *beer* itself, which has relatives in German and Dutch *bier*, French *bière*, Italian *birra*, and Rumanian *bere*, are not known for certain. One possibility is that it comes ultimately from Latin *biber* 'drink'.

beer-can chicken Beer-can chicken or, more earthily, *beer-butt chicken* is an American way with chicken that involves inserting an opened can of lager into the bird's cavity and roasting it 'standing up'. It is also called *drunken chicken*.

beerenauslese For those whose pockets do not stretch to the giddily expensive trockenbeerenauslese, beerenauslese offers a marginally cheaper opportunity to

appreciate the luscious sweetness which German and Austrian white wines can achieve. The term means literally 'berry selection', and denotes that each grape used in the wine has been individually picked to ensure that it has reached the perfect degree of over-ripeness, and also that it has been affected by the botrytis mould that further concentrates its juice (although not to the extent of shrivelling up, as in trockenbeerenauslese). *See also* AUSLESE, SPÄTLESE, TROCKENBEERENAUSLESE.

beestings Beestings, or *beastings,* is the first milk produced by a cow (or goat) after giving birth, which is thick and high in protein and antibodies. Humans have readily snatched it from new-born calves' lips, both for its supposed health-giving properties and for the way it sets when cooked (Florence White in her *Good Things in England* (1932) gives a Worcestershire recipe for 'beastings pudding' which 'was a baked custard made of beastings but without eggs'). The word, which goes back to Old English *bysting,* now has a rustic feel: the present-day terminology of animal husbandry favours *colostrum.*

beet The word *beet* is probably of Celtic origin. Latin borrowed it as *beta,* and passed it on to the prehistoric ancestor of the modern Germanic languages—hence German *beete* and Dutch and English *beet.* It is applied to a variety of related plants of the goosefoot family that are cultivated mainly for their large bulbous edible root. In British English the term is most usually reserved for the white-fleshed type from which sugar is made (the *sugar beet*), but in American English *beet,* or more fully *red beet,* commonly denotes the red-fleshed variety which in Britain is called the *beetroot.* The mangel-wurzel is also a type of beet, and there is a further variety, the *spinach beet,* more generally termed *Swiss chard,* which is grown for its edible leaves.

beetroot A red-fleshed variety of beet, known in American English as the *red beet,* or simply *beet.* Its stock in Britain, and in western Europe generally, tends to be low—for many people the memory of its inevitable presence in uninspiring salads, bought ready-cooked from the greengrocer or tinned in vinegary liquid, is as unpleasantly indelible as its lurid scarlet juice. In recent years, though, its stock has begun to rise, with chefs rediscovering its virtues, and different coloured 'heritage' varieties (orange-fleshed, for example, or with concentric rings of red and white) becoming available in supermarkets. In eastern Europe it is a valued vegetable, and is the main ingredient of the soup borscht.

Since at least the mid-nineteenth century the beetroot has been humorously symbolic of 'redness'. *All the Year Round* in 1859, for example, describes 'the smallest boy, with the whitest face, the most beetrooty nose, ever seen'; and to this day to 'go beetroot' or 'turn as red as a beetroot' is to blush.

beignet The French term for a fritter (descended from Old French *buignet*—*see* BUN), it has been adopted into American culinary vocabulary, where it denotes in particular a New Orleans speciality, a square of yeast-raised dough that is deep-fried and eaten hot sprinkled with icing sugar.

Belle Hélène Jacques Offenbach's operetta *La Belle Hélène* ('The Fair Helen'), about Helen of Troy, scored a great success on its Paris premiere in 1864, and several chefs were inspired to create dishes that they named after it. The one that became most widely known, and remains firmly in the repertoire, consists of poached pears served on vanilla ice cream, and coated with hot chocolate sauce. It is also called *poires Hélène.* Incidentally, the opera also gave its name to a railway station in Budapest: Szep Ilona.

Bellini An aperitif made from puréed peach and sparkling wine (in the original version, prosecco; for the well-heeled, champagne). It was created at Harry's Bar in Venice in the 1930s by the bar's owner, Giuseppe Cipriani, and named in honour of the painter Giovanni Bellini (?1430–1516), who was a native of the city. At least two versions exist of the reason for the choice of name. The more convoluted is that the drink's pink colour reminded Cipriani of the colour of a saint's robe in a painting by Bellini (if it be objected that puréed peach is not pink, the original Bellini was actually made with white peaches—still insisted on by purists—whose pink skins provide a blush of their own that can be augmented with a little raspberry or cherry juice if desired). The second, simpler but perhaps suspiciously similar to the *carpaccio* story, is that the occasion of the naming was a major exhibition of Bellini's work in Venice. Wherever it came from, the name is not recorded before 1948.

bell pepper An alternative term, reflecting its shape, for the sweet pepper. It appears at first to have been a generally used term (the first known reference to it comes in Sir Hans Sloane's *A Voyage to Jamaica* (1707)), but in modern usage it is mainly associated with American English.

Bel Paese The proprietary name of a firm-textured mild-flavoured Italian cows'-milk cheese. It was created by Egidio Galbani in 1906, and is still made by his family in Melzo, Lombardy. *Bel paese* means literally 'beautiful country', and reputedly comes from a book written by a friend of Galbani's, Abbot Antonio Stoppani.

benedictine A French herb-based liqueur. The recipe for it, which was supposedly devised by an Italian monk called Bernardo Vincelli who lived at the Benedictine Abbey of Fécamp in Normandy, was discovered and commercialized in 1863 by a local merchant, Alexandre Le Grand. He called it *benedictine*, in memory of Dom Vincelli's affiliations, and reinforced the liqueur's ecclesiastical connotations by printing DOM (standing for *Deo Optimo Maximo* 'to God, most good, most great') on its label.

A drier version of the liqueur, mixed with brandy, is known as *B and B* (benedictine and brandy).

bento The traditional Japanese form of packed lunch. It consists typically of rice and small portions of other foodstuffs, such as pickles, fish, raw or cooked vegetables, fruit, all simply but elegantly arranged inside a box, also called a *bento* or, in English, a *bento box*. The most familiar form of bento, known as *ekiben,* is that sold at Japanese railway stations, its contents reflecting the cooking of each station's region. The Japanese word is an adaptation of Chinese *biàndāng*, meaning 'convenient'.

Bercy *Sauce Bercy* is a velouté sauce made with the addition of shallots and white wine. It is served with meat or fish. It takes its name from Bercy, a southeastern district of Paris, which at one time was the site of the largest wine market in Europe. Local restaurants became famous for their fish dishes cooked in a wine sauce.

bergamot English has two apparently etymologically distinct words *bergamot,* both of culinary significance. The earlier, which appeared in the early seventeenth century, denotes any of a class of luscious yellow dessert pear. It came, via French and Italian, from Turkish *begarmudu,* meaning literally 'prince's pear'. The second, first recorded in 1696, is the name of a dwarf variety of Seville orange, whose rind yields an essential oil that is used in perfumery and as the key flavouring agent in Earl Grey tea. This bergamot gets its name from the northern Italian city and province of Bergamo, where presumably it was first grown (although now it mainly comes from Calabria in southern Italy). Its aroma is similar to that of various North American mints of the genus *Monarda,* which were named after it in the mid-nineteenth century.

best end A term (first recorded in 1728; in full *best end of neck*) denoting a cut of lamb or mutton (or occasionally veal) from the lower section of the neck, which contains the foreribs. Its greater proportion of meat to bone makes it superior to and more expensive than the upper section of the neck, the *scrag end*: 'I could only get scrag end this morning, aunt: the best end was sold', Mrs Henry Wood, *Master of Greylands* (1874). Especially when used as a roasting joint, it is alternatively known as a *rack*.

betel The Southeast Asian equivalent of chewing gum. The leaves of the betel plant (a member of the pepper family) are wrapped round some pieces of the seeds of the areca palm (known by association as *betel nuts*), together with lime obtained from shells, and chewed. The juices have a narcotic effect, stimulate the appetite, and also turn the chewer's teeth red. The word *betel* comes from Malayalam *vettila*.

beurre blanc A sauce made by adding large amounts of butter to a reduction of vinegar and chopped shallots. It was created, probably somewhere on the banks of the Loire in northwestern France, to accompany fish, but it also goes well with poultry, eggs, and vegetables. In French its name means literally 'white butter'.

beurre manié Butter that has had blended into it an equal amount of flour. It is used for thickening sauces, stews, etc. French *beurre manié* means literally 'handled butter' or 'kneaded butter'.

bhaji A bhaji (or *bhajia*) is an Indian vegetable fritter, eaten as a snack. One could have, for instance, aubergine bhajis, potato-skin bhajis, or (most commonly in Briticized Indian cuisine) onion bhajis. Hindi *bhaji* means literally 'vegetable'. *See also* PAKORA.

bhel puri Bhel puri, or *bhel poori*, is a crunchy Gujarati snack, widely consumed in the streets and on the beaches of Mumbai. It consists of puris (deep-fried puff pastries) with puffed rice, onions, spices, and hot chutney. Hindi *bhel* means 'mixture'; *see also* PURI.

bhindi The Hindi term for 'okra', the mucilaginous seed pods of a plant of the hollyhock family. It is quite commonly used in Indian cookery, and in that context is often referred to as *bhindi* in English.

bhuna A richly pungent type of Indian curry in which the sauce is vigorously reduced to a high degree of concentration.

Bibb lettuce A small variety of butterhead lettuce of American origin. It is named after Jack Bibb (1789–1884), the Kentucky vegetable-grower who developed it.

bibimbap A Korean dish consisting of a mixture of rice, vegetables, and meat, served with a raw or fried egg on top. The Korean word means literally 'mixed meal'.

biffin A variety of cooking apple with deep red skin, associated particularly with Norfolk. The name (first recorded in 1794) represents a dialectal pronunciation of the earlier *beefing*, a derivative of *beef* applied to the apple because of its colour: 'Norfolk Biffins, squab [i.e. plump] and swarthy, setting off the yellow of the oranges and lemons', Charles Dickens, *A Christmas Carol* (1844). Norfolk folk had a particular method of preserving the apples, which consisted of putting them, whole and unpeeled, in a warm oven and packing them down as they dried into flat wrinkled rounds—also called 'biffins'.

bigarade The French term for the Spanish bitter orange. Its familiarity as an international culinary term comes from *sauce bigarade*, an orange sauce served with duck (which nowadays is actually made with sweet rather than bitter oranges).

Big Mac *See* MAC.

bigoli In the Veneto in northeastern Italy, the name of a type of pasta in the form of long strands, 'like thick spaghetti with a rough-textured surface' (Caz Hildebrand and Jacob Kenedy, *The Geometry of Pasta* (2010)). The word may be related to Provençal *bigo* 'long thin beam'.

bigos Bigos is the Polish national dish. It is a stew made from alternate layers of sauerkraut and meat. Its name may be an adaptation of German *beigoss* 'sauce'.

bilberry Bilberries are the small purplish-blue berries of a bush (*Vaccinium myrtillus*) of the heath family. They are used for making tarts, flans, sorbets, etc. The name is probably of Scandinavian origin: Danish has the related *bøllebaer* 'bilberry', of which the first element seems to represent Danish *bolle* 'ball, round roll'. Alternative names for it include *whortleberry*, (in Scotland and northern England) *blaeberry*, and (in North America) *huckleberry*. In French the bilberry is known as the *myrtille* or *airelle*.

billi-bi A soup made from mussel stock with the addition of white wine and cream, very similar to the French mouclade. The term is said to come from the nickname of William B. Leeds Sr (1861–1908), an American in Paris for whom the dish was supposedly invented at Maxim's restaurant. An alternative account, however, has the dedicatee as one William Brand.

biltong Strips of lean meat salted and dried in the sun and carried as iron rations by trekkers in the South African veldt. Unappetizing but sustaining, it is made from any hunted animal that comes to hand, from buffalo to ostrich. The word is an Afrikaans compound, meaning literally 'buttocktongue': 'buttock' because originally made mainly from the animal's hindquarters, 'tongue' because of its supposed resemblance, in either appearance or taste, to cooked tongue.

Bing cherry A large, dark red variety of cherry, now the most widely grown sweet cherry in the US. It was developed in the early 1870s by the Oregon fruit-grower Seth Lewelling, and he named it after his Chinese orchard foreman Ah Bing, who may well have had a hand in creating it.

bird pepper A type of capsicum that has small, extremely hot red fruits. The name (first recorded in 1696) is said to have been inspired by the shape of the chilli when dried, curved like a bird's beak. An alternative term is *bird's eye chilli*.

bird's eye chilli *Bird's eye chilli*, or *bird's eye pepper*, is an alternative name for the bird pepper. According to Roger Owen in the *Oxford Companion to Food* (2006), it reflects the fact that the chillis 'are as small, vivid, and sharp as the eye of a bird'.

bird's nest soup A classic Chinese soup made from the gelatinous nests of various species of southern Asian swifts, combined generally with a chicken stock. Its Cantonese name is *ghuy yoong yien wan* (in Mandarin *ji yen wo tang*).

biriani A biriani, or *biryani*, is a highly spiced Indian rice dish flavoured with saffron and layered with meat, such as lamb or chicken. It is a festive dish, served on special occasions and sometimes garnished with silver leaf. The word is of Urdu origin. Urdu got it from Persian *biryāni*, a derivative of *biriyān* 'fried, grilled'.

biscuit Etymologically, *biscuit* means 'twice-cooked'. It comes, via Old French *bescoit* or *biscut*, from a hypothetical Latin adjective **biscoctus* (*coctus* was the past participle of *coquere* 'to cook', and turns up again in English *concoct*). Until the eighteenth century it was usually spelled as it was pronounced in English, *bisket*; only in the 1700s was the French spelling *biscuit* introduced.

Its name reflects the way in which it was once made. The original biscuit was a small flat cake made of wheat flour, sugar, egg yolks, and perhaps a little yeast. It was intended for long keeping, so to dry it out it was returned to the oven for a while after the initial cooking process had finished.

Until the late seventeenth century, biscuits were often called *biscuit bread*. This was a particularly appropriate term for the more heavily leavened variety, which were first baked in long rolls, then sliced up into rounds and dried out. The result was more like rusks than present-day biscuits.

The modern biscuit, in its myriad guises, is essentially a product of the nineteenth century. Mechanization enabled vast numbers to be produced at very low cost, and by the 1930s the biscuit had become a key item in the British diet. The ideal convenience food, portable and easily consumed, biscuits have established themselves as the archetypal partner to a cup of tea.

This in Britain; but in the US the story is very different. To a speaker of American English, the British sweet biscuit is a *cookie*; the word *biscuit* is reserved for dry savoury biscuits, and in particular for a completely distinct animal: a sort of flat round unsweetened cake, rather like a scone, popular especially in the South as an accompaniment to, for example, chicken.

The colloquial abbreviation *bicky* first appeared in the 1930s. On *take the biscuit*, *see* CAKE.

bishop A drink of mulled, spiced port apparently popular with undergraduates at Oxford and Cambridge in the eighteenth and nineteenth centuries. Boswell reports that Dr Johnson was very partial to it too. The first reference to it occurs in Jonathan Swift's *Women Who Cry Oranges* (1738), in which he gives a recipe: 'Fine oranges, well roasted, with sugar and spice in a cup, they'll make a sweet Bishop when gentlefolks sup.' An orange studded with cloves is a key element in the brew.

bishop's weed A name applied over the centuries to a variety of umbelliferous plants, perhaps most notably ground elder. In modern culinary contexts, it sometimes appears as a synonym of *ajwain*.

Bismarck herring A herring that has been pickled in vinegar with onion rings and other seasonings. The recipe originated with Johann Wiechmann, a brewer, trader, and fish-cannery owner of Stralsund, a port on the Baltic coast of northeastern Germany, or rather with his wife, who seems to have devised it in the 1850s. He was an admirer of the German chancellor Otto von Bismarck (1815–98), and would send him barrels of the herrings for his birthday. On the occasion of the founding of the German Empire in 1871 he asked for permission to name the fish after his hero, and the request was graciously granted.

bisque A thick rich soup, usually containing crustaceans such as lobsters, crabs, and crayfish. The word was originally borrowed into English from French as *bisk* in the mid-seventeenth century, at which time it still retained an early application, since lost, to 'soup made from poultry or game birds, particularly pigeons'. It is not clear where the word came from, although some have linked it with the Spanish province of Biscay.

Bisto The proprietary name of a British brand of gravy-browning and -thickening powder or, latterly, granules. It was first produced in 1908, by Cerebos Ltd. Its name is often said to have been concocted from the initial letters of *Browns Seasons and Thickens in One*, but there is no evidence to substantiate that, and it seems more likely to have been an arbitrary coinage. Bisto no doubt owed a significant part of its success to an inspired marketing creation, the 'Bisto Kids'. This pair, a bedraggled but friendly looking boy and girl, dreamed up in 1919 by cartoonist Wilf Owen, appeared in innumerable advertisements sniffing ecstatically at the aromas wafting from pot or plate and murmuring 'Ah, Bisto!'

bitter The traditional bitter beer of England gets its sharp taste from the addition of hops (*see* BEER). But the use of the noun *bitter* as a name for it seems to be by no means so traditional. In fact, the first unequivocal example of it is recorded as recently as the 1890s: 'a dozen pots of beer and a few glasses of bitter', George Moore, *Esther Waters* (1894).

bitter gourd A plant of the gourd family whose fruit resembles a hysterically knobbly cucumber. It is widely used in India (where it probably originated) and Southeast Asia as a vegetable. It is also called *bitter cucumber, bitter melon,* and, in India, *karela*.

bitters A bitters is a bitter-tasting highly concentrated alcoholic drink, used particularly for pepping up mixed drinks. Bitters can be made from fruit, but the better known sort are based on assorted herbs, roots, etc.: these include Angostura, Fernet Branca, and Underberg. The term *bitters* is first recorded in the early eighteenth century.

black and tan A drink consisting of half stout ('black') and half bitter beer ('tan'). The expression seems to have originated in the mid-nineteenth century as a term for a kind of terrier with black and yellowish-brown markings, but its use for the drink is first recorded in the 1880s. In the 1920s it was also applied to auxiliary members of the Royal Irish Constabulary recruited to suppress nationalist uprisings, who wore black and khaki uniforms.

black bean In East and Southeast Asian cookery, a soya bean that has been fermented and salted, softening it, and giving it a sharp pungent flavour. The beans can be standard soya or a black-skinned variety: if the former, the preservation process turns them black anyway. They are used as the basis of black bean sauce. *Black bean* is also the name of a black-skinned dried haricot bean widely used in Central and South America and in the southern states of the US to make black bean soup.

blackberry The very dark purple or black fruit of the bramble. Its name dates back to the Old English period. On the culinary distinction between the words *blackberry* and *bramble*, *see* BRAMBLE.

The BlackBerry range of smartphones, developed by the Canadian company RIM, first saw the light of day in 1999. The original idea for the trademarked name was 'Strawberry', said to have been inspired by a perceived resemblance of the phone's miniature buttons to the seeds on a strawberry. However, the idea of 'straw' was felt to be not cool enough. Someone suggested 'Blackberry' as an alternative, and the rest is history.

black bread Bread made from wholemeal rye flour. In its natural state it is more of a dark greyish-brown, but artificial colouring matter can be added to bring it closer to its name (which is first recorded in 1863).

black bun A traditional Scottish cake eaten at Hogmanay. It consists of a dark Christmas-pudding-like mixture of fruit and spices that is wrapped in a pastry crust and baked. The actual term *black bun* is not recorded before 1898, but recipes for what is essentially the same thing can be found from the early years of the nineteenth century, under the name *Scotch bun* and *Scotch Christmas bun*. *The Oxford Companion to Food* (2006) suggests that it was after Robert Louis Stevenson described the bun as 'a black substance inimical to life' that the name *black bun* came into use.

black butter The term *black butter*, a translation of French *beurre noir*, denotes a sauce consisting of butter fried until it turns a dark brown colour and then flavoured with a little vinegar, and sometimes capers. It is traditionally served with skate. It was sufficiently well known in the nineteenth century for Mrs Beeton to give a recipe for it in her *Book of*

Household Management (1861), although she called it *browned butter*, and described it as 'a French sauce'.

Earlier, the term seems to have been used as a synonym for *apple butter*, a sort of thick apple purée: in a letter of Jane Austen's dated 27 December 1808 we read 'Our black butter was neither solid nor entirely sweet . . . Miss Austen had said she did not think it had been boiled enough.'

In Cornwall, edible seaweed is known as *black butter*.

blackcurrant A variety of currant with black berries, widely used for making jams, syrups, and liqueurs (the latter the key component of kir). Its high vitamin C content is a main selling point for the commercial blackcurrant cordial brand known as Ribena (from the fruit's genus name *Ribes*). When blackcurrant cordial is mixed with an alcoholic drink it is often referred to colloquially as *black* (as in 'lager and black'). The fruit is not to everyone's taste: Jane Grigson in her *Fruit Book* (1982) notes that 'one French writer in 1722 wrote that black currants had a savour of bed bugs'.

black-eyed pea Black-eyed peas, or *black-eyed beans* as they are also called, are the seeds of a plant of the pea family, which are creamy-white in colour with a black mark on one edge. As their Latin name *Vigna sinensis* suggests, they originated in China, and are still widely used there for food, but they are now particularly associated with the southern states of the US. They were probably first planted there in the late eighteenth century (George Washington in his diaries mentions the 'small black eyed pea', which is presumably the same vegetable), and were much used as a forage plant (hence their alternative name *cowpea*, from their being fed to cattle) and as green manure. It is for their role in the soul food of the Deep South that they are best known now, though, and especially for their partnership with salt pork and tabasco.

The American pop group the Black-Eyed Peas was formed in 1995.

Black Forest gâteau Black Forest gâteau—in German *Schwarzwälder Kirschtorte*, 'Black Forest cherry-cake'—is a baroque confection based on chocolate sponge and decorated with whipped cream, cherries, and chocolate curlicues.

black pudding A sausage (*see* PUDDING) made from pig's blood with some thickening agent, such as cereal, and spices. Its name—a reference to the darkened colour of the cooked blood—is of long standing (in 1568 we find in Ulpian Fulwell's *Like to Like*, 'Who comes yonder puffing as hot as a black pudding?'). The synonymous *blood pudding* is equally ancient, but nowadays much less usual.

In England, the Midlands and the North are the great areas of black pudding appreciation; Bury in Lancashire is often claimed as the black pudding capital. But black puddings form an essential part of the basic peasant cuisine of many other European countries. In France, where they are known as *boudins noirs*, or simply *boudins*, they are usually lighter, less stodgy than the British variety, being made with pork fat, onions, and cream rather than cereal. An especially large version, made on special occasions using the pig's entire large intestine, is called a *gogue*. Elsewhere in Europe a black pudding is a *blutwurst* (Germany) or a *kashanka* (Poland). *Compare* WHITE PUDDING.

blackstrap The term *blackstrap* seems originally to have been applied, in the mid-eighteenth century, to an inferior type of port—harsh, overalcoholic, and oversweet, and impenetrably dark and viscous. Then, in the nineteenth century, a new application came along—to a beverage made from rum and molasses, with or without water. This also became known as *black stripe*. Neither usage is much met with nowadays, although the word is used of a type of molasses that remains after maximum extraction of sugar in processing.

black tea Tea that is fully fermented, giving the oxidized leaves a dark colour, before it is dried. It comes in numerous varieties, including bohea, congou, lapsang souchong, and pekoe, and is the tea that is found in ordinary everyday teabags. As a term *black tea,* first recorded in 1785, contrasts explicitly with *green tea* and *oolong*. It is also used to refer to tea served without milk.

black velvet A drink made from equal proportions of champagne and Guinness or other stout. It is said to have been invented in 1861 by a steward at Brooks's Club in St James's Street, London, in honour of the recently deceased Prince Albert. The Victorians were much attached to mourning black, so it would have been quite in keeping for them to apply the treatment to champagne, but there is no evidence of the name in print before the 1920s. It was clearly always a smart drink: 'Alastair had never come nearer to military service than in being senior private in the Corps at Eton. . . . It came as a shock to him now to find his country at war and himself in pyjamas, spending his normal Sunday noon with a jug of Black Velvet and some chance visitors. . . . Alastair came in from the bathroom. "How's the art tart?" He opened bottles and began mixing stout and champagne in a deep jug. "Blackers?" They had always drunk this sour and invigorating draught', Evelyn Waugh, *Put Out More Flags* (1942).

blaeberry A Scottish and northern English term for the bilberry, the small purplish-blue berry of a bush of the heath family. *Blae*, which in Scottish English means 'blue', comes from Old Norse *blár*.

blanc de blancs *Blanc de blancs,* literally 'white of whites', is a French term denoting white wine made from white grapes. And in case that sounds like a tautology, some white wine (and particularly champagne, to which the term is most familiarly applied) is made from red grapes: the pressed juice is not allowed to come into contact with the skins, and so no red pigment finds its way into the wine. In the case of champagne, the standard wine is a blend of juice from the pinot noir (a red grape) and the chardonnay (a white grape), but *blanc de blancs* champagne is made only from the chardonnay grape. Areas of France which make a still *blanc de blancs* include Provence, Béarn, and Limoux.

blancmange Blancmange has not always been the palely wobbling thing which until recently lurked behind jellies on Britain's tea tables. When the word first entered the English language, in the fourteenth century, it was used for a savoury dish. As its name implies (French *blanc* 'white', *manger* 'to eat'—the final *r* did not disappear until the nineteenth century) it was made from pale ingredients. Almonds, in some form or other—ground, fried, or as almond milk—were usually included, as was rice, either whole or as rice flour; these formed the basis of a thick gruel or pottage, to which was added chicken meat. The recipe is an ancient one: the Roman gourmet Apicius's *cibarium album* (again literally 'white eating') is essentially the same, although the direct antecedent of the blancmange eaten in the courts of medieval Europe was probably Arabic.

  The transformation of the chicken dish of the Middle Ages into the modern confection was a gradual one. Often the chicken was omitted, and a gelling agent added. By the eighteenth century it had become a sort of almond jelly, made with milk or cream. In the nineteenth century arrowroot was introduced into the recipe as a thickener, with flavourings such as lemon peel and cinnamon making it an appropriate dessert dish. This paved the way for the modern commercial cornflour-based version, which, in guises such as pink rabbits and chocolate-coloured castles (but scarcely ever, ironically, plain white), remained a mainstay among British puddings until the 1960s, when instant pre-prepared desserts started its demise.

A companion dish, popular in the nineteenth century, was *jaunemange* or *jaumange*, made with the addition of lemon juice and rind (French *jaune* 'yellow'). An alternative name for it was *Dutch flummery*.

blanquette In French cuisine, a blanquette is a stew of a white meat in a white sauce. Poultry and even lamb can be used for it, but its commonest main ingredient is veal (in French, *blanquette de veau*); Hannah Glasse introduced it to the British in her *Art of Cookery* (1747): 'Veal Blanquets. Roast a Piece of Veal . . . cut it into little thin Bits . . . put in some good Broth. . . . Keep it stirring.' Its name, which is virtually self-explanatory, is a derivative of French *blanc* 'white', and indeed it is virtually the same word as English *blanket*, which originally denoted a 'white or undyed woollen cloth'.

Blenheim Orange A type of eating apple with dull yellow and red skin. The original seedling was found near Blenheim Palace in Oxfordshire around 1740, whence its (eventual) name. It was raised by a local man by the name of George Kempster, and at first was known as *Kempster's Pippin*; the term *Blenheim Orange* is not recorded before 1862.

blini Blinis are small thick Russian pancakes made with buckwheat flour. They are usually served with salt herring, caviare, or smoked salmon, and sour cream and melted butter. *Blin* is Russian for 'pancake', but its plural, *blini*, has generally been taken in English as a singular form, and a new plural *blinis* has been created. *See also* BLINTZE.

blintze In Yiddish cuisine, blintzes are small thin pancakes that are folded round some such filling as cream cheese, mashed potato, or fruit. The word was borrowed into Yiddish from Russian *blinets*, a diminutive form of *blin* 'pancake' (*see* BLINI).

bloater The bloater was originally called the *bloat herring* (Samuel Pepys records in his diary for 5 October 1661: 'To the Dolphin, and there eat some bloat herrings'), and the originally colloquial form *bloater* did not appear until the early nineteenth century. It is a whole herring which is salted and then lightly cold-smoked (in contrast to red herrings, which are heavily smoked, and bucklings, which are hot-smoked). The precise derivation of *bloat* is not clear, although it is probably of Scandinavian origin: Old Norse had the expression *blautr fisk*, literally 'soft fish', which was applied to fresh rather than preserved fish, and Swedish has the parallel *blotr fisk*, meaning 'soaked fish', and so it has been conjectured that the term refers either to the fact that the preserved bloater is still moist (as opposed to the dried red herring), or to part of the process of preserving the fish, which in earlier centuries included steeping them in brine (they are now usually dry-salted). A further possibility is that it means simply a bloated—that is, 'swollen'—herring, since bloaters are much plumper than dry-cured fish, and 'soft, flabby' is not far removed semantically from 'puffy, swollen'; it may be no coincidence that the French word for a similarly cured herring is *bouffi*, literally 'swollen'.

blondie The pale cousin of the brownie. The same basic recipe is followed, but without the chocolate (although chocolate chips are usually added, either white or milk chocolate).

blood orange A variety of sweet orange with red or red-tinged flesh. The name is first recorded in 1855 (in Eliza Acton's *Modern Cookery for Private Families*), superseding the somewhat earlier *blood-red orange*.

Bloody Mary A cocktail made essentially of tomato juice and vodka, usually with the addition of a dash of Worcester sauce. It is said (by himself) to have been invented by a barman called Pete Petiot while he was working at Harry's New York Bar in Paris in 1921. The term *Bloody Mary*, however, is not recorded in print before 1947. It presumably comes, with reference to the drink's colour, from the nickname of Queen Mary I of England (1516–58), an enthusiastic executor of her Protestant opponents. A vodka-free version of the drink is known as a *Virgin Mary*. Replace the vodka with tequila and it becomes a *Bloody Maria*.

bloomer A long round white loaf with diagonal slashes across its top. Its linguistic history is obscure: there is no record of the term *bloomer* in print before 1937, and its derivation has never been determined for certain. The likeliest explanation is that, either before or after baking, the loaf expands, or 'blooms'—a reference perhaps to the widening of the slashes across the top, or to the fact that since the bloomer is not baked in a tin, it is free to expand in any direction it likes. In her *English Bread and Yeast Cookery* (1977), however, Elizabeth David puts forward several other theories, among them that *bloomer* refers to the 'bloom' or sheen on bread made from high-quality flour, and that it derives from a completely unrelated word *bloom*, meaning 'ingot of metal', on the basis of the loaf's shape.

BLT The abbreviated name by which a bacon, lettuce, and tomato sandwich is generally known. It originated in the US, probably in the early 1940s. The earliest known reference to it in print is in a 1952 issue of the journal *American Speech*, which reported a sighting of it in 1949. Jack Smiley, in his *Hash House Lingo* (1941), had described what is clearly the same sandwich, but called it, presumably by an oversight, a 'BMT'.

blueberry Blueberries are the purplish-blue fruit of various North American shrubs of the heath family (to which the wild European bilberry also belongs). They are used in pies, jams, and flummeries and on cheesecakes, or simply eaten raw.

Blue Vinny Blue Vinny is the yeti of the cheese world. A very firm white cheese, said to have been made in Dorset for many centuries from partly skimmed cows' milk, and marbled with veins of blue mould induced, according to tradition, by immersing bacteria-rich old harnesses in the milk, it certainly existed in the past (the first record of it is in William Barnes's *Glossary of the Dorset Dialect* (1863)). However, cheese buffs trying to hunt it down in the twentieth century have repeatedly failed to find it, and considerable doubts have been cast on whether cheeses that have turned up labelled 'Blue Vinny' in the shops are the genuine article. The word *vinny* is a descendant of Old English *fyne* 'mould'.

blush wine *See* ROSÉ.

bobby bean An alternative name for the FRENCH BEAN.

bobby veal *Bobby veal,* and the now apparently obsolete *bob veal,* are terms applied originally (in mid-nineteenth-century America) to veal from very young calves, specifically from unweaned calves slaughtered just after birth. They probably derive from *bob* in the sense 'cut short' (as in *bob* the haircut and *bobtail*); *bobby* itself is on record as being applied dialectally to the wren, on account of its short tail. Another connection, though, could be with dialect *staggering bob*, recorded from the late eighteenth century, which denotes a calf too young to walk steadily; there, *bob* may be a pet form of *Robert*. In more recent years the term has been used for veal from free-range calves (as opposed to calves that have been confined in 'crates'), but this usage too is now disappearing in favour of the marketing men's *rose veal*.

bobotie A South African dish consisting of minced beef or lamb blended with spices and other ingredients (such as rice or fruit) and baked under an egg-and-milk sauce topping. The word (stressed on the second syllable) is Afrikaans, and was probably adopted from Malay or Javanese. It is first recorded in 1870.

bock A rich strong type of German beer, typically dark in colour. *Bock* is short for *bockbier*, which in turn is an abbreviated version of *Eimbockbier*. This is an antique form of what in modern German is *Einbecker bier*, literally 'beer from Einbeck', a town in Hanover.

bohea The history of bohea tea (pronounced /bo'hee/) is a sad one. Originally it was one of the highest and most sought-after grades of black China tea (Richard Estcourt wrote in *The Fair Example* (1706) 'To dine at my Lord Mayor's, and after dinner be entertain'd with a dish of Bohea by my Lady Mayoress'), but by the nineteenth century the term was being used to designate the lowest-quality tea, made from the season's last crop of leaves ('the unsophisticated cup of bohea', Leigh Hunt, *The Seer* (1841)), and nowadays it has passed out of common usage. It comes from *Bu-i*, the name in the Fujian dialect for a range of hills in the north of the Fujian province of China (*Wu-i* in Cantonese) where such tea is grown.

boiled dinner Boiled dinner is roughly the North American equivalent of the French pot-au-feu: a dish of meat and vegetables simmered long and slow in a large pot. The usual meat ingredient, particularly in the celebrated 'New England boiled dinner', is a salted brisket of beef (known as 'corned beef' in American English). The earliest known reference to the term, in *Pocumtuc Housewife* (1805), shows that it was already a familiar dish: 'Directions for a Boiled Dinner may seem unnecessary.'

bok choy A variant form, used especially in American English, of PAK CHOI.

bollito misto Italian *bollito misto* means literally 'boiled mixed'. It denotes a dish consisting of a range of meats (the full list comprises a piece of beef, a shoulder of veal, a chicken, an ox tongue, half a calf's head, and a cotechino sausage) boiled in a large pot with vegetables. When served in restaurants, it is often wheeled around ceremoniously on a special trolley, with each type of meat in separate compartments, and assembled at the table. Its classic accompaniment is salsa verde.

bologna *See* POLONY.

bomba rice A Spanish variety of short-grain rice, used especially for paella. It is grown mainly in the Calasparra region of Murcia, in southeastern Spain.

Bombay duck The Bombay duck is a famous gastronomic red herring. It is not a duck at all, but a fish: an Indian fish (Latin name *Harpodon nehereus*) that is generally dried and eaten as a savoury with curry. The first element of its name is an alteration of *bombila*, which comes from the Marathi term for the fish, *bombīla*, presumably influenced by *Bombay*, a centre from which it was exported. The *duck* element remains a mystery, although some have speculated that it comes from the way the fish skim the surface of the water, like ducks. The name is first recorded in English in 1860.

An alternative term for the fish is *bumalo*, which also comes ultimately from Marathi *bombīla*.

Bombay mix The British name of a traditional Indian snack which in Hindi is called *chevda* or *chiwda*. It consists of a salted, mildly spicy mixture of dry ingredients including peanuts, gram-flour noodles, and fried lentils and chickpeas. It takes its name from the city and port of Bombay (since 1995 Mumbai) on the west coast of India, although its consumption is by no means restricted to that area. In the US it is generally known as *Punjabi mix*.

bombe The classic bombe, or more fully *bombe glacée* in French, is a hemispherical frozen dessert made from two separate contrasting layers of ice cream. It gets its name from its shape, which originally was more nearly spherical, reminiscent of the cannon-ball-like bombs (French *bombe*) of nineteenth-century anarchists. The word has not always been used for ice cream, however: the *Daily Chronicle* (1902) gave a recipe for a 'fish bombe', made in a cup-shaped mould with 'any kind of cooked white fish'.

bonbon A French word for 'sweet', *bonbon* was taken up by English towards the end of the eighteenth century ('Clarendel, lounging upon a chair in the middle of the shop, sat eating bon bons,' Mme D'Arblay, *Camilla* (1796)), and probably reached its heyday as a more delicate alternative to the foursquare *sweet* in the late Victorian and Edwardian eras, when bonbonnières (small decorated boxes for holding sweets) graced fashionable sideboards and tables. Nowadays the term is usually reserved specifically for soft sweets consisting of a fondant- or chocolate-coated fondant centre, often containing nuts, dried fruits, etc. *Bonbon* was originally a French nursery term, a reduplication of *bon* 'good', and hence is virtually the equivalent of English *goodie-goodie*.

bonne femme French *à la bonne femme* means 'in the style of a good housewife'. It is used to designate a wide range of recipes, mostly for fish dishes, stews, and soups, the common denominator of which is a relatively simple or even rustic method of cooking. Its most familiar application is *sole bonne femme,* in which the sole is cooked in a mixture of white wine and fish stock, to which chopped shallots and mushrooms have been added. The term has been used in English since at least the early nineteenth century: 'There was a goodly "soupe à la bonne femme"', Byron, *Don Juan* (1824).

bonnyclabber An Anglo-Irish term for a drink made by allowing milk to sour and coagulate. John Reader in his *The Untold History of the Potato* (2009) quotes a description of it as a delectable drink 'of very thick milk, . . . of yellow bubbling milk, the swallowing of which needs chewing'. The word is an Anglicization of Irish Gaelic *bainne clabair* 'thick milk'.

borage A plant of the forget-me-not family, borage is valued culinarily mainly for its vivid blue star-shaped flowers, which are used to decorate salads, and its cucumber-flavoured leaves, a common garnish for drinks such as Pimm's and cold punches. Its name may be of Arabic origin; it comes via Old French *bourrache* from medieval Latin *borrāgo*, which was perhaps adapted from Arabic *abū ʿāraq*, literally 'father of sweat' (borage was used by Arabic physicians to induce perspiration).

bordelaise *Sauce bordelaise*, in French literally 'Bordeaux sauce', is made by cooking chopped onions or shallots in a red wine reduction, then adding sauce espagnole (*see* BROWN SAUCE) and stock. It is served with roast meat.

borecole An alternative name, now rarely used, for 'kale', a vegetable of the cabbage family. It was borrowed in the early eighteenth century from Dutch *boerenkool*, which means literally 'peasant's cabbage'. The element *-cole* is of course the same word as *kale*, and it is also represented in the *caul-* of *cauliflower* and the *cole-* of *coleslaw*. Its ancestor was Latin *caulis* 'cabbage'.

börek A Turkish hors d'oeuvre consisting of small filo pastries filled with a spiced mixture of either feta cheese or minced meat. They are mainly made in either triangles or cigarette shapes (*sigara börek*).

borlotti beans Borlotti beans are among the most commonly used dried beans in Italy. Also known as *roso coco* beans, they are pinkish in colour with crimson speckles and streaks. Their name is probably a derivative of the northern Italian dialect base *borl-*, denoting something large and round.

borscht Borscht, variously spelled *borsch, borsht, borshch*, and even *botsch* since its introduction into Britain in the late nineteenth century, is a Russian and Polish beetroot soup (*borshch* comes closest to transcribing the Russian spelling, while the Polish form is actually *barszcz*—which not surprisingly has never caught on in English). Based on a meat stock and often containing other vegetables, especially cabbage, it is beetroot that is its defining ingredient, giving it its red colour. That this was not always so, however, is evident from its name: Russian *borshch* (a distant relative of English *bristle*) means literally 'cow parsnip', a plant of the carrot family which was the soup's original base.

The *borscht circuit* is a name given by American singers, comedians, etc. to the summer resort hotels of the Catskill mountains in New York state, whose cabarets were popular with their predominantly Jewish patrons.

Boston bean An alternative name for the HARICOT BEAN.

Boston cream pie A type of American sponge cake that has a custard or cream filling and typically a chocolate topping. The term is first recorded in 1855.

Boston strawberries A colloquial term in American English for baked beans, traditionally a popular item in the diet of Bostonians (Boston has the nickname 'Bean Town').

botargo A relish made from the roe of a tuna or red mullet. Hard to find on modern British supermarket shelves (although *boutargue* and *buttarga* are freely available in France and Italy respectively), it was once very popular in this country: on 5 June 1661 Samuel Pepys notes in his diary 'Drinking great draughts of claret, and eating botargo, and bread and butter'; and in 1730 Jonathan Swift mentions it in his *Panegyric on Dean*: 'And, for our home-bred British Cheer, Botargo, Catsup, and Caveer [caviare].' It has an adventurous linguistic history. English acquired it from Italian (it is first mentioned in English in *Epulario, or, the Italian Banquet* (1598)). The Italians borrowed it from Arabic *butarkhah*, which had in turn come from *outaraknon*, a word in the Coptic language of Egypt. Broken down into its constituent parts, this represented the definite article *ou* 'the' and *taríkhion*, a Greek word for 'pickle' (*see* TRACKLEMENTS).

boudoir biscuit A long, finger-shaped sponge biscuit with a crystallized sugar topping, used particularly as ballast in the making of fruity cream desserts: 'strawberry tiramisu with jelly and boudoir biscuits', *Time Out, London's Best Restaurants* (2011). A classic role is in forming the casing for a charlotte russe. The term originated in French, probably with reference to ladies consuming the biscuits in the privacy of their boudoirs. It has now largely taken the place of the earlier *Savoy biscuit*. An alternative name for such biscuits, particularly in American English, is *ladyfinger*.

bouillabaisse The classic Provençal fish stew, a speciality particularly of Marseilles, but made the length of the French Mediterranean coast. As with many traditional French dishes, its precise list of ingredients is a matter of often heated controversy, with different parties insisting on their own particular selection of fish. The one common denominator is the rascasse, a small unprepossessing Mediterranean scorpion-fish, *Scorpaena scrofa*, with red skin and dangerous spines; other commonly used species include sea bass, bonito, conger eel, John Dory, monkfish, gurnard, and crab. The fish is cooked briefly in fish stock with olive oil, assorted vegetables, including tomatoes, and herbs, notably saffron. Even the serving of bouillabaisse has an element of controversy. Traditionally the broth is served separately, as a soup, poured over slices of bread, followed by the fish as a distinct course, but often enough one finds that both fish and broth are brought to table in the same bowl.

The word *bouillabaisse* is a French version of Provençal *bouiabaisso*, literally 'boil and settle'—supposedly what the cook says to the cooking pot, which needs to boil for only a short period.

bouillon The stock produced by cooking a chicken, joint of meat, etc. in water. It is often used as a soup. The word is French, of course, a derivative of *bouillir* 'to boil', and in present-day English is commoner in America (where stock cubes are known as *bouillon cubes*) than in Britain.

boulangère Dishes (typically of lamb) described as *à la boulangère* are baked in the oven with an accompaniment of sliced potatoes and onions. The name, in French literally 'in the style of the baker's wife', reveals the source of the recipe, from the days when villagers would take dishes along to the baker's to have them cooked in the oven once the last batch of bread had been finished. The term is also applied simply to the potatoes themselves, oven-baked with onions: 'Meat-lovers . . . are also catered for with dishes such as a rump of lamb with garlic, anchovies, capers, and boulangère potatoes', *Good Food Guide* (2008). (In French the baker (*boulanger*) himself also lends his name to the dish (as in *gratin de pommes de terre boulanger*).)

boulette A French term meaning literally 'little ball', which is applied to a fairly whiffy soft cheese that is made in Belgium and French Flanders. It is produced in a variety of shapes—cylindrical, spherical, and conical—and generally coated with herbs and spices or a covering of leaves. The best known is the red-rinded *boulette d'Avesnes* (Avesnes is in French Flanders).

bouquet garni A bouquet garni (it means literally 'garnished bouquet') is a selection of herbs and other flavoursome plants tied in a bundle and added for flavouring to soups, stews, etc. while they are cooking. The precise composition of the bouquet varies according to the dish it is to be used with and what is available, but standard components include parsley, thyme, and bay, and a leek and a stick of celery are often also included. To the horror of traditionalists, powdered bouquet garni herbs can now be bought in little ready-to-use paper sachets, like teabags.

bourbon The term *bourbon* (pronounced /ˈbɜːbən/), which dates back to the mid-nineteenth century, denotes American whiskey distilled from a mash that contains at least 51 per cent maize (to qualify for the designation *corn whiskey* the maize content must be at least 80 per cent). The term comes from Bourbon county, Kentucky, a major centre of whiskey production in the US. For those who do not take it neat, a popular local tipple in the Deep South is *bourbon and branch water* 'whiskey and water' (*branch* here meaning 'stream').

Bourbon biscuit An oblong chocolate-flavoured sweet biscuit with a chocolate-cream filling It was originally produced in 1910 by the company Peek Frean, under the name *Creola*. This was later changed to *Bourbon*, presumably in unexplained honour of the ancient seigniory of Bourbon, from which came the dynasty that ruled France from 1272 to 1792.

bourride A fish stew or soup made along the French Riviera from a variety of white fish. After the fish is cooked, the broth is strained, mixed with aïoli, and served as a pale yellow soup, with the fish itself following as a separate course.

Boursin The proprietary name of a brand of soft white French cows'-milk cheese, available in varieties flavoured with garlic and herbs and with black pepper. It was launched in 1957 by François Boursin.

Bovril The proprietary name of a brand of concentrated beef essence developed in the 1880s by the Scottish industrialist John Lawson Johnston. It appears to have been coined in 1889, based on Latin *bōs, bovis*, 'cow, ox' and probably *vril*, the name of an imaginary form of energy invented by Edward Bulwer-Lytton for his novel *The Coming Race* (1871), presumably with intentional echoes of Latin *virilis* 'manly'. Bovril, which is used as the basis of hot drinks and in cookery, achieved considerable popularity during the first half of the twentieth century, notably as a quick and convenient source of nourishment to civilians and service personnel alike during the two world wars.

In the early twentieth century the association of Bovril with the concept of concentration led to the coining of the verb *bovrilize*, meaning 'to condense': 'Here is one of these "bovrilised" announcements..: "Wanted, Sit. as Comp. by Eng. Lady, 35; good Fr.; good refs.; would trav. R.R., 100", *Daily News* (1901).

During the 1930s and 1940s *bovril* was used as a euphemism for 'brothel': 'I had to take a job as a sort of dancing partner, and the place was practically a bovril', Rodney Ackland, *After October* (1936). And today the word is used colloquially in the waste-disposal trade for a 'ship which dumps sewage sludge in the open sea'.

boxty A type of Irish potato bread made with grated raw potato, mashed potato, and flour. The dough is formed into a circle, quartered and baked on a griddle (*compare* FARL). It is usually served as an accompaniment to meat. Its name comes from Irish Gaelic *bacstaí*, which has been variously derived from *arán bocht ti* 'poor house bread' and *bacús*, denoting something used for baking, such as an oven or griddle.

boysenberry A hybrid fruit which is a cross between the loganberry and various blackberries and raspberries. It is named after Rudolph Boysen, the twentieth-century American horticulturist who developed it.

bramble The bush on which the wild blackberry grows. Culinarily, a curious distinction in usage has grown up around it: when the fruit is used in pies, crumbles, tarts, etc. it is known as a 'blackberry', but make it into a jelly—of the sort spread on bread and butter, that is—and it becomes 'bramble'.

Bramley The Bramley, or in full *Bramley's Seedling*, is a large green-skinned cooking apple. It gets its name from Matthew Bramley, a butcher, in whose garden in Southwell, Nottinghamshire it is said to have been first grown, around 1850.

branch water An American term (first recorded in 1835) for plain water, as used for diluting spirits. Thus, a bourbon and branch water is (or rather was: the usage is no longer common) bourbon whiskey mixed with water (rather than with soda). The underlying idea is of water from a small clear stream or creek, for which *branch* is a US dialectal term.

brandade A brandade (or in full *brandade de morue* 'cod brandade') is a Provençal dish consisting at its most basic of salt cod mixed into a purée with olive oil and milk. In some versions garlic is added, and even potatoes. The word *brandade* is a derivative of the Provençal verb *brandar* 'to stir' (equivalent to French *brander* 'to tremble'), which in turn was formed from Provençal *bran* 'sword'—a reference to the long stirring with a wooden spatula which is historically a major feature of the making of brandade.

brandy A spirit distilled from the fermented juice of the grape or other fruit. It was the distillation part of this process that gave it its name. The wine is heated, or 'burnt', to separate out the alcohol, and so the Dutch called it *brandewijn*, literally 'burnt wine'. English borrowed the word in the early seventeenth century as *brandewine* or *brandwine*, but by the middle of the century this was already being altered to *brandy wine*, and the first recorded use of *brandy* on its own comes from as early as 1657 ('The late Dutch War occasioned the bringing in of such superfluity of brandy,' Samuel Colvil, *Whiggs Supplication*). The eighteenth century was the great age of brandy smuggling in England, when huge quantities were slipped ashore from France to satisfy the thirst of the middle and upper classes ('Brandy for the Parson, Baccy for the Clerk,' as Kipling wrote); the lower orders preferred gin. It was in 1779 that Dr Johnson apotheosized brandy: 'Claret is the liquor for boys; port for men; but he who aspires to be a hero must drink brandy.'

At that time, and still today, the word *brandy* without further qualification generally refers to grape brandy made in the Cognac region of southwestern France. But it can equally be applied not just to grape spirits from other parts of France (such as Armagnac) and elsewhere in the world (for example Spain, Germany, Greece, Australia), but also to spirits distilled from other fruits, so called 'fruit brandies' (such as Calvados from Normandy and North American applejack, made from apples, and the clear spirits made from cherries, raspberries, etc. in Alsace and Germany). In the seventeenth and eighteenth centuries, spirits distilled in Britain from malted corn were known as 'British brandy'. A further genre—more of a liqueur than a real brandy—is represented by such drinks as cherry brandy and apricot brandy, which are made from a base of sweetened grape brandy in which fruits are steeped.

brandy snap A crisp sugary buttery ginger-flavoured wafer, typically rolled up and filled with whipped cream. It dates from the early nineteenth century, and originally lived up to its name by having brandy in its recipe. Modern versions tend to dispense with that, not noticeably to the detriment of their flavour. They might more justly be called *ginger snaps*, but that term is used, mainly in North America, for a thin brittle ginger biscuit that is not rolled up (*see* GINGER NUT and JUMBLE).

Branston pickle The proprietary name of a British brand of sweet pickle originally produced by the firm Crosse and Blackwell in 1922. Its gets its name from the village of Branston, now a suburb of Burton upon Trent, Staffordshire, where the firm's factory then was and where also lived a certain Mrs Graham, who according to legend devised the original recipe in her kitchen.

bratwurst A type of pork sausage of German origin. The *brat*- element in its name goes back to Old High German *brāto* 'meat'; *wurst* means 'sausage'. The word began to become familiar to English speakers in the early twentieth century.

brawn Culinarily, brawn is a preserved preparation of pig meat, particularly from the animal's head, that is boiled, chopped up finely, and then pressed with its jelly into a mould (the American term for it is *headcheese*). The word has a fairly involved history, which starts and finishes in the kitchen but goes far afield in between. To begin at the beginning, its prehistoric Germanic ancestor was **bradon*, a word related to German *braten* 'to roast', which meant something like 'part suitable for roasting'. Often enough it would have been used with reference to an animal's hind leg, and by the time it was adopted by Old French as *braon* it had come to mean just that. It then broadened out to cover any fleshy or muscular part; that was its meaning when English acquired it via Anglo-Norman *braun* in the fourteenth century. English took it back to the table, first as any 'meat', then as 'pig meat', and finally (apparently around the eighteenth century) in the specific modern sense of a sort of meat loaf of pork spare parts.

The word's figurative connotations of 'beefy strength' seem to be a comparatively recent development.

Brazil nut Brazil nuts are the seeds (not, technically, the nuts) of the *Bertholletia excelsa*, a South American forest tree which grows to heights of up to 35 metres. They grow tightly packed together in globular capsules. We first hear of their name (applied for obvious reasons) in the early nineteenth century, although at that time it seems often to have been confused with other South American nuts, such as the *saouari*, and in early usage it appears also to have been called *almond of the Amazon*. Other names for it have included *creamnut, niggertoe*, and *paranut* (presumably from *Para*, a branch of the Amazon).

The name *Brazil*, for the record, comes from *brasil*, the Spanish term for 'brazilwood', a tropical American hardwood which produces a red or purple dye; this in turn was based on Spanish *brasa* 'glowing coals' (as in English *brazier*), from its colour.

bread As is only to be expected of a word for such a basic necessity of life, *bread* has an ancient ancestry, but in fact its use for 'baked dough' is comparatively recent. It seems originally to have meant 'piece, fragment' (the Old English plural *brēadru* meant 'pieces'), and possibly to have been related to Old English *breotan* 'to break'. (There is, though, another theory which links it etymologically with *brew*, based on the use of yeast to ferment the dough.) The standard word in the Old English period for 'bread' was *hlāf*, a word whose centrality to Anglo-Saxon society is signalled by its contribution to the words *lord* and *lady*, literally 'loaf-ward, bread-guardian' and 'bread-kneader' respectively (from Old English *hlāfweard* and *hlǣfdige*.) It was not until around 1200 that *bread* finally took over from it completely in the sense 'baked dough', leaving *loaf* to mean just 'individual mass of bread'.

The first bread was probably a rudimentary dollop of porridge-like dough made from toasted and roughly crushed corn baked over the fire, and it was not until about 3000 BC that flour-and-water loaves recognizably similar to modern flatbreads seem to have emerged. The ancient Egyptians are generally credited with the development of yeast-fermented dough, to give raised rather than flat bread. (The Hebrews, however, kept to unleavened bread, because, according to the biblical story, they left their leaven behind them in their haste to escape from captivity in Egypt, and flat bread remains popular in the eastern Mediterranean area.)

The web of metaphor spun around *bread* confirms its key place in the human diet. Its use in English as a general term for 'food'—no doubt reinforced by the 'give us this day our daily bread' of the Lord's Prayer—dates back at least to the fourteenth century, and to this day 'bread and water' is the proverbial minimal diet. (Latin *pānis* 'bread', incidentally, and its various Romance offspring, French *pain*, Italian *pane*, and Spanish *pan*—not to mention its English derivatives *pannier* and *pantry*—go back ultimately, as does English *food*, to an Indo-European base *pa-* denoting 'food, eating'.) The *staff of life*, now a cliché for 'bread', was inspired in the sixteenth century by Leviticus 26:26 'And when I have broken the staff of your life, ten women shall bake your bread in one oven.' And in the mid-twentieth century the universal necessity *bread* took its place beside *dough* as a slang term (originating in the US) for 'money.'

Sliced and packaged bread was first marketed, in the US, in 1924. Such a boon was it deemed to be to harassed twentieth-century citizens with no time to slice their own bread that eventually the expression *the greatest* (or *best*) *thing since sliced bread* took hold, denoting (sometimes ironically) a marvellous new idea, person, or thing. It is first recorded in 1969.

The collocation *bread and butter*, denoting sliced bread spread with butter, dates back at least to the early seventeenth century, and its metaphorical application to a person's livelihood or main source of income is first recorded in the 1830s. The expression *bread-and-butter letter*, meaning 'a letter of thanks sent to a host', originated in America at the end of the nineteenth century.

bread-and-butter pudding A dessert made by baking buttered slices of bread in a sweet custard mixture, traditionally enlivened with dried fruit. The earliest recorded recipe is in Eliza Smith's *Compleat Housewife* (1729).

breadfruit The large green spherical fruit of a tropical tree of the fig family, grown particularly on islands in the South Pacific, in India, and in the West Indies. Its starchy white flesh allegedly has the texture of new bread, hence the name: 'The Bread-fruit (as we call it) grows on a large Tree as big and high as our largest apple trees. . . . It is as big as a Penny-loaf, when Wheat is at five shillings the Bushel,' William Dampier, *A New Voyage Round the World* (1697). It  can be boiled like potatoes, and in the Caribbean it is often made into fritters. Ripe fruits that drop off the tree on to hard surfaces make an alarming thump.

bread pudding A rich, heavy cake or pudding made from pieces of bread soaked in milk and baked with eggs, sugar, dried fruit, and spices, eaten hot or cold. The first known reference to it is in John Nott's *Cook's and Confectioner's Dictionary* (1723).

breadstick The English equivalent of Italian *grissino* (*see* GRISSINI): a long thin crisp piece of baked dough, typically eaten as a pre-meal nibble. It is first recorded in 1909.

breast Culinarily, *breast* has two somewhat distinct applications in English. The earlier, dating back to the sixteenth century, is to a cut or joint of meat taken from the chest of an animal. It is used with reference to lamb and mutton, and to veal (the corresponding cut of beef is *brisket*, of pork, *belly*). The more recent is to flight muscles attached to the breastbone of a chicken, turkey, duck, etc. (in certain times and places the usage has seemed a little too sensational, and been replaced with the more discreet *white meat*).

bresaola In northern Italian cuisine, bresaola is dried salt lean beef, served in thin slices. Its name is a derivative of the dialect verb *brasare* 'to cook slowly'.

brewis *Brewis*, and the related *browis*, are now virtually obsolete terms that originally denoted a broth made from the liquid in which vegetables or meat had been boiled. This was often thickened with bread, flour, oatmeal, etc., and already by the fifteenth century the term had come to be used for the bread itself, soaked in broth or other liquid. It survived dialectally into the twentieth century, and Florence White in her *Good Things in England* (1932) gives a recipe, if such it can be called, for a particularly spartan version in which a crust of bread is soaked in hot water and then seasoned with salt and pepper. This recalls the *browis* of the traditional Sheffield Cutlers' Feast, a dish made by pouring boiling water on oatcakes mixed with dripping. The term *brewis* also lingered on in Newfoundland English, where it denotes a sort of hard bread eaten with fish. The word comes from Old French *broez*, as did its first cousin, the Scots *brose* (*see* ATHOLE BROSE).

brick cheese A type of American semi-soft cheese that has numerous small irregular holes and is usually fairly mild in flavour. It originated in Wisconsin, but is now widely made throughout the US and Canada. It is not clear whether its name comes from the shape in which it is made, or from the bricks that were originally used to weigh it down during the manufacturing process.

brick tea A tea of fairly basic quality that has been steamed and pressed into the shape of a small brick for ease of transportation. It is in wide use throughout northern Asia and Russia, and in former times served as a form of currency in Mongolia. The term is first recorded in 1827.

bridge roll Bridge rolls are small finger-shaped soft white bread rolls. They appear to be quite recent creations—the term is not recorded before 1926—but by the mid-twentieth century they had become omnipresent in Britain at occasions such as children's parties, their filling seeming almost invariably to be egg and cress. Since the 1960s they have gone into a decline. The origin of their name is not clear, but the likeliest explanation is that they were originally intended to be eaten at afternoon parties at which bridge was played.

bridie A Scottish meat pasty, traditionally semicircular and made of beef. It is not clear where the word comes from: attempts have been made to link the pasties with a woman called Margaret (or Maggie) Bridie, who at some ill-specified time in the past made or sold them, but probably the likeliest explanation is that it was originally *bride's pie*, that is, a pie made for a woman on her wedding day by her friends. It is particularly associated with Forfar in Angus in northeastern Scotland.

Brie A soft white French cows'-milk cheese made originally in the Brie region of the Île de France, to the east of Paris. It is an ancient cheese, dating back to at least the thirteenth century, and has long enjoyed a high reputation (at the Congress of Vienna in 1814 it won a cheese competition organized by the French representative Talleyrand). Since becoming better known in Britain after the Second World War, it has evolved into a staple of supermarket shelves—the demand now being met by non-French sources, such as Germany and England. Brie is traditionally named after the particular place where it was made, *Brie de Meaux* being the most famous (Meaux is a town just to the east of Paris). *See also* CAMBOZOLA, COULOMMIERS.

brik A Tunisian speciality consisting of an envelope of wafer-thin pastry that is deep-fried. The characteristic content of the envelope is an egg, perhaps with a little tuna or minced lamb added: this is the classic *brik à l'oeuf*. Brik is first cousin to Turkish börek, and their names are ultimately identical.

Brillat-Savarin A rich creamy cows'-milk soft cheese from Normandy. It was first made in the early 1970s, and was given its name, honouring the celebrated French writer and gastronome Jean-Anthelme Brillat-Savarin (1755–1826), by the doyen of French cheese-merchants, Henri Androuët.

brinjal The word used in Indian and African English for the aubergine. It is a descendant of Portuguese *beringela*, which comes from the same ultimate Arabic source as English *aubergine*. In West Indian English *brinjal* has become *brown jolly*.

brioche A soft roll or small loaf made from a rich yeast-raised dough made with flour, butter, and eggs. The word *brioche* originated as a derivative of the verb *brier*, a northern dialect variant of Old French *broyer* 'to knead'; this was a Germanic loanword, related to Old High German *brehhan* 'to break'.

brisket A cut of meat, particularly beef, taken from the animal's chest, between the forelegs. One of the cheaper cuts, in Britain it is usually boned and rolled, whereas in America it is sometimes roasted or pot-roasted on the bone. The origins of the word are not at all clear, but it probably comes ultimately from an Old Norse ancestor, a compound of either *brjóst* 'breast' or *brjósk* 'cartilage' and *ket* 'meat', and reached English via Old French and Anglo-Norman.

brittle A type of sweet made by melting and caramelizing sugar, spreading it out in a thin layer, usually with nuts incorporated (for example, peanut brittle), and letting it cool. Chunks can then be snapped off for consumption. Both the product and its name (a noun use of the adjective, first recorded in 1892) originated in America.

broad bean A large flat kidney-shaped bean that is usually eaten without its pod. Until the introduction of New World beans to Europe in the sixteenth century (*see* BEAN), this was what the word *bean* exclusively referred to, and the distinguishing term *broad bean* is not recorded before 1783. In the ancient world, broad beans were associated with the dead and were eaten at funeral feasts. In American English these are generally called *fava beans*. *See also* FUUL.

broccoli A plant of the cabbage family cultivated for its tightly bunched clusters of edible flower buds. These come in various colours—green, yellow, white, purple—but it is the purple variety, often known more fully as *purple-sprouting broccoli*, that until comparatively recently has been the main one grown in Britain. It was introduced from Italy, where it was originally produced, at the end of the seventeenth century (the Italian word means literally 'little shoots'), and soon caught on: John Evelyn, in his *Acetaria* (1699), refers to the 'Broccoli from Naples'. However, the majority of broccoli now commercially available has green flower buds. This variety was developed in Calabria in southwest Italy, hence its alternative name *calabrese*.

broccolini A vegetable that strongly resembles broccoli, but has longer thinner stalks and smaller florets. It is a hybrid of broccoli and Chinese cabbage, which was developed in Japan. The name, incorporating the Italian diminutive suffix *-ini*, is a registered trademark in the US, where the vegetable was launched on to the market in the mid-1990s.

broccoli raab *Broccoli raab*, or *broccoli rabe*, is the name commonly used in American English for the vegetable otherwise known as *cime di rapa* or *rapini*. First recorded in 1976, it is probably an adaptation of Italian *broccoli di rapa*, which means literally 'flowering tops of the turnip'.

broth Etymologically, *broth* is 'that which has been brewed'; the word comes ultimately from the same prehistoric Germanic source as modern English *brew*. From earliest times it was used for the 'liquid in which something is boiled', and the 'something' could be vegetable as well as animal ('Broth of the leaves [of broom] abateth swelling of the spleen,' John de Trevisa, *De Proprietatibus Rerum*, 1398). By the seventeenth century it was becoming largely restricted to the 'liquid in which meat is boiled', and more particularly to a thin soup made from this with the addition of vegetables, cereal grains, etc. (the term *Scotch broth* dates from at least the early eighteenth century), although memories of the earlier more general sense survived into the early twentieth century in *snow-broth* 'melted snow'.

The proverb 'Too many cooks spoil the broth' is first recorded in Sir Balthazar Gerbier's *Three Chief Principals of Magnificent Building* (1665).

browis *See* BREWIS.

brown Betty A pudding of American origin consisting of layers of fruit (typically apple) and buttered breadcrumbs that are baked in the oven until the top is brown and crisp: 'She had provided his favourite lunch—cold ham, boiled potatoes, and brown betty with thick cream', Josephine Tey, *The Franchise Affair* (1949). The identity of the 'Betty' in the name (which is first recorded in 1864) has never been established.

brown bread Bread of a darker colour than white bread. The term, which goes back to the fifteenth century, seems originally to have been applied to bread made from rye flour, or from a mixture of rye and wheat flour, but it was soon also being used, as it is today, for bread made from unsifted or unbleached flour. In the past such bread was cheaper and less desirable than white bread (Tobias Venner in his *Via Recta ad Vitam Longam* (1620) refers to 'a browne household bread agreeable enough for labourers'), but in the twentieth century the tables were turned: brown bread is now seen as wholesome and healthy, white bread (which is now cheaper) as denatured and potentially tasteless (*see also* HOVIS). The use of *brown bread* as Cockney rhyming slang for 'dead' is first recorded in 1973 (replacing the earlier *loaf of bread*).

brownie In America (originally, and now also in Britain), brownies are small, rich chewy squares of chocolate cake, typically containing nuts (or sometimes, from the hippie 1960s onwards, hashish or marijuana). The first mention of them in print comes from the end of the nineteenth century. In Australia and New Zealand, on the other hand, the term refers to a sort of sweet currant bread. *See also* BLONDIE.

brown rice Unpolished rice that has had only the husk of the grain removed. First recorded in 1916, the term has come to have strong connotations of homespun-clad sandal-shod vegetarianism.

brown sauce The term *brown sauce,* first recorded in 1723, has two fairly distinct applications in English. The more upmarket (and the only one in general use in America) is to what in French would be called *sauce espagnole* or *glace de viande*: a richly flavoured and coloured sauce made from reduced beef or veal stock, and often thickened with a flour and butter roux, which serves as the basis of other sauces (for instance, sauce bordelaise). The British vernacular *brown sauce* is a decidedly different animal. The term is an umbrella for a range of commercially produced bottled brown savoury relishes containing vinegar, sugar, various fruits, vegetables, and spices, and a selection of additives. Familiar under a variety of brand names (for example, *HP Sauce*, *Daddy's Sauce*) that have come and in most cases gone since the middle of the nineteenth century, they have established squatters' rights next to the tomato ketchup on many a British café table. Similar concoctions in America tend to be called *steak sauce*.

Brown Windsor Brown Windsor was the music-hall joke amongst British soups, an undistinguished meat broth—often the thinly disguised offspring of a stock cube—trotted out in seaside boarding houses, train restaurant-cars, and the like. The origins of the name are, perhaps deservedly, lost in obscurity—Mrs Beeton, for instance, does not mention it—but it may have some connection with a sort of transparent brown soap popularly known in the nineteenth century as *brown Windsor*. Even in the 1920s enthusiasm for it was perceptibly waning (Evelyn Waugh recorded in *Isis* (5 March 1924) that Gilbert Murray 'admitted that there were many things which were not as good as they used to be—Windsor soup, and marmalade and things like that'), and the easy availability of tinned and packet soup had virtually seen Brown Windsor off by the 1960s.

brunello An Italian red-wine grape, which is a clone of sangiovese. Its name in the Tuscan dialect means literally 'nice dark one'. Its highest-profile use is in Brunello di Montalcino, a red wine of exalted reputation and price produced around Montalcino, a town near Sienna in Tuscany.

bruschetta The now ubiquitous garlic bread is a lineal if somewhat debased version of the Tuscan bruschetta. This is a slice of bread toasted brown on each side and then moistened with a generous dribble of olive oil (it can also be rubbed with garlic, but this is optional). Its name reflects its original cooking method: it is a derivative of the Italian verb *bruscare* 'to roast over coals'. In the past two decades bruschette with various sorts of topping—mixed roasted vegetables, for example, tomato and basil, or baby artichokes—have become a popular antipasto and snack in Italian-style trattorie.

brussels sprouts Firmly ensconced as they now are, brussels sprouts (or *sprouts*—or indeed *brussels*—for short) seem to be a comparatively recent addition to the British table. The first recorded reference to them comes in Charles Marshall's *Plain and Easy Introduction to Gardening* (1796), and their description ('Brussels sprouts are winter greens growing much like boorcole [kale]') suggests that they may first have been valued for the tuft of leaves at the top of their tall thick stem rather than the small green buttons growing up it (*brussel tops* are still a source of winter greens). The first cookery writer to mention them seems to have been Eliza Acton, who in her *Modern Cookery* (1845) gives directions for cooking and serving them in 'the Belgian mode', boiled and with melted butter poured over them. But why *brussels sprouts*? They seem always to have been popular in Flanders and northern France, and market regulations for the Brussels area as long ago as 1213 mention them, but when the name was actually conferred on them is not clear. The French call them *choux de Bruxelles* 'Brussels cabbages'.

b'stilla An alternative spelling of BASTILLA.

bual A medium-sweet type of Madeira wine, sweeter than verdelho but less so than malmsey. Its name comes from the grape variety from which it is made, which in turn comes from Portuguese *boal*. According to Elizabeth David in the *Tatler* (1985), the bual imported into India in the nineteenth century to stock British and Indian army regimental messes came to be christened 'bull' by the troops.

bubble and squeak Nowadays this traditional English dish is typically made from left-over potato and cabbage fried together, with economy strictly in mind, but in its earliest incarnations in the eighteenth and nineteenth centuries cold meat usually took the place of potato. The first known reference to it comes in Thomas Bridge's *Burlesque Translation of Homer* (1772): 'We therefore cook'd him up a dish of lean bull-beef with cabbage fry'd, and a full pot of beer beside; bubble they call this dish, and squeak; our taylors dine on't thrice a week.' The generally accepted explanation of its name is that it refers to the sound of the ingredients frying, but Jane Grigson in her *Vegetable Book* (1978) suggests that it imitates the shrieks and gasps of its eighteenth-century eaters, when it was accompanied by fairly explosive sauces.

bubble tea A tea-based beverage created in Taiwan in the 1980s. It is mixed with fruit juice or fruit syrup and milk, and the most characteristic versions include large numbers of small chewy balls (called 'pearls') made of tapioca or other starch. These can be shaken up to produce a froth that gives the drink its name (and its alternative name, *foam tea*), and then sucked up through the distinctive wide straw with which the tea is served. In the early twenty-first century it is 'the drink of choice among eastern youth', *Time Out London, Eating and Drinking* (2009).

bucatini A type of Italian pasta in the form of long thin spaghetti-like tubes—spaghetti with a hole, in other words. Its name in Italian means literally 'little hollow ones' (*bucato* is Italian for 'pierced').

buckling Bucklings are whole herrings that have been lightly salted and then hot-smoked (in contrast to bloaters, which are cold-smoked). Their introduction to the English-speaking world is relatively recent: their first printed attestation is in 1909, in the American *Century Dictionary*. And like much preserved fish, they originated in northern Europe: the word *buckling* is borrowed from German *bückling*, a derivative of the verb *bücken* 'to bend'.

buck rabbit A Welsh rabbit with a poached egg on top. The earliest recipe in print seems to be in Jessie Lindsay and Vernon Mottram's *Manual of Modern Cookery* (1927). The name was no doubt inspired by *buck rabbit*, a term for a male rabbit. The dish is sometimes alternatively called a *golden buck*.

Buck's fizz Buck's fizz was the fashionable summer drink of the 1980s—refreshing, bubbly, and not excessively alcoholic. It consists of orange juice mixed with champagne or other sparkling white wine. The story goes that it was invented some time after the First World War by John McGarry, the barman of Buck's club (a London gentlemen's club just off Bond Street, founded in 1919 and named after Captain Herbert Buckmaster, whose idea the club was). Buck's can certainly take credit for the name, but in fact the drink itself was popular in Paris long before the First World War. *See also* MIMOSA.

The British pop group Buck's Fizz got its name because the drink was a favourite of Nichola Martin, one of the co-writers of the song 'Making Your Mind Up', who was instrumental in forming the group to sing the song in the 1981 Eurovision Song Contest (they came first).

buckwheat The seed of a plant of the dock family. Its three-sided shape recalls the seeds of the beech tree, and accordingly in the Low Countries (an area where it is still much eaten) it was in the Middle Ages named 'beech wheat'. English acquired the Middle Dutch word *boecweite* in the sixteenth century.

The plant seems to have been introduced to western Europe from Asia in the fourteenth century, and its various names in other European languages reflect this: in medieval Latin it was *frumentum Turcicum* 'Turkish corn', in German *heidenkraut* 'heathen plant', and in French *blé sarrasin* 'Saracen corn'. Czech has *pohanka*, literally 'heathen, Turkish', which may conceivably lie behind the alternative term *brank* which was used in English from the sixteenth to the nineteenth centuries.

The flour into which buckwheat seeds are ground is greyish with small black speckles. A particular use for it is in the making of pancakes. It is the main ingredient of the galettes of Brittany, of Russian blinis, and of American breakfast buckwheat cakes (a type of pancake).

Buddha's delight An alternative term for MONK'S VEGETABLES.

Buffalo wings Despite the inevitably conjured image of flying bison, Buffalo wings have no connection with any four-footed animal. They are chicken wings that have been deep-fried and coated in a spicy sauce, and are served with a blue-cheese dressing. The name derives from the fact that they hail from the city of Buffalo in New York state. It was there, in the Anchor Bar, that the recipe was developed in 1964.

builder's tea A British colloquial term (first recorded in 1996) for ordinary, bog-standard tea, typically brewed strong enough to stand a teaspoon up in, and served with milk and significant amounts of sugar. The implied contrast is with China tea and other effete varieties that would not satisfy the thirst of the honest but unsophisticated British artisan. 'Cinders asked if Abbey had any Earl Grey or jasmine tea. "Sorry, only your basic builder's tea, I'm afraid"', Sue Margolis, *Forget me Knot* (2009).

bulgar wheat Bulgar wheat, or *bulgur wheat*, is a cereal food made by boiling whole wheat grains, drying them, and then grinding them coarsely. It is widely used in vegetarian cookery, and a particular application is in the Lebanese tabbouleh salad. In American

English it is generally called *cracked wheat*. The word comes from Turkish *bulgur,* meaning 'bruised grain'. It is related to Persian *burghul,* which is also used in English for bulgar wheat (*see also* BURGOO).

bulgogi A classic Korean dish consisting of strips of beef marinated in a spiced soy sauce and then cooked on a special ridged grill plate over a charcoal fire. The Korean word means literally 'fire-meat'.

bullace A type of small plum, essentially a somewhat rounder variety of the damson. English acquired the word in the fourteenth century, probably from Old French *beloce,* but the ultimate etymology of that is obscure.

bullock's heart An alternative name, first recorded in 1866 and commonly in use in the West Indies, for the custard apple. It is justified by the fruit's size and shape and to some extent by its colour (reddish-brown on one side when ripe).

Bull's Blood A full-bodied Hungarian red wine originally made in and around the village of Eger, in the northern hills. The main grape variety used in it is the kadarka. Its name (in Hungarian *Egri bikavér* 'bull's blood of Eger'; first recorded in English in 1926) suggests a potency which modern examples scarcely live up to. It enjoyed something of a following in Britain in the 1960s and 1970s, but as its quality fell away, and other Eastern European wines became more widely available, it gradually disappeared from the off-licence shelves.

bull's-eye This large, round, typically peppermint-flavoured sweet has been popular since at least the early nineteenth century; Thomas Hughes mentions it in *Tom Brown's Schooldays* (1857). The name refers to its globular shape, and has no connection with the modern 'target' connotations of the word.

bullshot A mixed drink of American origin consisting of cold beef consommé and vodka roughly in the proportion two to one, generally enlivened with lemon juice, Worcester sauce, and Tabasco. It is said to have been invented in the early 1960s at the Caucus Club restaurant in Detroit, Michigan. There are those who swear by it as a hangover cure (decidedly in the 'hair-of-the-dog' category).

bully beef In modern usage the term *bully beef,* or *bully,* denotes virtually 'corned beef'—preserved beef in a tin—particularly as used for military or naval rations. But both its name (*bully* is an anglicization of French *bouilli* 'boiled beef', a noun use of the past participle of *bouillir* 'to boil') and early examples of its use indicate that originally it simply meant 'boiled beef'. Tobias Smollett, for instance, refers to it in his *Count Fathom* (1758): 'I could get no eatables upon the road, but what they called Bully, which looks like the flesh of Pharaoh's lean kine stewed into rags and tatters.' And Parson Woodforde, an avid recorder of his daily fare, noted in his diary for 18 September 1788, 'We had for Dinner some Hare Soupe, a couple of Chicken boiled and Ham—some Beef Bully, Stewed Pork—Partridges, etc.'

bumbo A drink concocted from rum, water (hot or cold), and sugar, and often flavoured with nutmeg. It was a popular tipple of buccaneers on the Spanish Main in the eighteenth century, and interest in it has been revived latterly by its frequent consumption by Captain Jack Sparrow (played by Johnny Depp) in the *Pirates of the Caribbean* films (2003–). Modern interpretations of the drink tend to be softened with fruit juice. The origins of the word (first recorded in 1748) are not clear, but it may be connected to Italian *bombo,* a child's word for 'drink'.

bun *Bun* is something of a mystery word. It suddenly appeared, out of the blue, in a 1371 text of the *Assize of Bread,* a statute fixing the weight and price of various sorts of loaf: 'Cum uno pane alba, vocato "bunne" [with a white loaf, called "bun"].' It is not known for certain where it came from, but it may have been an altered borrowing of Old French *buignet* 'fritter' (*see also* BEIGNET), which was a diminutive form of *buigne* 'swelling from a blow, bump on the head'. The probably related Spanish *buñelo* 'fritter' may also be part of the mix. To begin with, buns seem to have been simply small loaves. This central sense has remained current for several centuries, and is still in use in contexts such as 'burger bun', although much of its semantic territory has been taken over by *roll*. Increasingly the word has come to denote something sweet: in Scotland, for instance, *bun* (or more fully *black bun*) is a term for a rich dark fruit cake, while in England and elsewhere in the English-speaking world it signifies a small light sweet individual loaf, typically round. Several specific varieties have developed: the *Bath bun*, for example, the *Chelsea bun*, the *hot cross bun*, and the cream bun, proverbially beloved of schoolboys.

The use of *bun* for a 'tight round knot of hair at the back of a woman's head' dates from the 1890s (the term *bun penny* for a coin depicting Queen Victoria wearing such a 'bun' seems to have arisen not far short of a century after the coin's first minting in 1860). The colloquial *have a bun in the oven* for 'to be pregnant' appears to be post-Second World War, and New Zealand slang *do one's bun* 'to become very angry' is even more recent.

bun cha A Vietnamese dish consisting of fine rice noodles (*bun*) served in a fish-sauce-based broth with a topping of quickly grilled (*cha*) pork strips or small pork patties, and a green salad. This is street food, available on almost every corner in Hanoi.

bundt cake A cake that has been baked in a Bundt pan—that is to say, a baking mould with curved fluted sides and a hollow central tube. The term appears to be a partial translation of German *bundkuchen* (*kuchen* means 'cake', and *bund* may refer to a gathering of people, or to the way the dough is pressed or 'bundled' up against the central tube). *Bundt Pan* was registered as a trademark in the US in 1950.

bunny chow A South African takeaway food consisting of a hollowed-out half-loaf of bread filled with vegetable or meat curry. *Bunny* is probably an alteration of Hindi *banya*, from Gujarati *vāniyo* 'merchant, trader' (also the source of the tree name *banyan*); for the second element (*see* CHOW).

burdock A large-leafed plant of the daisy family that has prickly seed cases known as burrs (that accounts for the first part of its name (which dates back to the fifteenth century); the second comes from the dock plant, to which it is not related). Its main culinary claim to fame is that the root of the great burdock is used to make the drink dandelion and burdock (*see* DANDELION).

burger *See* HAMBURGER.

burgoo A culinary term of wide application. It comes from Arabic *burgul* (in Persian *burghu*, *see* BULGAR), and originally, in the eighteenth century, it denoted a sort of thick oatmeal gruel eaten by sailors. Subsequently, in the southern states of the US, it came to be used for a stew or thick soup containing a mixture of whatever meats and vegetables might be available. The term was applied especially to such a dish eaten at an outdoor gathering, such as a picnic or a political rally, and by extension came to be used of such gatherings themselves.

burnt cream The vernacular term for CRÈME BRÛLÉE. *See also* CAMBRIDGE BURNT CREAM.

burnt ends Crisp crusty morsels of meat cut from a piece of brisket that has been slow-smoked in the style of a Kansas City barbecue.

burrata A type of rich creamy Italian cheese made by shredding pieces left over from the production of provolone and similar cheeses, mixing them with cream, and enclosing the result inside an outer shell of mozzarella. It was probably first made at some time in the first twenty years of the twentieth century in the Puglia area of southeastern Italy. It began to be more widely known in the 1950s, and by the twenty-first century had become decidedly fashionable. Its name means literally 'buttered' in Italian.

burrito In Mexican cuisine, a small soft tortilla that is folded over and filled—most typically with cheese, beans, or scrambled eggs with chilli. In Mexican Spanish, *burrito* means literally 'little donkey'.

bush meat Originally, in the mid-nineteenth century, a term used especially in Africa for meat obtained from animals hunted for food (as opposed to sport); the *bush* in question is 'wild, uncultivated country'. Latterly, it has acquired more specific and somewhat euphemistic overtones, in application to meat from wild animals imported into the UK from Africa for sale to African immigrants: the 'monkey-meat in Ridley Road market' syndrome.

bush tea A generic term for any of a range of herbal teas (such as rooibos) made from the dried leaves and twigs of various shrubs, especially in southern Africa. First recorded in 1768, it is apparently based on *bush* in the sense 'shrub' rather than 'wild country'.

butter Butter probably originated amongst the nomadic peoples of central Asia—quite plausibly first discovered by accident after a hard day in the saddle during which the rider's neglected container of milk had been constantly churned. Its use gradually spread to India and Europe, although in Greece and Rome, both olive-oil cultures, it was at first treated with both suspicion and derision as an inferior foreign product: the Greek dramatist Anaxandrides patronized its barbarian manufacturers as 'your butter-eating gentry'. The first reference to it in classical times is by the Greek historian Herodotus, who described how it was made, but credit for recording its name goes to the physician Hippocrates, who called it *boútūron*. This was a compound formed from *bous* 'cow' and *tūrós* 'cheese', and is generally assumed to have been a translation of the term for 'butter' in some non-Indo-European language, probably Scythian. Latin borrowed it as *būtyrum*, which has since produced French *beurre*, Italian *burro*, Dutch *boter*, and English and German *butter*. (Of languages which have not taken up the Latin word, Swedish *smör* and Danish *smør* mean literally 'grease', while Spanish *manteca* is probably of pre-Romance origin.)

There are two main strands in the history of butter. In the Indian subcontinent it is preserved by melting it and straining off the impurities (*see* GHEE). (An exception to this pattern is Tibet, where rancid butter is preferred.) The European tradition, on the other hand, has been to preserve it with salt.

The use of the verb *butter* for 'to flatter' dates from the end of the seventeenth century, although *butter up* is not recorded until the early nineteenth century.

butter bean An alternative name for the lima bean, especially as found, dried or in tins, on the shelves of supermarkets and groceries. It is presumably based on the bean's creamy yellow colour. It is first recorded in the early nineteenth century.

butter bread *See* SPOON BREAD.

butter chicken A Punjabi dish in which tandoori chicken is served in a sauce made from a mixture of spices and tomato purée cooked in butter (it may have been an inspiration behind *chicken tikka masala,* to which it bears a marked resemblance). Its Urdu name is *murgh makhani,* literally 'chicken with butter'.

buttercream A soft mixture of butter and icing sugar used as a filling or topping for a cake, especially a sponge cake. The term seems to have originated in the 1890s.

butterhead lettuce Any of a general class of lettuce (for example cabbage lettuce or Bibb lettuce) that have soft leaves, grow in a loose head, and allegedly taste of butter. The name dates from around 1910.

buttermilk The liquid left after cream has been turned into butter by churning. It is used for making bread, scones, etc. (particularly for soda bread, where it reacts with the bicarbonate of soda to produce an aerating gas), and in Scandinavia it is popular as a drink. In the days when the peasantry of Ireland subsisted on potatoes, buttermilk was what they washed these down with ('the families of farmers, who pay great rent, living in filth and nastiness upon buttermilk and potatoes,' Jonathan Swift, *Short View of the State of Ireland* (1728)). The word is first recorded from the early sixteenth century, when Thomas Paynell enthused over buttermilk's nutritive value: 'Butter mylke.... Nothynge nourisheth more than this mylke when it is new, sopped up with new hotte breadde', *Regimen Sanitatis Salerni* (1528). *Churn-milk* is a now little-used alternative name.

butternut An alternative name, first recorded in the mid-eighteenth century, for the grey or white walnut of North America. Its brownish-grey hue came to be used as a colour term, applied particularly to the uniforms of the armies of the South in the American Civil War—indeed, Southern soldiers became known as 'butternuts': 'A "Butternut" is one who sympathizes with the South—one, in fact, who wears the uniform or livery of the Southern army', *The Times* (1863).

butternut squash A type of pear-shaped squash with light yellowish-brown rind and orange flesh. The name, which is first recorded in 1945, reflects its external coloration.

butterscotch A toffee-like confection of sugar and butter, is first heard of in the mid-nineteenth century. It presumably got its name from being originally manufactured in

Scotland, although its history is uncertain. The first known reference to it comes in F. K. Robinson's *Glossary of Yorkshire Words* (1855), where it is called *butterscot*.

butty *See* SANDWICH.

Byrrh A French red-wine-based aperitif, given a bitter taste by the addition of quinine. It was originally concocted in 1886 by the brothers Pallade and Violet Simon.

cabbage The cabbage, object of fear and loathing at the dinner table, forced down the unwilling throats of centuries of children because it is 'good for you', its cooking smells infiltrating every corner of the house (or institution), has a lot to live down in Britain, the land of the overcooked vegetable. William Connor ('Cassandra' of the *Daily Mirror*) summed it up in 1950: 'Boiled cabbage *à l'Anglaise* is something compared with which steamed coarse newsprint bought from bankrupt Finnish salvage dealers and heated over smoky oil stoves is an exquisite delicacy.'

Wild cabbages were probably eaten by Iron Age Celts on the Atlantic coast of Europe. Cultivated cabbages, of the green-leaved variety, were introduced into Britain by the Romans, and apparently relished by their Anglo-Saxon successors (they called it *cāwel* or *cāul*, as in modern English *coleslaw*, and in early Middle English the term was generally *colewort*, or simply *worts*; English did not acquire the word *cabbage* until the fourteenth century, from Old Northern French *caboche*, a variant of Old French *caboce* 'head', and until well into the seventeenth century it was frequently used not on its own, but in the phrase *cabbage cole*). The 1500s were in many ways the cabbage's red-letter century, for that seems to have been the period when the ordinary English green cabbage was joined from the Continent by such newcomers as the crisp compact white or Dutch cabbage and its cousin the red cabbage, favoured for pickling, and the crinkly-leaved Savoy cabbage.

cabbage lettuce A variety of lettuce in which the leaves form a cabbage-like head. The term is first recorded in 1562.

cabernet The family name shared by two major red-wine-producing grape varieties: *cabernet sauvignon* and *cabernet franc*. The former is the main red grape of Bordeaux: it is the major ingredient in the blend of grapes used to produce claret in the Médoc. It has been widely planted elsewhere in the world, notably California and Australia, and at the end of the twentieth century was easily the most fashionable and popular of the fine red-wine grapes. Cabernet franc generally plays only a minor part in the grape blend of red Bordeaux (although Château Cheval Blanc, the leading St-Emilion, is predominantly cabernet franc), but it is the main red-wine grape of the Loire valley, and it is also widely planted in Italy. The name *cabernet* originated in the Médoc dialect, but it is not clear where it came from. One suggested ultimate source is Latin *caput* 'head'.

cabinet pudding Cabinet pudding is redolent of a bygone age. In its most highly evolved and luxurious form, impregnated with liqueurs and decorated with crystallized fruits, it graced many a Victorian dinner table. The basic recipe called for sponge cakes crumbled up, to which was added a custard of eggs and milk, the whole being poached, steamed, or boiled in a mould (the ever economical Mrs Beeton suggested substituting bread and butter for the cake, and in fact that is the central ingredient in the first recorded recipe for cabinet pudding, published in Kitchener's *Cook's Oracle* (1821)). The name seems to derive from the political sort of cabinet, a supposition supported by an early synonym, *chancellor's pudding*, and by the practical identity of *diplomat pudding*.

Caboc A type of cows'-milk cream cheese, made in the Highlands of Scotland. It is Scotland's oldest cheese, said to date back to the fifteenth century. According to legend, it was first made by Mariota de Ile, daughter of the chieftain of Clan MacDonald of the Isles. She reputedly learned the recipe while taking refuge in an Irish nunnery and took it home with her to Scotland, where it has remained in her family ever since. A further embellishment of the Caboc story is that one day a cowherd found that the cheese in his knapsack had become covered with crumbs from his oatmeal biscuits, and to this day Caboc has been coated with toasted oatmeal (careless or absent-minded animal husbandmen tend to play a prominent role in the mythical history of cheese).

cachou Cachous are small scented tablets for sweetening the breath. They first appear to have come on the scene in the last quarter of the nineteenth century, and in 1898 the Army and Navy Co-operative Society price list gives a variety of options as to perfume, including 'white rose, violet, heliotrope, and citron.' The word is French, but comes ultimately from Malay *kâchou*. It originally stood for an astringent substance obtained from the bark of a variety of Asian trees and used, amongst many other purposes, as a spice: 'Cardamome, Long Pepper, Cachou, etc.', Wyndham Beawes, *Lex Mercatoria Rediviva* (1750); but the Latinized *catechu* is now usually used for this.

Caerphilly A pale yellow, crumbly, cows'-milk hard cheese made originally at Caerphilly, to the north of Cardiff, and in surrounding areas of the Vale of Glamorgan. Records of its manufacture go back to the early nineteenth century, but production was stopped by the Ministry of Food in 1940, and it has never picked up again in Wales. Most Caerphilly is now made in Somerset.

Caesar salad Caesar salad is a great American institution. It consists of cos lettuce leaves and garlic croutons dressed with a mixture of olive oil, lemon juice, raw eggs, Worcester sauce, Parmesan cheese, and seasonings (the dressing traditionally done in a flamboyant ceremony at table). It was invented in 1924 by Caesar Cardini, who ran a restaurant called Caesar's Place in Tijuana, northern Mexico.

Café de Paris butter A type of supercharged herb butter, typically served with steak. It blends butter with a mix of green herbs, standardly including thyme and parsley, and usually also garlic, mustard, anchovies, paprika, and curry powder. It seems to be a development of Café de Paris sauce, a herby sauce served with steak, which was invented at the Café de Paris in Geneva in the 1940s. Its precise recipe is secret, but it appears to be based on butter, cream, thyme, and chicken livers.

caipirinha A Brazilian mixed drink based on cachaça, a Brazilian spirit similar to white rum but made from pure sugar-cane juice rather than molasses. To it are added limes, lime juice, sugar, and ice. Brazilian Portuguese *caipirinha* means literally 'little yokel, little hick': so it is the drink of country folk and farmers.

cake The original dividing line between cake and bread was fairly thin: in Roman times eggs and butter were often added to basic bread dough to give a consistency we would recognize as cake-like, and this was frequently sweetened with honey. Terminologically, too, the earliest English *cakes* were virtually bread, their main distinguishing characteristics being their shape—round and flat—and the fact that they were hard on both sides from being turned over during baking. John de Trevisa (1398) gives an early definition: 'Some brede is bake and tornyd and wende [turned] at fyre and is called . . . a cake.' It is this basic shape that lies behind the transference of the name to other, completely different foods, such as fishcakes, pancakes, and potato cakes.

In Scotland, Wales, and parts of northern England *cake* early took on the specific meaning of a 'thin hard biscuit made from oatmeal' (what we would now specify more narrowly as an *oatcake*); from the seventeenth to the nineteenth centuries Scotland was known humorously as the 'Land of Cakes', and until comparatively recently Hogmanay was also known as 'Cake Day', from the custom of calling on people's houses at New Year and asking for cakes.

Meanwhile in England the shape and contents of *cakes* were gradually converging towards our present understanding of the term. In medieval and Elizabethan times they were usually quite small, but by the seventeenth century, a period which saw an increase in cake-making, larger sizes had become well established. Dried fruits were used freely in recipes of the time, and by the eighteenth century seed cakes (containing caraway seeds) had become very popular. It was around this period, too, that eggs finally took over from yeast as the main raising agent, defining the nature of the modern cake. Meanwhile, the notion that cakes were by definition round and flat had been dying out, a change perhaps signalled by the use of *cake*, without the indefinite article, as a general term for the substance of which cakes are made; the first evidence for this comes at the end of the sixteenth century. The icing of cakes had become fairly common by the middle of the eighteenth century.

Cake is a Viking contribution to the English language; it was borrowed from Old Norse *kaka*, which is related to a range of Germanic words, including modern English *cook*.

The proverb 'You can't have your cake and eat it' (or originally, and perhaps more logically, 'eat your cake and have it') first appears in the sixteenth century; John Heywood notes it in his *Proverbs and Epigrams* (1562). A 'piece of cake', however, meaning 'something simple', is much more recent; it is not heard of until well into the twentieth century. There may be some connection with *cake-walk*, used metaphorically with the same meaning since the First World War (it was originally, around the turn of the twentieth century, a strutting dance based on a promenade or walk, first popularized among black people in the southern US, in which the participants who performed the most complicated or outlandish steps won a cake as a prize). 'Take the cake', meaning more or less 'win first prize' (from the notion of cake as being something very special and desirable) dates from the 1880s, with its ironical overtones developing later. The alternative 'take the biscuit' seems to have come on the scene in the early 1900s.

French has borrowed the word *cake*, and applies it to various sorts of rich fruit cake.

calabrese A variety of green broccoli whose year-round import from warmer areas of Europe has in recent decades put the home-grown purple-sprouting broccoli into the commercial shade. It was originally developed in Calabria, in southwestern Italy (the word means literally 'Calabrian' in Italian), and seems first to have reached British shores at the end of the 1920s.

calamari Calamari are squid served as food. The word is Italian in origin, but half a century of exposure to British holidaymakers in the Mediterranean has propelled it into English. It is the plural of Italian *calamaro*, a descendant of medieval Latin *calamarium*, which meant 'pen case'; the metaphorical transfer was based on the squid's long tapering internal shell and its ink. The Spanish form of the word, *calamares*, has also come into English, sometimes in the Anglicized form *calamaries*.

caldo verde A Portuguese potato and cabbage soup, customarily ladled into its bowl over a slice of *chouriço* sausage (*see* CHORIZO). The name means 'green soup'.

California roll An American version of sushi in which crab (or crabstick), cucumber, and ginger are combined with avocado, in imitation of fresh tuna, and the whole is rolled up with cold cooked rice and seaweed. In was invented in Los Angeles in the 1960s by the sushi chefs Ichiro Mashita and Teruo Imaizumi.

calipash In the days (roughly from the mid-seventeenth to the late nineteenth century) when turtle meat was much prized by wealthy diners, *calipash* was the technical term for the flesh below the upper shell, which is of a dull green colour and a gelatinous consistency. The origin of the word is not clear: it was probably adopted from some

Caribbean language, but it does bear a more than passing resemblance to Spanish *carapacho* 'carapace'.

calipee The term, mirroring *calipash*, for the flesh above a turtle's lower shell, which is light yellow and gelatinous (Thomas Trapham in *A Discourse of the State of Health in the Island of Jamaica* (1679) reported that 'the Callapee, viz. the Belly-part so called, baked, is an excellent dish'). It may have originated as a fanciful alteration of *calipash*.

callaloo A Caribbean term applied both to a variety of edible greens, and to a soup made from them. The principal recipient of the name seems to be the leaves of the taro plant, but callaloo can also be spinach or various members of the cabbage family. As for the soup, its principal traditional ingredients apart from the greens are bacon or pig's tail, crab meat, okra, and coconut milk. It is widely made in the Caribbean, although it is commonly regarded as a Trinidadian speciality. The word, which first turns up in English in the mid-eighteenth century, is of unknown origin.

calzone The calzone—a Neapolitan speciality—is a sort of pizza turnover. On one half of a round of pizza dough is spread a filling—the classic is ham and mozzarella—and the dough is then folded over, sealed along one side, and baked. Italian *calzone* means literally 'trouser leg', and there is a certain resemblance.

Cambozola A German soft cheese that looks like Camembert from the outside and has blue veining like Gorgonzola. It was invented around 1900, but it was not until the 1970s, when it was patented by the German company Champignon, that it became widely known. Its name is essentially a blend of *Camembert* and *Gorgonzola*, but the intrusive *-bo-* probably comes from *Cambodunum*, the Roman name of Kempten, where Champignon's headquarters are situated. In the UK the cheese is often marketed as *Blue Brie*.

Cambridge burnt cream Essentially, crème brûlée. Florence White, in her *Good Things in England* (1932), gives an account of its ancestry: 'This recipe [for "Caramel Cream"] is given by Miss Eleanor L. Jenkinson, sister of the late Cambridge University Librarian, in *The Ocklye Cookery Book* [1909]. Miss Jenkinson says: "It is amusing to remember that this recipe, which came from a country house in Aberdeenshire in the 'sixties, was offered to the kitchens of Trinity College, Cambridge, by an undergraduate, and rejected with contempt. When the undergraduate became a Fellow, just thirty years ago (in 1879), he presented it again; this time it was accepted as a matter of course. It speedily became one of the favourite dishes of May week".' In the original version the arms of Trinity College were embossed on top with a branding iron, but nowadays that embellishment is generally dispensed with. The simple term *burnt cream* goes back to the seventeenth century, denoting a custard with a somewhat thicker caramelized sugar crust than the French crème brûlée, but the now virtually synonymous *Cambridge burnt cream* tends to be preferred on modern menus, no doubt for its heritage connotations.

Camembert A soft, pale yellow cows'-milk cheese with a white mould crust, made originally in the Auge region of Normandy. A similar cheese had no doubt been made in the area for many hundreds of years, and in the early eighteenth century there is a record of a *Camembert* cheese being mentioned by name. But the origin of the cheese in its modern form can be dated precisely to 1792, when a Marie Harel launched the version she had evolved. She passed her recipe on to her daughter, who set up a marketing operation in the village of Camembert, near Vimoutiers, to the south of Le Havre. It was tasted and liked by the Emperor Napoleon III, and its reputation has never looked back. The circular chipwood box invented for it in the 1890s by one M. Ridel enabled it to be successfully exported, since when it has become the epitome of French soft cheeses. But the majority of modern factory-made, pasteurized 'Camembert', some of it not even made in France, scarcely deserves to inherit the name.

Campari The proprietary name of a bright red Italian aperitif with an astringent taste. It is commonly mixed with soda water. It is named after Gaspare Campari, who invented it in Novara to the west of Milan in northwestern Italy in 1860.

canapé Canapés are small thin pieces of bread or toast topped with some sort of savoury garnish or spread, and served as snacks with drinks. The word *canapé* means literally 'sofa' in French (it comes ultimately from medieval Latin *canopeum*, source of English *canopy*), and the idea behind its gastronomic application is that the toppings—anchovies, caviare, smoked salmon, ham, etc.—sit on the pieces of bread as if on a sofa. It is a relatively recent introduction into English, first mentioned in *Mrs Beeton's Cookery Book* (1890).

candlenut The heart-shaped fruit of the candleberry tree, which grows in tropical Asia. It is rich in oil, and in the areas where it grows the nuts are strung together and used literally as candles. Gastronomically, they are employed as thickening agents in curries.

candy For American-speakers, *candy* is virtually any species of confectionery made with sugar (including, for instance, toffee)—roughly what British-speakers would call 'sweets'. In British English, however, the word tends to be restricted to certain types of sweet, particularly those made only from boiled sugar (though there is room for other ingredients, as in *coconut candy*) and striped in various bright colours, typically pink and white—hence *candy-stripes*. The word is a shortening of *sugar candy*, which is a partial translation of French *sucre candi*. This in turn was borrowed from Arabic *sukkar qandī*, the second element of which goes back to Sanskrit *khanda* 'sugar in pieces', from the verb *khand* 'to break'.

Candyfloss, the fairground confection of spun sugar, seems first to have come on the scene around 1900 (*floss* is fine filamentous material, as in *dental floss*). In American English *cotton candy* is the more usual term, in Australian English, *fairy floss*. The French call it *barbe à papa* 'dad's beard'.

canella A now obsolete term for cinnamon (or the similarly flavoured cassia bark). English acquired it in the seventeenth century from medieval Latin *canella*, which meant literally 'little cane'—an allusion to the fact that cinnamon comes in little rolls of bark, known in English as 'quills'. It survived into the nineteenth century (Flora Annie Steel and Grace

Gardiner in their *Complete Indian Housekeeper and Cook* (1888) give a recipe for 'cannella pudding', a sort of baked custard that includes cinnamon) but it has since died out. In the Middle Ages English had adopted the word via Old French as *canel*, which was in wide use, but it preceded *canella* into oblivion.

cannellini bean A creamy-white kidney-shaped bean of Italian origin. It resembles an oversized haricot bean, and like the haricot it is mainly sold either dried or tinned. Italian *cannellini* means literally 'small tubes'.

cannelloni Sheets of pasta that are wrapped round a meat or vegetable filling and baked. The Italian term (first recorded in 1851) means literally 'large tubes'.

cannoli A dessert of Sicilian origin consisting of cigar-sized tubes of deep-fried pastry filled with sweetened ricotta and typically chocolate chips and candied orange peel. The word comes from the plural of Italian *cannola*, which means literally 'small tube', but in America, where the dessert is popular, it has come to be treated as a collective singular.

cannon A long cylindrical cut of lamb consisting of a boned and rolled loin: 'roast cannon of lamb with bubble and squeak and rosemary jus', *Good Food Guide* (2008). Those familiar with the much longer established application of *cannon* to the lower part of an animal's leg, just above the foot—a knuckly joint with a discouraging proportion of bone to meat—may be disconcerted to find 'cannon of lamb' on a restaurant menu, but the new usage has now largely ousted the old. The inspiration for both is the same, the long round muscle of the loin and the long hollow bone of the leg both being held to resemble a literal cannon (although memories of the original metaphor no doubt reinforced the new one). The word's inherent spelling quandary—one *n* in the middle or two—affects this usage too: 'Canon of salt marsh lamb with fondant potatoes was accompanied by a basil mousse', *Time Out London, Eating and Drinking* (2008), perhaps compounded by the fact that the French for 'cannon' in this sense is *canon*.

canola A variety of the plant rape (*see* RAPESEED) developed in Canada in the 1970s whose oil is low in erucic acid and therefore more nutritious than the older varieties. The name is an acronym formed from 'Canada oil, low acid'.

Cantal A hard French cows'-milk cheese made in the Auvergne region of central France, and specifically in the department of Cantal. It is supposedly the oldest of French cheeses, records of it dating back to Roman times. In texture and flavour it is not dissimilar to Cheddar.

cantaloup When the cantaloup melon was introduced into Europe from Armenia, it was apparently first cultivated at Cantaluppi, a former summer estate of the popes near Rome.

Charles VIII brought it from Italy to France in the fifteenth century, and the name *cantaloup* became attached to it in French. Britain does not seem to have acquired the fruit until the early eighteenth century—the first record of it in English (somewhat idiosyncratically spelled) is in the 1739 edition of Philip Miller's *Gardener's Dictionary*: 'The Cantaleupt Melon: . . . the Flesh . . . is of a rich vinous Flavour.' The cantaloup has a distinctive ribbed skin and reddish-orange flesh.

cantucci Small almond biscuits which in Tuscany form the traditional accompaniment to vin santo: you dunk them into the wine before eating them. The word *cantucci* (singular *cantuccio*) is a diminutive form of Italian *canto*, which means literally 'corner', but is also used metaphorically for 'bit (of bread)', 'crust', and 'rusk'.

Cape Cod turkey Dried salt cod does not make the most exciting of dishes, and New Englanders who felt the need to glamorize it a little took to calling it facetiously *Cape Cod turkey* (after the peninsula in Massachusetts). A little sauce usually helped the masquerade along.

Cape gooseberry Another name for the PHYSALIS.

capelli d'angelo The Italian name (first recorded in 1941) for the type of pasta that in English is generally known by its direct translation, ANGEL HAIR.

caper Capers are the pickled young flower buds of a prickly low-growing shrub, *Capparis spinosa*, which grows in countries bordering the Mediterranean. They have been popular as a relish in Britain since at least the fifteenth century (the first reference in English to the plant on which they grow is by the fourteenth-century religious reformer John Wycliffe), and in Tudor and Stuart times they were imported by the barrel-load from southern Europe. Their classic use in English cookery is in caper sauce (Eliza Acton has a recipe in which chopped-up capers are simply added to hot melted butter, with a dash of vinegar) accompanying boiled mutton or fish. In France they are often used in salade niçoise, or in a black butter with skate. The best capers are reputed to be French, from around Toulon, particularly the varieties Capucine and Nonpareille.

A frequent alternative in the past when capers were unavailable were nasturtium seeds; they were pickled in vinegar with spices. In the sixteenth and seventeenth centuries, according to C. Anne Wilson in *Food and Drink in Britain* (1973), pickled broom buds often served the same purpose. And the ever frugal Mrs Beeton gives a recipe for a 'substitute' caper sauce which does not even contain these proxies; it is based simply on parsley.

The sharp, pungent taste of capers is said by some to recall the savour of goats, but this is probably only a piece of fanciful folk etymology; there is no evidence that the word *caper* is related to Latin *caper* 'goat' (from which we get English *capriole, Capricorn*, and the verb *caper* 'to dance'). It is derived directly from the Latin name of the plant, *capparis*, whose earliest English form, *capres*, was mistaken as plural, and 'singularized' to *caper*.

caperberry The fruit of the caper plant, which resembles a long-stemmed slightly pear-shaped olive. A product particularly of Spain, it is pickled and eaten much as an olive would be. It tastes very like the bud from which it grew.

capillaire Originally, in the eighteenth century, a syrup or infusion of maidenhair fern ('He used to pour capillaire into his port wine', James Boswell, *Life of Johnson* (1791)). Later the term was applied to a more palatable-sounding syrup flavoured with orange-flower water. It was adopted originally from French *capillaire* 'maidenhair fern' (from Latin *capillaris* 'of hair').

capon A capon is—or was, for the law no longer countenances it—a young male chicken which has been castrated, supposedly to improve its flavour. Generally speaking, the term was applied to birds between six and ten months which had been fattened on a special diet to be particularly choice for the table. In these days of mass-produced oven-ready chickens, *capon* has a quaintly old-fashioned air, but a fine plump roasted capon used to be an eagerly anticipated winter treat.

The word entered the language in Old English times (it was then *capun*), and medieval recipes for capons survive. The *Diuersa Seruisa* of around 1380, for instance, tells how to make 'capons in castles': 'Take capons and . . . open the skin at the head and blow them till the skin rise from the flesh, and remove the skin whole. Boil chicken meat, egg yolks, and spices, and make a stuffing, and fill the skin and parboil it, and put it on a spit and roast it, basting it with egg yolks. Take the capon's body and lard it, and roast it, and take almond milk and wheat starch and make a batter, and baste the roasting body, and serve it.'

The word's ultimate source is probably Latin *capo* (in its stem form, *capon*-). It is not clear where this came from, but it may well be based on a word for 'cutting' (Greek *koptein* meant 'to strike' or 'to cut'), from the operation of removing the unfortunate bird's testes. John de Trevisa, in his translation of Bartholomeus's *De Proprietatibus Rerum* (1398), described the process graphically: 'The capon is a cock made as it were female by carving away of his gendering stones.'

caponata A cold Italian hors d'oeuvre consisting of sliced aubergine, celery, onions, and tomato that are fried to a mush and allowed to cool, and then garnished with olives, anchovies, etc. It is a Sicilian speciality, and *caponata* is a Sicilian dialect term.

cappellacci An alternative name for TORTELLI.

cappelletti An alternative name for *tortellini* (*see* TORTELLI).

cappuccino An Italian term for coffee made with a head of hot frothy milk or whipped cream. The word means literally 'capuchin', and its application to coffee is generally taken to be a reference to the colour of the habit worn by monks of the Order of Friars Minor Capuchins, an independent branch of Franciscans, (the word *capuchin* itself is derived ultimately from Latin *cappa* 'hood', which comes from *caput* 'head'). *Cappuccino* probably established itself in English in the coffee bars of the 1950s (when the drink also went under the colloquial name *frothy coffee*).

captain's biscuit A British type of commercially produced hard biscuit typically eaten with cheese or other savoury foods. Coming on the scene in the 1840s, the late nineteenth century was its heyday (Flora Annie Steel and Grace Gardiner in their *Complete Indian Housekeeper and Cook* (1888) note that 'round captains' [*sic*] biscuits, daintily decorated with anchovy or maitre d'hotel butters, olives, &c., &c., are much liked' as 'supper dainties'), but in the twentieth century it faded from view.

carambola From a distance the carambola looks not unlike a lemon or a squat banana, but closer examination reveals five prominent ridges. Cut in half, it has a star-shaped cross-section, which has given it the alternative name *star-fruit*. It has waxy yellow skin and astringent slightly nondescript flesh, and in the West its role has not extended much beyond that of a decoration for fruit salads, but in its native Malaysia, and elsewhere in the East, it is far more widely used, in savoury as well as sweet dishes, and in pickles and chutneys. Its name comes via Portuguese from a Hindi word descended from Sanskrit *karmara* 'food-appetizer'.

caramel Sugar which has been cooked until it turns brown. The word *caramel* is a comparatively late introduction into English: it is first recorded in 1725. It came via French from Spanish *caramelo*, but its previous history is speculative; its most likely source is perhaps late Latin *calamellus*, a diminutive form of Latin *calamus* 'reed, cane' (the implied reference being to 'sugarcane'). The sweets *caramels*, a soft form of toffee, are made with sugar and milk, butter, or cream.

In France, caramel seasoned with salt is popular. It seems to have originated in Brittany (which produces an abundance of sea salt), and in the early twenty-first century has become a cheffy fashion in the UK too. It is reminiscent of the American saltwater taffy, a butterless form of toffee originally made with sea water, which was popularized in late-nineteenth-century Atlantic City, New Jersey.

carasau *See* CARTA DI MUSICA.

caraway Undoubtedly caraway's most important role in English cookery has been as the anonymous but crucial ingredient of seed cakes. These are first mentioned as early as the 1570s, when the caraway seeds would have been introduced into the cakes in the form of comfits—encrusted in a sugar coating. It does not seem to have been until the late seventeenth or early eighteenth century that the plain seeds were used, producing a cake whose popularity perhaps reached its apogee in Victorian times: 'I cut and handed the seed-cake,' Charles Dickens, *David Copperfield* (1850). And in fact caraway in general went through a popular phase at that time, probably as part of a general leaning towards all things German that followed Victoria's marriage to Albert: caraway seed has always been a much-used flavouring in Germany, and indeed in eastern Europe generally, and its essential oil is the key ingredient of the liqueur kümmel.

But even before their use in cakes, caraway seeds had been popular simply for chewing on their own, either in the form of comfits or plain. And indeed the word *caraway* came to mean 'caraway seed'; in Shakespeare's *Henry IV Part Two*, for instance, Justice Shallow offers Falstaff 'a last year's pippin of my own grafting, with a dish of caraways' (the combination of cheese, apples, and caraway seeds seems to have been popular in the sixteenth and seventeenth centuries). The usage survived longest in Scotland, where 'caraway' was called *carvy* (from French *carvi*): 'She had preserved, since the great tea-drinking . . . , the remainder of the two ounces of carvey, bought for that memorable occasion', *Blackwood's Magazine* (1820). The habit of chewing the seeds, whether as a digestive, to sweeten the breath after a meal, or simply to pass the time, had early crossed the Atlantic, and by the mid-nineteenth century we find caraway being mentioned among a range of so-called 'meeting-seeds', aromatic seeds chewed while away the more wearisome passages of sermons and similar addresses: 'Some people call it "caraway" and "aniseed," but we call it "meetin'-seed," 'cause we cal'late it keeps us awake in meetin'', *Knickerbocker* (1851).

The word *caraway* comes originally from Arabic *alkarawiyā* 'the caraway', which found its way into Spanish as *alcarahueya*; English borrowed it from Spanish. French *carvi* comes via a slightly different route from the same source.

carbonade A Belgian dish of beef and onions braised in beer. The word was probably borrowed into French from Italian *carbonata*, which goes back ultimately to Latin *carbō* 'charcoal' and referred originally to the way in which the meat was grilled over charcoal to seal it before being stewed. The Flemish name of the dish is *stoofvlees*.

carbonara In Italy, a dish of spaghetti or other pasta served *alla carbonara* comes with a sauce made from eggs, olive oil, cream, cheese (pecorino or Parmesan) and strips of bacon (or ham, coppa, or salt pork). The term may refer for some unexplained reason to the Carbonari, members of a nineteenth-century secret society working for a unified Italy, so-called because they disguised themselves as *carbonari* 'charcoal-burners' after being driven into hiding in the forest of the Abruzzi; on the other hand it might simply mean 'cooked in charcoal-burner's style', or 'cooked as if in a kiln' (Italian *carbonara* 'charcoal kiln'). *Carbonata,* an Italian term for a dish of charcoal-grilled salt pork, may well be lurking in the background, too.

cardamom This eastern spice, with its aromatic seeds, is a speller's nightmare. The *Oxford English Dictionary* lists seven different variants (including *cardumome* and *cardamony*) used since the word entered the language, but that was over 400 years ago, and spelling was less institutionalized then. Even today, though, many dictionaries list three alternatives: *cardamom* (usually regarded as the main one), *cardamum*, and *cardamon*. Yet as we struggle with its apparently intractable syllables, the word continues to defeat us; here, for example, is a shot at it by a writer in the *Observer* (1988): 'Every evening the only other customer was a corpulent Indian who sweated cardoman through his enormous pores.' Of all the various possibilities on offer, we should perhaps stick to *cardamom*, if only because it is closest to the word's source, which is Latin *cardamōmum*; this in turn derived from Greek *kardámōmon*, a blend of *kárdamon* 'peppergrass' and *ámōmon*, a variety of Indian spice.

cardinal A drink which combines red wine with blackcurrant liqueur—in other words, the red-wine version of kir. The name was suggested by the red robes of a cardinal. An alternative term is *communard*.

cardoon The cardoon is, like its close relative the globe artichoke, a member of the thistle family. It is cultivated for its leaves, and particularly for their (fairly) succulent stalks, which are blanched by earthing up in much the same way as celery. English acquired the word from French *cardon*, which is a derivative of French *carde*, meaning 'edible part of an artichoke'. This in turn came ultimately from Latin *cardus* or *carduus* 'thistle, artichoke', from which we also get the verb *card* 'to comb out fibres using a toothed implement.' English *chard* comes from the same source.

First mention of cardoons in English comes in Randle Cotgrave's *Dictionary of the French and English Tongues* (1611), and according to John Lindley and Thomas Moore's *Treasury of Botany* (1866) they were first actually cultivated in Britain in 1656.

carnaroli An Italian variety of medium-grained rice, used especially in the making of risotto. Its grains are rather longer than those of arborio rice. It is native to the province of Vercelli in northwestern Italy.

carob Carob has enjoyed a considerable vogue in recent years as a low-fat, low-calorie, low-caffeine alternative to chocolate. It is prepared from the pulp of the pods of an evergreen tree of the pea family which grows in warm areas and as well as being called the *carob*, it is known as *algarroba* or *locust* (because the pods of some species supposedly resemble locusts). The word *carob* comes via obsolete French *carobe* or *caroube* and medieval Latin *carrūbium* from Arabic *kharrūba*.

The long black seed pods are sometimes called *St John's bread*, from the erroneous supposition that St John the Baptist lived on them while preaching (what he in fact ate were locusts).

Carob beans were used in the ancient world as units of weight. The Greek name for them was *kerátion*, literally 'little horn'—from which English gets *carat*.

carpaccio An Italian antipasto consisting of raw beef fillet sliced extremely thinly, often served with olive oil, lemon, and small pieces of Parmesan cheese. It was apparently invented at Harry's Bar in Venice and named in honour of the Italian painter Vittore Carpaccio (*c*.1460–*c*.1525), but the small print of its origin and naming is not entirely clear. Giuseppe Cipriani, the owner of Harry's Bar, claimed to have first served it around 1950 for a customer who demanded raw meat, but its name is not recorded in print before 1969; Cipriani said it was inspired by the particular shades of red Carpaccio used, but given the dating, perhaps a more direct source was the painter's raised profile following an exhibition of his works in Venice in 1963. Over the decades the term has broadened out to cover any raw ingredient, including fish and even fruit, sliced thinly.

carpet-bag steak A mainly Australian and (perhaps originally) American way with a piece of rump steak which consists of cutting a slit in it (to make a receptacle like a carpet bag), stuffing it with oysters, and baking it. The term is first recorded in 1958.

carrageen Carrageen, or *carragheen*, is a type of edible seaweed with flat branching red fronds. It grows along the shoreline in both Europe and North America, but it is particularly associated with Ireland, and its name comes from Irish Gaelic *carraigín*, meaning literally 'little rock'. An alternative term for it is *Irish moss*.

carrot The Greeks were familiar with the carrot—they have bequeathed us its name, from Greek *karōtón*, and may well have originated the notion about it being good for the eyesight (a theory much embroidered in the Second World War, when, in order to encourage the consumption of carrots, one of the few foodstuffs not in short supply, the British authorities put it about that the pilots of night-fighter aircraft consumed vast quantities to enable them to see in the dark). The Romans had their *carōta*, too, and introduced it to Britain. We would be hard put to it, however, to recognize this dingy yellowish tough root as a carrot today. The modern orange carrot seems to have originated in a purple-rooted variety which was grown first in Afghanistan in the seventh century AD, and was gradually conveyed westwards by the Arabs. It travelled up via Spain to northern Europe, and it seems to have been in the Low Countries in the Middle Ages that an orange variant was cultivated. It crossed the Channel via France in the early sixteenth century, bringing its French name *carotte*, and was sufficiently well established by the late seventeenth century for expressions such as *carroty* and *carrot-head* to be in common use for red-haired people: 'The Carrotpate be sure you hate, for she'll be true to no man', *Roxburgh Ballads* (1680). The meaning 'inducement', from the notion of encouraging a reluctant donkey to move by dangling a tasty carrot in front of it, is first recorded in the 1890s.

carta di musica An extremely thin crisp Italian flatbread. Its name means literally 'music paper', and was presumably given to it because it resembles the sort of paper on which music is written (although it has also been suggested that the bread is so thin that music can be read through it). It is a speciality of Sardinia, and its local name is *carasau* (in full *pane carasau*). This comes from *carasatura*, denoting 'double cooking', which reflects the way in which it is traditionally made: after initial baking it is split in half and baked again, ensuring not only thinness and crispness but also a longevity useful for shepherds spending long periods out among the hills and needing to carry their food with them.

Cashel Blue A type of rich creamy blue cheese made from cows' milk at Fethard, near Cashel in County Tipperary, Ireland.

cashew The seed of a tropical tree, *Anacardium occidentale*, which originated in Central and South America (hence the name, which comes from *caju* or *acaju* in the language of the Tupi people of the Amazon basin), but is now grown extensively in Africa and India. The seed itself, which somewhat resembles a kidney-shaped peanut, grows as an incongruous-looking sprout at the extremity of a pear-shaped fruitlike receptacle (known as a *cashew-apple*); it was first described in English by William Dampier in *A New Voyage Round the World* (1703): 'The Cashew is a Fruit as big as a Pippin, pretty long, and bigger near the Stem than at the other end. . . . The Seed of this Fruit grows at the end of it; 'tis of an Olive Colour shaped like a Bean.'
   The shell of the nut has three layers, and its extraction is a highly labour-intensive business. The middle layer contains an acrid brown oil.

cassareep A staple condiment of West Indian cooking consisting of a syrupy liquid made by boiling down and seasoning the bitter juice of the cassava root. Its name is an alteration of an earlier *casserepo*, which comes from a local Cariban language; it is related to *kaseripu* in the Galibi language of French Guiana.

cassata A variety of Neapolitan ice cream which contains nuts and crystallized fruits. Its name comes from the oblong shape in which it is moulded: *cassata* is literally 'little case' in Italian. It is a comparatively recent introduction into English, first being mentioned in the February 1927 issue of *Harper's Magazine*.

cassava The cassava, a plant of the spurge family, provides a large proportion of the staple diet of the native peoples of South America. It has a large starchy root which is eaten as a vegetable (and is also, incidentally, the source of tapioca). The word *cassava* comes via French *cassave* from *casavi*, the name of the plant in the Taino language of Haiti. (An alternative term is *manioc* or *manioca*, which comes from Tupi *mandioca*.)

casserole Like many other cookery terms, *casserole* denotes both a receptacle and the dish cooked in it, the former being the primary sense. Of its involved etymological ancestry more later; but perhaps the most remarkable aspect of its history is the complete and sudden change in the dish it refers to that has taken place within the past hundred years. When English took it over from French at the beginning of the eighteenth century it meant a dish of cooked rice moulded into the shape of a casserole cooking pot and then filled with a savoury mixture, say of chicken or sweetbreads. It was also applied by extension to a border of rice, or even of mashed potato, round some such dish as fricassee or curry: Mrs Beeton's recipe for a 'savoury casserole of rice' describes such a rice border. Then some time around the 1870s this sense of *casserole* seems to have slipped imperceptibly but swiftly into a 'dish of meat, vegetable, and stock or other liquid, cooked slowly in the oven in a closed pot', its current sense. French meanwhile retains the original 'rice dish' connotations, although the term is now little used.
   Returning to the receptacle itself, a sturdy lidded ovenproof pot, usually sufficiently respectable-looking to be brought to the table, the word for it goes back ultimately to Greek *kuáthos* 'cup'. This had a diminutive form *kuáthion* 'little cup', which was borrowed into late Latin as *cattia* 'pan, basin'. In Provençal it became *casa*, and Old French took it over as *casse*. This in turn was made into a diminutive, *cassole*, of which French *casserole* is a later unexplained extension.
   The word seems not to have been used as a verb in English until after the First World War: 'It seemed a shame to casserole [the chicken], for it would 'ave roasted beautiful', Dorothy Sayers, *Strong Poison* (1930).

cassia Cassia, or *cassia bark*, is the aromatic bark of an East Asian tree related to the cinnamon. It is dried and used to produce an inferior sort of cinnamon, which is sometimes used to adulterate true cinnamon. Ground up, it is reddish brown in colour, rather than the pale tan of true cinnamon. Its name comes via Latin and Greek from Hebrew *qěsī·āh*.

cassoulet The precise recipe for cassoulet, the rich stew of haricot beans and assorted meats from southwestern France, is a subject over which families have feuded and friendships foundered over the centuries. There are three towns in Languedoc which claim to produce the only 'authentic' version: in Castelnaudary, which claims to have invented it, they make it with fresh pork, ham, and pork sausages; in Toulouse, they put in Toulouse sausage and preserved duck or goose; and in Carcassonne they opt for pieces of mutton. However, as Paula Wolfert explains in *The Cooking of Southwest France* (1987), 'these regional distinctions are now completely blurred'. The word is a diminutive of French dialect *cassole* 'saucepan', and shares a common ancestry with *casserole*.

castor sugar Castor sugar, or *caster sugar*, a British term for white sugar with finer grains than those of granulated sugar, dates from the mid-nineteenth century. It comes, of course, from the suitability of such sugar for use in a castor, a small pot with a perforated lid, used for sprinkling or 'casting' the sugar on to food. The nearest American equivalent is *superfine sugar*, or *Baker's Special*, which has grains slightly smaller than the average 0.25 millimetres of castor sugar.

caudle A caudle is—or was—a hot drink made from sweetened wine or beer mixed with eggs, bread, and spices. Its main role was as a comforting or nourishing pick-me-up given to invalids or to women about to give birth. But it was also used simply as a nightcap, if the title of Douglas Jerrold's *Mrs Caudle's Curtain Lectures*, published in book form in 1846, is anything to go by (a *curtain lecture* is, to quote Dr Johnson's definition, 'a reproof given by a wife to her husband in bed', and *caudle* was used humorously as a verb in the mid-nineteenth century, on the basis of Jerrold's creation, to denote such admonishment: 'The mother is easily convinced . . . she must Caudle her husband into the same conviction', *Tait's Magazine* (1845). The word *caudle* comes via Old Northern French *caudel* from a hypothetical medieval Latin *caldellum, a diminutive form of Latin *caldum* 'hot drink', and is thus related to French *chaud* 'hot'. It goes back to the thirteenth century, when Robert of Gloucester recorded an ironic little aphorism in his *Chronicle* (1297): 'As they say, when I am dead, make me a caudle.'

cauliflower England was introduced to the cauliflower towards the end of the sixteenth century. It seems originally to have been developed by the Arabs, and had not actually arrived in mainland Europe until earlier in the same century. This accounts for its lack of an ancient, 'ancestral' name. The words for it in most European languages are variations on the notion 'flowering cabbage': German *blumenkohl*, for instance, Spanish *coliflor*. The Italian version is *cavolfiore* (*cavolo* is Italian for 'cabbage', and is related to English *kale* and *cole*); this seems to have been adapted in French to *chou fleuri*, and passed on to English, where the native *cole* 'cabbage' replaced *chou* (in the earliest printed reference to it, in John Gerarde's *Herbal* (1597), it is spelled *cole florie*). In the seventeenth century the unfamiliar element *florie* was changed to *flower*, producing in due course *cauliflower* (a similar development led to modern French *chou-fleur*). Mark Twain described the vegetable as 'nothing but a cabbage with a college education'.

The expression *cauliflower ear*, referring to an ear swollen and distorted from years of taking punches, is first recorded in 1909.

cava Spanish sparkling wine, made mostly in the area of Penedès, to the west of Barcelona, from the macabeo, parellada, and xarel-lo grapes. The sparkle is introduced by a second fermentation in bottle. This is the same method as is used for champagne, and since they started making the wine in the 1870s the Spanish had called it *champaña*. However, champagne-producers, ever jealous of their name, eventually objected, and in 1970 the term *cava*, which means literally 'cellar' in Spanish, was adopted in its stead.

caveach *See* ESCABECHE.

caviare *Caviare*, or *caviar*, has a complicated linguistic history in English. When it was first introduced, in the late sixteenth century, it seems to have been borrowed simultaneously from a number of different European languages: Italian *caviale*, Spanish *cabial*, French *cavial*, and Portuguese *caviar* (all of them derived ultimately from Turkish *khâvyâr*). And what is more, to begin with it was pronounced with four syllables, following the Italian. So in the sixteenth and seventeenth centuries, an anarchic array of spellings such as *chauiale*, *cavery*, and *cauiarie* existed. As early as 1625 it was becoming a three-syllable word, with the final -*e* being dropped, at least in speech (pronounced *caviair*), and in the eighteenth century, according to Jonathan Swift, it was often elided to just two syllables: he spells it *caveer*, to rhyme with *cheer*. The modern pronunciation is probably due to French influence.

It is of course the roe of the sturgeon, and it comes in three main grades depending on the size of the fish. The largest comes from the white sturgeon, the *beluga* (a derivative of Russian *belyi* 'white'); the next is from the *sevruga* (Russian *sevrjuga*), about 1.25 metres long, which some consider gives the finest caviare; and finally comes the common sturgeon. In addition there are *oscietra*, which is usually golden-brown in colour and comes from albino fish, and *keta*, which is obtained from the dog salmon, and is a good deal cheaper. It is, incidentally, rather ironic that this most Russian of delicacies, which has introduced this wealth of Russian terminology into the language, is not itself designated by a Russian word: in Russian, 'caviare' is *ikra*, a term which enjoyed a brief life in English in the sixteenth and seventeenth centuries as *ikary*.

The exclusivity of caviare, and the fact that it is rather an acquired taste, has long been recognized. It lies behind the familiar lines from Shakespeare's *Hamlet*: 'For the Play I remember pleas'd not the Million, 'twas Cauiarie to the Generall: but it was an excellent Play'; that is to say, its subtle pleasures are lost on the ignorant multitude. 'At a concluding vodka and caviare reception hosted by the Russians [at the 1945 Potsdam conference], [Ernest] Bevin [the British Foreign Secretary, and staunchly working-class] is reputed to have said to Stalin, "'Ere, Joe, this jam tastes fishy"', D. R. Thorpe, *Supermac* (2010).

A cheap substitute for caviare is made, especially in Denmark and Iceland, by dyeing black the roe of the lumpfish, a North Atlantic seafish. It is termed *lumpfish caviare*. A vegetarian version is also made from puréed aubergine: 'Scallop ceviche with aubergine and lemon "caviars" was .. an exercise in the yin-yang balance of coolness and piquancy', *Time Out, London's Best Restaurants* (2011).

A more recent metaphorical application of the word (1890–1920) is to the censoring of a section of text by overprinting it with a pattern of black-and-white diamond-shapes, supposedly reminiscent of the appearance of black caviare spread on bread and butter.

cavolo nero A Tuscan variety of kale that has long, narrow, very dark green leaves with a knobbly, bubbly surface ('savoyed' in the trade, after the wrinkly leaves of the savoy cabbage). It came to wide international notice towards the end of the twentieth century, with the rise in popularity of 'real' Italian cuisine. Its name in Italian means literally 'black kale'.

cawl A Welsh dish consisting of a broth containing meat and vegetables, which can be eaten either with the broth or as a separate course. The word, which rhymes with *fowl*, probably comes ultimately from Latin *caulis* 'stem, stalk', with reference to the stalks of cabbages and other vegetables that the dish contains.

cayenne This pungent spice consists of the finely ground flesh and seeds of dried red peppers (*Capsicum frutescens*). It is the seeds that make the difference; without them you have the relatively mild paprika, but cayenne is distinctly hot. It first found its way to British tables in the eighteenth century, and early spellings (*chian, kayan, kian*) reflect its source in the language of the Tupi peoples of South America—they called it *kyinha*. It was not long though before, by the process of folk etymology, it became assimilated to the name of the chief town of French Guiana—Cayenne. Other names given to it include *chilli pepper, red pepper*, and, from the sixteenth to the nineteenth centuries, *guinea pepper*.

cecil A superannuated term for a type of rissole or meatball: minced meat (generally the cold remains of a roast) mixed with chopped onions, breadcrumbs, and seasonings, rolled into balls and fried. The meat seems usually to have been beef (Mrs Rundell in her *New System of Domestic Cookery* (1819) gave a recipe for beef cecils). The word is presumably an application of the personal name, but the reason for it is unknown.

cedrato An Italian word for the citron, occasionally used in the past in English (*Mrs A. B. Marshall's Cookery Book* (1888) has a recipe for chestnut and cedrati [the plural of *cedrato*] ice cream). It is a derivative of *cedro* 'citron' (from Latin *citrus*). English also acquired the word via French as *cedrat* or *cedrate* in the late eighteenth century, but it did not survive much beyond the middle of the nineteenth century.

celeriac A bulbous-rooted form of celery that was introduced in the 1720s by the garden designer and seedsman Stephen Switzer. Jane Grigson, in her *Vegetable Book* (1978), conjectures that he may even have invented the name, which is simply *celery* with the arbitrary addition of the suffix -*ac* to give it a learned sound.

celery The term *celery* did not enter the English language until the mid-seventeenth century, when the plant began to be grown in Britain for food. Cultivated celery was introduced from Italy, and the name came with it, via French (where it was called *sceleri d'Italie* in the seventeenth century). The ultimate source is Greek *sélinon* 'parsley'. Celery was initially regarded as highly exotic in Britain, and instructions had to be given on how to eat it. The naturalist John Ray provided them in 1673; under the heading 'Italian food' in his *Journey in the Low Countries* he notes 'Selleri, the young shoots whereof they eat raw with oyl and pepper.' The seventeenth-century diarist John Evelyn recommended using the leaves and the blanched stalks, peeled and cut up, in salads. In a later century, though, Mrs Beeton, with her customary concern for her readers' delicate digestions, cautions that 'in a raw state, this plant does not suit weak stomachs'.

But apart from the cultivated celery, there is a wild form that has always grown in Britain: a bitter, less succulent plant called *smallage*. Its name comes from Middle English *small ache; ache* was in former times the general term for plants of this genus, and comes ultimately from Latin *apium* (the Latin name for 'celery' is *Apium graveolens*).

cellophane noodles An alternative name for GLASS NOODLES, based on the transparency of cellophane.

cendré A French cover term for a range of small soft cheeses that are covered in a layer of wood ash (*cendré* means literally 'ashy'). Such cheeses come in various shapes—discs, truncated pyramids, etc.—and are particularly associated with the Champagne region.

cep A large fragrant fleshy mushroom, *Boletus edulis*, is widely used in French cookery. Its name (in modern French *cèpe*) comes from Gascon dialect *cep*, which goes back to Latin *cippus* 'stake'. In Victorian England ceps were often called *penny buns*, from their brown bun-shaped cap. *See also* PORCINI.

cervelat A spicy smoked sausage made either from pork or from a mixture of pork and beef. The word was borrowed from the now obsolete French *cervelat* (modern French has *cervelas*), which in turn came from Italian *cervellata*. This gives a clue to the sausage's original ingredients, for it is a derivative of *cervello* 'brain'. (The English word *saveloy* is an alteration of *cervelat*.)

ceviche Ceviche, or *seviche*, is a classic Spanish-American dish made by marinating or 'cooking' fish or shellfish in a mixture of lime juice and olive oil, tomato, onions and chilli. The name, first recorded in English in 1951, comes from South American Spanish *seviche* or *cebiche*. The origin of that is not known, but given the similarity of form and referent, it has been speculated that it may have come from Spanish *escabeche* (*see* ESCABECHE; in ceviche the fish is raw before the application of the acidulated marinade, in

escabeche it is cooked). Another possible derivation is via Spanish *cebo* 'fodder, food, bait' from Latin *cibus* 'food'.

The basic technique—of 'cooking' fish in an acidic liquid—is found independently in other parts of the world: in the Philippines, for example, where it goes under the name *kinilaw,* and in the islands of the South Pacific.

chaat Chaat, or *chat,* is an Indian street snack, widely sold from stalls and carts in Indian cities. It consists of a variety of small savoury goodies: the standard mix includes yoghurt-soaked fritters, pieces of potato, and various spicy sauces and chutneys. The term is a specialization of Hindi *cât,* which means literally 'tasting, a delicacy', and is derived from *câtnâ* 'to lick'.

challah A challah, or *challa,* or *chollah* (pronounced /ˈhahlə/) is a loaf of bread made with eggs and white flour, typically plaited in form and sprinkled with poppy seeds, traditionally baked to celebrate the Jewish sabbath. The word comes from Hebrew *hallah,* which is probably a derivative of *hll* 'hollow, pierce', perhaps referring to the original form of the loaf. In South African English the loaf is termed *kitke.*

Chambertin A soft cows'-milk cheese with an orange rind, made in the Burgundy region of France. It was developed around 1950 by the cheesemaker Raymond Gaugry. Its name—in full *ami de Chambertin,* 'friend of Chambertin'—reflects the idea that it makes a perfect partner for the finest red burgundies, and especially no doubt for Chambertin itself, a rarefied grand cru which was reputedly Napoleon's favourite wine.

champ A simple Irish dish made from mashed potato with plenty of milk and butter, and flavoured with chopped-up onions or spring onions. It is traditionally eaten on Hallowe'en (31 October).

chanterelle A type of edible wild mushroom that grows in woods, has a yellow funnel-shaped cap and smells faintly of apricots. Its name came into English from French in the late eighteenth century. The French word evolved from modern Latin *cantharellus,* which meant literally 'little drinking vessel'. In present-day France the mushroom is more usually called *girolle* than *chanterelle. See also* TROMPETTE DE MORT.

Chantilly Chantilly cream, or in French *crème Chantilly*, is a sweetened whipped cream used in a wide assortment of desserts (Eliza Acton in her *Modern Cookery* (1845) gave a recipe for 'Chantilly Basket, filled with whipped cream and fresh strawberries'). It was named after the chateau of Chantilly, near Paris, where in the mid-seventeenth century the celebrated chef Vatel worked, although the cream does not seem to have any actual connection with the chateau.

Chaource A soft French cows'-milk cheese produced in cylindrical form. It takes its name from the small town of Chaource, to the south of Troyes in the Champagne region, where it is made.

chapati Chapatis (or *chapattis,* or *chappatis,* or *chupattis*—there are a variety of spellings) are a sort of flat unleavened wholewheat Indian bread. The term is an Anglicization of Hindi *capati,* a descendant of Sanskrit *carpati* 'thin cake', which itself was derived from the adjective *carpata* 'flat'. It first found its way into English in the early nineteenth century.

Quentin Crewe, in his *International Pocket Food Book* (1980), reports that in India 'elephants are commonly fed with chapatis the size of a car wheel.'

char In Mandarin Chinese, the word for 'tea' is *ch'a*—and when English-speakers first encountered tea in the late sixteenth century, this was the term they adopted for it, in various spellings such as *chia* and *chaw*: 'Water mixt with a certaine precious powder which [the Japanese] use, they account a daintie beverage; they call it Chia', Robert

Johnson, *The World* (1601). It was *t'e*, in the Amoy dialect of southeastern China, which was eventually to provide the standard word for 'tea' in English, but *char* or *cha* has continued as a colloquial British alternative, particularly as reinforced by Hindi *cā* during the British occupation of India (whence the British military institution, a 'cup of char').

charcoal biscuit A crisp non-sweet biscuit of which powdered charcoal is an ingredient, giving it a dark grey colour. The charcoal, which makes a negligible flavour impact, was originally introduced (in the late nineteenth century) to counteract fermentation or to act as a deodorizer, but its presence is now purely cosmetic (although its advocates claim it aids digestion). The biscuits are typically eaten with cheese.

charcuterie A collective term for cold cooked meat products, especially from the pig: hams, salami, brawn, and the like. The French term was based on *char* (a now obsolete form of *chair*) *cuite* 'cooked flesh'. It began to be used in English in the 1850s.

chard The name *chard* comes ultimately from Latin *carduus* 'thistle', and is thus related to *cardoon*. However, the plant chard is not a member of the thistle family, to which the cardoon and globe artichoke belong: it is a beet. The reason for the association of names is that, as with cardoons, it is the enlarged midrib of the leaf which is eaten. English acquired the word in the seventeenth century, from French *carde*. It is first recorded in 1658, in John Evelyn's *French Gardener*, in the sense 'leaf-stalk of an artichoke', but within less than a decade had settled to its present meaning 'beet leaf.' The initial *ch-* may derive from French *chardon* 'thistle'.

Chard has been alternatively known since at least the early eighteenth century as *Swiss chard*, apparently from an association of the vegetable with Switzerland by the Dutch. Similar, but with slightly larger stalks, is the *seakale beet*, known in Australia and New Zealand as *silver beet*.

chardonnay A grape variety that characteristically produces full-bodied dry white wines. There is a village called Chardonnay in the Mâconnais area of southern Burgundy. It is not clear whether the grape was named after the village or the village after the grape, but either way the location is appropriate, for Burgundy produces the most outstanding chardonnay wines—from austere Chablis in the north to the richer, often buttery Meursaults, Pulignies, etc. in the southern Côte d'Or. But in recent years, the New World has caught on to the chardonnay: California, Australia, etc. are producing more exotic wines from the grape, with lush, tropical-fruit flavours. At the beginning of the twenty-first century it was the second most widely planted white grape in the world. 'Glossy, rich, and loud in flavour [chardonnay] was as closely identified with the 90s and early 2000s as Britpop, Blair, and Bridget Jones ... It came to dominate sales of white wine, its cultural reach so profound that it briefly became a popular girls' name', David Williams, *Observer Food Monthly* (2011).

Charentais *See* MELON.

charlotte A hot pudding consisting of fruit, typically apple, baked within a case of bread, sponge cake, etc., in a characteristically deep round mould. It first appears on the scene at the end of the eighteenth century (in a poem called *Hasty-Pudding* by J. Barlow: 'The Charlotte brown, within whose crusty sides a belly soft the pulpy apple hides'), and it has been speculated that it was named after Queen Charlotte (1744–1818), wife of George III, who apparently was an enthusiastic patron of apple growers. The coincidence of names is probably fortuitous, but what is certain is that as early as the first decade of the nineteenth century recipes for the dish had begun to appear; this from Mrs Rundell, *A New System of Domestic Cookery* (1807): 'Cut as many very thin slices of white bread as will cover the bottom and line the sides of a baking dish, but first rub it thick with butter. Put apples, in thin slices, into the dish.'

The apple charlotte has on the whole remained a British dish, but the charlotte has achieved wider renown in the shape of the *charlotte russe*, literally 'Russian charlotte', a cold pudding in which custard replaces the fruit. It was supposedly invented by the French chef Antonin Carême in 1802, who, so the story goes, initially named it *charlotte à la parisienne*, but later changed it to *charlotte russe* in honour of his employer, Czar Alexander of Russia.

char siu A Chinese method of preparing and cooking pork: the meat is cut into strips, marinated in a mixture of honey, soy sauce, hoisin sauce, and five-spice powder (and sometimes also artificial colouring), which has the effect of turning it dark red, skewered on long forks (the name means literally 'fork burnt' or 'fork roasted' in Cantonese), and cooked in the oven or over a fire.

chartreuse One of the most ancient and celebrated of French liqueurs. Brandy-based, it is flavoured with a secret combination of herbs probably invented by the Carthusian monks of Vauvert, near Paris, in the seventeenth century. They passed the recipe on to their brothers at the Grande-Chartreuse (the 'Great Charterhouse') near Grenoble in 1735, where it has been produced commercially since 1835. Today it comes in two basic varieties: the original green Chartreuse, and the sweeter, slightly less alcoholic yellow version introduced in 1840. A much stronger *élixir* is also produced. The use of *chartreuse* as a colour term (based on the green rather than the yellow type) dates from the late nineteenth century.

The term *chartreuse* also denotes a dish consisting of layers of vegetables and meat or game (typically partridge) cooked in a mould. The original version seems to have been meatless, and is said to have reflected the vegetarian diet of Carthusian monks.

In Britain *chartreuse* is pronounced /shar'trerz/, in American English generally /shar'trooz/ or /shar'troos/.

chasseur A dish designated *chasseur* (for instance *chicken chasseur* or *veal chasseur*) is served with a sauce of mushrooms, shallots or onions, tomatoes, and white wine. In French, *chasseur* means literally 'hunter', and the recipe probably originated as a way of serving game. The equivalent term in Italian cookery is *cacciatore*.

chateaubriand A thick steak cut from a beef fillet. It was named after the French writer and statesman François René, Vicomte de Chateaubriand. The original application of the term appears to have been to a particular method of preparing steak—grilled and served with béarnaise sauce—which was invented by the chef Montmirail in 1822, when the Vicomte de Chateaubriand was French ambassador in London; but by the 1870s, when it was introduced into English, it had been transferred to the steak itself: 'The steak which had formerly been served . . . under the name of *filet de boeuf* was now always announced as a Chateaubriand,' E. S. Dallas, *Kettner's Book of the Table* (1877).

chaudfroid French *chaudfroid* means literally 'hot–cold', and that describes fairly accurately what the dish is: meat, poultry, fish, etc. cooked and allowed to go cold before serving (typically covered in a stiff sauce made of stock and gelatin, known as a *chaudfroid sauce*, or in aspic). Chaudfroids often formed the basis of elaborate cold-buffet dishes in nineteenth-century French haute cuisine, and the descendants of these, decorated with painstakingly shaped pieces of truffle, mounds of chopped aspic, etc., can still be encountered.

chayote A green pear-shaped tropical fruit of the squash family. It has a single large seed and tastes somewhat like cucumber. It is usually eaten cooked. Its name, first recorded in 1884, came via Spanish from Nahuatl *chayotli*. It goes under a number of other appellations in various parts of the world, including *chocho, choko, christophene,* and *mirliton*.

Cheddar The epitome of English-style hard cheese. It has long since left its humble origins behind it, taking its name to wherever in the temperate world English-speaking people and their dairy cattle have spread. Indeed, the word *Cheddar* has become virtually synonymous with *cheese*—as in the exclamation *hard Cheddar!*

Cheesemaking has been going on in and around the Somerset village of Cheddar since at least Elizabethan times, and its product has consistently enjoyed a high reputation—at least until the twentieth century, when mass-produced copies have often taken its name in vain. The distinctive feature of Cheddar's production is the process that has become known as 'cheddaring', in which the finely chopped curds are formed into blocks and stacked, so as to coagulate.

cheese Cheese no doubt emerged in Neolithic times. Once human beings had domesticated animals and started to milk them, it would not have taken long before it was found that milk left around fermented and thickened into something quite palatable. It may have been the nomads of Central Asia who, keeping milk in containers made from animal stomachs, discovered the coagulating properties of rennet. Until about 2,000 years ago northern Europeans probably knew only fresh cheeses, consisting of moist unripened curds. The Germanic peoples called it **justaz*, a word related to Latin *jūs* 'juice', which survives today in the Swedish and Danish term for cheese, *ost*, and was borrowed into Finnish as *juusto*. Then, however, increasing contact with the northwardly mobile Romans brought an awareness of the harder cheeses of southern Europe. Their Latin name was *cāseus* (whence Spanish *queso* and Welsh *caws*). This the West Germanic tribes borrowed as **kāsjo*, which has subsequently dispersed to Dutch *kaas*, German *käse*, and English *cheese*. (For some reason the people of Gaul did not adopt *cāseus*; they preferred instead to adapt Vulgar Latin **formāticus* 'cheese made in a form or mould' into a new word for cheese, *fromage*.)

The use of *cheese* to denote a confection made by boiling down a sweetened purée of fruit (notably damson but also quince, apple, apricot, etc.) until it reaches a firm cutting consistency dates from at least the sixteenth century. *See also* COTIGNAC, MEMBRILLO.

The widening of the lips involved in saying the word *cheese* had led by the 1930s to its use (now beyond a cliché) by photographers to get their subjects to smile. *Hard cheese* as a British slang expression of commiseration dates from the 1870s. Along with its more specific synonym *hard Cheddar*, it now has a distinctly dated air. The origin of *cheesed off* 'fed up', first recorded in the 1940s, is not known.

cheesecake The word *cheesecake* is an old one, dating back to the early fifteenth century. At that period it meant a 'cooked tart made from curd cheese, with the addition of ingredients such as eggs, sugar, spices, etc.'. That basic idea survives in, for instance, today's Yorkshire curd cheesecake tarts; but the term *cheesecake* has been applied to some very different animals over the past 600 years. In the seventeenth century, it was used for what was virtually a custard tart, made from a cooked mixture of eggs, butter, cream, and flour, and a little later for tarts filled with lemon curd. The recipes given by Alexis Soyer in 1853 and Mrs Beeton in 1861 perpetuate this notion of the *cheesecake*, and it seems not to have been until the twentieth century that the traditional curd-cheese cheesecake was widely reintroduced, probably in the first instance by eastern European immigrants in the US. This would not do for the chill-cabinets of supermarkets, however, and so a new convenience cheesecake was developed in America. It is made of soft cheese, cream, and eggs, uncooked, but set with gelatine, on a base of biscuit crumbs, and topped with fruit such as blackcurrants, cherries, and strawberries.

The colloquial use of the term *cheesecake* for the titillating display of scantily clad women arose in America in the early twentieth century. A number of fanciful theories about its origins have been put forward, none of which carry sufficient conviction to bear repeating. The answering *beefcake*, in which dishy men take the place of dishy women, was coined in the late 1940s.

cheese football A snack consisting of a small wafer-biscuit sphere filled with a cheese-based paste. It was introduced by the British biscuit manufacturer Jacob & Co. in the 1960s.

cheese straw A snack consisting of a thin strip of pastry flavoured with cheese. The term is first recorded in 1874.

Chelsea bun A sweet currant bun whose characteristic feature is that it is made from an oblong piece of dough that is rolled up into a coil. They were first made at the Chelsea Bun House, a bakery opened near Sloane Square, London (which survived until 1839), in the late seventeenth or early eighteenth century. The earliest known reference to them (and not at all a complimentary one) is by Jonathan Swift in his *Journal to Stella* (2 May 1711): 'Was it not *Rrrrrrrrrare Chelsea buns* [a street vendor's cry]? I bought one to-day in my walk; it cost me a penny; it was stale, and I did not like it.' It is not clear, however, whether this disappointing article was a Chelsea bun as we now know it or a hot-cross bun (for which the Bun House was also famous) left over from Easter.

chenin blanc A type of wine grape that produces a white wine—often tart and undistinguished, but capable, when conditions are favourable, of being lusciously memorable (as in the case of the great botrytized sweet wines of Vouvray and elsewhere in the middle Loire in particularly fine years). Apart from France, it is also widely grown in California and South Africa. It gets its name from Mont-Chenin in the Touraine.

cherimoya The fruit of a tropical American tree of the custard-apple family. Its scaly patterned green skin became an increasingly common sight on the market stalls and even the supermarket shelves of Britain in the late twentieth century. This conceals a sweet white juicy pulp similar to that of its close relative, the custard apple, and also many smooth black seeds, from which it gets its name (originally an American Spanish adaptation of *chirimuya*, a word meaning 'cold seeds' in the Quechua language of Peru).

chermoula In North African cookery, a marinade of fragrant herbs and spices (a typical mix would be coriander, parsley, cumin, and paprika) with garlic, olive oil, and lemon juice: 'Main courses feature . . . chamoula [sic]-marinated pork steak', *Good Food Guide* (2008).

cherry The cherry was first cultivated in the Near East, and the word for it in the Akkadian language of Mesopotamia was *karsu*. When the fruit reached Greece, it brought its name with it, in the form *kerasós* 'cherry-tree', and in due course this passed into Latin as *cerasus* (Pliny has a story of the great Roman gourmet Lucullus introducing the cherry to Italy from Pontus, a kingdom to the south of the Black Sea, around 65 BC, but it is probably apocryphal). The Latin word was borrowed into the Germanic languages in prehistoric times, where it eventually produced modern German *kirsche* (from which English gets the word for cherry eau-de-vie). It also gave the Anglo-Saxons their word for cherry, *ciris*, but this died out in the early Middle English period, and was replaced in the fourteenth century by *cherise*, the Old Northern French descendant of Latin *cerasus*. It did not take English-speakers long to misinterpret *cherise* as a plural, and so the new singular *cherry* was coined.

(The modern French term *cerise*, incidentally, gave English an adjective meaning 'bright red' in the nineteenth century.)

The colloquial use of *cherry* for 'hymen' appears to be a twentieth-century development. The expression *lose one's cherry*, meaning 'to lose one's virginity', is first recorded in 1928.

cherry tomato A small round variety of tomato, typically with a strong flavour. The term originated in America. It is first recorded in 1859.

chervil Two distinct and only distantly related plants share the name *chervil*. The more familiar (and the original possessor of the name) is a plant of the parsley family that is used as a herb. Its leaves, which are more delicate and feathery than those of parsley, have a subtly liquorice-like taste, and have a wide range of culinary applications as both garnish and flavouring. The other sort of chervil, also an umbellifer, is valued for its root (*chervil root*), which is like a small grey carrot, and usually eaten boiled; its leaves are mildly poisonous. English borrowed the word *chervil* in Anglo-Saxon times from Latin *chaerephyllum*; this in turn goes back to Greek *khaírephullon*, which may have been a compound of *khaírein* 'to greet' and *phúllon* 'leaf'.

Cheshire A hard but crumbly English cows'-milk cheese made in Cheshire and the neighbouring counties of Shropshire and Clwyd. It comes in two main varieties: 'white', which is actually very pale yellow, and 'red', which is dyed with annatto. A blue-veined variety is also made; in past centuries, when the veining occurred by accident and was unwelcome, the cheese was known as 'green fade', but now it is deliberately manufactured, under the name *Blue Cheshire*. Cheshire is the oldest named cheese produced in the British Isles; it is referred to in the Domesday Book.

chess pie A speciality of the Deep South of the US: a pie or tart baked with a simple filling of eggs, butter, and sugar, sometimes with additional flavourings. The name, first recorded in 1932, may incorporate an alteration of *chest*.

chestnut The British have never exploited the versatility of the chestnut to the same extent as the French (*see* MARRONS GLACÉS) and other inhabitants of southern Europe (who at times in the past have subsisted on them), but they have always had a soft spot for hot roasted chestnuts, which are one of the few survivals of traditional British street food.

The *chest-* of *chestnut* traces its history back to Greek *kastanéā*, which some etymologists think denoted originally 'nut from Castanea' (in Pontus, Asia Minor) or 'nut from Castana' (in Thessaly, Greece)—although a likelier derivation may be from Armenian *kaskeni*. This passed into Latin as *castanea*, which English originally acquired in the Anglo-Saxon period as *cisten*. However, *cisten* seems to have died out in the eleventh century, and it was not until the fourteenth century that English reborrowed the word, via Old French, as *chesteine*. *Chesteine-nut* in due course became *chestnut*. (The Spanish descendant of Latin *castanea*, incidentally, is the source of *castanet*, an allusion to the instrument's chestnut-shell-like shape.)

The term was first applied to the unrelated and inedible horse chestnut in the mid-sixteenth century, when the tree was introduced into Britain.

chewing gum Chewing gum, a flavoured rubbery substance made usually from chicle (the coagulated juice of the sapodilla plant) and used as the masticatory equivalent of worry beads, originated in the US in the middle of the nineteenth century: the *Chicago Daily Democrat* (1850) announced 'Chewing gum! A new and superior preparation of Spruce Gum.' A refinement on the original idea, *bubble gum*, which with practice could be inflated into large bubbles by the chewer, was brought out just before the Second World War.

chicken à la king A dish consisting of cooked breast of chicken in a cream sauce with mushrooms and peppers. It is said to have been created, probably in the last quarter of the nineteenth century, at the Brighton Beach Hotel, New York, and named in honour of Mr and Mrs E. Clark King III. Alternative accounts, however, name the Wall Street broker James R. Keene or his son Foxhall P. Keene as the dedicatee. The term is first recorded in 1912.

chicken-fried steak In the US, a thin slice of beef which is lightly egged and floured and fried until crisp. The method is associated particularly with the South and Midwest, and the name (first recorded in 1952) reflects the local way of frying chicken. *See also* KIEV.

chicken Maryland Chicken Maryland, or *Maryland chicken*, or, with a little French polish, *chicken à la Maryland,* is a dish in which pieces of chicken are coated with beaten egg and breadcrumbs and fried. Cream or milk is added to the pan juices at the end. Legend has it that it was introduced to the New World by Lord Baltimore (c.1580–1632), who obtained the original grant of land for the North American colony that later became Maryland, but there is no record of the actual term *chicken Maryland* before the 1890s.

In Australian English, the term is applied to a chicken portion comprising the whole leg: thigh and drumstick.

chickpea Chickpeas have no etymological connection with chickens. To the Romans the small hard pealike seed was *cicer* (the orator and statesman Cicero took his cognomen from it—an ancestor evidently had a facial wart that looked like a chickpea). In French this became *chiche*, which English took over in the fourteenth century as *chich*. It was most commonly encountered, naturally, in the plural (John Wycliffe's 1388 translation of 2 Samuel 17:28, for example, has 'fried chichis and honey', where the Authorized Version has 'parched pulse and honey'), and continued in use until the twentieth century. From the sixteenth century, however, on the model of French *pois chiche*, the seed began to be called *chich pea*; and in the eighteenth century, whether by folk-etymological substitution of a more familiar word or simply through a misprint, this was altered to *chickpea*.

An alternative name for the 'chickpea' is *garbanzo bean*.

chicory Chicory and endive are closely related plants (both belonging to the genus *Cichorium*), and the use of their names is diametrically opposite on the two sides of the Atlantic. In Britain, the word *chicory* is used for *C. intybus*, which produces attractive blue flowers and is also called *succory*. In cultivation, its young shoots are blanched by depriving them of sunlight, which produces white bullet-shaped 'chicons' that are eaten raw in salads. An alternative name for these is *witloof*, and Americans call the vegetable *endive* or *Belgian endive* (the method of blanching was pioneered in Belgium in the 1840s). The Italians have specialized in producing red-leaved varieties of chicory, which became popular in Britain in the 1980s under the name *radicchio*.

There is another variety of chicory, known as *Magdeburg chicory*, which has very large roots that can be roasted, ground, and used as a coffee additive or substitute.

The word *chicory* itself comes via early modern French *cicorée* and Latin *cichorium* from Greek *kíkhora*, and entered English in the fifteenth century (*succory* is ultimately the same word, filtered through Dutch and Low German).

chilli Chillis (or *chilis,* as the word is more usually spelled in American English) are the extremely pungent red fruits of a plant of the capsicum family. They are used for spicing up fiery dishes from their native Central and South America, and have also become incorporated into the cuisines of other parts of the world to which the plant has been exported—India, for instance. Spanish explorers had brought it back to Europe in the seventeenth century, but in Britain it remained something of an exotic rarity ('"Try a chili with it, Miss Sharp," said Joseph, really interested. "A chili," said Rebecca, gasping; "oh yes!" She thought a chili was something cool, as its name imported,' William Thackeray, *Vanity Fair* (1848)), its only common role being as a pickling spice. Its name comes via Spanish *chile* (sometimes also used in English) from Nahuatl *chilli*, and has no connection with the name of the country Chile.

Dried ground chillis are cayenne pepper; but confusingly *chilli powder*, or *chili powder* as it is also spelled, is a mixture of cayenne with other spices, particularly cumin.

The heat of a chilli is calibrated in Scoville Heat Units. The scale was developed by the American pharmacist Wilbur Scoville (1865–1942) and introduced in 1912. At one extreme, sweet peppers would score 0; at the other, habaneros and Scotch bonnet peppers, among the hottest widely available chillis, can reach 350,000, while the naga jolokia chilli from northeastern India has been clocked at over a million.

chilli con carne *Chilli con carne* (a partial Anglicization of Spanish *chile con carne*, which means literally 'chilli with meat') is one of the kingpins of Tex–Mex cuisine. It is a stew of minced beef with onions, fried up with chillis or chilli powder and other spices, and often eked out with red kidney beans. The earliest known reference to it in English is in the title of a work by one S. Compton Smith, *Chile con Carne, or the Camp and the Field* (1857). Originally a standby of the pioneers in the southwestern US, it had by the late twentieth century become an item on the universal fast-food menu, turning up as a filling or topping for such unlikely companions as baked potatoes, pizzas, and even Yorkshire puddings.

chimichanga In Mexican cuisine, a tortilla rolled round a savoury filling and deep-fried. The name in Mexican Spanish means literally 'trinket'.

chimichurri A traditional Argentinian and Uruguayan accompaniment to beef, that can serve as a marinade, dressing, or dipping sauce: 'The steaks were impeccable . . . A dip of chimichurri sauce completed the experience', *Time Out London, Eating and Drinking* (2009). It is a variation on a basic salsa verde, incorporating parsley, garlic, chilli flakes, oil, and vinegar. In the absence of a plausible etymology, the word *chimichurri* has been subjected to a number of fanciful derivations, mostly revolving round the name of an English-speaking colonist in South America: the one most often cited is a no-doubt apocryphal Irish settler in Argentina called Jimmy McCurry.

China chilo A nineteenth-century English dish consisting of mutton stewed with lettuce, peas, and onions, and served with a border of rice. The *China* presumably alludes to the oriental origins of the rice (Mrs Beeton described the rice garnish as being 'the same as for curry'), but the origins of the rather odd *chilo* are lost.

chine An animal's chine is its backbone: to a butcher and a cook, it is a joint of meat, especially from a pig, containing all or part of this (in pork butchery, it is specifically the portion of a bacon pig remaining when the sides have been cut off for making into bacon). The word came into English in the fourteenth century from Old French *eschine,* which was apparently based on a blend of Latin *spina* 'spine', with an ancient Germanic word related to English *shin*, meaning 'something long and narrow'. The usual treatment of a chine is to stuff it: its most notable manifestation is a stuffed Lincolnshire chine, in which a cut of pork from between the shoulders and across the backbone is cured in brine, sliced across, stuffed with chopped parsley, lengthily simmered, and served cold. *Chine* is also used as a verb, meaning 'to cut (meat) across or along the backbone': 'And the Pigge you shall chine [and] divide into two parts', Gervase Markham, *English Housewife* (1615).

Chinese artichoke Chinese artichokes, the edible tubers of a plant of the family Labiatae, are among the most bizarrely shaped of vegetables, resembling the central section of a string of discoloured and rather misshapen pearls. As their name suggests, they are of oriental origin (although perhaps Japanese rather than Chinese), and they were introduced to western Europe in the early 1880s. They were very popular from about 1890 to 1920, but subsequently their popularity nosedived, and they are only just beginning to make a comeback. In France, they were first cultivated at Crosne, to the southwest of Paris, and the French have called them *crosnes* ever since (in common with other vegetables and fruit being repopularized in Britain through French influence, there are signs that the French name, here *crosne*, is going to take over from the almost-forgotten English one).

Chinese cabbage *Chinese cabbage*, or *Chinese leaf*, is a cover term applied to two oriental vegetables of the cabbage family that started to become widely available in Britain in the 1980s. It is most frequently used for the *pe-tsai* (transliterated in the pinyin system *báicài*, literally 'white vegetable'), an elongated pale green cabbage (*Brassica pekinensis*) that looks rather like a cos lettuce, and can be eaten raw in salads or cooked. It is also known as *Pekin cabbage* or *snow cabbage*. The other *Chinese cabbage* is the *pak choi* or *bok choy* (the Cantonese equivalent of *pe tsai*, and similarly meaning 'white vegetable'). Also known as *Chinese greens* or *Chinese chard*, it does not form a compact head like the *pe-tsai*. Its dark green leaves bunch loosely on their massive riblike stalks (both leaves and stalks are eaten). Its Latin name is *B. rapa chinensis*.

Chinese chives A type of chives originating in East Asia. Its leaves are longer, wider, and flatter than those of the related European chives, and have a hint of garlic in their flavour—hence their alternative name *garlic chives*. They are sometimes also called *kuchai*, which is a Malay alteration of their Cantonese name *gau choi*.

Chinese gooseberry The original English name of the fruit now almost universally known as the *kiwi fruit*. The fruit comes from China, and was introduced into New Zealand in the early years of the twentieth century; the name *Chinese gooseberry* was hence almost certainly coined in New Zealand, and it is first recorded in an October 1925 issue of the Auckland *Weekly News*.

Chinese vermicelli An alternative name for GLASS NOODLES.

chip The humble chip—a strip of potato either shallow- or now usually deep-fried—seems first to have surfaced in the middle of the nineteenth century, having crossed the English Channel from France. Charles Dickens mentioned it in his *Tale of Two Cities* (1859): 'husky chips of potatoes, fried with some reluctant drops of oil'. The Edwardian restaurant critic Lt.-Col. Newnham-Davis (1854–1917) noted that in his youth it was a novelty, and that 'the great Lord Salisbury had a fondness for a chop and chips'. At first it was longwindedly called *potato chip* or *chipped potato*, but by the end of the century the abbreviated *chip* had arrived, and has been with us ever since. The word never really caught on with Americans, however—what they call *potato chips* the British would call *potato crisps*—and they have always preferred the term *French fries*. Since the Second World War this has been making determined inroads into the British *chip*, particularly in fast-food outlets (in the late 1980s Buxted changed the name of their ready-meal 'Chicken and Chips' to 'Chicken and Fries'). Meanwhile a minor outflanking move on British usage has been made by French *pommes frites*, or their abbreviation *frites*, in upmarket establishments where the *chip* would be infra dig (*see also* PONT-NEUF POTATOES). To complicate matters further, in Australian English *chips* are crisps, and chips are *hot chips*. In Indian English chips are known as *finger chips*. *See also* OVEN CHIP.

The chip's main role remains, as it has always been, in its symbiotic partnership with fried fish. The notion of frying fish in batter had been introduced into Britain by Jewish immigrants in the late eighteenth century, but the fish was usually eaten with bread; in the early nineteenth century, potatoes as street food meant baked potatoes. However, once chips had appeared on the scene, it did not take them long to join forces with fish: Joseph Malin opened his fish-and-chip shop in Bow in the East End of London in 1860, and a similar establishment opened in Mossley, Lancashire in 1863 by a 'Mr Lee' set the Oldham area on the road to being an early centre of fish-and-chip consumption. The phrase *fish and chips* itself is first recorded in 1876. By the 1880s the introduction of refrigerated transport had vastly increased the amount of cheap cod being brought into Britain from Icelandic waters, further cementing the fish-and-chip marriage that was to provide a major contribution to working people's diet until well after the Second World War (the middle classes, who found the notion of fish and chips a little vulgar, even if they liked eating it, could disguise it as a *fish supper*—served, of course, on a plate, not wrapped in newspaper). The fish-and-chip shop as an institution is now well over 150 years old, its affectionate abbreviation *chippy* perhaps a third of that.

chipolata Chipolatas have nothing to do with chips; their name comes, via French, from Italian *cipollata*, meaning 'flavoured with onion' (the Italian for 'onion' is *cipolla*, which is related to English *chives*). These small sausages make their first appearance in English in 1877, in *Kettner's Book of the Table*, but over the succeeding century they have secured a particular niche for themselves as accompaniments to Christmas turkey and as party nibbles.

chipotle A smoked jalapeño pepper, used in Mexican cooking. It is usually dried and used in stews and sauces, but it can also be pickled and eaten as an appetizer. The word comes via Mexican Spanish from a Nahuatl compound formed from *chil-* (as in *chilli*) and *poctli* 'smoke'. It is first recorded in English in 1950.

chitterling Chitterlings are the intestines of pigs used as food. They can of course be used as casing for sausages, but they also form a delicacy in their own right, typically sold precooked to be eaten cold or fried. Chitterlings served with collard greens (a sort of kale) are a noted speciality of the southern US (where the pronunciation of the word is reflected by the spelling *chit'lins*). The word *chitterling* first appears in English in the late thirteenth century, but its origins are obscure; it may go back to a hypothetical Old English **cieter* 'intestines', and it is possible that there is some connection with German dialect *kuttel*, which has the same meaning.

chives Chives are the smallest member of the onion family used in the kitchen. Their tubular green leaves are chopped up and sprinkled as a flavouring garnish on soups, salads, etc. Their name comes via a dialectal variant of Old French *cive* from Latin *cēpa* 'onion', source also of English *chipolata*.

chocho In Jamaica and other English-speaking islands of the Caribbean, the name given to the chayote. First recorded in 1756, it came via Spanish from an Amerindian language of Brazil. *See also* CHOKO.

chocolate The ancient Aztecs and Maya of Central America made a drink by mixing ground cacao seeds with water, which they called *cacaua-atl*—'cacao-water'. The Spanish Conquistadores quickly developed a liking for it, and appear to have introduced an innovation in its preparation by substituting hot water for cold (which the Aztecs used) and adding various flavourings. This drink was called *chocolatl,* which may have been a compound formed from Maya *chocol* 'hot' and Aztec *atl* 'water'. English acquired the word probably towards the end of the sixteenth century ('The chiefe vse of this Cacao is a drinke which they call Chocolate', Edward Grimstone, *Acosta's Historie of the West Indies* (1604)). The drink was enormously popular and fashionable in Europe in the seventeenth century (*see* COCOA). By the middle of the century, however, the solid confection made from roasted ground cacao seeds was becoming familiar, and over the centuries this has ousted the drink (which is now generally specified in British English as *drinking chocolate*) as the main application of the word.

Chocolate made with milk solids, which is of a relatively pale brown colour, is termed *milk chocolate* (first recorded in 1723). Darker chocolate, made without milk and generally less sweet, is called in British English *plain chocolate* (1737). In American English the term *bittersweet chocolate* is used.

The use of *chocolate* to refer to an individual sweet made from or covered with chocolate dates from the 1880s. The abbreviated form *choc*, as in 'a box of chocs', emerged in the last quarter of the nineteenth century. *Choc ice,* denoting a brickette of (usually vanilla) ice cream covered with chocolate, is first recorded in 1951.

chocolate mud cake An extremely rich, virtually flourless chocolate cake that comes under the general category of 'death by chocolate'. Its chief ingredients are chocolate, butter, sugar, and eggs, and it is iced with ganache. The term dates from around 1990.

chocolate nemesis An extremely rich flourless chocolate cake which originated as a speciality of the River Café, London. Its 'rise' is provided by beaten eggs. It belongs to the generic type known as 'death by chocolate', which no doubt inspired the name as well as the recipe. A version without sugar is called *chocolate oblivion*.

choko An alternative form of the term CHOCHO, used in Australia and New Zealand.

cholent In Jewish cookery, a stew or casserole of beans, vegetables, and often meat. Traditionally it is prepared on Friday evening, cooked slowly in the oven overnight, and eaten on the Sabbath. The word, first recorded in 1903, is an Anglicization of Yiddish *tsholnt* or *tshulnt,* which itself probably came from a hypothetical Old French **chalent* 'being hot', a descendant of the Latin present participle *calens* (related to English *calory*).

chollah An alternative form of CHALLAH.

chop The *chop* as a concept emerged in the seventeenth century. Slices of meat the size of individual portions, they were in their way forerunners of hamburgers, served up to busy city dwellers in the London chophouses that proliferated from the 1690s onwards. Right from the start *chop* seems usually to have been applied to cuts containing a bone and chopped from the loin, shoulder, or particularly ribs. It did, though, take a little time to bed down as a solo term: at first people spoke of 'a chop of mutton', for instance, rather than simply 'a chop' (on 9 July 1663 Samuel Pepys recorded 'Had a chop of veale'). In modern usage, *chop* is applied to cuts of lamb, pork, or veal, but not of beef (a corresponding section of which would be too big to form a single portion that could fit on to the average plate).

The term *mutton-chop whiskers* for long bushy sideboards on a man's face that are narrow at the top and broad and rounded at the bottom, somewhat in the shape of a chop, dates from the 1860s.

chop suey A Chinese dish consisting of small pieces of meat or chicken cooked with bean sprouts and other vegetables such as onions and bamboo shoots and served with rice. It is commonly said to have originated in the US, invented by Chinese chefs to suit American tastes. In fact, it is an indigenous Cantonese dish, which was brought to the West Coast of America by Cantonese immigrants in the second half of the nineteenth century. The term *chop suey* is first recorded in the October 1888 issue of *Current Literature*, an American publication. It represents a slightly mangled rendition of Cantonese Chinese *shap sui* 'odds and ends', literally 'miscellaneous bits'.

chorizo A spicy Spanish pork sausage whose key flavouring ingredient, paprika, gives it a red colour. It can be eaten either fresh or dried. In Mexico the term is applied to the sausage meat mixture itself, unencased. It is first recorded in English in 1846.

The Spanish word, which comes ultimately from medieval Latin *salsicia* 'sausage' (also the ancestor of English *sausage*), is pronounced /chə'reethoh/ or /chə'reesoh/, but in recent years many British speakers have taken to importing into it a generalized 'foreign' *z*-sound /ts/, presumably based on the pronunciation of Italian *zz* or German *z*: /chə'ritsoh/ (or even /kə'ritsoh/). (Curiously, *Ibiza* seems to present no such problems— although large numbers of British speakers now defiantly Anglicize the initial vowel from /i/ to /eye/— reinforcing the old linguistic adage that 'Chaque mot a son histoire'.)

In Portugal, the sausage is *chouriço*.

Chorley cake A small round cake made of unsweetened shortcrust pastry with a sugary filling of currants and sometimes candied peel. It takes its name from Chorley, a town to the northwest of Manchester. It is not far from Eccles, in the Lancashire cake-making belt, and the cake resembles a somewhat plainer version of Eccles cake.

chota peg *See* PEG.

choucroute *See* SAUERKRAUT.

choux pastry A type of pastry made from flour, milk, butter, and eggs. Its most typical application is in the making of small round buns (as used for profiteroles) known in French as *choux*, literally 'cabbages', from their shape—hence *pâte à choux*, the pastry used for making them. The first reference to the term in English comes in the 1706 edition of Edward Phillips's *New World of English Words*: *Petits Choux*, a 'sort of Paste for garnishing, made of fat Cheese, Flour, Eggs, Salt, etc., bak'd in a Pye-pan, and Ic'd over with fine Sugar.' But it was not really until the late nineteenth century that it achieved any sort of general currency in English.

chow A slang term for 'food', *chow* originated in the Pidgin English of the Chinese trading ports of the late eighteenth and early nineteenth centuries. Its probable source was Cantonese *chaau* 'to fry, cook,' although a more picturesque explanation offered has been that it was short for *chow-chow*, the name of a sort of Chinese dog, on the basis that they formed part of the Chinese diet (a theory perhaps supported by the fact that the earliest known reference to the word, in the glossary of a volume of reminiscences about China published in 1795, is in the form *chow-chow*).

chow-chow *Chow-chow* originated as Pidgin English for 'mixture,' probably based on Mandarin Chinese *cha* 'miscellaneous', and hence has come to be applied variously to a sweet Chinese preserve composed of ginger, fruits, orange peel, etc. in a heavy syrup, and (in America) to a relish consisting of chopped vegetables pickled in mustard—what in Britain is called *piccalilli*.

chowder *Chowder*, the name of a thick American fish soup, commemorates the pot in which it was once cooked. For it comes from French *chaudière*, 'stew pot', a descendant of late Latin *caldāria* (a close relative of which produced English *cauldron*). The soup seems to have originated in Newfoundland, where any fish that came to hand (notably cod, of course) went into it. The central ingredient of modern versions is likely to be clams. It is usually made in New England with milk (the Rhode Island version uses clear broth, and

Manhattan chowder features tomatoes), and other things that go in to thicken and flavour it include bacon, onions, and potatoes. Chowders can also be non-fishy—you can, for example, have a corn chowder.

chow mein A southern Chinese dish consisting of stir-fried noodles served usually with a thick meat-, vegetable-, or fish-based sauce (in the Pekinese dialect of Chinese *chao miàn* means literally 'fried dough'). Whereas the majority of Chinese culinary terms in English have become established since the Second World War, with the rise of the Chinese restaurant, *chow mein* belongs to an earlier stratum, introduced via the West Coast of America in the early years of the twentieth century, and institutionalized in the 1920s and 1930s as the archetypal Sino-American dish.

chrain In Jewish cookery, a pungent horseradish-based sauce. It comes in two forms: red chrain with beetroot, and white chrain, without, but in practice 'chrain' usually denotes the former. It is traditionally served with cold fish ('There's a good choice of fish . . . , ranging from gefilte fish with chrain to more elegant dover sole', *Time Out London, Eating and Drinking* (2009)). The name is a Yiddish adoption of the Slavic term for 'horseradish'—Russian *khren*, for example.

Christmas pudding Steaming fragrant black cannonballs of suet, raisins, currents, spices, sugar, eggs, etc., lambent with brandy flames and top-knotted with holly, have made Britain's Christmas tables (and no doubt sometimes diners) groan since at least the eighteenth century, but the name *Christmas pudding* appears to be a comparatively recent coinage, first recorded in Anthony Trollope's *Doctor Thorne* (1858). The association of dishes containing mixed dried fruit and spices (and formerly also meat) with Christmas is a longstanding one, though. Most of them originally contained dried plums, or prunes, but long after these had been replaced by raisins the term *plum* lingered on: so traditional British Christmas fare included *plum broth*, a thick beef soup enlivened with dried fruit and spices; *plum porridge*, an oatmeal mixture with similar ingredients; *plum pie*, a forerunner of today's mince-pie, which as early as the seventeenth century was known as *Christmas pie* ('It is a great Nostrum the composition of this Pasty ["Christmas Pye"]; it is a most learned Mixture of Neats-tongues, Chickens, Eggs, Sugar, Raisins, Lemon and Orange Peel, various kinds of Spicery, etc.', Henri Misson, *Memoirs* (1719)); and of course *plum pudding*. Nowadays served only at Christmas, and so called exclusively *Christmas pudding*, this was formerly a common year-round pudding (albeit not always as rich as the festive version); indeed, in 1748 Pehr Kalm, a Swedish visitor to England, noted that 'the art of cooking as practised by Englishmen does not extend much beyond roast beef and plum pudding'. And in 1814, one of the traditional English delicacies introduced to the French by Antoine Beauvilliers in his *L'art du cuisinier* was *plomb-poutingue*.

chuck A cut of beef from the animal's forequarters. Its precise demarcation varies in different parts of the English-speaking world. In America, for instance, it usually covers the upper fore-end of the animal from the neck to the ribs, including the shoulder blade (and this is its earliest recorded application in British English too, as quoted in Georgina Jackson's *Shropshire Word-book* (1881)); in current British English, however, it is usually reserved to a much smaller area, namely the three ribs nearest to the neck. The usage appears to be a specialization of an earlier *chuck* which meant simply 'lump', and was a variant of *chock*; the word *chunk* is probably also related.

The Western American term *chuck* 'food, grub' (most familiar to British audiences from the *chuck wagon* of Westerns) may come from this general sense 'lump', which was often applied to foodstuffs such as bread and cake; the earliest occurrences of *chuck* 'food', from the mid-nineteenth century, suggest that it originally meant 'bread' or 'ship-biscuit'.

chudleigh A small round cake made from plain white dough. Served hot, it is split and eaten with butter or cream and jam. Similar to, but smaller than a Cornish split, it is a speciality of Devon, and presumably takes its name from the Devonshire town of Chudleigh. Florence White in her *Good Things in England* (1932) describes a cricket tea in Tiverton at which the schoolboys 'stuck a spoonful of luscious strawberry jam in the centre of a split Chudleigh already thickly spread with scalded (or as Londoners call it, clotted) cream before closing it with another half on top and digging their strong white teeth into the chosen "tuck".'

chufa The plant, a type of sedge, whose tubers are eaten as *tiger nuts*. It is grown particularly in marshy parts of Spain and Italy, and the name comes from Spanish. It is also applied, especially in the US, to the tuber itself.

chump The chump, or *chump end,* is the rearward end of a loin of mutton or lamb, just before it meets the hind leg. Nowadays, it is most familiar sliced into *chump chops* (first recorded in 1883), but it also makes a useful small roasting joint in its own right. The term is a metaphorical extension of the original sense of *chump,* 'thick lump of wood', which dates from the early eighteenth century (and which also yielded the slang meaning 'fool'). The word itself probably started life as a blend of *chunk* and *lump* or *stump*.

churro In Spain, Portugal, and Mexico, a street and bar snack consisting of a ribbed curled baton of sweet dough that is deep-fried like a doughnut. It is dredged with sugar or cinnamon sugar, and commonly eaten for breakfast with coffee or hot chocolate. The original Spanish term (first recorded in English in 1929) may be related to the adjective *churro,* meaning 'coarse, rough'.

chutney Chutney made the journey from India to Britain in the early nineteenth century, and in the process changed out of all recognition. Indian *chatni* is standardly a relish made from fresh fruits with their appropriate spices, whereas the British variety, whether commercially bottled or made at home to stem a rising tide of apples or tomatoes from the garden, resembles more what the Indians would call a pickle, with its generous dollop of malt vinegar for long keeping. By the time Eliza Acton published her *Modern Cookery for Private Families* in 1845 *chatneys* (as she still called them) had become a well-established part of British cuisine. She gives three recipes for them, and notes 'all Chatneys should be *quite thick*, almost of the consistence of mashed turnips or stewed tomatoes, or stiff bread sauce. They are served with curries; and also with steaks, cutlets, cold meat, and fish.'

ciabatta A type of Italian loaf made from a dough that includes olive oil as one of its ingredients. Its long, flat, vaguely shoe-like shape earned it its name—Italian *ciabatta* means literally 'slipper' (it is probably a borrowing, via Turkish, of Persian *ciabat*). It gives every appearance of ancient ancestry but in fact, in its present form and under the name *ciabatta,* it is a relatively recent creation, dating from the early 1980s. It is reputed to have been the brainchild of Arnaldo Cavallari, a miller from the Veneto, who was inspired by the desire for a native Italian bread that would turn back the invasion of the French baguette.

cider Cider-making in England is largely a consequence of 1066. No doubt apple juice had been fermented to make an alcoholic drink in Anglo-Saxon times, but it was the Normans who introduced it in a big way. At first much of it was imported from Normandy (still a centre of cider production), but soon cider-apple orchards were being planted in Kent and Sussex, and it was not long before the apples, the technology, and the taste for the drink spread throughout the more southerly parts of England, and particularly to the

West Country. The Normans brought the word with them too: *cider* (or *cyder*, as it is sometimes spelled in Britain) comes from Old French *sidre*, which was adapted from medieval Latin *sícera*. This in turn came from Greek *síkéra*, an approximation used in the Septuagint for Hebrew *shekār* 'strong drink', a derivative of the verb *shākar* 'to drink heavily'. As this potted history suggests, *cider* denotes etymologically any intoxicating beverage, and indeed that meaning survived in English as late as the fifteenth century, particularly in biblical contexts (Proverbs 31:6, for instance, 'Give strong drink unto him that is ready to perish, and wine unto those that be of heavy hearts,' was translated by John Wycliffe in 1382 as 'Give cider to mourning men'). The specific application of the word to 'drink made from apples' developed in Old French.

The term *scrumpy* for 'rough unsweetened cider', first recorded in 1904, is a dialect word derived from *scrump*, meaning 'small or withered apple' (which was also the source of the verb *scrump* 'to steal apples'); the origin of *scrump* is not known for certain, although it is no doubt related to Swedish *skrumpen* 'shrivelled' and German *schrumpfen* 'to shrivel'. A drink made by watering and repressing the pulp from which the original apple-juice for cider was pressed was known in former times as *ciderkin* or *water-cider*. In American English, 'cider' is commonly called *hard cider*.

cigar A roll of filo pastry with a sweet or savoury filling. It is a speciality of Mediterranean cookery, from Morocco to Greece and Turkey, and it has also been incorporated into the Jewish culinary repertoire.

cilantro An alternative name for the herb coriander. It comes from Spanish, which acquired it from late Latin *coliandrum*, an alteration of Latin *coriandrum* (*l* and *r* are phonetically close, and are often swapped over).

cime di rapa The Italian term (literally 'turnip tops') for the edible leafy stalks of rapini, a Mediterranean variety of turnip. They are especially popular in Rome.

cinnamon A spice obtained from the inner bark of a tropical Asian tree, cinnamon has been known in Britain since the early fifteenth century, when it was brought from the Middle East by returning travellers (in 1460 John Russell, in his *Book of Nurture*, was advising 'Look that your sticks of cinnamon [he spelled it *synamome*] be thin'). It caught on straightaway, and since it was comparatively inexpensive as spices went in medieval times, it was quite widely used, in meat dishes as well as sweet ones. The source of the term *cinnamon* is Semitic, perhaps Hebrew *qinnāmōn*; this was borrowed into Greek as *kúnnamon*, later *kinnámōmon*, which found its way via Latin *cinnamōmum* and Old French *cinnamome* into Middle English as *sinamome*. This was gradually reformulated from the sixteenth century onwards into modern English *cinnamon*, on the basis of the original Greek form. *See also* CANELLA.

Cinzano The brand name of an Italian vermouth. It comes in red and white varieties, sweet and dry, and latterly also rosé. Its name comes from its originators, the brothers Giovanni Giacomo and Carlo Stefano Cinzano, who introduced it in Turin in 1757. The drink's profile was raised in Britain in the 1970s by a popular series of television advertisements featuring Joan Collins and Leonard Rossiter. Previously, Cinzano had become the first product ever to appear on a neon advertising sign in Paris in 1913.

citron A large citrus fruit (*Citrus medica*) which resembles an elongated, knobbly lemon. It is now mainly valued for its thick peel, which is preserved in sugar and put into cakes and puddings. The term *citron* was first used in English (as a French borrowing) in the early sixteenth century, when it was applied to lemons and limes as well as citrons (it remains the word for 'lemon' in French), but by the seventeenth century it was being reserved specifically to the citron. The French word *citron* was modelled (using the final syllable of *limon* 'lemon') on Latin *citrus* 'citron tree', which has of course provided the generic name for oranges, lemons, and their allies. Nothing is known for certain of its ultimate linguistic antecedents, but it was probably acquired by Latin from a non-Indo-European language—perhaps from the same source as Greek *kédros*, from which English gets *cedar*.

From the sixteenth to the early nineteenth centuries the pomelo (a large citrus fruit resembling the grapefruit) was called *pome-citron*. And a more recent application of the word *citron* has been to a small inedible watermelon, *Citrullus vulgaris citroides*, whose rind is candied and used in much the same way as that of the original citron.

civet A thick rich game stew. It is made from any furred game—wild boar, venison, rabbit—but perhaps the commonest ingredient is hare. The meat is cooked slowly in red wine, which is subsequently thickened with the animal's blood. Historically a key ingredient is small green onions, in French *cives* (a close relative of English *chives*), which give the dish its name. English first tentatively borrowed the term *civet* from French in the eighteenth century.

clafoutis A French batter pudding generously dotted with black cherries (or, in non-classic versions of the dish, other fruits). It is a particular speciality of the Limousin region of central France. The word is a derivative of the dialect verb *clafir* 'to fill'.

clanger A type of cylindrical pasty that is a speciality of Bedfordshire—indeed it is often called a *Bedfordshire clanger*. Made with suet crust, it has a savoury filling at one end and a sweet one at the other, with a partition between. There is also a Buckinghamshire version, which contains just a savoury filling: bacon, potato, and onion.

clapshot A Scottish term of uncertain origin for potatoes and turnips mashed together—a classic accompaniment for haggis.

claret Now firmly associated with the red wines of Bordeaux, *claret* was originally a descriptive term for any light-coloured wine, including white wine. The word comes from Old French *claret*, a diminutive of *clair* 'clear, light, bright', and until at least the end of the sixteenth century referred to wine midway between full-bodied red and out-and-out white—that is, palish red, rosé (made by blending red and white), or even yellowish-white: 'The seconde wine is pure claret, of cleare lacent or Yelow choler,' William Bullein, *Bulwarke of Defence Against All Siknesse* (1562). The first record of its specific application to red Bordeaux is in 1565, by one Edward Tremaine. It retains that meaning in British English today, although it has never really caught on in other varieties of the language: American English, for instance, prefers simply *red Bordeaux*.

Memories of the word's earlier use survive in modern French *clairette*, the name of a group of grape varieties which produce a range of fairly undistinguished wines, mainly white (the best, and best-known, is *Clairette de Die*, a usually sparkling wine made in the Rhône valley). And a wine called *clairet*, pale red verging on rosé, is still made in Bordeaux.

Claret's establishment in English as unequivocally a word for 'red wine' is confirmed by its metaphorical use for 'blood', particularly as drawn by fisticuffs; the usage now has a very dated air, conjuring up the bare-knuckle fights of the eighteenth century, but it dates back to the early seventeenth century: 'This should be a Coronation day: for my head runs claret lustily', Thomas Dekker, *The Honest Whore* (1604). And at about the same time, it began to be used as a pure colour term, meaning 'reddish-violet'.

The word is now pronounced pretty much as it is spelled, but Auberon Waugh told a story about his father, the novelist Evelyn Waugh, which reveals an earlier pronunciation 'clart'. Waugh, under the impression that this superannuated pronunciation was one most suited to his station as country gentleman, used it constantly. But then a friend poked fun in print at this harmless eccentricity of his, and he henceforth foreswore claret, drinking only burgundy for the rest of his life.

clary An aromatic plant related to sage, in former times put to culinary use: Hannah Glasse, in her *Art of Cookery Made Plain and Easy* (1747), gave a recipe for clary fritters which she described as 'a pretty heartening dish for a sick or weak person'. It is now mainly an ornamental plant. English adopted the word in the fourteenth century from Old French *clarie*, which came from medieval Latin *sclarea*.

clementine A small almost seedless citrus fruit that is a cross between a tangerine and a Seville orange; it combines the peelability of the former with the bittersweetness of the latter. It was first cultivated around 1900 near Oran, Algeria, by a French priest, Père Clément. The name *clémentine* was adopted for it in French, and first promulgated by Louis Trabut in a 1902 volume of the *Revue horticole*. It is first mentioned in an English text in 1926.

clod A British English term for a rather gristly cut of beef taken from the animal's neck. Presumably coined from its being a solid and unpromising lump of meat, it is first recorded in *Queen Elizabeth's Household Book* (1601): 'He hath for his fee two cloddes, one little rumpe, chine of beefe, of every oxe that is sent to the Queene's house.'

clotted cream A thick cream obtained by heating milk slowly in shallow pans and then allowing it to cool while the cream content rises to the top in clots or coagulated lumps. It has a minimum fat content of 55 per cent. It is particularly associated with southwest England, and visitors to Devon and Cornwall are certain to have large quantities of the creamy-yellow cholesterol-rich substance pressed on them, either as part of the traditional cream tea, to be dolloped liberally on jammy scones, or in little tubs to be taken home or posted to friends; Cornish clotted cream has the EU's PDO (Protected Designation of Origin) status. Until the nineteenth century it was known as *clouted cream* (Edmund Spenser in his *Shepherd's Calendar* (1579) records how Dido would give the shepherd boy 'Curds and clouted Creame'), in which the *clout* represents a now obsolete word for 'lump, clod' that came from the same Germanic base as *clot* and was actually used in the plural in Middle English for 'cream curds': 'Put thereto cream, and if it be in clouts, draw it through a strainer,' directs a cookery book of around 1430.

cloudberry Cloudberries are the amber-coloured berries of a plant of the raspberry family, which grows in northern regions of the world. They are widely used in Scandinavia in the making of liqueurs and jams. The origins of the romantically mysterious-sounding name, which dates back to the late sixteenth century, are uncertain, but it may incorporate a now obsolete sense of *cloud*, 'hill'.

cloud ear A type of greyish-brown tree-growing mushroom that is widely used, dried, in oriental cooking. The name is a literal translation of Chinese *yún ěr*. In Japan it is called *arage kikurage*, literally 'tree jellyfish'.

cloutie dumpling A Scottish version of Christmas pudding. It is a suet pudding containing a mixture of sultanas, raisins, treacle, and spices, wrapped in a cloth or *clout* (hence the name) and steamed. It is traditionally eaten at Hogmanay.

clove Etymologically, a *clove* is a 'nail'. English acquired the term for this dried unopened aromatic flower bud of a tree of the eucalyptus family in the thirteenth century from Old French *clou de girofle*, which meant literally 'nail of the clove-tree' (an allusion to the shape of the clove, with its bulbous head and thinner body). English took the term over originally as *clow of gilofer* (*gilofer* was subsequently 'englished' to *gillyflower*, which at first was used for 'clove', and only later came to be applied to clove-scented pinks, wallflowers, etc.); but by the end of the fourteenth century *clove* was being used on its own for the spice. Cloves were popular in medieval Europe, and were used as extensively in both sweet and savoury dishes as their considerable expense would allow—the journey from their original home in the Spice Islands (now the Moluccas, in Indonesia) was long and risky. Their particular shape allows them to be pressed into oranges, onions, etc. like little studs, producing two flavouring agents in one.

The *clove* of garlic, incidentally, is a completely different word, which comes from the same Germanic source as the English verb *cleave*.

club cheese An American term for a cheese-based dairy product, in which cheese is pounded and mixed with butter and other ingredients. It is the precursor of commercially produced processed cheese.

club sandwich A sandwich of American origin made from three slices of bread or toast and two layers of filling—typically chicken or turkey with lettuce, tomato, mayonnaise, and now usually bacon—often secured with a cocktail stick. 'Some believe that it was originally only a two-decker, perhaps matching the two-decker "club cars" running on US railroads from 1895', Alan Davidson, *Oxford Companion to Food* (2006). Its invention has been attributed to the Saratoga Country Club in upstate New York. The term is first recorded in 1903.

club soda A now largely American term for soda water. It began life as a trademark, originally registered in Ireland in 1877, but it is now a generic term.

cob A small round brown loaf. The word *cobbe* in Middle English was a general term for any round lumpy object, and was applied specifically to a range of round things, including 'heads', 'pieces of coal', and 'testicles'. The earliest record of its use for a 'loaf' is a metaphorical one, from Shakespeare's *Troilus and Cressida* (1606), where Ajax calls Thersites 'Thou cobloaf!'—not a complimentary reference. The *cob* of *cobnut* is the same word.

cobbler[1] A long iced drink consisting of a spirit, liqueur, or fortified wine mixed with sugar and citrus fruit. It is not clear where the name came from, although it may be short for *cobbler's punch*. The first record we have of it is from the first decade of the nineteenth century, by the American author Washington Irving, and by the middle of the century Charles Dickens was introducing it to British readers: 'This wonderful invention, Sir . . . it is called a cobbler. Sherry cobbler, when you name it long; cobbler when you name it short', *Martin Chuzzlewit* (1844).

cobbler[2] A sort of fruit pie made with a thick scone-like crust (supposedly resembling cobble stones). It originated in the western states of the US in the mid-nineteenth century.

cobbler[3] *See* VIETNAMESE RIVER COBBLER.

Cobb salad An American dish consisting of cold chicken or turkey with bacon, tomatoes, lettuce, and other salad leaves, cheese, avocados, and hard-boiled eggs, tossed in a vinaigrette, and topped with crumbled blue cheese. It was created at the Brown Derby restaurant in Hollywood in the 1930s, and named after the restaurant's owner, Robert Howard Cobb.

cobnut An alternative name for the hazelnut (*hazel* is by far the older term). Its original form, first recorded in the fifteenth century, was *cobble-nut* (*cobble*, as in *cobble-stone*, was originally a diminutive form of *cob* 'round lump', now used for a sort of loaf), but *cobnut* is probably of equal antiquity, although documentation of it has not survived.

The term *Kentish cob* is actually something of a misnomer, for it is applied to a variety of filbert, a slightly different species from the native hazelnut. It was first raised by a Mr Lambert of Goudhurst in Kent in 1830.

Coburg A round loaf with two cuts made in the top at right angles, so that it opens out in baking (a similar loaf without these cuts is called a *cob*). It is reputed to have been named shortly after the marriage of Victoria to Prince Albert of Saxe-Coburg in 1840, which would fit in well with the first known use of the word in 1843 (in a letter from Dante Gabriel Rossetti).

Coca-Cola The proprietary name of a brown-coloured American carbonated soft drink, widely available. The mix of ingredients that give it its particular flavour is secret (the original recipe is locked away in a bank vault in Atlanta, Georgia), but it certainly contains coca flavouring, obtained from the leaves of the coca tree (a tropical American shrub), and extract of cola nut (*see* COLA). It may originally from time to time have contained a tiny amount of cocaine, which also comes from coca leaves, but any possibility of this was removed when the manufacturing process was overhauled in 1903. The drink's immediate ancestor was an alcoholic beverage concocted by John Pemberton, a drugstore-owner of Columbus, Georgia. He called it 'Pemberton's French Wine Coca'. In response to prohibitionist legislation he produced a non-alcoholic version in 1886. Named *Coca-Cola*, this went on to conquer the world, and such a prominent symbol has it become of the global reach of American culture that it inspired the (usually hostile) expression *coca-colonization* (first recorded in 1950): 'Let's not forget the "coca-colonisation" of Africa, as

Kenyan historian Ali Mazuri has so aptly termed it', *BBC Wildlife* (1990). The forward march of the drink's progress faltered only once, in 1985, when its makers introduced 'New Coke' with a different formula. Drinkers did not like it at all, and the Coca-Cola Company hurriedly reverted to the original version (under the name 'Coca-Cola Classic'). *See also* COKE.

cock-a-leekie This sustaining broth of chicken and leeks is firmly associated with Scotland, although something similar appears in other parts of Britain, and indeed of Europe. In its earliest medieval versions, it was a chicken stew with onions, and also raisins or prunes. The chicken would often have been eaten separately, and the stewing liquor drunk as soup. Adapted to Scottish conditions, leeks replaced onions, and by the nineteenth century the prunes seem to have disappeared, leaving the cock-a-leekie (or, in an earlier spelling, *cocky-leeky*) we are familiar with today.

cocktail The word *cocktail* first appeared at the beginning of the nineteenth century, in the US, but in its early days it was used for fairly unadventurous mixtures of spirits with bitters and often sugar. It was not until the 1920s (the cocktail decade par excellence) that the bewildering, and bizarrely named, array of concoctions we are now familiar with began to proliferate. The origins of the name remain obscure and much disputed. Many more or less plausible derivations have been suggested over the years, including, for example, *kaketal,* a West African word for a scorpion, and *coquetier,* a French term denoting a double eggcup. A number of stories involve a nineteenth-century Pennsylvania (or Virginia) innkeeper called Betsy (or Betty) Flannigan and what she did with a mixed drink and a rooster's tail feathers. Several of the suggestions are demonstrably false, and none of the rest can be conclusively proved. Probably the least unlikely is a link with another early nineteenth-century sense of *cocktail,* 'a horse with a docked tail (which sticks up somewhat like a cockerel's tail)'. This treatment was usually given to ordinary working horses, such as coach-horses and hunters, and so the term came to be applied in racing slang to a racehorse whose pedigree was not pure thoroughbred, but had one or more of these lesser beasts in it. This notion of 'adulteration' or 'mixture', the case goes, underlay the application of the term to the drink.

With the 1920s also comes the cocktail party, an institution which has given rise to a curious new breed of miniaturized food: the *cocktail sausage*, for instance (first heard of in a Fortnum and Mason catalogue of 1938), and the *cocktail onion*. And this was the decade, too, which saw the first application of *cocktail* to edible rather than drinkable mixtures: in 1928 came the *fruit cocktail* (a posh name for 'fruit salad'), and the late 1950s saw the rise of the *prawn cocktail*, in the 1970s Britain's most popular hors d'oeuvre. In the 1980s we acquired the *cocktail* of drugs, and even of chemical constituents: 'Mix together a cocktail of oxidised itrium, barium, and copper and you have a sort of ceramic through which electricity can flow without loss of energy due to resistance', *Observer* (1988).

cocoa *Cocoa*, a brown powder produced by grinding the roasted seeds of a tropical American evergreen tree, has had a chequered linguistic history, owing to its confusion with the *coconut*. When the Spaniards first encountered cocoa in Central America in the early sixteenth century, they named it *cacao*, an adaptation of *cacaua*, the term for 'cocoa bean' in the local Nahuatl language. English adopted the Spanish word in the mid-sixteenth century, and used it quite happily for the next 150 years or so. But then, around 1700, we begin to see the first signs of *cacao* and the *coco* of *coconut* (a word of equal antiquity) becoming associated in speakers' minds. Early intermediate forms were *cacoa* and *cocao*, which were still pronounced with three syllables, but by the end of the eighteenth century *cocoa* seems to have become firmly established, its *-oa* spelling revealing its exotic origin, but its pronunciation showing its complete phonetic assimilation to *coco*.

The drink made from the product of the cocoa tree was originally called *chocolate* (and it was extremely fashionable in England in the second half of the seventeenth century, 'much used in England, as Diet and Phisick with the Gentry,' John Chamberlayn, *The Manner of Making Coffee, Tea and Chocolate* (1685)). The term *cocoa* was not widely applied to it until the end of the eighteenth century: 'The General, between his cocoa and his newspaper, had no leisure for noticing her,' Jane Austen, *Northanger Abbey* (1798). And the drink we would recognize as cocoa today appeared later still. The process of manufacturing it, by removing a large proportion of the fat content (*cocoa butter*) to produce a lighter drink, was invented in 1828 by the Dutchman Coenraad Van Houten. This cocoa, often adulterated with flour, potato starch, and even earth, became a staple beverage of the nineteenth-century British working class, enthusiastically promoted by the temperance societies.

coco bread A starchy, slightly sweet type of bread eaten in the English-speaking Caribbean, and especially Jamaica. It is usually split, like an outsize burger bun, and stuffed with some kind of filling. Its name reflects the fact that a small amount of coconut milk was part of the recipe, though that is seldom the case nowadays.

coconut The coconut gets its name from the small dark depressions in its base, which reminded fifteenth- and sixteenth-century Spanish and Portuguese travellers of the mischievous face of a monkey. The Spanish and Portuguese term for a 'grin' or 'grimace' was *coco*, and so this fruit of the tropical palm tree *Cocos nucifera* became known colloquially as the *coco*. The term reached English (in which, as in other languages, the fruit had been known as the *Indian nut*) in the mid-sixteenth century, and from the early seventeenth century was gradually supplanted by the compound noun *coconut*. On the whole, temperate Europe has never seen enough in the coconut to import it in large quantities, although Mrs Beeton in her *Book of Household Management* (1861) was confident enough of its availability to give a recipe for coconut soup, and by the late

Victorian period the coconut shy had become a familiar feature of fairgrounds. It is the dried shredded flesh of the nut—desiccated coconut—that has probably been its most significant contribution to Western cookery. It is particularly favoured in Australia, where it seems few cakes can escape having the little white flakes sprinkled over them (see LAMINGTON). (The *coconut* has no etymological connection with *cocoa*, by the way, although the confusion between the two—encouraged by Samuel Johnson's *Dictionary* (1755), in which by accident entries for *coco* and *cocoa* got run together—is understandable.)

cocoyam *Cocoyam* is the common West African name of the taro, a tropical and temperate plant widely cultivated for its large starchy edible tubers. Its name, which is first recorded in 1922, may be an allusion to the appearance of the larger tubers, which look like yams with the fibrous outer coating of a coconut. The abbreviated *coco* is often used in the Caribbean.

codlin *Codlin,* or *codling,* is a now seldom encountered apple name. Originally, in the Middle Ages, it was applied to a hard type of apple, not suitable for eating raw—a cooking apple, in other words. It was also used as a generic term for any unripe apple. Later it came to refer more specifically to an elongated variety of cooking apple that tapered towards the eye. The original form of the word was *querdling,* which may have come from Anglo-Norman *quer de lion* 'lion's heart'—perhaps a reference to the shape or firmness of the fruit. In past centuries roasted apples were sold on the streets of London, to vendors' cries of 'Hot codlins!': 'A little old woman, her living she got, By selling hot codlings, hot, hot, hot', *Popular Song,* early nineteenth century.

Nowadays the word is mainly familiar in the name of the codlin moth or codling moth, a small greyish moth whose larva feeds on apples.

coeurs à la crème In French literally 'hearts of cream', these little confections are made of curd cheese, cream, egg whites, and sugar, mixed together and put into heart-shaped moulds that have drainage holes in the bottom. They are served either on their own, with cream, or with fruit. An alternative French name for them is *crémets.*

coffee The shrub from whose seeds (known since the seventeenth century as *beans*) we make coffee is indigenous to Ethiopia and the Sudan. But its local name is *būn*; so where did the term *coffee* come from? We can trace it back as far as Arabic *qahwah,* but beyond that all is uncertainty. Arab etymologists have traditionally explained *qahwah* as a term for 'wine', deriving it from the verb root *qahiya* 'to not be hungry', and it has been speculated that it may originally have referred to an alcoholic drink made by fermenting the pulp of the tree's ripe fruits. Others, however, see its source in *Kaffa,* name of a part of the plant's native Ethiopia. But whatever the true facts about the word's birth, its subsequent history has followed fairly closely the spread of the drink coffee from the Middle East to Europe.

The practice of infusing ground roasted coffee beans in water seems to have begun in Arabia in the fifteenth century (the first coffee-house opened in Mecca around 1511). By the 1530s coffee-drinking had reached Turkey, where the Arabic word for the new beverage was rendered as *kahveh.* Word of the drink reached Britain around 1600, and early references to it are all in spellings fairly close to the Arabic and Turkish forms: *chaoua, cahve, caffe,* and *kauhi.* It was not until the middle of the century, however, that the habit of coffee-drinking began to establish itself (the first English coffee-house opened in Oxford in 1650, and the first in London was set up by a Turkish merchant in St Michael's Alley in 1652), and the form of the word then adopted—*coffee*—was filtered through Dutch *koffie.* (The intermediate source of French *café* and German *kaffe* is Italian *caffè.*)

Coffee was immensely fashionable in the second half of the seventeenth century. This period saw the opening of innumerable coffee-houses in London, many of which were later to metamorphose into venerable City clubs and institutions such as Lloyd's. Coffee became a domestic drink too, ousting beer at the breakfast table. The eighteenth century, however, saw the introduction of the much cheaper tea, and while coffee remained popular with the gentry, it went into a decline as a mass drink from which it has only slowly been recovering over the past sixty years. In the US, of course, things have been different. The tax on tea which led to the Boston Tea Party always encouraged the drinking of coffee, a tendency reinforced by waves of coffee-loving immigrants from Europe.

Café was borrowed from French as a term for a 'coffee-house' in the early nineteenth century. *Cafeteria* was originally an American Spanish word for 'coffee-house', derived from Spanish *cafetero* 'coffee seller'.

Cointreau The proprietary name of a brand of French orange-flavoured liqueur, manufactured in Angers. It was first made in the 1840s by the brothers Adolphe and Edouard Cointreau.

Coke The secondary proprietary name of Coca-Cola. It originated in the first decade of the twentieth century as a colloquial abbreviation, quite possibly given a nudge by the use of *coke* as a shortening of *cocaine,* which emerged at about the same time: 'the propensity of a large proportion of those who regularly drink Coca-Cola to call for their favourite drink as "dope" or "coke" or "koke"', *Printers' Ink* (1915). It was registered as a trademark in 1944.

In colloquial American English, *Coke-bottle spectacles* are ones with very thick lenses, a usage inspired by the thick round bottom of the iconic curvaceous Coca-Cola bottle.

cola The cola, or *kola*, is a small evergreen African tree that produces large seeds (known as *cola nuts* or *kola nuts*) containing caffeine. In Africa the nuts are chewed raw, or dried, ground up, and made into a drink. An extract of the nut is used for flavouring commercially produced carbonated drinks (including, it is presumed, Coca-Cola and Pepsi-Cola), and since around 1920 *cola* has been employed as a generic term for such drinks (including artificially flavoured ones): 'She ordered a cola and sipped it idly, watching her reflection in the mirror', *Family Circle* (New York) (1948). The word *cola* itself is an Anglicization of *k'ola,* the name of the cola nut in the Temne language of Sierra Leone.

colcannon An Irish dish similar to English bubble and squeak. It is made from cabbage and potatoes sliced up small, mixed together, and fried into a sort of cake, crisp on the outside. It is eaten particularly at Hallowe'en, when tradition demands that a ring, a coin, an old maid's thimble, and a bachelor's button be hidden in it, which will indicate the finder's future. The word comes from Gaelic *cal ceannan,* which means literally 'white-headed cabbage' (*cal* derives from Latin *caulis* 'cabbage' and *ceannan* from Old Irish *ceann* 'head'). American English has Anglicized the word to *cale-cannon.*

cold duck An American term, first recorded in 1969, for a drink consisting of a sweetened mixture of champagne and sparkling burgundy. The idea for the drink originated in southern Germany, where the waste-not-want-not practice developed in the nineteenth century of pouring the dregs from nearly finished wine bottles into champagne (or sekt). The resulting concoction was called *kaltes ende* 'cold end', which was waggishly transmogrified into *kalte ente*—literally 'cold duck'.

coleslaw *Coleslaw* means literally 'cabbage salad'. English borrowed and adapted the word from Dutch *koolsla* at the end of the eighteenth century, probably from Dutch settlers in the US, and the first printed example of it shows its outlandishness tamed to *cold slaw*—a folk-etymological modification often repeated in later years. English does however have its own equivalent to Dutch *kool* 'cabbage', namely *cole*. Like *kool*, this comes ultimately from Latin *caulis* 'cabbage', whose underlying etymological meaning is 'hollow stem'. It is the source of the *cauli-* of *cauliflower*, of the *-cole* of *borecole*, and of the mainly Scottish *kale*, not to mention French *chou*. *Cole* is now largely obsolete, but it has been used since Old English times for plants of the genus *Brassica*, such as cabbage and rape, and it was available to be substituted for Dutch *kool*. *Sla*, however (which represents a phonetically reduced form of *salade* 'salad'), proved more intractable. An early effort at reproducing it was *slaugh*, soon abandoned in favour of *slaw*.

The frequent equation of the first element of *coleslaw* with *cold* has led to *slaw* being regarded, particularly in American English, as an independent term for a 'cabbage dish'. And not just for a salad of raw dressed cabbage, either; *cold slaw* has spawned *hot slaw*: 'It was customary in his family in his boyhood to serve a "hot slaw" with turkey, the slaw consisting of cabbage cooked with vinegar and sugar', *Sun* (Baltimore) (1944).

collar A joint of pork or especially, in modern use, bacon, taken from the animal's neck (hence *collar*), and boned and rolled. The term dates back to the early seventeenth century, and over time the focus of its usage has changed from the original piece of pig to the method of preparation, and from noun to verb: taking out the bones, rolling up the meat (or even fish), and tying it with string (J. T. Hewlett, for example, in his *Parsons and Widows* (1844), refers to 'a collared eel, which would have provoked the appetite of an anchorite'). A further complication is that at an early stage *collar* was commonly used in conjunction with *brawn*, at a time when *brawn* meant simply 'pig-meat', and the association continued when *brawn* moved on to denote chopped-up pig-meat pressed into a mould. *Collar* took over elements of the new meaning, and so we find, for instance, Mrs Beeton (1861) giving directions for 'collared pig's face (a breakfast or luncheon dish)', which essentially involved stuffing a boned-out pig's head with chopped pork and ham. All these verbal elaborations have now faded away, and *collar* is back where it began, as a single joint.

collards *Collards*, or *collard greens*, is the name used in the US for a smooth-leaved variety of kale. It is associated particularly with the soul food of the Deep South, where typically collards are boiled with a piece of bacon or salt pork. The word, first recorded in 1755, is an alteration of *colewort*, an old name for a plant of the genus *Brassica*, especially kale (*see* COLESLAW).

college pudding A traditional English plum pudding—that is, a suet pudding with currants, raisins, and candied peel, as served in times gone by to members of Oxford and Cambridge colleges. The name is first recorded in print in 1829.

collop *Collops* was the medieval term for 'bacon and eggs' (in William Langland's fourteenth-century poem, Piers the Plowman complains 'I have no salt bacon, ne no kokeney [small eggs, literally 'cock's eggs'] by crist coloppes forto maken'). It probably came from a Scandinavian word which meant literally 'jumping on coals' (Swedish has *kalops* 'meat stew', which goes back to an Old Swedish *kolhuppadher*, a compound based on *kol* 'coal' and *huppa* 'to jump'; the underlying idea is the same as that of French *sauter*, which also means literally 'to jump'). By the sixteenth century it was being used for the slices of bacon alone, but the association with eggs was still strong, and the day before Shrove Tuesday was often called *Collop Monday*, from the tradition of eating bacon and eggs then. The broadening of meaning continued, and nowadays, especially in American English but also dialectally in Britain, it is used for any 'slice of meat (or indeed fish)': 'Main courses pick up the theme by offering collops of monkfish with leek and pancetta risotto', *Good Food Guide* (2008).

colocassi A Cypriot version of the taro, a tropical and temperate plant with large starchy edible tubers. In the case of the colocassi, the tubers are comparatively elongated and slender, with a characteristic stalk-like stump, so that they rather resemble an unfamiliar but suspicious species of tall mushroom. Their name is an alteration of *colocasia*, the Latin genus name of the taro; this in turn came from Greek *kolokasía*, a term originally applied to the edible root of the Egyptian water-lily.

colza An alternative name, first recorded in English in the early eighteenth century, for the plant rape (*see* RAPESEED). It was borrowed from Walloon French *kolza,* which came from Dutch *koolzaad,* a compound formed from *kool* 'cole' (*see* COLESLAW) and *zaad* 'seed'. The edible oil obtained from it can be called *colza oil. See also* CANOLA.

comfit Comfits are sugary sweets—literally as well as etymologically 'confections'. Originally, in the Middle Ages, they appear to have been what today would be called *crystallized fruits*: pieces of fruit preserved by being boiled in sugar. But by the sixteenth century the term had moved on to denote a 'sweet consisting of an aniseed, caraway seed, almond, etc. encrusted in a sugary coating'. It comes via Old French from Latin *confectum* 'preparation', a derivative of *conficere* 'to prepare' (from which English gets *confectionery*).

Comice A large, juicy, late-ripening dessert pear with yellow skin. Its name is short for *Doyenné du Comice.* It was developed in the mid-nineteenth century by a gardener called Hilaire Dhommé, who worked for a certain M. Millet de la Turtaudière, a gentleman of Angers. *Doyenné* itself is an abbreviation of French *poire de doyenné*, literally 'deanery pear'; and *Comice* reflects the fact that M. de la Turtaudière was president of the local *Comice Horticole* 'Horticultural Society'.

commanderia A strong sweet dessert wine made in Cyprus. It has probably been produced for over 3,000 years, but the name *commanderia* dates from more recent times, and comes from the Commandery, a district of Cyprus ruled by the Knights Templars from 1191. Ancient production methods—such as burying amphorae in the ground to age the wine in—still obtain locally, but commercially exported commanderia is made with more up-to-date techniques.

communard An alternative name for cardinal, a combination of red wine and blackcurrant liqueur. It was inspired by the Communards, members of the revolutionary Paris Commune of 1871, who are traditionally pictured wearing red.

compote Unpromisingly, *compote* is ultimately the same word as *compost*. Both go back to Latin *composita*, the feminine past participle of the verb *componere* 'to bring together, unite' (source of English *compound*). In Old French this became *composte*, which was used for a dish of fruit stewed in syrup. English used *compost* in this sense when it first borrowed it (a mid-fifteenth-century cookery book, for instance, gives a recipe for 'pears in compost': 'take pear Wardens, pare them and seethe [boil] them, and cast them to the syrup.... And then pare clean rasings [roots] of ginger and cast them to the pears in compost'). By the end of the sixteenth century, however, the modern sense of *compost* was developing fast, and not surprisingly 'stewed fruit' died out. It was replaced in the seventeenth century by *compote*, a later French form of Old French *composte*.

Comté A French cows'-milk hard cheese, yellow in colour. Until the middle of the twentieth century it was made with large holes, rather like Emmental, but modern Comté is holeless. It is made in Franche Comté (literally 'Free County'), a region of eastern France—hence its name.

conchiglie Pasta in the form of small shells. The Italian term (first recorded in 1964) means literally 'conch shells'.

condensed milk Thick sweetened milk that has had some (usually about 60 per cent) of its liquid removed by evaporation. It is usually sold in tins, and has a somewhat caramelized taste. The process was developed in the mid-nineteenth century by the American Gail Borden, and in the second half of the century Switzerland became a main centre of production (*see also* SWISS MILK): 'Don't run away with the idea that the Swiss do nothing but yodel and make condensed milk', P. G. Wodehouse, *Over Seventy* (1957). The term is first recorded in 1863. *Compare* EVAPORATED MILK.

Conference A variety of dessert pear developed by Messrs. Rivers, whose nurseries at Sawbridgeworth, Hertfordshire contributed so much to the British fruit and vegetable garden in the late nineteenth century, and introduced by them in 1894. Its name commemorates a horticultural conference of the time. It is the most widely grown pear in Britain.

confit *Confit* is the past participle of French *confire* 'to preserve'. It is used culinarily to denote food that has been cooked very slowly in fat. Its initial impact in English was as a noun, applied to pieces of meat—typically goose, duck, pork, or turkey—cooked in this way and then stored in a pot, again covered in their own fat. Thus preserved, they can be kept for quite a long time, all the while tenderizing, and developing their flavours. For eating they can either be used on their own, hot or cold, or incorporated into a dish such as cassoulet or garbure. Towards the end of the twentieth century, usage began to move on: not only is the noun now applied to non-meat items, with the accent on slow preservation irrespective of the cooking medium: 'Confit of sea trout was beautifully juxtaposed with spring truffle and a deeply green-tasting purée of lovage', *Guardian Weekend* (2011), but the original French adjectival use is now increasingly common in English: 'guinea fowl with confit cabbage . . . seared rare tuna with niçoise salad, and confit lemon', *Good Food Guide* (2008); 'warm breast of wood pigeon salad, puy lentils, girolle mushroom, redcurrants, and confit grapefruit', *Sunday Times* (2011).

congee Congee or, in a now obsolescent spelling, *conjee* is a simple East Asian porridge made from rice and water or stock. It can be eaten as it is, or enlivened with various additions, such as soy or fish sauce, pickles and nuts, or pieces of meat. The British in India during the Raj regarded it as invalid food, and even used it to starch their shirt-fronts—it became a verb: 'his stiff, full cravat of former days . . . surmounted with a well congied modern shirt collar', *The Bengalee* (1829). The word *congee* came into English in the late seventeenth century, possibly via Portuguese, from Tamil *kanji*.

congou A kind of black (i.e. fermented) China tea. Its name is probably an alteration of Chinese *kong-hu*, meaning 'pains taken', the implication presumably being that the tea is the product of work done. It began to appear in England in the 1720s (the *London Gazette* in 1725 advertised 'Next Week will be sold, a large Parcel of Bohee, with some Congou and Green Tea'), and in early use its name often morphed into *congo*.

consommé In French, *consommé* is literally something that has been 'consummated'— that is, by boiling down, the flavours of meat, vegetables, or whatever have become completely concentrated. The word comes from the past participle of the verb *consommer*, which means both 'to accomplish, finish, consummate' and 'to consume', in the eating sense—not to be confused with *consumer*, which means 'to consume' in the destructive sense. Originally, the word seems to have been applied to any rich broth which was the product of long, slow cooking; but by the mid-nineteenth century the current signification 'clear soup' was well established. One of the earliest references to *consommé* in English is by Byron, who in *Don Juan* (1824) laments 'Alas! I must leave undescribed the *gibier*, / the *salmi*, the *consommé*, the *purée*, / all which I use to make my rhymes run glibber / than could roast beef in our rough John Bull way.'

cooked water Cooked water, or in Italian *acquacotta*, is a traditional Tuscan soup. It consists of a vegetable broth, containing in autumn plentiful quantities of wild mushrooms, which is served poured over slices of toast.

cookie The usage of the word *cookie* varies markedly in different parts of the English-speaking world. The usual British perception is that it is the American equivalent of *biscuit*, but it is not quite so simple as that. To be sure, it is used in the US and Canada for 'biscuits', but only sweet biscuits; and it also includes slightly leavened biscuits that attain a partially raised shape which would almost qualify them in Britain for the term *cake*. In this particular sense *cookie* has to some extent established itself in British English, helped no doubt by the sale in the United Kingdom of various brands of American-style chocolate-chip cookies. The word was introduced into the US in the late eighteenth century by Dutch immigrants, and comes from Dutch *koekje*, a diminutive form of *koek*, 'cake'. Dutch influence is no doubt responsible also for the parallel use of the word in South African English. In Scotland, however, the situation is markedly different; there, *cookie* signifies a 'plain bun', and there must be some doubt as to whether it comes from the same source as the American word.

   The colloquial use of *cookie* for 'guy, fellow' (as in a 'smart cookie') dates from 1920s America. Less internationalized is the US expression *toss the cookies*, meaning 'to vomit'. *How the cookie crumbles* for 'the way things are' originated in the US too, apparently in the late 1950s. In present-day computer jargon, a *cookie* is a packet of data sent by an Internet server to a browser, which is returned by the browser each time it subsequently accesses the same server, thus identifying the user or tracking their access to the server. The term, a shortening of the original *magic cookie,* originated around 1994.

cooler A long cold drink, particularly a mildly alcoholic one based mainly on fruit juice or other soft drinks. A roughly equivalent term in South African English is *cooldrink*.

Copha The proprietary name in Australia for a vegetable fat made from coconut oil. It is used, especially mixed with chocolate, in the making of confectionery, toppings for cakes, etc. In New Zealand it is known as *Kremelta*.

coppa An Italian pork product consisting of raw cured collar (meat from the animal's neck) pressed into the shape of a sausage. The Italian usage (first recorded in 1863) probably comes from an earlier meaning, 'back of the head', which was in turn a metaphorical use of *coppa* 'cup'.

coq au vin A casserole of chicken pieces cooked in red wine. The French term, which began to be used in English in the 1930s, means literally 'cockerel with wine', but nowadays the dish is almost always made with a standard (female) chicken. It is no doubt an age-old method employed by French country cooks to send off a venerable rooster that had outlived any other usefulness, but it was not 'discovered' and entered into the pantheon of French haute cuisine until the early years of the twentieth century.

coquille St Jacques The French term for a scallop, literally 'St James's shell' (it refers to the use of the shell of the mollusc, which used to be found in huge numbers on the coast of northwestern Spain, as a badge by medieval pilgrims travelling to Santiago de Compostella, the shrine of St James). In France, scallops are commonly cooked on the half-shell, often with a cream and wine sauce, covered in breadcrumbs with grated cheese and browned under the grill, and *coquilles St Jacques* has come to denote this recipe in English.

coral Gastronomically, coral is the unfertilized roe of a lobster, which turns red when cooked. The usage dates from the mid-eighteenth century, and in more recent times has been extended to the beak-shaped orange roe of the scallop.

cordial In British English, a sweet typically fruit-flavoured drink (for example, *blackcurrant cordial*). Originally, in the fourteenth century, the term denoted a medicine that invigorates the heart and stimulates the circulation, reflecting its origin in medieval Latin *cordialis* 'of the heart', from Latin *cor* 'heart'. The present-day usage does not seem to have emerged until the early nineteenth century: 'the closet which held the peppermint-water and other cordials', Thomas de Quincy, *The Spanish Military Nun* (1847). In American English the word means 'liqueur'.

cordon bleu The original cordon bleu was a blue ribbon that formed part of the insignia of members of the French *Ordre des Chevaliers du Saint-Esprit* 'Order of the Knights of the Holy Spirit', instituted in the late sixteenth century. The term was later applied to an award given to female cooks for culinary excellence, and subsequently by extension to any highly skilled cook. English had acquired it by the early nineteenth century: '"How good this is!" said Popjoy, good-naturedly. "You must have a *cordon bleu* in your kitchen",' W. M. Thackeray, *Pendennis* (1849), and later used it more broadly as a designation of superior (and by implication, French-style) cookery: 'The wife's cooking is described by a member as "Cordon Bleu",' Raymond Postgate, *Good Food Guide* (1959). It was fair game for adoption as the name of a dish, and this seems to have happened in America in the 1950s when a dish of veal escalopes enclosing a filling of cheese and ham, covered in breadcrumbs and fried, became *veal cordon bleu*. Veal is something of a minority attraction, but chicken is another matter, and *chicken cordon bleu* (the term is first recorded in 1967) soon became a supermarket ready-meal staple.

coriander Coriander is amongst the most cosmopolitan of herbs. It is popular throughout Asia, in South America (the members of one Peruvian tribe are said to be such coriandophiles that their skin gives off its characteristic pungent scent), and in the Middle East (it is mentioned in the Bible: 'And the house of Israel called the name thereof Manna: and it was like coriander seed, white,' Exodus 16: 31). There is evidence that coriander was imported into Britain from southern Europe in the Bronze Age, but it was the Romans who brought the name for it, *coriandrum*, which they in turn had got from Greek *koríannon*. R being a slippery consonant, however, the Anglo-Saxons changed this later to *cellendre*, and it was not until the fourteenth century that the present *r*-form was reacquired via Old French.

It continued to be a popular herb in Britain, for both its seeds and its parsley-like leaves, throughout the medieval and Elizabethan period and right into the nineteenth century (the term *coriander seed*, or simply *coriander*, was even used as a colloquialism for 'money': 'You must shell out your corianders!', Maria Edgeworth, *Moral Tales* (1801)). Essex was a centre of coriander growing. In the later nineteenth and early twentieth centuries it went into a decline, but increasing familiarity with foreign cuisines since the Second World War has given it a renewed boost.

corkscrew A cocktail concocted from rum, dry vermouth, and peach brandy.

corn The sharp distinction in usage of the word *corn* on either side of the Atlantic—British English tends to apply it to any sort of cereal grain, whereas American English uses it more specifically for 'maize'—seems to have originated around the end of the seventeenth century. It was a predictable enough development, of course, since maize is the natural cereal crop of the Americas, and remained the most abundant until the plains were covered with wheat. In the US, cereals in general are called *grain*, which in fact is distantly related to the word *corn*. Both go back ultimately to an ancient Indo-European *grnóm*, which meant literally 'worn-down particle'. *Corn* reached English via a Germanic route, whereas *grain* came through Latin *grānum*. The original notion of 'small particle' survives in *corned beef*, where *corned* refers to the grains of salt used for preserving the meat, and even the more restricted sense 'seed' is not completely confined to cereal seeds—we still speak of *peppercorns*, for example. It is noticeable that although the American usage has made its presence felt in British English in various compounds, such as *cornflour* and *popcorn*, it has not encroached on the word's central sense. *See also* MAIZE.

The colloquial use of the word for 'hackneyed joke, music, etc.', which originated in America between the two World Wars, was probably to begin with an allusion to the supposed lack of sophistication of corn-growing country areas, although another ingenious theory once put forward was that it referred to old American seed catalogues, which often included hoary jokes and riddles interspersed between the advertisements for seed corn. (*Corn* on the foot, incidentally, is a completely different word, related to English *horn*.)

corn dodger *See* DODGER.

corn dog A variant on the 'hot dog' theme in which a frankfurter is dipped in cornmeal batter, fried, and served on a stick. The concept is said to have been invented by Neil Fletcher in 1942 for the Texas State Fair, but the actual term *corn dog* is not recorded before 1967.

corned beef In Britain, corned beef is cooked beef preserved in brine and saltpetre (which give it its pink colour), chopped up and pressed, and sold in characteristic oblong tins narrower at the top than at the bottom. It is typically imported from South America (the best-known source is probably Fray Bentos in Uruguay). Its name comes from its being preserved with *corns* or 'grains' of salt, and dates from the seventeenth century: 'Beef . . . corned, young, of an Ox,' Robert Burton, *Anatomy of Melancholy* (1621). Until the nineteenth century the adjective *corned* was applied to pork as well as beef.

In American English, such meat is called *canned pressed beef*. The term *corned beef* is used for 'salt beef', especially from the brisket.

cornflakes Cornflakes, a commercially manufactured breakfast cereal made from toasted maize, originated in the US in 1894. This was when William Kellogg (1860–1951) discovered a process for making the maize into flakes. In 1906 he set up a company to market the result, and since then cornflakes have spread to every corner of the civilized world. They soon arrived in Britain, and in *Summoned by Bells* (1960) John Betjeman recalled breakfast of 'cornflakes, bread, and tea' at his prep school during the time of the First World War.

cornflour A very fine flour ground from maize. The term originated in the US, where 'maize' is standardly called *corn*, but became established in British English in the second half of the nineteenth century (American English now generally uses *cornstarch*). It has also been applied to other sorts of fine flour, made from, for example, rice.

cornichon The French word for a small gherkin, which occasionally is used in English (it is first recorded in the 1820s). It is a diminutive form of *corne* 'horn', a reference to the shape of a gherkin.

cornmeal Flour made from corn. In American English the term refers to maize flour (less finely ground than cornflour), in Scottish English to oatmeal. It is first recorded in 1749.

corn pone In the southern states of the US, corn pone is a sort of bread made with maize flour and milk and cooked by either baking or frying. It is eaten with such homely dishes as hog-jowl. The *pone* element comes from a Native American word for 'bread'; it is related to Delaware *äpân* 'baked'.

corn salad. An alternative name for LAMB'S LETTUCE.

coronation chicken A cold dish of cooked chicken served in a curried mayonnaise sauce, typically flavoured with apricot purée. It was created by the cook Rosemary Hume in honour of Elizabeth II's coronation in 1953 (inspired, it would seem, by a very similar dish served eighteen years before for George V's Silver Jubilee) and first served at a coronation lunch held for Commonwealth heads of government. On that occasion it was accorded the fancy French name *poulet reine Elizabeth,* but it is as *coronation chicken* that it has since become a familiar light-lunch or sandwich-filler option, widely available ready-made in supermarkets.

cos A crisp long-leaved variety of lettuce. The earliest known pictorial record of a lettuce, from an ancient Egyptian carving, shows the tall leaves characteristic of the cos, but the plant that now bears the name seems to have originated in Turkey and adjacent islands (including Kos): the earliest record of it in English, in John Evelyn's *Acetaria* (1699), refers to the 'Coss Lettuce from Turkey'. It was probably brought westwards via Rome, for *Roman lettuce* was an early name for it in Britain, and in the US it is still generally known as the *romaine*. Another term occasionally used for it in Britain is *Manchester lettuce*.

cosmopolitan A vodka-based cocktail made with an orange-flavoured liqueur, such as Cointreau or Triple Sec, cranberry juice, and lime juice. It seems to have been created in all its essentials in the 1970s, in the US, but it was in the late 1980s that it (and its name) gained international recognition, in the hands of Manhattan mixologist Tony Cecchino, with a definitive recipe established by the Florida bartender Cheryl Cook. In the 1990s it became the cocktail of choice for trendy young women, its profile enhanced by frequent appearances on the US television programme *Sex and the City*: 'I picture inviting her to a girls' night out . . . where we'd drink cosmopolitans and chatter', Claire Berlinski, *Loose Lips* (2003). The name is often shortened to *cosmo*.

cotechino A type of large Italian pork sausage made in the region of Emilia-Romagna, and particularly in Modena. It is traditionally served hot with lentils. Its main characteristic ingredient is pork rind (Italian *cotica*, a descendant of Latin *cutis* 'skin'), from which it gets its name.

Cotherstone A blue-veined cows'-milk cheese made on two specific farms near Cotherstone, to the west of Darlington in County Durham. Such cheese has been made in this area since Norman times, but the actual name *Cotherstone* is not recorded in print before 1911. The cheese used also to be known as 'Yorkshire Stilton'.

cotignac A clear, firm, pink sweet jelly made in France from quince juice. It is traditionally sold in round wooden boxes. It is particularly associated with Orléans in central France, and larger boxes have the image of Joan of Arc, the 'maid of Orléans', imprinted on the jelly. The French word *cotignac* goes back ultimately to late Latin *cotōneum* (*see* QUINCE). English borrowed it in the sixteenth century, as *codiniac,* and produced several of its own versions of the word, including *cotiniate, quiddany,* and *quidiniac,* but all these have long since died out, and English now happily embraces the French term. *See also* MEMBRILLO.

Cotswold *See* LYMESWOLD.

cottage cheese Despite its traditional sound, *cottage cheese* is in fact a comparatively recent term; it is first recorded in John Bartlett's *Dictionary of Americanisms* (1848), and before the twentieth century seems largely to have been restricted to the US. It originally appears to have been used for any soft cheese suitable for spreading, but it now refers specifically to a lumpy moist unripened low-fat curd cheese made from skimmed milk. The word is presumably a reflection of the cheese's origins in farm-cottage kitchens.

cottage loaf A traditional English type of loaf, now seldom seen, consisting of a large round base surmounted by a smaller round topknot of bread. It is presumably of some antiquity, although the actual name is not recorded before the mid-1800s: the artist John Constable, for instance, wrote in 1832 in a letter to a friend 'I send you a cottage loaf for Sunday,' and Charles Dickens included it in his mouthwatering account in *Barnaby Rudge* (1841) of the tea produced by Mrs Varden for Dolly and Joseph Willet, 'for whose delight, preserves and jams, crisp cakes and then pastry, short to eat, with cunning twists, and cottage loaves, and rolls of bread both white and brown, were all set forth in rich profusion.' From the account given by Eliza Acton in her *English Bread Book* (1857) it can be deduced that at that time it was the commonest shape in which loaves were baked—simply, one presumes, for aesthetic reasons, for it is certainly not the easiest of loaves to make, as its decline over the past sixty years attests. Although cottage loaves are standardly round, they can be of the more conventional oblong loaf shape; these are—or were—known as *cottage bricks*, and they were particularly common in the London area.

cottage pie In present-day English, *cottage pie* is an increasingly popular synonym for *shepherd's pie*, a dish of minced meat with a topping of mashed potato. Its widening use is no doubt due in part to its pleasantly bucolic associations, in part to the virtual disappearance of mutton and lamb from such pies in favour of beef (or textured vegetable protein). But in fact, *cottage pie* is a much older term than *shepherd's pie*, which does not crop up until the 1870s; on 29 August 1791 we find that enthusiastic recorder of all his meals, the Reverend James Woodforde, noting in his diary 'Dinner to day, Cottage-Pye and rost Beef' (it is not clear precisely what he meant by *cottage pie*, however).

coulibiac A coulibiac, or *koulibiac* as it is also spelled, is a Russian fish pie. As well as its main ingredient (which could be eel, salmon, or even sturgeon—and sometimes chicken is substituted for the fish) it contains rice, hard-boiled egg, and vegetables. This filling is encased in a crust of either puff pastry or brioche dough, which is usually simply wrapped around it to form a sort of pillow shape, rather than being baked in a dish.

coulis A thin purée or sieved sauce made typically of vegetables or fruit (*tomato coulis* is a common manifestation of it). Nouvelle cuisiniers' penchant for using fruit coulis, especially made from raspberries, at every opportunity made the term familiar to English-speakers in the 1980s, but in fact it had first crossed the Channel nearly 600 years ago, in the form *cullis*. This was a sort of strained broth or gravy made originally probably from chicken, but subsequently from any meat or even fish, and used as a basis for sauces or simply poured over meat dishes. The word originated in Old French as a noun use of the adjective *coleis* 'straining, pouring, flowing, sliding', which in turn came ultimately from Latin *cōlāre* 'to strain' (source of English *colander*). A memory of the old form is preserved in *portcullis*, which means literally 'sliding door'.

Coulommiers A Coulommiers is essentially a Brie made in a small size. Its flavour is usually somewhat less fruity than that of the larger version. It takes its name from the town of Coulommiers to the southeast of Meaux in the Île de France.

courgette A variety of vegetable marrow eaten when comparatively immature and small (its name is the diminutive form of French *courge* 'gourd'). It has white flesh and usually green skin, although a yellow-skinned variant has been produced. It is a staple vegetable in Italy, southern France, and other parts of the Mediterranean, but it was virtually unknown in Britain until after the Second World War. In North America it is known as *zucchini*, a term given to the language by Italian immigrants.

court bouillon A court bouillon (in French literally 'short bouillon') is a light stock used mainly for poaching fish or shellfish in. It is made from water and the usual mixture of stock vegetables (onions, carrots, celery) and herbs, with the optional addition of white wine or (particularly for freshwater fish) vinegar. The term has been used in English texts since the early eighteenth century, but Eliza Acton in her *Modern Cookery* (1845) made it clear that cooking with court bouillon was still far from an everyday event: 'court bouillon—a preparation of vegetables and wine, in which (in expensive cookery) fish is boiled.'

couscous A North African dish consisting originally of coarsely ground wheat, now often of semolina pasta in granular form, steamed over boiling water or more usually over a broth in which meat and vegetables (in Morocco traditionally 'seven vegetables', which vary from season to season) are cooked. The ground wheat or semolina pasta (themselves called *couscous* too) is then served with the broth, meat, and vegetables poured over it. The dish was introduced to Europe by the French in the sixteenth century, and the word *couscous* reached English via French (it is of North African origin, from Arabic *kuskus*, a derivative of the Arabic verb *kaskasa* 'to grind small, pulverize'). English readers first encountered it in John Pory's translation of Leo's *Geographical History of Africa* (1600): 'In winter they [the people of Fez] have sodden [boiled] flesh, together with a kind of meat called couscous'.

couverture Chocolate made with extra cocoa butter to give a high gloss, used for covering sweets and cakes. The term was introduced into English from French (where it means literally 'covering') in the 1930s, and has subsequently also been used, to the chagrin of real-chocolate aficionados, to denote an inferior product in which hydrogenated fat takes the place of most of the cocoa butter.

cowheel The foot of a cow or ox, used as food. This bony and horny appendage is standardly boiled, either to be eaten, if it is all you can afford, or to produce a savoury broth or jelly (*calf's-foot jelly*, if the animal in question is young enough). Either result was valued in the past as food for invalids (Thomas Muffet and Christopher Bennet in their *Health's Improvement* (1655) note that 'also a tender Cow-heel is counted restorative').

cow pea An alternative name for BLACK-EYED PEA.

Cox's orange pippin The Cox's orange pippin (its name is commonly shortened to *Cox*) is a crisp sweet eating apple with a red-tinged skin (the 'orange' in the name refers to the skin colour, not the apple's taste). It was originally propagated some time in the first half of the nineteenth century by a Mr Richard Cox, a brewer and amateur gardener of Colnbrook, near Slough, and first distributed in 1850 by Charles Turner.

crab apple No one is too sure where this term for the small sour wild apple came from. All that is clear is that it has no connection with the crustacean of the same name. It first appears in the late fourteenth century, and the northern and Scottish form *scrab* suggests that it may be of Scandinavian origin (there is a Swedish dialect word *skrabba* for 'wild apple'). *Crabbed* and *crabby* 'cantankerous' probably derived from *crab* the animal, which had a reputation for bad temper and perversity, but have subsequently become linked with the sourness of crab apples.

crabeye bean An alternative name for the pinto bean, a pale pinkish-brown speckled bean popular in the Caribbean and the southern US, presumably given to it from a supposed resemblance to the beady bean-shaped eye of the crab.

crabstick The original crabstick, which came on the scene in America in the mid-1950s, was a finger-shaped portion of crabmeat (or pseudo-crabmeat) coated in batter or breadcrumbs for frying: in other words, a sort of crabby fish finger. The name was later usurped, however, by what many regard as an altogether more dubious article: a stick of white minced-up fish masquerading as crustacean beneath an exterior dyed a lobsterish pink (an alternative, and less misleading name for it—but still one with the whiff of euphemism—is *ocean stick*). The underlying concept comes from Japanese *surimi*, literally 'minced meat', which denotes a paste made from minced fish (or sometimes meat) and used for fish sticks and the like. It originated in pre-refrigeration days as a method used by Japanese fishermen to keep their catch in eatable condition on the way home.

cracker As a term for a crisp savoury biscuit, *cracker* dates back to the early eighteenth century. Most of the earliest examples of its use are American, and for the most part it seems to have stayed on that side of the Atlantic (the exception is the *cream cracker*, a British term for a type of crisp biscuit usually eaten with cheese, which is first mentioned in the 1906 edition of Mrs Beeton's *Book of Household Management*). American country stores would have a barrel containing crackers for their customers to dip into while (in more leisured days) they chatted and no doubt put the world to rights: hence the term *cracker-barrel philosopher* for someone who expresses homespun, unsophisticated views.

crackling Cracklings originally were the crisp residue left after animal fat, and particularly lard, had been rendered down for tallow. They were usually fed to dogs. It is not until as late as the 1880s, in fact, that we find the word *crackling* being used in its present-day sense 'crisply browned pork skin', although the antiquity of the near-synonymous and probably related *scratching*, and the now obsolete *cratchen* and *cracon*, suggest that it is far older than that. The slang *bit of crackling* for 'attractive girl or woman' dates from the Second World War or immediately afterwards.

From the sixteenth to the nineteenth centuries *crackling* was also used for what we would now call *cracknel*.

cracknel A cracknel was originally a hard crisp biscuit, although nowadays *cracknel* is probably more familiar as a term for a sort of brittle nut-filled toffee used as a filling for chocolates. The word probably comes from Old French *craquelin*, which derived ultimately from the Middle Dutch verb *krāken* 'to crack'. English acquired it in the fifteenth century, and later the translators of the King James version of the Bible had recourse to it in I Kings 14:3: 'And take with thee ten loaves, and cracknels, and a cruse of honey, and go to him.'

cranachan A Scottish dessert consisting in its original and simplest form of oatmeal mixed with cream—in fact, a more luxurious version of crowdie (and *cream crowdie* is an alternative name for it). Nowadays it is usually further boosted with honey, soft fruits, especially raspberries, and often whisky. The name came from Scottish Gaelic *crannachan*, which denoted a dish of half-churned cream traditionally eaten on Halloween. Its earlier, more literal referent was a type of crane or churn, and it probably came from *crann* 'beam, bar, tree' and the diminutive suffix *-achan*.

cranberry Cranberries grow in Britain, but in medieval times they went under a variety of names such as *marsh-wort, fen-wort, fen-berry*, and *moss-berry*. The term *cranberry* did not appear until the late seventeenth century, in America. It was a partial translation of *kranbeere*, literally 'craneberry,' brought across the Atlantic by German immigrants (the German word is an allusion to the plant's long beaklike stamens). It was the Germans and Scandinavians, too, who probably popularized the notion of eating cranberries with meat in the English-speaking world, which led to today's pairing of turkey with cranberry sauce. The berries have also been widely used in pies and tarts, though, even receiving royal approval: 'the dinner ending with a good tart of cranberries', Queen Victoria, *Journal of our Life in the Highlands* (1868).

The cranberry achieved its fifteen minutes of fame in 1995, when a recommendation by the television cookery presenter Delia Smith led to the stripping of supermarket shelves, and Britain faced an acute Christmas cranberry shortage.

crappit heids A Scottish delicacy consisting of haddocks' heads (*heids*) stuffed with a seasoned mixture of oatmeal, suet and onion, and boiled. *Crappit* means 'filled, stuffed'; it may represent a borrowing of Dutch *krappen* 'to fill the crop of (a bird), cram'.

cream The main source of the term *cream* was late Latin *crānum*, a word of unknown origin. It merged with late Latin *chrisma* 'ointment' (source of English *chrism*) to produce Old French *cresme* or *craime*. English borrowed this in the fourteenth century, and it gradually ousted the native word *ream* (a relative of German *rahm* and Dutch *room* 'cream'), which survived dialectally into the twentieth century.

The notion of *cream* as the choicest part separated out from the rest (of the milk) has been metaphoricized since at least the sixteenth century ('the gentleman, which be the creame of the common,' Richard Mulcaster, *Positions for the Training up of Children* (1581)), and reinforced since the mid-nineteenth century by the borrowing of French *crème de la crème*, 'cream of the cream, élite'. The verbal use *cream off* 'to remove the best' dates from the seventeenth century.

cream cheese A soft unripened cheese made from unskimmed milk and cream. The term is first recorded in 1583.

cream cracker A British term for a crisp unsweetened biscuit, typically eaten with cheese. It was first recorded at the beginning of the twentieth century (the 1906 edition of Mrs Beeton's *Book of Household Management* notes 'Cream Crackers' at 6d a pound); *cream* is said to refer to the way the ingredients (which certainly do not include cream) are 'creamed' together before baking. Jacob's, the biscuits' original British manufacturer, introduced them from America in the 1880s.

British *cream-crackered* as rhyming slang for 'knackered' (i.e. tired out) is a relatively recent development, probably dating from the 1970s: 'I didn't see anybody else walk at all, which is staggering, you're absolutely cream-crackered by then', *Harrow: the School on the Hill*, ITV (2001).

creamed potato *See* MASHED POTATO.

cream puff A small light puff-pastry (or, in North America, choux-pastry) cake filled with whipped cream. The term dates from the 1880s (in America), its colloquial application to an ineffectual or 'wet' person, particularly an effeminate man, probably from the 1930s. In American English it is also a slang expression for a second-hand car in excellent condition.

Creamsicle The trademarked name in the US for a type of ice lolly with a central core of ice cream surrounded by a layer of fruit-flavoured water-ice (the equivalent product in Britain has the proprietary name *Mivvi*). It blends the *cream* of *ice cream* with *Popsicle*.

cream soda In the US, and increasingly in Britain, a cream soda is a sweet fizzy drink flavoured with vanilla, originally made from soda water. *The American Agriculturist* (1854) was in on the beginning of its career: 'A recipe has been sold all over the country for making "cream-soda".'

crème brûlée A dessert consisting of a custard made with cream and eggs, topped by a layer of caramel. Superficially it resembles *crème caramel*, but the difference resides in the method of achieving the caramel topping: in the case of *crème brûlée*, sugar is sprinkled over the surface of the cooked custard, and it is then put under a hot grill to caramelize. The result is quite crisp and bubbly. *Crème brûlée* has been popular in Britain since the seventeenth century under its English name, *burnt cream* (see CAMBRIDGE BURNT CREAM), but it was not until the end of the nineteenth century that the French term (a direct equivalent) came into vogue.

crème caramel One of a species of French custard desserts known as *crèmes renversées*, literally 'creams turned upside down'. They are made in moulds and then turned out. In the case of *crème caramel* (also known in English as *caramel custard*), a coating of caramel is put in the bottom of the mould before the egg and milk custard mixture is poured in; when it is cooked and taken out of the mould the caramel forms a topping which runs down the side of the custard. *Crème caramel* should not be confused with *crème au caramel*, which is a caramel-flavoured cream dessert.

crème de menthe Literally 'mint cream', *crème de menthe* is a syrupy mint-flavoured liqueur of French origin. Its standard colour, a lurid emerald green, has become synonymous with vulgarity (colourless *crème de menthe* is also made).

crème fraîche A type of lightly fermented thick cream. It is the basic form of cream in France, where it is usually referred to simply as *crème* (*crème fraîche* means just 'fresh cream'). There it is thickened naturally by the action of bacteria, but crème fraîche sold in the UK, where it began a rise to popularity in the 1990s, is fermented with the addition of buttermilk, sour cream, or yoghurt.

crêpe English took over *crêpe*, the French term for a 'thin pancake', in the late nineteenth century, but mainly in the context of *crêpe Suzette*. Its acceptance as a word in its own right had to wait until the 1970s and 1980s, when the upsurge of interest in French food spawned crêperies in shopping precincts nationwide. French *crêpe* itself comes ultimately from Latin *crispus* 'curled' (source of English *crisp*), and as applied to 'pancakes' is short for *galette crêpe* 'curled or wrinkled pancake' (the underlying meaning of English *crumpet* is very similar). Crêpes are popular throughout France, but one particularly famous variety is the *crêpe dentelle*, literally 'lace pancake', which is made in Quimper in Brittany, and is actually more of a crisp biscuit than a pancake.

crêpe Suzette A light pancake served rolled up or folded over in an orange sauce, sprinkled with an orange-based liqueur or brandy and flambéed at table. It seems to have come on the scene at around the turn of the twentieth century, but its precise origins and the reason for its name are not clear. The chef Henri Charpentier made great play with having invented the dish at the Café de Paris, Monte Carlo in 1896 for the Prince of Wales, and named it after the young lady who was the prince's companion on that particular occasion, but his claim has been shown to be an imposture. Contemporary evidence suggests that its most likely creator was a head waiter at Restaurant Paillard in Paris in 1889, and that it was named in honour of an actress in the Comédie Française who played the part of a maid serving pancakes. The first known reference to such crêpes in print comes in Auguste Escoffier's *Modern Cookery* (1907), in which he refers to them by the English name *Suzette pancakes*. Less often encountered nowadays, they were for perhaps the first two thirds of the twentieth century the epitome of the luxurious, expensive, and exclusive dessert—found, for instance, on all the best ocean liners: 'Crêpes Suzette are pancakes raised by Cunard to a remarkable point of perfection', *Vanity Fair* (1928).

cress A general term for a range of plants of the cabbage family with small peppery-flavoured leaves used in salads. They include the *watercress*, its terrestrial counterpart the *land cress* or *American cress*, and the *garden cress*, whose seedlings form one half of the partnership *mustard and cress*. The word *cress* comes from a prehistoric West Germanic **krasjon*, and has been in the language since the Old English period. Close relatives include German *kresse* and Dutch *kers*.

crisp Crisps—in full *potato crisps*—very thin slices of potato fried until they are crisp and curly, then usually given some distinctive flavouring and packaged up to be eaten cold, appeared on the scene in the middle of the nineteenth century. Their invention has been attributed to George Crum, chef at Moon's Lake Lodge in Saratoga, in upstate New York, allegedly after a customer in 1853 sent back some fried potatoes for being too large and soggy (Funk's *Standard Dictionary* of 1893 records them as *Saratoga chips,* and American English-speakers still call them *potato chips*). The early market leader in Britain was Smith's crisps, made by a company founded in Cricklewood, in northwest London, by Francis Leigh Smith after the First World War. Its plain unvarnished crisps had a small blue-paper twist of salt inside the packet that enabled eaters to season them to their own taste. After the Second World War Henry Walker, originally a Nottinghamshire butcher, turned his talents to manufacturing crisps in Leicester. Over the following decades, marked by the introduction of flavoured crisps (salt and vinegar, chicken tikka, etc.; the first British example was cheese and onion, produced by Golden Wonder in 1962), Walker's increasingly dominated the British crisp market, and in the 1990s Smith's crisps finally disappeared. A relatively recent trend in the world of crisps is to produce ones made from other sorts of root vegetable—sweet potatoes, parsnips, carrots, beetroot, etc.

crispbread Crispbread in its original Scandinavian form is made exclusively from rye flour, although most modern commercial versions contain a proportion of wheat flour too. It first appeared on the scene in Britain in the 1920s, when brands such as Ryvita and Vita-wheat were introduced. The earliest known reference to it is in the Army and Navy Stores catalogue for 1926–7.

croccante An Italian sweetmeat made from almonds and caramelized sugar, similar to praline. Its name is a derivative of the verb *croccare* 'to crack, creak'—presumably imitative of the sound made when eating it.

croissant These new-moon-shaped puff-pastry rolls seem first to have been introduced to British and American breakfast tables at the beginning of the twentieth century. Their name—literally French for 'crescent'—reflects their form, and in fact there has always been a certain amount of interchangeability between the two terms: in the sixteenth and seventeenth centuries *croissant* was often used in English for what we would now call a *crescent*, and when croissants themselves first came on the scene, *crescent roll* was an alternative name for them. (In defiance of the name many modern croissants, especially large ones or ones made with a purely butter-based dough, tend to be distinctly straight.)

The popular version of how croissants first came to be made relates that the bakers in an eastern European city being besieged by the Turks towards the end of the seventeenth century (some say Vienna 1683, some Budapest 1686) heard the sound of the attackers digging a tunnel under the city walls and as a reward for raising the alarm were granted the right to make rolls in the form of the Islamic symbol, the crescent. All this is complete moonshine, however, and appears to have been invented in the 1930s by the Swiss doctor and scholar Alfred Gottschalk (1873–1954) for the first edition of *Larousse gastronomique* (1938), of which he was co-editor. As for the term *croissant* itself, it is not recorded in this general sense in French before 1853, and the earliest known recipe for a modern-style puff-pastry croissant dates from 1906.

cromesqui The French form of KROMESKI, which is also sometimes used in English: 'Entrecôte of veal . . . came topped with a dazzling piece of cromesquis [sic] made with the veal meat', *Good Food Guide* (2008).

croquembouche A spectacular cone-shaped confection constructed of scores of small choux-pastry buns. In France it traditionally forms a centrepiece at celebrations such as weddings and first communions. The whole edifice is usually glazed with caramelized sugar—hence the name, literally 'crunch in the mouth'.

croque-monsieur The French name for what in English would be called a 'toasted cheese-and-ham sandwich'. It first crops up around the end of the nineteenth century (legend has it that the dish was first served under that name in a café on the Boulevard des Capucines in Paris), but where the term comes from is not clear; it means literally 'crunch-sir' or 'munch-sir' (*croquer* being French for 'to crunch'). A more recent refinement, with a fried egg on top, has been dubbed *croque-madame*.

croquette Croquettes, small shaped masses of some savoury (or occasionally sweet) substance deep-fried, typically in a coating of breadcrumbs, get their name from their crisp exterior: for *croquette* is a derivative of the French verb *croquer* 'to crunch'. The range of potential ingredients is limitless—meat, rice, cheese, fish, pasta, vegetables have all been pressed into service—but undoubtedly the croquette's commonest filling today is mashed potato. It is far from new to the English kitchen; it is mentioned in the 1706 edition of Edward Phillipps's *New World of English Words*: 'In Cookery, Croquets are a certain Compound made of delicious Stuff'd Meat, some of the bigness of an Egg, and others of a Walnut.'

crosne An alternative name for the CHINESE ARTICHOKE.

crostini In Italian cuisine, crostini are small rounds of toasted or fried bread topped with any of a range of foods such as cheese, pâté, anchovy paste, bone marrow, chicken livers, etc., and served, usually hot, as antipasti. The name is a derivative of Italian *crosta* 'crust'.

crottin A small individual French goats' cheese, in the shape of a flattened ball. The best known is *crottin de Chavignol*, from the Berry region of central France. The name is probably a metaphorical application of French *crottin* 'animal dropping, dung': there is a certain resemblance, once the cheeses have matured and become darker in colour.

croûte A dish that is served *en croûte* comes literally 'in a crust'—which usually means 'in a pastry case', but can also turn out to be 'surrounded by slices of bread'. French *croûte* comes via Old French *crouste* (source of English *crust* and also of *custard*) from Latin *crusta* 'rind, shell' (source of English *crustacean*, 'shelled creature' and related to *crude* and *crystal*).

crouton A crouton is literally a 'little crust'. The term was borrowed in the early nineteenth century from French *croûton*, a diminutive form of *croûte* 'crust'. It denotes a small piece of toasted or crisply fried bread, used to give contrasting texture to soups or as a general garnish.

crowdie The Scots term *crowdie* has two distinct applications. It denotes a sort of porridge made from oatmeal and water or buttermilk (this is by far the older usage, dating back at least to the late fifteenth century, but it is now an archaism). It is also used for a type of soft skimmed-milk cheese (this not recorded before the early nineteenth century, but still very much alive, the making of the cheese having been revived in the 1960s). The origins of the word are obscure. Its original meaning has suggested some connection with *groats* 'crushed cereal grains' or with Icelandic *groutr* 'porridge', but neither connection has been established. The later one strongly indicates a link with *curd*, which would heighten the suspicion that the two usages represent separate and unrelated words.

crown roast In the original application of the term (first recorded in the first decade of the twentieth century, and probably an American coinage), a crown roast is an eye-catching roasting joint consisting of two racks of lamb sewn or skewered together in a circle, with the exposed rib-bones pointing upwards. The term can also be applied to a similar construction of pork (or even veal) ribs. Its transference to a joint of turkey or other poultry consisting only of the breast section is a much more recent development. *Compare* GUARD OF HONOUR.

crubbeen Crubbeens are an Irish way with pig's trotters, and especially the front feet. They are cured in brine and boiled for some time, and generally eaten cold with vinegar. *Crubbeen* is an Anglicization of Irish Gaelic *crúbín*, which means literally 'little hoof'.

crudité In French, *crudité* literally means 'rawness'. Hence its application, in the plural, to an hors d'oeuvre dish of small pieces of raw vegetable, such as celery, cucumber, carrot, peppers, or cauliflower, served with a dip of mayonnaise or similar cold sauces. Its introduction into English is comparatively recent.

cruller A small cake made from a sweet dough twisted into a ring or plaited shape and then deep-fried. First mentioned in the early nineteenth century by Washington Irving, it is essentially a North American phenomenon, and its linguistic origins (Dutch *krulle*, derived from the adjective *krul* 'curly') probably reflect its introduction into American cuisine by early Dutch settlers.

crumb *Crumb* is an ancient word, probably descended from an unidentified Indo-European ancestor (related forms with the same meaning are Greek *grūméā* and Albanian *grime*), and its basic underlying signification has always been 'small particle of bread'. The more generalized application to 'small particle of anything', as metaphorically in 'crumbs of comfort,' is a comparatively late development. Its use for the 'inside part of bread', as opposed to the *crust*—that is, the part that can be reduced to crumbs—dates from the fifteenth century.

crumble A British dessert in which raw or stewed fruit (commonly apple) is topped with a layer made from flour and fat rubbed into the texture of breadcrumbs, and baked. The term is first recorded in 1947, but the technique itself seems to have been a product of Second World War culinary making-do.

crumpet The origins of the crumpet are mysterious. As early as 1382, John Wycliffe, in his translation of the Bible, mentioned a *crompid cake*, whose name may be the precursor of the modern term, but the actual 'cake' itself does not bear much resemblance to the present-day crumpet. It seems to have been a thin cake cooked on a hot griddle, so that the edges curled up (*crompid* goes back to Old English *crump, crumb* 'crooked', and is related to modern English *crumple*). The inspiration behind its naming thus seems to be very similar to that of *crêpe*, which means literally 'curled'. Earliest recipes for crumpets, from the late seventeenth century, continue this theme, standardly using buckwheat flour, and it is not until nearly a hundred years later that crumpets as we know them today begin to emerge. Elizabeth Raffald, in *The Experienced English Housekeeper* (1769), was the first to describe their making: 'Beat two eggs very well, put to them a quart of warm milk and water, and a large spoonful of barm: beat in as much fine flour as will make them rather thicker than a common batter pudding, then make your bakestone very hot, and rub it with a little butter wrapped in a clean linen cloth, then pour a large spoonful of batter upon your stone, and let it run to the size of a tea-saucer; turn it, and when you want to use them roast them very crisp, and butter them.' During the nineteenth century the crumpet—toasted before the fire, its honeycomb of cavities filled with melting butter—established itself as an indispensable part of the English teatime scene, so that in 1912 E. H. Ryle could write, in giving advice to athletes, that 'the usual indigestible concomitants of a heavy tea—buttered buns and crumpets—ought to be eschewed'.

The use of *crumpet* as a collective term for sexually attractive young women seems to have emerged in the 1930s. Its origins are not clear, but it may be more than a coincidence that in the second half of the nineteenth century the crumpet's constant companion, the muffin, was used in Canadian English as a word for an attractive young female companion. In the 1980s sexual equality caught up with the crumpet, and the term is now applied to sexually attractive men too (as in 'Paul Newman—the older woman's crumpet,' *Double First*, BBC1 (1988)).

Cuba libre A combination of white rum with a cola drink, with an optional splash of lime juice or wedge of lime: what in more down-to-earth parlance would be a 'rum and Coke' or a 'Bacardi and Coke'. *Cuba libre*, literally 'free Cuba', was the war cry of Cubans fighting for the independence of their island from Spain, which was achieved in 1898. The earliest known use of it to name a drink comes from the very same year, but that was for a simple mixture of water and brown sugar. However, cola drinks seem to have arrived in Cuba in the wake of US troops around 1900, and it is likely that the transference of the name took place not long afterwards.

cucumber *Cucumber* was *cucumer* in the English of the Middle Ages, a direct borrowing from Latin *cucumer-*, *cucumis*, and it is not until the late fifteenth century that we start to find examples with the *b* included (resulting from a reborrowing from Old French *coucombre*). By the sixteenth century it had become quite commonly *cowcumber* (by the same sort of folk etymology that produced *sparrowgrass* from *asparagus*) and this colourful variant established itself as the main form over the next two hundred years, so that in 1798 the grammarian John Walker could write that 'in some counties of England, especially in the west, the word is pronounced as if written *Coocumber* . . . But . . . it seems too firmly fixed in its sound of *Cowcumber* to be altered.' A reaction soon set in, however, consequent on the spread of education and the greater regard paid to the spelling of words, and in 1836 Benjamin Scott reported in his *Pronouncing Dictionary of the English Language* that 'No well-taught person, except of the old school, now says *cow-cumber* . . . although any other pronunciation . . . would have been pedantic some thirty years ago.'

We are used these days to considering the cucumber only as a vegetable to be eaten raw, either in salads or in those cornerstones of the genteel English tea, cucumber sandwiches, but in the past it was often cooked (Mrs Beeton, for instance, has recipes for fried and stewed cucumber), and present-day chefs are re-exploring the options for applying heat. Smaller varieties are usually pickled, the smallest of all under the name *gherkin*.

The cucumber has its positive side—'cool as a cucumber' has been used approvingly for a display of sang-froid since at least the early eighteenth century—but it cannot be denied that it has gained a reputation for causing flatulence. Eliza Acton, however, had some advice for those who could not stomach it: 'The vegetable, though apt to disagree with persons of delicate habit, when sauced in the common English mode, with salt, pepper, and vinegar only, may often be eaten by them with impunity when dressed with plenty of oil.'

The colloquial half-a-cucumber, *cuke*, is first recorded from 1903, and provoked Ogden Nash to complain: 'Who coined these words that strike me numb? . . . The cuke, the glad, the lope, the mum.'

cullen skink A Scottish smoked haddock soup, thickened to a greater or lesser extent with potatoes (and cream) according to taste. *Skink* is a Scots word for 'broth'—originally specifically broth made from shin of beef. It probably comes from Middle Low German *schinke* 'thigh, ham', source of modern German *schinken* 'ham' and related to English *shank* (which meant 'shin-bone' in Anglo-Saxon times), and therefore etymologically denotes 'soup made from shin-bones'. Cullen is a small fishing port on the southern shore of the Moray Firth, and so not surprisingly makes its skink from fish rather than meat. Altogether, the name suggests ancient Scottish ancestry, but as Jane Grigson points out in her *Fish Book* (1993), there is no record of the dish before the 1920s, and it may be a relatively recent creation.

Cumberland sauce A piquant English sauce based on redcurrant jelly, with the addition of orange juice and peel, port, and mustard. It is typically served with cold meat. It seems to have arisen from a combination of two distinct sauces popular with game dishes in the eighteenth century, one based on redcurrant jelly, the other on port or claret. The earliest printed evidence we have for a blend of the two is in William Kitchener's *Apicius Redivivus, or the Cook's Oracle* (1817), which gives a recipe for a 'wine sauce for venison or hare' which includes 'claret or port wine', stock, and 'currant jelly'. In the form in which we now know it, however, it was probably the introduction of the French chef Alexis Soyer, whose recipe for a 'German' sauce to go with boar's head, printed in his *Gastronomic Regenerator* (1846), specifies oranges and mustard as well as port and redcurrant jelly. The actual name *Cumberland sauce* does not seem to have been conferred on it until the 1870s (the first record of it is in Short's *Dinners at Home* (1878)), and the reasons for its choice are not clear. One theory is that it was bestowed in honour of Ernest, Duke of Cumberland, brother of George IV, who in 1837 became the last independent king of Hanover. This would be appropriate in view of the sauce's 'German' origins intimated by Soyer, but the gap between Cumberland's death in 1851 and the first known reference to the sauce is suspiciously large.

Cumberland sausage A type of British sausage made originally in the former county of Cumberland, in what is now the northern part of Cumbria. Its distinctive features are that it is made from coarsely cut pork (originally from the now defunct Cumberland breed of pig) and that it is sold not twisted into links but in a continuous length, characteristically formed into a spiral. It is no doubt of some antiquity, but there is no written description of it on record before 1911.

cumin Cumin, or *cummin*, is a plant of the carrot family whose small pungent crescent-shaped seeds (like caraway seeds but bristly) are widely used in Middle Eastern and Indian cookery. Its name originated in Greek *kúmīnon*, which was probably borrowed from a Semitic language (Hebrew has *kammōn*). This passed into Latin as *cumīnum*, and English originally acquired it in the Anglo-Saxon period as *cymen*, which if it had survived to the present day would have become *kimmen*. However, it appears to have died out, and was reborrowed via Old French *cumin* in the twelfth century. Kümmel, the caraway- or cumin-flavoured liqueur, gets its name from the German word for 'cumin', a descendant of Latin *cumīnum*.

The ancient Greeks and Romans used the metaphor of 'dividing a cumin seed' much as modern English uses 'skinning a flint', to denote a stingy person, and learned English writers of the seventeenth, eighteenth, and early nineteenth centuries adopted the usage: 'a sneaking, pitiful, cummin-splitting fellow,' Thomas Mitchell, *Comedies of Aristophanes* (1822).

cupcake The term *cupcake* originated in the US in the early nineteenth century (it is first recorded in Eliza Leslie's *Receipts* of 1828). It arose either because such cakes were made in cups or cup-shaped containers, or because their ingredients were measured out in cups. In modern usage it denotes an individual cake baked typically in a crimped paper cup, and usually with a topping of fondant icing.

Curaçao A generic term for liqueurs flavoured with sweet or bitter oranges (such as Cointreau or Triple sec). It comes from *Curaçao*, the name of a Dutch island off the coast of Venezuela, and was chosen either because the liqueur was first made there, or because it was made from oranges grown there. The word is of Spanish origin (Curaçao was a Spanish possession from 1527 to 1634, when the Dutch West India Company annexed it). Its use for the liqueur is first recorded in English in the early nineteenth century: Thomas Moore's rhyme in his *Intercepted Letters* (1812) ('And it pleased me to think at a house that you know / Were such good mutton cutlets and strong curaçoa') already shows the anglicized pronunciation which led Moore himself and thousands after him to spell the word *curaçoa*.

Today Curaçao is made in various parts of the world, notably Latvia. It is standardly colourless or yellow, but it also comes in green, pink, and even blue.

curd The thick protein-rich solid component of milk that separates out following coagulation, and is used for making cheese. It has always been used as a food in its own right (often in combination with cream or—as in the case of little Miss Muffet—with whey, the liquid part of milk). Today the word appears most familiarly in the context of *curd cheese*, a somewhat indeterminate term for a soft mild cheese made from skimmed milk curds, distinguished from cottage cheese by being smooth rather than granular. Its other main application, dating from the mid-nineteenth century, is to a confection made with butter, eggs, sugar, and citrus juice, most commonly lemon (*lemon curd*, also known as *lemon cheese*). It is used as a spread or filling.

The word *curd* first turns up in the fourteenth century as *crud* ('"I have no penny," quoth Piers, "pullets forto buy, nor geese nor pigs, but two green cheeses, a few cruds and cream",' *Piers the Plowman* (1362)), a form which survives in various colloquial senses such as 'incrustation of filth' and 'disgusting person or thing'. In its central meaning it was metathesized (had its *r* and *u* reversed) to *curd* in the fifteenth century. It is not altogether clear where the word came from in the first place, but it may be connected with Gaelic *gruth* 'curds'. The verb *curdle* was derived from *curd* in the sixteenth century.

currant The original currant was the small blackish dried grape, as used now in fruit cakes, buns, and puddings; but when various fruit bushes of the genus *Ribes* were introduced into Britain from northern Europe in the late sixteenth century, the popular misconception arose that the familiar dried currants were made from their fruits, and so the name was transferred, and today we have *blackcurrants*, *redcurrants*, etc. (*white currants* and *pink currants* are closely related to the red, and are first cousins to the gooseberry). One of the first references to them in English is made in the *Niewe Herball or Historie of Plantes* (1578) translated by Henry Lyte who, realizing that they are members of the gooseberry family,

calls them 'beyond-seas gooseberries'. But he could not forbear to mention that the name 'currant' was already catching on—'bastard currants' was his term. At first purists, linguistic and horticultural, tried to discourage the usage—the sixteenth-century herbalist John Gerard disapproved of it, and John Parkinson wrote, in *A Garden of Flowers* (1629), 'Those berries . . . usually called red currans are not those currans . . . that are sold at the Grocers'—but by the late seventeenth century it had become firmly established.

'Dried-grape' currants were originally called *raysons of coraunce* in English. The term derives from Old French *raisins de Corinthe*, denoting grapes that had been imported from Corinth in Greece. They seem first to have been introduced into Britain in the early fourteenth century, and over the next three hundred years they became extraordinarily popular, not just in cakes and sweet dishes, but also accompanying meat and fish: C. Anne Wilson, in *Food and Drink in Britain* (1973), quotes the Venetian ambassador writing home in 1610, when there was a possibility of a significant reduction in Greek currant exports: 'Such a thing cannot take place without discontenting the entire population of England, which consumes a greater amount of this fruit than all the rest of the world; being accustomed to the luxury and loving it so dearly that individuals have been found who, from lack of money to purchase it on certain high days and holy days when it is customary fare, are said to have gone out and hanged themselves.'

curry Curry in its present-day manifestation—a meat or occasionally vegetable stew flavoured with commercial curry powder—is essentially a British dish. To be sure a basically similar dish is made in India, using a mixture of freshly ground spices, *garam masala* (literally 'hot spices') whose components vary from region to region, but it is not called *curry* (the word actually comes from Tamil *kari*, which means 'sauce'). It became popular in the eighteenth century with employees of the East India Company, who would vie with each other to see who could eat the fieriest one (still a test of machismo in some quarters). They brought the dish back to Britain with them, naming it after the sauce with which it was dressed, and by 1747 we find Hannah Glasse giving a recipe for making 'Currey the Indian way' in her *Art of Cookery* (it was a sort of chicken fricassee spiced with turmeric, ginger, and pepper 'beat very fine'). Eliza Acton writing in 1845 gave six different curry recipes (including curried macaroni), attesting to the enormous popularity curry achieved in Victorian Britain, but she was still insisting that for the best results the spices should be ground and mixed at home (she attributed the 'great superiority of the oriental curries over those generally prepared in England' to the lack of proper fresh spices). Less than twenty years later, however, the pragmatic Mrs Beeton made no bones about stating that commercially made curry powder, 'purchased at any respectable shop is, generally speaking, far superior [to home-made], and . . . very frequently more economical'. The first restaurant in Britain to offer such fare, the Hindoostanee Coffee House, opened in Marylebone, London in 1809. It was not a great success, but its twentieth- and twenty-first-century successors have established themselves firmly on the nation's high streets. In the Caribbean, meanwhile, and especially Jamaica, *curry goat*—that is, curried goat, or goat curry—is a celebratory dish.

Curry leaves (*kari patta*) are the bay-like leaves of a southwest Asian plant related to the lemon. They are used, preferably fresh, as a flavouring element in many Indian dishes, notably in the South.

In Australian English, to 'give someone curry' is to abuse or scold them.

cush-cush *See* YAM.

cushion A term dating back at least to the early eighteenth century for the fleshy part of a domestic animal's buttock. In modern culinary usage it is more often encountered in the phrase *cushion of veal*, denoting a topside cut of veal that has been rolled and tied into a neat parcel.

custard In medieval times a *custard* was an open tart rather like a modern quiche, with meat, fish, etc. covered in a rich egg mixture which solidified on cooking. *The Forme of Cury*, a fourteenth-century collection of recipes, gives this version containing meat: 'Take peiouns [pigeons], chykens, and smale briddes [birds]; smyte hem in gobettes, and sethe hem alle ifere [together] in god broth and in gres with veriows [verjuice].... Make a crust in a trap [dish], and pynche it, and cowche the flesh therinne; and cast therinne raisouns, coraunce, powdour douce [ground spices] and salt. Breke ayren [eggs] and wryng hem thurgh a cloth and swyng [mix] the sewe [pieces] of the stewe therwith, and helde [pour] it vppon the flessh. Couere it and bake it wel, and serue it forth.' At this time the form of the word varied between *custard* and *crustade*, which betrays its connection with pies; it derives from Anglo-Norman *crustade*, which in turn was based on Old French *crouste* 'crust'.

   The custard as pie survived at least until the end of the seventeenth century (the modern *custard pie*, incidentally, does not appear until the early nineteenth century, and its application to slapstick comedy is a twentieth-century development), but over the centuries the term came to be applied to the eggy component of the filling. This dish, a simple mixture of eggs, milk, and often sugar, baked, held the field until the middle of the nineteenth century, when a Birmingham chemist named Alfred Bird experimented with a custard based on cornflour rather than eggs, to which his wife was allergic. An astute businessman, he marketed the result, and in the ensuing century bright yellow custard made from custard powder colonized the tables of Britain, inevitably accompanying trifles, jellies, apple pies, and any other dish with which a less straightlaced nation might have partnered cream. The French call custard *crème anglaise,* literally 'English cream'.

   The *custard* of the children's taunt 'Cowardy, cowardy, custard,' incidentally, was originally *costard*, the name of a type of apple.

custard apple The yellowish-white-fleshed fruit of a small tropical tree of the genus *Annona*. It has a rough green skin, which ripens to a blackish-brown. It got its name in the seventeenth century, from the supposed resemblance of its sweet juicy pulp in colour and taste to custard (William Dampier gave an early account of it in his *New Voyage Round the World* (1699): 'Full of a white soft Pulp, sweet and very pleasant, and most resembling a Custard of any thing ... From whence properly it is called a Custard-Apple by our English'). To eat it one can simply cut it in half and spoon out the flesh.

   Alternative terms for it are *sweetsop*, *sugar apple*, and *bullock's heart*; in India it is called *sharifa*, and the French know it as *anone*.

   Custard apple has also been used as a name for the papaya.

custard cream A British type of sweet sandwich biscuit with a vanilla-flavoured cream filling. Its exterior is traditionally covered with a pattern of curlicues redolent of the Edwardian era when it probably originated (the name is first recorded in print in 1916).

cutlet Despite the fact that it is so close in meaning to *chop*, *cutlet* has no direct etymological connection with *cut*. It was borrowed into English in the eighteenth century from French *côtelette*, which was in origin a double diminutive of Old French *coste* 'rib'. It was at first sometimes spelled *costelette* or *costelet*, but it was not long before English *cut*-was drafted in. For the first two hundred years or so the term seems to have been reserved for cuts of meat, usually a small slice from the neck region, but then it began to branch out to a 'cross-sectional slice cut from a large fish', and even to cutlet-shaped concoctions made of non-meat ingredients—notably the vegetarians' notorious *nut cutlet*, first recorded in F. E. George's *Vegetarian Cookery* (1908).

cymling An alternative American term, first recorded in 1779, for a pattypan squash. It is probably an alteration of *simnel*. The *c* is pronounced /s/.

Cynar A bitter Italian aperitif, the chief ingredient of which is artichokes (globe). The Latin genus name of the artichoke is *Cynara*.

dacquoise A type of French gateau in which layers of meringue are sandwiched together with whipped cream or buttercream, often with the addition of fruit. It originated as a speciality of the town of Dax in southwestern France (French *dacquois* means 'of Dax').

daikon *See* RADISH.

daiquiri A cocktail made from rum, lime juice, and sugar which seems to have originated towards the end of the nineteenth century: the first known reference to it in print comes in Scott Fitzgerald's *This Side of Paradise* (1920). 'Legend tells us that American mining engineer Jennings Cox invented the Daiquiri for visitors in 1896, naming it in honor of the nearby village of Daiquiri in eastern Cuba', Sharon Tyler Herbst and Ron Herbst, *The Ultimate A-to-Z Bar Guide* (1998).

daisy An American mixed drink in which bourbon is diluted with fruit syrup (often grenadine) and soda water, and usually served on ice. It originated in the 1850s.

dal An alternative spelling of DHAL.

damper An unleavened loaf or cake of flour and water baked in wood ashes. The term is mainly characteristic of Australian and New Zealand English, and conjures up the world of nineteenth-century bushwackers: 'I particularly like the name given to one such dish: they called it "The Old Thing", and it consisted only of mutton and damper, a light, flat bread about two inches thick and eighteen inches wide, which if poorly cooked in the campfire was heavy enough to be known as "buggers on the coals"', Richie Benaud, *Over But Not Out* (2010). First recorded in 1825, it was inspired by the idea of something that 'dampens' or takes the edge off the appetite.

damson In medieval times damsons were *damascenes*, which reveals the origin of their name: plums of Damascus, in Syria. The term has been applied over the centuries to a variety of plums other than the small-fruited *Prunus institia*, and in fact a distinction between the *damson* and a subvariety called the *damascene* survived long enough to be the subject of a lawsuit in 1891, in which a Nottinghamshire greengrocer complained that he had ordered one and been supplied with the other. Damsons have always been recognized as rather tart and indigestible when eaten raw (C. Anne Wilson, in *Food and Drink in Britain* (1973), quotes a fifteenth-century schoolboy: 'I ate damsons yesterday, which made my stomach so raw that I could eat no manner of flesh'), and cookery books concentrate on methods of preserving them as jams and otherwise cooking them with

sugar (Dr Johnson, for example, in the *Rambler* (1750) wrote on 'The art of scalding damascenes without bursting them').

dan dan noodles Street food from the Szechwan province of west central China, consisting of noodles cooked in a spicy sauce that typically includes Szechwan pepper. *Dan dan* refers literally to the carrying-pole used by street vendors.

dandelion A common yellow-flowered plant of the daisy family that owes its name to its jagged leaves (it was acquired in the fourteenth century from French *dent-de-lion,* which itself was a translation of medieval Latin *dens leonis* 'lion's tooth'). For most of the twentieth century its most familiar culinary application in Britain was probably in *dandelion and burdock*, a non-alcoholic or mildly alcoholic drink made by boiling up dandelion flowers and burdock leaves; the epicentre of dandelion-and-burdock production is the north of England. During the Second World War its roots were sometimes used to make ersatz coffee (but its bitter leaves were eschewed. The French have no such qualms, however. They tame the bitterness by blanching the growing leaves, and eat them mainly raw, especially with bacon: *salade de pissenlit au lard* (the French name *pissenlit,* literally 'piss in bed', refers to the plant's diuretic properties; many English dialect names for it, such as *Jack-piss-the-bed, pissy beds, tiddle-beds,* and *wet-the-bed,* carry the same message). In the late twentieth century the leaves began to find their way on to British restaurant menus, but they have yet to make the breakthrough on to supermarket salad shelves. In North America they are known as *dandelion greens*.

Danish blue A blue-veined cheese made, unsurprisingly, in Denmark. It was invented in the early twentieth century as a cheaper alternative to Roquefort, and in the post-Second World War period was very successfully marketed in Britain. Lately, however, it has faced stronger competition from other continental blue cheeses. Its Danish name is *Danablu*.

Danish pastry The Danish pastry (or *Danish,* as it is often abbreviated in American English) is a comparatively recent introduction from continental patisserie; the first reference to it in English does not appear until 1934. And the connection of this rich confection of yeast dough with Denmark is fairly tenuous; it seems to have originated in Vienna, and the Austrians for some unexplained reason associated it with Scandinavia. The Danes, paradoxically, refer to it as *Wienerbrod*—'Viennese bread'.

dariole A small cup-shaped mould in which are made sweet or savoury puddings, cakes, jellies, cream desserts, etc. (which in their turn are called *darioles*). It takes its name from a small French puff-pastry bun of somewhat similar shape, so called because of its golden-brown exterior (Old Provençal *daurer* meant 'gild', the equivalent of French *dorer*—the name of the fish *John Dory* comes from the same source).

dark meat The meat from the legs of chickens and turkeys. The term seems to have been coined in the nineteenth century to save the sensibilities of those who would not sully their lips with the lascivious *leg* or, even worse, *thigh. See also* DRUMSTICK, JOINT, and *compare* WHITE MEAT.

darne A thick section cut from a substantial fish, such as salmon or tuna. The word is French (*darne de saumon* might be roughly translated as 'salmon steak'), but it comes originally from Breton *darn*, which means 'piece'.

dasheen Another name given, particularly in the Caribbean, to a cultivated variety of the taro, a tropical plant with very large starchy edible tubers. It is not recorded until as recently as 1899, and its origins are not altogether clear, but it has been speculated that it comes from French *de Chine* 'from China' (taro seems to have come to the West from China, although it probably originated in northern India). *See also* EDDOES.

dashi A stock which forms the basis of most Japanese soups. It is most commonly made from shavings of dried bonito fillet and a type of dried kelp (seaweed). Instant dashi granules, known as *dashi-no-moto*, are commercially available.

date The word *date* is Greek in origin: it comes ultimately from Greek *dáktulos*, which meant 'finger' or 'toe' as well as 'date'. It is usually assumed that the name comes from the resemblance of dates to fingers, and they have even been likened to the dusky toes of Arab boys, but the more prosaic truth is probably that the leaves of the date-palm look like fingers. A staple of the Middle East for perhaps as long as 50,000 years (the date-palm is said to have 360 different uses—not all of them culinary), the date was known of, and probably known, in Britain by the end of the thirteenth century.

  The now rather dated application of the word to a foolish person (as in 'soppy date') seems to have originated in the second decade of the twentieth century. Joseph Manchon records it in *Le slang: lexique de l'anglais familier et vulgaire* (1923): 'You date! *que tu es drôle!*'

daube A rich southern French dish of beef braised in red wine, and liberally seasoned with herbs. Its name is a specific application of a wider term, *en daube*, which denotes such a cooking method for meat. It was probably borrowed by French from a Spanish **doba*, never actually recorded but assumed to have been derived from the verb *dobar* 'to stew'. It found its way into English as long ago as the early eighteenth century: Hannah Glasse, for instance, gave a recipe in her *Art of Cookery* (1747) for 'Beef *à la Daub*. You may take a Buttock of Beef, lard it, fry it . . . put it into a Pot . . . stew it.'

Death by Chocolate A cover term for any of a range of very rich chocolate-based confections. Now a trademark in the UK and the US, it was invented in 1984 by Erik Russell while he was working for a London-based dessert manufacturer. Its implication is that the cake, dessert, etc. is so engorged with fat, cholesterol, and the like that its eater is in imminent danger of succumbing to a heart attack or stroke or, in the longer term, hardening of the arteries. It has been applied to a dessert featuring brownies, a chocolate mousse, and even an ice cream, but its iconic embodiment is a chocolate cake—either a layer cake or more especially a flourless cake made with eggs, butter, and sugar (for instance, chocolate nemesis).

demerara A designation originally given (in the mid-nineteenth century) to a type of partly refined, light brown sugar made in Demerara, a region of northeastern South America in what is now Guyana (it takes its name from the Demerara river). Modern demerara sugar is generally made by adding a little molasses colouring to refined white sugar. The name is also applied to a type of dark rum fermented from molasses, made in Guyana.

demi-glace A rich glossy brown sauce from which the liquid has been partially evaporated, typically flavoured with wine, and served with meat. The French term means literally 'half-glaze'. English adopted it early in the twentieth century, and has also deployed the Anglicized form *demi-glaze*.

Denver omelette An alternative term for WESTERN OMELETTE, namechecking the city in Colorado, in the US.

deoch an doris *Deoch an doris* (pronounced /doken'doris/) is a Scots and Irish term for a 'parting drink', and particularly a 'parting dram'. In Gaelic it means literally 'drink at the door'. It is traditionally taken standing up (if possible).

Desirée A variety of main-crop potato with a pink skin. It was originally developed in the Netherlands in the early 1960s.

devil's food cake A rich chocolate cake. The term, first recorded in 1905, suggests a deliberate contrasting of the dark 'wicked' chocolate cake with the lightness and pale 'innocence' of angel's food cake (*see* ANGEL CAKE). It is mainly used in American English.

devils on horseback Devils on horseback are an adaptation of angels on horseback, a hot savoury consisting of oysters wrapped in bacon and grilled. The diabolical version replaces the oysters with prunes or plums. The name first appears in the early twentieth century, and right from the beginning it seems often to have been used simply as a synonym for *angels on horseback*.

dhal Dhal, or *dal* as it is sometimes spelled, is the pealike seed of a tropical shrub that is widely eaten in Africa, India, and the Caribbean (where it is usually called the *pigeon pea*). Its Hindi name, *dāl*, derives ultimately from the Sanskrit verb *dal* 'to split', an allusion to the fact that the seeds are split and dried for keeping. English originally acquired the word in the late seventeenth century, in the form *doll*: 'At their coming up out of the Water they bestow the largess of Rice or Doll (an Indian Bean),' John Fryer, *New Account of East India* (1698).

In Indian cookery the term is applied more widely to a range of dried and split pulses (*moong dal*, for example, is dried and split mung beans), and also to dishes made with dhal, onions, and spices.

dhansak A speciality of Parsee cuisine, from western India. It is a casserole of various meats, vegetables, and lentils, served with rice. Its name comes from Gujarati *dhaan* 'rice' and *sak* 'vegetables'.

Diane The gastronomic invocation of Diana, the Roman goddess of hunting, began in nineteenth-century France, where dishes of venison and other game were served *à la Diane*—that is, with a rich and peppery cream and truffle sauce. It is not clear what connection if any this has with *steak Diane*, which burst on the scene in New York in the mid-1950s and remained a firm restaurant favourite for the next twenty years. It consists of thin slices of steak fried with seasonings, especially Worcester sauce, and, in the sort of restaurant that does that sort of thing, flambéed at table.

digestif A drink of neat spirits, usually brandy or a liqueur, taken after a meal in the perhaps optimistic expectation that it will aid digestion. The term is French, and English adopted it at the beginning of the twentieth century in the much broader sense 'any substance that promotes digestion': 'My husband thought a cigarette an excellent digestif,' *Daily Chronicle* (1908)—for which in fact the Anglicized form *digestive* already existed. The more specific 'postprandial drink' became established in the 1930s.

digestive biscuit The digestive biscuit, a slightly sweet biscuit made from wholemeal flour, seems first to have come on the scene in the 1870s, produced by the firm of Huntley and Palmers. Its name, no doubt intended to convey the idea of easy digestibility, evidently came to be regarded by the marketing men as too spartan-sounding to promote a biscuit that itself lacked excitement, and from the 1950s many manufacturers substituted *sweetmeal biscuit* or *wheatmeal biscuit* (obligatorily so in the US, where *digestive* is banned as misleading). Those terms have never really made the leap from the biscuit packet to the general language, though, and if anything ensured the continuing existence of the digestive biscuit, it was the post-Second World War practice of covering it with chocolate.

dill The quintessential northern European herb, its feathery green fronds dot the grey fishmarkets of Sweden, Finland, etc., bearing witness to its symbiosis with fish in Scandinavian cookery. Its name is appropriately Germanic, too; it comes from a hypothetical West Germanic word **diljo*, and is found throughout the Germanic languages (English, German, Swedish *dill*, Dutch *dille*, etc.). It found its way early to North America, and has established a particular niche there as the key ingredient in dill pickles: small cucumbers pickled in dill-flavoured vinegar, eaten with such New York specialities as pastrami on rye.

Dill is a versatile herb; most of its component parts can be put to culinary use. The wispy, threadlike, bluish-green leaves go well in soups, with potato salad, etc., as well as with fish (when the leaves alone are being referred to, the herb is often termed *dill weed*), while the seeds can be chewed on their own, as digestives (they were one of a range of 'meeting seeds', early American precursors to chewing gum—*see* CARAWAY).

dim sum A Cantonese speciality consisting of a miscellany of small snacks eaten for breakfast or lunch. They come most commonly in the form of filled dumplings, steamed or deep-fried, containing, for example, pork, prawn, crab, or shark's fin, but non-dumpling items also feature, such as chicken feet, meatballs, and small cubes of chopped pork spareribs, and also sweet dishes. The Cantonese term is *tim sam*, from *tim* 'dot' and *sam* 'heart'.

dip Dips became all the rage in the 1960s. Suddenly every hostess wanted to offer her guests a thick savoury sauce (a chickpea dip, perhaps, or a sour cream and chive dip, or, for the more adventurous, a garlic dip) to dunk pieces of raw vegetable (crudités) or other food into: 'Have a trolley of savouries and "dips" ready to wheel in', *Woman's Own* (1962). The term has not always had such (would-be) sophisticated connotations, though: in the nineteenth century it denoted a sauce for serving with a main course or especially a sweet sauce used for lubricating puddings, and in the early twentieth century it was applied to the fat and juices left in the pan after meat has been cooked, which can be soaked up and eaten with pieces of bread: 'Jam-butties one day and bread and dip the next', *Spectator* (1960). The current usage is probably a new coinage rather than a direct development of earlier ones, inspired by the cuisine of the eastern Mediterranean: 'The cooking of the eastern Mediterranean was once memorably summed up in a four-word dismissal: "Dips and burnt meat"', John Lanchester, *Guardian Weekly* (2011).

diplomat pudding A dessert of the Victorian era, identical in all its essentials to cabinet pudding. The political inspiration behind the names is presumably broadly the same too, although it is not clear what it was. The English *diplomat pudding* may well have originated as a rendering of French *diplomate*, which refers to a similar dessert.

dirty rice A Cajun dish from Louisiana, in the US, consisting of white rice cooked with minced or chopped meat (traditionally chicken livers and gizzards) that gives the rice a discoloured look: 'You'll love the huge pork chop, served up heartily with dirty rice and red-eye gravy', *Chile Pepper* (2004). The term is first recorded in 1949.

Discovery A variety of dessert apple with crisp flesh and bright red skin. It was created by crossing the Worcester Pearmain with another variety, perhaps Beauty of Bath.

dock pudding A dish traditionally made and eaten in northern England during Lent. It uses the leaves of the plant known there as 'dock', but this is not to be confused with the sort of dock whose leaves are used to soothe nettle stings. It is a completely unrelated plant, called in southern England (and hence in botany textbooks) 'bistort'. The leaves are cooked together with oatmeal, eggs, and other green leaves (typically nettle and dandelion), either by baking or by frying in bacon fat. 'Varieties of dock pudding have been eaten on a local basis in the north Pennines for centuries, but began to attract national attention in 1971, when the "World Championship Dock Pudding Contest" was inaugurated in the Calder Valley, around the villages of Hebden Bridge and Mytholmroyd', Richard Mabey, *Flora Britannica* (1996).

dodger Originally, from the early nineteenth century, a type of cake made from cornmeal that is baked hard or fried, eaten especially in the southern states of the US. It is generally termed more fully a *corn dodger*. At the end of the century the term was taken over by Australian English and subsequently found its way into British services' slang. It has been used mainly to denote 'bread', but also more specifically 'a sandwich' and more generally 'food': 'None of your sliced bread here, but proper hunks of dodger', John Hepworth and John Hindle, *Boozing out in Melbourne Pubs* (1980). It is not clear where the original usage came from, but there may be some connection with Northern English dialect *dodge* 'lump'. *See also* JAMMY DODGER.

Dolcelatte The proprietary name of a variety of smooth, creamy blue-veined Italian cheese, somewhat similar to Gorgonzola but milder. It means literally 'sweet milk'.

dolly mixture An assortment of small sweets in various colours, flavours, and shapes. The term, which is presumably an allusion to the sweets' size, seems to have originated in the 1920s or 1930s.

dolmades Dolmades are stuffed vine leaves (the singular is *dolma*). The dish is popular all over the eastern Mediterranean, and particularly in Greece and Turkey. It consists of grapevine leaves blanched and then wrapped around a filling (typically cooked rice and herbs, and often minced lamb as well), braised, and usually served cold as part of a mezze, or mixed hors d'oeuvres. The word *dolma* itself is of Turkish origin, and is a derivative of the verb *dolmak* 'to fill'; *dolmades* is the Greek plural form.

donburi A Japanese rice-bowl dish consisting of some sort of fish, meat, or vegetable cooked and served on top of rice (for instance, salmon teriyaki donburi). The term in Japanese means literally 'bowl'.

döner kebab A Turkish speciality consisting of slices of marinated lamb or mutton which are packed in a cylindrical mass on a vertical spit and then grilled as they revolve. Slices are cut from the surface as it reaches the required degree of 'doneness', and are typically eaten with pitta bread or rice. Its Westernized fast-food format, consisting of a sort of pitta-bread sandwich filled with slices of kebab, some lettuce or other salad, and a spicy sauce, was invented by Turkish immigrants in Germany around 1970, who found that their German hosts did not much like the plain unvarnished meat. It spread to many other parts of Europe, and the döner kebab house has become a familiar part of the British inner-city scene. The term means literally 'turning roast meat', incidentally (*döner* derives from the verb *dönmek* 'to turn, rotate'); and the Turkish letter ö is pronounced similarly to German ö (the closest English sound is *er*). The Arabic word for the dish is *shawarma*.

doorstep A humorous colloquialism, first recorded in 1885, for a thick slice of bread, or a sandwich made from such slices: 'Won't you slice me a doorstep please?', *Listener* (1969).

Dorito A US brand of tortilla chip first produced in 1964. Its name in Spanish means literally 'little golden one'.

dosa A thickish pancake made in southern India from rice flour. It is a versatile component of southern Indian cuisine, appearing at breakfast, as a between-meals snack, and at main meals. The word comes from Tamil *tōcai*. Its English plural is *dosas* or *dosai*.

Double Gloucester An English cows'-milk hard cheese with a strong but mellow flavour. It was originally made from milk of the Gloucester breed of cattle. Its most distinctive feature is its orangey colour. This is produced artificially, originally by the addition of carrot juice or saffron, but now with annatto. At first only the cheese destined for the markets of London and other centres was coloured (city innocents associated high colour with high flavour), while the product for local consumption was left in its natural yellow state. But now the dyeing is virtually universal.

The 'double' in the name refers to the fact that full-cream milk from two milkings is used in making the cheese (the term *Double Gloucester* is first recorded as long ago as 1772). There is also a *Single Gloucester*, which in 1997 was accorded the European Union's Protected Designation of Origin (PDO) status. This is also made from the milk of two milkings, but one of them is skimmed. It is not dyed.

dough *Dough*—which denotes an uncooked mixture of flour and liquid—is one of those words that take one back to the very roots of our language, several millennia BC. Its Indo-European antecedent has been reconstructed as **dhoigh-*, **dheigh-*, **dhigh-*, which meant something like 'smear' or 'knead', and was also used for 'clay'. By various circuitous linguistic routes, this Indo-European form has given rise to such apparently unlikely English words as *figure, fiction*, and the final syllables of *paradise* and *lady* (-*dy* comes from a word that meant 'knead', and so the whole compound was literally 'loafkneader').

The use of *dough* as a colloquial synonym of *money* (perhaps actuated by the perception of it as a basic necessity, as later with *bread*) is first recorded in the mid-nineteenth century, in the US, and it does not seem to have crossed the Atlantic until the First World War, with the *doughboys* (American soldiers: the word originally meant 'small dumpling', and it has been conjectured that it was applied to the large globular brass buttons on infantrymen's uniforms, and hence to the soldiers themselves).

Spelled according to its former northern pronunciation, *dough* also gives us *duff* (*see* PLUM DUFF).

doughnut Doughnuts first surface in the US around the beginning of the nineteenth century, when they were also called *oly-cooks* (the word comes from Dutch *oliekoek* 'oilcake', and gives a clue to the Dutch origins of the doughnut). In those days they were still simply small dumplings. The development of the ring-shaped doughnut seems not to have come about until much later in the century, and the two shapes continue to form a culinary divide between Britain and the US. Britons on the whole continue to favour the sugar-encrusted bun with more or less jam inside, depending on the generosity of the maker, while Americans tend to prefer their doughnuts, or *donuts*, toroidal (although cream- or jam-filled doughnuts are also common in the US). The extent to which the latter are now generally considered to be prototypical doughnuts in World English can be gauged from the variety of ring-shaped objects to which the word *doughnut* has been metaphorically applied, including the toroidal vacuum chamber of a particle accelerator. *Doughnutting*, the clustering of members round a speaker in a parliamentary debate, especially in order to give the impression to television viewers that the speaker is well supported or to conceal low attendance, is thought to have originated in Canada. The term enjoyed a brief vogue in Britain after the televising of proceedings in the House of Commons began in 1989.

The word is presumably an allusion to the small, rounded shape of the original doughnuts; the element *-nut* is used similarly in *gingernut* and its now obsolete synonym *spicenut*.

In Britain, the doughnut seems in the nineteenth century to have been a particular speciality of the Isle of Wight, candied peel sometimes taking the place of jam in local recipes. And in Hertfordshire, according to William C. Hazlitt in 1870, children used to call Shrove Tuesday *Doughnut day* rather than *Pancake day*, because doughnuts were specially made on that day.

dragée A term applied in modern usage to various types of sweet, particularly sugar-coated almonds or other nuts or fruits, tiny hard round balls of sugar (often silvered) used as cake decorations, and chocolate drops. The word appears to come ultimately from Greek *tragemata* 'sweets', plural of *tragema*, which was derived from the verb *trōgein* 'to gnaw'. These Greek sweets consisted typically of aromatic seeds, such as aniseed or fennel, coated in honey, and this was the association the word *tragemata* carried with it into Latin, and thence into Old French as *dragie*. This was borrowed into English in the fourteenth century as *dredge*, by which time sugar had replaced honey as the outer coating. *Comfit* soon replaced *dredge* as the English term for such sweets, but in the nineteenth century English reborrowed the French word, which by then had become *dragée*.

dragon fruit The fruit of a Central and South American cactus of the genus *Hylocereus*, which has a scarlet exterior and edible white flesh dotted with tiny black seeds. Sweet but fairly bland, this is considerably less exciting than the fruit's appearance. Bract-like appendages suggesting green flames issuing from the mouth of a red dragon have earned it names meaning 'dragon fruit', or variations on it, in various East and Southeast Asian countries where it is now widely cultivated (for instance, Malay *buah naga* and Laotian *mark mang gohn*), and when it began to appear on British supermarket shelves towards the end of the twentieth century, marketers seized on *dragon fruit* as more attention-grabbing than its original name in the now extinct Taino language of the Caribbean, *pitahaya*, which first came into English (via Spanish) in the early eighteenth century.

Drambuie The proprietary name of a golden-coloured Scottish liqueur made from whisky and an unspecified range of herbs. It traces its history back to 1745, when Bonnie Prince Charlie supposedly presented the recipe for it to a Mackinnon of Skye as a reward for services rendered, but it was not marketed on a commercial scale until the 1890s. The name comes from Gaelic *dram buidheach* 'satisfying drink'.

dripping The rendered-down fat which falls in drops from roasting meat, and particularly beef, has long been regarded both as useful in the kitchen, for basting and frying—Mrs Beeton gives two ways of clarifying it for this purpose—and as a cheap but deliciously savoury alternative to butter for spreading on bread. By the end of the twentieth century, however, the ratio of expense had reversed itself, and this, together with the steady trend towards leaner meat, has seen almost the demise of dripping. The first known mention of it comes in an Act of Parliament in Edward IV's reign, where it figures in a list of utensils: 'hammers, pinsons [pincers], firetongs, drippingpans' (1463). The usual American English version of the word is *drippings*.

drop scone A small thick pancake of Scottish origin, made by dropping spoonfuls of batter on to a griddle or other heated surface. The term is first recorded in 1899. An alternative name for the same thing is *girdle cake*.

drumstick The first known reference to poultry thighs as 'drumsticks' comes in the *Mayor of Garret* (1764), a play by the now almost forgotten dramatist Samuel Foote (1720–77), known to his contemporaries as 'the English Aristophanes': 'She always helps me herself to the tough drumsticks of turkeys.' They get their name, of course, from their shape, bulbous at one end, with the bone protruding sticklike at the other. *See also* JOINT.

A culinary *drumstick* rather less familiar to Westerners is the seedpod of the Indian tree *Moringa oleifera*. Its name was given to it by the British in India, on account of its long thin shape (unlike the chicken leg, it has no bulbous extremity). The tree's familiar English name, *horseradish tree*, gives a strong hint as to the pod's flavour.

drunken chicken A speciality of Shanghai cuisine: pieces of chicken cooked in Shaoxing wine (a type of rice wine made in the Shaoxing region of eastern China), allowed to cool, and eaten cold. Its Chinese name is *zui ji*, which translates more accurately as '(rice) wine chicken', but the catchier *drunken chicken* is now firmly established in English. In American English, the term is also used as an alternative name for beer-can chicken.

Dublin Bay prawn A name widely used in English for a large long-clawed variety of prawn (known in French as *langoustine*) until it was ousted by *scampi* in the 1960s. It refers back to a time when the crustaceans were little-considered leavings in the nets of Irish fishing fleets, sold off cheaply in the markets of Dublin. It is not recorded in English before 1949, although an earlier *Dublin prawn* dates from 1911. An alternative name is *Norway lobster*, and Americans call it *saltwater crayfish*.

Dublin lawyer A luxurious Irish dish in which lobster is cooked in a heady mixture of cream and Irish whiskey. The origins of the name are unknown, but a waggish (but surely libellous) explanation has it that the lawyers of Dublin are rich (lobster), fat (cream), and drunk (whiskey). Flora Annie Steel and Grace Gardiner gave directions for a slightly more restrained version of the dish for sahibs and memsahibs in *The Complete Indian Housekeeper and Cook* (1888): 'One tin of lobster, two units of butter, five of sherry, red pepper, and salt to taste, with a squeeze of lemon. Heat all together in a silver dish over a spirit lamp. Excellent for breakfast'.

Dubonnet A sweet red-wine-based French apéritif, which contains a small amount of quinine. It was a favourite tipple (with a dash of gin) of Her late Majesty Queen Elizabeth the Queen Mother, and her elder daughter is said to be quite partial to it too. It was the result of a competition held by the French government in the mid-1840s to produce a drink that would entice French Foreign Legionaries in North Africa to take quinine, to counteract the threat of malaria. The competition was won by Joseph Dubonnet.

duchesse potatoes Duchesse (or occasionally *duchess*) potatoes are mashed potatoes formed into croquettes or small cakes, or piped into fancy shapes, and then baked or fried so as to acquire a crisp surface. The term (a partial translation of French *pommes duchesse*) was not used to any extent in English until after the First World War.

dukkah Dukkah, or *duqqa*, is an Egyptian spice mix consisting of cumin and coriander seeds crushed together with sesame seeds, salt, and pepper, and sometimes chopped hazelnuts. It is either sprinkled on meat or vegetables, or eaten with bread dipped in olive oil, as an appetizer or snack. The word is a derivative of an Arabic verb meaning 'to pound'.

dulce de leche A thick, sweet, light-brown sauce or spread made from caramelized milk. It originated in Argentina, and its American Spanish name (first recorded in 1884) means literally 'sweet of milk'. It is now popular throughout Latin America (in Brazil it is called in Portuguese *doce de leite*). The earliest record of the term in English is from 1923, but dulce de leche had to wait until the twenty-first century to become a fashion item among

Anglophone foodies: 'Ubiquitous Menu Items of 2002: aïoli, artisanal chèvre, champagne cocktails, dulce de leche, fava beans', *enRoute* (2002).

dulse *See* LAVER.

dumpling In the days when people regularly baked their bread at home, dumplings came naturally; a little of the yeast dough was kept back, rolled into balls, and slipped into boiling water to cook. Nowadays, though, they have a leaden reputation. The derivation of the word is obscure: dumplings are particularly associated with Norfolk, so it may come from some now-lost East Anglian dialect term, or it may be associated with *dumpy* 'short and fat' and its obsolete synonym *dump* (but as far as we can tell from written evidence these are both eighteenth-century in origin, whereas *dumpling* goes back to the sixteenth century). Another possible connection that has been canvassed is with *lump*.

Dumplings as a sweet dish containing fruit, usually apple, have a history almost as long as their savoury counterparts. They too are now taboo in a weight-watching age, but they once enjoyed considerable popularity; Samuel Coleridge even went so far as to say, according to Charles Lamb, that 'a man cannot have a pure mind who refuses apple-dumplings'.

Dundee cake A rich fruit cake decorated on top with almonds. Despite its traditional-sounding name, it does not seem to be of any great antiquity: the first printed recipe for it appears in 1892, in T. F. Garrett's *Encyclopedia of Practical Cookery*. It is said to have originally been made as a way of keeping the Keiller's factory in the Scottish city of Dundee on the Firth of Tay, in work at times of the year when it was not producing marmalade.

Dundee marmalade A type of rich dark marmalade originally made in the Scottish city of Dundee on the Firth of Tay. As early as 1856 Charles Dickens, in *Household Words*, was writing of it as the acme of marmalades: 'anchovy paste, Dundee Marmalade, and the whole stock of luxurious helps to appetite'. The term was registered as a trademark by James Keiller and Son in 1880.

Dunlop A Scottish hard cheese made from cows' milk, not dissimilar to Cheddar. It originated in the Ayrshire village of Dunlop in the late seventeenth century, and the circumstances of its birth are quite well documented: a certain Margaret Gilmour settled in the village in 1688, having apparently learned the techniques of whole-milk cheesemaking in Ireland, and the products of her creamery went down well with Scots used hitherto only to skimmed-milk cheeses.

durian In an age when exotic fruits from around the world have become clichés on Western supermarket shelves, one fruit retains its aura of mystery and unattainability: the durian. And the reason is simple—its appalling smell. The taste of its flesh sends its eaters into ecstasies (and it has the reputation of being an aphrodisiac), but its aroma is so terrible as to daunt even the most adventurous marketing man, and local airlines where it grows, in Southeast Asia, ban passengers from taking it on board, so there is little chance of stray examples reaching the outside world. In Anthony Burgess's *Malayan Trilogy* it is described as being 'like eating sweet, pink raspberry blancmange in the lavatory'. Its shape is oval, and it has a hard spiny rind (hence its name, a derivative of Malay *duri* 'thorn').

duxelles A mixture of finely chopped, lightly sautéed mushrooms and shallots, used, for example, as a stuffing or in sauces. It was probably named after the Marquis d'Uxelles, whose chef, La Varenne (1618–78) is said to have created the recipe.

Earl Grey tea A blended tea based, at least originally, on China tea with the addition of bergamot oil (nowadays much Earl Grey contains other teas, and substitutes for bergamot oil). The story goes that the recipe for it was given to the second Earl Grey in the 1830s by a grateful Chinese mandarin whose life had been saved by a British diplomat. The blend was soon taken up commercially, and has since become the epitome, especially among Americans, of the genteel end of the British tea spectrum. It was said in the 1980s that the advance of middle-class British farmhouse- and cottage-buyers in Tuscany could be accurately gauged by the increasing availability of Earl Grey in the local shops.

Easter eggs The custom of giving eggs as Easter presents is a widespread and longstanding one (the underlying symbolism of rebirth and renewal is fairly clear). All over Europe since at least the fifteenth century, the shells of hard-boiled hens' eggs have been dyed or painted or otherwise decorated, and presented to mark the most solemn of all Christian festivals. It is associated particularly with the Slavic countries, including Russia, where in the late nineteenth and early twentieth centuries, Carl Fabergé produced intricately bejewelled and enamelled metal Easter eggs for the imperial family, but there is also a long tradition in Britain. The chocolate versions with which we are familiar today first came on the scene in France and Germany in the early nineteenth century. The term *Easter egg* is not recorded before 1804, but probably for some centuries before that *pace egg* had been in use (*pace* being an alteration of *pasch* 'Easter', from Old French *pasche,* which was a descendant ultimately of Hebrew *pesakh* 'passover').

eau de vie *Eau de vie*, in French literally 'water of life', is a generic term for alcoholic spirits distilled from the fermented juice of fruits. Broadly speaking, it is a synonym for *brandy*, although in present-day English it tends to be used not so much for grape brandy (cognac, armagnac, etc.) as for brandy made, particularly in Alsace, from other fruits, such as cherries, raspberries, etc. (what the French usually term *alcools blancs*). The term, which has been used in English since the eighteenth century ('We were treated at breakfast with chocolate and *l'eau de vie* by our paramours,' Tobias Smollett, *Roderick Random* (1748)), goes back to Latin *aqua vitae*, inspirer of Swedish and Danish *akvavit* and equivalent to English *whisky*, a descendant of Gaelic *uisge beatha* 'water of life'.

Eccles cake A small round cake made of buttery flaky pastry with a sugary filling of currants and sometimes candied peel. It takes its name from Eccles, a town in Greater Manchester (a notable cake-baking area), and was reputedly invented by the cookery writer Elizabeth Raffald (1733–81), who spent most of her working life in Manchester. The earliest known reference to the cake by name dates from the early nineteenth century, when two Eccles bakers, James Birch and his one-time apprentice William Bradburn, disputed the role of its creator.

éclair The primary meaning of *éclair* in French is 'lightning', and one (not very convincing) explanation advanced for its application to these cream-filled choux-pastry temptations is that it was suggested by the light gleaming from their coating of fondant icing. The word did not put in an appearance in English until the middle of the nineteenth century. The *éclair* is the subject of one of the few extant lexicographic jokes: in the *Chambers Dictionary* (1998), it is defined as 'a cake, long in shape but short in duration'.

Edam Instantly recognizable from the coating of scarlet wax on exported examples, Edam is a mild, pale yellow cows'-milk cheese produced in cannonball shapes. It originated over six centuries ago in the Dutch town of Edam on the banks of the Ijsselmeer, to the northeast of Amsterdam.

edamame Fresh green soya beans in their pod, which in Japanese cuisine are boiled or steamed, seasoned with salt, and served as a snack or appetizer (the finished dish is also called *edamame*). The Japanese term means literally 'twig bean', reflecting how the young pods are harvested with their attachment to the plant intact. It is first recorded in English in 1951.

eddoes Eddoes are the starchy edible tubers of a tropical plant, the taro (in practice the term seems to be applied to the smaller, potato-sized tubers; very large ones, which have to be sliced up for cooking, are simply called *taro*, or alternatively *dasheen*). They resemble a hairy cross between potatoes and dahlia tubers. The name, which seems to come from a West African language, first crops up as long ago as 1685 (predating the more general *taro*). This was in *The English Empire in America* by Richard Burton, who describes eddoes and potatoes as 'a substantial and wholesome nourishing root'. In *The Natural History of Barbadoes* (1750) Griffith Hughes notes that 'the different species of eddoes are distinguished into the blue eddoes, the scratching eddoes, and the roasting eddoes'.

Edinburgh rock Scottish confectionery in the form of small sticks of boiled sugar that has been processed and pulled so as to produce a lot of very small crystals, giving the rock a characteristic friable texture (unlike the more solid conventional seaside rock). It is made in pastel shades (white, pink, yellow, beige) that correspond to particular flavours. It was introduced in the early nineteenth century by the Edinburgh confectioner Alexander Ferguson.

egg The egg, nature's own pre-packed food, centrepiece of more simple suppers than anyone has had hot dinners, essential ingredient of countless sauces, cakes, puddings, etc., symbol of wholesomeness (until the great salmonella-in-eggs scandal of the late 1980s), traces its name back to a prehistoric Indo-European source related to words for 'bird' (such as Latin *avis*). The Old English term was *ǣg*, which survived in Middle English as *ey* (plural *eyren*). But in the fourteenth century the related *egg* was borrowed from Old Norse. For a time the two forms competed with each other (William Caxton, in the prologue to his *Book of Eneydos* (1490), asked 'What should a man in these days now write, eggs or eyren, certainly it is hard to please every man'), and the Norse form did not finally emerge as the winner until the late sixteenth century. Human beings have no doubt been consuming wild birds' eggs since prehistoric times, but it was the domestication of the Indian jungle fowl and its gradual spread westward that brought the egg as we now know it, a standard dietary item, to Europe. The Romans brought it to Britain. Since then, of course, a variety of different birds' eggs have continued to be eaten at different seasons and places—ducks, geese, plovers, and gulls have all been popular sources, and quails' eggs enjoyed a vogue at the end of the twentieth century—but the chicken, now a scarcely animated egg-producing machine, leaves all competitors out of sight. The institution of an egg for breakfast is largely a Victorian idea.

egg bread *See* SPOON BREAD.

egg cream An American soft drink consisting of milk and soda water, flavoured with syrup, especially chocolate syrup. It has been a favourite at New York soda fountains since it first appeared in the early 1950s. It does not contain any egg: the name comes from the froth produced by the soda water, somewhat similar to beaten egg whites.

egg foo yong *See* FOO YONG.

eggplant Used in present-day English chiefly by American speakers as a synonym for the aubergine, *eggplant* was originally applied specifically to the white-skinned, egg-shaped variety of the vegetable. This was in the mid-eighteenth century (available evidence suggests that the term predates *aubergine* by about 30 years). By the middle of the nineteenth century *eggplant* had come to be used for the purple-skinned aubergine, and subsequently over the past hundred years, the split between American and British usage has developed.

egg roll The usual American term for a SPRING ROLL. It is first recorded in 1938.

eggs Benedict An American dish consisting of poached eggs and grilled ham placed on the split and toasted halves of the sort of buns known in the US as 'English muffins', and then covered with hollandaise sauce. More than one account of its origin exists. Perhaps the most widely believed is that a certain Lemuel Benedict ordered it at the Waldorf–Astoria Hotel, New York City, as a hangover cure. Alternatively, 'it originated at Manhattan's famous Delmonico's Restaurant when regular patrons, Mr and Mrs LeGrand Benedict, complained that there was nothing new on the lunch menu. Delmonico's maitre d' and Mrs. Benedict began discussing possibilities and eggs Benedict was the result', Sharon Tyler Herbst, *Food Lover's Companion* (2001). The term is first recorded in 1898.

eggy bread A homely British alternative term for FRENCH TOAST: 'Start the day on a "full Welsh" breakfast: eggy bread with crispy bacon and maple syrup', *Good Food Guide* (2008). It is first recorded in the early 1960s.

Egremont russet A variety of tawny-skinned russet apple, the most commonly encountered in Britain. It was raised by (or under the auspices of) the Earl of Egremont at Petworth in Sussex, and introduced in 1872.

einkorn An ancient variety of wheat that has small bearded ears and spikelets that each contain one slender grain. It was used as animal fodder in prehistoric times, but is now little grown. English acquired its name in the early twentieth century from German, where it means literally 'one seed'. *See also* EMMER, KHORASAN, SPELT.

eiswein It seems scarcely plausible that anyone should wish to make wine from frozen grapes, but that is essentially what eiswein is. In the Rhine and Mosel valleys, certain selected grapes are left on the vines until the depths of winter, and gathered in the early morning when they—and the picker's fingers—are congealed with cold. The theory is that when the water content is frozen, only the concentrated essences of the grape are released when it is pressed, and in practice it does produce a deliciously sweet white wine. The craze for making it began in the mid 1960s, when it was dismissed in many quarters as a gimmick, but now German law requires that it should be made from grapes of at least beerenauslese quality.

elder¹ A small tree or shrub of the honeysuckle family that bears flat clusters of small white flowers (*elderflowers*), used to make wines, cordials, tisanes, and other drinks, and also fritters, followed by bluish-black or red berries (*elderberries*), used for making wines and jellies. The name is a descendant of Old English *ellærn*.

elder² The udder of the cow, which in less squeamish times and places has been used and perhaps even relished as food. In Britain its consumption seems to cling on only in the tripe-producing centres of West Yorkshire and eastern Lancashire. The word itself, which is first recorded in the late seventeenth century, may be directly descended from a prehistoric Germanic noun derived from the verb **alan* 'to nourish', or it may be a borrowing from Dutch (Middle Dutch had the noun *elder* with the same meaning).

émincé An émincé is a French way of dealing with left-over cooked meat. The meat is sliced thinly (*émincer* is French for 'to mince'), covered with a sauce, and heated through. As Escoffier noted in his *Guide to Modern Cookery* (1907), 'an unalterable principle governs the preparation of émincés and hashes, which is that the meats constituting these dishes should never boil if it be desired that they be not too hard'.

Emmental The Emmental (or *Emmenthal*) is a valley (German *t(h)al* 'valley') in Switzerland near Berne. It has given its name to a firm cows'-milk cheese with large round holes in it which was first made there, but whose production has since spread far and wide in Europe (more is made in France than in any other country).

emmer An ancient variety of wheat that has small bearded ears and spikelets that each contain two grains. It is now grown mainly for animal fodder and breakfast cereals. English acquired its name in the early twentieth century from German, where it is a descendant of Old High German *amer* 'spelt'. *See also* EINKORN, KHORASAN, SPELT.

empanada In the Spanish and Portuguese culinary traditions, a type of turnover or pasty. It usually has a savoury filling of meat and vegetables, but it also comes in sweet versions, with a fruit filling. It has its roots in Spain, Galicia, and Portugal, but it went with their colonists around the world, to Latin America and the East Indies (the usually chilli-hot Mexican version is said to have been introduced by Cornish miners working there, but it is likely to have been there well before they arrived). The word *empanada* comes from the feminine past participle of the Spanish verb *empanar* 'to roll in pastry', which was based on *pan* 'bread'. It is first recorded in English in the early 1920s.

enchilada A Mexican dish made from a tortilla that is fried in oil and then rolled round a filling (meat, cheese, vegetables, or any combination thereof). It is served with a chilli sauce, which gives it its name: *enchilada* is the feminine form of Mexican Spanish *enchilado* 'seasoned with chilli'.

The colloquial phrase *the whole enchilada* means 'the whole lot, everything': 'It began with the Mexican furore and, if that wasn't the whole enchilada, things reached their personal low point in October when he [Jeremy Clarkson] lifted an injunction on his first wife', *Observer* (2011). It originated in America in the 1960s. Of similar provenance but slightly later vintage (early 1970s) is *big enchilada*, meaning 'the most important or powerful person or thing'.

endive Few culinary terms cause such confusion as *endive* and *chicory*. The basic problem is that what the British call *endive* the Americans call *chicory*, and what the British call *chicory* the Americans call *endive* (the French side with the Americans: British *endive* translates as French *chicorée*).

In Britain, then, the endive is a lettuce-like salad plant of the daisy family whose leaves have a distinctive bitter taste. There are a number of different varieties under cultivation. The commonest is the curly endive, a shock of spidery leaves that are yellowish-white at the heart and deepen to green towards the edges; its usual French name, *frisée*, is becoming established in English. Then there is the escarole, or batavia, which has more conventional lettuce-style leaves. And in France the pointedly bitter leaves of the wild endive are widely eaten.

American speakers reserve the word *endive* for the blanched shoots of *Cichorium intybus* (a plant of the same genus as endive), for which the British term is *chicory*.

The actual word *endive* comes via Old French from medieval Latin *endiva*. This was a variant of classical Latin *intibus* or *intibum* 'chicory', which in turn was borrowed from Greek *entúbioi*, a word possibly derived ultimately from Egyptian *tybi* 'January', in allusion to the time of year when the plant is in season. It was introduced into English in the fifteenth century, and at first referred only to the chicory (*Cichorium intybus*); but in the sixteenth century the endive (*C. endivia*) arrived in Europe from Asia, and the terminological anarchy began.

entrecôte As its name implies, an entrecôte is a beefsteak taken from the long strip of tender muscle underlying the ribs (the word means literally 'between the ribs' in French), usually from the sirloin area. The novelist Thackeray, a noted gourmet, was perhaps responsible for introducing the term into English: 'Whenever you go to Paris, call at once for the *entrecôte*; the fillet in comparison is a poor *fade* lady's meat'. In America it is known as a *rib steak*.

Époisses A soft cows'-milk cheese made in Burgundy. It has a slightly orangey crust, which is washed in the local white wine or marc. It gives off a pungent aroma, and it is banned on pubic transport in France. It takes its name from a village near the Côte d'Or, to the west of Dijon.

eryngo Eryngo, or *eringo*, is the root of the sea holly, which in former times was candied, or pickled, and used as a sweetmeat or in recipes. Dorothy Hartley in *Food in England* (1954) reports old recipes for 'eryngo conserve', 'eryngo jelly', and 'eryngo toffee'. It also had a reputation as an aphrodisiac: Falstaff in his ill-starred amorous quest in Windsor Park called on the sky to 'hail kissing-comfits and snow eringoes', *Merry Wives of Windsor* (1598). The word is probably an alteration of Italian and Spanish *eringio,* from Latin *eryngion* 'sea holly' (which is also the source of the plant's modern Latin genus name, *Eryngium*).

escabeche A dish of Spanish origin consisting typically of fish that has been fried and then soaked in a marinade of seasoned vinegar (another main ingredient can replace the fish). It is usually served cold. The Spanish word came from Arabic *sikbāj,* which in turn came from a Persian compound formed from *sik* 'vinegar' and *bā* 'broth'. It is first recorded in English in 1699. The dish is popular in the Caribbean, especially Jamaica, where it goes under the name *escovitch* (from the earlier Spanish form of the word, *escaveche*). In former times the eroded form *caveach* was current in the West Indies, and in the eighteenth century it was taken up in English as a verb, denoting this sort of marination: Elizabeth Raffald in *The Experienced English Housekeeper* (1778) told her readers how 'to caveach Soles'. In a further twist, in England the noun came to be applied to the vinegary marinade itself: the poet Thomas Gray (1716–71), for example, in a marginal jotting in his copy of William Verrall's

Complete System of Cookery (1759), gives a recipe for 'caviche', which is a spiced vinegar 'to be used, as Catchup, in small quantities as a sauce for cold meats'. *See also* CEVICHE.

escalope A thin boneless slice of white meat, typically cooked by frying. The term is most usually applied to veal, but it can also be used for turkey, and even salmon. It was acquired in the early nineteenth century from French *escalope* (also the source of English *scallop*), which may have originated as a blend of *écale* 'shell' and *envelope* 'envelope'.

escarole A variety of endive, a lettuce-like salad vegetable. Its bitter-tasting leaves are curly (though not as curly as those of its close relative, the curly endive or *frisée*) and crisp. Its alternative name is *batavia*.

Etymologically, the word means 'something edible'. It comes from late Latin *escariola*, which is derived ultimately from the Latin verb *edere* 'to eat'. English originally acquired it in the fourteenth century in the Italian form *scariola*; *escarole* is a later borrowing via French.

espresso In Italian, *caffè espresso* is coffee that has been literally 'pressed out' or 'expressed'—that is, made by forcing steam at high pressure through finely ground beans. In Italy it is served without milk or cream, and so in English the term *espresso* has become synonymous with 'black coffee' (as opposed to *cappuccino*, which contains milk). Its proliferation dates from the coffee-bar culture of the second half of the 1950s, although it is first recorded in English in 1945.

espuma The Spanish word for 'foam'. Its use in English in the culinary sense (*see* FOAM) reflects the fact that it was the Catalan chef Ferran Adrià of the famed El Bulli restaurant, who launched the concept at the end of the twentieth century.

Est! Est!! Est!!! An Italian white wine from the southern part of Latium which is more distinguished for the curiosity of its name than for any inherent quality. The story goes that when a certain Bishop Fugger was on his way to Rome, he sent a servant on ahead of him to check on the wine served at hostelries en route. If the wine was good, he was to write *Est!* 'It is' on the door; if it was not up to scratch, *Non est!* 'It is not'. Apparently when he got to the town of Montefiascone, he found the wine so marvellous that he wrote *Est!* on the inn door in triplicate. It fails to make such an impression these days. A red wine is made under the same name, but it is seldom seen outside its locality.

Eton mess A dessert consisting of whipped cream, pieces of meringue, and fruit, typically strawberries, mixed together in a freeform style, that is traditionally served at the annual Eton College versus Winchester College cricket match. It dates back at least to the late nineteenth century (the name is first recorded in 1893, when 'Eton mess aux fraises' was served at a Marlborough House garden party to mark the marriage of the future George V to Princess May of Teck), but it largely kept itself to itself in the twentieth century. It was not until the early twenty-first century that it began to be more widely known and appear on restaurant menus, propelled at least partly no doubt by a certain snob appeal of the name. The original version of the pudding seems to have consisted only of strawberries (or bananas) and cream (or ice cream): 'Retainers at the Carlton Club remind Conservative peers and MPs that "Eton mess" is available. It turns out to be orthodox strawberries and cream', *Times* (1965). The meringue is a comparatively recent addition. It is not clear whether the *mess* of the name means 'something in a disordered state', which would not be inappropriate, or whether it harks back to the earlier sense, 'a prepared dish'. The fact that in Eton jargon 'messing together' denotes commensality (For Collegers [at Eton], their year of election was the key unit, as each year messed together (had tea in each other's rooms)', D. R. Thorpe, *Supermac* (2010)), tends to support the latter explanation.

evaporated milk Processed milk that has had some of its liquid content removed by evaporation. It differs from condensed milk in being unsweetened. The term is first recorded in 1870.

Eve's pudding An English sweet baked pudding, consisting typically of a layer of stewed apple topped with a sponge cake mixture. It appears to be a lineal descendant of an earlier boiled suet pudding with a filling of apple, which was called *Duke of Cumberland's pudding*. The name of the rather more genteel modern version, which also appears as *Mother Eve's pudding*, was no doubt inspired by Eve's involvement with a fruit, retrospectively identified as an apple, in the Garden of Eden.

Explorateur A soft creamy cows'-milk cheese made in the Île de France, the region surrounding Paris. It was invented in the 1960s to honour the explorer Bertrand Flornoy, who was mayor of the town of Coulommiers.

faggot Faggots are a traditional British product of the pig. The animal's liver, lights, heart, and spleen are minced up, mixed with belly of pork, onion, and usually breadcrumbs, moulded into billiard-ball shapes (covered preferably with the pig's caul fat), and then braised in stock. *Faggot* appears to be the same word as *faggot* 'bundle of sticks', and its application to this rissole-like dish presumably comes from the faggot being thought of as an agglomeration or aggregation of bits of meat. The first record of it in this sense is in Henry Mayhew's *London Labour and the London Poor* (1851). *Faggot* meaning 'bundle' was borrowed in the thirteenth century via Old French from Italian *fagotto* (which now also means 'bassoon'). Before that it has been traced back through Vulgar Latin *facus* to Greek *phákelos* 'bundle'.

In recent times faggots have had an image problem. As if their humble origin and sometimes dubious contents were not enough, they have had to contend with the adoption of *faggot* as a derogatory American slang term for 'homosexual' (dating from the early years of the twentieth century). A few firms (particularly in the West Country, a traditional pig area, and Wales) continue bravely to market them, although one cannot have helped its cause in the 1970s with an advertising campaign based on the slogan 'Surprise your husband with a faggot!' The West Midlands also traditionally likes its faggots, and until the advent of the Balti Triangle, the signature dish of Birmingham could have been said to be faggots and peas.

Faggot-like products are common to most areas of Europe where the pig is an important food animal. In Brittany they are known as *boullettes*, in Provence and the Ardèche as *gayettes* (no pun intended, of course).

fairy cake A small dainty individual sponge cake topped with icing and usually some other sort of decoration, such as a minute slice of crystallized fruit. The earliest record of the winsome term in print comes from 1895.

fairy floss The Australian term for candyfloss (*see* CANDY). It is first recorded in 1945.

fajitas A key dish in Tex–Mex cuisine, consisting of strips of spiced beef or chicken, chopped vegetables, and grated cheese, wrapped in a soft tortilla, and often served with sour cream. The word comes from Mexican Spanish, where it means 'little strip, little belt' (it is a diminutive of Spanish *faja* 'strip, belt', a descendant of Latin *fascia* 'band').

falernum The original falernum was a white wine produced in ancient Roman times on the southern slopes of Monte Massico, a range of hills on the west coast of Italy. It seems to have been of a fairly high alcoholic strength: 'one curious claim was that it was the only wine which could be set alight', Jeremy Paterson, in *The Oxford Companion to Wine*, ed. Jancis Robinson (1999). Its name appears to come from the vineyard in which its grapes were grown, the *ager Falernus*. In evocations of classical times, English naturalized it to *falerne* or *falernian*: 'Vineyards famous for the old Falernian', Edward Bulwer-Lytton, *Zanoni* (1842).

In modern usage, the name is applied to a commercially produced sugary liquid made and used in the West Indies for sweetening rum punches and similar drinks. The earliest record of it is from the 1930s.

falooda Falooda, or *faluda,* is a cold drink or dessert widely consumed on the Indian subcontinent. It is made from rose water, sugar, and milk or water. The addition of a setting agent, such as agar-agar, turns it from a drink into a dessert. The name is Urdu.

farce *See* FORCEMEAT.

farfalle Pasta in the form of small butterflies. Its name (first recorded in Italian in 1952) comes from the plural of Italian *farfalla* 'butterfly'.

farl A thin, traditionally triangular cake made of oatmeal or wheat flour. Its name reflects its shape: for originally it was *fardel*, literally 'fourth part', from *ferde* 'fourth' and *del* 'deal, part'. As the oatmeal hints, it comes from Scotland ('an farls bak'd wi' butter', Robert Burns, *Holy Fair* (1787)), but they also make versions of it in Ulster, either in the form of soda bread or as something called 'fadge', made with mashed potato and white flour. It is mainly in these latter forms that it has become more widely known in recent years, via British supermarkets.

farro Grains of wheat, usually emmer wheat, that in Italy are dried and then soaked for use in soups or salads or to accompany meat dishes. It is not dissimilar to pearl barley or couscous. The Italian word is descended from Latin *far* 'corn', source also of English *farinaceous*.

fasoulia *Fasoulia* is the Greek word for 'beans' (it is a descendant of ancient Greek *phaselos,* which was taken over into Latin as *phaselus,* source of Italian *fagiuolo,* Spanish *frijol,* German *fasole,* and Russian *fasol',* and now the taxonomic genus name of most types of bean; its ultimate source is uncertain, and it may have been a pre-Greek loanword, but its first syllable is probably identical with that of Latin *faba*—*see* FAVA BEAN). Seen on a Greek menu, it refers to a salad made by soaking dried haricot beans, simmering them for some time in olive oil and water, and allowing them to cool.

fat hen The British name of a plant of the goosefoot family whose leaves can be (and have been since prehistoric times) used as a green vegetable. It appears to have been inspired by the fact that the plant's seeds were eaten by farmyard poultry (which presumably grew fat on them). In America it is known as *lamb's quarter* or *pigweed*.

fava bean The usual American name for the broad bean, dating back to the 1920s. *Fava* comes from Italian *fava,* a descendant of Latin *faba* 'bean'. This has relatives in several Slavic languages (for example, Russian and Czech *bob*), and may be traceable back to a prehistoric Indo-European ancestor with the underlying meaning 'swell'. The American name was familiarized among British audiences by the cannibalistic psychopath Hannibal Lecter in the film *Silence of the Lambs* (1990): 'A census taker once tried to test me. I ate his liver with some fava beans and a nice chianti'.

feather steak Feather steak, or *feather blade,* is a tender cut of beef taken from the shoulder blade. It gets its name from the pattern of its muscle fibres, fanning out from a central shaft.

feijoada A pork stew that has a claim to be called Brazil's national dish. Its standard ingredients are black beans and a variety of pig products, including fresh pork and cured pork, sausages, pig's trotters, and sometimes pig's ears and tails. Its name is a derivative of Portuguese *feijão* 'bean', which is descended from Latin *phaseolus* 'bean'.

felafel Felafels, or *falafels*, are small vegetarian rissoles popular in the Middle East. In Egypt, where they supposedly originated, they are made with broad beans, but in Syria, the Lebanon, and Israel they are made with chickpeas. It is via Israel that they have become popularized in the West. In Egypt, their name is *felafel* in Alexandria, but in Cairo they are called *ta'amia*.

fennel Etymologically, *fennel* means 'little hay'. It comes ultimately from Latin *feniculum*, a diminutive form of *fenum* 'hay'. It was originally borrowed into English in Anglo-Saxon times as *fenol* or *finul*, which was subsequently reinforced in Middle English by Old French *fenoil* (another descendant of Latin *feniculum*). A close relative of the celery, with an aniseed-like taste, fennel is a highly versatile plant in the kitchen: the bulbous base of its stalks can be eaten as a vegetable, either raw or cooked (so used, it is often called *Florentine fennel*); its feathery green leaves (perhaps the origin of the epithet 'little hay') are used as a herb, particularly for flavouring fish; and its aromatic seeds can be included in sauces, baked in bread, etc. In medieval times it was an emblem for flattery, and was said to be the food of snakes.

fenugreek A plant of the pea family whose chief contribution to cookery is its hard aromatic yellow-brown seeds. It is one of the main spices used in Indian food. There is evidence of its culinary use by the ancient Egyptians, but the name comes from a quite different application of the plant in classical times: it was commonly dried and used for animal fodder, and the Romans termed it *fenum graecum*, literally 'Greek hay'. English borrowed the word from Latin as early as AD 1000, as *fenogrecum* (a book of Anglo-Saxon *leechdoms*—remedies—recommends the use of the plant to relieve stomach ache), but the modern English form is a Middle English readoption from French.

Fernet Branca A very astringent brown Italian bitters, often pressed into service as a cure for a hangover or a *crise de foie*. It was developed in Milan in the 1840s by an apothecary called Bernardino Branca. He is said to have invented a Swedish doctor by the name of 'Fernet' to add a specious authority to his creation.

feta A white semi-hard Greek cheese made from ewes' or goats' milk. It is widely used in Greece (in Greek salad, for instance), and indeed demand outstrips local supply, and a lot has to be imported from Denmark (where it is made from cows' milk).

fettuccine Pasta in the form of long ribbons. It is the central Italian equivalent of the northern Italian tagliatelle. Its name in Italian (first recorded in 1897) means 'little slices, little ribbons'.

fidget pie An ancient English pie containing bacon, onions and apples. Its name has nothing to do with restless movement. *Fidget* is a variant of *fitchet*, a now obsolete dialect name for the polecat. This in turn was a diminutive form of *fitch* 'polecat', which was a borrowing of Middle Dutch *visse* or *fisse*. The application of the polecat to the pie hopefully had nothing to do with the pie's smell. It was probably more a matter of colour. *Fitchet-coloured* used to be applied to things the colour of a polecat, and a *fitchet cat* had brown and black fur—perhaps the colour of an overcooked pie.

fig The fig is a native of, and was first cultivated in, western Asia, but since ancient times has been one of the key fruits of the Mediterranean seaboard. Over the centuries it has accumulated a heavy freight of symbolism. Its leaves, of course, have come to connote prudery, following Adam and Eve's recourse to them as makeshift cache-sexes in the Garden of Eden, but its fruits' metaphorical associations lie in the diametrically opposite direction. The crimson interior revealed by opening a fig has since time immemorial been likened to the external female sex organs. And the link is embodied in the very name of the fruit itself. This goes back to a pre-Indo-European (possibly Semitic) language of the Mediterranean area, whose word for 'fig' gave Greek *súkon* (source of English *sycamore*, etymologically 'fig-mulberry', and *sycophant*, of whose derivation more presently) and Latin *ficus* (from which, via Old French *figue*, English got *fig*). Now Greek *súkon* was used figuratively for 'cunt', and Italian *fico* 'fig' has a derived feminine form *fica* which is employed in the same way. English borrowed this in the sixteenth century as *fig* or *figo*, in the sense 'indecent gesture made by putting the thumb between two fingers or into the mouth' ('The figo for thee then!' says Pistol to the disguised king in Shakespeare's *Henry V* (1599)). To return to *sycophant*, it means literally 'fig-shower', but the 'fig' is not the fruit but the gesture: originally in ancient Greece someone who denounced a criminal was said to 'show them the fig', and gradually from denoting an 'accuser' the term passed via 'informer' to 'flatterer'.

figgey The figgey pudding of 'We wish you a merry Christmas' originated in the Middle Ages. It was a dish of dried figs stewed in wine and very often served in Lent, along with the fish course. The fourteenth-century cookery book *Diuersa Seruicia* gives a recipe: 'Take figs and boil them in wine, and pound them in a mortar with bread. Mix it up with good wine; boil it. Add good spices and whole raisins. Dress it; decorate it with pomegranate seeds on top.'

fig newton An American biscuit consisting of a purée of dried figs surrounded by pastry–what in Britain would generally be called a 'fig roll': 'I'm not used to eating just a box of fig newtons for supper. Back home we used to have enormous meals', Rona Jaffe, *The Best of Everything* (1958). The trademark name is a tribute to the town of Newton, Massachusetts, near which the biscuit was originally manufactured. In the late 1950s the punningly inclined began to substitute *fig newton* facetiously for *figment* (as in 'It was no fig newton of my imagination'), a usage which survived into the twenty-first century.

filbert The nut of the cultivated hazel (*Corylus maxima*), which was introduced to Britain from southeastern Europe several centuries ago. The generally accepted derivation of its name is that it comes from St Philibert (died 684), a Frankish abbot whose feast day, 22 August, falls at around the time when hazel nuts are gathered. An alternative suggestion, though, based on earlier spellings such as *filberd*, is that it is a corruption of 'full beard', a reference to the long husk which almost completely covers the nut. This husk distinguishes the filbert from the wild hazel of the hedgerows (*C. avellana*), whose nut, the cobnut, is seated in a much shorter green cup. The distinction has not always been applied linguistically, however. An improved variety of filbert developed by a certain Mr Lambert of Goudhurst in 1830 was christened the *Kentish Cob*; this name has now virtually cornered the market for all varieties of cultivated hazel nut, and *filbert*, once so common (it was used as an epithet for perfectly formed fingernails, and even featured in a music-hall song, 'Gilbert the filbert, the colonel of the nuts') is now little more than a memory.

filé Ground-up dried leaves of the sassafras, a tree of the laurel family. It is used in the Creole cookery of Louisiana to flavour and thicken soup, especially gumbo. The word is of Louisiana French origin, from the past participle of French *filer* 'to twist, spin'.

filet mignon A small round tender cut of beef from the centre of the fillet, similar to the tournedos. The term, which in French means 'dainty fillet', has been in fairly common use in American English since the beginning of the twentieth century, but never seems to have caught on to the same extent in British English.

fillet The word *fillet* originally denoted a narrow band or strip in general, and particularly a headband. English borrowed it in the fourteenth century from Old French *filet*, which in turn came from a diminutive form of Latin *filum* 'thread'. Its original culinary application, which dates from the fifteenth century, was to the lean tender strip of meat beneath an animal's ribs: 'Take fillets of pork and partly roast them,' *Liber Cocorum* (1420). In the case of pork, *tenderloin* has replaced *fillet*, but we still speak of *fillet* of beef (and in French *filet* still applies to pork and lamb). It has also been used for an analogous choice portion of meat from either side of the breastbone of a bird, although this is now more usually called the *supreme* (for chicken) or *magret* or *aiguillette* (in the case of duck). Then in the eighteenth century we find *fillet* being applied to a boneless slice cut from fish, roughly similar in shape to meat fillets, and also, harking back to the original sense of Latin *filum*, to a boned joint of meat tied up with string. The link with string has now broken, and the term is now used for a lean cut of veal, lamb, or pork from the top of the hind leg. In all these culinary senses, Americans usually spell the word *filet*, and pronounce it *à la française*, /fiˈlay/.

filo Filo, or *phyllo*, is a type of pastry used in Greece and the Near and Middle East, made in extremely thin, almost transparent sheets. It has become familiar in the West in dishes such as baklava, and in the last quarter of the twentieth century was increasingly incorporated into European cuisine. The term is a modification of modern Greek *phyllon* 'leaf', hence 'sheet of pastry'. In Turkey the pastry is known as *yufka*.

financière In classic French haute cuisine, a dish prepared *à la financière* is garnished with a rich mixture of chicken quenelles, cock's combs, and mushrooms in a Madeira and truffle sauce—affordable no doubt only by financiers. The term should not be confused with *financier* (also from French), which denotes a cake made with a mixture of flour, ground almonds, and whisked egg whites.

fines herbes The French term for a mixture of chopped fresh herbs used in cooking. The standard elements of the mix are parsley, chives, tarragon, and chervil, but it is common to find others included, such as thyme or rosemary. Alexis Soyer, the French chef who worked in England and had a crucial influence on Victorian cookery, may have introduced the concept of *fines herbes* to the British, and by the mid-nineteenth century it was well enough established for Mrs Beeton to give a recipe for whiting aux fines herbes in her *Book of Household Management* (1861) (she does not specify which herbs to use). But probably its most familiar application in Britain is to flavour the *omelette aux fines herbes*. (The *-s* of *fines*, incidentally, is pronounced /z/.)

finger chip The Indian English term for a chip.

finger food Food suitable for conveying to the mouth with the fingers. The term, first recorded in 1949, is applied specifically to small savoury items, such as canapés and slices of quiche, that can be eaten standing up without the aid of cutlery, and are served at social functions, such as receptions, where a sit-down meal would be thought *de trop* (or too expensive). It has an air of niminy-piminy genteelness, as if the little finger at least will be raised primly in the air. So too does *finger buffet*, as such arrangements are described.

fingerling potato A general term for any variety of potato with a thin, cylindrical, vaguely fingerlike shape. It is probably an adaptation of *fingerling* 'small fish', although that originally had nothing to do with the size and shape of the fish: it was first applied to the salmon parr (an early stage in the salmon's life cycle, before it heads out to sea), on account of the finger-shaped markings on its side.

finnan haddock   Finnan haddock, or *finnan haddie*, as the Scots often call it, is a haddock that is split open and then smoked to a pale yellow colour. It is of Scottish origin, and the name derives from Findon, a village near Aberdeen. Mrs Beeton gives us an early glimpse of the industrialization of food processing: 'In London, an imitation of [finnan haddock] is made by washing the fish over with pyroligneous acid, and hanging it up in a dry place for a few days.' Jane Grigson, in her *Fish Book* (1993), quotes Sir Walter Scott as claiming that 'a Finnan haddock has a relish of a very peculiar and delicate flavour, inimitable on any other coast than that of Aberdeenshire'. The Scottish soup made from finnan haddock, incidentally, is cullen skink. *See also* SMOKIE.

fino   The two basic types of sherry are fino and oloroso. The distinctive feature of fino is that it develops in a barrel beneath a blanket of naturally occurring yeasts known as *flor* (literally 'mould, flower'). This performs the dual function of protecting the sherry from oxidation by the air, and imparting fino's distinctive yeasty taste. Fino (the term means simply 'fine' in Spanish) is naturally pale in colour and austerely dry, although most commercially available finos receive a very slight sweetening with sugar.

A fino that is aged sufficiently long in cask to acquire a deeper colour and nuttier taste is known as an amontillado.

fir apple   A variety of potato with long thin knobbly tubers. It got its name (first recorded in 1906) from a perceived resemblance to a fir cone (*fir apple* is an old eighteenth-century term for a fir cone). Because of the colour of its skin it is generally referred to as the *pink fir apple*. In the early 1920s it was described as a 'curiosity', but over the past twenty years it has become fairly common on British supermarket shelves.

firewater   A colloquial term, dating back to the early nineteenth century, for strong alcoholic liquor, especially rough whisky, that has a burning effect on the drinker's throat. From the first it was often applied to such drink consumed by Native Americans: 'His Canada fathers . . . taught him to drink the fire-water, and he became a rascal', James Fennimore Cooper, *Last of the Mohicans* (1826), and it is said to be a literal translation of the Ojibwa word for 'whisky', *ishkodewaaboo*.

firmity   An altered version of FRUMENTY.

fish and chips   *See* CHIP.

fishcake   A round flat mixture of shredded fish and mashed potato, typically coated in breadcrumbs or batter and fried. It is traditionally a receptacle for left-over or non-premium-grade fish, but in the latter part of the twentieth century the more up-market salmon fishcake enjoyed a vogue. Examples made from crab meat tend to be called *crabcakes*. The term *fishcake* is first recorded in 1854.

fish finger   The fish finger—a small breadcrumbed ready-to-cook oblong originally of a single chunk of fish, nowadays more usually of reconstituted fish—is perhaps the archetypal frozen food, symbolic of the revolution which overtook Western food production and eating habits in the 1950s. It was introduced by Birds Eye in 1953. The equivalent American English term is *fish stick*.

fish maw   An alternative name, first recorded in the fifteenth century, for the swim bladder of a fish, which is an internal gas-filled sac that maintains and controls the fish's buoyancy (*maw* originally meant 'stomach', and has been applied to various other hollow internal organs over the centuries, including the uterus and a bird's crop). Gastronomically, it is associated with Chinese cuisine, which esteems it a delicacy: 'Joy King Lau . . . Highlights included . . . spongy, slithery fish maw stuffed with springy minced prawn', *Time Out London, Eating and Drinking* (2009).

five-spice A mixture of five spices commonly used in Bengali and Bangladeshi cookery. The standard ingredients are equal proportions of cumin, black mustard, fennel, fenugreek, and nigella seeds. Its name is a translation of Hindi *panch phoran*.

The term is also applied to a ground spice mixture used in China and parts of Southeast Asia, typically containing fennel seeds, cinnamon, cloves, star anise (whose flavour predominates), and Szechwan pepper.

fizz A long drink with a spirit base (typically gin) diluted with soda water. Sugar and lemon juice are added, and often also other ingredients, such as liqueurs, egg whites, or cream. *Fizz* has also been used since the mid-nineteenth century as an affectionate colloquialism for champagne or similar sparkling wines. *See also* BUCK'S FIZZ.

flageolet Flageolets are a variety of haricot bean, grown for their small pale green seeds. They were developed in 1872 by Gabriel Chevrier in the Arpajon region of Brittany, and in France are often termed *chevriers* in his honour. The French word *flageolet* itself is an alteration of Provençal *faioulet*, whose ancestor was Latin *phaselus* 'kidney bean'. It appears to have no etymological connection with *flageolet* 'small flutelike instrument', which probably comes ultimately from Latin *flāre* 'to blow'.

flan The word *flan*, for an 'open tart', is a surprisingly recent introduction into English; the first we hear of it is in Alexis Soyer's *Gastronomic Regenerator* (1846): 'A Flan of Puff Paste . . . Have a plain round or oval flan mould.' However, there is much more to its history than this. Middle English had a word *flawn*, which apparently signified some sort of custard tart or cheesecake (it actually survived into the nineteenth century: 'The flawns and the custards had all disappeared,' Richard Barham, *Ingoldsby Legends* (1840)). This was borrowed from Old French *flaon* (whose modern descendant gave English *flan*), which in turn came from medieval Latin *flādō*, itself acquired by Middle English as *flathon* with the same meaning as *flawn*. And there are further twists. Latin got the word from a prehistoric Germanic base **fladu-*, which also produced German *fladen* 'flat cake' (and 'cowpat') and Dutch *vlade* 'pancake', and is probably related ultimately to Sanskrit *prthús* 'broad', Greek *platús* 'broad', and English *flat*.

In Spanish, *flan* denotes a baked custard pudding cooked in a mould (harking back to the English word's earlier meaning), which has taken many a British holidaymaker by surprise.

flank A cut of beef (or veal) from the lower side of the animal, between the front and rear legs. It is usually divided into the *forequarter flank,* which contains some ribs (these can also form a separate cut, termed *short ribs*), and the *hindquarter flank,* immediately below the sirloin. There is also the *thick flank,* which comes from immediately above the hind leg and is also called the *top rump*. All these are best suited to slow cooking. Lean meat from the inside of the flank can be cut as *flank steak* (also known as *bavette* or *goose skirt*), which, given fairly lengthy marination, can be cooked more quickly.

flapjack The term *flapjack* has had a variety of designations in the course of its career. Originally it denoted a sort of thick pancake ('a Flapiack, which in our translation is called a Pancake,' John Taylor, *Jack-a-Lent* (1620)), and that is how it is still used in the US. *Flap* in this context means 'toss'. According to the *Oxford English Dictionary* a *flapjack* used also to be a sort of apple tart or apple turnover (called *apple-jack* in dialects of eastern England). And in the 1930s we see the first evidence of the word's present-day British usage, for a biscuit made from rolled oats, syrup, and butter.

flare A butcher's and cook's term for the internal fat of a pig, especially from inside the loin around the kidneys. It is also known as *leaf fat*. Rendered down it produces the finest grade of lard, sometimes called *leaf lard*, but it can also be used in its raw state as a cooking fat: 'Flare-cakes are round cakes, made of flour and "unrendered" (unmelted) lard, and stuck over freely with currants', Henry Mayhew, *London Labour and the London Poor* (1851). The term is first recorded in 1847, but its origins are not known.

flatbread Flat, thin bread that is typically unleavened. The word is first recorded in English in 1762, apparently as a translation of German *fladenbrot*.

flat white In Australian English, a cup of coffee made by adding steamed milk to an espresso, producing a relatively negligible head of foam. The term is first recorded in 1971.

flead *Flead*, or *fleed*, is a term formerly used in southeast England for the internal fat of a pig, especially as viewed as a culinary resource. The fat would standardly be rendered down into lard, but it could also be used in its raw state as a cooking fat: Florence White in her *Good Things in England* (1932) quotes recipes for 'flead cakes' from Kent and Surrey. *See also* FLARE.

flip Originally, *flip* denoted a mixed drink of beer and spirits, heated with a hot iron (known as a *flip-dog*). The term goes back at least to the late seventeenth century, and may have originated in the notion of 'flipping', or stirring up, the drink to produce a foam. Its use in *egg-flip*, as a synonym for *egg-nog* (*see* NOG), is a late nineteenth-century development.

floating island Floating island (in French *île flottante*) is a cold dessert consisting of a round flat baked meringue 'island' floating on a sea of custard. The earliest references to it in English come from America: Benjamin Franklin, for instance, reported in a letter of 1771 'At dinner had a floating island.' It is very close in conception to, and sometimes confused with, the French dish *oeufs à la neige* 'snow eggs', in which the beaten egg whites are formed into small individual masses, not one large one, poached rather than baked, and then placed on top of a light egg custard.

florentine Nowadays the term *florentine* denotes a large flat biscuit made from nuts and candied fruits and covered on one side with chocolate, but formerly things were very different. In Renaissance times, and up until the nineteenth century, a florentine was a sort of meat pie or tart: 'B. E.' in his *New Dictionary of the Canting Crew* (1700), describes it as a 'made Dish of Minced Meats, Currans, Spice, Eggs, etc., Baked,' and Eliza Smith's *Compleat Housewife* (1750) gives a recipe for a 'Florentine of a kidney of Veal.' It is not clear what its associations with the Italian city of Florence were.

In French cuisine, *à la florentine* denotes dishes cooked with spinach, usually in a mornay sauce. The term is applied particularly to eggs, and also to fish and white meat. Florentine cooks are said to have introduced spinach into the French diet in the sixteenth century.

flour *Flour* is historically the same word as *flower*, and the distinction in spelling between the two only became firmly established in the nineteenth century. The usage goes back to the early Middle Ages. When grain was milled, the most highly valued part, the meal, was characterized as the 'flower', the finest portion, as contrasted with the husks or bran. In most cases this was wheat meal—hence the Middle English phrase *flour of wheat* (perhaps an echo of French *fleur de farine* 'fine wheat flour'). And in modern usage the term *flour* implies 'wheat flour' unless further qualified (which it can be not just by other grass cereal names, such as *rye* and *rice*, but also by *buckwheat, chestnut, corn*—the compound *cornflour* dates from the mid-nineteenth century—and even *potato*; the only exception to the general rule is *oats*, which usually teams up only with *meal*).

Fluffernutter *See* NUTTER.

flummery In Britain, flummery is a dish of yesteryear. Originally it was a sort of sticky pap made by boiling oatmeal and then straining it; Gervase Markham in his *English Hus-wife* (1615) gave directions: 'From this small Oat-meal, by oft steeping it in water and cleansing it, and then boiling it to a thick and stiff Jelly, is made that excellent dish of meat which is so esteemed in the West parts of this Kingdom, which they call Wash-brew, and in Cheshire and Lancashire they call it Flamerie or Flumerie.' But by the end of the seventeenth century the term was also being used for a dish of cream or almond milk set with some gelling agent such as isinglass and served as a dessert with more cream or wine poured over it. In 1747 Hannah Glasse gave recipes for 'Hartshorn Flummery' and 'French Flummery' in her *Art of Cookery*, and as recently as 1861 Mrs Beeton's *Book of Household Management* was recommending a 'Dutch flummery', a sort of jellified custard made with generous amounts of sherry or Madeira. Nowadays the dish only crops up as a historical curiosity, but the bavarois is its natural successor. The term *flummery* itself comes from Welsh *llymru*, a word of unknown origin. Its main present-day use in British English is a metaphorical one, for 'flattery, humbug', which dates from the mid-eighteenth century, but in America berry flummeries are still popular. *See also* SOWANS.

foam Culinarily, a froth produced by introducing the gas nitrous oxide at high pressure into an edible liquidized substance (for instance, mushroom foam). The concept was launched in the 1990s by the Catalan chef Ferran Adrià at his restaurant El Bulli, at Roses on the Costa Brava. The rationale behind it was to fill something of the role of a sauce in a dish without the use of eggs and cream (not far removed from the mission of the earlier Nouvelle Cuisine). It was taken up by Adrià's disciples, including the English chef Heston Blumenthal, and in the early twenty-first century spread virally through restaurant cuisine. *See also* ESPUMA.

focaccia An Italian bread made from pizza dough, baked in thin squares or rounds and then cut into slices. Its name is a descendant of late Latin *focacia*, which was derived from Latin *focus* 'fireplace': such bread would have been baked on a metal plate over the embers of a fire.

foie gras Foie gras—literally 'fat liver' in French—is the oversized liver of geese or ducks that have been force-fed to fatten them. It was popular in the ancient world—the Egyptians and the Romans used dried figs on the unfortunate birds—but it is in France that it has achieved its modern apotheosis. In the Landes, in Alsace, and particularly around Périgord, the unwilling goose's assimilation of fistfuls of maize is translated into a melting unctuous delicacy that, along with caviare, has become synonymous with sybaritic eating. Its most ringing testimonial was Sydney Smith's declaration that his friend Luttrell's idea of heaven was eating pâté de foie gras to the sound of trumpets (in French, *pâté de foie gras* denotes the whole foie gras encased in pastry, but in English it is used for a paste made from the liver, and often flavoured with truffles).

fondant Fondants are sweets made from a paste produced by boiling sugar syrup and then kneading it until it is soft, creamy, and smooth. The same sort of paste is also used as a filling for 'soft-centre' chocolates and as the basis of icing for cakes (*fondant icing*). The term comes from the present participle of French *fondre* 'to melt', and is probably an allusion to fondant 'melting in the mouth'.

Other uses of the term that have recently become more familiar in English are *chocolate fondant*, referring to a sort of chocolate sponge pudding with chocolate in the centre, that melts when it is heated, and *fondant potatoes* (in French, *pommes de terre fondantes*), denoting potatoes that are cooked slowly in butter.

fondue The original fondue is a Swiss dish in which cheese is melted in a pot with white wine and other flavourings over a heat source (*fondue* is the feminine past participle of French *fondre* 'to melt'), and chunks of bread are dipped into it on long-handled forks and then eaten. Inspired by the same general notion of do-it-yourself gobbets of food plucked from a heated bowl, the term has also been applied to a dish of Burgundian origin, in which cubes of beef are individually cooked in a pot of hot oil. (The same basic principle is used in many Chinese and Southeast Asian dishes, where small pieces of meat, fish, etc. are cooked in heated stock.)

fontina A firm mild cows'-milk cheese made originally in the Val d'Aosta, in the Alps, but now more widely the speciality of Piedmont. The origins of its name are not known.

fool Gastronomically speaking, a fool is a cold dessert made from puréed or stewed fruit mixed with cream or custard. In theory it can be made with any fruit, but the Victorians seem to have been inordinately fond of gooseberry fool: Edward Lear celebrated it in a limerick: 'There was an old person of Leeds, / whose head was infested with beads; / she sat on a stool, / and ate gooseberry fool, / which agreed with that person of Leeds'; and that is the fruit which fool is most commonly associated with today. The first known recipe for gooseberry fool is given in Hannah Glasse's *Art of Cookery* (1747), and Mrs Beeton in 1861 refers to it as 'a very old-fashioned and homely dish'. It has been suggested that the word is related to French  *fouler* 'to press, crush' (from the crushing of the fruit), but this is ruled out by the fact that the sixteenth- and seventeenth-century predecessors of fruit fools were in fact simple custard dishes. Randle Holme described them in his *Academy of Armory* (1688): 'Foole is a kind of Custard, but more crudely; being made of Cream, Yolks of Eggs, Cinamon, Mace boiled: and served on Sippets with sliced Dates, Sugar, and white and red Comfits, strawed thereon'. The likeliest explanation of the name is that, like *trifle*, *whimwham*, etc., it was a reallocation of a word for something light-headed or frivolous to a light dessert.

foo yong See FU YONG.

forcemeat The Latin verb for 'to stuff' was *farcīre*. English acquired it in the fourteenth century via Old French *farser* as *farce* (a fifteenth-century cookery book instructs 'Broach thy pig [put it on a spit]; then farce him'). This did not survive beyond the early eighteenth century; but the variant form *force* had arisen, and in the late seventeenth century this was combined with *meat* to form *forcemeat*, denoting 'minced or chopped meat used for stuffing' (Randle Holme, in his *Academy of Armory* (1688), defined the term as 'meat with a stuffing of herbs, or other things made to that purpose'). In present-day English it has passed out of common usage, supplanted by the more general *stuffing* or the more specific *sausage meat* (which in practice is what most forcemeat was).

The use of *farce* for a variety of comic play, incidentally, came from the application of Latin *farcīre* to the 'stuffing' or 'padding out' of religious plays with humorous interludes.

formity An altered form of FRUMENTY.

fortune cookie In America, and particularly in American Chinese restaurants, a wafer biscuit that while still warm and pliable is folded round a slip of paper containing a prediction, a wise maxim, or a 'witty' saying. When it cools down it becomes crisp, and the recipient must break it to retrieve the contents. The term is first recorded in 1926.

fourme A general term for any of a range of cows'-milk cheeses produced in central France. It is an Auvergne dialect word, descended via Provençal *forma* 'a cheese' from Latin *forma* 'a cheese mould' (ultimate source also of modern French *fromage* 'cheese'). The best-known fourme is *fourme d'Ambert*, which is similar to Stilton. It is made in a tall sturdy cylinder shape, and traditionally cut horizontally.

four spices A direct translation of *quatre-épices*, the French term for a mixture of four powdered spices, typically pepper, nutmeg, cloves, and cinnamon. It is used in stews, pâtés, etc.

fragrant meat As Hugh Rawson points out in his *Dictionary of Euphemisms and Other Double-talk* (1981), *fragrant meat* is what the Chinese call a 'hot dog'—but in this case it is no sausage, but a real dog! The eating of dogs is an ancient Chinese tradition, but evidently a sufficient cause of embarrassment to give rise to this delicate circumlocution.

fraise A type of thick pancake typically incorporating pieces of bacon. Conceptually it is perhaps closer to an omelette, but made with batter rather than beaten eggs and butter. It is now largely a thing of the past, although sweet versions containing fruit survived into the twentieth century: Florence White in her *Good Things in England* (1932), quotes a recipe for an 'apple fraize'. The term, which also occurs in the form *froise*, dates back to the early fourteenth century. It probably came from an unrecorded Old French **freis* or **freise*, which would be traceable back ultimately to *frixum*, the past participle of the Latin verb *frigere* 'to fry'.

Frangelico A yellowish-brown hazelnut-flavoured Italian liqueur. Its name was inspired by the legend of an Italian hermit called Fra Angelico (*fra* is short for *frate* 'brother', and is prefixed to the names of monks and friars) who created his own unique recipes for liqueurs. It comes in a bottle that has a passing resemblance to a monk in his habit, complete with a rope-belt round its middle. Its profile has been raised in the twenty-first century, not least because of its espousal by the cookery writer Nigella Lawson ('I'm . . . very keen on a snifter of espresso liqueur to which a drop or two of Frangelico has been added', Kitchen (2010), and it has become a fashionable sweet-course flavouring (Desserts continue the theme, with a chocolate malva pudding teamed with frangelico ice cream', *Good Food Guide* (2008)).

frangipane The connection between *frangipane*, a variety of almond-flavoured confectioner's custard used in cakes, pastries, etc., and *frangipani*, the red jasmine or its perfume, is a sixteenth-century Italian marquis, Muzio Frangipani. At some time when he was living in Paris this nobleman, evidently a man of the most refined tastes, created a perfume for scenting gloves, based on bitter almonds (the word started off in the French compound *gants de frangipane* 'Frangipani's gloves'). Its similarity to the scent of red jasmine flowers has led to the term being applied to that plant. The perfume evidently scored a considerable success in sixteenth-century Paris, for the local pastrycooks were moved to try to capture something of its savour (and cash in on its popularity) by adding almonds to their confectioner's custard (made with milk, sugar, flour, eggs, and butter) and calling it *frangipane*.

frankfurter The true frankfurter is a cold-smoked sausage made of pork and salted bacon fat, although over the years the name has come to be applied to sausages with a variety of sometimes dubious ingredients, whose common denominator is a smoky flavour. The frankfurter's popularity was born in the US (source also of its colloquial name, *frank*), and it is the quintessential sausage of the hot dog. But it originated, of course, in Germany, or more specifically in Frankfurt-am-Main. It was at first called *Frankfurt sausage* in English, or simply *frankfurt*—it is first mentioned in *Kettner's Book of the Table* (1877)— but by the end of the nineteenth century the German term *frankfurter* (short for *Frankfurter wurst* 'Frankfurt sausage') had entered the language. The naming of sausages after their cities is quite common in German, and was the source of some bemusement amongst Germans when John Kennedy made his famous remark on a visit to Berlin, 'Ich bin ein Berliner': he was literally saying 'I am a sausage' (or alternatively 'I am a doughnut', which *Berliner* can also mean; but either way the audience no doubt got the message).

frappé *Frappé* is the past participle of French *frapper*, which means literally 'to hit', and hence metaphorically 'to chill'. English has been using it since the mid-nineteenth century in the general sense 'cooled', but latterly it has been virtually exclusively applied to drinks (as in 'a crème de menthe frappé'). It has also been turned into a noun, broadly referring to an iced drink (a usage first recorded in 1903): specifically, either a soft drink that has been frozen down into a semi-liquid mush, or a liqueur that is served over crushed ice. In addition, in the US, and particularly in New England, the term can denote a thick milk shake. American English also uses an accentless version of the noun, *frappe*, which can be pronounced /frap/.

Frappuccino A trademarked name used by the Starbucks chain of cafés for a drink of iced coffee, typically topped with whipped cream. It was introduced in 1995, and in an evolutionary leap, in the second decade of the twenty-first century coffee-less Frappuccinos were marketed, flavoured with vanilla, strawberries and cream, chocolate, and the like. The word is a blend of *frappé*, presumably in the sense 'iced drink', and *cappuccino*.

freedom fries A polemical but short-lived alternative name proposed in the US for French fries (i.e., chips) as a sign of America's grave displeasure with France for declining to support its invasion of Iraq in 2003 (the French themselves were widely characterized at the time as 'cheese-eating surrender-monkeys'). It was coined by Republican Congressman Bob Ney (and soon followed by *freedom toast* for *French toast*). *See also* LIBERTY CABBAGE.

fregola Fregola, or *fregula*, is a Sardinian type of pasta in the form of very small balls, not dissimilar to couscous: 'We liked the tomato-based fish stew strewn with doughy balls of fregola', *Time Out, London's Best Restaurants* (2011). The name is a derivative of Italian *fregare* 'to rub', a reference to the way the pasta is made.

French bean A mainly British name for any of a range of beans of New World origin that are cultivated for their pods, which are eaten when green as a vegetable. It is first recorded in 1552, and probably originated as a way of distinguishing these exotic new beans (*see* BEAN) from the traditional 'British' broad bean.

French bread A generic English term for white bread made from dough containing soft flour and relatively little water and baked in long thin loaves with a crisp golden-brown crust and a light crumb with large holes in it. Such loaves are usually known in English as *French sticks*, or just *French loaves*, but in their native France they are more specifically designated according to size and thinness as *ficelle, flûte, baguette*, etc. (the last now increasingly used as a synonym for *French loaf* in English). There are many other sorts of bread made in France than this, of course—indeed, it is a comparative newcomer, dating from the mid-nineteenth century when the introduction of the steam-injected Viennese oven made its manufacture possible—but for English-speakers, if it's *French bread*, it's long, thin, and crusty. Since the 1950s it has become increasingly easily available in Britain, as part of the general continentalization of British eating habits, and is now often to be found (in form if not in soggy debased content) as the superstructure of pub sandwiches or (somewhat ironically) as the carbohydrate component of the 'traditional British' ploughman's lunch.

French dressing In British English, an alternative name for vinaigrette (in American English it denotes a creamy salad dressing made from mayonnaise, oil, and ketchup).

French Fancy The British brand name of a type of small individual sponge cake topped with vanilla cream and covered with fondant icing—in effect, a variety of fairy cake. It was introduced in the mid-1960s by Rank Hovis McDougall, and presumably named to suggest a certain self-indulgent naughtiness, although that perhaps sat rather ill with the wholesome image of 'Mr Kipling', under whose cakey umbrella French Fancies were soon brought.

French fries *French fries* is the usual American term for chips, first recorded in 1902. It is a curtailed version of *French fried potatoes*, which dates back at least to the 1850s. Since the Second World War it, and its further abbreviated form *fries*, have been making determined inroads into British usage, particularly in fast-food outlets (in the late 1980s Buxted changed the name of their ready-meal 'Chicken and Chips' to 'Chicken and Fries'). Anything going under this name is likely to be thinner than the traditional British chip, but individual bulk is usually more than made up for by numerical quantity. The fancy terminology reflects the French origin of this method of cooking potatoes (Mrs Beeton referred to it in 1861 as the 'French fashion'), and may also be a memory (at a certain remove in time) of the chip's introduction to America: Thomas Jefferson is said to have enjoyed fried potatoes so much when he was America's Commissioner in Paris that when he became president (1801–1809) he had them served at a dinner at the White House. *See also* FREEDOM FRIES, HOME FRIES.

French stick *French stick*, or more vaguely *French loaf*, is an English term for a long thin loaf of French bread, particularly the type known in French (and increasingly in English) as a *baguette*. It is first recorded in 1959.

French toast Nowadays, the term *French toast* refers to a slice of bread soaked in milk, dipped in beaten egg, and fried. However, the French toast our ancestors knew was a more robust affair. In a seventeenth-century cookery book, Robert May's *The Accomplisht*

Cook (1660), we find this recipe: 'French Toasts. Cut French Bread, and toast it in pretty thick toasts on a clean gridiron, and serve them steeped in claret, sack, or any wine, with sugar and juice of orange.' This is essentially the dish which survived into the early twentieth century as *poor knights pudding*.

In France, French toast is known as *pain perdu*, literally 'lost bread'—that is, bread smothered in eggs, milk, etc. so as to disappear—a term adopted by Middle English as *payn purdew*, *panpardie*, or *panperdie*.

fricandeau A dish made from a good-quality cut of veal, typically from the upper part of the leg or the shoulder, which is larded with strips of pork fat and then braised or roasted. It is usually finished off by having the cooking juices poured over it and glazed in the oven. The word, which is a derivative of *fricasser*, was borrowed into English from French in the eighteenth century: Elizabeth Raffald, for example, in her *Experienced English Housekeeper* (1769), mentions a 'fricando of beef'.

fricassee A dish consisting typically of a white meat (such as chicken, veal, or rabbit) cut up, stewed in stock, and served usually in a white sauce. The word *fricassee* is of course of French origin (it comes from the past participle of *fricasser*, which originally meant 'to fry' and may have been formed from *frire* 'to fry' and *casse* 'ladle, dripping pan'—source of *casserole*), but English took it over as long ago as the sixteenth century. Around 1600 it was applied metaphorically to a sort of early shrapnel bomb.

fridge cake A cake whose semi-liquid mixture of ingredients (typically chocolate-based) are solidified by cooling in a refrigerator rather than baking in an oven. 'There are many baffling aspects to the royal wedding, but perhaps the most baffling of all is the news that Prince William has asked McVitie's . . . to bake [sic] him a vast chocolate "fridge cake"', *Observer Food Monthly* (2011).

fries *See* FRENCH FRIES.

frisée A French term recently introduced into English for the 'curly endive', a salad plant with the appearance of a straggly, unkempt lettuce. It has suffered considerably in the past from a confusion of nomenclature—in Britain it is called *endive*, in America *chicory*—and if the new name goes some way to remove this confusion it will have more than earned its place in the language. (In French it is short for *chicorée frisée*, literally 'curly chicory').

frittata An Italian dish made with beaten eggs and usually some sort of filling, fried until cooked through and served flat—in effect, an Italian version of a Spanish omelette (*see* OMELETTE): 'We liked the idea of a main course frittata (organic eggs, ricotta, and courgette) too', *Time Out London, Eating and Drinking* (2009). The Italian word is a derivative of *fritto*, the past participle of *frittere* 'to fry'.

fritter Fritters are portions of food—fruit, vegetables, seafood—coated in batter and deep-fried. The name reflects the method of cooking: it was borrowed in the fourteenth century from Old French *friture*, which came ultimately from Latin *frigere* 'to fry'. The cooking method itself is said to have been introduced from the Middle East by Crusaders returning to Western Europe. The fourteenth-century cookery book *Diuersa seruicia* gives a recipe for apple fritters: 'Take flour and eggs and grind pepper and saffron and make thereto a batter; and pare apples and cut them into broad pieces, and cast them therein, and fry them in the batter with fresh grease and serve them forth.' The Japanese equivalent to fritters is tempura.

fritto misto The Italian equivalent of Japanese tempura. It consists of an assortment of bite-sized ingredients—pieces of meat, fish, vegetables, etc.—covered in flour or light batter and deep-fried (the name means literally 'mixed fry'). Probably the version most familiar to Britons is *fritto misto di mare*, containing a selection of seafood.

fromage frais Fromage frais (literally 'fresh cheese' in French) is an unripened cheese made by curdling pasteurized skimmed milk with rennet, lactic acid, or a bacteria culture. Soft, almost semi-liquid in consistency, it is traditionally eaten in France as a dessert with fresh fruit (a particular use is in *coeur à la crème*, in which the fromage frais is mixed with beaten egg white and sugar, put into heart-shaped moulds, and served perhaps with cream or fruit). In the mid 1980s a sweetened, fruit-flavoured version of fromage frais became widely available in Britain, and quickly established a sizable foothold in the yoghurt-style dessert market.

Froot Loops The trademarked name of a wheat- and oat-based ring-shaped breakfast cereal made by Kellogg's. It was introduced in 1963. The small rings come in various bright colours and assorted fruit flavours. In 1980s American English the name (its spelling usually normalized to *fruit-loop*) was adopted as a colloquial term for a crazy or eccentric person, presumably inspired by *fruitcake* 'crazy person' and *loopy* 'crazy': 'If our study of self-esteem is to be taken seriously, we can't afford to be seen as a bunch of fruit-loops', Gary Trudeau, *Doonesbury* (1987). It is also used to mean 'an effeminate homosexual male'.

fruitcake A cake containing dried or crystallized fruits, particularly grapes (in the form of raisins, sultanas, currants), but also potentially including candied peel, cherries, dates, etc. Nuts are often an ingredient too, which gave rise in the early years of the twentieth century to the colloquial expression *nutty as a fruitcake,* meaning 'crazy'. From there it was a short step to using *fruitcake* itself to mean 'crazy person', an application first recorded in 1945. Both the usages began in American English and spread to British English, but *fruitcake* as a derogatory term for an effeminate homosexual male has largely stayed in America.

frumenty A dish of former times that was essentially a porridge made from wheat. Grains of wheat had their outer covering removed and were then cooked slowly in milk. The result was flavoured, often with cinnamon or nutmeg, and sweetened. The word goes back to the fourteenth century, when it was acquired from Old French *frumentee,* a derivative of *frument* 'grain'. That in turn was a descendant of Latin *frumentum*. It was subject to a series of metamorphoses: the Old French form *fourmentee,* with metathesized *r* and *u,* produced English *furmenty,* and this was further eroded to *furmity, formity* and *firmity* (Mrs Rundell in her *New System of Domestic Cookery* (1816) gave a recipe for 'Somersetshire firmity').

fry A euphemistic term referring to an animal's embarrassing internal organs, and particularly its testicles, as prepared for eating—typically by frying. It is applied mainly to the testicles of young sheep—'lamb's fries'. The French euphemize edible testicles as *rognons blancs,* literally 'white kidneys'. *See also* PRAIRIE OYSTER.

fry-up A simple and often ad-hoc dish or meal made in a frying-pan. Typical ingredients would include fat-rich pork products, such as bacon and sausages, and cold left-overs, such as potatoes and baked beans. The name is a British one, first recorded in 1967: 'Then lunch. More often than not a "fry-up"—I became a dab hand with a frying-pan', John Wainwright, *The Take-over Men* (1969). *See also* ULSTER FRY.

fudge *Fudge*, which denotes a sort of soft, somewhat toffee-like sweet made by boiling together sugar, butter, and milk, is a mystery word. It first appeared, in the US, at the end of the nineteenth century, when it was used for 'a kind of chocolate bonbon', and by 1902 the journal *The Queen* was recording that 'the greatest "stunt" among college students is to make *Fudge*'. It is generally assumed to have been an adaptation of the verb *fudge*, in the sense 'to make inexpertly, botch', but this merely begs the question, as the origin of the verb, too, is uncertain.

ful *Ful,* or *fuul,* is the Arabic word for 'bean'—the Old World broad bean, that is, not the New World haricot bean. Regional practice is to let the bean come to full maturity and then dry it, which gives the main local variety's buff skin a still darker hue. They are used to make what can reasonably be claimed to be Egypt's national dish, *ful medames* (or *ful mudammes*): the soaked beans are simmered for a long time and then mashed with oil, lime or lemon juice, and often garlic, onion, tomato, parsley, and cumin, and the resulting mixture is typically eaten with bread for breakfast or as part of a mezze. *Medames* may ultimately be a derivative of Egyptian Arabic *dims* 'ashes', reflecting the way the pot of beans is traditionally cooked over coals.

full English Short for *full English breakfast,* a calorie-rich collation centred on fried eggs and bacon, typically accompanied by any or all of sausages, black pudding, fried or grilled tomatoes and mushrooms, baked beans, and fried bread, washed down with tea, and rounded off with toast and marmalade. The explicit contrast is between this hearty (if not heart-stopping) fare for English trenchermen and the effete 'Continental breakfast' of rolls or croissants and coffee. The institution is not so steeped in history as this would seem to suggest, however. In former times English people broke their fast with an eclectic range of foods, including hot or more usually cold meats and game. As early as the seventeenth century, Sir Kenelm Digby suggested that 'two poached eggs with a few fine dry fried collops [i.e. rashers] of pure bacon are not bad for breakfast' in *The Closet of Sir Kenelm Digby Knight Opened* (1669), but it was not until the late Victorian period (by which time the price of eggs had fallen considerably) that eggs and bacon became the norm. *See also* ULSTER FRY.

The elements of the full English breakfast make for a reasonably filling meal at any time of day, which has led latterly to the concept of the 'all-day breakfast': 'Glenn Branson . . . stood in the corridor outside the briefing room, a cup of coffee in one hand and an All-Day Breakfast egg, bacon, and sausage sandwich in the other', Peter James, *Dead Tomorrow* (2009).

fumet The French word *fumet* means literally 'aroma', and originally in English it was used for the 'smell of well-hung game': Dr Johnson, in his *Dictionary* (1755), giving it in the form *fumette*, described it as 'a word introduced by cooks, and the pupils of cooks, for the stink of meat,' and Tobias Smollett in his *Adventures of Ferdinand Count Fathom* (1753) describes a 'roasted leveret very strong of the fumet.' As recently as 1877, E. S. Dallas in his *Kettner's Book of the Table* was advising that 'pheasant requires to be kept until the *fumet* is fully developed'. In classical French cuisine, however, the term had come to mean a concentrated stock used for adding flavour to a sauce, particularly one made from mushrooms or fish, and nowadays *fish fumet* is frequently loosely used simply for 'fish stock'.

furmenty or **furmity** An alternative version of FRUMENTY.

fusilli Pasta pieces in the form of short spirals. The name in Italian (first recorded in 1952) means 'little spindles'.

fu yong *Fu yong,* or *foo yong,* or *fu yung,* designates a Chinese dish made with egg as a main ingredient. In particular, in Chinese–American cuisine the somewhat tautological *egg fu yong* is the name of a sort of Spanish omelette made with eggs and a range of fillings that typically include bean sprouts, water chestnuts, spring onions, and a meat element, such as ham or chicken. In Cantonese, *fúyúng* means 'hibiscus', which can have flowers the colour of egg yolks.

gado-gado An Indonesian dish consisting of a mixture of cooked vegetables, typically including potatoes, beans, beansprouts, cabbage, and cucumber, and also hard-boiled eggs, served with a spiced chilli and peanut sauce. Its name comes from a Javanese verb meaning 'to eat curried food (as opposed to rice)'.

galangal A Chinese plant whose dried ground root has a gingery-peppery taste which makes it much valued as a flavouring in East Asian cookery. It has been known and used in the West for over a millennium, but the history of its name has one or two unexpected twists and turns. It goes back ultimately to Chinese *gāo liáng jiāng*, which means literally 'good ginger from Gaozhou (a city in Canton now called Maoming)'. This came westwards via Arabic *khalanjān*, and passed into medieval Latin as *gallingar* (which Old English adopted as *gallengar*). In French the Arabic term became *galingal*, and Middle English took this over as *galingale*. By the sixteenth century, however, this name was also being applied to a European plant of the sedge family whose root had roughly similar properties to those of the oriental galingale, and as the latter gradually dropped out of culinary use in Britain with the passing of the Middle Ages, so the native plant came more and more to take over the name *galingale*, and the oriental spice had to make do with the variant form *galangal*.

galantine The term *galantine* originally signified 'jellied juices of meat or fish'. But since the juices generally served as the basis of a sauce, with thickenings and spices, it came to stand for the sauce itself (the fourteenth-century cookery book *Forme of Cury* gives a recipe for 'lampreys in galantine', in which the galantine is made from the lampreys' blood and cooking juices together with wine, vinegar, breadcrumbs, raisins, ginger, galingale, and cloves). The inclusion of the spice galingale (a standard medieval ingredient of the sauce) may give a clue to the form of the word. For to begin with it had no *n* before the *t*. It came originally from medieval Latin *galatīna*, which probably derived from Latin *gelāre* 'to freeze' (if so, *galatine* would be a parallel formation to, or possibly even the same word as, *gelatine*). This developed in Old French to *galatine*, and it seems likely that the later French form *galantine* (as borrowed into Middle English) arose by association with the word *galingale*.

English galantine sauce survived well into the seventeenth century, although it had by then become simply a dark spicy sauce, without its original meat jelly: 'When it is baked make a galentine of Claret-wine and Cinnamond and sugar, and poure it on the Pye,' Sir Theodore Mayerne, *Archimagirus Anglo-Gallicus* (1658). But then, at the beginning of the eighteenth century, a new sort of galantine came on the scene from France, clearly descended from the galantine sauces of old but significantly different. This was a dish of pieces of white meat (chicken, veal, etc.) mixed with forcemeat and seasonings, shaped (galantine of chicken is often made in the bird's re-formed skin), boiled, and served cold, coated in aspic or its own jelly (here is the link with the original 'jellied meat juices'). And that is what *galantine* on a twenty-first-century menu signifies.

gala pie A pork pie which contains at its centre a hard-boiled egg. Such pies are typically long and rectangular, and served in slices, and yet a portion of egg of identical shape and size usually appears in each slice. This piece of sleight-of-hand is achieved by cooking a mix of yolks in a long tube, then putting the result in a wider tube, filling it up with egg white, and cooking again: result, a very long hard-boiled egg. The name suggests a pie suitable for a festive occasion.

galbi jjim Galbi jjim, or *kalbi jjim*, or *kalbi chim*, is a Korean dish of slowly braised beef (or pork) short ribs. *Galbi* is Korean for 'short ribs'; the term *jjim* originally denoted a dish made by steaming marinated meat or fish, but this method has now largely been replaced by simmering in broth.

galette In France, *galette* is a general term for a 'round flat cake'. And not just a sweet cake, either (although one of the best known is the traditional puff-pastry *galette des Rois* 'Kings' cake,' baked on Twelfth Night). The word is also used for thin fried cakes made from potato, or for pancakes. It comes from Old French *galet* 'pebble'.

galia melon *See* MELON.

Galliano A yellow Italian liqueur that is a key ingredient of the Harvey Wallbanger cocktail. It was created in 1896 in Livorno, Tuscany by the distiller Arturo Vaccari, and named in honour of Giuseppe Galliano, a hero of the Italian–Ethiopian war of 1895–6. It is marketed in a characteristic tall bottle, and its colour, which is produced by tartrazine, is said to be symbolic of the gold rushes of the 1890s.

gamay A grape variety used for producing red wine. Once widely planted in Burgundy, it has been systematically ousted from the Côte d'Or by the more noble pinot noir, and its great stronghold is now Beaujolais. Here it produces typically a light, easily quaffable red wine with a characteristic 'boiled-sweet' flavour. It takes its name from a tiny hamlet in the commune of Saint Aubin, in the Côte d'Or.

gammon English acquired the word *gammon* in the fifteenth century from Old Northern French *gambon*, a derivative of *gambe* 'leg' (its modern French descendant is *jambon* 'ham'). At first it was used generally for the 'hind leg or haunch of a pig', but during the sixteenth century it came more and more to be applied specifically to the cured or salted animal rather than the live one. Hence the word's modern use for 'bacon from the hindquarters, and particularly the hind leg, of the pig'.

ganache A soft sweet paste made by mixing melted chocolate with cream, and used for covering cakes, filling tarts, making sweet truffles, etc. It is said to have been created around 1850 at the Pâtisserie Siraudin in Paris. The origins of its name are unknown.

gaperon Gaperon (or *gapron*) is a soft cows'-milk cheese, flavoured with garlic and usually pepper, that is made in the Auvergne region of central France. It is shaped like a sphere with the bottom cut off. Its name is a derivative of *gape*, a local dialect word for 'buttermilk'.

garam masala A standard mixture of ground spices used in Indian cookery. Ingredients vary, but the blend standardly contains cinnamon, cardamom, cloves, cumin, coriander, and pepper. The term means literally 'hot spice'.

garbanzo bean The term used in the context of Spanish and Latin American cuisine for 'chickpea'. It comes from Spanish *garbanzo*, which English originally took over in the seventeenth century as *garvance*. It was gradually Anglicized to *calavance*, and over the years came to be used more and more loosely for any kind of bean or pulse: 'When I was in the Navy, haricot beans were in constant use as a substitute for potatoes, and in Brazil and elsewhere were called calavances,' Sir Joseph Hooker (1880). The original Spanish became re-established in the nineteenth century, mainly through American Spanish. It is an alteration (presumably influenced by *garroba* 'carob') of Old Spanish *arvanço*, which itself was borrowed from a prehistoric Germanic word for a plant of the pea family that may ultimately be of Asiatic origin.

garbure A rich vegetable broth of southern France and northeastern Spain, somewhere between a soup and a stew in consistency. It is based on vegetable stock, and contains a wide variety of ingredients, depending on where it is made: potatoes, cabbage, onions, beans, tomatoes, courgettes, maize, together with garlic and herbs. Added flavour may be given with a ham bone or piece of bacon, or, in the Béarn region, confit of goose, and it is usually thickened with dry bread. The source of the word is disputed: some derive it from French *gerbe* 'bunch' (a descendant of Frankish *garba*), the notion being that it is made from a 'bunch' of vegetables, while others claim that it comes from Spanish *garbías* 'stew'.

Garibaldi A type of British biscuit with a layer of currants inside. Little seen nowadays, it was popular in the first half of the twentieth century. It was named after Giuseppe Garibaldi (1807–82), the Italian nationalist leader, but the reason for this remains unclear. He visited England in 1854, staying for a while on Tyneside on his way from the US back to Italy, but whether this was still ringing bells when the biscuit was originally manufactured in 1861 (by Peek Freans), is not known. Its colloquial nickname, *squashed-fly biscuit* (coined from the appearance of the currants), dates from at least the first decade of the twentieth century; it is mentioned by H. G. Wells in *Tono-Bungay* (1909): 'instead of offering me a Garibaldi biscuit, she asked me with that faint lisp of hers, to "have some squashed flies, George".'

garlic The garlic has a very long pedigree in British cookery, a fact confirmed by the Anglo-Saxon origins of its name. In common with so many other potherbs, it was introduced by the Romans, and it remained popular throughout the medieval and Elizabethan periods, but by the seventeenth century there began to be mutterings about its excessive pungency and its unsuitability in polite society. John Evelyn, in his *Acetaria* (1699), notes: 'We absolutely forbid it entrance into our Salleting [salad], by reason of its intolerable Rankness, and which made it so detested of old, that the eating of it was . . . part of the Punishment of such as had committed the horrid'st Crimes. To be sure, 'tis not for Ladies Palats, nor those who court them, farther than to permit a light touch on the Dish, with a Clove thereof.' And Mrs Beeton sums up the Victorian attitude: 'The smell of this plant is considered offensive, and it is the most acrimonious in its taste of the whole of the alliaceous tribe. . . . On the continent, especially in Italy, it is much used, and the French consider it an essential in many made dishes.' It is only with the explosion of interest in other countries' culinary traditions since the Second World War that the British have ceased to regard garlic with almost vampire-like aversion.

The second syllable of the word is essentially *leek*, which in Anglo-Saxon times was used for many members of the onion family: *ynneleac* was an 'onion', *potleac* was a 'leek'. The first element, *gar*, is Old English for 'spear', a reference to the spearhead-like shape of the cloves. The word *clove*, incidentally,

comes from Old English *clufu*, which is related to the verb *cleave*; there is no connection with *clove* the spice.

garlic chives An alternative name for CHINESE CHIVES.

garum Garum (also known as *liquamen*) was a powerfully pungent condiment used in ancient Greece and Rome. It was made from small fish such as sardines, anchovies, red mullet, etc. which were fermented together with the intestines of larger fish such as tuna, and it was included in a wide range of recipes. Its name was derived from a Greek term for a sort of fish, *gáros*.

gâteau English borrowed *gâteau* from French in the mid-nineteenth century, and at first used it fairly indiscriminately for any sort of cake, pudding, or cake-like pie—indeed as late as 1932 the *Edinburgh Book of Plain Cookery Recipes* was telling its readers how to make a 'gâteau of fish'. Since the Second World War, however, usage of the term has homed in on an 'elaborate cream cake': the cake element, generally a fairly unremarkable sponge, is in most cases simply an excuse for lavish layers of cream, and baroque cream and fruit ornamentation. (In French, *gâteau* continues to designate more broadly 'cake'.)

The word *gâteau* is the modern French descendant of Old French *guastel* 'fine bread', which is probably of Germanic origin. In its northeastern Old French dialect form *wastel* it was borrowed into English in the thirteenth century, where it survived until the seventeenth century: a Privy Council edict of 1638 ordered that 'no Baker shall bake or make to be sold any other . . . sorts of bread (except Simnel, Wastel, and Horsebread [bread made of beans, bran, etc. as food for horses])'.

gazpacho A Spanish vegetable soup whose chief characteristic is that it is served ice-cold. Its main ingredients are tomatoes, peppers, onions, cucumber, olive oil, and usually breadcrumbs, but there are many additional regional variations within Spain. It is traditionally cooked in a large clay bowl, and brought to the table with garlic croutons and small bowls of raw vegetables. Its name is of Arabic origin, and means literally 'soaked bread'.

gefilte fish A classic of Jewish cookery consisting of chopped fish mixed with matzo meal, egg, and seasoning, shaped into balls or oval fishcakes, and simmered in fish stock. It is usually served cold. Yiddish *gefilte* means 'filled'.

geitost An alternative form of GJETOST.

gemelli Pasta shapes in the form of a spiral, made by twisting two strands together. The name in Italian means 'twins'.

genepy Genepy, or *génépi*, is a herbal liqueur of the western Alps, which takes its name from its main ingredient, an alpine species of artemisia (wormwood). It owes its wider fame largely to the attraction of the French Alps for winter sports enthusiasts. The word comes from the Savoyard dialect, but its ultimate etymology is unknown.

Genoa cake A type of rich fruit cake, typically topped with almonds. The name presumably reflects some sort of connection with the Italian city and port of Genoa, but it is not known what it is.

Genoese pastry Genoese pastry, or *Genoese sponge,* is a type of rich light sponge mix made with flour, sugar, eggs, and butter. It is used for making cakes, large and small (also termed *genoese sponge*), petits fours, Swiss rolls, etc. *Genoese* is a direct translation of the French term *génoise* (literally 'of Genoa'), which is also used in English ('Soigné ladies. . . changed into gorgeous tea gowns at five o'clock to gossip over dainty pieces of Madeira or . . . *génoises*—delicate fancy sponges flavoured with liqueurs, whimsically coloured and iced,' Kate Colquhoun, *Taste* (2007)), but beyond that, the reason for any connection with Genoa, Italy remains, as with *Genoa cake,* unknown.

gewürztraminer A name given to a particular form of the grape variety *traminer*. German *gewürz* denotes literally 'spice', but in fact the main attribute of the white wines made from the grape is a perfumed quality: the most commonly invoked comparisons are with rose petals and with lychees. It produces its finest wines in Alsace, where its name appears on labels in the French form *gewurztraminer*, without the umlaut.

ghee The Hindi term for semi-fluid clarified butter. Made from cows'-milk or buffalo-milk butter, it is a main source of fat in Indian cookery (although by no means the only one; vegetable oil is also widely used). The word comes from Sanskrit *ghritá*, a derivative of the verb *ghri* 'to sprinkle', and may be related to Middle Irish *gert* 'milk'.

gherkin Gherkins are first encountered in English in the pages of Samuel Pepys's diary: in the entry for 1 December 1661 he notes: 'We opened . . . the glass of girkins . . . which are rare things.' The word for these miniature pickled cucumbers has a particularly involved history. English borrowed it from an assumed (but not actually recorded) early modern Dutch **gurkkijn*, which was a diminutive form of *gurk*. Somehow or other, Dutch had acquired this word from a Slavic language (probably Polish *ogurek*), but Slavic had in turn got it from medieval Greek *angoúrion* (the French term for 'gherkin' used to be *angourie*, but *cornichon* is now generally used). This may have come from classical Greek *ágouros* 'youth'—in which case *gherkin* would mean etymologically something like 'little unripe one'.

'The Gherkin' is a nickname bestowed by Londoners on the glass-clad bullet-shaped tower office block officially known as the 30 St Mary Axe Tower, which was erected in the City to the design of Norman Foster in 2002–3. Its resemblance to a gherkin stops short of curling to one side.

giblets The edible internal organs of poultry, including the heart, liver, kidneys, and gizzard. Historically the term has also been taken to include various extraneous external bits, such as wingtips and feet, but that is no longer current usage. The word comes from Old French *gibelet* 'game stew', a derivative of *gibier* 'game', and when it first entered English in the fourteenth century it seems to have been used solely in the sense 'unessential appendage': John de Trevisa, for instance, in his translation of Ranulph Higden's *Polychronicon* (1387), writes 'They put no giblet [rendering Latin *appendicia*] to the hours of God's service.' But this was presumably just a metaphorical extension of the underlying culinary meaning, which first surfaces in English in the sixteenth century, in an idiomatic expression 'set the hare's head against the goose giblets', meaning 'use one thing as a set-off to another'. Giblets were once highly prized in Britain as food, as they still are in France (Henry Fielding in his *Grub Street Opera* (1731) warns 'take particular care of the giblets, they bear a very good price in the market'), but today, if not consigned immediately to the rubbish bin in their neat plastic packet, they are usually reserved for the stockpot.

Gibson A cocktail consisting of gin and vermouth garnished with a cocktail onion: in effect, a martini with an onion. The name is first recorded in 1930, at the height of the cocktail age, but the identity of the original Gibson has not been preserved. It may have been Charles Dana Gibson (1867–1944), the American artist and illustrator who inspired the fashionable 'Gibson girl' at the turn of the twentieth century.

gigot A gigot is the hind leg of a meat animal—in current usage, French as well as English, restricted to lamb, but formerly used also for veal, venison, etc.: 'Turkeys and hens we had roasted; a gigget of young goat,' Richard Ligon, *A True History of Barbadoes* (1657). English borrowed the word in the early sixteenth century from French *gigot*, a diminutive form of the dialectal *gigue* 'leg', which was derived from the verb *giguer* 'to hop, jump'.

gimlet A cocktail made from gin or vodka with lime juice. It originated in the US in the great days of cocktails, the 1920s. It was presumably named for its penetrating quality (although a no doubt apocryphal story has been told of a Royal Naval surgeon named T. O. Gimlette who in the 1870s came up with the idea of mixing the sailors' compulsory lime-juice ration with gin, and it has also been suggested that the drink was named after the implement used in former times to puncture kegs of lime juice).

gin A colourless to pale straw-coloured alcoholic drink made from grain or molasses spirit and flavoured with juniper berries and a variety of herbs and spices. It was first made in Holland in the late sixteenth century, and the Dutch named it *genever*, a word borrowed from Old French *genevre* 'juniper'. English soldiers, sailors, and merchants soon brought it across the Channel from the Low Countries, and adapted its slightly unusual name to a word they were more familiar with, *Geneva* (the Swiss town). This was a fairly highly flavoured aromatic drink still produced to this day in the Netherlands, although now in English it is more usually referred to as *Hollands gin*, *Hollands*, or just plain *Dutch gin*, than as *geneva*; it is usually sold in stone bottles, and drunk neat. It caught on very quickly in England, and between 1690 and 1727 annual consumption soared from half a million to five million gallons. It was around this time that the abbreviated version of the name *geneva* appeared: *gin*. The first record of it in print comes from 1714: 'The infamous liquor, the name of which deriv'd from Juniper-Berries in Dutch, is now, by frequent use . . . from a word of middling length shrunk into a Monosyllable, Intoxicating Gin' (Bernard Mandeville, *Fable of the Bees*). And gin was indeed now running riot in England, being downed by the poor in such quantities that it led to a national malaise. Successive Gin Acts in the 1730s and 1740s did nothing to cure it. In London alone twenty million gallons per year were being distilled in the late 1740s, and so cheap was it that in the famous phrase you could get 'drunk for a penny, dead drunk for tuppence'. The squalor and degradation that resulted were memorably depicted by William Hogarth in his engraving *Gin Lane*. However, more realistic taxation and better supervision of distillation in the 1750s gradually eased the problem. One of the results of the higher production standards was a less coarse, more subtle type of gin, originally made in London, and now generically known as *London gin*. It is drier and less assertively flavoured than Dutch gin, and is usually used as the basis of mixed drinks rather than consumed neat. Its most familiar present-day companion is of course tonic water, but the combination of gin and tonic (or *G and T* for short) is not in fact recorded before the 1930s. A much older partnership is gin and bitters, whose modern descendant is *pink gin*, made with angostura bitters. And of course gin served as the basis of many of the novel concoctions of the Cocktail Age in the 1920s and 1930s: horse's necks, white ladies, gimlets, and so on. The other type of British gin is *Plymouth gin*, which is fuller in flavour than London gin.

The derogatory term *gin palace* for an ostentatiously decorated pub seems to have originated in the 1830s. Its application to luxurious motor cruisers is a much more recent development.

gin and it An abbreviation for 'gin and Italian vermouth', a mixed drink popular between the 1930s and 1960s.

ginger So complex is the linguistic history of *ginger* that A. S. C. Ross (formulator of U and non-U) wrote an 74-page monograph on it. It goes back ultimately to a Sanskrit word *srnga-veram*, literally 'horn-body', a reference to the branching antler-shape of its root. The name has been borrowed in a bewildering array of forms into most languages in the world in the course of the millennia, but suffice it to say that the immediate source of the versions in most western European languages is Greek *ziggiberis*. This gave Latin *zingiber*, later *gingiber*, which was borrowed into Old English as *gingifer*.

As a spice, ginger is common in all of tropical Asia, and it was early exported to Europe (the Roman cookery writer Apicius refers to it, and Pliny gives a recipe for cooking beaver's tail with it). In medieval times three main types were recognized: beledi ginger and Quilon ginger (or 'columbine'), both from India, and ginger from Mecca. It was then a common spice, used with about equal frequency to pepper, but over the centuries it has rather lost ground in Britain. It has been retained in powdered form for use in cakes and biscuits, and its crystallized root (*stem ginger*) makes a regular appearance at Christmas, but the fresh root (*green ginger*) has up until recently been regarded as an Oriental oddity (slightly ironically, since the best comes from Jamaica), and is only now regaining ground with the explosion of interest in Asian food.

Ginger's pungency has long made it synonymous with truculent vigour. Benjamin Disraeli was one of the first to use *ginger up* in print: 'Whether they were gingered up by the articles in the "Times" or not I can't say' (1849)—the expression may derive from the practice of putting a piece of ginger into a horse's anus to make it buck its ideas up—and the *ginger group* first appeared in the 1950s.

The word's application to the colour of hair is first recorded in East Anglian dialect of the early nineteenth century, but by the middle of the century it had become common enough for Dickens to take it up in *Our Mutual Friend* (1865): 'mature young gentleman with too much ginger in his whiskers'. To begin with the reference was evidently to the orangey-brown colour of preserved ginger, but over the years *ginger* has come to be used over the whole spectrum of red-headedness.

gingerbread The cakelike consistency of gingerbread bears little resemblance to bread, so it comes as no surpirise that *gingerbread* has no etymological connection with *bread*. It was originally, in the thirteenth century, *gingebras*, a word borrowed from Old French which meant 'preserved ginger'. But by the mid-fourteenth century, through the process known as folk etymology (the substitution of a more familiar for a less familiar form), *-bread* had begun to replace *-bras*, and it was only a matter of time before sense followed form. One of the earliest known recipes for it, in the early fifteenth-century cookery book *Good Cookery*, directs that it be made with breadcrumbs boiled in honey with ginger and other spices. This is the lineal ancestor of the modern soft cakelike gingerbread in which treacle has replaced honey. It is made either in a raised cake shape or in flat biscuits, which are commonly baked in fanciful shapes, such as people (*gingerbread men*) or animals. In former times these would be decorated with gold leaf—hence the expression 'take the gilt off the gingerbread' (not recorded before the late nineteenth century).

ginger nut In the eighteenth century, sweet ginger-flavoured biscuits were known as *gingerbread nuts* ('We beg the receipt of your gingerbread nuts,' wrote Joseph Jekyll in a letter dated 1775). Around the middle of the nineteenth century, however, *gingerbread nut* was superseded by *ginger nut*. The element *nut* presumably refers to the biscuits' smallness and roundness (ginger nuts seem originally to have been smaller than their twenty-first-century descendants). It also appears in *spice nut*, a now obsolete synonym for *ginger* *nut* ('to induce you to purchase half a pound of the real spice nuts,' Charles Dickens, *Sketches by Boz* (1836)), and of course in *doughnut*. The nearest American equivalent (thinner and crisper) is called a *ginger snap*.

ginseng The forked aromatic root of a Chinese plant of the ivy family that is dried and used in various traditional remedies and tonics. It is said to have the power of prolonging life. This and other supposed properties have given it a following in the West since at least the eighteenth century: 'I took some of the tincture of ginseng,' Tobias Smollett, *Humphry Clinker* (1771). The word itself comes from Mandarin Chinese *rén shen* (in the older Wade-Giles transcription *jen-shen*); *rén* means 'man' (presumably, like *mandrake*, an allusion to the manlike shape of the forked root) and *shen* is the Chinese word for 'ginseng'.

girdle cake An alternative name for a drop scone: a small thick pancake baked on a heated flat metal plate. The term (first recorded in 1802) comes from Scotland and northern England, where such a plate is a *girdle*. That is a metathesized version of *griddle*, and accordingly in the rest of England the pancake is a *griddle cake* (first recorded in 1783).

girolle The usual French term for the yellow trumpet-shaped mushroom generally known in English as the *chanterelle*. As its culinary use in Britain increases, so does the word *girolle* come increasingly into play in English to name it.

gjetost Gjetost, or *geitost*, is a Norwegian cheese made from the whey of goats' milk (Norwegian *gjet* or *geit* means 'goat', *ost* means 'cheese'). The whey is boiled down to a solid brown mass which is fairly sweet.

Glamorgan sausage A meatless skinless Welsh sausage of which the main ingredients are cheese (typically Caerphilly or Cheddar) and leeks (or spring onions). Jane Grigson (*Observer Guide to British Cooking*, 1984) quotes George Borrow: 'The breakfast was delicious, consisting of excellent tea, buttered toast, and Glamorgan sausages, which I really think are not a whit inferior to those of Epping' (*Wild Wales*, 1862)—Epping sausages were skinless but contained meat. The meatlessness recalls another cheesy Welsh simulacrum of meat, Welsh rabbit.

glass noodles Extremely thin noodles, used in East Asian cooking. They are white in colour, but turn transparent when cooked, whence their name (and its main alternative *cellophane noodles*). Their commonest Chinese names are *fěn sī*, literally 'powder thread', and *dōng fěn*, literally 'winter powder' ('powder' probably refers to the starch from which the noodles are made, which is usually obtained from mung beans). The English term is first recorded in the late 1970s. Another alternative English name is *Chinese vermicelli*.

globe artichoke A term coined in the mid-nineteenth century to distinguish the edible thistle, original owner of the name *artichoke*, from the Jerusalem artichoke (*see* ARTICHOKE). It is a reference to the spherical mass formed by the edible bracts surrounding the immature flower head.

glögg Glögg (also spelled *glogg* in English) is a Scandinavian winter warmer—a hot punch containing red wine, brandy, and sugar, and typically garnished with almonds, raisins, and orange peel. The word is a derivative of the Swedish verb *glödga* 'to burn' (a relative of English *glow*).

glühwein The German version of 'mulled wine'. The word means 'glow-wine'.

gnocchi Small Italian dumplings made either from flour, semolina, or potato starch. They can be cooked in a variety of ways—boiled, baked, or grilled—*gnocchi alla romana*, for instance, is baked in the oven with butter and Parmesan cheese. *Gnocchi* is the plural of *gnocchio*, which is an alteration of *nocchio* 'knot in wood, lump', perhaps of Germanic origin. The dish is first mentioned in an English cookery book in 1891, in A. B. Marshall's *Larger Cookery Book of Extra Recipes*.

gobstopper This hard globular sweet—large enough to inhibit conversation until sucked to manageable proportions—was a great favourite amongst British schoolboys between the wars, but since the 1950s seems to have gone into something of a decline. The first reference to it in print comes in Walter de la Mare's anthology of verse for children, *Come Hither* (1928).

goji berry Goji berries, or *gogi berries*, are the bright red berries of the goji plant, which is a variety of the wolfberry. They have a high vitamin content, and are widely cultivated in China (their name is a version of Chinese *gouqi*). They were introduced to the West from Taiwan in the late 1990s, and quickly established a reputation as the latest must-eat wonder health food, panacea, and preserver of life: 'One of my favourite stories is the legend of . . . a Chinese man who faithfully ate gojis and lived to the ripe old age of 252,' Heidi Swanson, *Super Natural Cooking* (2007).

golden berry A name sometimes applied to the *physalis* or Cape gooseberry, particularly by grocers and the producers of tinned fruits. It describes accurately enough the colour of the pale orange fruit inside its calyx. It is first recorded in 1951.

Golden Delicious A variety of dessert apple that appeared in America around 1900. It has yellowish-green skin and flesh that is often described as bland or insipid ('delicious' can seem a decided misnomer). It is a heavy cropper, which made it popular with twentieth-century growers, and it became a focus of obloquy for those who deplored the crowding out of traditional varieties of apple by a few supermarket-friendly types.

golden syrup The term *golden syrup* first turns up in the mid-nineteenth century, applied to the thick sticky liquid obtained as a by-product of boiling down sugar-cane syrup to produce sugar. Nowadays, however, most golden syrup is made by turning refined sugar—usually beet sugar—back into a liquid and adding a little original sugar syrup for colour.

Golden syrup is not familiar to Americans, who do not use it; their nearest equivalent is perhaps corn syrup. The British, meanwhile, often refer to it as *treacle*, although technically treacle is made only from sugar-cane syrup.

goldwasser A liqueur originally made in Danzig, East Prussia (now Gdańsk, Poland). It is typically flavoured with caraway, but its most immediately obvious characteristic is the small particles of gold leaf suspended in it, which float around like a snowstorm toy when the bottle is shaken (they are quite harmless to the drinker). The German name means 'goldwater'.

goober See PEANUT.

good King Henry A European plant of the goosefoot family with large pointed dark green edible leaves that can be used like spinach, cooked or raw. Its name dates back at least to the late sixteenth century, when it was plain *good Henry*. This had equivalents in other languages, such as German *der gute Heinrich* and French *bon-Henri*, and it was rendered into medieval Latin as *Bonus Henricus*. German seems a likely starting point for this nexus, as it has several other *Heinrich*-based plant names (such as *der böse Heinrich* 'wicked Henry' and *der stolze Heinrich* 'proud Henry'). The English version had laid claim to royal status

before the end of the sixteenth century, no doubt as an affectionate nod
to the late King Henry VIII (1491–1547).

gooseberry Gooseberries have long been more popular in Britain than
elsewhere. There are records of their cultivation as early as the thirteenth
century, and by the sixteenth century gooseberry sauce had become
established as a favourite accompaniment to mackerel (this is the only
use to which the French deign to put the fruit, as witness their name for
it, *groseille à maquereau*). Then in the early eighteenth century comes
the first appearance of that quintessential English pudding, gooseberry
fool—according to Mrs Beeton 'a very old-fashioned and homely dish'
but 'when well made, very delicious, and if properly sweetened, a very

suitable preparation for children'. Gooseberry growing became quite a fad in the Midlands
and the North of England in the nineteenth century, and a few of the annual competitive
gooseberry shows of that era survive today; but overall, with the increasing importation of
luscious exotic fruits, the sourish gooseberry has undergone a decline in popularity since
the nineteenth century.

The origin of its name is far from clear. The fact that in Tudor and Elizabethan times
gooseberries were frequently used in stuffing geese makes it more likely than not that the
word is simply a compound of *goose* and *berry* (it first appeared in print in 1532). However,
it is also possible that it may have been an adapation of French *groseille*, which was
certainly borrowed into English in the 1500s and survived for several centuries, in Scotland
and northern England as *groser* or *groset* and in other local areas as *gozell*. What does seem
clear is that before the name *gooseberry* was adopted, the fruit was called *thevethorn*
(a word applied originally, in Anglo-Saxon times, to the 'bramble'), and that *thevethorn*
survived dialectally well into the nineteenth century, both as *theabe*, *thepe*, and *thape* in
Scotland, Yorkshire, and East Anglia and in the slightly altered forms *feaberry* and *dayberry*.

The humorous alternative name *goosegog* seems to have started life as yet another
dialectal variant: it is first recorded in glossaries of East Anglian words in the early
nineteenth century. The origin of *gog* is if anything even more obscure than that of
gooseberry, although there are records of a presumably related word, *horse-gog*, used
dialectally for various sorts of plum. Australian slang *goog* 'egg' and dated American slang
gogs 'spectacles' are probably adapted from *goosegog* rather than going back to a previous
common ancestor.

The role of the *gooseberry* as an embarrassingly superfluous third person spoiling the fun
of a courting couple, as in 'play gooseberry' (first recorded in a glossary of Devonshire
dialect words in 1837), perhaps contains some reference to the unwelcome tartness of
gooseberries, although there may alternatively be a connection with *gooseberry-picker*, a
nineteenth-century euphemism for 'chaperone' (perhaps originally someone sent along to
keep an eye on a young couple on the pretext of gathering gooseberries). The notion
of concealing the realities of childbirth from inquisitive children by saying that babies
are found under gooseberry bushes is much more recent; it does not appear in print
before 1944.

goose skirt An alternative name for a flank steak (*see* FLANK). *Goose* may have been
suggested by the muscle fibres of the steak, which somewhat resemble the texture of
goose meat. *See also* SKIRT.

Goosnargh cake A type of shortbread made with minimal sugar and flavoured with
caraway seeds. Its name comes from the village of Goosnargh in Lancashire to the north of
Preston, where it achieved great popularity in the nineteenth century. The village is also
famous for its local breed of duck, a cross between the Aylesbury and the Peking. Its profile

was considerably raised at the end of the twentieth century by its espousal by the local (and internationally renowned) chef Paul Heathcote.

gordita A type of small thick tortilla which serves as a base for various toppings, such as beans, meat, chorizo, or salsa. Its name in Mexican Spanish means 'little fat girl'.

Gorgonzola A sharp-flavoured blue-veined creamy Italian cows'-milk cheese. Its rather alarming name comes from nothing more fierce than the village of Gorgonzola, near Milan, where it was first made. Legend has it that it originally acquired its blue veins accidentally after being stored longer than intended in local innkeepers' cellars.

gorp An alternative informal American term for TRAIL MIX. It is first recorded in 1968, but its origins are unknown.

Gouda Gouda is a town to the northeast of Rotterdam that has given its name to one of the two best known of Dutch cheeses. Pale yellow, mild in flavour, and with holes of various sizes, it is produced in a flat round shape and often given a protective coating of wax. It dates from the thirteenth century.

gougère A savoury French choux pastry containing cheese, such as Gruyère or Emmental. It is usually baked in a ring, but sometimes also in individual portions. It is a particular speciality of Burgundy.

goujon In French cuisine, a goujon is a narrow boned strip of fish, typically sole, that is deep-fried. The French word means literally 'gudgeon', which is the name of a small freshwater fish.

goulash This rich Hungarian meat stew seems not to have impinged on the British consciousness until the middle of the nineteenth century (it is first quoted in English in a letter from the Crown Princess of Prussia, 1866). The classic goulash is made of beef (or veal, pork, or lamb) with lots of onions—generally the same amount of onions as meat—bulked out with potatoes, seasoned generously with paprika, and finished off with a slick of sour cream.

Terminologically, though, things are not so straightforward. In Hungary itself, the dish is called either *paprikás* (*see* PAPRIKASH), if the sour cream has been added, or *pörkölt* (a derivative of the verb *pörköl* 'to singe'), if it has not. Hungarian *gulyás* means literally 'herdsman', and in Hungary it is mainly applied to a soup (in full *gulyás leves* 'herdsman's soup'), a thick meat broth with the characteristic flavouring of onions and paprika and often a little cumin. Reduce the liquid content and add potatoes and you have the stew for which English has co-opted the name *goulash*.

In the 1920s bridge players hijacked the word, applying it to the practice of redealing unshuffled cards, which produces rather odd hands (the notion behind this seems to be that goulash, like hash, is thought of as a confused or undifferentiated mixture).

graham In the US, the term *graham* designates bread, biscuits, etc. made from wholemeal flour: 'It's got graham crackers instead of crust,' John Steinbeck, *The Wayward Bus* (1947). It comes from the name of Dr Sylvester Graham (1794–1851), an American physician who expounded various theories of dietary reform. He was an ardent advocate of vegetarianism (in mid-nineteenth-century America vegetarianism was named *Grahamism* after him), and laid great emphasis on the importance of eating flour made from the whole unrefined grain, including particularly the bran. His old house in Northampton, Massachusetts, is today a health-food restaurant.

grains of paradise The aromatic pungent seeds of a tall West African plant of the ginger family. They resemble those of cardamom, and are often used as a cardamom-substitute. The name is first recorded in the fourteenth century, and may have originated as a translation of French *graines de paradis*. Other terms for the spice are *Guinea grains* and *malaguetta*.

gram An alternative name for the chickpea, now little used except in the expression *gram flour*, a flour made from chickpeas used particularly in India and the Middle East. The word was borrowed in the eighteenth century from Portuguese *grão* (then often spelled *gram*), a descendant of Latin *grānum* 'grain, seed'.

grana An Italian term for a type of hard cows'-milk cheese with a somewhat granular texture (the word means 'grain') that makes it suitable for grating. It is standardly made in the form of a large drum. The most highly renowned example is *Parmigiano Reggiano* (*see* PARMESAN), but *grana Padano* from Lombardy (*Padano* means 'of the Po (Valley)'), which has a creamier, crumblier texture than Parmesan (and is cheaper), also has its adherents.

granadilla *See* PASSION FRUIT.

Grand Marnier A proprietary French brandy-based liqueur flavoured with orange. Invented in 1880, its name is that of its manufacturers, Marnier-Lapostolle.

granita A type of Italian water ice or sorbet whose texture of ice crystals is slightly more granular than that of the standard sorbet (hence the name, which means 'grained' or 'granular'). Mark Twain first recorded it in English in his *Innocents Abroad* (1869): 'people at small tables [in Venice] . . . smoking and taking *granita* (a first cousin to ice-cream)'. It soon caught on in America to such an extent that its name was Anglicized to *granite* (the name of the rock *granite* comes from the related Italian *granito*): 'Granites . . . must be frozen without beating, or even much stirring, as the design is to have a rough, icy substance', *New York Tribune* (1887).

Granny Smith A green-skinned crisp-fleshed variety of dessert apple, developed in Australia in the late nineteenth century. Its name commemorates 'Granny' Smith, the nickname of Maria Ann Smith (died 1870), the Australian gardener who first grew it, at Eastwood, Sydney.

granola A breakfast food consisting of a mixture of oats (and sometimes other grains) with nuts and dried fruits, usually eaten with milk or yoghurt. The origins of its name can be traced back to the US in the early 1860s, when Dr James C. Jackson, director of a health spa in New York State, developed a breakfast cereal made from slow-baked wholemeal flour and water ground up small, which he called 'Granula' (from late Latin *granula* 'small grain'). A little over a decade later J. H. Kellogg marketed a similar cereal under the same name. The makers of the original naturally objected, so Kellogg changed the name to 'Granola' (using a popular American suffix for commercial products, *-ola*). The cereal was a success, but over time it was eclipsed by cornflakes, and the trademark lapsed. It was revived in the 1970s as a generic term when the grain/nut/fruit mix became popular (not least because of its heavily promoted healthiness), and in the early twenty-first century showed signs of making inroads into the standard British English term *muesli* (the significant difference between the two foods is that granola is usually baked as part of its manufacturing process, whereas muesli is not). And, like *muesli*, it has come to be used as patronizing shorthand for liberal or Green political views or lifestyles, stereotypically held by people who eat health foods: 'In the American media mind, we've made anti-globalization out to be a granola sort of thing,' *New York Magazine* (2001).

grape It was perhaps to be expected that in Britain, never more than a marginal grower of grapes even in the most favourable climatic periods, the terms for the fruit current in more southerly parts of Europe did not catch on. In the Old English period the grape was known as *winberige*, literally 'wineberry', and *grape* represents a thirteenth-century borrowing of Old French *grape* 'bunch of grapes' (this was a back-formation from the verb *graper* 'to gather grapes with a vine-hook', which in turn was derived from the noun *grape* 'hook', a relative of English *grapnel*). This is not an isolated semantic development, however; in fact, the majority of the surprisingly diversified range of words for 'grape' in the European languages originally meant 'bunch': French *raisin* (source of English *raisin*) came from Latin *racemus* 'bunch of grapes' (from which English gets *raceme*); German *traube*, Dutch *druif*, Swedish *druva*, and Danish *drue* go back to a Germanic source which meant 'clump, heap, etc.'; Rumanian *strugure* was to begin with a 'bunch', as were Lithuanian *keke* and Latvian *k'ekars*; and the *-grono* of Polish *winogrono* signifies 'bunch, cluster'. The only major exceptions are Italian and Spanish *uva*, descendants of Latin *ūva*, which probably originally meant 'berry', and Russian *vinograd*, literally 'vineyard'.

The use of *grapevine* for the 'route by which rumour is conveyed' goes back to mid-nineteenth-century America, where it was also applied to the 'rumour' itself.

grapefruit The grapefruit has, of course, no direct connection with grapes; it was named from the way it hangs in clusters, like bunches of grapes. The fruit of the *Citrus paradisi*, it is a comparatively recent addition to the Western fruit bowl; much more recent than, for example, the related pomelo, of which it was once thought to be a hybrid or sport. The first reference to it comes in 1814, in John Lunan's *Hortus Jamaicensis*, and it was not produced in commercial quantities until the 1880s, in Florida. When the relevant volume of the *Oxford English Dictionary* was published, in 1900, it could still refer to *grapefruit* as an American word for a small variety of pomelo, but in the *Daily Chronicle* (1904) we read that the grapefruit 'is gradually growing in popularity in England', and references in the 1926–7 Army and Navy Stores catalogue to such recondite items of cutlery as grapefruit knives, grapefruit spoons, and grapefruit forks suggest that by then the social conventions for consuming grapefruit (slicing it through the middle and extracting the half segments, and probably also regarding it as an hors d'oeuvre rather than as a dessert dish—a role shared among fruit only by the melon) had already solidified.

Grape-Nuts The US proprietary name (registered in 1898 by the Postum Cereal Company) for a breakfast cereal made from wheat in the form of small crisp grains. Its inventor, Charles W. Post, chose the name because he thought, mistakenly, that the cereal contained dextrose, which at that time was widely known as *grape sugar*.

grappa An Italian alcoholic spirit distilled from the juice extracted from skins, pips, and other residue left after the pressing of wine grapes. It is the Italian version of *marc*. The word means 'grape-stalk' in Italian.

grasshopper A cocktail consisting of equal amounts of green crème de menthe, white (i.e. colourless) crème de cacao, and cream, the overall effect being suitably green. The so-called 'flying grasshopper' substitutes white crème de menthe for the crème de cacao and (a rather larger amount of) vodka for the cream.

grass jelly Grass jelly, or *leaf jelly*, is a jellylike dessert popular in China and Southeast Asia that is made by boiling the stems of a plant of the mint family. Its Chinese name is *xian cao*.

gratin Nowadays, *gratin* is commonly applied to a dish with a topping of grilled grated cheese—a usage deplored by purists who insist that it is the crisply baked topping (which could be of breadcrumbs as well as cheese) that is the criterion of the *gratin*. In fact, though, there need not be any substance on top of the gratin, simply the crisped surface of the main ingredient (the most celebrated gratin, for instance, the *gratin dauphinois*, a dish of sliced potatoes baked in cream, classically has no additional topping—it originated in the Dauphiné, a region of southeastern France famous for its cream). The French word *gratin* originated as a derivative of the verb *grater* 'to grate', but it referred not to the grating of cheese or any other substance to make a topping, but to the scraping of the burnt crispy bits from the bottom of the pan.

gravlax A Scandinavian dish consisting of salmon marinated with dill. It originated as a pre-refrigeration method of preservation in which the raw fish was sprinkled with salt and dill and then buried in the ground (*grav* is Swedish for 'grave' or 'pit') for a period varying from a few days to, for a highly fermented result, as much as three months. The modern way is to keep the fish marinating in the fridge for a maximum of three days; it is then scraped free of its salt and dill, sliced thinly, and served in the manner of smoked salmon, usually with a mustard sauce (*gravlaxsas*). The verb *grava* has evolved in Swedish, meaning 'to preserve raw', and its past participle *gravad* is applied not just to salmon (*gravad lax* is an alternative term for *gravlax*, *lax* being Swedish for 'salmon'—*compare* LOX): *gravad makrel*, for example, is a cheap alternative.

gravy The gravy that was eaten in the fourteenth century bears little resemblance to the sludgy brown liquid, as likely as not made from stock cubes or freeze-dried gravy granules, usually served up in Britain at the beginning of the twenty-first century. It was a sort of sauce or dressing for white meat or fish, and was made from their broth with some sort of thickening agent, typically ground almonds, and spices (the name itself appears to be of Old French origin, coming either from *graine* 'meat', or from *grané*, an adjective derived from *grain* in the sense 'grain of spice', with in either case a misreading of *n* for *u* or *v* in early manuscripts; the former etymology would relate it to *grenade* or *grenadine*, now obsolete terms for small stuffed fillets of veal or poultry). The *Forme of Cury*, a late fourteenth-century cookery book, gives a recipe for oysters in gravy: 'Shell the blanched oysters and cook them in wine and in their own broth; strain the broth through a cloth. Take blanched almonds; grind them and mix them up with the same broth, and mix it with rice flour and put the oysters in. Put in powdered ginger, sugar, mace, and salt'. A more elaborate version of the sauce, known as *gravy enforced*, was enriched with boiled egg yolks and cheese, while the inferior *gravy bastard* seems to have been made with breadcrumbs rather than ground almonds.

The common denominator between this and what we now call 'gravy' is the juice given off by meat in cooking; and the critical change between obtaining this in the form of broth, from boiling the meat, and in the form of juices produced by roasting, seems to have taken place in the sixteenth century. In 1615 we find George Chapman writing, in his translation of the *Odyssey*: 'There are now at fire two breasts of goat: both which let Law set down before the man . . . with all their fat and gravy.' In the seventeenth century, the practice was to make cuts in a joint when it was part-roasted, to allow the juices to escape (a special press was even invented, to squeeze them out). Later, it became more usual to make gravy separately from a different, inferior cut of meat—typically from *gravy beef*, part of the leg used for that purpose (Hannah Glasse (1747) has a recipe which calls for laying 'a pound of gravy beef over your chickens').

Nowadays, as the eating public becomes increasingly familiar with a greater variety of sauces, the Great British Gravy, traditional lubricant of meat and two veg, seems démodé.

But its metaphorical use for 'something desirable, easily or unexpectedly obtained' (probably derived from gravy's being regarded as something 'additional' to the food it accompanies) arose as recently as the early years of the twentieth century (*gravy train* is first recorded in 1927).

Greek coffee *See* TURKISH COFFEE.

Greek salad A salad consisting of tomatoes, cucumbers, olives, and feta cheese, often enlivened with an assortment of herbs. Its Greek name is *khōriattikisalata*, which means 'country-Attic-salad' (Attica is the area round Athens).

green cheese The term *green cheese* has been used with various different applications over the centuries. Probably the earliest, dating back to the Middle Ages, is 'unripened or unmatured cheese', which relies on the use of *green* to mean 'young' or 'unripe'. However, it has also been used to refer to cheese made from skimmed milk or whey, and to cheese that is literally coloured green (typically with sage—*see* SAGE DERBY). It is not clear which of these is being invoked in the idea of the Moon being made of green cheese, which dates back at least to the early sixteenth century. The fact that belief in it is equated with naivety suggests that unripened cheese is being suggested as lunar material, but it could also be that the blurry marbling of sage cheese is held to resemble the Moon's surface seen from Earth.

green eggs and ham An American dish that is essentially ham and eggs coloured green—for example with basil oil or pesto, or simply with some sort of green food dye. Its profile was raised in 1960 when Dr Seuss published his simple reading primer called *Green Eggs and Ham*.

greengage A small green variety of plum. The *Hortus Collinsonianus* (1759) tells the story of its introduction into Britain: 'On Plums. *Mem*. I was on a visit to Sir William Gage, at Hengrave, near Bury [St Edmunds]: he was then near 70. He told me that he first brought over, from France, the *Grosse Reine Claude*, and introduced it into England; and in compliment to him the Plum was called the *Green Gage*; this was about the year 1725.' In the eighteenth century the element *gage* seems to have been generalized to any 'plum,' so that one could speak of *blue gages, purple gages*, etc. ('Plum; of the many sorts, the following are good: Green and blue gages, Fotheringham, etc.,' Charles Marshall, *Introduction to Gardening* (1796)); and the abbreviation *gage* for *greengage* is still heard, particularly in the greengrocery trade.

As the above passage mentions, in French the fruit is termed *reine-claude*. The name comes from Claude (1499–1524), the wife of King François I, who was keen on horticulture and encouraged its introduction into France from Italy.

greens The use of *greens* as a general term for the green parts of a plant (now obsolete) dates from the seventeenth century, but its application to otherwise unspecified leafy vegetables is an eighteenth-century development: 'fresh provisions . . . such as roots, greens, hogs, and fowls,' Daniel Defoe, *A New Voyage Round the World* (1725). A number of plants have hidden behind the name over the centuries. In southern England, at any rate, it has traditionally been applied to various manifestations of the cabbage family—the upper leaves of the brussels sprout (*brussel tops*) and young cabbages which have failed to form a heart (*spring greens*)—but there are many regional variations, and in America the term usually refers to such items as spinach and beet leaves. Whatever the word stands for, however, greens have the reputation of being good for you but unpalatable, of being *par excellence* the foodstuff with which mothers cajole and threaten their offspring: 'If you don't eat up your greens, you won't get any pudding!' There are signs of rehabilitation, though: with the vastly increasing range of leafy salad vegetables over the past couple of decades, *greens* is being more and more pressed into service as a cover term for them.

green tea Tea made from unfermented leaves that is pale in colour and slightly bitter in flavour. It is produced mainly in China and Japan. According to legend it was discovered in 2737 BC by the Chinese Emperor Shen Nung when tea leaves accidentally fell into the water he was boiling to drink. It comes in numerous varieties, of which one of the best known is gunpowder. Its reputation as a health-giving beverage has considerably increased its popularity in the West in recent decades. In Japan it is used for the tea ceremony. As a term *green tea*, first recorded in 1704, contrasts explicitly with *black tea* and *oolong*.

gremolada Gremolada, or *gremolata*, is a traditional accompaniment to the Italian dish *osso bucco*, consisting of a mixture of chopped parsley, garlic and grated lemon peel. The word may be a derivative of the verb *gremire* 'to stuff'.

grenache A red wine-producing grape that is the world's second most widely planted variety. It may have originated in northern Spain, where it is known as the *garnacha* and forms an important part of the blend for the wines of Priorat and Rioja, but it has also been claimed that it was brought to Spain from Sardinia. It certainly spread from Spain to southern France, where it is a mainstay of Côtes du Rhône and one of the permitted varieties for Châteauneuf-du-Pape, and it is also responsible for much of southern France's rosé. It is also widely grown in Australia. Its French name is an alteration of Spanish *garnacha*, and that in turn may have come from *vernaccia*, the name given to any of a range of Italian grape varieties (*see* VERNACCIA).

grenadine A sweet, thick, deep red syrup made from pomegranates (and, nowadays, various other things). It is used in cocktails and other mixed drinks, and also as a drink on its own, well diluted with water (known in France as a *grenadine*). The word comes from French, where it was originally a derivative of *grenade* 'pomegranate'.

gribiche *Sauce gribiche* is essentially a version of mayonnaise in which the raw egg yolk is replaced by the pounded yolk of a hard-boiled egg. Capers, herbs, and the chopped white of the egg are added to it, and in French cuisine it is standardly served with calf's head or cold fish. The origins of French *gribiche* are unknown.

griddle cake *See* GIRDLE CAKE.

grinder An alternative term for a SUBMARINE SANDWICH. First recorded in 1954, it is mainly used in New England, but it also crops up further afield in the US, including Ohio and California. Its origins are unclear, but given that it is often applied to a heated or toasted sandwich, it could simply refer to the masticatory effort needed to eat it.

griskin An antique British term for the lean part of the loin of a bacon pig, redolent of the days when country folk kept a pig and relied on its cured meat throughout the year. First recorded towards the end of the seventeenth century, it was probably based on *grice*, an obsolete word for a young pig (from Old Norse *gríss*), with the diminutive suffix -*kin*.

grissini Long thin sticks of crisply baked bread, familiar as pre-meal nibbles to anyone who has ever eaten in an Italian restaurant. The singular form of the Italian word is *grissino*, which came from a Piedmontese dialect term deriving ultimately from *ghersa* 'file, line'. It made its way into English in the mid-nineteenth century: 'Crisp grissins . . . they make so

162 | **grits**

pleasant a noise between the teeth', Edward Bulwer-Lytton, *My Novel* (1851). The vernacular term is *breadstick*.

grits *See* HOMINY.

grog A naval beverage consisting approximately of one part rum to three parts water. The term comes from *Old Grog*, the nickname of the British admiral Edward Vernon (1684–1757), who in 1740 ordered that his men should be given diluted rather than full-strength rum to stop them getting drunk on duty (the nickname derived from Vernon's habit of wearing a cloak made from grogram, a coarse fabric). The success of his edict may be gauged by the fact that by the 1770s *groggy* had become a colloquial term for 'drunk'.

The Royal Navy's rum ration was abolished in 1970, but the word *grog* remains in use; indeed in Australia and New Zealand it has become a general term for 'alcoholic drink', and American English uses the expression *food and grog* for 'tavern fare'.

gros plant The name given in the Nantais region, towards the mouth of the river Loire, to a grape variety known elsewhere in France as *folle blanche*. It is also applied to the wine made from it locally, which is white, light, and often tooth-strippingly dry. It means literally 'large sapling'.

groundnut An alternative name—used by botanists rather than consumers—for the 'peanut'. Dating from the mid-eighteenth century, it alludes to the fact that its seedcase burrows down into the earth to ripen (it has nothing to do, despite the way the word is sometimes pronounced, with grinding nuts). Culinarily, the term is most commonly encountered in *groundnut oil*, a tasteless oil pressed from peanuts which is widely used in the catering industry and, in recent times, domestically, but it is probably forever tarred with the brush of the notorious Groundnut Scheme, an expensive but abortive plan set up by the British government in 1947 to grow peanuts in East Africa.

To American-speakers, the word *groundnut* denotes the small edible tuber of an American climbing plant, also of the pea family, the *Apios tuberosa*.

gruel A term for a thin porridge. Nowadays it is used to conjure up visions of a watery tasteless mixture served up to invalids (unable to stomach anything stronger) or prisoners (as a punishment), but originally it was not coloured by any such associations. It was borrowed in the fourteenth century from Old French *gruel*, which originally meant 'flour'. This in its turn went back to Vulgar Latin **grūtellum*, a diminutive form derived from prehistoric Germanic **grūt-* (to which English *groats* 'grain, especially as made into porridge' is closely related).

Gruyère A firm, pale yellow cows'-milk cheese with fairly small holes, produced in a wheel-shape. It originated in Switzerland in the twelfth century, in the town of Gruyères (to the east of Lausanne), but much of it is now made in France, where *Gruyère* is a cover-term for three distinct cheeses: Beaufort, Comté, and Emmental.

guacamole A Mexican dish consisting of puréed avocado, typically with onions, tomatoes, and seasonings, used as a dip or hors d'oeuvre. The name is a Mexican Spanish version of Nahuatl *ahuacamolli*, a compound of *ahuacatl* 'avocado' and *molli* 'sauce, stew'.

guard of honour A roasting joint of lamb consisting of two racks facing each other with the exposed rib-ends intersecting (suggesting the raised and intersecting swords of a literal guard of honour). *Compare* CROWN ROAST.

guards' pudding An English steamed pudding of which the main ingredients are breadcrumbs, eggs, butter, sugar, and jam (no flour). The provenance of the dish and its name has not been established, but given the popularity of nursery-style puddings in English male institutions, it is quite plausible that this one could have first seen the light of day in one of the messes of the Brigade of Guards.

guava The fruit of a tropical American tree of the eucalyptus family; it has yellow skin and sweet-sharp pink flesh. English readers first heard of it in the mid-sixteenth century, in Richard Eden's *Decades of the New World* (1555): 'They nourish a tree which they call *Guaiaua*, that beareth a fruit much resembling the kind of citrons which are commonly called lemons, of taste somewhat sharp mixed with sweetness.' Eden's spelling *guaiaua* was an early attempt at rendering Spanish *guayaba*, which came from one of the now extinct Arawakan languages of the Caribbean.

Gubbeen A rind-washed cows'-milk cheese that has been made by Tom and Giana Ferguson at Gubbeen Farm in County Cork, Ireland since 1979.

Guinea grains An alternative name for GRAINS OF PARADISE, first recorded in 1858. It reflects the fact that the spice was originally shipped to Europe from Guinea in West Africa (which in the late Middle Ages was often known as the 'Grain Coast').

gulab jamun An Indian sweetmeat made from flour, butter, and yoghurt, rolled into a little ball, fried, and soaked in syrup. Bengali *gulāb* means 'rose water', and *jāmun* means 'fruit'.

gumbo A thick soup—or thin stew, depending on your point of view—of the southern states of the US, whose characteristic ingredient is okra. (The original meaning of *gumbo* was 'okra', and it is still so used in American English. The word is of Bantu origin, and related to *ochinggombo*, the term for 'okra' in the Umbundu language of Angola; it was of course brought to America by Africans transported as slaves, and first appears in English at the start of the nineteenth century.) The mucilaginous okra pods give gumbo its distinctive smooth thickness, but the main flavour is provided by seafood—shrimps, oysters, etc.—by ham, or by chicken, or sometimes by a combination of these: J. F. Watson noted in 1805 that 'shrimps are much eaten here [in the Deep South]; also a dish called *gumbo*. This last is made of every eatable substance, and especially of those shrimps which can be caught at any time.'

The term *gumbo* is also applied to a mixture of French and various African languages spoken by blacks in some parts of Louisiana and the French West Indies, but this is probably a different word, derived from *nkombo*, meaning 'runaway slave' in the Bantu language of the Kongo people of Zaire.

gumdrop The use of a sweetened, usually fruit-flavoured gelatine mixture called *gum* as a basis for small hard sweets is first recorded in the early nineteenth century, but the term *gumdrop* for an individual sweet does not emerge until the middle of the century (the *North-West*, of Port Townsend, Washington, reported 'Candies, gum drops, mottoes' for sale in 1860).

The use of *goody gumdrops* as a childish alliterative exclamation of delight is first recorded in 1959: 'Buttered toast, and cherry cake, as well as Marmite. Goody, goody gumdrops', Nicolas Freeling, *Strike Out Where Not Applicable* (1967).

gungo pea The name used in the West Indies for a variety of pigeon pea with light-coloured seeds, and also more broadly as a synonym for *pigeon pea* itself. It is probably an alteration of the earlier *Congo pea* (first recorded in 1866), which reflects the fact that the legume was brought to the New World (presumably on slave ships) from the Congo, a territory of western central Africa.

gunpowder A type of green China tea in which the leaves are rolled up tightly into tiny balls so that it has a granular appearance, somewhat like gunpowder. The term is first recorded in 1771.

gyro A sandwich made with slices of spiced minced meat (typically lamb) cooked on a vertical spit, served with salad in pitta bread. Its name comes from modern Greek *guros* 'turning', and its use in English (dating from the 1970s) maps on to areas with significant numbers of Greek immigrants—the US and Australia—whereas British English has adopted that of its Turkish first cousin, *döner kebab*. It would appear that the Greeks did not acquire this 'turning kebab' (from the Turks) until the 1920s.

habanero The American English term (first recorded in 1972) for a SCOTCH BONNET pepper. In Spanish it means 'of Havana'.

haggis Haggis, nowadays the classic Scottish dish, consumed on Burns Night with its traditional accompaniment of bashed neeps (mashed swedes) or clapshot and whisky, was in fact widespread south of the Border up until the early eighteenth century. By 1771 Tobias Smollett could write, in *Humphrey Clinker*, 'I am not yet Scotchman enough to relish their singed sheep's-head and haggice', but against this dialect glossaries show that something called *haggis* was still eaten in country areas of England, such as Gloucestershire and Shropshire, in the nineteenth century.

The quintessential Scottish haggis, apostrophized by Burns as 'great chieftain o' the puddin'-race', consists typically of sheep's heart, liver, and lungs, cooked and then chopped up with onions, oatmeal, and seasonings and stuffed sausage-like into a sheep's stomach. The origin of its name (which is first recorded in the early fifteenth century) is something of an enigma. One explanation put forward is that it is the same word as *haggess*, a seventeenth-century term for 'magpie' (which came from Old French *agace* 'magpie'). Implausible as this might seem, it would mirror the possible derivation of *pie* 'baked pastry case with a filling' from *pie*, another archaic word for 'magpie', thought to be based on the idea that a pie contained a miscellaneous collection of (edible) odds and ends similar to that said to be assembled by the acquisitive magpie. On this view, the haggis would be named from its assortment of ingredients. Other candidates for its source, however, are the northern Middle English verb *haggen* 'to chop', and French *hachis*, from which English gets *hash*.

haloumi Haloumi, or *halumi*, is a mild salty Cypriot cheese made from goats', ewes', or cows' milk. A common way of serving it is to cut it in slices and fry it or grill it. It is widely encountered around the eastern Mediterranean, and its name is of Egyptian origin (in Coptic it was *ialom*).

halva Halva (or *halwa*) is an eastern Mediterranean sweet made from crushed sesame seeds and honey. The word comes, probably via Yiddish *halva* or Turkish *helva*, from Arabic *halwa*, which means literally 'sweetmeat'. English actually borrowed the Arabic form of the word as long ago as the seventeenth century, and it surfaced again in the form *halawi* in the nineteenth century, but twentieth-century Jewish, Turkish, and Greek immigration established *halva* as the standard English term.

ham In Anglo-Saxon times the word for the part of the leg at the back of the knee (from which we get *hamstring*), *ham* was later extended in meaning to 'thigh' generally, and in

the seventeenth century came to be applied to the thigh of an animal dried, salted, and often smoked for eating. Typically it is a pig's thigh, but mutton hams, venison hams, and even bear hams were common fare in the eighteenth and nineteenth centuries, and the French *jambon d'aile de canard* (literally 'duck-breast ham'; *see* GAMMON) beloved of 1980s nouvelle cuisine reminds us that the term need not necessarily be confined to 'thigh meat'—here, it is the method of preservation that is the criterion for applying the name.

In current British usage *ham* typically connotes preserved meat that has been cooked (usually by boiling, but also by baking) and is then eaten cold, but this is by no means the only use to which it can be put. In many cuisines it is eaten uncooked (Parma ham from Italy, for example, and Bayonne ham from France—in fact cured at Orthez, near Bayonne, in the southwest tip of France); and in the classic dish of ham and eggs, still eaten across the Atlantic, it is fried. Mrs Beeton gives a recipe for this, warning that 'if the ham be particularly hard and salt, it will be found an improvement to soak it for about 10 minutes in hot water, and then dry it in a cloth'. In *The Wind in the Willows* (1908) 'the good-natured mole, having cut some slices of ham, set the hedgehogs to fry it, and returned to his own breakfast'.

Ham meaning 'actor who goes over the top', incidentally, is short for *hamfatter*, 'bad actor', from the African American minstrel song 'The ham-fat man'.

hamburger The original hamburger was a German sausage called after the city where it was created—the port of Hamburg (*compare* FRANKFURTER)—but of course the concept of a small cake of minced beef, grilled or fried, is an ancient one, and was simply waiting for a new name. The particular version that became the hamburger seems to have originated in the Baltic area, or perhaps in the Russian *bitock*, a beef cake. This was adopted as a conveniently packaged form of meat by the seamen of Hamburg, who took it with them when they emigrated to the US. When it first turned up in English texts, in the late 1880s, it was called a *Hamburg steak* or a *Hamburger steak*, but by the early twentieth century the abbreviated *hamburger* had come into use (*see also* VIENNA STEAK). This coincided with what was probably the big boost which was decisive in propelling the hamburger towards its eventual status as the quintessential American fast food: the 1904 St Louis World's Fair, whose visitors devoured it in droves. This status was confirmed when it was adopted as the main staple dish in the new US chain restaurants; the White Castle chain was the first to open, in 1921, and the movement came of age when McDonalds started up in 1940 (*see* MAC) (by this time, of course, the classic way of serving a hamburger, between two halves of a toasted bun, was firmly established). After the Second World War, the spread of American culture took the hamburger to virtually every inhabited nook and cranny in the world (including, post-perestroika, the former Soviet Union), and has donated the word to other languages (French has *le hambourgaire*, for instance).

Not surprisingly, the misapprehension soon arose that hamburgers were in some way connected with ham, and that the element *-burger* had some sort of independent status as a word element. From this it was a short step to the coining of new forms based on *-burger*. *Beefburger* seems to have been the first, around 1940—supposedly a synonym for *hamburger*, but in reality often merely a second-rate version of it—but the late 1950s saw an explosion of *cheeseburgers, baconburgers, eggburgers, steakburgers, porkburgers, lamburgers, chefburgers, jumboburgers, monsterburgers,* etc. (some of them referring to the composition of the meat cake, some to its toppings, some to its size) which has been reverberating more and more fancifully ever since: 'There's no better way to cook a lamb chop, kebab, or lamburger than over charcoal', Hugh Fearnley-Whittingstall, *The River Cottage Meat Book* (2004). Many of the new variations on the theme do not even contain meat—*nutburger, veggie burger* (*Vegeburger* is the trademarked version of the term).

The other upshot of this linguistic re-analysis of the hamburger is that *burger* has become a word in its own right: 'He kept thinking of food, of meaty burgers with thick-cut fries and ketchup', Peter James, *Dead Simple* (2005). This development was first reported in the journal *American Speech* in 1946, but again did not really blossom until the 1960s.

Hamburg parsley A variety of parsley with a large white root that resembles a small parsnip in appearance and celery in taste; the tops can be used like ordinary parsley. It originated in Germany in the sixteenth century. Its English name is first recorded in 1796.

hand In British English, a *hand of pork* is a cut comprising the first joint of the pig's front leg and the lower part of the shoulder. If some of the forepart of the belly (including ribs) is also included, the joint is termed a *hand and spring* (*spring* is an old word for 'pork belly', which now survives only in this collocation).

hand roll A variety of sushi in which the cold rice and other ingredients are contained within a small ice-cream-cone-shaped wrapper of greenish-black seaweed (*nori*). Its Japanese name is *temaki*.

hanger steak An American term for what in France—and increasingly in British English—is called *onglet*: a cut of beef consisting of muscles that support the diaphragm. The name may reflect the idea of the diaphragm 'hanging' by these muscles from the backbone.

hard sauce A mixture of butter and sugar beaten together, usually with the addition of brandy, rum, or vanilla flavouring. When served with Christmas pudding or a similar hot dessert the butter melts, producing the desired sauce-like effect. The term, which is first recorded in 1880, is still widely used in American English, but British English prefers *brandy butter, rum butter,* etc.: 'To travel in Kent without visiting Canterbury is rather like eating plum pudding without brandy butter,' Lord Clonmore, *Kent* (Shell Guides, 1935).

hard tack Hard, dry saltless bread or biscuit, especially as handed out in former times as rations for soldiers or sailors (if for use at sea, it could alternatively be termed *ship's biscuit* or *sea biscuit*). The term (which uses *tack* 'equipment' in the dismissive metaphorical sense 'fare, food') is first recorded in the 1830s.

haricot bean A general term for a wide variety of beans (all of the species *Phaseolus vulgaris*) which originated in America, and were brought to Europe in the sixteenth century. They include the flageolet and the red kidney bean, but in isolation the term *haricot* is usually applied to the small white variety which is used for baked beans. It has a circuitous linguistic history. It was originally applied in fourteenth-century French to a stew or ragout, typically of mutton. It was probably a derivative of the verb *harigoter* 'to cut up', and in the seventeenth century was borrowed into English in this sense (it survived well into the nineteenth century: Mrs Rundell, for example, in her *New System of Domestic Cookery* (1806), gave a recipe for a 'Harrico of Veal'). The Aztec name for the beans that were now finding their way across the Atlantic was *ayacotl*, and it seems that by the mid-1600s this tongue-twister had, by the process of folk etymology, become transformed into the familiar *haricot*. An alternative name for the small white haricot is *pea bean*, and in America it is also known as the *navy bean* or *Boston bean*.

harissa A hot sauce or paste used in North African cuisine, made from chilli peppers, paprika, and olive oil. The word comes from Arabic, where it means 'pounded'.

hartshorn Shavings from the antlers of a deer (*hart* is an old word for an adult male deer). It is a rich source of ammonia, and nowadays the term, if it is remembered at all, conjures up the pungent liquid (*spirit of hartshorn*) made by steeping the shavings in water and used for reviving fainters and swooners. However, it also has gelling properties, and it was widely used culinarily in the seventeenth, eighteenth, and nineteenth centuries (Mrs Rundell, for instance, in her *New System of Domestic Cookery* (1816) has a recipe for 'Hartshorn jelly' which also includes orange and lemon juice and sugar).

Harvey's sauce The proprietary name of an anchovy-based savoury sauce widely consumed in Britain from the late eighteenth century. It was produced by Elizabeth Lazenby and Company, and in 1959 the firm offered this account of its origins: 'The history of Elizabeth Lazenby can really be dated from 1760. In that year, a Mr Peter Harvey, owner of an inn called the 'Black Dog' in Bedfont, Middlesex, invented a thin sauce known as 'Harvey's Sauce'. So good was it that many of his customers endeavoured to obtain the recipe, and one of them, a certain London grocer named M. Lazenby, offered to buy it, but Peter Harvey refused to part with his secret. Mr Lazenby . . . married Harvey's sister Elizabeth. As a wedding present, Peter Harvey gave Elizabeth . . . the recipe for his famous sauce.' It was soon on the most fashionable tables: 'Buy in gross . . . Ketchup, Soy, Chili vinegar, and Harvey,' Lord Byron, *Beppo* (1817).

Harvey Wallbanger A cocktail consisting of orange juice mixed with vodka or gin; strictly accurate versions have an Italian liqueur, such as Galliano, floated on top. This is a comparatively recent creation (from the US, the home of the cocktail), not mentioned in print until 1970, but for a brief period it was the 'in' drink. The reasons behind the bizarre name are not known. The *Wallbanger* is presumably just a compound of *wall* and *banger*, perhaps suggestive of the effects of the drink on the drinker (who has been identified, not very convincingly, as a Californian surfer called Harvey). It seems more plausible that both the drink and the name were a clever advertising promotion on the part of the makers of Galliano.

hash Etymologically, a *hash* is a dish consisting of 'cut-up' bits, for the word comes ultimately from French *hacher* 'to chop up', a derivative of Old French *hache* 'axe' (source of English *hatchet*). The noun based on *hacher* is *hachis*. This remains the French term for 'hash', and it was borrowed into English in the early seventeenth century as *hachee* or *hachy* (*The Closet of Sir Kenelm Digby Opened* (1648) speaks of a 'juicy hachy of rabit, capon, or mutton'). But before the century was up the native form *hash*, based on the related verb *hash*, had all but replaced it (Samuel Pepys, for instance, writing in his diary for 13 January 1663, reports a dinner party at which he was served 'at first course, a hash of rabbits and lamb, and a rare chine of beef'). In modern use the term refers to a dish of roughly chopped or minced meat (typically precooked or preserved—corned beef is a frequent ingredient), often mixed with vegetables or potatoes, cooked in the oven. (The notion of re-using already cooked meat lies behind *rehash*, an early nineteenth-century coinage.) It has greater currency in American than British English, where it has spawned a variety of more-or-less derogatory food-related expressions, such as *hash-house* for a 'cheap eating house' and *hash-slinger* for a 'waiter or waitress'.

The idea of a *hash* being a 'mess' rather than a 'mixture of re-used bits' seems first to have taken root in the eighteenth century, and the expression 'make a hash of something' followed in the early nineteenth century ('Froude writes up to me we have made a hash of it,' J. H. Newman, in a letter written in 1833). Also early nineteenth-century is 'settle someone's hash', meaning 'to finish off someone's chances completely'.

hash brown Hash browns are an American way with potatoes. Cooked potatoes are chopped up small, generally formed into small rissole-like cakes, and then fried until they are brown. The original name of the dish (first recorded in 1900) was *hashed brown potatoes*, and this full form remained current for many decades (a 1917 publication called *Mrs Allen's Cook Book* used an alternative *hash browned potatoes*). H. L. Mencken in his *American Language* (1945) noted 'mash potato' and 'hash-brown potatoes' as examples of a tendency to omit -*ed* in past participial adjectives, but the element *potato* still remained, and *hash brown, tout court*, is not recorded in print until 1969 (although no doubt it was common in the spoken language long before then).

Hash browns in the 1970s and 1980s became a standardized part of the American fast-food package, familiar in outlets worldwide.

They should not be confused with *hash brownies*, a punning name for cakes (*see* BROWNIE) liberally spiked with marijuana or 'hash'.

hashmagandy A superannuated Australian and New Zealand colloquialism for a meat stew, first recorded in 1919. The first syllable is presumably *hash* 'dish of cooked chopped meat', and the rest of the word may well have been suggested by *salmagundi*.

haslet Originally, *haslet* was the internal organs of the pig (or occasionally other animals) used as food, typically in a fry-up. Hannah Glasse in her *Art of Cookery* (1747) gives this definition: 'In a hog . . . the haslet which is the liver and crow [abdominal lining], kidney and skirts [diaphragm].' Now, though, the term is generally applied to a meat loaf made from such offal, and typically cooked in caul fat. It derives from Old French *hastelet*, a diminutive form of *haste* 'piece of roast meat', which was borrowed from Low German *harst*.

hasty pudding As its name suggests, hasty pudding is a pudding that can be assembled at very short notice. Its exact ingredients vary from place to place, but in essence it is a sort of porridge made from crushed or ground cereal grains and milk. In Britain, where the term originated in the late sixteenth century, it traditionally refers to a sweet milk pudding made with flour, semolina, or tapioca. In the US it is made with the main indigenous cereal, maize, which is often sweetened with maple syrup or brown sugar.

haunch English acquired *haunch* in the thirteenth century, from Old French *hanche* (its ultimate origin was probably Germanic). It referred to the part of the human body that includes the hip, buttock, and thigh, a usage now familiar only in the plural (as in 'squat down on one's haunches'). Already by the fifteenth century it was being applied to a roughly corresponding part of a quadruped, as divided up by a butcher: the hind leg and loin. At first it was a fairly broad term, applicable, for example, to sheep meat, but over the centuries its focus has narrowed down to one thing: a *haunch of venison*. In practice in modern usage it is generally restricted still further, to the hind leg, which is admittedly cheaper and easier to handle: 'Leg or haunch of venison is leaner [than loin] and more likely to become dry,' Anne Willan, *Reader's Digest Complete Guide to Cookery* (1989); 'The prime roasting cuts of venison are the leg (often referred to as the haunch) and the saddle,' Hugh Fearnley-Whittingstall, *The River Cottage Meat Book* (2004).

Havarti A mild semi-soft Danish cheese with lots of small irregular holes. Its name commemorates the farm of Hanne Nielsen, the nineteenth-century Danish cheesemaker who popularized it.

haver-cake A now more or less obsolete northern English term for 'oatcake'. *Haver* is an ancient Germanic word for 'oats', current in English from the fifteenth to the eighteenth centuries, which now survives only in *haversack* (etymologically a 'sack for oats').

hazelnut The hazel is one of the ancestral trees of the ancient Indo-European homelands, and its name can be traced back to a prehistoric **kosolos* or **koselos*. Its nut, with its smooth round hard shell, has no doubt been providing human beings with useful autumn and winter food ever since. Its alternative English names are *cob* and (for a slightly different species) *filbert*.

The use of the word *hazel* as a colour term, to describe a yellowish brown, dates back to the Old English period.

headcheese The rather unappetizing North American name for brawn (in the sense 'a jellied mould of pig meat'). *Head* reflects the leading role played in the dish by meat from the pig's head; *cheese* refers to the form into which the meat is pressed, like a cheese. The term is first recorded in 1841.

    heart of palm An alternative name for PALM HEART.

    hedgehog A dessert dish poplar in England in the eighteenth and nineteenth centuries in which a vaguely hedgehog-shaped cooked base made from eggs, butter, cream, sugar, and ground almonds had sharp slivers of almond inserted all over its surface, giving the appearance of erinaceous spines. The concept survived into the twentieth century, reapplied to cakes: *Good Housekeeping's Cookery Book* (1960), for example, gave a recipe for 'Hedgehog cake'. *Compare* PORCUPINE.

    hedgerow jam A term of recent coinage for jam made from a range of uncultivated, typically autumnal fruits foraged from the countryside. A pot might contain a mixture of, say, crab apples, blackberries, sloes, and rosehips.

    herb The word *herb* comes via Old French from Latin *herba*, which meant 'growing vegetation, green plants, grass'. By the time it reached English in the late thirteenth century, it had developed along two distinct semantic lines: 'any plant with a non-woody stem (as opposed to a *shrub* or *tree*)' and 'such a plant whose leaves are put to a particular human use, medicinal or culinary'. The former remains in technical botanical use, but in non-specialist language is now familiar only in the derived adjective *herbaceous*, as in 'herbaceous border'. And in the case of the latter, medicinal connotations have now largely given way to gastronomic ones. As contrasted with *spice*, which broadly speaking denotes a 'flavouring substance obtained from the seeds, fruits, bark, etc. of a plant grown in warm areas of the world', *herb* is used for a 'plant—such as mint, parsley, thyme, sage, rosemary, chervil—whose leaves (or sometimes stalks) are used fresh or dried for flavouring food'. In American English pronunciation of the word, the *h* is silent.

English *arbour* began life in Old French as a derivative of *herbe*.

herb bennet A yellow-flowered woodland and hedgerow plant of the rose family (also known as *wood avens*) with a clove-flavoured root that was used in former times for food (and in herbal medicine). English acquired its name in the Middle Ages from Old French *herbe beneite*, a translation of medieval Latin *herba benedicta* 'blessed herb', which was probably a tribute to the plant's supposed ability to ward off the Devil.

hero An alternative American term for a SUBMARINE sandwich. First recorded in 1955, the name presumably reflects the size of the sandwich or of its eater's appetite.

highball A long drink of spirits (typically whisky) diluted with water, soda water, etc. and served iced in a tall glass. The term, which originated in the US in the 1890s, is generally taken to be a reference to the tall glass.

hindle wakes A supposedly traditional Lancashire dish consisting of a chicken stuffed with breadcrumbs, prunes, and herbs, and eaten cold. The story attached to it is that it was brought to northwest England by Flemish weavers in the fourteenth century, and named, in a mixture of French and English, *hen de la wake* 'hen of the wake'—that is, a chicken sold at an annual parish fair, known formerly as a 'wake'. However, ancient as the dish itself may well be, there is no documentary evidence for the term *hindle wakes* before the twentieth century, and it could well be, as Jane Grigson suggests in her *English Food* (1974), that it was inspired by Stanley Houghton's play *Hindle Wakes* (1912) about doings during wakes week (the annual holiday week) in the imaginary Lancashire town of Hindle. It is, though, worth noting that in the Middle Ages *hindal*, or *hindheal*, was a name used for 'wild sage', and that sage is one of the herbs traditionally used in hindle wakes.

hing The Hindi word for ASAFOETIDA, used in the past in English.

hoagie One of a whole range of synonyms for *submarine*, a sandwich of American origin made from a long roll or piece of French bread. First recorded in 1955, it is associated particularly with Philadelphia. It has shown some signs of crossing the Atlantic as a term for a 'long roll'. It is not known where the word comes from.

hobo steak An American term for a method of cooking a steak that involves encasing it in salt and baking it. Fillet steak might be beyond the means of tramps (*hobo* is American English for 'tramp'), but the technique is a familiar one among travelling people without the standard range of domestic cooking pots (as in the legendary gipsy dish of hedgehog baked in a crust of mud).

hock¹ An animal's hock is the area around the lowest joint in its leg, corresponding to the ankle in humans. Culinarily it is most often applied to a sinewy bony cut of pork from below this joint and above the trotter. It is commonly cured, smoked or unsmoked, as bacon or ham: William Verrall had a recipe for 'ham hock with peach fritters' in his *Complete System of Cookery* (1759). The cured version is also known as *knuckle*. Hock is also applied to a cut of beef from around the lowest joint of the back leg (although *leg of beef* is the more usual present-day term for it). It is a direct descendant of Old English *hōh*, meaning 'heel'. By the Middle Ages that had become *hough*. In southern England it evolved further to *hock*, but in the North and Scotland it remained as *hough*. The two are now pronounced the same, but the distinction in spelling remains ('potted hough' is a classic Scottish spiced beef paste).

hock² A term traditionally applied in British English to German white wines, and specifically to those produced beside the river Rhine, as opposed to those from the river Mosel (to distinguish them hocks come in brown bottles, whereas Mosels—or Moselles—come in green bottles). The word is a shortening of *hockamore*, a seventeenth-century Anglicization of German *Hochheimer*, wine from the vineyards of Hochheim. This town is actually not on the Rhine itself, but a little further east, to the north of the river Main, but for classification purposes its wines are always included with those of the Rheingau (the area to the south and west of Wiesbaden). In the nineteenth and early twentieth centuries hock was immensely popular and indeed fashionable in Britain: W. G. Grace regularly refreshed himself between innings with hock and seltzer; Oscar Wilde, awaiting his arrest at the Cadogan hotel, 'sipped at a weak hock and seltzer as he gazed at the London skies', according to John Betjeman; and so fond of hock was Queen Victoria alleged to be that a local proprietor named a Hochheim vineyard after her, the *Königin Viktoria Berg*. The Queen still resolutely serves it at State banquets, but on the whole in recent years, despite the continued commercial success of liebfraumilch, the reputation of hock has gone into something of a decline, as tastes have switched to drier white wines. As with the product, so with its name: *hock*, never adopted to any extent in American English, has come to be regarded as a rather parochial term, and is increasingly being replaced by *Rhine wine* (harking back to *Rhenish wine*, in use from the fourteenth to the nineteenth centuries).

hoecake A small coarse square cake made from maize flour. The term originated in America in the 1740s, apparently reflecting the original method of baking, on the blade of a hoe. Hoecakes are essentially the same as (American) johnnycakes.

ho fun A wide flat variety of Chinese rice noodle.

hoisin sauce A sweet, spicy dark-red sauce made from soya beans, vinegar, sugar, garlic, and various spices. It is widely used in southern Chinese cookery. In the Cantonese dialect, the word *hoisin* means 'seafood'; it is a compound of *hoi* 'sea' and *sin* 'fresh'.

hokey-pokey In the late nineteenth and early twentieth centuries *hokey-pokey* was a British English term for a cheap sort of ice cream sold by street-vendors: 'Three hokey-pokey ice-cream hand-carts, one after another, turned the corner of Trafalgar Road,' Arnold Bennett, *Clayhanger* (1910). It presumably came from the cry with which the vendors hawked it, although what this originally was is not known (one suggestion put forward in the 1880s was Italian *O che poco!* 'Oh how little!'—a reference to price, presumably, rather than quantity—which is given some plausibility by the fact that many ice-cream sellers at that time were Italian).

Nowadays the word is used in New Zealand for honeycomb (a crunchy spongy confection), and also for ice cream containing little pieces of honeycomb.

hollandaise sauce A hot creamy sauce made from egg yolks and butter, usually with a dash of lemon juice or vinegar. It is typically served with fish or with vegetables, such as asparagus. French *sauce Hollandaise* translates as 'Dutch sauce', and that in fact is the name under which the sauce was known in Britain as long ago as the sixteenth century: 'Will you eat of a pike with a high dutch sauce?', Claudius Hollyband, *French Schoolmaster* (1573). The French term began to be adopted in the middle of the nineteenth century, but *Dutch sauce* survived well into the twentieth century. The sauce was presumably thought of as originating in the Netherlands, although the circumstances of its naming are not known.

Hollands A now little-encountered term for a variety of gin originally made in the Netherlands. It is of a slightly higher strength than British and American gin, and also has a more pronounced flavour, so it tends to be drunk neat rather than serving as the basis for cocktails and mixed drinks. It is often sold in stoneware bottles. The word came into use in English during the great age of gin-drinking, the eighteenth century, but has now, along with its synonym *geneva*, largely died out; when people want to refer to the drink these days, they usually call it simply 'Dutch gin'.

holy basil An Asian species of basil, *Ocimum sanctum* (or *O. tenuiflorum*). It is venerated as a sacred plant by Hindus, and grows in the grounds of many an Indian temple. It is widely used in Southeast Asian cookery for its clove-like savour (but it should not be confused with *Thai basil*). Its English name is first recorded in 1880; in India it is called *tulsi*.

home fries An American term, first recorded in 1951, for fried sliced potatoes, roughly corresponding to British English *chips*.

The term perhaps emphasizes their all-American status, as opposed to the foreignness of *French fries*.

hominy The coarsely ground kernels of maize with the husks removed, prepared as food by boiling it in water or milk. The word is of Native American origin, and Algonquian *appuminnéonash* 'parched corn' has been suggested as a source: this is a compound of *appwóon* 'he bakes' and *minneash* 'grains, corn'. It is first mentioned in an English text by Captain John Smith, an early English colonist in North America, in 1629: 'Their servants commonly feed upon Milk Homini, which is bruised Indian corn pounded, and boiled thick, and milk for the sauce.' Ground more finely, it is known as *hominy grits*, or sometimes just *grits*: 'Breakfast was on the table . . . . There were grits and gravy, hot cakes, and buttermilk', Marjorie Rawlings, *The Yearling* (1938). Etymologically, *grit* in this sense is the same as *grit* 'small stones', but their use diverged in prehistoric Germanic, before they became recognizably 'English' words. The *grits* of *hominy grits* originally meant 'bran, chaff', and was applied from the late sixteenth century to coarsely ground oatmeal; hence its American use for 'ground maize'. *Groat* is a relative.

honey Until the nineteenth century, when the price of sugar fell to a point where it came within reach of the general public, honey was the most commonly used sweetener. And indeed, before the eleventh century, when the first crusade set off the initial trickle of sugar from the Middle East to western Europe, it was virtually the only substance available for adding sweetness (apart from naturally occurring sugars in fruits and certain vegetables, such as parsnips).

Honey is an ancient word, but it does not come from the primeval term for 'honey'. That was Indo-European **melit-*, which has come down to many modern European languages, including French and Spanish *miel*, Italian *miele*, and Welsh *mel*, and has also contributed to English *mellifluous*, *mildew*, and *molasses*. *Honey* and its Germanic relatives, German *honig*, Dutch *honing*, Swedish *honung*, and Danish *honning*, go back to a prehistoric West and North Germanic **khunagom* or **khunanggom*, which may originally have described the colour of honey (it has been linked with Greek *knèkós* 'pale yellow' and Sanskrit *kāñcana-* 'golden').

The use of *honey* as a term of endearment goes back a long way too; in Chaucer's *Miller's Tale*, for instance, the carpenter refers to his wife Alison as his 'honey dear'. And it is this meaning that probably lies behind the use of the Geordie dialect form *hinny* for the cake known as a *singing hinny*.

The term *honeymoon* dates from the sixteenth century. *Moon* is probably used here in the sense 'month', with the implication that the first month after marriage is the sweetest, although it has also been suggested that the underlying meaning is that love, like the moon, will wane.

honeycomb A term with (alongside its core meaning, 'the wax storage cells of honeybees') two widely divergent culinary applications: the earlier, dating from the beginning of the eighteenth century, is to tripe from the second stomach of a ruminant, which has a reticulated, honeycomb-like pattern; more recently, it has denoted a crisply crunchy confection with many small holes, made by boiling sugar in water and then adding bicarbonate of soda (the usual American name for it is *sponge toffee*, and New Zealanders call it *hokey-pokey*).

honeydew melon See MELON.

hooch *Hooch*, a largely American colloquialism for 'cheap fiery alcoholic spirits', originated among the ethnic peoples of

Alaska. A small tribe that lived on Admiralty Island called itself *Hutsnuwu* 'grizzly bear foot' (a name variously transcribed by Europeans as *Hootzenoo, Kootznahoo, Hoochinoo*, etc.). It seems that they distilled their own brand of liquor, which American trappers and traders got to know as *hoochinoo*, or *hooch* for short: 'Whenever whisky runs short the Yukoner falls back upon a villainous decoction known as "hootchinoo" or "hootch",' c.1898, quoted in Pierre Berton, *Centennial Food Guide* (1966). Hence, by the early twentieth century, any old improvised spirits that came to hand were known as *hooch*.

hop Hops are what give bitter beer its particular tang—indeed the original distinction, now blurred, that developed between beer and ale in the fifteenth century was that beer was flavoured with hops and ale was not. They are the dried female flowers of a climbing plant of the hemp family (a distant relative of cannabis, in fact). Herbs had been used to flavour beer in Britain from earliest times, including no doubt hops (which the Anglo-Saxons called *hymele*), but it was the continental Germanic peoples who in the early Middle Ages really cottoned on in a big way to their value both as a taste-enhancer and as a preservative. The Flemish in particular were very keen on hopped beer, and those who settled in England in the fifteenth century brought it with them (together with their word *hoppe*, whose ultimate origin is not known). English beer-drinkers were duly impressed, and a thriving import trade in hops developed; and in the sixteenth century Flemish emigrés began to raise the plants in Kent, which has been the hop-garden of England ever since, dotted with the conical-roofed oasthouses in which hops are dried.

hopper A type of saucer-shaped pancake characteristic of southern India and Sri Lanka. Its yeast batter, made from rice flour, is cooked in a bowl-shaped pan, which gives the hopper its particular form: thick in the middle, thin and lacy towards the edge. Often a whole egg is cooked in the centre. Its name in Tamil is *appam* (probably a descendant of Sanskrit *apupa* 'fried delicacy'), and a variant form of this, *appa*, was folk-etymologically transformed in Anglo-Indian English into *hopper*. *See also* STRING HOPPER.

hopping John A dish from the Caribbean and the Deep South of the US: a stew of rice with black-eyed peas, and salt pork or bacon. The term is first recorded in 1838. For that authentic touch, spell it *hoppin' John*. There is no record of who 'hopping John' was, and efforts to explain the name (that it came from an invitation to guests at a meal to 'hop in, John', or from a domestic ritual of children hopping once round the dining table before sitting down to eat) range from the desperate to the bizarre.

horchata Horchata, or *orchata,* is a Spanish drink made by steeping nuts or grains in water. In the original form of the beverage, which comes from Valencia, tiger nuts are used, but in Latin America and the US, where it has also become popular, almonds or rice are the usual principal ingredient. Its name is ultimately a descendant of Latin *hordeum* 'barley', which is also the ancestor of English *orgeat*.

horehound A white-flowered plant of the dead-nettle family, with a strong smell and hairy leaves. Its bitter juice has been used since prehistoric times in the treatment of coughs and colds, and its distinctive flavour has also been put to culinary use. Its name goes back to Old English *hāre hūne,* where *hūne* was the specific term for the plant and *hāre* meant 'greyish white'.

Horlick's A proprietary beverage made by adding hot milk to a powder made from malt extract and milk. First manufactured in 1883, it was named after William Horlick (1846–1936), a British-born American industrialist who ran the firm which made it. Its popularity as a comforting and nourishing nightcap took off after the First World War (along with that of the similar Ovaltine). In the 1930s the advertising claim that it warded off 'night starvation' raised the odd snigger.

In the latter part of the twentieth century the expression 'make a Horlick's of something', meaning 'to make a mess of it', enjoyed some currency in British upper-crust slang. In this context *Horlick's* may represent a euphemistic substitution for *bollocks*.

hors d'oeuvre French *hors d'oeuvre* means literally 'outside of work'—hence, a 'dish served outside of the ordinary set of courses in a meal, side dish'. As this suggests, an hors d'oeuvre was originally served as an extra relish at any point in a meal, but the tendency to reserve the term to a small savoury first course seems to have developed fairly early on. It is also now used for small snacks served with drinks before a meal. The first person to use the word in English seems to have been Alexander Pope, in his *Dunciad* (1742): 'The stews and palace equally explor'd, intrig'd with glory, and with spirit whor'd; try'd all *hors-d'oeuvres*, all *liqueurs* defin'd, judicious drank, and greatly daring din'd.' *See also* ANTIPASTO.

horseradish The lengthy, contorted root of the horseradish plant, *Armoracia rusticana*, with its explosive pungency that can make the ears of the unwary steam, has long been a favourite of British cuisine. In former centuries it was often scraped over oily fish, such as salmon or mackerel, a use to which it is still frequently put in other northern European countries and which is now being rediscovered in Britain, but horseradish sauce established itself early as the condiment to accompany beef: in 1669 the *Closet of Sir Kenelm Digby Knight Opened* gave a recipe involving grating the horseradish and adding  vinegar and a little sugar to it. It was put to more unexpected uses, though: Samuel Pepys, in his diary for 16 September 1664, notes 'there met Mr Pargiter, and he would needs have me to drink a cup of Horseradish ale, which he and a friend of his, troubled with the stone, have been drinking of.'

The chef Alexis Soyer in his *Culinary Campaign* (1857) gives a mind-bogglingly fiery recipe for a 'Universal Devil's mixture' which partners horseradish with mustard, chillis, cayenne, and pepper. But horseradish has not been universally popular with the French; Alexandre Dumas pronounced that 'Horseradish has the same disadvantage as the French turnip. It is equally apt to bring on flatulence, causes a heaving of the stomach and even provokes headaches, when too much of it is eaten.'

The *horse* element in the name was once widely applied to a large, coarse variety of something; it was used freely in a host of plant and animal names (*horse cucumber, horse ant, horse parsley*, etc.), and it survives today in *horse chestnut, horse mackerel*, and also very likely *horse laugh*.

horse's neck A mixed long drink consisting of ginger ale, a twist of lemon peel, and spirits, generally brandy, served on ice. Like most highballs and cocktails, it originated in the USA in the 1920s, but it appears to have been named after an earlier and less sophisticated concoction, a rough-and-ready mixture of moonshine whiskey and dry cider drunk in the backwoods around the turn of the nineteenth century, and also known as a *horse's neck*.

hot and sour soup A warming soup widely consumed in northern and western China (its name in Mandarin is *suan la tang*). To a pork or chicken broth base are added chilli (for heat) and vinegar (for sourness), mushrooms and any of a range of other vegetables, and noodles. Variations on the same basic theme are found throughout Southeast Asia, notably in Thailand and Laos, where the soup is called *tom yum*.

hotchpotch *See* HOT-POT.

hot cross bun The practice of eating special small cakes at the time of the spring festival seems to date back at least to the ancient Greeks, but the English custom of eating spiced buns on Good Friday was perhaps institutionalized in Tudor times, when a London byelaw was introduced forbidding the sale of such buns except on Good Friday, at Christmas, and at burials. The first intimation we have of a cross appearing on the bun, in remembrance of Christ's cross, comes in *Poor Robin's Almanack* (1733): 'Good Friday comes this month, the old woman runs, with one or two a penny hot cross buns' (a version of the once familiar street-cry 'One-a-penny, two-a-penny, hot cross buns'). At this stage the cross was presumably simply incised with a knife, rather than piped on in pastry, as is the modern commercial practice. As yet, too, the 'name' of such buns was just *cross buns*: James Boswell recorded in his *Life of Johnson* (1791): '9 Apr. an. 1773 Being Good Friday, I breakfasted with him and cross-buns.' The fact that they were generally sold hot, however, seems to have led by the early nineteenth century to the incorporation of *hot* into their name.

hot dog *Hot dog* originated as a term for a long thin cooked sausage (typically a frankfurter), especially as served with mustard in a soft bun, in the US at the end of the nineteenth century. How all this came about, however, has excited much speculation and controversy down the decades. The version of events that held sway over many years was that frankfurters in a roll were originally sold at the Polo Grounds, the then home of the New York Giants baseball team, by a stall-holder called Harry Stevens at the beginning of the twentieth century, and that the cartoonist T. A. ('Tad') Dorgan called them 'hot dogs' in the caption to a cartoon he drew of the scene for the *New York Journal*. All this has been shown to be wide of the mark, however, particularly by research carried out by Barry Popik of the American Dialect Society. The real starting point of the story seems to be the colloquial use of *dog* to mean 'sausage' in American English from around the middle of the nineteenth century (partly as a not entirely facetious reference to the origin of the meat to be found in many examples). There is evidence from 1894 of students at Yale University referring to carts on which hot sausages in a bun were sold as *dog wagons*, and in an October 1895 issue of the *Yale Record* we find the first known printed reference to *hot dogs*: 'How they contentedly munched hot dogs during the whole service'. It can scarcely be coincidental that the colloquial use of *hot dog* for 'someone particularly or flamboyantly skilled or excellent' arose virtually contemporaneously in America, and perhaps originally the hot dog was subconsciously regarded as a sort of 'super' sausage sandwich. It has also been speculated that the name reflects some perceived resemblance between the sausage and the dachshund (although the term *sausage dog* for 'dachshund' is not actually recorded before the 1930s). As far as the notion of serving the sausage in a long thin bun is concerned, it probably came to America with German and other Central European immigrants in the mid-nineteenth century; attempts to pin the idea down to one individual have foundered on the rock of facts.

Whatever its origins, though, over the past century and more the hot dog has established itself as a key component in the US street-food/fast-food pantheon (albeit not universally approved of: the American journalist H. L. Mencken censoriously described the hot-dog sausage as 'a cartridge filled with the sweepings of abattoirs'). *See also* TUBE STEAK.

hot-pot Originally, in the eighteenth century, the term *hot-pot* denoted a sort of hot punch—a heated and spiced mixture of ale and spirits (the *New Dictionary of the Canting Crew*, of around 1700, defines it as 'Ale and Brandy boiled together'). Its modern application to a meat stew is not recorded until the mid-nineteenth century. The first writer known to have used it in print is, appropriately enough, Elizabeth Gaskell, in *North and South* (1854)—appropriately, since the hot-pot is quintessentially a northern dish, associated particularly with Lancashire. Mr Thornton, a northern mill-owner, records how the mill-hands offered him a share in their hot-pot: 'It was a very busy day, but I saw that the men would be hurt if, after making the advance, I didn't meet them half-way, so I went in, and I never made a better dinner in my life. I told them . . . how much I'd enjoyed it; and for some time, whenever that special dinner recurred in their dietary, I was sure to be met by these men, with a "Master, there's hot-pot for dinner today, win yo' come?".' The traditional Lancashire hot-pot is made of mutton or lamb (although historically other sorts of meat have been used as available) layered with vegetables and finished with a topping of sliced potatoes which crisps and browns.

So far so straightforward, but *hot-pot* as a word for a meat stew probably has a much longer anterior history than at first sight appears. In the fifteenth century the term *hotchpot* appeared, denoting a dish with multiple ingredients, usually including meat: a cookery text of *c.*1440, for instance, mentions 'Goos in Hochepot'. It was adopted from French *hochepot*, which meant literally 'shake-pot'—presumably a reference to the way in which the ingredients were mixed together. Over the centuries it, and its slightly altered form *hotchpotch*, narrowed down in focus specifically to a meat stew with vegetables. Mrs Rundell, for example, in her *New System of Domestic Cookery* (1815), gave a recipe for 'an excellent Hotch-potch' which answers that description. Nowadays, we are mainly familiar with *hotchpotch* in the metaphorical sense 'an ill-assorted mixture', but the culinary application of both it and *hotchpot* survived well into the second half of the nineteenth century, and *hot-pot* is almost certainly a folk-etymological rationalization of them.

hough *See* HOCK.

Hovis A proprietary name for a type of brown flour with added wheat germ, commonly used also for bread made from such flour. Both seem to have originated in the 1880s, manufactured by the firm Richard Smith of Macclesfield in Cheshire (to begin with the bread was called 'Smith's Old Patent Germ Bread'), but the name *Hovis* did not emerge until the mid-1890s. It was apparently a blend of Latin *hominis vis*, literally 'strength of man'.

howtowdie A Scottish dish consisting of a boiled chicken served with poached eggs and spinach. The earliest known reference to it comes in the work of the Scottish poet Allan Ramsay (1686–1758): 'They all, in an united Body, Declar'd it a fine fat How-towdy'. The word comes from Old French *hetoudeau* or *estaudeau* 'fat young boiling fowl'.

HP Sauce The proprietary name (registered in 1912) of a spicy-sweet bottled brown sauce that over the decades has graced British dining tables both high and low, adding a mild kick to underpowered chips, fry-ups, cold cuts, sausage sandwiches, and the like, and becoming something of a national treasure in the process. The sauce appears to have been originally concocted in the late nineteenth century by Nottingham grocer F. G. Garton. He named it 'HP' because, he said, it was used in the restaurants of the Houses of Parliament. The recipe was taken over by Edwin Samson Moore, who began to produce the sauce commercially at his factory in Aston in the West Midlands. He marketed it vigorously and it has never looked back, its label image of the Houses of Parliament achieving almost iconic status. Its mass appeal may be gauged by the fact that the former British Prime Minister Harold Wilson was at pains never to deny the suggestion that he was an HP fan: it buttressed his 'man of the people' image.

huckleberry The term *huckleberry* denotes both the small glossy black berry of a North American shrub of the heather family, and also in American English a similar and closely related fruit usually known in British English as the *bilberry*. It is thought to have originated as an alteration of *hurtleberry*, a now obsolete synonym of *bilberry*. Mark Twain's use of it for the name of the eponymous hero of his novel *The Adventures of Huckleberry Finn* (1884) has ensured its familiarity with millions who have never seen let alone tasted the fruit itself.

huevos rancheros A Mexican breakfast dish consisting of fried or poached eggs accompanied by fried corn tortillas, and a tomato-and-chilli sauce. The Spanish name (first recorded in English in 1901) means literally 'ranchers' eggs', reflecting the dish's supposed origin as a mid-morning refuelling stop for cowboys and farmhands.

huff Simple basic pastry used as a crust for baking meat, fruit, etc., and not officially intended to be eaten. The term, first recorded in 1787 and now long out of use, reflects the fact that the crust 'huffs' or puffs up into a dome in cooking.

huffkin A small yeast-raised sweet roll or teacake that is a speciality of Kent. It is typically oval in shape with a hole in the middle, and cut in half and buttered for eating. The term is first recorded in 1790, and suggests a certain light puffiness (*compare* HUFF).

humbug The use of the word *humbug* for a stripy peppermint-flavoured boiled sweet seems to date from the nineteenth century: the *Oxford English Dictionary* notes it as being 'remembered in common use in Gloucestershire' in the 1820s, while Elizabeth Gaskell in *Sylvia's Lovers* (1863) explained: 'He had provided himself with a paper of humbugs for the child—"humbug" being the north-country term for certain lumps of toffy, well-flavoured with peppermint.'

The word *humbug* itself first appeared as a popular slang term of the 1750s, and like most colloquial neologisms aroused a good deal of disapproval (the January 1751 issue of *The Student* declared it 'a blackguard sound . . . a fine make-weight in conversation' which 'some great men deceive themselves so egregiously as to think they mean something by it'). It originally meant 'practical joke, hoax' rather than the present, more earnest 'hypocritical sham', and its application to an article of food may be of similar inspiration to *trifle*.

hummus Hummus, or *hoummos*, is an hors d'oeuvre made from crushed or mashed chickpeas with the addition of sesame paste (tahini), garlic, and lemon juice. It is characteristic of the cuisine of the Middle East and the eastern Mediterranean (the term entered English via Turkish), but with the explosion of interest in foreign cuisines in Britain over the past sixty years (due in no small measure to the writings of Elizabeth David, whose *Book of Mediterranean Food* (1955) contains the first recorded reference to *hummus* in English) it has now established a place on supermarket shelves.

hundreds and thousands These tiny pieces of coloured sugar, used in myriads as decorations on cakes and puddings, seem to have been around since at least the beginning of the nineteenth century; the *Oxford English Dictionary* quotes an unnamed source as vouching for their existence in the 1830s, but gives no documentary evidence. The vogue for them seems now to have passed, but until well after the Second World War they pervaded the British tea table: '"Cooks nearly always put hundreds and thousands on trifle, dear," she said. "Those little pink and white sugar things",' Agatha Christie, *Thirteen Problems* (1932). In the US they are usually called *sprinkles*, *jimmies*, or *nonpareils*.

hundred-year-old egg A less inflated, but still highly exaggerated alternative name for a THOUSAND-YEAR-OLD EGG.

Huntsman An invented name for an invented English cheese, consisting of layers of Double Gloucester and Stilton sandwiched together.

hush puppy In America, hush puppies are a variety of individual fried-batter roll, made in finger-shape from cornmeal, milk, and egg. Their name supposedly comes from their being thrown to excitable dogs to quieten their barking.

hydromel *See* MEAD.

iceberg A crisp compact round variety of lettuce developed in the US at the end of the nineteenth century. It has very pale green to white leaves.

ice cream Ice cream is reputed to have been made in China as long ago as 3000 BC, but it did not arrive in Europe (via Italy) until the thirteenth century, and Britain had to wait until the late seventeenth century to enjoy it (hitherto, iced desserts had been only of the sorbet variety). The first written reference we find to it in English dates from 1671, when it was called *cream ice,* a term which survived into the twentieth century: 'So exquisitely rare at the time that it might have been part of the Crown Jewels, a single sweetened cream ice was served to Charles II at the Garter Feast of 1671 at St George's Hall', Kate Colquhoun, *Taste* (2007). This was followed by *iced cream,* first recorded in a 1688 issue of the *London Gazette*: 'all such fruits, iced creams, and other such Varieties as the Season afforded'. The term *ice cream* itself first appeared in print in 1744, and by the time Hannah Glasse and Elizabeth Raffald were giving recipes for it in the mid-eighteenth century, it was evidently well established. At first, ice cream was simply as its name suggests: cream, perhaps sweetened, set in a pot nestling in ice to cool it down. But before long recipes became more sophisticated, the technique of periodic stirring to prevent the formation of ice crystals was introduced, and ice cream was set on a career of unbroken popularity. As early as 1821 we find mention of 'ice-cream gardens' in New York, and gradually now-familiar ways of serving ice cream appear: ice-cream sodas in 1886, for instance, and in 1909 ice-cream cones. The use of plain *ice,* usually in the plural, for ice cream (as well as sorbets and the like) dates from the eighteenth century: 'Do you notice that nobody speaks of ices any more, always ice-cream', Nancy Mitford, letter to Evelyn Waugh (1952).

Since introducing ice cream to Europe in the Middle Ages, Italy has never relinquished its lead in this field, and over the centuries the manufacture of ice cream has in many countries been the province of Italian emigrés. Indeed, so familiar a figure was the Italian ice-cream vendor in Britain that in the early twentieth century *ice-creamer* was used as a derogatory term for an Italian: 'I remembered that there are Chinks and Japs and Fuzzy Wuzzies and Ice Creamers and Dagos, and so on', Nancy Mitford, *Pigeon Pie* (1940).

In America, a type of frozen dessert with a lower butterfat content than standard ice cream is known as *ice milk* (the term is first recorded in 1947).

icing In medieval times, icing—a sprinkling of sugar—was put on top of savoury as well as sweet foods: fish pies, for instance. But the iced cakes we are familiar with today started to emerge in recognizable form in the seventeenth century; in those days, once the sugar had been applied (either directly, or to a layer of beaten egg white), the cake was returned to the oven for a while for the icing to harden. That was still the case in the eighteenth century, when the term *icing* is first actually recorded, in Elizabeth Raffald's *Experienced English Housekeeper* (1769): 'Tarts that are iced require a slow oven, or the icing will be brown.' And a hundred years later, Mrs Beeton was describing very much the same method. For the last century or so, however, the tendency has been to go for a softer icing, which requires no cooking at all.

The term *icing* has also in the past been applied to marzipan, as used for topping cakes: Mrs Beeton gives a recipe for this 'almond icing'.

Of roughly equal antiquity with the term *icing* is *frosting*, which is the preferred word in American English. The term *icing sugar*, denoting finely powdered sugar used to make icing, is first recorded in 1889; American English also uses *confectioners' sugar*.

The metaphorical use of *icing on the cake* for 'desirable extras' first crops up in print in a 1969 issue of the *Listener*, but is probably earlier.

idli Idlis are southern Indian cakes made from rice and gram flour, typically served for breakfast with a spicy sauce. They are whitish in colour, and are cooked by steaming. The word is of Tamil origin.

imam bayildi Imam bayildi is a Turkish dish consisting of aubergines stuffed with onions and tomatoes, and the name means 'the imam [priest] fainted'. The usual explanation given for the name is that once upon a time a Turkish priest, when presented with such a dish by his wife, swooned with pleasure at its exquisite flavour, but another less charitable account claims that he fainted when he heard the cost of the ingredients.

Indian corn *See* MAIZE.

India Pale Ale A type of light-coloured beer similar to bitter, originally produced in Britain in the early nineteenth century for export to India and other British colonies (the term is first recorded in 1835). It had a higher alcohol and hop content than standard pale ale, to preserve it on its journey to the tropics. Latterly its abbreviated name, *IPA*, has been commonly applied by brewers to beer products that are effectively standard bitter.

injera A soft, spongy, somewhat sour-tasting yeast-leavened Ethiopian and Eritrean flatbread. In its original and most authentic form it is made from teff flour, but wheat, barley, oats, or cornmeal can also be used. The word comes from Amharic.

involtini An Italian savoury dish consisting of a covering, typically of thinly sliced meat (ham, for example, or veal, or beef), rolled tube-fashion round a filling. It can be either raw (as an antipasto) or cooked. The Italian name means literally 'little bundles'; it is a derivative of *involgere* 'to wrap up'.

IPA *See* INDIA PALE ALE.

Irish coffee Irish coffee, also known as *Gaelic coffee*, is a beverage concocted from black coffee, sugar, and Irish whiskey, with a layer of cream carefully floated on the top. Despite its traditional-sounding name, it does not appear to be of any great antiquity, the first recorded references to it being from around 1950. It is said to have been invented at Shannon airport, near Limerick. Marketing managers of middle-brow restaurant chains seized on the concept in the 1970s, producing an array of variants based on other spirits (such as *Caribbean coffee*, with rum).

Irish moss An alternative name, first recorded in 1845, for CARRAGEEN. To modern eyes *moss* is a misnomer, but in fact there is reliable evidence from the sixteenth to the late nineteenth century of *moss* being used to mean 'seaweed'; *Irish* reflects the plant's particular association with Ireland.

Irish stew The popularity and availability of Irish stew have waned in step with those of its main ingredient, mutton. Long a mainstay of institutional and domestic menus in Britain, it faded from the scene in the second half of the twentieth century, perhaps little regretted by those who remember watery versions meagrely eked out with bony mutton. It is composed of mutton (Mrs Beeton gives a recipe using loin or neck, or a more economical one with breast) packed in alternate layers with sliced potatoes, pearl barley, and onions, covered with water, and boiled or baked—so essentially it is the same dish as Lancashire hot-pot. The recipe is no doubt many centuries old, but the name *Irish stew* itself first turns up in 1814, in Byron's *Devil's Drive*: 'The Devil . . . dined on . . . a rebel or so in an Irish stew.'

Irn-Bru The proprietary name of a sweet orange-coloured Scottish carbonated drink with a citrussy tang. Drinks of this sort began to be produced in Scotland at the beginning of the twentieth century under the generic name *iron brew,* which was no doubt meant to suggest that they were a source of dietary iron and were generally good for you. Post-Second World War legislation frowned on such a name for a product that in fact contained a vanishingly small amount of iron and could not, in any strict sense of the word, be said to have been brewed, so in 1946 the leading manufacturer A. G. Barr changed *iron brew* to *Irn-Bru.* Since then the drink has never looked back, and today occupies a place in the Scottish potable pantheon second only to whisky. It has been claimed facetiously that if their internal organs were examined post mortem, those of many Scots would be found to be dyed Irn-Bru orange.

it *See* GIN AND IT.

jabugo ham A ham produced in Jabugo in the Huelva province of western Andalusia. It is the best-known variety of *jamon Ibérico* 'Iberian ham', which is a cured ham made from the native Spanish black pig (*cerdo ibérico*). *See also* SERRANO HAM.

Jack cheese An alternative American term, now little used, for MONTEREY JACK cheese.

jacket The notion of describing potatoes baked in their skins as *jacket potatoes* or *potatoes in their jackets* seems to date from the latter part of the nineteenth century. In Italy, the slightly more risqué *in veste da camera* 'in their nightshirts' is used in the same sense.

jackfruit The roughly spherical, edible fruit of a tropical Asian tree, similar to but larger than the breadfruit. The *jack-* element of its name, which goes back to the seventeenth century, is a folk-etymological alteration of Portuguese *jaca*, which itself came from Malayalam *chakka*.

Jacob's ladder A British term for a cut of beef more widely known as *short ribs*. It has a certain ladder-like appearance, with the ribs representing rungs, which prompted the allusion to Jacob's dream of a ladder reaching to heaven, described in Genesis 28:12.

Jaffa cake A sponge biscuit with an orange-flavoured jelly and chocolate topping, originally produced by the firm of McVitie's in 1927. *Jaffa* signifies 'orange'—it is the proprietary name of a large thick-skinned variety of orange, which originated in the mid-nineteenth century near Jaffa, a port on the coast of Israel—but *cake,* paradoxically, has proved a more problematical term. In 1991, HM Customs and Excise set out to establish that Jaffa cakes were not cakes but biscuits and hence, according to the rules, subject to Value Added Tax. Eventually their cakey status was officially admitted grudgingly: the makers' case turned on the assertion that when they get stale cakes go hard and biscuits go soft, and that Jaffa cakes go hard; on the other hand, it must be conceded that in most supermarkets, Jaffa cakes are to be found on the biscuit shelves.

jaffle An Australian term for a toasted sandwich: '"Aren't you eating with us, Nigel?" . . . "No way . . . I had a couple of jaffles and a malted earlier",' Chris Wallace-Crabbe, *Splinters* (1981). It comes from the proprietary name of the device in which the sandwich is toasted, a jaffle-iron, which is a hinged mould with a long handle that enables it to be held over an open fire.

jaggery The term commonly used in India and Southeast Asia for a type of coarse brown sugar made by evaporating the sap of various palm trees, especially the palmyra and kithul palms. Despite its Dickensian sound, its immediate source (in the late sixteenth century) was Portuguese *xagara* or *jagara*. The Portuguese got it from Malayalam *cakkarā*, which in turn came from Sanskrit *śarkarā* 'sugar' (*see* SUGAR). In the West the substance is usually more prosaically termed *palm sugar*.

jalapeño A medium-hot green chilli pepper, used especially in Mexican-style cooking. Mexican Spanish *chile jalapeño* means 'chilli from Jalapa', which is a city in east central Mexico (the name is a Hispanicized form of Aztec *Xalapan*, literally 'sand by the water').

jalebi An Indian sweetmeat consisting of a coil of batter that is deep-fried in ghee and then soaked briefly in syrup. The Hindi word is related to, and may have come from, *zalābīya*, a term for a frittered doughnut in Persian and Arabic. It is first recorded in English in 1868.

jalfrezi A medium- to very hot curry of northeastern India and Bangladesh featuring meat, fish, or vegetables cooked in a sauce made with onions, tomatoes, and fresh chillies. It became familiar in the UK in the last quarter of the twentieth century thanks to the growing popularity of 'Indian' restaurants (in 2011 it came top in a poll of popular curries conducted by *Chaat!*, the magazine of the British Curry Club, ousting the old favourite tikka masala). However, old India hands had been aware of it long before that: E. S. Poynter, for example, in her *What and How?* (1904), written for British expats in the Indian subcontinent, gave a recipe for 'Jhal Frezee' which essentially amounted to cold meat, onions, and chillies. The word itself is a Bengali colloquialism compounded from Bengali *jhāl* 'spicy food' and Urdu *parhezī*, denoting food suitable for someone on a diet.

jam *Jam* remains one of the unsolved mysteries of culinary etymology. No conclusive evidence has been found for the origin of the word, but most authorities agree that the likeliest explanation is that it describes the way jam is made by crushing or 'jamming' fruit together. Two early references seem to support this: first Hannah Glasse in her *Art of Cookery* (1747), using a curious Italianate spelling: 'To make Rasberry Giam. Take a pint of this Currant Jelly, and a quart of Rasberries, bruise them well together, set them over a slow fire . . .' And then Mrs Boscawen in 1781: 'The trotting of his horse will make my strawberries into jam before they reach the hand of my fair niece.'

The word begins to emerge in the 1730s; the first record of it is in the *Dictionarium Britannicum* (1736) of Nathan Bailey, who essays a fanciful derivation from French *j'aime*, 'I love it', on the grounds that that was what 'children used to say . . . formerly, when they liked any Thing'. Before that, other words used for fruits preserved in sugar included *conserva*, a borrowing from Italian or medieval Latin, first recorded in 1502, *comfiture* (1558), and the still current *conserve* (1530) and *preserve* (1600). Nor is it just a matter of fruits: the process and the word *jam* have been applied to other parts of plants, such as flower petals, and to plants which we would more readily classify as vegetables—notably marrow and tomatoes: 'Tortas de barros, a creamy sheeps' milk cheese . . . is served with tomato jam to fabulous effect', *Time Out, London's Best Restaurants* (2011).

Nowadays we take jam with bread as a matter of course, but until comparatively recently it was a luxury, to be occasionally indulged in with, or instead of, butter (hence such expressions as 'wanting to have jam on it', which seem to have arisen in the 1910s, and hence too, very probably, *jammy* in the sense 'lucky'—its other meaning, 'easy', perhaps comes from 'money for jam'). Up until the nineteenth century, fruit preserves might just as often be eaten on their own, as a dessert: a sumptuous breakfast, for example, described by Thomas Peacock in *Headlong Hall* (1816), includes rolls, toast, muffins, bread, and butter, but no jam; and Mrs Beeton, in listing the necessary ingredients for a picnic (6 medium-sized lobsters, 18 lettuces, 1 piece of collared calf's head, 1 large cold plum pudding, 2 sponge cakes . . .) stipulates bread and butter, but not jam. *See also* JAM TART.

jambalaya A paella-like Cajun dish from Louisiana, US. It consists of rice cooked with a variety of other ingredients including shrimps, sausage, chicken, and ham, seasoned with chilli powder and cayenne. The word is Louisiana French, and comes from Provençal *jambalaia*, a chicken and rice stew. According to Rita and Richard Collins's *New Orleans Cookbook* (1979), the town of Gonzales in Louisiana is the jambalaya capital of the world.

jammy dodger A biscuit consisting of two pieces of shortbread with jam sandwiched between them. The classic version, produced by Burton's Foods under the proprietary name *Jammie Dodger*, contains raspberry-flavoured plum jam which can be glimpsed through a heart-shaped hole in the top of the biscuit. The second half of its name probably comes from an early twentieth-century British slang term for a sandwich (*see* DODGER).

jam tart An open pastry case filled with jam and baked. The term is typically applied to a small individual tart, which is part of the traditional British pantheon of teatime cakes and pastries, but it can also refer to a larger tart. Such a simple confection might be assumed to have a long history, but in fact the earliest record of the term *jam tart* is from the early 1840s. Were the tarts stolen by the Knave of Hearts jam tarts? The original nursery rhyme, published in 1782, gives no clue, but in John Tenniel's illustrations to Lewis Carroll's *Alice's Adventures in Wonderland* (1865) the tarts (small-sized) do look suspiciously jammy.

In Cockney rhyming slang, *jam tart* has stood in over the years for *heart* (mainly in the playing-card sense) and *sweetheart* (female). In the latter application it seems to have rapidly broadened out in meaning in the late nineteenth century to 'young woman'. This usage survives in Australian English: 'The Pope's a Jew if that jam tart doesn't root like a rattlesnake', *Private Eye* (1969). In Britain it has died out, but it may well be that *tart* 'prostitute' is its legacy (*see* TART).

Jansson's temptation A Swedish dish (in the original Swedish, *Janssons frestelse*) which is essentially a fishy version of gratin dauphinois (*see* GRATIN): sliced potatoes, salted sprats, and onions are baked in cream (in default of salted sprats, difficult to obtain outside Scandinavia, anchovies can be used). There is naturally no shortage of suggestions as to the identity of Jansson—one frequently mentioned candidate is the famous Swedish bass-baritone Pelle Janzon (1844–89)—but as Jane Grigson asks in her *Fish Book* (1973), 'as Jansson is a Swedish equivalent of Smith or Jones, why look any further for a meaning than "Everyone's Temptation"?'

Jargonelle An early-ripening variety of pear. The name is seldom heard nowadays, but it was familiar enough in the eighteenth and nineteenth centuries: Mrs Rundell, in her *New System of Domestic Cookery* (1816), gave instructions on how 'to preserve Jarganel Pears most beautifully'. It was borrowed from French, where it is a diminutive of *jargon*, the name of a type of gemstone (probably related to English *zircon*).

Jarlsberg The proprietary name of a hard yellow Norwegian cows'-milk cheese with many small holes and a mild, nutty flavour. It was originally made in the 1850s in Jarlsberg, an old county to the south of Oslo, in imitation of Emmenthal, which had been introduced to Norway by Swiss cheese-makers in the 1830s. It was revived and launched commercially in the 1960s.

jasmine rice A type of long-grain rice with a flavour reminiscent of the fruit of the screw pine or pandanus. It comes from Thailand, and is widely used in Thai cooking. An alternative name for it is *Thai fragrant rice*. In Thai, it is *kao horm mali*.

jeera Jeera, or *zeera* (Hindi *jīrā*), is an Indian term for cumin.

jelly The word *jelly* comes ultimately from Latin *gelāre* 'to freeze'—hence its underlying notion is of a liquid substance that 'congeals' into a semisolid. The original jellies were meat jellies, made by boiling down the gelatinous portions of animals—calves' foot jelly, etc. These still survive today, of course, in the savoury jellies underlying the crust of patés and pork pies, in aspics (introduced into Britain from France in the 1770s), and in the jelly of jellied eels. The notion of fruit-flavoured jellies was first mooted by the seventeenth-century food writer Robert May, but it did not really catch on in a big way until the early nineteenth century (Eliza Acton, in her *Modern Cookery* (1845), advised her readers that a 'great variety of . . . excellent jellies for the table may be made with clarified isinglass, clear syrup, and the juice of fresh fruit'). In concert with blancmange, it came to dominate Anglo-Saxon tea-tables in the early twentieth century (in America it came to be known by the proprietary name *Jell-o*), but the 1970s and 1980s saw a decline in the face of ready-made desserts, yoghurts, etc. A parallel development in the use of the word is for a clear variety of jam, made from such fruit as apple, blackberry, redcurrant, etc., and set with pectin rather than gelatine (it is more widely used in American English than in British English).

Jelly babies, small gelatinous sweets shaped like babies, are a product of 1940s Britain, but *jelly beans*, favourite sweetmeat of former US president Ronald Reagan, go back further, to early twentieth-century America. They are baked-bean-shaped, with a hard sugar coating and a soft chewy centre. A *jelly-roll* to American-speakers is what British-speakers would call a *Swiss roll* (the *jelly* here refers to the jam sandwiched between the sponge cake). It has a variety of salacious metaphorical applications in the Black English of the southern states, to the 'female sex organs' and to 'sexual activity,' and it was these rather than the cake which inspired the nick-name of the American jazz pianist Ferdinand 'Jelly Roll' Morton (1885–1941).

jerk *Jerk* has a complicated history and prehistory as an English word, which is best approached by going back to its starting point, *echarqui*. This was a noun in the Quechua language of northern South America meaning 'dried flesh' (the Quechua people preserved meat—typically pork—by cutting it into strips and drying it in the sun). The word was

taken over by Latin American Spanish as *charqui*, and this was in turn acquired by English (originally in the US) in the late nineteenth century, its spelling Anglicized to *jerky*. It was applied to strips of meat preserved to a state of hardness by air-drying and used as iron rations, for example, by hunters in the wild or on board ship. The meat is usually beef, but there are other

options (Hugh Fearnley-Whittingstall, for instance, in his *River Cottage Meat Book* (2004) gives a recipe for venison jerky). Meanwhile, back in South America the Spanish had spun off from *charqui* a verb, *charquear*, denoting the preserving of meat in this fashion, which English took over in the eighteenth century as *jerk*: 'Killing cattle; more for the sake of their hides, and tallow, than their flesh; of which, nevertheless, they jerk great quantities for the use of such ships as sail from Pernambuco', *Juan and Ulloa's Voyage to South America* (translation, 1758). In recent years, however, *jerk* has come to refer not so much to a method of preserving meat as to a method of cooking it: marinating typically pork or chicken in a mixture of spices and barbecuing it over a wood fire. This is a quintessentially Caribbean way with meat—it provides the standard item of fast food on the streets of Jamaica—and in the second half of the twentieth century it found its way to the UK. The verb is mainly used as a past participial adjective, as in 'jerked chicken', but increasingly (as with *mash potato* for *mashed potato*, *skim milk* for *skimmed milk*, and *curry goat* for *curried goat*) *jerk* replaces *jerked*: 'There's a vaguely Caribbean beach-bar look here . . . Jerk chicken . . . was undercooked, even if the zippy peanut sauce covered it up a bit', *Time Out London, Eating and Drinking* (2009).

The Quechua, incidentally, had their own verb, *echarquini*, which may have been the source of the now-obsolete English noun and adjective *jerkin*: 'as drie as their ierkin beefe in the West Indies', John Smith, *Map of Virginia* (1612).

Jersey cabbage An eccentric variety of brassica grown on the island of Jersey. It bears a topknot of leaves that are edible at a pinch, but its main raison d'être is its sturdy stalk, which grows up to two metres tall and is fashioned into decorative walking sticks.

Jersey Royal The proprietary name of a variety of thin-skinned, typically kidney-shaped potato that is generally harvested as new potatoes. It was the accidental result of experimentations in the 1880s by the Jersey farmer Hugh de la Haye. It is the island of Jersey's biggest crop export.

Jerusalem artichoke The Jerusalem artichoke—a plant of the sunflower family grown for its knobbly potato-like tubers and not to be confused with the globe artichoke—has no connection whatsoever with the city of Jerusalem, and does not even have first claim on the name *artichoke*. It is a native of North America, and when Europeans first encountered it and brought it home in the early seventeenth century they were apparently struck by a resemblance between its taste and that of the globe artichoke—and so they called it *artichoke*. It was first cultivated in Europe at the Farnese gardens in Rome around 1617, and when it was exported it took its Italian name *girasole* 'sunflower'—literally 'turning to the sun'—with it. The English, however, could make little of this outlandish term, and so they immediately transformed it into something more manageable—familiar enough to pronounce, and yet suggestive of foreign parts: *Jerusalem*: 'Artichocks of *Ierusalem* is a roote vsually eaten with butter, vinegar, and pepper,' Tobias Venner, *Via Recta* (1620).

The French term for the 'Jerusalem artichoke' is the delightful *topinambour*, which apparently was originally the name of a small Brazilian tribe.

joe An American slang term, especially among sailors, for coffee. It is first recorded in 1930. Its origins are not known for certain: one speculation is that it was inspired by the Stephen Foster song 'Old Black Joe' (1853).

John apple An alternative name for an APPLE-JOHN.

johnnycake In America, where it originated (it is first recorded in 1739), the term *johnnycake* denotes a type of corn bread typically eaten for breakfast with butter or maple syrup. In Australia it stands for a thin wholemeal cake, typically cooked over the ashes of a campfire or fried in a pan, and in the West Indies for a sort of scone or dumpling. It is probably based on the name *Johnny*, but it has also been suggested that *johnny* may be an alteration of *journey* (from the notion of a foodstuff easily prepared by travellers) or even of *Shawnee* (suggesting a Native American origin, although others claim that the bread was originally made by African Americans in the southern states).

joint In British English, a joint is a large piece of meat for cooking—and has been since the sixteenth century. It typically contains a bone (a leg, a rib, a shoulder), and is roasted. But in nineteenth-century America, the word was used for something rather different. This was the Victorian era, when direct reference to 'legs' was taboo. This was awkward when one wished to request that particular portion of the anatomy of a cooked chicken, turkey, etc. to be given to one. The solution was to euphemize the leg of such a fowl as a *joint*. Apparently it caused a certain amount of confusion among British visitors. *Compare* DRUMSTICK.

jollof rice A deep red West African stew made with rice, chilli peppers, tomato paste or palm oil, and meat or fish. *Jollof* is a variant of *Wolof*, the name of a people of Senegal and Gambia. According to Jenny Macarthur in the *Oxford Companion to Food* (2006), jollof rice is 'possibly the best-known African dish outside Africa'.

'Jollof rice is a subject of great debate in West Africa. Every country has its own version, and abhors "inauthentic" variations. In Ghana, it is eaten on its own or with fried ripe plantains. The addition of green, leafy plants is much frowned upon there. Nigerians

purport to have the most authentic recipe and sigh wearily at preposterous notions such as adding garlic, bell pepper, carrots, green beans, or cabbage. Likewise, a stunned silence would greet anyone adding seafood to jollof rice in ... Liberia ... Meanwhile, our French-speaking cousins in Cote D'Ivoire, Senegal, and Mali would see the use of okra or nuts as heresy', Reina Yaidoo, *Guardian* (2011).

Jonagold A variety of dessert apple with greenish-gold skin and crisp flesh. It was developed in America in the 1960s as a cross between the Jonathan (a bright red apple named after Jonathan Hasbrouk, a nineteenth-century American lawyer) and the Golden Delicious, and its name came about by a similar process.

Jordan almond *See* ALMOND.

jostaberry A fruit that is a cross between various species of *Ribes*, especially the blackcurrant and the gooseberry (it looks like an oversized blackcurrant). It was developed in Germany in the early twentieth century, but plants were not marketed to the public until 1977. Its original German name is *jostabeere*: the *jo* comes from *johannisbeere* 'blackcurrant' and the *sta* from *stachelbeere* 'gooseberry'.

jujube Although now little heard of, the jujube was common in the nineteenth and early twentieth centuries as a fruit-flavoured gum or lozenge, often medicated to allay coughing. The first account of it in print comes in Peter Simmonds's *Dictionary of Trade Products* (1858): 'The term jujube is ... very generally applied by chemists and confectioners to a thickened mucilaginous lozenge.' However, this was merely a secondary application of the term, which originally denoted an edible berrylike fruit of a tree of the buckthorn family (the word *jujube* is a corruption of its original Greek name *zizyphon*). The fruit, which has a red skin and sweet yellowish flesh, was perhaps used to flavour the lozenges which became known as *jujubes*; or alternatively the transfer of names may have been based on a similarity of shape.

julep To twenty-first-century drinkers a julep is a product of the Deep South of the US (made famous in the song 'One mint julep'): a strong but refreshing mixture of Kentucky bourbon or rye whiskey and sugar, poured over ice, and flavoured typically with sprigs of fresh mint. It was not always so, however. Originally, a julep was any sweet syrupy drink, often one used as a vehicle for medicine (William Buchan's *Domestic Medicine* (1789) mentions 'cordial julep, expectorating julep, and musk julep'). In that sense, the term has long since passed into limbo, but it may survive dialectally in the slightly altered form *jollop* 'medicine'. The word *julep* comes via Arabic *julāb* from Persian *gulāb*, which meant literally 'rose-water'.

julienne Julienne vegetables are vegetables (such as carrots, celery, or peppers) cut into long thin strips. The term presumably comes from one or other of the French proper names *Jules* or *Julien*, but the reason for the application is not known. It first crops up in the 1722 edition of *Le cuisinier royal*, and from earliest times was commonly used in the phrase *potage à la julienne*, denoting a vegetable soup. In fact when the word was first borrowed into English in the mid-nineteenth century, it was in the sense 'vegetable broth': 'The best part of a pint of julienne . . . is very well for a man who has only one dish besides to devour,' William Thackeray, *Miscellaneous Essays* (1841).

jumble A jumble or *jumbal*, is, or was, a small thin crisp sugared biscuit or cake. Jumbles were generally given flavourings such as rose water, cinnamon, or orange zest, and made in particular shapes. In the seventeenth century these might be anything that took the cook's fancy, such as a knot or a letter of the alphabet, but by the nineteenth century a ring shape had become standard. By then, too, the word had largely died out in Britain, but it remains in use in the US. Its origins are unclear: it appears to have no connection with *jumble* 'muddle', but it may be related to *gimmal* (or *gimbal*) 'two-part (or three-part) finger ring'.

jungle curry A type of Thai curry (in Thai, *gaeng pah* or *kaeng pa*) that originated in the northern forests of Thailand. Its defining characteristic is not that it contains various denizens of the jungle—Keith Floyd, tongue in cheek, claimed 'snake, frog, wild boar, assorted birds, and unspecified furry creatures' as ingredients in *Far Flung Floyd* (1994)—but that, unlike most other Thai curries, it contains no coconut, which does not grow in northern jungles. It is usually gaspingly chilli-hot.

juniper berry The aromatic dark purplish-blue to black berry-like cone of the common juniper, an evergreen shrub or small tree of the northern hemisphere. It is often used for its resinous tang in game cookery, and it is the key flavouring ingredient of gin (indeed the word *gin* comes ultimately from the French name for juniper; *see* GIN).

junket A dessert made from sweetened milk that has been curdled with rennet and then allowed to set to a jelly-like consistency. It is typically served with clotted cream. The word comes from Old French *jonquette*, a derivative of *jonc* 'rush', which originally meant 'basket'; evidently junkets made in medieval times were often broken up and laid in such rush baskets to drain before being served. By the middle of the seventeenth century, however, it had become customary to leave the curds undisturbed.

As early as the sixteenth century the word had taken on a more general application, to any sweet dish or delicacy, and before even this, around 1450, the word *junkery* appears, meaning 'feasting and merrymaking', foreshadowing modern English *junketing*.

jus A thin gravy or sauce made from the natural juices exuded from meat while cooking, especially roasting: 'roast cannon of lamb with bubble and squeak and rosemary jus', *Good Food Guide* (2008). The term was borrowed originally in the 1840s from French, where it is essentially shorthand for *jus de viande* 'meat juice' (it is thus a doublet of *juice*, which was taken from the same French word six centuries earlier). It retains an air of French polish, and its use latterly to inject an element of would-be sophistication into descriptions of humble gravy, and by extension of any thin, non-creamy sauce ('A tiny bonne bouche of melon, grape, and kiwi in raspberry jus', *Daily Post* (Liverpool) (2003)), has made it a butt of satire.

kabanos A type of long thin dry Polish pork sausage with a smoky flavour. The name is a derivative of Polish *kaban* 'young male pig'.

kabinett In former centuries the monastic wine-growers of the Rhine and Mosel used to put aside bottles of their very best wine in special closets, or *kabinetts*, in their cellars, for their own particular future use. Hence the present-day term *kabinett*, which denotes a German wine of high quality—specifically, of the basic grade in the classification *Qualitätswein mit Prädikat* (the earliest record of its appearance on a wine label is on a bottle of Steinberger Auslese 1811). Kabinett wines are finer than humble *tafelwein* or *landwein*, but do not have the cachet of the more expensive *spätlesen* and *auslesen*.

kadaif At first glance, kadaif looks like slimmed down shredded wheat. It is an eastern Mediterranean confection made from a leavened flour-and-water batter sieved into very thin strands which are rolled round a filling of chopped nuts, baked, and then soaked in syrup. *Kadaif*, or *kadayif*, is its Turkish name. In Greece it is *kataifi*. Both come from Arabic *qata'if*, which refers to a type of pancake. In Arab countries, particularly Egypt and Syria, the vermicelli-pastry confection, which is made from the same batter as kadaif, is known as *kunafa*.

kaffir lime A type of Southeast Asian citrus tree that produces small knobbly pear-shaped fruit. Their exiguous juice is too bitter to be of much culinary use, but their rind and the tree's glossy aromatic two-part leaves (like a figure of eight) are a different matter: both are widely used in Thailand and Indonesia to add their particular tang to curries and other cooked dishes, and the leaves can be shredded and eaten raw in salads. The name *kaffir lime* presents something of a conundrum. *Kaffir* is a South African word. Derived from Arabic *kāfir* 'infidel', it was originally used (from the late sixteenth century) to denote a member of the Xhosa people. It was soon being applied indiscriminately to any black South African, and by at least the middle of the nineteenth century it had become an insulting term indicative of contempt (its use is now illegal in South Africa). It was widely used in the nineteenth century to name various wild or indigenous southern African plants and animals—for instance, *kaffir cattle, kaffir orange, kaffir plum*. However, *kaffir lime* does not appear to be from this stable, perhaps not surprisingly, as the tree is not a South African one: it is not recorded, for example, in the authoritative *Dictionary of South African English* (1996). The plant's traditional name in Thailand is *makrut,* and a possible vector for a South

Africa-to-Thailand transmission of *kaffir lime* is Cape Malays, South Africans (mainly in the Western Cape) of South and Southeast Asian ethnic origin.

Kahlúa The proprietary name (first recorded in 1945) of a dark brown coffee-flavoured Mexican liqueur. Its origin is not known.

kaiseki A style of traditional Japanese cuisine in which a series of small, refined, intricate dishes are prepared, served typically as the edible element of the tea ceremony: 'A range of fixed-price kaiseki menus . . . starts at expensive, rising to the special Kyoto sushi kaiseki menu for which the old maxim applies—if you have to ask the price you can't afford it,' *Good Food Guide* (2008). The Japanese word (first recorded in English in 1920) is ostensibly a compound formed from *kai* (from *kaichu* 'kimono pocket') and *seki* 'stone'. The rationale behind this somewhat gnomic metaphor is the Zen custom of putting a heated stone next to the stomach to allay hunger: it is a discrete reference to the frugality of the meal. In fact, though, *kaiseki* is an alteration of the earlier, original term *kwaiseki*, meaning 'seating for a social gathering, especially a tea or poetry party', formed from *kwai-* 'meeting' and *seki* 'seat'. All the elements of these compound words were originally adopted into Japanese from Middle Chinese.

kaiser roll A North American term (often abbreviated to *kaiser*) for a crisp bread roll with cuts in the top radiating from the centre. It was originally made by folding the corners of a square of dough into the middle before baking. It originated in Vienna and was named *kaisersemmel* 'emperor roll', apparently in honour of Emperor Franz Josef (1830–1916). It is often used for sandwiches: 'Sliced ham on a kaiser', *Waterloo* (Ontario) *Chronicle* (1986).

Kalamata olive A purplish-black rich-flavoured variety of olive named after its place of origin, Kalamata, on the southern coast of the Peloponnese in Greece. It is standardly slit along the side before being marinated in vinegar and brine.

kalbi jjim *See* GALBI JJIM.

kale Essentially, *kale* is the same word as the *cauli-* of *cauliflower*, the *cole-* of *coleslaw*, and the *kohl-* of *kohlrabi*. It originated as a northern and Scottish version of *cole*, a now virtually obsolete word for cabbage. This goes back ultimately to a Latin word for 'cabbage', *caulis*, which etymologically meant 'hollow-stemmed vegetable', and has provided the term for 'cabbage' in a wide variety of European languages (such as French *chou*, Italian *cavolo*, Spanish *col*, German *kohl*, Dutch *kool*, and Welsh *cawl*). *Kale*, or *kail*, as it is also spelled, remains a general Scottish word for 'cabbage', and also for 'cabbage soup'; indeed, so common a feature has it historically been of the  Scottish diet that the term *kailyard* (literally 'cabbage-garden') was applied at the end of the nineteenth century to a school of Scottish fiction describing (over-romantically) the life of the ordinary people. South of the border, *kale* has come to be applied more specifically to an open-headed variety of cabbage, whose crinkly leaves have given it the added name *curly kale*. Another synonym, now little used, is *borecole*. It should not be confused with *seakale*, which is an entirely different vegetable.

In American English, *kale* is a slang term for 'money'—an allusion to its green crinkliness.

kapitan A Nyonya (Chinese–Malaysian) dish made with a curry paste compounded typically of chillies, shallots, garlic, ginger, lemongrass, turmeric, five-spice, and shrimp paste. The name refers to the high-ranking Chinese official (the *kapitan* or 'captain') who in the past acted as the go-between between the Chinese communities in Malaya and the Malay rulers.

karela The Hindi name used in Indian cookery for the BITTER GOURD.

kasha An eastern European dish made from crushed buckwheat (the word is Russian). It is prepared in various ways: it can, for instance, be made into a thick gruel or porridge, or alternatively shaped into small pancakes. Fashion designers, always on the look-out for a novel colour term, appropriated *kasha* for a particular shade of beige: 'She had an outfit made . . . in a new colour called "kasha"', Mary McCarthy, *Memories of a Catholic Girlhood* (1957).

kataifi See KADAIF.

Kate and Sidney British rhyming slang (and also a partial spoonerism) for *steak and kidney* (usually pudding, but also applicable to the pie). It is first known in print from 1914, and the earliest record of *steak and kidney* itself is only from the 1860s, when Mrs Beeton gave a recipe for the pudding. 'Beefsteak pudding? Phew! A pity Johnny's not here, Ma! Remember how he used to go for your Kate and Sidney?', Marguerite Steen, *Twilight on the Floods* (1949).

kebab In Turkish, *kebap* simply means 'roast meat' (*see also* DÖNER KEBAB). A *şiş kebabiu*, however, is meat grilled in small chunks on a skewer (*şiş* is Turkish for 'skewer'). English adopted the term as *shish kebab* in the second decade of the twentieth century, and has since shortened it to simply *kebab*. A shish kebab is a traditional Turkish dish, typically made from mutton; the vegetables with which the pieces of meat are often interspersed are an inauthentic detail, added to jazz the kebab up in Westernized versions. (The Georgian version of the shish kebab, which has spread to other parts of western Asia and eastern Europe, is the *shashlik*, whose name derives ultimately from Turkish *şiş*.)

English originally acquired the term in the late seventeenth century, via Hindi *kabāb* (hence probably the current English spelling, in preference to the original Turkish form). At first it was spelled *cabob* or *kabob*, and it took a long time to settle down orthographically; indeed in American English *kabob* remains the preferred spelling.

The term *shish kebab* is used metaphorically in chemistry for a type of crystalline structure in which minute platelike crystalline bodies grow out from a central rod.

kedgeree Hindi *khichrī* is a dish of boiled rice with lentils or other pulses, and seventeenth-century European contacts with India brought reports of it back to England. The 1662 translation of the *Travels of Mandelslo from Persia into the East-Indies*, for instance, notes: 'their ordinary Diet being only Kitsery, which they make of Beans pounded, and Rice, which they boile together . . . Then they put thereto a little butter melted.' It is not until the beginning of the nineteenth century that we get wind of the transformation that was to make kedgeree one of the mainstays of the Victorian breakfast table. Eliza Acton's 1845 recipe includes flaked fish with the rice (and no lentils, of course), but she adds her eggs raw, beaten, and still regards it as a 'foreign' dish, and she even recommends chutney with it. By Mrs Beeton's time (1861) however, chopped hard-boiled eggs had established themselves as an essential ingredient. Aficionados of the quintessential kedgeree insist that it should be made with smoked haddock.

keema The Indian term (Hindi *kīmā*) for minced meat.

kefalotyri A type of salty Greek ewes'- or goats'- milk cheese made in the form of a round shallow drum. When young it is eaten raw, and as it hardens with age it can be used in cooking (for example, it commonly forms the cheese component of the topping sauce for a moussaka). Its name means 'hat cheese' (modern Greek *kepháli* means 'head', and hence by extension 'hat'); the shape of the cheese supposedly resembles a round brimless hat.

keftedes In Greek cookery, small herby meatballs made with minced lamb or pork. Modern Greek *kephtedes* is the plural of *kephtes,* which came via Turkish from Persian *koftah* 'pounded meat' (also the source of English *kofta*).

Kendal mint cake A hard peppermint-flavoured sweet which is sold in flat rectangular blocks and is popular with ramblers and hill climbers. It has been made at Kendal in Cumbria in the English Lake District since at least the late 1860s. It received its biggest publicity boost in 1953, when it was used by the successful British Everest expedition.

ketchup When the term *ketchup* first entered the English language, at the end of the seventeenth century, it stood for something very different from the bottled tomato sauce of today. At that time tomatoes were an expensive rarity, and ketchups were long-keeping, often vinegar-based sauces flavoured with mushrooms, anchovies, onions, lemons, oysters, pickled walnuts, etc. They formed the essential ingredient of the proprietary sauces so popular with the Victorians, of which Worcester sauce is virtually the only survival. It was not until the early twentieth century, with the importation of cheap tinned tomatoes from America, that tomato ketchup began to encamp itself firmly in the centre of British meal tables.

The word *ketchup* itself comes, probably via Malay, from Chinese *koechiap,* literally 'fish juice'; this was a sort of relish made from pickled fish. The original spelling was *catchup,* and as early as the 1730s this produced a spin-off version *catsup,* possibly from some sort of erroneous or humorous association with 'cats' and 'supping'. We first hear of it in Jonathan Swift's *Panegyric on Dean* (1730): 'And, for our home-bred British cheer, botargo, catsup, and caveer' (it was clearly still an exotic commodity); *catsup* is still seen in American English, and has even given rise to a spelling pronunciation. The spelling *ketchup* began to appear around 1710.

Key lime pie An American pie containing a lime-flavoured custard topped with meringue. It is traditionally made from Key limes, which are a yellowish variety of lime grown especially in the Florida Keys, a string of coral islets off the south coast of Florida. The term is first recorded in 1954.

khorasan An ancestral variety of wheat with very large grains. It has been claimed that it was known in ancient Egypt, but its name is that of a historic region covering parts of modern-day Iran, Afghanistan, Turkmenistan, Uzbekistan, and Tajikistan.

kibbeh A Middle Eastern dish of ancient ancestry and many variations, consisting essentially of a mixture of bulgar wheat, chopped onions, and minced lamb, beaten to a paste and eaten raw, fried, or grilled.

kibbled wheat Wheat whose grains have been coarsely ground. Although the advocacy of vegetarians has brought it to recent prominence (it is now commonly found in muesli, for instance, and is sprinkled on the top of bread and rolls), the verb *kibble* seems to be of some antiquity. It is first recorded in the late eighteenth century, but it may well be much older. It is not clear where it comes from, although there may be some connection with the Middle English noun *kible* 'stout cudgel' (perhaps as used for crushing the grain) or even with *cobble* (from a resemblance of the crushed grain to small stones).

kickshaw A seventeenth- and eighteenth-century term for any dainty or elaborate dish characteristic of high-falutin 'foreign' cuisine (as opposed to solid English fare). It is an Anglicization of French *quelque chose* 'something'. Its first appearance is in Shakespeare's

Henry IV Part Two (1597), in which Justice Shallow gives orders to his servant Davy for a meal to be prepared for Falstaff, including 'some pigeons . . . a couple of short-legged hens, a joint of mutton, and any pretty little tiny kickshaws'. As an indication of the wide diversity of dishes to which the word was applied, a recipe for kickshaws by Gervase Markham in *The English Housewife* (1615) describes a rich highly spiced omelette containing assorted pig's offal, but by the time Hannah Glasse is writing of them in 1747 they have become small fruit pies.

kidney bean The roughly kidney-shaped seed of the cultivated bean plant *Phaseolus vulgaris*, which is a native of Central America. The term (first recorded in 1548) is potentially wide in application, and certainly encompasses cannellini beans, which are also called *white kidney beans*, but in practice it usually refers to a dark-red-skinned variety of the bean, which might be said to resemble a kidney in colour as well as shape. It is mainly procurable dried or tinned, and is a key component of chilli con carne.

Kiev A culinary term boosted to wide familiarity by *chicken Kiev* (or, in its Sunday best form, *chicken à la Kiev*), which is a boned chicken breast coated with breadcrumbs and stuffed with garlic- and parsley-infused butter that bursts out incontinently when the chicken breast is broached. The precise nature of the dish's connection with Kiev, the capital city of the Ukraine, is unclear. It appears to have no long-standing place in traditional Ukrainian cuisine (in Ukrainian it is *kotleta po-kyivsky* 'cutlet Kiev-style'), and although it has been claimed that it was invented in the early 1960s to mark the opening of the Moscow Hotel in Kiev, another version has it that it was created in the kitchens of the Moscow Merchants' Club early in the twentieth century. Whatever its origins, its easy packagability made it a natural for the new genre of supermarket ready-meals in the mid-1970s, and it has retained its popularity ever since. So familiar has its name become that *chicken* can be omitted, and the choice of fillings has spread beyond garlic butter: so 'leek-and-bacon Kievs' can be bought, and 'cheese-and-ham Kievs' (the latter muscling aside the designation *cordon bleu*). This nomenclature presupposes that for the consumer, *Kiev* means 'chicken', but non-meat-eaters are now catered for too, with 'vegetarian Kievs' made from beans.

Kilpatrick *Oysters Kilpatrick* is an Australian recipe for cooking oysters: after being poached they are returned to their shells, covered with a gratin of brioche crumbs and finely chopped bacon, and flashed under the grill. The precise origins of the name are unknown, but it could be an alteration of *oysters Kirkpatrick*, which denotes a fairly similar American recipe also featuring bacon. That was created by Ernest Arbogast, chef at the Palace Hotel, San Francisco, and named in honour of Colonel John Kirkpatrick, manager of the hotel between 1894 and 1914.

kimchi The national dish of Korea: a pungent fermented vegetable pickle seasoned with garlic, chilli, ginger, etc. which appears at virtually every meal, eaten as an accompaniment to rice. The vegetable component is most commonly Chinese cabbage, but there are

many other possibilities, including turnips and cucumber. Most Korean households make their own kimchi, burying it in a sealed jar during the winter so that it keeps better. The word, first recorded in English in 1898, comes from Korean *kimch'i*.

king, à la *See* CHICKEN À LA KING.

king crab The American name of a type of long-legged, relatively small-bodied North Pacific crab that resembles the North Atlantic spider crab. In recent years the term has shown signs of emigrating to British English, and often turns up on restaurant menus (perhaps welcomed as a more user-friendly alternative to the potentially off-putting *spider crab*): 'A king-crab cocktail had lots of pearly fresh meat, as it should do at £15 a pop', Jay Rayner, *Observer Magazine* (2011). A further ground for confusion is that *king crab* is another name (of many centuries' standing) for the horseshoe crab, which is not actually a crab at all.

King Edward A variety of main-crop potato that has a white skin mottled with red. It was developed in Northumberland at the beginning of the twentieth century, and named in honour of King Edward VII (1841–1910).

king rabbit There are strict religious laws forbidding Jews to eat pork. Nevertheless, the odd porker is raised for food in Israel, and an alternative to *pork* is needed to disguise its presence on menus. Among the euphemisms used is *king rabbit*, chosen presumably because the rabbit's cooked flesh is similar in colour to that of the pig (*see also* WHITE MEAT). Another euphemistic gastronomic application of the term *rabbit* was to cats and kittens during the siege of Paris in 1870–71.

kipper The kipper has a mysterious past. The first record of the word in English, from about AD 1000, refers to a male salmon or sea trout during the spawning season, and this usage is still current among fishermen. It is not at all clear, however, whether this is really the same word as now applies to the familiar kippered herring, and indeed if it is true that our kipper (split and then brined and smoked, in contrast to the bloater, which is preserved whole) derives ultimately from Old English *cypera* 'copper', in reference to its 'coppery' colour, then they could well be quite distinct. But even so, in the early days of kippering we are still in the realm of salmon and trout; Daniel Defoe, in his *Tour of Great Britain* (1724–6), describes how the process was carried out in the eighteenth century: 'Preserving Salmon by making it into what they call Kipper: This is done by dividing it in the Middle from Head to Tail, and drying it slowly before a fire.' In effect, kippers were once what we would now call smoked salmon, and the kippered herring did not come into its own until about 120 years ago (Mrs Beeton does not mention it). It is said first to have been produced on the Northumbrian coast early in the first half of the nineteenth century (John Woodger of Seahouses is credited with the original idea of applying the salmon curing method to herrings, in the 1840s), and by the end of the century had become firmly established as part of the traditional English breakfast.

   The kipper tie, incidentally, a very wide tie symptomatic of the swinging sixties, was named partly from its shape, but was also partly suggested by the name of Michael Fish, a leading English clothes designer of the period.

kir Though the French still tend to stick to the term *vin blanc cassis* (or *blancass* for short), the name *kir* has spread the fame of this blend of dry white wine and crème de cassis (blackcurrant liqueur) far beyond the borders of France. It comes from Canon Félix Kir, a Second World War resistance hero and for several years mayor of Dijon, who developed a particular brand of the drink. As the Dijon connection suggests, it was originally a Burgundian speciality, and the classic formulation is a glass of the rather sharp white wine made from the local aligoté grape, with just enough sweet crème de cassis to take the edge off the wine's acidity and give it kir's distinctive pink colour. (Crème de cassis too is a noted product of Burgundy—the Côte d'Or heads the league table of blackcurrant-growing départements in France—and should on no account be replaced by blackcurrant cordial or other inauthentic substitutes.) Over the past two or three decades kir has achieved considerable popularity in Britain and elsewhere as a summer aperitif (it can now be bought ready-bottled in supermarkets), and a more luxurious version made with sparkling wine has been developed, known as kir royale (in French *kir royal, kir* being masculine).

Those who prefer it can substitute red wine for white; the resulting drink is known as a *cardinal*. And numerous permutations of liqueur are possible, of course; crème de framboise (raspberry) and crème de mure (blackberries) form the basis of delicious drinks, and in Provence *myro*—white wine with a dash of crème de myrtilles (bilberries)—is a combination of long standing, said to have been originally a shepherd's drink. But whatever the ingredients, the wine/crème mixture seems to have a beneficial effect on the health: Canon Kir died in 1968, having achieved the impressive age of 92.

kirsch A colourless spirit distilled from cherries. The word *kirsch* is German for 'cherry', and as applied to the fruit brandy is short for *kirsch(en)geist* 'cherry spirit' or *kirsch(en)wasser* 'cherry water' (which is sometimes taken to apply to a superior grade made in the Black Forest area); the same drink made in Alsace is known by the French term *eau-de-vie-de-kirsch. Kirsch* itself is related to English *cherry* via a common ancestor, Latin *ceresia*.

Kirschenwasser was the earliest term for the drink to be adopted in English (Sir Walter Scott refers to it in *A Legend of Montrose* (1819): 'We had drunk about two mutchkins of *kirschenwasser*'); the abbreviated *kirsch* is not recorded until 1869.

Kirsch, which is dry, should not be confused with the sweet dark sticky *cherry brandy*.

Kit Kat The proprietary name of a wafer biscuit covered with chocolate, introduced in Britain by Rowntree's in 1935 (originally as *Rowntree's Chocolate Crisp*; it became *Kit Kat* in 1937). Today it sells around the world in a myriad of different flavour variations. The name itself was originally used in the 1920s (in the form *Kit Cat* or *Kit Kat*) for boxed chocolates. Its ultimate ancestor was the Kit Kat Club, a Whig club founded in the reign of James II (which in turn got its name from a shorthand form of *Christopher Catling*, the name of the owner of the pie-house near Temple Bar, London where the club originally met). It is doubtful whether the confectionery got its name directly from this, but *Kit Kat* was a voguish term in Britain in the post-First World War Jazz Age (there was a nightclub called the Kit Kat in the West End of London, for example, and in Glasgow, patrons of St Andrew's Halls danced to Charlie Harkinn and his Kit Kat Band), and it is said that the nightclub was the immediate source of Rowntree's inspiration. Bolstered by the success of the slogan 'Have a break . . . have a Kit Kat!' (introduced in 1957), the term has for the most part avoided any possible confusion with *Kitekat*, the name of a brand of cat food.

kitke The term used in South African English for CHALLAH. It may come from Hebrew *kikkār* 'loaf'.

kiwiberry A fruit that resembles a small green or purple smooth-skinned version of its close relative, the kiwi fruit. Cut open, it reveals a similar pattern of small black seeds surrounded by green flesh. It is a native of northern China and Siberia.

kiwi fruit The kiwi fruit originated in China (hence its earliest English name *Chinese gooseberry*). It was brought to New Zealand in the early years of the twentieth century, and began to be grown on a commercial scale in the 1940s. Exports started in the early 1950s, and by the 1980s the kiwi fruit had a place on virtually every supermarket shelf in the Western world, its vivid green flesh flecked with black seeds beloved of the colourists of Nouvelle Cuisine. Its original name was not inappropriate, considering its shape and colour, but it seems not to have been acceptable to the American market in the 1960s, perhaps for political reasons, so an alternative was sought. What more apt name could have been chosen for one of New Zealand's most high-profile exports, particularly in view of the passing resemblance of the fruit's brown furry exterior to a kiwi, their national bird. An early move in this direction seems to have been inspired by the closely related kiwiberry—the *New Zealand News* (1968) notes 'New Zealand exports of Chinese gooseberries will enter the United States—where they are called "giant Kiwi-berries"— almost duty-free from next season'—but *kiwi fruit* is first recorded in the mid-1960s, and by the 1970s had become the established version. (The French, incidentally, took to calling the fruit *souris végétales*, 'vegetable mice'.)

kleftiko A Greek–Cypriot dish consisting of lamb on the bone (often shoulder or shank) slowly pot-roasted with flavourings of oregano and other herbs. The term, first recorded in English in 1968, comes from a noun use of the modern Greek adjective *kléphtikos*, meaning 'of the klephts'. These were mountain-dwelling outlaws, who fought for Greek independence in the 1820s. Although they reverted to banditry after the war of independence (the word comes ultimately from Greek *kleptēs* 'thief', which is also the source of English *kleptomaniac*), they retained enough charisma to inspire the name of the dish.

klipfish Cod that has been preserved by splitting the fish open, boning, salting, and drying it. The term (first recorded in 1835) is probably a partial translation of Danish *klipfisk*, which means literally 'rock fish' (a reference to laying the fish out on rocks to dry them). Confusingly, it is also used as the name of fish of the Clinidae family, small fish often found in rock pools.

knackwurst A type of short fat German sausage made from pork and/or beef, and generously seasoned with garlic and cumin. It is cooked by boiling or grilling, and typically eaten with sauerkraut. The German name is composed of the onomatopoeic verb *knacken* 'to crackle' (presumably a reference to the noises produced either by the cooking process—as with English *banger*—or by eating) and *wurst* 'sausage'. In American English the variant form *knockwurst*, first recorded in 1929, is if anything commoner.

knickerbocker glory An elaborate ice-cream dessert consisting of layers of ice cream, jelly, fruit, and cream served in a tall glass. It has no connection with nether garments; the term was presumably inspired by Diedrich Knickerbocker, the mock-Dutch name invented by Washington Irving for the fictitious author of his *History of New York* (1809). This subsequently became synonymous with the descendants of the original Dutch settlers in New Amsterdam, and eventually with New Yorkers in general—so a knickerbocker glory is essentially a tribute to New York. The term is first recorded in the 1930s.

knish In Jewish cookery, a dumpling of flaky dough with a savoury filling that is baked or fried. The word, first recorded in English in 1916, comes via Yiddish from Polish *knysz* and Russian *knysh*, denoting a kind of bun or dumpling.

knockwurst An alternative form of KNACKWURST.

knuckle A cut of meat consisting of the lowest joint in an animal's leg together with the adjoining parts. First recorded in 1625, the term is usually used with reference to bacon or ham—'the tea-things, including . . . a cold knuckle of ham', Charles Dickens, *Old Curiosity Shop* (1840)—to veal, and to pork (though for uncured pork, *hock* is usually preferred).

Kobe beef A type of high-quality (and highly priced) tender marbled beef with a high proportion of saturated fat, produced from the Tajima breed of Wagyu cattle that have been raised in the area around Kobe, the capital of the Hyogo Prefecture in Japan. The cattle are reared on a special diet that includes rice, beans, and beer, and are regularly massaged to promote tenderness. The standard Japanese term is *Kōbe-gyū*, which means 'Kobe cattle', but *Kōbe-*

biifu is also used (*biifu* being the Japlish version of *beef*).

koeksister A twisted or plaited doughnut soaked in syrup, popular in South Africa. The origins of the Afrikaans word (first recorded in English in 1891) are unclear. The first element looks like Dutch *koek* 'cake', but it could also be from Malay *kuih* 'cake, sweetmeat'; the second may be derived from Dutch *sissen* 'to sizzle' with the agentive suffix *-er*.

kofta In Indian cookery, the term *kofta* denotes a spiced meatball, or a similarly shaped mass of chopped fish or vegetable, cooked in a spicy sauce. In Urdu (and Persian), the word *koftah* means 'pounded meat'.

kohlrabi The kohlrabi is not a promising vegetable—globular and pale green, with a few spindly stalks protruding from it and something of the flavour of a turnip—but eaten young and small enough it can be succulent. It is the swollen stem of a plant of the cabbage family, and its name betrays its family connections. *Kohlrabi* was acquired by English in the early nineteenth century from German, which in turn got it from Italian *cavoli rape*. This is the plural of *cavolo rapa*, which means literally 'cabbage turnip'. The first element, *cavolo*, comes ultimately from Latin *caulis* 'stem, stalk, cabbage', which is also the source of English *kale* 'cabbage', the *cauli-* of English *cauliflower*, the *cole-* of English *coleslaw*, and indeed German *kohl* 'cabbage', with which the Germans replaced the *cavoli* of *cavoli rape*. The second element, *rapa*, comes from Latin *rāpa* 'turnip'. This also produced English *rape*, which formerly denoted 'turnip' but is now used only for a related yellow-flowered plant cultivated for its oil-rich seeds. An alternative name for the kohlrabi is *turnip cabbage*.

kola See COLA.

korma A mildly spiced Indian curry made from meat or fish marinated in yoghurt or curds. The Urdu term, first recorded in English in 1832 (in the form *qoorma*), comes from Turkish *kavurma*, which means 'cooked meat'.

koumiss Koumiss, or *kumiss*, is fermented mare's or ass's milk, as drunk by the nomadic peoples of west and central Asia. The standard brew is fairly inoffensive, at only about 2 per cent alcohol, but a more potent drink, also called *koumiss*, can be distilled from it. English acquired the term (which originated as Tatar *kumiz*) in the late sixteenth century, but to begin with it was frequently confused with *cosmos*: 'As the Arabians, so they [Tatars] delight in sour milk, or cosmos', Robert Johnson, *The World, or an historicall description of the most famous kingdomes or commonweales therein* (1601). In late Victorian England there was a sudden craze for koumiss on account of its supposed medicinal properties. Mare's milk was in limited supply, even in those days of horse-drawn transport, so cow's milk koumiss was made instead, a sovereign remedy for anaemia, phthisis, and 'catarrhal infections': 'The koumiss cure is growing greatly in popularity. . . . Sometimes patients spend six or seven summers at the koumiss establishments', *Pall Mall Gazette* (1884).

kreplach A Jewish version of ravioli: small triangles or squares of pasta-like dough filled with chopped meat or cheese and served with soup. The word, first recorded in English in the 1890s, comes from the plural of Yiddish *krepel*, which was adapted from German dialect *kräppel* 'fritter'.

kriek A cherry-flavoured Belgian beer, made by adding sour morello cherries to lambic beer (*kriek* is the Flemish term for such cherries).

kromeski Kromeskis are croquettes made by binding chopped-up meat in a thick sauce, letting it cool, and shaping it into rolls or rectangles that are battered and fried. They originated in Poland, but the word, which is a fanciful alteration of Polish *kroméczka*, literally 'little slice', no doubt with a pseudo-Slavic ending *-ski* cobbled on to it, came into English in the 1840s via French, and the French spelling *cromesqui* is sometimes used in English.

kuchai An alternative term for CHINESE CHIVES.

kugelhopf A cake made from a yeast-based brioche-like dough in a characteristic shape, rather like an inverted flower pot with a hole down the middle; it usually contains raisins and currants and is dusted with icing sugar. As its name suggests, it originated in Germany and particularly Austria (where it is usually called a *gugelhupf*), but it is now perhaps chiefly associated with Alsace. There are several no doubt equally apocryphal stories concerning its introduction to France from further east, one of which implicates Austrian-born Marie-Antoinette's partiality for such cakes (it was she who on hearing that the people of Paris were starving for want of bread said, probably more out of naivety than malice, 'Qu'ils mangent de la brioche'—usually mistranslated as 'Let them eat cake'). The word *kugelhopf* is based on German *kugel* 'ball'.

kulfi Indian ice cream, made from sweetened condensed milk and generally flavoured with cardamom and topped with chopped almonds and pistachios.

kumiss *See* KOUMISS.

kümmel A sweet colourless liqueur flavoured with caraway and cumin seeds (*kümmel* is German for 'caraway seed', and is related to English *cumin*). It is said to have originated in Amsterdam in the late sixteenth century, but it quickly spread across northern Europe as far east as Russia. The British, however, do not seem to have taken to it until the mid-nineteenth century: 'Caraways in palpable form have now disappeared from our tables, but only to return in the spirit—in Russian bottles labelled Kümmel', E. S. Dallas, *Kettner's Book of the Table* (1877).

kumquat A miniature orange, smaller than a golf ball, which is eaten whole, peel, pips, and all. It comes from China, and its name is Cantonese for 'golden orange'. It first appeared in the West in the seventeenth century: William Dampier, in his *New Voyage Round the World* (1699), wrote: 'The Oranges are of divers sorts, and two of them more excellent than the rest. One sort is called Camchain, the other is called Camquit . . . The Camquit is a very small round Fruit.' The spelling with an initial *k* has gradually ousted that with initial *c*.

kunafa *See* KADAIF.

kvass A mildly alcoholic Russian drink somewhat similar to beer. It has a sweet-sour taste and is made by fermenting rye, barley, etc. Its inherent insipidity is often mitigated by flavourings such as peppermint or fruit. The Russian word *kvas* comes ultimately from an Indo-European **kwāts-*, denoting 'fermentation', which also produced English *cheese*. England first heard of the drink from Richard Chancellor, who sailed on a pioneering trading voyage to Muscovy in the mid-sixteenth century: 'Their drink is like our penny ale, and is called Quass' (1553).

kye A term used in the Royal Navy for cocoa, and in particular the strong thick drinking chocolate used to sustain sailors on watch in bitter high latitudes. First recorded in 1943, it is not clear where it came from. The logic of a connection with nautical slang *kye* 'a contemptible or miserly person' or with English dialect *kyish* 'dirty' is not immediately apparent.

labne In Middle Eastern and especially Lebanese cuisine, labne, or *labneh,* or *lebne,* is a type of cream cheese made by straining yoghurt: 'a salad of labne, pistachio nuts, and herbs was a breath of fresh spring air', *Time Out London, Eating and Drinking* (2009).

lady's fingers An alternative English name for okra, the mucilaginous seed pods of a plant of the hollyhock family. Quaintly ancient as it sounds, the term, or at least its application, appears to go back no further than the early twentieth century. First mention of it comes from the US, restricted in sense to a particular small variety of the vegetable, but it has since broadened out in meaning to cover okra generally. Another plant, however, has a far more ancient claim to the name: the kidney vetch (*Anthyllis vulneraria*), whose closely bunched head of small thin flowers might be held to resemble a dainty hand (it has been claimed that the 'lady' is specifically Our Lady, that is, the Virgin Mary, but there is no conclusive evidence for this). It had the name in the seventeenth century, probably earlier, and held the field apparently unopposed until the later nineteenth century, when a positive cornucopia of fruit and vegetables suddenly started being called *lady's fingers*, including in the US types of potato and apple, and in Australia the banana and a variety of grape. Okra seems to have been only one among the bunch, but it has stayed the course better than the others.

One other type of food has shared the name: a sort of small finger-shaped sponge cake: '"Fetch me that Ottoman, and prithee keep your voice low," said the Emperor; "and steep some lady's-fingers nice in Candy wine"', John Keats, *The Cap and Bells* (1820). But here must be mentioned the orthographic uncertainty that has beset the word: a confusing medley of *lady's fingers, ladies' fingers, lady-fingers*, and others has been used over the centuries. It seems now as established as anything can be that okra is *lady's fingers* and that, at least in American English, the sponge cake is a *lady-finger*.

lager Lager has revolutionized the British beer scene over the past fifty years. In 1959 it accounted for only 2 per cent of beer sales, but since then it has muscled aside traditional beers such as light ale and bitter. It was supposedly first made in Munich (*lager* is German for a 'store', and the name refers to the maturation of the beer by long storage), but this original German lager was dark in colour. The light beer we are now familiar with comes from Pilsen in the Czech Republic.

laksa A Malaysian and Indonesian dish of Chinese origin consisting of thick rice noodles served in a curry sauce or spicy soup with meat, vegetables, or seafood. Its Malay name comes from Persian *lakhsha* 'noodle', which originally meant 'slippery' (although many

Malays interpret it as an adoption of Sanskrit *laksha* 'many', referring
to the multiplicity of flavourings).

lambic beer A type of Belgian wheat beer made in the area to the
southwest of Brussels using wild yeasts. Several different fruit-
flavoured versions are produced, including raspberry, strawberry,
blackcurrant, and especially cherry (*see* KRIEK). Its name probably
comes from Lembeek near Halle, southwest of Brussels.

Lambrusco A frothy, fruity red sparkling wine made in the Emilia-
Romagna region of northern Italy from the Lambrusco grape (its Italian name means
literally 'grape of the wild vine'). It can be made dry or off-dry, but the majority of
Lambrusco is a fairly sweet amiable quaffing wine. It was the latter that took off
commercially in a big way in America in the late 1970s, giving rise to a range of laboratory-
inspired white, pink, and low-alcohol versions that have given Lambrusco a bad name.

lamb's lettuce A small plant of the genus *Valerianella* with soft long roundish leaves eaten
raw in salads. It has been known in Britain for many centuries: John Gerard mentions it
in his *Herbal* (1597), but it was only in the 1980s, with an increasing interest in exploring
a wider range of salad leaves, that it started to become widely available commercially.
The French, who call it *mâche*, have always known its worth. The origins of its name,
which may be a translation of Latin *lactuca agnina*, are not known for certain, but it
presumably reflects a supposed partiality of lambs for the leaves. An alternative name,
used particularly for the wild variety, is *corn salad*, an allusion to the plant's growing
commonly in corn fields.

lamb's wool Lamb's wool is a traditional English drink, now long departed but popular
from the sixteenth to the nineteenth century, which consisted of heated beer, sweetened
and spiced, in which the soft fluffy white pulp of baked apples was mixed. On 9 November
1666 Samuel Pepys noted in his diary, 'Being come home, we to Cards till two in the
morning; and drinking lamb's wool, to bed.'

lamington An Australian goodie: a square of sponge cake coated in chocolate and
desiccated coconut. It seems to have originated in the 1920s, and was named after Lord
Lamington, governor of Queensland from 1895 to 1901.

Lancashire hot-pot *See* HOT-POT.

langue de chat A langue de chat, in French a 'cat's tongue', is a flat, thin finger-shaped
sweet biscuit with rounded ends, typically served with desserts and sweet wines. Its name
no doubt comes from its shape.

Lapsang Souchong Souchong is a high-grade variety of black China tea (Cantonese *siu
chung* means 'small sort', a reference to its fine leaves) familiar in Britain since the mid-
eighteenth century: in 1760 the *Annual Register* reported the shipping of 62,900 pounds
from China by the East India company. Lapsang Souchong, however, a smoky-flavoured
version of souchong, does not put in an appearance until the early 1880s, in a Junior Army
and Navy Stores catalogue (*Lapsang* appears to be simply an invented commercial name).
By the 1930s it had established itself as the epitome of refined China tea.

larb Larb, or *laab*, is a type of Thai and Laotian salad composed of minced meat, cooked
or raw, mixed with lime juice, chilli, onion, and herbs, and usually eaten with sticky rice.

lard Originally, *lard* was bacon or fat pork, a meaning it still has in French; the sense
'rendered pig fat' did not become firmly established until the eighteenth century (the

French for 'lard' in this sense is *saindoux*). The word comes ultimately from Latin *lardum* or *laridum*, which may be connected with Greek *lārīnós* 'fat'. Its appearance as a verb, meaning 'insert small strips of fat bacon into meat before cooking', actually predates the noun in English, first occurring in 1330. The strips of bacon or other fat so used are called lardons or lardoons. This word (the original French *lardon* is nowadays more frequently encountered in cookery books than the Anglicized *lardoon*) has been around since at least the mid-fifteenth century, but has never perhaps become an everyday term; Hannah Glasse complained in 1747 'when I bid them lard a Fowl, if I should bid them lard with large Lardoons, they would not know what I meant: But when I say they must lard with little Pieces of Bacon, they know what I mean.' (Larding, incidentally, is not to be confused with barding, which is the placing of a thin sheet of pork fat, or a rasher of fat bacon, over a piece of meat to keep it moist during cooking. The word probably comes from Arabic *barda'ah* 'stuffed packsaddle', and was used in fifteenth-century English for 'horse armour'.)

The highest grade of lard is made from the fat beneath the pig's skin and under its ribs, and also from the mesentery, part of the intestinal wall. These are cooked over a very slow heat to produce lard. Lard used to be kept in a pig's bladder; hence the expression *bladder of lard* for a very fat person.

The word *larder* is a derivative of *lard*. A larder was probably originally a room in which bacon was stored. In previous centuries it was also called a *lard house* and a *lardry*.

lardy cake A rich, lethally fattening English cake made from white bread dough with lard, sugar, mixed fruit and peel, and often spices. The dough is rolled out flat, lard and other ingredients are spread on it, the whole is folded over and rolled out again, and so on for several turns, rather like making puff pastry. Nowadays it is particularly associated with Wiltshire, but there are many traditional recipes from other parts of England, such as Hampshire, Suffolk, and Northumberland, and Sussex and Surrey, among other counties, had lardy rolls. In the days when sugar was expensive, lardy cake was made only on special occasions, such as harvest time, and many versions of it are called *harvest cake*. The first known reference to it comes in *Magnum Bonum* (1879) by the Hampshire novelist Charlotte Yonge: 'hot tea and "lardy cake" tendered for his refreshment'.

lasagne Etymologically, *lasagna* means 'chamber pot'. That was what a Greek *lasanon* was, and the Romans borrowed the word as *lasanum*, applying it with wry humour to a 'cooking pot'. Its Italian descendant *lasagna* (first recorded in 1282) came to stand, in its plural form *lasagne*, for a particular sort of dish cooked in such a pot, flat sheets of pasta layered with minced meat and tomatoes, and topped with Parmesan cheese. The singular form *lasagna* is applied to this variety of pasta itself and also, in English, to the dish made with it (the final vowel in both forms of the word is pronounced in English as an indistinguishable /ə/). *Lasagne verdi* 'green lasagne' are coloured with spinach; the method is a speciality of Bologna. A slimmer version, about twenty millimetres wide, is known as *lasagnette*.

lassi A refreshing cold drink of Indian origin made from yoghurt or buttermilk. It can be salty or sweet. Its name is Hindi.

latke In Jewish cuisine, latkes are crisp pancakes made from grated potatoes. The word *latke* is Yiddish, and comes ultimately from Russian *latka* 'a pastry'.

latte A drink made by adding a shot of espresso coffee to a glass or cup of frothy steamed milk (if it is made with skimmed or semi-skimmed milk it is a *skinny latte*; the use of *skinny* in that sense is first recorded in 1969 in America). The name comes from Italian *caffè latte*, literally 'coffee milk'.

laver *Laver* was originally a Latin word. It was used by Pliny for an (unspecified) water plant, apparently as a synonym of Greek *síon*, which denoted variously the 'water parsnip', the 'water pimpernel', and the 'watercress'. Both terms were taken over by English herbalists. William Turner, for instance, in his *Herbal* (1562), writes: 'Sion otherwise called lauer is found in waters with a fat bushe ryght vp with brode leues.' Then suddenly, at the beginning of the seventeenth century, we find *laver* being used for 'seaweed', and by the 1800s it had become established as a term for 'edible seaweed' (typically of the genus *Porphyra*): John Arbuthnot, in his *Rules of Diet* (1732), mentions 'Laver, which is the Lactuca Marina or Sea-Lettuce', and Christopher Anstey's *Bath Guide* (1766) reports the selling of it in the streets with the cry 'Fine potted Laver, fresh Oysters, and Pies!' It is clear that until comparatively recently the consumption of seaweed was common amongst coastal communities in all parts of the British Isles, but the Gaelic origin of alternative names for laver and other species, such as *dulse* and *slawk*, clearly suggest that it has always been more acceptable to the Celtic palate than to Anglo-Saxon ones, and in the twentieth century laver came to be very closely associated with Welsh cuisine. The main reason for its fame has no doubt been *laverbread*, a particular way the Welsh have with the seaweed. White Kennet, in *Cowell's Interpreter* (1701), reported on this strange dish with all the detachment of an anthropologist: 'In Glamorganshire and some other parts of Wales, they make a sort of Food of a Sea plant, which seems to be the Oyster-green or Sea-liver-wort. This they call Laver-bread.' In recent years, however, Welsh proselytism and an increased interest in British regional cuisine have gained a wider audience for laverbread—which is boiled laver mixed with oatmeal and fried in bacon fat, butter, etc.

In Cornwall, edible seaweed is known as *blackbutter*.

Laxton's Superb An English variety of green eating apple with a red blush. It is a cross, based on the Cox's orange pippin, created in Bedford in 1897 by the Laxton family of nurserymen and horticulturists.

leaf fat Dense fat occurring in layers round the kidneys of some animals, especially pigs, and used culinarily as suet or for making lard. The term dates from the early eighteenth century, and at that time, when it was in commoner use than it is now, it was often abbreviated to *leaf*: 'To make Black Puddings . . . The next day take the leaf of the hog and cut into dice', Hannah Glasse, *The Art of Cookery Made Plain and Easy* (1747). It probably refers to the overlapping layers or lobes of the fat.

leaf jelly An alternative name for GRASS JELLY.

lebkuchen A type of gingerbread-style biscuit popular in Germany and Switzerland. Its principal flavourings are cinnamon and cloves, and it is often made with honey. It is typically glazed and made in decorative shapes—for hanging on Christmas trees, for example, or for constructing a 'gingerbread house' (in imitation of the one encountered by Hänsel and Gretel). German *kuchen* means 'cake', but the origin of *leb-* is uncertain.

leek Leeks were eaten in ancient Sumer, in the fifth millennium BC, and their consumption in Britain certainly dates from prehistoric times. The Romans liked them, sometimes in startling combinations—leeks and quinces stewed in honey, for instance. And in medieval England they were particularly a vegetable for Lent: C. Anne Wilson, in *Food and Drink in Britain* (1973), quotes from Thomas Tusser's *Five Hundred Points of*

Good Husbandry (1590): 'Now leeks are in season, for pottage full good, and spareth the milchcow, and purgeth the blood: These having with peason [peas], for pottage in Lent, thou sparest both oatmeal and bread to be spent.' In the seventeenth century the leek seems to have begun to go out of fashion in England, certainly in London and the South (although the history of monster-leek growing contests in Northumbria attests to its continuing popularity in the North), and did not really return to respectability until after the the Second World War. In Scotland and Wales, however, it has never been away: the Scots have their cock-a-leekie soup, and for the Welsh of course it is the national vegetable, associated with St David, who is reputed to have sustained himself by eating wild leeks.

The word *leek* is a strictly Germanic one, with relatives in German (*lauch*) and Dutch (*look*). It forms the second syllable of *garlic*, and its prehistoric Germanic ancestor was borrowed into Russian as *luk* 'onion'. The words for 'leek' in the Romance languages (French *poireau*, Italian *porro*, Spanish *puerro*) come from Latin *porrum*; *poree*, the Old French ancestor of the modern French word, gave English *porray* or *porrey*, a now obsolete term for a thick soup made from green vegetables.

In former times to *eat the leek* signified 'to swallow one's pride, submit to humiliation': 'It was whispered the Whigs meant to swallow the Corporation leek' wrote Benjamin Disraeli in a letter dated 20 August 1835.

lemon The lemon is a close relative of the lime, and it is appropriate that their names should come from the same source: Arabic *līmah* 'citrus fruit'. The term travelled west with the fruit, from Persia and the Middle East to Europe, and reached English at the end of the thirteenth century via Old French *limon* (which in modern French means 'lime'). The lemons came, no doubt, with the recommendation of the Crusaders, who had first encountered them in the Holy Land in the late twelfth century, but to begin with they were naturally a rare and expensive luxury (39 bought for Queen Eleanor in 1290 cost a pound). From the end of the fourteenth century, however, supplies became more regular and plentiful, and the lemon began to establish itself as an essential item in the kitchen. It was particularly valued for the drinks that could be made with it, refreshing but also good for you ('I drank water and lemons, by physician's advice,' wrote Lady Russell in 1594). Indeed, it was towards the end of the sixteenth century that the usefulness of lemons and limes in preventing scurvy began to be realized. The British Admiralty did not act on this knowledge for two hundred years, however. It was not until 1795 that lemon juice was officially issued to British sailors, and in the following twenty years no less than 1.6 million gallons of it were drunk. Around the same time we begin to see the first signs of the use of *lemon* as a colour term, for a pale yellow—probably an indication of the increasing familiarity of the fruit itself.

Modern slang has not used the lemon kindly, with senses alluding more to the sour taste of the fruit. In the US a *lemon* is 'something defective or disappointing' (hence the expression 'The answer is a lemon', denoting that no satisfactory reply was given) or an 'informer, stool pigeon', while in Britain and elsewhere it is a 'gormless person'. To 'hand someone a lemon' is to swindle or trick them, and in Australia and New Zealand to 'go lemony at someone' is to get angry with them.

The lemon of *lemon sole*, incidentally, was probably adapted from French *limande*, and does not appear to have any etymological connection with the fruit.

lemonade From its simple seventeenth-century beginnings as a drink made from lemon juice and water, usually with sugar, lemonade has diversified widely. The homemade product is still usually called *lemonade*, but commercial lemonade is now often a carbonated drink (commonly known as *fizzy lemonade* to distinguish it from the still version). This can be either yellow and tasting more or less of lemon (known in American

English as *lemon soda*), or completely transparent with a barely discernable lemon flavour (what Americans call *lemon-lime*). The commercial approximation to homemade lemonade, produced in concentrated form so that the consumer has to dilute it, is usually called *lemon squash* rather than *lemonade*.

The term is an adaptation of French *limonade*, a derivative of *limon* (which used to mean 'lemon' but is now restricted to the 'lime'). It was the first example in English of a word for a fruit drink ending in -*ade* (*orangeade* followed in the eighteenth century), but it was not really until the late nineteenth century that the suffix took on a life of its own with new formations such as *cherryade*, *gingerade*, and *limeade*: 'Gingerade is not really the liquor with which roast beef and plum pudding ought to be associated', *Illustrated London News* (1887). It originally signified 'product of', and came into French via Provençal -*ada* from Latin -*āta*, the feminine past participial ending of verbs in -*āre*.

lemon curd *See* CURD.

lemon grass A species of tropical grass which, as its name suggests, has a strong savour of citrus. It is widely used as a flavouring in Southeast Asian cookery. In Indonesia it is known as *sereh*, in Malaysia as *serai*, and in Thailand as *takrai*.

lentil Lentils are an ancient source of human food: there is evidence of their cultivation in Neolithic times, around 6000 BC, and cultures in most parts of the world have included them as part of their diet. The Latin word for the lentil is *lens* (subsequently applied, from the lentil's shape, to a piece of glass with two curved surfaces); its diminutive form *lenticula* gave French *lentille*, and hence English *lentil*. In the sixteenth and seventeenth centuries the word was applied in English to 'freckles': 'Wheat flour cleanseth the face from lentils and spots', John Woodall, *The Surgeon's Mate* (1617).

Lentils come in an assortment of shapes and sizes. For most of the twentieth century the most familiar in Britain was the *orange lentil*, sometimes known as the *Egyptian lentil*. It is simply the dehusked version of the *brown lentil*, known in Hindi as *masoor dhal* (*dhal* or *dal* is the general Hindi term for lentils). In recent years, however, other varieties have come to the fore. There are the larger, slightly flatter *green lentils*, also called *continental lentils*. And above all is the *Puy lentil,* esteemed by gourmets as the king of lentils: it is about the same size as the orange lentil, has a dark green skin with blue marbling, and is grown particularly around Velay in the Auvergne, central France.

lettuce The lettuce is named from the milky-white juice it exudes when its stem is cut. From Latin *lac* 'milk' was derived *lactūca* 'lettuce', which English acquired via Old French *laitués*, the plural of *laitué*. Lettuce juice was used as a medicine in ancient times, and the plant itself was noted for its soporific qualities. It was introduced to Britain by the Romans, who commonly ate it cooked rather than raw. This tradition continued into and beyond the Middle Ages (and still survives in France), but by the seventeenth century the memory of it was dying out (John Evelyn, for instance, in his *Acetaria* (1699) is extravagant in his praise of lettuce as a raw salad vegetable, but of cooked lettuce he notes only as an afterthought 'Lettuce boil'd and Condited [seasoned] is sometimes spoken of'). Since then lettuce  has taken its place as the ubiquitous, taken-for-granted, background salad green, noticed only to be dismissed as 'rabbit food' (an expression first recorded in the 1930s).

liberty cabbage During the First World War any reference in the US to things German was deemed unpatriotic, and this included foodstuffs. An alternative name had therefore to be found for sauerkraut, and the choice fell on *liberty cabbage*. The image appealed to was presumably of America as the land of the free, defending the liberty of the world against German tyranny. Similar inspirations were *liberty sandwich* for 'hamburger sandwich' (*compare* SALISBURY STEAK) and, beyond the gastronomic sphere, *liberty measles* for 'German measles'. *See also* FREEDOM FRIES.

Liebfraumilch *Liebfraumilch*, nowadays a generic term for any fairly sweet German white wine made in the Rhine area (used essentially for the British export market, incidentally, not in its homeland), used in the nineteenth century to be applied more specifically to wine made around the Rhineland city of Worms, near Mannheim. There is a church there called the *Liebfrauenkirche* 'church of Our Lady', which has a small vineyard beside it, and legend has it that the wine made from grapes grown there was originally called *Liebfraumilch*, literally 'Our Lady's milk' (it is nowadays called *Liebfrauenstiftswein* 'wine from the foundation of Our Lady'). It first became well known in Britain in the mid-nineteenth century: Alfred Tennyson noted in a letter (1846) that 'Dickens was very hospitable, and gave us biscuits and a flask of Liebfraumilch.'

lights The lungs of pigs, sheep, etc. used as food. In Britain they are usually served only to pets, although in other times and cultures people have happily consumed them, and they lurk in many a pâté and sausage. The word is of Anglo-Saxon origin, and until comparatively recently it meant 'lungs' in general. And these two words are etymologically connected: lights were so named because they weigh very little, and *lung* is traceable back to a hypothetical Indo-European root **lnggh-* from which English *light* 'not heavy' is ultimately derived. Some Celtic languages show a similar association of meanings; the Old Irish word *scaman*, for instance, was used for both 'lungs' and the adjective 'light'.

Lillet The proprietary name of a wine-based French aperitif originally made in the early 1870s in Podensac, in the Bordeaux area of southwestern France, by the brothers Paul and Raymond Lillet. Bordeaux wine is used in its making, and its particular flavour characteristics are imparted by citrus liqueurs.

lima bean A large flattish variety of edible bean that originated in South America. When immature the beans are pale green, but as they ripen they develop a creamy-yellow colour which gives them their alternative name (more familiar than *lima bean* in British English) *butter bean*. They contain minute traces of cyanide. The term *lima bean*, first recorded in the early nineteenth century, is a reference to the bean's Peruvian origins (its pronunciation—/limer/ rather than /leemer/—reflects an earlier age's more cavalier attitude to the rendering of 'foreign' words). Another synonym is *Madagascar bean*, from its extensive cultivation there.

Limburger A soft cheese with a not altogether deserved reputation for pungency and whiffiness. Originally made in the Belgian province of Limburg, it has since the nineteenth century been essentially a German cheese, widely made in the Allgau, on the Swiss-German border. In the English-speaking world it is much better known in the US than in Britain.

lime The lime is the lemon of the tropics, fiercer in flavour, usually smaller and thinner-skinned, and better able to stand up to hot growing conditions. The two fruits are closely related, of course, and their names come from the same ultimate source, Arabic *līmah* (*lemon* reached English via Old French *limon*, whereas *lime* took a route via Spanish *lima*, Provençal *limo*, and French *lime*, and arrived in English in the seventeenth century). By the nineteenth century Britain had built up a considerable empire in the Caribbean, and so lime-juice began to be issued to the Royal Navy as an anti-scorbutic, replacing lemon-juice. In consequence, American sailors took to referring to their British counterparts as *lime-juicers*, a term also applied to British immigrants who had come on the long sea voyage out to colonies in Australia and elsewhere. This was abbreviated towards the end of the nineteenth century to *limey*, which remains current—just—as a derogatory Americanism for a British person. (In fact, limes are less rich in vitamin C than lemons, so it would have been better to stick with lemon juice.)

There is no etymological connection, incidentally, between *lime* the fruit and *lime* the tree, whose name is an unexplained seventeenth-century alteration of *line*, a variant form of *lind*, from which we get *linden*. The tree's only culinary application is in the making of lime-blossom tea (as drunk by Aunt Léonie in Proust's *Du côté de chez Swann*).

limoncello A lemon-flavoured Italian liqueur. The Italian word means literally 'little lemon'.

Lincolnshire Poacher An English cows'-milk cheese made at Alford, to the east of the Lincolnshire Wolds, by Simon and Tim Jones. It is similar to Cheddar in appearance. Its name is taken from the title of a well-known folk song (and unofficial Lincolnshire anthem) 'The Lincolnshire Poacher', which celebrates the joys of poaching.

lingonberry The edible dark red sharp-tasting berry of a low-growing shrub of the heather family which grows in northern upland habitats. It is related to the cranberry. Its traditional English name, dating from at least the late eighteenth century, is *cowberry*, bestowed because cows like eating it (that also inspired the Latin name of its genus, *Vaccinium*, a derivative of *vacca* 'cow'). *Cowberry* was probably thought to have image problems, and in the 1950s the term *lingonberry* was introduced, combining *berry* with *lingon*, the Swedish name of the fruit (it is much used in Swedish cookery).

linguine Small pieces of pasta in the form of narrow ribbons, with a cross-section in the shape of a flattened ellipse. The name in Italian (first recorded in 1952) means literally 'little tongues'.

Linzertorte An Austrian style of cake consisting of a flan-type shortbread base covered with raspberry jam and then latticed with pastry. It takes its name from the Austrian city of Linz and is said to be the oldest cake recipe on record, dating from 1696. The first mention of it traced in English is in the 1906 edition of Mrs Beeton's *Book of Household Management*, in which it is glossed as 'German Gâteau'.

liquamen An alternative name for GARUM.

liqueur *Liqueur* is essentially the same word as *liquor*. It comes from the same ultimate source (Latin *liquor*, a relative of English *liquid*), and was acquired in the eighteenth century from French *liqueur*, the equivalent of English 'liquor' as well as 'liqueur'. It denotes any sweet spirit-based drink, flavoured with herbs, spices, fruit, flowers, coffee, chocolate—the list of possibilities is almost endless—and typically drunk at the end of a meal. Many modern commercial liqueurs had their origins in late medieval France, their recipes often devised by monks, and it is common for such recipes to remain an obsessively guarded secret.

liquor Old French *licor* 'liquid' was taken over by English in the thirteenth century (the spelling *liquor* is a later reversion to its ultimate Latin roots). It was soon being used to mean 'a drink', although the very specific application to distilled spirits does not seem to have established itself until the nineteenth century. In the fifteenth century it began to denote liquid involved in various food preparation processes, including a liquid in which something has been steeped or cooked, and the liquid which drains from food during cooking: 'When you boil a leg of pork or a good piece of beef, save the liquor', Hannah

Glasse, *The Art of Cookery Made Plain and Easy* (1747). These usages now have a rather antiquated air, but one slightly left-field offshoot that survives (just) is the application to the green parsley sauce that traditionally accompanies meat pie and mash in the East End of London.

liquorice Liquorice (or *licorice*, as it is usually spelled in North America) is the pungent root of a small European plant of the pea family. It was used as a flavouring in ancient times (the name is Greek in origin, meaning literally 'sweet root'—*glykyrrhiza*, as in 'glucose' and 'rhizome'), and has been known in Britain since at least the early thirteenth century, introduced via Spain from the Arabs. In medieval times and up until the seventeenth century it was commonly used, either whole or ground up, for flavouring cakes, puddings, drinks, etc., and the tradition of using it in savoury dishes has been revived at, for instance, L'Ousteau de Beaumanière restaurant in Provence and Heston Blumenthal's Fat Duck at Bray. Nowadays, however, it is far more familiar in the form of a black sweet, made from the evaporated juice of the liquorice root. Earliest examples of this include the pontefract cake, a small disc-shaped pastille of liquorice, but over the past hundred years a far more varied repertoire of liquorice sweets has emerged, including the *liquorice bootlace*: 'doughnuts an' trifle an' liqu'rice bootlaces,' Richmal Crompton, *William and the Space Animal* (1956). They are summed up, of course, in *liquorice allsorts*, a mixture of liquorice sweets in assorted shapes, many of them with fondant fillings or exteriors (the term *allsort* is first recorded in 1928). These are said, probably apocryphally, to have come into the world in 1889 when Charlie Thompson, sales rep for the sweet manufacturer Bassett's, dropped a tray of samples so that they all got mixed up.

The use of *liquorice stick* as a jazz musician's slang term for a clarinet appears to have originated in the US in the 1930s.

Little Gem A type of small lettuce that is a compact variety of cos. In everyday usage the name is often simplified to *gem*: 'crispy lemon sole with plum tomato, gem salad and tartare sauce', *Good Food Guide* (2008); 'I went with the halibut with little peas in the French manner, lardo, radish, baby gem lettuce, and Jersey royals, which the waiter recommended', A. A. Gill, *Sunday Times* (2011).

Livarot A soft cows'-milk cheese made in the Livarot area of the Calvados region of Normandy. It is made in small wheel-shapes with an orangey-brown crust. It smells and tastes quite strong.

liver sausage A large ready-to-eat sausage containing a paste of cooked liver, or a mixture of liver and pork. First recorded in 1855, the name may well be a translation of German *leberwurst*. In American English a semi-translated version, *liverwurst,* is in common use; it dates from the 1860s.

loaf In Anglo-Saxon times, *loaf* meant 'bread' in general as well as a 'single unit of bread'. The word is common to many Germanic languages (German has *laib*, with the same meaning), and probably was borrowed millennia ago from Slavic *chleb*. It forms the first element of *lady*, which in Old English was *hlǣfdige*, literally 'breadkneader'. And a *lord* was a *hlǣfweard*, a 'guardian of the bread'.

The word began to be used for a conical mass of sugar as long ago as the fourteenth century, but the *meatloaf* is a comparative newcomer. There is an apparent reference to it in a letter from Lady Newdigate dated 1787: 'We made a Dinner upon our Cold Loaf,' but it does not start to appear in cookery books until the end of the nineteenth century.

The colloquial use of *loaf* to mean 'head' (as in 'use your loaf') is probably from rhyming slang *loaf of bread*, but it may also owe something to a now obsolete application of the word to the round head of a cabbage.

lobby An abbreviated form of *lobscouse*, used both in its native Merseyside and in Staffordshire. The dish and the word no doubt found their way from Liverpool to Stoke-on-Trent on the narrow boats plying the Trent and Mersey Canal.

lobscouse A dish famous for its contribution to the English language rather than memorable in its own right—from its name comes the term *scouse* 'Liverpudlian', which has come into wide use since the Second World War. The dish itself is a fairly standard meat stew—typical contents would be neck of mutton, potatoes, and root vegetables. The landlubber's version might be thickened with barley, but its classic thickener, ship's biscuit, gives away its nautical origins: this was to begin with a seaman's stew. Liverpool's strong seafaring connections account for the city's association with the dish. Its linguistic origins are less clear. It clearly has links with Danish, Norwegian, and German *lapskaus*, and Dutch *lapskous*, which suggests a seafaring community centred on the North Sea and the Baltic having a similar diet and sharing the words for it, but the elements of these compounds remain obscure. It may be that the first, *lob-* or *lap-*, has some sort of onomatopoeic origin. This could be represented in the English dialect verb *lob* 'to bubble, boil,' which was applied particularly to porridge, and it may also occur in the now obsolete *loblolly*, a dialectal term for a sort of thick gruel. *See also* LOBBY.

lockshen In Jewish cookery, egg noodles that are boiled and then served in soup: 'chicken soup rich with lockshen and knaidlach [i.e. matzo balls]', *Time Out London, Eating and Drinking* (2009). The word comes from Yiddish, where it is the plural of *loksh* 'noodle'. It is first recorded in English in 1892.

loganberry A loganberry looks like a slightly elongated raspberry. It is a cross between the raspberry and the blackberry, first raised in 1881 by the American lawyer and horticulturist J. H. Logan in Santa Cruz, California.

lollipop The word *lollipop* is first recorded in 1784, in a January issue of the *London Chronicle*: 'She confessed that a certain person had enticed her to commit [the robbery], and given her sweetmeats, called lolly-pops.' At this stage, as this passage suggests, lollipops were simply 'sweets' (a meaning the abbreviated *lolly* retains in Australia and New Zealand), and it does not seem to have been until the early twentieth century that they gained their now quintessential characteristic, the stick (their typical shape, a disc supported on a thin stick, is the basis of the 'lollipop man' metaphor dating from the late 1950s, the children's traffic attendant who carries a round 'stop' sign on a long pole). *Lolly* is first recorded in the mid-nineteenth century, and was the version of the word adopted when water-ices on sticks (*ice lollies*, or sometimes *iced lollies*) were first widely marketed in the 1940s; its slang use as a term for money also seems to date from the 1940s. As for the origin of *lollipop* itself, that is not altogether clear; the explanation usually given is that it was based on *lolly*, an obsolete northern dialect term for the tongue (so called because it *lolls* out).

lollo rosso A variety of lettuce with deeply divided red-edged leaves. It began to appear in strength on British supermarket salad shelves in the 1980s. Its Italian name means literally 'red husk, red chaff'.

lomo In Portuguese and Brazilian cookery, cured loin of pork rubbed with paprika. It is a traditional ingredient of Brazilian feijoada.

London broil An American term for a flank steak (*see* FLANK) that has been grilled (American English *broil* means 'grill') and is served cut diagonally across the grain into thin slices. The term is first recorded in 1946, but the reason for the attribution to the capital of the UK is unclear. The dish is not known there.

London gin London gin, or *London dry gin* in full, is a light unsweetened variety of gin originally distilled in London in the eighteenth century, but now produced in various parts of the world. As a type it is usually contrasted with *Plymouth gin*, which is fuller in flavour.

longan A fruit that is similar to the related but larger lychee in having a rough, thin, brittle shell enclosing milky-white flesh with a shiny black seed at its centre. White encircling black suggested to the Chinese a dragon's eye, which is what Chinese *lóngyǎn* literally means. English adopted the word in the early eighteenth century.

long pig The macabre term *long pig* for 'human flesh used as food' dates from the mid-nineteenth century. It is supposedly a translation of an expression used in the language of a cannibal people of the southwestern Pacific rim.

loquat Loquats are the yellowish-orange plumlike fruits of a tree of the rose family. They come originally from China and Japan, and indeed their alternative name is *Japanese medlar* (in French *nèfle du Japon*, in Italian *nespola giapponese*, both of which mean 'Japanese medlar'; the medlar is a relative). *Loquat* itself comes from Cantonese *lō-kwat*, literally 'rush orange'. The fruit was probably first introduced into Europe in the eighteenth century.

lotus A large red-flowered Asian water lily, of which the root, seeds, leaves, and flowers are widely used in East and Southeast Asian cookery: 'A stir-fried dish of pork with crunchy lotus roots . . . was every bit as flavoursome as expected . . . Sticky rice was appropriately fragrant from being encased in lotus leaf wrappers', *Time Out London, Eating and Drinking* (2009). (It should not be confused with the plant whose fruit, in Greek mythology, induced lethargy and a dreamy forgetfulness—'How sweet it were, hearing the downward stream / With half-shut eyes ever to seem / Falling asleep in a half-dream! / . . . Eating the Lotos day by day', Alfred Tennyson, 'The Lotos-Eaters' (1832)—which was probably the jujube, a Eurasian shrub or small tree that produces edible berry-like fruit.)

lovage A herb of the carrot family, closely related to the celery, whose dark green leaves have a flavour that combines those of celery and lemon. The word originated in Latin *ligusticum*, which meant literally 'plant from Liguria' (a region of northwest Italy). By post-classical times this had become *levisticum*, which passed into Old French as *levesche* or *luvesche* (the modern French term for 'lovage' is *livèche*). English speakers of the fourteenth century took the second syllable of this to be the equivalent of *ache*, a Middle English term for the parsley and allied plants (which survives in modern English *smallage* 'wild celery'), and so they changed Old French *luvesche* to *lovache*, as if it meant 'love-parsley'. The modern English spelling was well established by the fifteenth century.

love apple *See* TOMATO.

love in disguise A toe-curling name (based on the symbolism of the heart for 'love') for what seems to modern sensibilities a fairly disgusting Georgian and Victorian dish: a calf's heart wrapped up in minced veal, coated in a layer of crushed vermicelli (apparently to suggest rough prickles), and then baked. But perhaps we should not take it all too seriously: Florence White in her *Good Things in England* (1932) called it 'an eighteenth-century jest'.

lox The Jewish version of smoked salmon. It finds its soulmate in cream cheese and bagels, ring-shaped rolls—hence the classic New York breakfast of lox and bagels. The word itself comes from Yiddish *laks* 'salmon', which is one of a group of related terms which constitute one of the most widely distributed of all Indo-European word 'families'. Cognate forms include not just words for 'salmon' (German *lachs*, for example, Swedish *lax*—hence *gravlax*—and Russian *losos*'); in areas where salmon are not found, the word has been used for another sort of fish, or for fish in general: Tocharian, for instance, an extinct Indo-European language of central Asia, had *laks* for 'fish'. In Old English the word for 'salmon' was *læx*; its descendant, *lax*, survived in local dialects until the seventeenth century, although since the thirteenth century it had been fighting a losing battle against the Latin-based *salmon*.

Lucozade The proprietary name of a sweet fizzy drink created in 1927 by a Tyneside chemist called William Turner. It was intended to aid the recovery of his sick daughter, so its key ingredient was energy-giving glucose. When it was marketed commercially it was named *Glucozade* (the *-ade* presumably on the model of *lemonade, orangeade,* etc.). This was changed to *Lucozade* in 1929. Its bottle, with its characteristic yellowish-orange cellophane wrapper (introduced by Beecham's in 1938 and intended as a protective light filter, but perhaps also suggesting the drink's mildly citrussy taste), became a familiar sight by sick-beds, in hospitals, etc. In the early 1980s it radically altered its marketing strategy: out went the cellophane wrapper, and instead of being aimed at the convalescing sick, its target became the bouncingly healthy, supposedly in need of even more energy.

luganega Luganega (or *luganiga*) is a type of raw Italian pork sausage that is made in Lombardy. Its classic seasoning is cloves and cinnamon, but it can also feature fennel seeds. It is produced in long coils. Its name means literally '(sausage) of Lucania' (Lucania was a Roman province in southern Italy, corresponding to modern Basilicata).

lumache A type of Italian pasta consisting of a short section of curled ridged tubing flattened at one end. Its name means literally 'snails'.

luncheon meat After the grandiosity of its name, the reality of luncheon meat is a severe let-down—a precooked mixture, mainly of meat (commonly pork), formed into a dull pink block and preserved in a can. The term is a relic—nowadays comparatively little encountered—of Second World War euphemism, when the shortage of real meat was in part mitigated by the substitution of this semi-meat (which in fairness must by law have a meat content of at least 80 per cent). Inherently an intractable foodstuff, probably best simply sliced and left to its own devices, luncheon meat was nevertheless subjected to all the wiles of 1940s and 1950s cookery-book writers, who found 1,001 uses for it: 'Dice luncheon meat and use it as a filling for bread', Elizabeth Craig, *Collins Family Cookery* (1957). Probably the most celebrated variety of luncheon meat is Spam.

lychee The lychee, or *litchi*, a fruit with a thin knobbly pinkish shell enclosing translucent white juicy flesh, which in turn surrounds a large brown stone, is of Chinese origin. Its name, which comes from Cantonese *lai ji*, was first borrowed into English in the sixteenth century as *lechia*: 'They have a kinde of plummes that they doo call Lechias', Robert Parke, *Mendoza's History of the Kingdome of China* (1588). Wine made from the gewurztraminer grape is often said to have a distinctive savour of lychees.

Lymeswold There is not a place called Lymeswold: the name was dreamed up by the marketing men to designate a newly invented 'French-style' English cheese, launched in Britain by Dairy Crest, a subsidiary of the Milk Marketing Board, in 1982. Probably suggested by *Wymeswold*, the name of a village in Leicestershire, it conjures up the English pastoral landscape in *wold*, with its echoes of the touristically successful *Cotswolds* (*Cotswold* itself had already been taken as a cheese-name, by the inventors of a rather unsubtle mixture of Double Gloucester with chives), and overall it makes an appeal to bucolic traditionalism. It is certainly more atmospheric than *Aston* (the site of the creamery in Cheshire where the cheese was actually made). Unfortunately, this all cut little ice in the vital export market. It was discovered that the French, for instance, were quite unable to pronounce *Lymeswold*. So abroad, it became *Westminster Blue*.

The cheese itself was soft, creamy, and mild, with restrained blue veining. The concept behind it seems to have been to produce something that looked French (cashing in on the sophisticated but popular image of Brie, Camembert, and the like) but was free from the hairier aspects of French cheeses (smelliness, runniness, etc.) that were perceived as being a mass-market turn-off. The whole exercise was reminiscent of the introduction of the so-called 'pale cream' sherries (see SHERRY), which look sophisticatedly dry but taste sweet. But it did not work. Critics found the cheese bland, and the public never really took to it. It was quietly withdrawn in the early 1990s.

lyonnaise In French cuisine, any dish described as *lyonnaise*, or *à la lyonnaise* (literally, 'in the style of Lyon', a city and gastronomic centre situated in eastern central France) is cooked, and particularly fried, with onions. Probably the commonest dish so named is lyonnaise potatoes, apparently first introduced to the British by the proselytizing French chef Alexis Soyer in his *Gastronomic Regenerator* (1846).

mac An abbreviation that around the world conjures up the McDonald's chain of fast-food outlets. This had its beginnings in a drive-in hamburger restaurant opened in 1940 in San Bernardino, California by brothers Richard and Maurice McDonald. They were joined in the mid-1950s by Ray Kroc, a former jazz pianist, who masterminded the franchising of the McDonald's brand across the US. He bought them out in 1961, and in succeeding decades McDonald's spread around the globe, its 'golden arches' logo a worldwide symbol of American consumerism. It has enthusiastically exploited its Scots patronymic prefix, most notably perhaps in *Big Mac,* the proprietary name of a large McDonald's hamburger introduced in 1967, but also for other items on its menu, such as 'Chicken *McNuggets*', '*McMuffins*', '*McRib*' sandwiches, '*McFlurry*' (a vanilla ice-cream dessert), and even in Asia, McRice. It also uses it for different types of outlet—'*McCafé*', for example, and '*McStop*', modelled on the idea of a truck stop. It has not been able to keep it entirely to itself, however. Others have used it, often with decidedly negative connotations and polemical intent (*McMansion*, for instance, for a large and tastelessly ostentatious house). The best-known example is probably *McJob,* popularized at the beginning of the 1990s by the writer Douglas Coupland for a low-paid or menial job with minimal prospects (of the sort, it is implied, available in McDonald's restaurants). Then there is *mac out,* an American teenage slang expression of the 1980s, meaning 'to overeat'. None of the above should be confused with *mac* the colloquial American abbreviation of *macaroni* (as in *mac and cheese*—what in Britain would be *macaroni cheese*).

macadamia nut The fruit of an Australian evergreen tree (genus *Macadamia*) named after John Macadam (1827–65), a Scottish-born engineer. It is more or less spherical, the size of a large hazelnut, and grows inside an extremely hard pale-brown shell. In Asia it is used as an ingredient in stews, but in Europe, where its scarcity keeps its price high, it is most commonly encountered salted, as an upmarket alternative to peanuts. Alice B. Toklas ordered some sent from the US to Paris when she read of them in the *New Yorker*.

macaroni Macaroni first found its way from Italy to Britain at the end of the sixteenth century, but at that time it was small pasta dumplings or gnocchi. Tubular pasta was developed in the south of Italy, and at first it was called *macaroni siciliani,* to distinguish it from other types. Gradually, though, the tubes took sole possession of the name. In Britain, they have become thoroughly Anglicized over the centuries: un-Italian dishes such as *macaroni cheese* (mentioned as long ago as 1769 by Elizabeth Raffald in her *Experienced English Housekeeper* and now an unexpected Barbadian favourite; American-speakers call it *macaroni and cheese*) have become firmly established in British cuisine, although sweet *macaroni pudding* made with milk is now seldom encountered. Its name has been naturalized, too: when English acquired it, it was *maccaroni* (a derivative ultimately of Byzantine Greek *makaría* 'barley-broth'), but the spelling with one *c* finally became generally accepted in the nineteenth century, while in modern Italian the northern form *maccheroni* has superseded *maccaroni*. An undercurrent of foreignness has remained though: 'No single cricket club have we ever heard dieted either with frogs, sour crout, or macaroni', James Pycroft, *The Cricket Field* (1851).

In the second half of the eighteenth century the term was applied to a 'fashionable dandy', perhaps because such people were thought to have a taste for foreign food.

In Australian English, *macaroni* is a colloquialism for 'nonsense'.

macaroon Macaroons are small round cakes made from ground almonds, sugar, and egg whites, generally lined on the bottom with rice paper. They appear to have originated in Venice in the fourteenth or fifteenth centuriy, and their English name comes from *macaron*, the French descendant of early modern Italian *maccaroni* 'macaroni'. The French *macaron*, incidentally, is a more refined, delicate, and sophisticated article than the British *macaroon*, smaller and produced in a wide array of colours and flavours. The idea of sandwiching two together with a layer of ganache or buttercream was introduced by the Parisian bakery Ladurée in the 1930s. The result is known as a *gerbet* (although it is usually loosely referred to as a *macaron*).

macchiato A drink of espresso coffee with a dash of frothy steamed milk. The term comes from Italian *caffè macchiato*, literally 'stained coffee' (*macchiato* is the past participle of *macchiare* 'to mark, stain', a distant relative of English *immaculate*).

mace The dried fibrous outer covering which partly encloses the nutmeg. It is ground up and used as a spice (typically dark yellow) which is similar to but rather less intense than nutmeg. It is commonly employed for giving a nutmeg-like taste to savoury dishes, such as pâtés and terrines. The word *mace* comes ultimately from Greek *makir*, which was the name of a sort of Indian bark used as a spice. Latin took it over as *macir*, which metamorphosed on its way to Old French into *macis*. This was the form in which English originally acquired it in the fourteenth century (the *Abingdon Accounts* of the mid-fourteenth century, for example, refer to 'In macys ijs. xd.'), but before long this came to be mistaken for a plural, and the new 'singular', *mace*, was formed. (French still has the form *macis*.)

macedoine A macedoine of vegetables is a mixture of different varieties of vegetable diced very small, served either hot or cold. The term is also applied to fruit salads made of finely chopped fruit. The term is of French origin, and is probably a reference to the proverbially heterogeneous mixture of races in Macedonia (a region in the Balkans) in the time of Alexander the Great. Since it was acquired by English in the early nineteenth century, it has been used sporadically in the metaphorical sense 'medley, assortment': 'Such is the tattle of our beaus. These simple elements compose . . . The Macedoine of London-talk', Henry Luttrell, *Advice to Julia* (1820).

Maconochie In British services' slang of the first half of the twentieth century, tinned meat and vegetable stew, especially as supplied to soldiers on active service: 'They sat in the door of the dugout and ate Maconochies', A. S. Byatt, *The Children's Book* (2009). The term came from the name of the stew's manufacturers, Maconochie Brothers of London.

Madeira cake Madeira cake first begins to appear in recipes in the eighteenth century. In those days it was frequently indistinguishable from an ordinary sponge cake or pound cake (still the preferred term in American English), but gradually it became established as a rather richer cake, with plenty of eggs, and usually flavoured with lemon rind. It gets its name from the genteel practice of eating a slice with a glass of Madeira wine in the mornings.

madeleine The madeleine, a small rich cockleshell-shaped sponge cake, is probably the most celebrated of all literary cakes. Its fame rests on its use by Marcel Proust, in *Du côté de chez Swann* (1913), as a symbol of the power of a fleeting sensory impression to conjure up a flood of memories of the past. He describes how his aunt Léonie would have a lime-blossom tisane prepared for her; and then 'presently my aunt would dip a little madeleine in the boiling infusion, whose taste of dead leaves or faded blossom she so relished, and hand me a piece when it was sufficiently soft'. In later years the taste of a madeleine dunked in lime-blossom tea had the capacity to revive with great immediacy scenes and incidents associated with the original gustatory experiences. 'The sight of the little madeleine had recalled nothing to my mind before I tasted it....' But 'as soon as I had recognized the taste of the piece of madeleine soaked in her decoction of lime-blossom which my aunt used to give me ... immediately the old grey house upon the street, where her room was, rose up like a stage set to attach itself to the little pavilion opening on to the garden which had been built out behind it for my parents....'

Madeleines are made from a mixture of sugar, flour, and eggs, and baked in small ribbed moulds which give them their seashell-like appearance. The source of the term is not known for certain. Legend has it that they were named after Madeleine Palmier, a nineteenth-century French pastry-cook of Commercy. Like many legends, this probably has no basis in fact, but it is at least true that madeleines are particularly associated with Commercy, a town in Lorraine, where they seem to have originated in the eighteenth century.

The English have their own version of the madeleine, but its connection with the true French madeleine, and the reason for its hijacking of the name, are obscure. It is a small individual sponge cake in the shape of a truncated cone, covered in jam and desiccated coconut, and surmounted with a glacé cherry.

magret A fillet of breast meat from a duck, standardly prepared with the skin left on. The French word originated in the Gascon dialect as a diminutive form of *magre* 'lean' (corresponding to standard French *maigre*), the breast being the leanest portion of a duck fattened up to produce *foie gras*.

maid of honour Maids of honour are small almond-flavoured custard tarts. A story, probably apocryphal, goes with their name: Anne Boleyn is said to have invented them while she was lady in waiting to Catherine of Aragon, and Henry VIII liked them so much that he called them *maids of honour* (a maid of honour being literally a queen's unmarried female attendant). The first record of them in print, however, is not until 1769: 'Almond and Lemon Cheesecakes, Maid of Honour, Sweetmeat Tarts', *Public Advertiser*. Richmond-upon-Thames used to be particularly noted for its maids of honour.

mai tai A cocktail based on light rum, curaçao, and fruit juice. It has been claimed that it was invented in 1944, but there is no authenticated record of it before about 1950. Its name probably comes from a Tahitian expression meaning literally 'good, nice, pleasant'.

maître d'hôtel butter *Beurre maître d'hôtel* is a simple French classic consisting of butter into which lemon juice and chopped parsley have been incorporated. It can be served with grilled or fried meat or fish, or with vegetables. Its English translation, *maître d'hôtel butter*, is first recorded in 1861 in Mrs Beeton's *Book of Household Management*. (It had been preceded in 1845, in Eliza Acton's *Modern Cookery for Private Families*, by *maître d'hôtel sauce*, which has the same lemon-and-parsley theme; its French original, *sauce à la maître d'hôtel*, is first recorded in 1803). A maître d'hôtel is the man in charge of a restaurant or a hotel dining room—a sort of head waiter plus. There is no direct English equivalent, which is why the French term has been imported whole (in American English, cut down to *maître d'*).

maize A cereal plant of Central American origin which produces large grains set in rows on a cob. Its name entered English in the mid-sixteenth century from Spain *maíz*, which in turn came from Taino *mahiz* (Taino is an extinct Caribbean language). Its nomenclature is by no means straightforward. In North America, before the plains were covered with wheat, it was the main cereal crop, and it is commonly referred to as *corn*. British English, however, tends to use that term for wheat or (in Scotland) oats, so an alternative strategy was needed. The more specific *Indian corn* (first recorded in 1617) is unambiguous, and has been used in both British and American English, but it is now handicapped by the unacceptability of *Indian* in the context of Native American culture. Maize with grains of a high sugar content, which is grown for human consumption and harvested when slightly immature, is generally called *sweetcorn* (the term dates from the mid-seventeenth century); cooked and eaten with the grains still attached to its central woody core it is *corn on the cob* (first recorded in 1867). *Maize* itself tends to be used, especially in British English, with a wider reach, encompassing all varieties of the plant, including those grown for stockfeed and for various sorts of processing (although the name for the product of the processing usually reverts to *corn: corn oil, cornmeal, cornflour, cornflakes, popcorn,* etc.). Australian and New Zealand usage mainly follows American.

makhani In North Indian cuisine, a dish designated *makhani* is cooked in a rich sauce made with butter or ghee and usually onions, tomatoes, and cream. Probably the best known exemplar is *murgh makhani,* which translates into English as *butter chicken*. The Hindi term is a derivative of *makkhan* 'butter'.

maki A type of sushi in which the rice and other fillings are wrapped in nori (dried seaweed). There are various subcategories: *hosomaki* 'thin-rolled', *futomaki* 'thick-rolled', and *temaki* 'hand-rolled'. The term itself is short for Japanese *maki zushi*: *maki* is a derivative of *maku* 'to roll up'. It is first recorded in English in the 1970s

malaguetta Malaguetta, or *malagueta,* is an alternative name for GRAINS OF PARADISE. English probably adapted it in the mid-sixteenth century from French *malaguette,* which in turn may have been based on a diminutive form (unrecorded) of Italian *melica* 'millet'.

Malibu The proprietary name of a rum-based coconut-flavoured liqueur. It invokes the name and hip image of a beach resort in southern California, popular with surfers.

malmsey A dark brown, tangily sweet fortified dessert wine, the sweetest of the four standard types of Madeira. It inherited its name from that of a strong sweet white wine imported into England via Venice from Greece and various eastern Mediterranean islands from the fifteenth century (that was probably the wine in the 'butt of malmsey' in which the Duke of Clarence was reputedly drowned in the Tower of London in 1478). That in turn came, probably via Middle Dutch *malemeseye* and an unrecorded Old French *malmesie,* from medieval Latin *malmasia,* an alteration of Greek *Monemvasia,* the name of a port in the Peloponnese, Greece from which the wine was exported. The Italian name of the port, *Malvasia,* was given to the grape variety from which the wine was made. Nowadays the Malvasia, in its various forms—white and red, dry and sweet—is widely grown around the Mediterranean, especially in Italy (but relatively rarely in Greece); the main types used for malmsey are Malvasia Candida and Malvasia Babosa. *See also* BUAL, SERCIAL, VERDELHO.

Malteser The proprietary name of a sweet consisting of a small ball of malt-flavoured honeycomb (a sugary confection with many small holes) covered in milk chocolate. It is a blend of *malt* and *teaser* (and has nothing to do with the island of Malta). The sweets were invented in 1936 by Forrest Mars, begetter of the Mars Bar, and were originally called *Energy Balls*. Their advertising over the following decades made remarkable play with the notion that they were non-fattening, or could even help eaters lose weight.

manchego A firm Spanish cows'-milk cheese made in La Mancha, a region of central Spain, from which it gets its name.

Manchester lettuce An alternative name for the cos.

Manchester pudding An English dessert similar to (and perhaps the ancestor of) queen of puddings. Its middle is the same—a baked breadcrumb and custard mixture—but it differs in having a puff pastry base and no layer of meringue on top.

manchet A term used between the fifteenth and nineteenth centuries for a round loaf of soft white bread made from the finest wheat flower—decidedly the preserve of the wealthy. Its likeliest source is probably Old French *manchette,* literally 'little sleeve', which was applied to the sleeve of a habit. The fact that the fifteenth-century *maincherin,* possibly another derivative ultimately of French *manche* 'sleeve', was used for a type of loaf might tend to support that view, and the limb-covering metaphor is also in evidence in Italian *calzone,* the name of a sort of pizza turnover, which means literally 'trouser-leg'. However, another strong possibility is that it is a compound formed from obsolete English *maine* 'flour of the finest quality' (short for *pandemaine,* a term for a high-quality loaf, from Anglo-Norman *pain demeine,* literally 'Lord's bread') and *cheat* 'wheat bread of the next-to-highest grade' (of unknown origin).

'For soups and stews and choice ragouts Nell Cook was famous still; Her manchets fine were quite devine, her cakes were nicely brown'd'. R. H. Barham, *Ingoldsby Legends* (1840).

mandarin A small loose-skinned somewhat flattened variety of orange (*Citrus reticulata*) that originated in China. The first reference to it in English comes in 1771, in J. R. Foster's translation of *Osbeck's Voyage to China:* 'Here are two sorts of China oranges. . . . The first is that called the *Mandarin-o,* whose peel is quite loose.' English acquired the word, via French, from Spanish *mandarina,* where its application to the fruit probably arose from the resemblance of its colour to that of the yellowish-orange robes of Chinese imperial officials—mandarins (this term is not Chinese in origin, incidentally; it first arrived in Europe as a Portuguese borrowing from Malay *mantri* 'counsellor', which was itself a Hindi loanword that originated in Sanskrit *mantrin*).

mangetout In French the term *mangetout* (literally 'eat-all') usually refers to young French beans, which are eaten pods and all. In English, however, it has been applied (largely since the 1950s) to a variety of pea, previously known exclusively as the *sugar pea,* which is cultivated for its edible pods (it is generally termed by the French *pois gourmand*). These pods have no hard inner skin, like ordinary pea pods, and are picked before the peas inside grow large enough to swell their flatness. They have been around for nearly 300 years (John Mortimer, in his *Whole Art of Husbandry* (1707), writes: 'The Sugar Pease, which being planted in April is ripe about Midsummer, its Cods [pods] boiled with the unripe Pease in them is extraordinary sweet', but it is only in the last thirty years that they have become fashionable and widely available in Britain. The term *sugar pea,* and its alternative *sugar snap,* tend still to be used for a variety of mangetout with thicker and more rounded pods.

In American and Australian English the mangetout is commonly termed the *snow pea*.

mango The mango is a native of India—its name comes ultimately from Tamil *mānkāy*, a compound formed from *mān* 'mango-tree' and *kāy* 'fruit', and reached English via Malay *manggā* and Portuguese *manga* (*mango* is a later Dutch form). It has been cultivated in the East for several millennia, and so there are several different varieties, in colours ranging from green through yellow-orange to red. Three main types are commonly available in the West. The summer mango and the Alphonso mango are eaten raw for the sake of their flesh—succulent, tasting faintly of turpentine, and notoriously juicy. The earliest writers referred to this *embarras de jus*: 'The Mangas is inwardly yealowish, but in cutting it is waterish', William Phillip, *J. H. van Linschoten his Discours of Voyages into ye Easte and West Indies* (1598). And modern marketers have cashed in on it with the advice to eat mangoes in the bath—with a friend (a note of luxury and voluptuousness appropriate for a fruit whose shape has been said to resemble that of a woman's breast). The other type is smaller, greener, and sharper in taste, and is the appropriate sort to use in Indian dishes, and also for pickling. Thanks to the Raj, mango was an institution in Britain long before post-Second World War Asian immigration brought the actual fruit to our markets, and the jars of pickled mango that reached Britain from India in the second half of the seventeenth century led to the term *mango* being adopted for 'pickle' in general. John Evelyn, for instance, in his *Acetaria* (1699) gave recipes for 'mangoes' of walnuts and of cucumbers: 'Boil [the cucumbers] in the Vinegar with Pepper, Cloves, Mace, &c . . . And when all is cold, add a good Spoonful of the best Mustard . . . and you have an excellent Mango.' And he added 'When you have occasion to take any out, make use of a Spoon, and not your Fingers.' In the eighteenth century *mango* was even used as a verb: 'To mango Cucumber. Cut a little Slip out of the side of the Cucumber . . . ', Eliza Smith, *Compleat Housewife* (1728).

mangosteen The mangosteen is a curious fruit. It looks like a knob on top of a wooden bedpost: globular, dark reddish-brown, and surmounted with a slightly over-exuberant finial (which in fact is its calyx). But inside, sheltering in a matrix of pink pith, are five or six segments of white juicy flesh which give the mangosteen its reputation among cognoscenti as being one of the most delicious of all fruits. Word of it as part of the prodigious fruit bounty of the East Indies reached the West as early as the sixteenth century ('There are yet other fruites, as Brindoijns, Durijndois, Iamboloens, Mangestains, and other such like fruites,' William Phillip, *J. H. van Linschoten his Discours of Voyages into ye Easte and West Indies* (1598)), but it is not until very recently that it has begun very slowly to appear on British supermarket shelves. The word comes from a former Malay term *manggustan* (now replaced by *manggis*). In Barbados it is used for the jujube fruit.

Manhattan A cocktail made from sweet vermouth, whisky, and usually a dash of angostura bitters. It is said to have been created in 1874 by a barman at the Manhattan Club in New York City for a party hosted by Lady Randolph Churchill, mother of Sir Winston. The earliest evidence of it crossing the Atlantic is its appearance in the 1906 edition of *Mrs Beeton's Book of Household Management*.

manioc An alternative name for CASSAVA.

manzanilla A type of fino sherry made at Sanlucar de Barrameda, about 20 kilometres northeast of Jerez. Sanlucar is near the sea, on the estuary of the River Guadalquivir, and it is said that the sea breezes are responsible for the distinctive salty bitter tang of manzanilla. In Spanish *manzanilla* means literally 'camomile'; it is a diminutive form of *manzana* 'apple' (camomile has apple-scented leaves).

A manzanilla that is aged sufficiently long in cask to acquire a deeper colour and a nuttier taste is known as a *manzanilla pasada*.

maraschino Originally, the term *maraschino* referred to a sweet Italian liqueur distilled from the juice of bitter wild cherries, particularly those grown in Dalmatia. Such cherries are known in Italian as *marasce* (*marasca* is a reduced form of *amarasca*, a derivative of the adjective *amaro* 'bitter'), and the diminutive form *maraschino* was used to name the liqueur. It first became familiar in Britain towards the end of the eighteenth century, no doubt from reports of those returning from the European Grand Tour: in 1796, for example, Mrs Mary Robinson writes in her novel *Angelina*: 'After they had drank their mareschino [sic], Lady Selina ordered tea.' The secondary application of the term to a cherry preserved in either real or imitation maraschino, and used typically as a garnish for cocktails or on fruit, seems to have originated around the beginning of the twentieth century. (In Italian, incidentally, the consonant cluster *sch* is pronounced /sk/, but in present-day English /sh/ is the more usual rendering.)

marble cake A cake with a mottled appearance, made of light and dark sponge. The term is first recorded, in American English, in 1871, and the technique was probably brought to the US from Germany, where it has a long tradition.

marc A brandy-like drink distilled from the fermented juice extracted from the residue of skins, pips, stalks, etc. left after wine-grapes have been pressed. It is made in virtually all wine-growing areas of France, but probably the best known to the outside world is *marc de Bourgogne*, Burgundian marc. The primary application of the word is to the grape residue itself, and it is a derivative of French *marcher* 'to walk'—the underlying notion being that the residue is what is left after the grapes have been 'trodden'. The final -*c* is silent in French, and when the word was originally borrowed into English (in the sense 'residue') in the seventeenth century, it was often spelled *marre*.

Marengo A dish named *Marengo*—usually *chicken Marengo* or *veal Marengo*—is sautéed and then cooked in a sauce of white wine, tomatoes, mushrooms, and garlic. The term is said to have come from a chicken dish cooked for Napoleon by his chef Dunand, from the only ingredients to hand, immediately after the battle of Marengo, in north Italy, on 14 June 1800. It soon found its way to Britain: Mrs Beeton gives a recipe for 'fowl à la Marengo' in her *Book of Household Management* (1861) in which she refers to it as a 'well-known dish . . . a favourite with all lovers of good cheer'.

margarine Margarine was invented in France in 1869 by the food technologist Hippolyte Mège-Mouries, who won a competition to find a butter substitute with a concoction made from cow fat. When first introduced into Britain it was called *butterine*, but this incensed the butter producers, and a new name was sought. In 1887, by solemn act of Parliament (the Margarine Act), *margarine* was enshrined as the legal term (the act was repealed in 1928). It was coined from *margaric acid*, a name given by the biochemist Michel-Eugène Chevreuil to a fatty acid which he postulated (erroneously) as one of the main constituents of animal fats. He based the name on Greek *margarītēs* 'pearl', from the pearly lustre of the acid's crystals. Another of Chevreuil's fatty acids was oleic acid, and in fact originally the butter substitute was called *oleo-margarine*, being made from the glycerides of the supposed oleic and margaric acids. The name did not last very long in Britain, but it has continued in use in American English, where it is often abbreviated to *oleo*.

Margarine was quick to earn a downmarket reputation, and in the 1890s it was used as a metaphor for any second-rate or bogus substitute: 'Take care you do not get margarine Liberalism,' *Daily News* (1897). But before the end of the nineteenth century it had become a staple food among poorer people, and although a fall in butter prices between the First and Second World Wars led to a slump in sales, improved manufacturing techniques, with more palatable vegetable oils replacing animal fats, have established it firmly in the market place.

The pronunciation of the word has aroused considerable controversy. The spelling and derivation suggest a hard /g/ sound, but it is clear from examples of the abbreviation *marge* as early as the 1920s that the pronunciation with /j/ is of long standing. Margarine with a /g/ stayed in the fight for a long time, and produced its own shortened form, *marg*, but there is no doubt that the /j/ pronunciation has won the day.

margarita A cocktail made from tequila, an orange liqueur, and lemon or lime juice, and usually drunk in a glass whose rim has been coated with salt. More than is usual with cocktails, its origin and that of its name have been the subject of intense speculation. It is usually cited as Mexican, but California and other parts of North America have also put in claims. It is often said to date from the 1930s, but no written evidence for it has been found from before around 1950. As for *margarita,* there have been several claimants to be its inspiration, perhaps most notably Margarita Sames, a Texan lady who asserted that she created the drink for guests while living in Acapulco in 1948, but none have been verified. Another avenue of exploration leads us to the daisy, an American mixed drink of mid-nineteenth-century vintage based on a spirit, lemon juice, and fruit syrup: the Spanish for 'daisy' is *margarita*.

margherita A term designating a pizza topped with tomatoes, mozzarella cheese, basil, and Parmesan. The topping is said to have been created and named by Rafaele Esposito of the Pizzeria di Pietro e Basta Cosi to commemorate the visit by Margherita di Savoia (1851–1926), queen of Italy, to Naples in 1889—the red, white, and green of the main ingredients being the national colours of Italy.

Marie A type of plain sweet biscuit: 'He swollowed his tea and eat a Marie biscuit hastilly', Daisy Ashford, *The Young Visiters* (1919). The term (first recorded in 1878) presumably comes from the female forename, but what the original inspiration was is unknown.

Marie Rose sauce A cold sauce made from mayonnaise and tomato purée which is the classic vehicle for that iconic starter of the 1960s and 1970s, prawn cocktail. The term, first recorded in 1973, incorporates the female forename *Marie Rose,* but the anonymous coiner probably did not have any particular female in mind; more likely, *rose* was suggested by the sauce's pink colour.

marinade In modern usage, *marinade* denotes a liquid (typically containing a varying mixture of wine, vinegar, and oil with vegetables and seasonings) in which meat or fish is steeped to tenderize and flavour it before cooking. The 'cooking' element is a comparatively recent development, however. Originally the term signified a pickle in which fish (either raw or already cooked) was preserved and then eaten without further cooking. To begin with the medium was evidently brine, for the ultimate source of the word, the Spanish verb *marinar,* is related to English *marine.* From the seventeenth century, *marinade* and *marinate* have been used fairly indiscriminately as the verb to describe the process of soaking in a marinade, although nowadays *marinate* is the generally preferred form.

The term *marinade* is also sometimes applied to a dry mixture of flavourings, usually containing salt, which is applied to meat or fish and has a similar effect to that of liquid marinade.

marinara Pasta served *alla marinara* comes with a sauce made from tomatoes, garlic, basil, and olive oil. In Italian it means literally 'in sailor's style', but despite what this might lead one to suspect, the sauce contains nothing fishy. It is a Neapolitan speciality.

Maris Piper A variety of potato with white skin, creamy flesh, and smooth oval tubers, widely used for making chips. It was named after Maris Lane, the original site of the Plant Breeding Institute in Trumpington, Cambridge where it was developed in the 1960s. *Piper* was chosen arbitrarily as a word beginning with *p-* for *potato*.

marjoram A cover-term for a wide range of aromatic small-leaved herbs of the genus *Oreganum*. The main varieties are the *sweet marjoram*, sometimes also called *knotted marjoram*, which has a comparatively mild flavour, and is extensively used throughout Europe; the *wild marjoram* or *oregano*, which is more pungent and is popular particularly around the Mediterranean; and the *pot marjoram* or *French marjoram*. In addition to these there are several sub-varieties with variegated or yellow leaves, small or crinkly leaves, etc. The sweet marjoram was introduced into Britain by the Romans, and it has had a small but consistent niche in the national cuisine since then (John Evelyn, for instance, in his *Acetaria* (1699), recorded *marjoran*, as he spelled it, as being 'of faculty to comfort and strengthen', and Mrs Beeton in 1861 noted that it was a 'favourite ingredient in soups, stuffings, etc.'). The origins of its name are something of a mystery. English acquired the word via Old French from medieval Latin *majorana*, but it is not known where *majorana* came from.

marmalade The word *marmalade* originally signified 'quince jam'. It comes via French from Portuguese *marmelada*, a derivative of *marmelo* 'quince'. This in turn goes back ultimately to *melímēlon*, a Greek term, meaning literally 'honey-apple', which was applied to the fruit of an apple tree grafted on to a quince (the second element, *mēlon* 'apple', is the source of English *melon*). In the fifteenth and early sixteenth centuries such quince preserve was known in English as *chare de quince* or *chardecoynes* (from an Anglo-Norman term meaning literally 'flesh *or* pulp of quince'), but in 1524 we find the first reference to *marmalade*, in an account of the presentation of 'one box of marmalade' to the king by a certain 'Hull of Exeter'. Throughout the sixteenth century its main ingredient appears to have remained quince, but the seventeenth century saw a sudden diversity, with fruits such as plums, damsons, and even strawberries and dates being used for marmalade (at this time citrus fruit preserved in sugar was still generally called *succade*, a word of French origin but uncertain etymology). In 1767, Hannah Glasse gave a recipe for 'marmalade of cherries' (and also for a curious concoction called 'Marmalade of Eggs the Jews Way', which involved the slow cooking of 24 beaten egg yolks with a pound of sugar), and as late as 1845 Eliza Acton in her *Modern Cookery for Private Families* was giving directions on how to make a 'marmalade' for an apple Charlotte: 'Weigh three pounds of good boiling apples . . . let these stew over a gentle fire, until they form a perfectly smooth and dry marmalade.' As this last phrase implies, marmalade was from earliest times not the soft spreadable confection of today, but a firm sweetmeat that could be cut with a knife, and was eaten as part of the dessert course of a meal. Vegetables could be turned into marmalade too, by stewing them in a sweet-and-sour mixture of sugar and vinegar: the *Farmer's Magazine*, for example, in 1776 gave a recipe for carrot marmalade. The concept was shunted on to history's back burner in Britain, but it made a triumphant return at the end of the twentieth century in the form of the newly fashionable *onion marmalade*: 'There's an Irish slant to proceedings, with the likes of crubbeens with onion marmalade', *Time Out London, Eating and Drinking* (2009).

The use of citrus fruits for marmalade seems to have begun in the seventeenth century, and in the middle of that century we find the first references to the addition of sliced peel. But it is not really until the middle of the nineteenth century that this ingredient had so ousted all others that it became safe to assume that *marmalade* meant, essentially, 'orange marmalade' (a development confirmed in due course by the emergence of the metaphorical use of *marmalade* for the colour orange, as in 'marmalade cat', not recorded before the 1920s). In other European languages, such as French and German, the word still means generally 'jam' or 'preserve', but the notion of 'citrus preserve' has become so firmly ensconced in English that in 1981 an EC edict declared that the term *marmalade* could not be applied to a product other than with oranges, lemons, or grapefruit. Hence *ginger marmalade*, perhaps the only non-citrus marmalade to survive, had to be officially renamed 'ginger preserve' on its labelling.

In recent years the popularity of marmalade has declined and sales have fallen, probably reflecting the increasingly beleaguered status of the traditional English breakfast, of which toast and marmalade forms a key part.

marmite In French, a *marmite* is a two-handled covered earthenware or metal cooking pot used for stews and soups. The term is said to come from an Old French word for 'hypocrite', the notion being that the pot conceals its contents.

In the early years of the twentieth century, a new savoury spread was developed, made from yeast extract. It was given the proprietary name *Marmite*, presumably on account of its resemblance in colour and flavour to the juices produced by cooking beef in a marmite (a picture of which appears on the label). It soon caught on with the public, and has remained popular up to the present time. It has carved a particular niche for itself in the Australian culinary scene (*see also* VEGEMITE). In 2011 its sale was banned in Denmark, because of concerns about the health effects of the extra vitamins and other additives it contains.

Marmite is supposedly something you either love or hate. No doubt there are many (conceivably a silent majority) who are merely indifferent to it, but in the early twenty-first century its name has been increasingly invoked as a symbol of polarized opinion: 'Every comedian is Marmite. You have that reflex action whereby you laugh or you don't. You either love us or are left lost', Jimmy Carr, *Observer Magazine* (2011).

Maroilles A soft French cows'-milk cheese with a reddish rind, made in squares. It gets its name from the abbey of Maroilles, just to the south of the Belgian border, where it was first made in the tenth century.

marquise A chilled chocolate dessert, like a very smooth rich mousse in consistency. Its ingredients, apart from chocolate, are butter, eggs, and sugar. French *marquise* means literally 'marchioness'.

marrons glacés *Marron*, the French word for the 'sweet chestnut', has crossed the Channel twice. It was first acquired in the sixteenth century (Robert Ashley in his translation of Loys le Roy 1594 mentioned 'dates, chestnuts, and marrons') and by the seventeenth century it was being spelled *maroon*: 'roasted maroons, pistachio, pine-kernels,' John Evelyn, *Acetaria* (1699). It survives, of course, as a colour term, originally applied in French to the colour of the chestnut's internal shell. The word made a second appearance in the 1870s in the expression *marrons glacés*, literally 'iced chestnuts', which are peeled sweet chestnuts that are poached in syrup and then coated with sugar. A main centre of their production is Privas, in the Ardèche in France. The French word *marron* itself came via Italian *marrone* from medieval Greek *máraon*.

marrow The primary application of *marrow* (an ancient word, which has been traced back to the hypothetical Indo-European base **mozgho-*) is to the tissue that fills bone cavities. Traditionally this has been a considerable culinary delicacy (special long thin 'marrow spoons' were made from the seventeenth to the nineteenth centuries to extract it from the bones—typically long beef bones—at table), and it remains so in many cultures. In the twentieth century the British seem largely to have relegated it to pet food ('enriched with marrowbone jelly', to quote a well-known dog-food ad), but latterly, thanks largely to the advocacy of the chef Fergus Henderson, it has made a minor comeback.

In the eighteenth and nineteenth centuries it was a common practice to find 'vegetable' analogues to animal products (salsify, for instance, became known as *vegetable oyster*, and a variety of tropical nut as *vegetable ivory*). And at the beginning of the nineteenth century we see the first evidence of the term *vegetable marrow* being applied to a variety of monster-sized gourd, presumably on the grounds of some perceived similarity in texture or colour. Before long this was shortened to simply *marrow*. In American English, where the abbreviated form is rare, the vegetable is commonly known as the *summer squash*.

marrowfat pea A particularly large variety of pea, first described in Philip Miller's *Gardener's Dictionary* (1733). The name (*marrow pea* was a former synonym) is an allusion to the succulent fatty substance in bone cavities, widely regarded as a delicacy. The peas are mostly sold processed and tinned.

Mars Bar The proprietary name of a confectionery bar covered with milk chocolate and containing soft nougat and caramel. Such a sweetmeat was originally produced in the US in 1923 by a company founded in 1911 by Franklin C. Mars (1883–1934). It was called *Milky Way*. It was not a success (although its name was later redeployed for a slightly different product), but it was not forgotten by Franklin's son and business partner Forrest Mars (1904–99). The two fell out and parted company, and Forrest moved to Britain. He set up a factory in Slough, and having trademarked the name *Mars Bar* (probably inspired by an earlier Mars product, the *Mar-O-Bar*), started to produce Mars Bars in 1933. It has been in continuous production ever since. Its most celebrated advertising slogan, 'A Mars a day helps you work, rest, and play', debuted in 1959.

Towards the end of the twentieth century the conceptual enormity that is the deep-fried Mars Bar appeared: a Mars Bar coated, like fried fish, in batter and plunged into a deep-fat frier. The original version is said to have been created at the Haven Chip Bar in Stonehaven near Aberdeen in 1995, and it has since risen to cult-like status as a symbol of the depravity of the Scottish diet.

In Cockney rhyming slang a *Mars Bar* is a 'scar': 'He said "J" had given the doctor a Mars bar (slang for scar)', *Observer* (1987).

marshmallow Marshmallows are small round spongy sweets made from sugar, starch, and gelatine and typically coloured white or pink. In the US they are often toasted, giving them a crisp exterior. Americans also use a marshmallow mixture as a topping or filling for cakes and desserts. Originally, in the nineteenth century, marshmallows were made from a mucilaginous extract of the root of the marsh mallow plant—hence their name. In the twentieth century the word has come to be used metaphorically for anything or anyone frivolous or overly sentimental: 'The situations are witty, the songs as true, her eyes as mistily, romantically happy as I remembered. Perhaps it is just that I am more of a marshmallow than I was as a teenager', *Punch* (1966).

marsh rabbit In New England, a euphemistic name for the muskrat (a semi-aquatic rodent with a musky smell) when brought to market for the table.

Martini First and foremost, *Martini* is the proprietary name of a brand of Italian vermouth produced by the company Martini and Rossi. But since the 1890s it has been used for a cocktail made from dry vermouth and gin. The vermouth need not be Martini: indeed the story goes that the cocktail was originally named after a New York barman called Martinez who first concocted it, and only subsequently became *martini* through association with the brand of vermouth. However that may be, it was certainly one of the earliest of the classic mixed drinks, well predating the post-First World War cocktail age, and it even rated a mention in the 1906 edition of Mrs Beeton's *Book of Household Management*. The *dry martini*, the version favoured by sophisticates, contains a higher proportion of gin (about four parts, or even more, to one of vermouth) than the ordinary martini. Ian Fleming's James Bond had his own meticulously elaborate version: 'In a deep Champagne goblet, three measures of Gordon's [gin], one of vodka, half a measure of Kina Lillet [a citrussy aperitif]', *Casino Royale* (1953)—shaken and not stirred, of course. To achieve a 'dirty martini', add a small amount of brine from an olive jar.

Maryland chicken *See* CHICKEN MARYLAND.

marzipan Marzipan, a paste made from ground almonds, was originally called *marchpane* in English—or *martspane*, or *mazapane*, or *marchpan*. These were the best efforts English-speakers could make at the word when it was borrowed, either via early modern French *marcepain* or from its source, Italian *marzapane*, at the end of the fifteenth century (*marchpane* continued in use until the early twentieth century). The Italian word has long been a source of puzzlement to etymologists. One complex and highly tenuous early twentieth-century suggestion was that it came ultimately from Yemeni Arabic *mawthabān*, literally 'king who sits still', a term applied derisively by the Saracens at the time of the Crusades to a Venetian coin which had a representation of the seated Christ on it. This was adopted into the Italian dialect of Venice as *matapan*, which supposedly in due course (transformed into general Italian *marzapane*) came to be used for a measure of weight or capacity; then for a box of such capacity; then for such a box containing confectionery; and finally for the contents of such a confectionery box. Another conjecture derived it from Arabic *makšabān* 'wooden box', hence 'sweetmeat' (based on *kašab* 'wood'). A common theme in these theories is that the name of the container is transferred to the thing it contains, and that is the case too with the etymology that is now generally preferred. In Burma (now officially Myanmar) there was a town on the north bank of the Thanlwin river called *Martaban* (its name is now Mottama), which was renowned in the Middle Ages for the fine glazed jars of preserves and fruit which were exported from there to the Middle East and Europe; the jars came to be known as *martabān* in Arabic and Persian, and the word appears to have been adopted into Venetian Italian as *marzapane*, which in due course came to be applied to the sweetmeats within. This solution cannot be said to be conclusively proved, but what can at least be said for certain is that (despite the modern French form *massepain*) the word has no etymological connection with Latin *pānis* and French *pain* 'bread'. Paradoxically, though, its present-day English form, *marzipan*, relies on an assumption that it has. It was borrowed in the nineteenth century from German *marzipan*, an alteration of Italian *marzapane* based on the notion that it came from Latin *marci pānis* 'Mark's bread'. (And indeed, in the late Middle Ages the term *marchpane* was often applied to an early sort of gingerbread, made from ginger, honey, and breadcrumbs, and bearing no resemblance to modern marzipan.)

masala A mixture of ground spices used in Indian cookery. There are many different sorts, of which the best known is the North Indian *garam masala*. The term is also applied to a dish flavoured with masala (as in *chicken masala*). It comes from Urdu *masālah*, which was based on Arabic *masālih*. That originally meant 'matters, interests', hence 'necessities', hence 'seasonings'. The word's obvious metaphorical possibilities have been fully exploited in Indian English: it is used to mean 'a varied mixture of elements', and applied specifically to a type of Bollywood musical characterized by a variety of interwoven, usually predictable themes; and it can also denote 'pep, vigour': '"The Prime Minister . . . said he wanted to have vigilant MPs like me in Parliament. I still have a lot of *masala*," Jain cackles into the telephone', *Pioneer on Sunday*, Delhi (1992).

A *masala dosa* is a thin pancake or dosa stuffed with spiced potato or other filling. The term is first recorded in English in 1957.

mascarpone A very soft, unsalted cream cheese made in the Lombardy region of Italy. It is typically eaten as a dessert with fruit or flavoured with sugar, cinnamon, chocolate, etc. or a liqueur. Its name is a derivative of Lombard dialect *mascarpa*, a word of unknown origin.

mashed potato Pounding them to a purée is a long-standing method of dealing with boiled potatoes: Hannah Glasse in her *Art of Cookery Made Plain and Easy* (1747) gives a lengthy recipe for it which includes butter and milk. The first record of the homely abbreviation *mash*, coupled with its traditional partner 'sausages', comes from the early twentieth century. For those for whom the terms *mashed potato* or *mash* seemed a little vulgar, the twentieth century also came up with the genteel alternative *creamed potato* and the sophisticatedly French *pommes purées*, and in the US it is sometimes called *whipped potato*.

The popular dance known as the *Mashed Potato* originated in the US in the late 1950s, and became a brief craze in 1962. It was similar to the Twist. The reason for the name is not known: there is no obvious connection with any slang sense of *mash* or *mashed* (for example, 'under the influence of drink or drugs'), and it could simply be that the dance moves are being likened to the action of mashing potatoes.

maslin A term used between the fourteenth and nineteenth centuries for a mixture of cereal grains, especially rye mixed with wheat. It came from Anglo-Norman *mestilun* or *mestilon*, an alteration of Old French *mesteillon*. That in turn came from late Latin *mistilio*, a derivative ultimately of Latin *mixtus* 'mixed'. Over the centuries it has appeared in a truly bewildering array of orthographic disguises, including *machelson, mashlum, masseling, mastcleyne, mescelin, misleden, misselane, mixtelyne*, and *musselgeom*.

matcha A type of finely ground Japanese green tea. It is the mainstay of the traditional tea ceremony, but it is also put to a range of other uses—as a flavouring for ice cream, for example.

matchstick A thinly sliced strip of a vegetable. The term is used prenominally, as in 'matchstick chips': 'She went back to cutting vegetables. How bored I am . . . Matchstick carrots. Bitter thoughts', Hilary Mantel, *Eight Months on Ghazzah Street* (1988). It is first recorded in 1971.

maté A tealike, slightly alcoholic beverage made in South America from the dried leaves and shoots of an evergreen tree of the holly family. Its name comes from Quechua *mati*, which was altered in American Spanish to *maté* (helped no doubt by an association with Spanish *té* 'tea'). Other names for it include *Paraguay tea* and *yerba maté* (*yerba* is Spanish for 'herb').

matelote As its name might suggest (it originated as French *plat de matelots* 'sailors' dish'), a matelote is a fish stew. Paradoxically, though, it is rather more usual in France to find a matelote made from freshwater fish than from sea fish: the classic ingredient is perhaps eel (the Irish writer Thomas Moore salivates in *The Fudge Family in Paris* (1818) over 'the bliss of an eel *matelote*'). The word came into English at a comparatively early date (it is entered in Nathan Bailey's *Universal Etymological English Dictionary* (1730)), and was even turned into a verb by Thackeray, who knew his food

and wine: 'I have tasted [eels] charmingly matelotted with mushrooms and onions', *Greenwich* (1844) (onions and mushrooms are the matelote's traditional garnish). But early English sources show that the term was often extended to cover non-fishy ingredients: Hannah Glasse, for instance, in her *Art of Cookery* (1747), mentions a 'Pig Matelote'.

matjesherring A term used fairly broadly for any herring fillet or salted herring. It is a partial Anglicization of Dutch *maatjesharing*, which means 'young herring'—that is, a herring in which the roe is not yet fully developed. The first element of the word is descended from a diminutive form of Middle Dutch *maget* (modern Dutch *maagd*) 'maid'.

matzo A brittle wafer of unleavened bread eaten by Jews during Passover (and indeed at other times). The word comes via Yiddish *matse* from Hebrew *massāh*. Its ancestral plural is *matzoth* or *matzot*, but the Anglicized *matzos* is often used.

matzo ball In Jewish cookery, a small dumpling made from seasoned *matzo meal* (crumbs made by grinding up matzos) bound together with egg and chicken fat, typically served in chicken soup.

mauby In Barbados and elsewhere in the West Indies, mauby is a bitter-sweet frothy drink made from an extract of the bark of trees or shrubs of the buckthorn family. Mauby girls dispensing it from a container carried on their head were once a common sight in the streets of Bridgetown. The word *mauby*, first recorded as long ago as 1790, in J. B. Moreton's *Manners and Customs of the West India Islands* ('Cool drink or mauby is a delicious nectar to them in the morning'), seems to have been taken over from the name of a drink made from the sweet potato (*mabi* meant 'sweet potato' in the local Carib language).

mayonnaise Mayonnaise sauce has the simplicity of a classic: egg yolks blended with olive oil, and seasoned according to taste with salt, pepper, mustard, and lemon juice. In Britain, until recently, it has laboured under the disadvantage of an impostor, the commercially made salad cream, that has stolen its honourable name. But in the 1970s and 1980s increased consumer-awareness of authenticity prompted manufacturers to market 'real' mayonnaise. Its most familiar role is to accompany salads, cold meats, etc., but the term *mayonnaise* can designate a dish in its own right (an *egg mayonnaise*, for instance, is hard-boiled egg covered with mayonnaise).

The derivation of the word *mayonnaise* has always been a matter of some controversy. Among suggestions put forward in the past are that it is an alteration of *bayonnaise*, as if the sauce originated in the town of Bayonne, in southwestern France; that it was derived from the French verb *manier* 'to stir' (this was the chef Carême's theory); and that it could be traced back to Old French *moyeu* 'egg yolk'. But the explanation now generally accepted, based on the early spelling *mahonnaise*, is that it originally meant literally 'of Mahon', and that the sauce was so named to commemorate the taking of Port Mahon, capital of the island of Minorca, by the duc de Richelieu in 1756 (presumably Richelieu's chef, or perhaps even the duke himself, created the sauce). English borrowed the word from French in the 1840s (its first recorded user was that enthusiastic gastronome, William Makepeace Thackeray).

mead Mead, a fermented mixture of honey and water, is one of mankind's most ancient alcoholic drinks. The word for it is widespread amongst the Indo-European languages (with the significant exception of Greek and Latin): German has *met*, for instance, Swedish *mjöd*, Welsh *medd*, Russian *med*, and Sanskrit *madhu-* (the latter signifies only 'sweet alcoholic drink'). And the similarity with Chinese *myit* suggest a common Eurasian origin. The ancestor of the Indo-European forms was **medhu-*, which also produced Greek *méthu* 'wine', source of English *methyl, methylated spirits*, and *amethyst* (the amethyst was formerly thought to be capable of preventing drunkenness). In northern Europe mead was widely drunk since at least the Bronze Age, and in Anglo-Saxon England it was the warrior's drink (the great hall of the chieftain was known as the 'mead hall'). But as the Middle Ages passed it gradually retreated into country areas, replaced in fashionable circles by sweet wine from southern Europe, and eventually died out. It is not clear how far modern commercially-made 'mead', which attempts to capitalize on the drink's 'Olde Englishe' connotations, resembles the rustic brews of past centuries. Latterly, mead's profile has been raised by the revelation that it is a favourite tipple of Rubeus Hagrid, hirsute Keeper of Keys at Hogwarts in the 'Harry Potter' stories of J. K. Rowling.

The post-classical Greek word for 'mead' was *hudrómeli*, a compound formed from *húdōr* 'water' and *méli* 'honey'. It was adopted by Latin as *hydromeli*, and its modern descendants include French *hydromel*, Italian *idromele*, and Spanish and Rumanian *hidromel*. *Hydromel* has been used in English, either as a synonym for *mead* or as a term for an unfermented mixture of honey and water, since the fifteenth century. *See also* METHEGLIN.

meal Edible ground grain (or pulses). In Scottish English the term denotes ground-up oats, and in American English it can mean 'maize flour', but in English at large, where its place has for the most part been usurped by *flour*, it mainly survives in compounds: *cornmeal*, *oatmeal*, *wholemeal*, etc. It comes from Old English *melu* or *meolo*, a word of Germanic origin which can be traced back to a prehistoric Indo-European ancestor meaning 'grind' that also produced (via Latin) English *mill*, *molar*, and *emolument* (and the words for flour in German (*mehl*), Dutch (*meel*), Danish (*mel*), Swedish (*mjöl*), Lithuanian (*miltai*), and Welsh (*blawd*)). It has no etymological connection with English *meal* 'occasion for eating'. *Mealy-mouthed* 'lacking frankness', first recorded in the sixteenth century, probably arose from the idea of the softness of meal.

mealie The South African English term for maize. It was adapted (possibly influenced in spelling by English *meal* 'ground grain') at the beginning of the nineteenth century from Afrikaans *mielie* (a form which is often used in English as well). The provenance of this is disputed. It may have come from Dutch *milie* 'maize', which was borrowed from Old French *mil*. However, this had become obsolete by the late seventeenth century (modern Dutch now uses *maïs*), and it may be that Portuguese *milho* 'maize, millet' is a more likely candidate. In either case the ultimate source is Latin *milium* 'millet' (reflecting the fact that before words (including English *maize*) based on Taino *mahiz* became widely established, a perceived resemblance between a corn cob and the seed head of millet inspired names for maize).

Flour made from maize is *mealie-meal* (first recorded in 1846, this may be a compound formed from *mealie* and English *meal*, or a direct translation of Afrikaans *mieliemeel* 'mealie flour'). It is widely used in South Africa for making *mealiepap*, a maize-flour porridge (Afrikaans *pap* 'porridge' comes from Dutch): 'Mieliepap for every taste: Have you tried it with meat and gravy? . . . Mieliepap—a good South African name for a great South African custom!', *Fair Lady* (1968). *Mealie rice* is crushed maize kernels, used as a cheap substitute for rice.

meat The central modern meaning of *meat*, 'the flesh of animals used as food', developed in the fourteenth century, but originally, in Anglo-Saxon times, the word meant simply 'food in general', and that sense has continued to the present day in certain fixed expressions such as 'meat and drink' and 'what's one man's meat is another man's poison'. It used also to mean 'a particular dish or article of food', from which derived such compounds as *bakemeat* 'pie', *milkmeat* 'cheese or other dairy products', and the still (just) current *sweetmeat* 'a sweet, or other sugary delicacy'. *See also* MINCEMEAT.

Further back in time, the ultimate origins of the word *meat* are disputed. Its likeliest ancestor is the Indo-European base *met- 'measure', which also lies behind English *immense*, *measure*, and *moon*. On this theory, its etymological meaning is 'portion of food measured out'. But another possibility is that it can be traced to an Indo-European base *med-, meaning 'be fat' or 'flow.' Various other derivatives of this, such as Greek *madarós* 'wet' and *mastós* 'breast' and Latin *madere* 'to be wet,' would build up a picture of *meat*— 'food, nourishment'—as something that flows from the mother's breast. Part of this same word-family are *mast*, the fruit of forest trees, such as beech, used as food for animals, and *muesli*.

The precise semantic borderlines of *meat* in current usage are actually quite fuzzy. It is clear that it does not include fish (although that was not always the case), but what about birds? There seems to be a general perception that any recognizably muscular tissue is meat, and of course there is the dark meat and white meat of turkeys, chickens, etc., but on the other hand the well-established distinction between *meat* (that is, the 'red meat' of cattle, sheep, etc.) and *poultry* survives—a distinction enthusiastically espoused by the new breed of demivegetarians, who restrict their animal-tissue intake to fish and poultry. And then there is the question of internal organs (*see* OFFAL), a grey area in more ways than one. There seems to be a relationship between frequency of consumption and membership of the category *meat*: the British would perhaps be more inclined to call liver *meat* than brains.

meatloaf A baked dish consisting of minced meat moulded into the shape of a loaf. The term is not recorded before 1892, but there is an apparent reference to the dish in a letter from Lady Newdigate dated 1787: 'We made a Dinner upon our Cold Loaf'. At the beginning of the twenty-first century it is probably best known as the stage name of the US rock musician and actor whose real name is Michael Lee Aday (born 1947). It is said to have originated either as a childhood nickname or as a reproach for pudginess administered by Aday's high-school football coach.

mebos A South African English term for a preserve made from dried apricots and other fruit, pulped or flattened. It was adopted around the end of the eighteenth century from South African Dutch, which probably got it from Japanese *umeboshi* 'plums pickled in salt and dried'.

medlar Gastronomically, the medlar is an unpromising-looking fruit. Wizened and brown, its wide but puckered circular extremity earned it in Old English the name *openarse* (which persisted dialectally into the twentieth century) and the French have called it *cul de chien*, literally 'dog's arse'. The politer *medlar*, introduced from French in the fourteenth century, comes ultimately from Greek *méspilon*. Medlars are not ready for eating until late autumn, when they are fully ripe, or overripe ('bletted' is the term for this state of incipient decay); the seventeenth century had a simile 'as useless as openarses gathered green'.

The loquat is sometimes called the *Japanese medlar*, a name which dates from the mid-nineteenth century. It is not very closely related to the medlar, although both belong to the rose family, and nor are their fruit very similar.

Melba The Australian soprano Nellie Melba (1859–1931)—actually a stage-name; her real name was Helen Porter Mitchell—was no great cook, but she was the cause of much cooking. The best-known dish she inspired is *peach Melba*, created in her honour by the illustrious chef Escoffier in 1892. The version he served her with was somewhat different from the peach Melba we now know. It consisted of a swan carved out of ice, bearing some vanilla ice cream on which reposed peaches surmounted with a net of spun sugar. This was a little too labour-intensive to reproduce on a daily restaurant menu, even in those expansive days, and so in 1900 Escoffier came up with a simpler version in which raspberry sauce replaced the swan as the main foil to the peaches. By 1907 Escoffier's 'Melba sauce'—sweetened raspberry purée—was being commercially marketed.

Another of Dame Nellie's culinary contributions is very thin crisp toast, known as *Melba toast* or *toast Melba*. The story goes that when she was staying at London's Ritz hotel in 1897, having returned in poor health from a tour of America, she was put on a stern dietary regime in which such toast figured. Never slow to spot an opportunity, the manager César Ritz declared 'Call it *toast Melba!*' It is made by toasting a slice of ordinary bread, which is then split and the two halves toasted again.

Melba is also used for a garnish of small tomatoes stuffed with diced chicken, truffles, and mushrooms in a velouté sauce.

melitzanosalata A Greek mezze dish consisting of a purée of chargrilled aubergines (similar to the Turkish *baba ganoush*). Modern Greek *melitzana* 'aubergine' (and its Italian cousin *melanzana*) probably come ultimately from Arabic *badhinjan,* which is also the source of English *aubergine* (although it would be pleasant to believe the earlier theory that they can be traced back to the Latin term *mala insana,* 'apple of madness', which was apparently once applied to aubergines).

melon The Greek word *mēlon* meant 'apple' (it is related to Latin *mālum* 'apple', from which English gets *malic acid*). But combined with *pépōn* 'ripe' it produced *mēlopépōn* 'melon'. This passed into Latin as *mēlopepō,* but in post-classical times the second element was dropped, leaving *mēlō,* which reached English via Old French in the late fourteenth century. At this stage melons were rare luxuries in Britain, imported individually from abroad, but by Elizabethan times native melons were being grown, and in the eighteenth and nineteenth centuries they became one of the most important products of the gentry's hothouses. They were usually known generically as *musk melons* (as distinct from *water melons*)—a not particularly appropriate term, probably adopted from an oriental variety of melon (in Dutch, the *muscus-meloen*) which really did have a scent reminiscent of musk. Nowadays, however, we are more aware of individual types: the *cantaloup*; the green-skinned *Charentais,* developed in the Charentes area of western France; the pale yellow *honeydew,* introduced and named in California around 1915; the small *ogen,* with its brownish-orange skin, brought in in the 1960s and named after the Ha-Ogen kibbutz in Israel where it was first commercially developed; and the even more recent *galia,* related to but larger than the *ogen,* and christened with the name of the daughter of the man who produced it.

melt¹ An animal's melt is its spleen. As a culinary item it is usually reserved for pets in Britain, but pig's melt is often used in sausages, and ox melt can be stuffed. An alternative form of the word used to be *milt* (the *Oxford English Dictionary,* in a section published in 1906, makes this the main form, and calls *melt* 'dialectal'), and it is related to, or perhaps even identical with, *milt* meaning the 'roe of a male fish'.

melt² A sandwich, hamburger, or other dish containing or topped with melted cheese: 'The Americans pair tuna with cheese in their classic toasted tuna-melt sandwich', Niki Segnit, *The Flavour Thesaurus* (2010). The term is first recorded, in the US, in 1956.

melting moment Any of various kinds of soft light shortbread biscuit. The term is first recorded in 1946.

membrillo A firm, sweet, deep-red quince preserve made in Spain. It is often served with cheese: 'sharp spears of salty manchego on chargrilled toast married beautifully with sweet cubes of membrillo', *Time Out London, Eating and Drinking* (2008). The Spanish word (first recorded in English in 1920) means 'quince'. It came ultimately from Greek *mélimélon,* the name of a variety of sweet apple, which was also the source (via Portuguese) of English *marmalade.* Its development in Spanish appears to have been influenced by *mimbre* 'willow'. *See also* COTIGNAC.

merguez A beef and lamb sausage spiced with harissa, which gives it a reddish colour. It originated in parts of North Africa, and it spread from there to the local colonial power France, where it has become incorporated into the national cuisine. The word *merguez* is French too, an adaptation of Arabic *mirkâs* or *mirqâs.*

meringue The name for this confection of sugar and beaten egg white is a direct borrowing from French *meringue,* but beyond that its origins are obscure. Legend has it variously that it was named after the town of Meiringen in central Switzerland or after the Saxon town of Mehrinyghen, seat of operations of the Swiss pastrycook Gasparini who supposedly invented it there in 1720. However, the fact that the word had even entered the English language before this (it is first mentioned in Edward Phillips's dictionary *The New World of English Words,* in John Kersey's 1706 edition) casts considerable doubt on the story.

In fact, mixtures of beaten egg white and sugar cooked in a slow oven had been popular since the early seventeenth century (they were called *Italian biscuit*), and it was the great increase in the proportion of egg white which marked the inception of the superlight meringue towards the end of the century.

merlot A grape variety used for producing red wine. It is a major constituent in the blend of claret grapes: in the Médoc and Graves it plays a subservient role to the firmer, more austere cabernet sauvignon, but on the right bank of the Gironde (St-Emilion, Pomerol, etc.) most red wines are merlot-based. It is also widely cultivated in Italy. It is generally accepted that its name is derived from French *merle* 'blackbird', but the reasons behind the application are obscure. Among the (somewhat desperate) suggestions are that blackbirds are particularly fond of eating this particular variety of grape, and that when they are ripe, the grapes are of a blackbirdish colour.

merrythought An obsolescent British term for the wishbone of a chicken, turkey, or other edible bird. It is first recorded at the beginning of the seventeenth century (much earlier than *wishbone*), and presumably refers to the thought processes of the person lucky enough to secure the longer (or, in some versions of the superstition, shorter) of the two broken clavicles: 'I . . . have seen a Man in Love grow pale and lose his Appetite, upon the plucking of a Merry-thought', Joseph Addison, *Spectator* (1711).

mescal Mescal, or *mezcal,* is a clear strong alcoholic drink distilled from the sap of an agave (a type of New World succulent plant with narrow spiny leaves). It originated in Oaxaca, a state in southeastern Mexico. Its name comes via Spanish from Nahuatl *mexcalli* 'agave'.

mesclun A type of French salad consisting of an assortment of different leaves—for example, endive, rocket, lamb's lettuce, dandelion, and purslane. It is a southern dish in origin, and the word *mesclun* comes from the Nice dialect term *mesclumo* 'mixture'.

metheglin A variety of mead that has been invigorated with additional spices—originally for medicinal purposes. The word comes from Welsh *meddyglyn,* a compound of *meddyg* 'medicinal' (which was borrowed from Latin *medicus*) and *llyn* 'alcoholic liquor'. As the derivation of its name suggests, it was originally a drink of the Celtic fringe, but it seems to have achieved wider popularity in the sixteenth and seventeenth centuries (Samuel Pepys, for instance, recorded on 25 July 1666: 'I drinking no wine, had metheglin for the King's own drinking').

methi The Indian English term for fenugreek. Hindi *methī* was borrowed from a Dravidian language.

meunière In French classical cuisine, food cooked *à la meunière* (literally 'in the style of the miller's wife') is lightly coated in flour, fried in butter, and sprinkled with lemon juice, melted butter, and chopped parsley. The method is used mainly for fish, but it can also be applied to brains, roes, scallops, etc. According to legend, it was invented at a mill in Royat, near Clermont Ferrand, which is now a hotel called La Belle Meunière.

meurette On a French menu, anything described as *en meurette* has been cooked in a red wine sauce. *Oeufs en meurette,* eggs poached in a red wine sauce, is a classic recipe, as is a casserole of freshwater fish in red wine in the region centred on Lyon. The word *meurette* is a descendant of Old French *muire* 'pickling brine', which in turn came from Latin *muria* 'brine'.

mezze Mezze, or *meze*, is a course consisting of assorted hors d'oeuvres served in Greece and the Near East. Typical components include hummus, tarama, tzatziki, small spicy sausages, stuffed vine leaves, baba ganoush, grilled cheese, and kebabs. As this suggests, mezze can easily grow into a meal in its own right, and that is what it has almost become in the Cypriot tradition imported into the Greek restaurants of Britain. It started off, however, as little more than an appetizer, a few snacks, such as a bowl of olives and some cubes of cheese, served with a drink of ouzo or raki in a bar (much the same as the Spanish *tapas*). And that is what it remains in the Near East and in mainland Greece (where it is called *mezedes*). The word *mezze* comes from Turkish *meze* 'snack, appetizer'.

microgreens A term of American origin, first recorded in 1997, for young small shoots of celery, rocket, lettuce, etc. used to make salads and other dishes: 'beautifully judged braised pork cheek subtly infused with cardamom, with buttered asparagus and modish microgreens', *Good Food Guide* (2008). They are said to provide a more concentrated version of the flavour of their full grown counterparts.

Midori The proprietary name of a green melon-flavoured Japanese liqueur. Japanese *midori* means 'green'.

milk The milk of other species of mammal is one of humankind's most ancient foods—it was in fact the most significant single contribution of the Neolithic peoples' domestication of animals to the human diet. Over the millennia most species of livestock have been milked, including in various parts of the world horses, donkeys, camels, buffaloes, and yaks (the only major exception is the pig, although nutritionally its milk is very close to that of human beings), but today in the West the term *milk*, unless further qualified, is generally taken to refer to cow's milk. It is also applied to vegetarian substitutes, such as soya milk.

The urbanization following the Industrial Revolution saw a decline in both the quantity and the quality of milk drunk in Britain (much of it watered down and disease-laden). But by the 1860s the spread of the railways and the development of cooling methods enabled fresh milk to be brought from the country to the town. Pasteurization followed towards the end of the nineteenth century, and milk has never looked back. Consumption rose from two pints per head per week around 1900 to five pints per head in the mid 1970s. A key feature in this growth was the introduction of doorstep deliveries in the early part of the century, giving birth to that familiar British institution, the *milkman* (also known, particularly in Australia, as the *milko*). The period from the 1930s to the 1950s, in particular, saw a vogue for milk among the young, and milk bars, selling milk shakes and similar drinks, became a familiar part of the scene. This was followed up in Britain in 1958 by a strong National Dairy Council advertising campaign to get people to drink more milk, spearheaded by the slogan 'Drinka pinta milka day.' *Pinta* (representing 'pint of') soon took on a life of its own as a term for a 'pint of milk'—and indeed a 'pint of beer'—provoking much apoplexy amongst linguistic purists.

The word *milk* is ancient too. It can be traced back to our Indo-European ancestors, who used a verb something like **melg-* for 'wiping' or 'stroking'. Since the action of milking involved pulling the hand down the animal's teat, this verb eventually came to mean 'milk'. But it was the Germanic languages that picked it up, in the form **meluks*, as a noun. Its modern descendants include German *milch*, Dutch and Danish *melk*, Swedish *mjölk*, and English *milk*. (The words for 'milk' in the Romance languages, such as French *lait*, Italian *latte*, and Spanish *leche*, as well as Welsh *llaeth*, come from Latin *lac*—source of English *lactation, lactic*, etc., and ultimately also of *lettuce*—which is related to Greek *gála*, source of English *galaxy* 'Milky Way'.)

milk shake The concept of the milk shake, a beverage made by whisking up milk with a fruit syrup or other flavouring (often with the addition of ice cream), seems to have originated in the US in the 1880s. It was introduced to Britain just before the Second World War (the first known British reference to it is in a caption in the *Daily Herald* (1937), to a photograph of an unnamed woman 'sampling a milk-shake after she had opened a milk bar in Tottenham Court Road'), and in the 1940s and 1950s it reached a peak of popularity from which it has since rapidly declined as its principal consumers, teenagers, have turned to stronger stuff. *See also* SHAKE.

'The 1081-calorie bacon milkshake at US burger chain Jack in the Box contains bacon-flavoured syrup, vanilla ice cream, and a maraschino cherry', *Guardian* (2012).

milk stout Milk stout is, or was, a stout of creamy consistency sweetened with the addition of lactose, a sugar derived from milk. The term is now legally disallowed in Britain as being misleading.

mille-feuille A cake, typically a small square one, made of layers of puff pastry filled with cream (there are also savoury mille-feuilles, usually filled with seafood). Its name, literally 'thousand-leaf' in French, is a reference to the multiple strata of the puff pastry.

millet Any of a range of cereal plants of the family Gramineae which produce a large crop of small seeds on elongated seed heads, or 'panicles' (the word comes ultimately from Latin *panus* 'stalk', which is also the source of *Panicum,* the genus name of the most common millet of temperate regions). In the UK until comparatively recently it has been known almost exclusively as a food for cagebirds, but it is widely grown in warm countries and regions with poor soil. Its seeds are chiefly used to make a coarse flour. English acquired its name in the fifteenth century from French *millet,* a diminutive form of *mil,* which in turn came from Latin *milium* 'millet'.

mimolette The cheese sold as *mimolette* in France is basically the same as Dutch Edam—indeed, much of it is made in the Netherlands. It is said to have been created in the late seventeenth century, in response to a demand from Louis XIV for a French version of Edam. It comes in larger balls than standard Edam, with flattened top and bottom, and it is dyed orange with annatto. It is sold either young, when it is fairly soft, or matured for up to eighteen months. Its name comes from the feminine form of the French adjective *mollet* 'soft', with the addition of the prefix *mi-* 'partly'. The profile and popularity of mimolette were raised in the 1960s when President de Gaulle (the man who memorably commented on the impossibility of governing a country that made 246 different types of cheese) said it was his favourite cheese.

mimosa A mixed drink consisting of champagne and orange juice—essentially, the American equivalent of Buck's fizz. First recorded in 1936, the term perhaps suggests the frothiness of the mimosa tree's heads of small yellow flowers. That association certainly lies behind a completely different culinary application of *mimosa*, to a garnish made by passing the yolks of hard-boiled eggs through a sieve: 'Our [lunch] included delicately stuffed baby turnips with organic egg "mimosa" and kalamata olives', *Time Out London, Eating and Drinking* (2008).

mincemeat The modern distinction between *mince* 'minced meat' and *mincemeat* 'dried fruit mixed with spices, suet, and often some sort of alcohol' arose only gradually. *Mincemeat* originally meant simply 'minced meat' (it is first recorded from the mid-seventeenth century, in the metaphorical sense of 'making mincemeat of someone'—'chopping him up or annihilating him'—which still survives), and we do not have any unequivocal evidence of its being used in its current sense until the mid-nineteenth century.  But in the Middle Ages and into Renaissance times and beyond it was commonplace to spice up or eke out meat with dried fruit, and it seems likely that the earliest mincepies contained a generous measure of such raisins, currants, etc. The reduction in meat content was a slow but steady process (still not complete, of course, for the inclusion of beef suet is a remnant of it). The growing need to draw a lexical distinction between plain minced meat and *mincemeat* was signalled around 1850 by the introduction of the term *mince* for the former (Edward Lear's owl and pussycat, who 'dined on mince and slices of quince', were born in 1871).

American English, incidentally, prefers the term *ground meat* to *minced meat*.

mincepie We first hear of mincepies in the early seventeenth century: Richard Johnson, in his *Pleasant Conceites of Old Hobson* (1607), writes of 'cramming their bellies with minced pyes' (*minced pie* for *mincepie* seems to have survived longer in the USA than in Britain). Even at this early stage it seems clear that the mincemeat they contained was not simply minced meat, but contained a significant quantity of dried fruits, spices, sugar, etc. (the meat content has since shrunk, of course, to a little beef suet). Dishes containing a mixture of currants, raisins, spices, and originally meat have long been traditional Christmas fare in Britain (*see* CHRISTMAS PUDDING), and mincepies are no exception: as early as 1662, for instance, Samuel Pepys was writing in his diary for 6 January (Twelfth Night) 'We have, besides a good chine of beef and other good cheer, eighteen mincepies in a dish, the number of years he [Sir William Penn] hath been married.' Indeed, from the mid-seventeenth century they were often called *Christmas-pies*, a name which survived into the nineteenth century: 'Please to say Christmas-pie, not mincepie; mincepie is puritanical', Chambers *Book of Days* (1864). But in 1747 Hannah Glasse in her *Art of Cookery* was still giving directions for 'Lent Mince Pies'.

The rhyming-slang use of *mincepies* (or *minces* for short) for 'eyes' dates from the mid-nineteenth century.

minestrone A thick Italian vegetable soup. Its proportion of solids to liquid is high: it includes a wide variety of chunky vegetables (the precise mixture varies from region to region of Italy, but usually includes tomatoes, courgettes, onions, beans, and celery) and also pasta or (in Milan) rice. It probably originated in Genoa. Its name is a derivative (formed with the suffix *-one*, denoting 'largeness') of *minestra*, a thinner, less filling, more orthodox sort of vegetable soup. This in turn comes from the verb *minestrare* 'to serve, dish out'.

minneola A variety of tangelo, a citrus fruit with thin deep-reddish skin and a characteristic neck or knob at its stem end. It is named after a town in Florida, near which it was developed in the mid-twentieth century.

mint *Mint* is a cover term for various plants of the genus *Mentha*. Without further qualification it is used for the *garden mint*, or *spearmint* (so named perhaps from the pointed shape of its leaves), possibly the most widely used and popular of all herbs in Britain, which comes into its own in mint sauce served with lamb and also as a flavouring for young boiled potatoes and peas. Its name comes via prehistoric West Germanic **minta* and Latin *menta* from Greek *mínthē*, which according to legend was applied to a nymph beloved of Pluto, who turned her into a mint plant. It has no etymological connection, incidentally, with the *mint* where coins are made, which comes ultimately from Latin *monēta* 'money'.

   The other main sort of mint of culinary interest is the peppermint, presumably so named (towards the end of the seventeenth century) from the hotness of its taste. The first known references to sweets flavoured with it come from the end of the eighteenth century.

minute steak A thin slice of steak that can be cooked very quickly (*minute* is pronounced /ˈminit/, not /myˈnyoot/). The term is first recorded in 1921.

mirabelle A type of small sweet yellow plum, often with a reddish blush when ripe. The French name (first recorded in English in 1706) probably comes from the place-name *Mirabel*, of which there are several examples in southern France.

mirch The Hindi term for 'chilli'. It is also used for 'chilli powder'. 'Mirch Masala' is a favourite name for Indian restaurants in Britain.

mirepoix A mixture of finely chopped vegetables, typically onion, carrot, and celery, fried in butter and used for flavouring stews and other meat dishes, as a base for sauces, and as a garnish. It was reputedly devised in the eighteenth century by the cook to the Duc de Lévis-Mirepoix, a French field marshal.

mirin A Japanese alcoholic drink, pale golden in colour and sweet, made from fermented rice—essentially a sweeter version of sake. It is used mainly in cooking.

mirliton The French word *mirliton* means 'reed pipe' (it probably originated as an imitation of the sound made by the instrument). But it also has culinary applications. It can denote a type of small puff-pastry tartlet, in which sense it has made fitful appearances in English (Flora Annie Steel and Grace Gardiner, for example, in their *Complete Indian Housekeeper and Cook* (1898), give a recipe for 'mirletons' [sic], 'made in patty-pans lined with the trimmings of puff paste, and filled with various mixtures'), and in the US state of Louisiana it is the usual term for the chayote, a fruit of the gourd family.

miso A savoury or sweet paste made from fermented soya beans and barley or rice malt, used in Japanese cookery—for example, as a dressing for salads, as a flavouring for pickles, and in marinades: 'The menu also features . . . more adventurous options such as miso-glazed baby back ribs', *Time Out, Eating in London* (2008). The Japanese term is first recorded in English in the early eighteenth century.

Mississippi mud pie A calorific American dessert consisting of a rich mousse-like chocolate cake. The name originated in the 1950s.

mixed grill A dish consisting of various items of grilled meat, typically a chop (usually lamb or mutton), kidneys, sausages, and bacon, with an accompaniment of grilled tomatoes and mushrooms. It is something of an endangered species now (too much saturated fat, no doubt), but for much of the twentieth century it was a staple of British cafés and hotel dining rooms. First recorded in 1913, the term was also put to metaphorical use, denoting a haphazardly heterogeneous mixture: 'a stale mixed grill of underdone gothick, underdone chinoiserie', Stanley Morison, describing the typography of *The Times* in the early 1930s, quoted in Juliet Gardiner, *The Thirties: An Intimate History* (2010).

mizuna An oriental plant of the cabbage family with finely cut, feathery leaves that are used raw in salads. Its name is Japanese, and means literally 'water greens'.

mocha A term applied to coffee of a high grade, particularly and originally a rich and pungent variety of Arabian coffee. It comes from Mocha, a seaport in the Yemen, at the entrance to the Red Sea, from which it was once exported. It has been known in Britain since the late eighteenth century. In the US the word is often applied to a combination of coffee and chocolate flavouring.

mocktail A term of American origin, blending *mock* and *cocktail*, for a non-alcoholic drink consisting of a mixture of fruit juices or other soft drinks. It is first recorded in 1936.

mock turtle When John Tenniel drew the Mock Turtle for Lewis Carroll's *Alice in Wonderland*, he gave him a turtle's shell but a calf's head, hind legs, and tail—and appropriately so. West Indian green turtles were the luxury food of the eighteenth and nineteenth centuries, valued for their meat and for the soup made from it. But only aristocrats could afford them when they were first imported in the 1750s, and so the search began for a substitute suitable for shallower middle-class pockets. The answer was veal, and more particularly the calf's head. Hannah Glasse in her *Art of Cookery* (1747) has a recipe in which a calf's head is stewed in stock laced with Madeira, and then served with its broth in a turtle's shell. Margaret Dods's *Cook and Housewife's Manual* (1826) mentions 'Mock Turtle, or Calf's Head', but thereafter, not perhaps surprisingly, the head itself largely disappeared from the table, leaving the soup as the counterfeit reptile's main contribution to English cuisine.

Interestingly, as conservation worries have led to the virtual demise of real turtle soup, the urge to mimic it inexpensively seems to have gone too.

mode, à la In French cuisine, *à la mode* (literally 'in the fashion') refers to a dish of beef braised with vegetables and served either hot in a rich brown sauce or cold in aspic. It had some currency in English in the eighteenth and nineteenth centuries in the compressed form *alamode beef*. In the US, however, *à la mode* denotes a dish (such as apple pie) served with ice cream.

mojito A cocktail (pronounced /mə'heeto/) of Cuban origin consisting of white rum, lime or lemon juice, sugar, mint, ice, and carbonated or soda water: 'Havana's Bodeguita del Medio started life as an ordinary bar, busy with local bohos and rough sailors knocking back cheap beers and mojitos . . . But Hemingway dropped by for a few litres of daiquiri and the bar became a tourist trap', *Time Out London, Eating and Drinking* (2008). The Cuban Spanish word was based on *mojo,* with the diminutive suffix *-ito.*

mojo A Cuban sauce or marinade containing garlic, olive oil, and sour oranges. The word is probably a reapplication of the Spanish adjective *mojo* 'wet'. In English it is pronounced /'mo-djo/ or /'mo-ho/.

molasses The dark brown sticky liquid that remains after cane sugar syrup has been boiled down to produce sugar. The more it is boiled, the more sugar is removed, and therefore the less sweet it is. What remains—including minerals such as iron and calcium—gives the molasses its colour, so the less sweet, the darker. (Treacle, on the other hand, has had very little sugar removed, and so is paler and sweeter.)

Etymologically, the word can be traced back to the Latin for 'honey', *mel* (as in *mellifluous*). A derivative of this, *mellaceum* 'grape juice', was borrowed into Portuguese as *melaco*, and English acquired it in the sixteenth century. It was taken over in the plural form, which has since come to be regarded as a singular.

In the eighteenth and nineteenth centuries the Scots had a drink which they called *molass*, a fierce rumlike spirit distilled from molasses. 'The common people have got so universally into the habit of drinking this base spirit, that when a porter or labourer is seen reeling along the streets, they say, *he has got molassed*', William Buchan, *Domestic Medicine* (1789).

mole A highly spiced Mexican sauce (pronounced /ˈmolay/) made chiefly from chilli peppers, ground almonds, and, in its most familiar form, bitter chocolate (the chocolate adds richness, depth, and colour). It is served with meat. Its most famous incarnation is in *mole poblano*, a stew of turkey in a chocolate mole sauce which is an iconic item of Mexican cuisine. Its full name in Mexican Spanish is *mole poblano de guajolote*: *guajolote* means 'wild turkey'; *poblano* refers to the variety of chilli used (see POBLANO); and *mole* itself comes from the Nahuatl word *molli*, meaning 'mixture, sauce, stew'. Legend has it that the dish was invented in the sixteenth century by nuns of the convent of Puebla, to the east of Mexico City. See also GUACAMOLE.

monkey bread A type of bread composed of small roughly shaped balls of dough, dipped (in the standard sweet version) in melted butter, sugar, and cinnamon, and moulded into a loaf shape. This gives a marbled effect when the baked bread is cut. It first appeared in the 1950s, in America, and its profile received a boost in the 1980s when Nancy Reagan, wife of US President Ronald Reagan, incorporated it into the White House Christmas celebrations. The reason for its name is not known: perhaps there is some notion of the haphazard result of a monkey assembling a loaf. Alternatively it has been suggested that the bread looks like a pack of monkeys jumbled together.

monk's vegetables In Chinese cuisine, an assortment of stir-fried vegetables and other non-meat ingredients served in a soy-sauce-based liquid. The components vary widely, but will typically include various types of mushroom, water chestnuts, carrots, peanuts, bamboo shoots, bean curd, and noodles. The monk in question is a Buddhist monk, who is of course a vegetarian. The Chinese name of the dish is *luóhàn zhāi*: *luóhàn* means 'enlightened person', and is used as an epithet of the Buddha; *zhāi* means 'vegetarian food'. An alternative English term for it is *Buddha's delight*.

Mont Blanc A classic French chestnut pudding consisting of a mound of sweetened chestnut purée topped with a summit of whipped cream, supposedly resembling a snow-capped mountain. The direct inspiration for the name was presumably Mont Blanc (literally 'Mount White'), an Alpine peak on the French/Italian border, though there is no suggestion that the dish was originally specifically intended to resemble that mountain. In Italy it is known as *Monte Bianco*.

Monterey Jack A type of mild American cheese that comes in two varieties: semi-soft, and a harder Cheddar-like version. It is also known as *Monterey cheese* and, in America, as *Jack cheese*. *Monterey* comes from the name of Monterey County, California, where it was originally made in the 1880s; *Jack* comes from its creator, a Scottish-born Californian cheese-maker called David Jacks (1822–1909; his original surname was Jack). *Jack cheese* is first recorded in 1912, *Monterey Jack* not until the early 1940s.

Montmorency A variety of sour cherry with bright red skin. It originated in a valley of that name in the Île-de-France. Dishes, sauces, etc. with *Montmorency* in their name include these cherries: 'slow-roast glazed duck with cherry brandy and montmorency sauce', *Time Out London, Eating and Drinking* (2009).

mooli *See* RADISH.

mooncake A round cake-like confection eaten in China at the time of the Moon Festival in the autumn. They are made from pastry with a sweet filling (such as a paste made from dates or adzuki beans) and embossed with a special design on top. The name (which is a direct translation of Chinese *yuèbǐng*) is first recorded in English in 1938.

moonshine *Moonshine* has been used since the late eighteenth century—the great days of smuggling—for spirits illegally distilled or imported: 'The white brandy smuggled on the coasts of Kent and Sussex is called moonshine', Francis Grose, *Dictionary of the Vulgar Tongue* (1785). The name comes from the secretive nocturnal circumstances of its production or acquisition (it was also called *moonlight* in the nineteenth century). The term has largely died out in Britain, but in American English it continues in use with reference to illegally distilled whiskey (as opposed to smuggled whiskey, which is *bootleg*).

   Another culinary use of the term has disappeared altogether: in the mid-eighteenth century, Hannah Glasse in her *Art of Cookery Made Plain and Easy* (1767) gave a complicated recipe for a dessert dish called 'moonshine' in which a 'sky' of blancmange or custard was diversified with a half-moon and stars in clear jelly.

Morbier A French cows'-milk cheese made in Franche-Comté. Its chief distinguishing feature is a greyish-black line that runs through the middle of it. This is the product of a layer of soot put on the curds made from the morning milking to protect them, and later covered by the curds from the evening milking. The cheese is named after the commune in the Jura where it was originally made.

morcilla A Spanish version of black pudding. Its name is probably derived from the same source as Spanish *morcon* 'black pudding', but the identity of that is unknown.

morel Morels are edible mushrooms with long pointed spongy caps (an alternative name is *sponge mushroom*). The word *morel* (first recorded in the seventeenth century) comes via French *morille* from Dutch *morilje*.

morello A name given to a range of comparatively dark-skinned varieties of cherry, with fairly bitter flesh. It was acquired by English in the seventeenth century from Italian *morello*, which means 'black, dark', and came ultimately from Latin *Maurus* 'Moor'. Morello cherries are used particularly for making jam, but they are also often steeped in brandy, either to be eaten in their own right or to make cherry brandy.

Moreton Bay bug A type of marine crustacean of northeastern Australian waters, valued for its edible tail flesh. The first part of its name comes from the bay at the mouth of the Brisbane River, Queensland, which was bestowed on it by Captain Cook in honour of James Douglas, 14th earl of Morton (1702–68), a distinguished patron of scientific research and president of the Royal Society from 1764 (the spelling *Moreton* arose by mistake). *Bug* seems to have been a term used by Australian fishermen for this and related species of flat lobster as a word vaguely applicable to any jointed, insect-like creeping creature. *Moreton Bay bug* is not recorded before 1970, at a time when more such crustaceans were being taken by prawn trawlers and becoming more widely available commercially, but the related *Balmain bug* (named after a suburb of Sydney) had got its name by the early 1950s.

Mornay *Sauce Mornay*, a béchamel sauce flavoured with cheese, seems to have been created at the end of the nineteenth century. There are conflicting accounts as to whom its name commemorates. Some give the honour to the seventeenth-century French Huguenot writer Philippe de Mornay, others to the son of its inventor, Joseph Voiron of the restaurant Durand in Paris, who was supposedly called Mornay.

morning glory There are many species of morning glory, a climbing plant of the convolvulus family with trumpet-shaped flowers. The one that is of culinary interest is the semi-aquatic *Ipomoea aquatica*, also known as *water spinach*, whose pointed leaves are used as a green vegetable in East and Southeast Asia: 'We preferred the fresh, flavourful stir-fried morning glory with garlic and chilli', *Time Out London, Eating and Drinking* (2009). The term is also applied to a whisky- and brandy-based cocktail made with Cointreau, Pernod, and bitters.

mortadella A large lightly smoked Italian sausage, eaten cold. It is typically made of pork, although other mixtures of meat are possible, and originally it was flavoured with myrtle (hence the name, which comes ultimately from Latin *murtum* 'myrtle'), but nowadays its additional features are usually parsley, pistachios, or green olives. The first record of the word in an English text is in a letter from John Chamberlain dated 9 September 1613: 'The duke of Savoyes ambassador . . . hath brought . . . a present from his wife of salaccioni, cervellate, mortadelle'.

morteau A type of smoked pork sausage that is a speciality of the Morteau region in Franche-Comté, eastern France.

mortrews A medieval dish, possibly of Provençal or Catalan origin, consisting of meat, poultry, or fish pounded into a paste, then cooked in broth or milk, usually with breadcrumbs, eggs, and various spices, to form a sort of thick soup. The word comes from Old French *mortreux*, the plural of *morterel* (which was also used in English), a derivative of *mortier* 'mortar' (the vessel in which the dish's main ingredient was pounded).

Moscow Mule A cocktail consisting of vodka, lime or lemon juice, and ginger beer. It was developed in California in the late 1940s as part of an advertising campaign for Smirnoff vodka. *Moscow* subtly suggests the Russianness of vodka and *mule* the kick that the drink can administer. The latter element has been spun off to include other ingredients: 'Swanky cocktails are mixed to perfection, and include classics with a twist (lychee mojitos, strawberry and basil mules), and quirky originals', *Time Out London, Eating and Drinking* (2009).

mostarda di Cremona An Italian condiment consisting of a mixture of candied fruits (such as cherries, plums, figs, small oranges, slices of pear) in a mustard-flavoured syrup. It is traditionally eaten with cold boiled meat, but it also goes well with cheese and charcuterie. It originated in the northern Italian city of Cremona, to the southeast of Milan, but there are other versions from other places: *mostarda di Mantova*, for instance, from Mantua, which features small green apples.

mouclade A French dish consisting of mussels cooked in white wine and served in a sauce thickened with cream. It comes from Aunis and Saintonge, on the west coast, and *mouclade* is an Aunis dialect word, derived from *moucle*, the local variant of French *moule* 'mussel'.

mountain chicken A colloquial name in Caribbean English for the South American bullfrog, a large terrestrial frog which is eaten as a delicacy in certain West Indian islands, notably Dominica and Montserrat. *Compare* PADDY CHICKEN.

mountain wine A term used in the eighteenth and nineteenth centuries for a rich, raisiny fortified wine made in the hills around Málaga, a Mediterranean port city in southern Spain. It was often abbreviated to simply *mountain*: 'Women love white best.—Boy, bring half a pint of mountain', Henry Fielding, *Rape upon Rape* (1730). Mildew and phylloxera dramatically reduced production in the mid-nineteenth century, and the name died out. Since production revived (in a relatively small way) in the second half of the twentieth century, the wine has generally been termed simply *Málaga*.

mousetrap A colloquial British term for inferior or unpalatable cheese, usually of a (broadly) Cheddar type, presumed to be fit only for baiting mousetraps: 'The tasty local cheese—what a change after the eternal "mousetrap"!', Frank Smythe, *Again Switzerland* (1947). The usage is first recorded in 1936. In New Zealand the term denotes something rather different: slices of bread spread with tomato relish and a mixture of beaten eggs, grated cheese, chopped onion, bacon, etc., and browned in the oven.

moussaka Moussaka, or *mousaka*, is an eastern Mediterranean dish consisting of minced lamb alternating in layers with sliced aubergines and tomatoes and onions, and often thickened and topped off with a béchamel sauce. English acquired the word in the mid-nineteenth century from modern Greek *mousakas* or Turkish *mussaka*, and knowledge of it has been spread by returning holidaymakers from Greece and Turkey, but in fact moussaka is eaten throughout the Middle East, and the term probably originated in Arabic *musaqqâ*, which means 'moistened'.

mousse A light frothy dish, usually eaten cold, consisting of a sweet or savoury purée whipped up and set in a mould with beaten egg whites, cream, or gelatine. English took the term over from French as recently as the 1890s. There, it originally meant 'moss', and indeed *moss* and *mousse* probably share a common prehistoric source (whose ancestral sense was probably 'bog'). The possible etymological connections with *applemose*, a now obsolete term for a dish made from stewed and pulped apples, are not clear; the semantic similarities are striking, but the likelier explanation is perhaps that the element *-mose* comes from a primitive Germanic word for 'soft food' (represented also in *muesli*).

mousseline In French cuisine, *mousseline* is a rather general term denoting a light fluffy dish, particularly one made in a mould from finely minced poultry, fish, etc., which is given a mousse-like consistency by the addition of whipped cream. The resemblance of the word to *mousse*, however, is purely fortuitous, for the primary sense of French *mousseline* is 'muslin', and its application to this dish is merely an allusion to the lightness and delicacy of the fabric.

A *mousseline sauce* is a hollandaise sauce with whipped cream mixed into it.

moutabal An alternative name widely used in the Middle East for BABA GANOUSH.

mozzarella A soft white Italian curd cheese, now generally made from cows' milk, but originally a buffalo-milk cheese. It has achieved worldwide fame as a melted topping for pizzas, but in Italy it is just as commonly eaten on its own, with just a little salt, pepper, and oil, and perhaps some olives and tomatoes. It is made all over Italy, and is traditionally sold in small balls that are kept moist in a bowl of whey. Its name in Italian means literally 'little slice'. It is a diminutive form of *mozza* 'slice, slice of cheese', a derivative of the verb *mozzare* 'to cut off', which perhaps came ultimately from Latin *mutilāre* (source of English *mutilate*).

muesli This Swiss dish of cereal, fruit, and nuts, eaten with milk or yoghurt, made its first appearance in Britain as early as 1926, but until the 1960s its consumption was largely restricted to the health-food fringe. Since then, however, as high-fibre has been transformed from a fad to a multi-million pound business, muesli has inundated the nation's breakfast tables, and given rise to the 'muesli belt', a shorthand collective term for the *Guardian*-reading middle classes concerned with issues like ecology and healthy eating. And the 1980s even saw the rise of so-called 'muesli-belt malnutrition', a condition in which children fed on a diet high in fibre but low in fat and sugar, suitable only for adults, lose weight, and have their growth stunted.

Muesli is a Swiss-German diminutive form of *mus* 'pulpy food, purée'; it is related to an Old English word for 'food', *mōs* (*see also* MEAT). When it was first introduced into Britain it was often called *Birchermuesli*, after its proponent Dr Bircher-Benner, who served it to patients in his 'natural health' clinic in Zürich. *See also* GRANOLA.

muffin The muffin-man with his bell, selling his wares in the street at a halfpenny a time, is a part of English folklore. But what exactly did he have in his tray? He seems to have disappeared from the scene by the 1930s, and the evidence for what his wares were is contradictory. Elizabeth David, in her *English Bread and Yeast Cookery* (1977), surveys the sources from the mid-eighteenth century to the 1950s and finds almost as many variations as recipes. A large part of the problem is that the muffin has a Siamese twin in the crumpet, and the two terms have often been confused (there is a regional dimension, too, the north of England once using *muffin* for what in the south tended to be called *crumpets*). It does seem to be the case that muffins in former times were often made from a leavened batter of flour and milk similar to that used for crumpets, the difference being that the finished muffin did not have such large airholes as the crumpet. The end result was a round flattish spongy cake eaten warm for breakfast or tea, usually buttered. These muffins do not appear to have borne much resemblance to the revived muffins on sale in British supermarkets and bakeries since the 1970s. These are what Americans call *English muffins*. They are the same shape as earlier muffins, but are made of a soft bread-like dough. As a further contribution to terminological confusion, to American speakers the term *muffin, tout court*, denotes a sort of cup-shaped bun or cake made from a flour, milk, and egg batter, usually with some sort of additional flavouring element, such as blueberries or chocolate chips. This sort of muffin became more familiar in Britain from the late twentieth century.

English probably got the word *muffin* from *muffen*, the plural of Low German *muffe* 'cake'.

The metaphor underlying the colloquial *muffin top*, or *muffin* for short, meaning 'a roll of fat visible above the top of a pair of tight-fitting low-waisted trousers', is based on the way the top of an American-style muffin puffs out over the edge of the container it is baked in: 'I hated my muffin top and was desperate to slim down', *Daily Star* (2010).

muffuletta A very large sandwich made with a whole round Italian-style loaf (for example, focaccia). Its defining ingredient is 'olive salad', a mixture of olives with garlic, capers, various herbs, olive oil, and vinegar, but other fillings are likely to include ham, salami, and provolone cheese. It is said to have been created by Salvatore Lupo, proprietor of the Central Grocery on Decatur Street in New Orleans, in the first decade of the twentieth century, and it remains a New Orleans speciality. Its name, which is not recorded before 1967, comes from a Sicilian dialect word meaning 'round hollow-centred loaf'. That in turn was probably a diminutive derivative of standard Italian *muffola* 'muff, mitten'.

muggety pie A mercifully obsolete dish containing the intestines of a calf or sheep. The origins of *mugget* 'such intestines' are lost in history.

muktuk The skin and blubber of a whale, typically the narwhal or the beluga, used as food by the Inuit. The word comes from Inuit *maktak*.

mulberry Mulberries, most luxurious of fruit, dark crimson, bursting with juice, raspberry-like in shape, and so fragile when ripe that there is really nothing to be done with them but eat them raw, trace their name back to Latin *mōrum* (source also of French *mûre*—which confusingly means 'blackberry' as well as 'mulberry'). Our Anglo-Saxon ancestors took the term over as *mōrberie*, but some time around the fourteenth century the first *r* metamorphosed into an *l*.

The mulberry tree on whose leaves silkworms dote, incidentally, is the white mulberry, which produces rather unexciting fruit. As far as human beings are concerned, the black mulberry is gastronomically superior.

England owes many of its mulberry trees to James I. He had a plan to establish an indigenous silk industry, and to that end ordered the importation of mulberry trees. Unfortunately, what he got were not white mulberries but black ones, which have produced many offspring over the centuries.

mule *See* MOSCOW MULE.

mulligan In America, a mulligan is a hotch-potch of a hot-pot, a stew composed of any spare vegetables and pieces of meat that happen to be to hand. This extract from *Collier's Magazine* (1913), nine years after the word's first known appearance in print, gives something of its flavour: 'I suppose you never have eaten any "Mulligan".... The recipe calls for canned Willie, spuds, onions, canned tomatoes, all mixed up together' ('canned Willie' is corned beef). The origin of the name is obscure, but it seems to come from the proper name *Mulligan*.

mulligatawny This hot spicy soup first entered British cuisine at the end of the eighteenth century; it had found favour with employees of the East India Company on station in the subcontinent, and when they returned home they brought it with them—although the soup it has evolved into in British hands, heavily dependent on commercial curry powder, bears little resemblance to its aromatic South Indian original. The name comes from Tamil *milakutanni*, a compound of *milaku* 'pepper' and *tanni* 'water'. It standardly includes meat or meat stock, but Eliza Acton gives a vegetarian version made from marrows, cucumbers, and apples or tomatoes.

In the early nineteenth century the word, or its abbreviation *mull*, was used in Anglo-Indian slang for members of the government service in Madras: 'A well-known Mull popp'd out his head. *Note* An abbreviation for Mulkatany, a common appellation for Madras officers', 'Quiz', *The Grand Master; or Adventures of Qui Hi? in Hindostan* (1816).

mung bean The mung bean, or *moong bean*, as it was originally spelled in English, is a small widely-cultivated olive-green Oriental bean. It is perhaps most familiar in the West as the source of edible bean sprouts. The name comes from Hindi, and is a shortening of *mungo*; this in turn was borrowed from Tamil *mūngu*, which came ultimately from Sanskrit *mudga*.

Munster A semi-soft cows'-milk cheese made in and around Munster in Alsace, France. It is said to have been originally made by Irish monks who settled in Alsace in the seventh century. Its aroma can be disconcertingly pungent, but its flavour is relatively mild. In Alsace it is often paired with boiled potatoes.

murgh On an Indian menu, *murgh* is 'chicken' (as in *murgh massalam*, a marinated then casseroled chicken dish, and *murgh makhani*, 'butter chicken'). The word is Urdu, from Persian *murg* 'bird, fowl'. It is first recorded in English in 1976.

Murphy This now distinctly passé slang term for the potato seems to have originated around the beginning of the nineteenth century (it is first recorded in the *Lexicon Balatronicum, A Dictionary of Buckish Slang, University Wit, and Pickpocket Elegance* (1811)). It is perhaps most familiar to recent generations through the 'stunning murphies' baked by Sally Harrowell in Thomas Hughes's *Tom Brown's Schooldays* (1857). It is, of course, a would-be jocular reference to the predominance of the potato in the eighteenth- and nineteenth-century Irish diet, Murphy being a common Irish surname. (A similar inspiration lies behind the use of *mickey* in American English in the mid-twentieth century for a roasted potato sold by a street vendor.)

muscadet The name of a grape variety that has become synonymous with the wine made from it in a particular part of France—the area around the mouth of the river Loire. Here it produces a light, very dry white wine which goes well with the seafood of the region. *Muscadet sur lie* is muscadet that has been matured on its lees, and is somewhat richer in flavour. The name is a derivative of French *muscade* 'nutmeg'. The grape, but not the wine, is alternatively known as the *melon de Bourgogne*.

muscat Any of a range of white, red, or black grapes that have a characteristic musky scent. They are used for making wine or raisins, or as table grapes. Most varieties used for wine are white, and are usually turned into sweet or fortified wines, most notably in France (*muscat de Beaumes-de-Venise, muscat de Frontignan, muscat de Rivesaltes*) and Australia, but some are fermented out dry (for example in Alsace). English acquired the word in the sixteenth century from French, which in turn got it from Provençal *muscat*, a derivative of *musc* 'musk'.

muscatel Nowadays, the commonest application of *muscatel* is to raisins made from muscat grapes (this dates from the seventeenth century). Formerly, though, it was also used for a sweet wine made from these grapes ('At the same time shall men sing of the vineyard of Muscatel,' Miles Coverdale's 1535 translation of Isaiah 27:2—which in the Authorized Version is rendered 'In that day sing ye unto her, A vineyard of red wine'). The word was borrowed from Old French *muscadel* (which used to be a common spelling in English), itself a diminutive form of *muscat* (see MUSCAT).

muscovado A dark-brown unrefined sugar extracted from boiled sugar cane by centrifuging. English borrowed the term in the seventeenth century from the Portuguese phrase *açucar mascavado* 'unrefined sugar'. The Portuguese verb *mascavar* 'to adulterate' came from a probable Vulgar Latin **minuscapare* 'to make less'. The English form *muscovado* no doubt comes from unconscious association with such words as *muscovy* and *muscatel*.

Muscovado is sometimes also called *Barbados sugar*.

mushroom Culinarily, the term *mushroom* generally refers, if not further qualified, to the common cultivated mushroom, *Agaricus bisporus*, or its wild relative the field mushroom, *Agaricus campestris*. These are graded into three sizes: the smallest, 'button' mushrooms; medium-sized 'cups'; and the largest, 'flat mushrooms' or 'open mushrooms'. This

exclusivity in the face of the scores of other species of edible mushrooms available in the countryside reflects a traditional British unadventurousness when it comes to fungi, but since the Second World War continental varieties such as ceps, morels, and girolles, and even the oriental shiitake, have become better known.

The word *mushroom*, first recorded in the early fifteenth century, was borrowed from Old French *mousseron*. This has been traced back to a late Latin *mussiriō*, a word of unknown origin. *See also* SHROOM.

mushy peas Marrowfat peas that have been cooked until softened to a purée and are served in their own juice. They originated in the north of England, notably as an accompaniment to fish and chips, but in the latter part of the twentieth century their fame spread southwards. The term is first recorded in the 1960s.

mussaman Mussaman, or *massaman,* is a fairly mild Thai curry made with coconut milk, potatoes, peanuts, and a curry paste typically including lemongrass, cardamom, cinnamon, garlic, chilli, and shrimp paste. It originated along the Thai border with Malaysia, where many of the population are Muslims. Its name may be an alteration of obsolete English *Mussulman* 'Muslim'.

mustard Mustard was originally made by mixing the roughly crushed hot-tasting seeds of various plants of the cabbage family with unfermented grape juice, or 'must'—hence its name, which comes from Old French *moustarde*, a derivative of Latin *mustum* 'must'. The Romans were very fond of it, and it was they who introduced it to Britain. It remained popular during the medieval period and beyond, not the least of its attractions being its cheapness compared with other hot spices that had to be imported from far-distant lands. In those days Tewkesbury gained a reputation for producing the finest mustard in England. But mustard-eating really took off in a big way in the nineteenth century when Colman's of Norwich started marketing yellow mustard powder in tins for the masses. Henceforth a dab of made-up mustard sauce became almost as automatic an addition to British main courses as pepper and salt. English mustard is usually made from the brown and white varieties of seed (the vivid yellow colour is 'assisted'—with turmeric or some such substance). But other countries' mustards are differently constituted. French mustards (the best-known of which comes from Dijon) are made from brown and black seeds; those containing whole or slightly crushed rather than finely ground grains have enjoyed a vogue in recent years. And American mustard, the traditional accompaniment of the hot dog, is made from white seeds. (It is white mustard, incidentally, whose seedlings form the mustard of the salad garnish *mustard and cress*.) In consequence of all these possible permutations, commercially produced mustards come in a range of colours, from pale or vivid yellow to dark brown; but it is to a sort of mid-way brownish-yellow that *mustard* has become attracted as a colour term: 'She stared at the large poster of Marie Kendall . . . Mustard hair and dauby cheeks', James Joyce, *Ulysses* (1922).

The metaphorical application of mustard's piquancy to 'zeal' or 'zest' dates back to the seventeenth century in such expressions as 'keen as mustard', although its adjectival use is an early twentieth-century development ('That fellow is mustard', Edgar Wallace, *King by Night* (1925)) as is the American *cut the mustard*, meaning 'to meet or surpass expectations'.

mustard greens The peppery leaves of any of a range of wild and cultivated mustard plants, used as a vegetable. In the US, they are a feature of the 'soul food' of the Deep South. In China, Japan, and Southeast Asia thick-stalked varieties are widely used, cooked or pickled.

mutton In Anglo-Saxon times one ate simply *sheep*, and British accession to the EU brought about a return to such blunt terminology—whether from the lamb or the adult sheep, all is *sheepmeat* (*The Times* (1978) explained that 'The word "sheepmeat" with which Brussels refers to mutton and lamb is translated from the official French term, *Viande ovine*'). In the late thirteenth century, however, in what might be interpreted as the first instance of French oneupmanship over the gastronomically illiterate British, the Old French word *moton* was drafted into the language, introducing for the first time the possibility of a distinction between the live animal and its flesh used for food. (In fact *mutton* was from early on used for live sheep as well, and this continued until comparatively recently; and the distinction from *lamb* as the flesh of young sheep does not appear to have developed until the seventeenth century.) Old French *moton* itself came from medieval Latin *multo*, which in turn was probably borrowed from a Celtic language of Gaul (several modern Celtic languages have cognate forms, such as Welsh *mollt* and Cornish *mols*).

In the sixteenth century the word came to be used as a collective euphemism for sexually promiscuous women, or 'food for lust', as the *Oxford English Dictionary* resoundingly defines it, and in Shakespeare's time *laced mutton* was a prostitute: 'Ay, sir; I, a lost mutton, gave your letter to her, a laced mutton' *The Two Gentlemen of Verona* (1593). By the twentieth century it had become virtually synonymous with the female sexual organs, in the phrase 'hawk one's mutton', meaning 'to solicit'. And *mutton*'s unflattering connotations have culminated in 'mutton dressed as lamb', the crushing judgment on an older woman trying to look younger than her age, first recorded in James Joyce's *Ulysses* (1922).

Mutton was once a mainstay of the British diet: Mrs Beeton refers to it as 'undoubtedly the meat most generally used in families', and Victorian cookery books are stuffed with recipes for mutton pies and puddings, broiled mutton chops and cutlets, braised legs of mutton, Irish stew, and other now less well remembered dishes—China chilo, for example, a rather unappetizing stew of minced mutton. The assertive flavour of mutton is now, however, out of fashion, and it is hard to find a butcher who stocks it.

nacho A tortilla chip (that is, a small crisp piece of tortilla) topped with melted cheese and chopped chillis, served as a snack or with dips. The origins of its name (first recorded in English in 1948) are disputed: it may come from Mexican Spanish *Nacho* (a pet form of *Ignacio*), which was supposedly the name of the chef credited with inventing the nacho; alternatively it could be from Spanish *nacho* 'flat-nosed', perhaps inspired by a triangular-shaped chip.

nage In French cuisine, a nage is a light white-wine-based vegetable stock in which scallops and small crustaceans, such as crayfish, are cooked. The name comes from the description of such dishes as *à la nage*, literally 'swimming'.

nam pla The classic Thai fish sauce, a thin pungent salty liquid made by fermenting small fish in brine and maturing the resulting fluid in the hot sun (Thai *nam* means 'water' and *pla*, 'fish'). It is used in a wide variety of dishes, fulfilling much the same role as soy sauce does in Chinese and Japanese cookery. In Vietnam it is called *nuoc mam*.

nan Nan, or *naan*, is a type of flat but puffy leavened Indian bread. The name is Hindi.

Nantua Any dish cooked *à la Nantua*, or served with a *sauce Nantua*, contains crayfish or crayfish tails as its chief flavouring element. Perhaps the one most often found on menus today is *filets de sole Nantua*, sole fillets garnished with a ragout of crayfish tails and covered with *sauce Nantua*, a béchamel flavoured with crayfish. Nantua is a small French town to the northeast of Lyon, near the Swiss border.

nashi pear The nashi pear, or simply *nashi*, is the crisp apple-shaped fruit of a tree of the same genus as the pear, that is native to China and Japan (*nashi* means 'pear' in Japanese) and cultivated in Australia and New Zealand. It started to become more widely known in the West in the 1960s. An alternative name for it is *Asian pear*.

nasi goreng In Malay, *nasi* denotes 'cooked rice' and *goreng* 'fried', but there is more to *nasi goreng* than fried rice. It is a composite Dutch–Indonesian dish in which any of a selection of ingredients, typically including cooked pork, chicken, or seafood, are added to the rice. It is served with sliced omelette.

navarin A sort of stew of lamb or mutton containing vegetables. During the winter months these will standardly be potatoes and onions, but in the spring the new season's vegetables (carrots, turnips, beans, peas, etc.) are used to make a *navarin printanier* ('spring navarin'). The French for 'turnip' is *navet*, which is probably the source of *navarin*. E. S. Dallas's comment in *Kettner's Book of the Table* (1877) suggests that the term was not of great antiquity: 'Navarin is a stupid word which has arisen from a desire to get rid of the unintelligible and misleading name, Haricot de mouton, without falling back on the vulgar phrase, Ragoût de mouton.'

navel orange A large seedless orange of a variety that has a depression at the top containing a small secondary fruit. This evidently struck some observers as bearing a passing resemblance to a human navel, and so the fruit got its name (first recorded in 1856).

navigator British rhyming slang (often abbreviated to *nav*) for 'potato'. It dates back at least to the 1850s. In the nineteenth century, street sellers used to cry out 'Nav scot!' (= potatoes hot) to advertise their baked potatoes. The navigator the original rhymer had in mind was presumably not a nautical one, but one of the labourers (*navvies* for short) who built the canals and railways of Victorian Britain. Large numbers of them were Irish, and the connection with the potato, thought of as the stereotypical Irish vegetable, is no doubt not fortuitous.

navy bean The American name for the small white haricot bean, the bean used for baked beans. It presumably arose from the bean having formed an important element in the navy's shipboard diet.

Neapolitan Neapolitan ice is a block of ice cream made in layers of different flavours and colours: a typical combination is strawberry, vanilla, and chocolate. The name seems to have come simply from the high reputation Italians, and particularly Neapolitans, had as ice-cream makers in the nineteenth century. It first appears in English in the 1890s, and to begin with is found only in American texts.

neat An old word of Germanic origin for an ox or cow (it is related to Danish *nød* and Swedish *nöt*, both with the same meaning, and to Austrian German *noss* 'livestock', and its underlying etymological signification is 'useful property'). It has long since gone out of solo use, but it lingered longer in the names of cattle-related products. The main ones of culinary relevance are (or were) *neat's foot jelly* and *neat's tongue*.

nectarine A smooth-skinned variety of peach. It seems first to have appeared in Britain in the early part of the seventeenth century. Its name is generally taken to be a nominal use of the adjective *nectarine* 'sweet as nectar', perhaps influenced by German *nektarpfirsich* and Dutch *nektarperzik*, literally 'nectar-peach'.

neep A standard Scottish term for the 'turnip' or 'swede': *bashed neeps*, 'puréed swede', is a classic accompaniment to haggis. It is the same word as the second syllable of *turnip*, and comes ultimately from Latin *nāpus* (source also of French *navet* 'turnip').

Negroni A cocktail composed of equal parts gin, vermouth, and Campari. The story goes that it was invented in 1919 by a Florentine barman in response to a request by Count Camillo Negroni to strengthen his Americano by substituting gin for soda water.

negus An eighteenth- and nineteenth-century version of hot punch made usually with port, sweetened, and flavoured with lemon and nutmeg. It was invented by Colonel Francis Negus (died 1732).

neroli An essential oil distilled from the flowers of the Seville orange. Its main use is in perfumery, but it is also used for flavouring a range of culinary items, from creamy desserts through confectionery to liqueurs. It is said to have been originally popularized in France in the 1670s by Marie Anne Orsini, née de la Trémoille (1642–1722), French-born Princess of Nerola, Italy, and it took its name from her. *See also* ORANGE FLOWER WATER.

nesselrode A cold pudding made from custard cream with chestnut purée and usually mixed candied fruits. It belongs to the rococo period of nineteenth-century French haute cuisine, and is seldom seen nowadays. It is said to have been invented by Monsieur Mouy, chef to the Russian statesman Count Karl Nesselrode (1780–1862). Nesselrode was Russian foreign minister from 1816, and worked vigorously for European federation; indeed, Jane Grigson sees the ingredients of the nesselrode as a reflection of the count's cosmopolitan background: chestnuts for his family's German origins, raisins for his place of birth, Lisbon, and Greek currants as a covert reference to his anti-Turkish stance. Eliza Acton, however, attributes the recipe to the famous French chef Antonin Carême.

Neufchâtel A soft French cows'-milk cheese, originally made in Neufchâtel-en-Bray in Normandy.

Newburg A designation given to a method of cooking lobster by sautéing it with cream and fish stock, with the addition of sherry or brandy. The recipe was created around 1876 by Ben Wenburg, head chef at the New York restaurant Delmonico's, but already by the 1890s the *w* and *n* of his name had been transposed to give *Newburg* (according to one version, because Mr Wenburg had fallen into bad odour with the owners of the restaurant). In common with other lobster dishes, it has gained a reputation of being the preserve of sybaritically self-indulgent plutocrats: in the 1930s A. D. Lindsay, Master of Balliol College, Oxford, banned it from college menus to show solidarity with the unemployed.

New England boiled dinner *See* BOILED DINNER.

New York steak An alternative name in America for a STRIP STEAK.

Nice biscuit A thin sweet biscuit containing coconut and sprinkled with sugar. It rhymes with *geese* (as opposed to *mice*), so it was presumably named after the fashionable town on the Côte d'Azur, France, but the reason for the connection is unknown. It is first recorded in 1895.

nigella The small black pungent seeds of the eastern Mediterranean plant *Nigella sativa* (a close relative of love-in-a-mist), that are widely used in Indian and Middle Eastern cookery. The name is a modern Latin creation, meaning literally 'little black one'. The seeds are often alternatively called *black cumin* and *black onion seeds*, though the plant is in no way related to either cumin or onion.

nightcap The use of *nightcap* for a 'drink taken on going to bed' dates from the early eighteenth century—the notion being that, like a literal nightcap, it warms you up and helps you to sleep. Originally it was strictly alcoholic: 'A pint of table beer (or Ale, if you make it for a "Night-Cap")', *The Cook's Oracle* (1818). Non-alcoholic nightcaps do not appear on the scene until the 1930s; the first known reference to this abstemious version is in a 1930 advertisement for Ovaltine: 'Ovaltine . . . the world's best "night-cap" to ensure sound, natural sleep.'

nigiri sushi A type of sushi consisting of a small ball or rectangle of cold rice, smeared with wasabi paste and topped with raw fish or other seafood. The term comes from Japanese *nigiri zushi*: *nigiri* is a derivative of the verb *nigiru* 'clasp, clench, roll in the hands'. This sort of sushi, which is typical of Tokyo, is the one that has spread around the world, so that for Westerners, *sushi* and *nigiri sushi* are virtually synonymous.

nog Originally, an East Anglian term (of unknown ancestry) for a sort of strong beer—in 1693 we find one Humphrey Prideaux writing in a letter of 'a bottle of old strong beer, which in this country [Norfolk] they call "nog"'. Not until the early nineteenth century was it applied (in full as *egg nog*) to a drink made from milk and beaten eggs mixed with rum, brandy, or wine. An alternative name for it is *egg flip*.

nonpareil French *nonpareil* 'unequalled, peerless' was originally adopted by English in the late fifteenth century. Its has various specific noun uses, including two culinary ones that have achieved some currency in English: it refers to a type of small round pickled caper; and it is also applied to small coloured pellets of sugar used for decorating cakes and desserts. The latter (what in Britain would be *hundreds and thousands*) is used in American English, where the term has also been extended to embrace a flat round disc of chocolate covered with white sugar sprinkles.

noodle Thin flat strips of pasta made from wheat flour, rice flour, mung bean starch, etc., crop up in many cuisines around the world, from Europe to China. They are commonly used as thickeners for soups. Familiar Italian varieties include tagliatelle and fettuccine. English borrowed the word from German *nudel* (whose origin is unknown), but it did not become a familiar term in the language until the mid-nineteenth century, when German immigrants brought it to the US; earlier, in her *Journal* (October 1779), Lady Mary Coke recorded her puzzlement at it: 'A noodle soup—this I begged to be explained and was told that it was made only of veal with lumps of bread boiled in it.'

nori A seaweed of the laver type which in Japan is pressed into greenish-black sheets and dried. It is used in sushi.

nougat This soft or hard chewy preparation of nuts, sugar, and honey is now usually made commercially with hazelnuts, but its name reveals its original ingredient to have been walnuts. It comes, via Old Provençal *noga*, from Latin *nux*, which meant not simply 'nut' but, if not further qualified, 'walnut'; and to this day the oil-cake made from the residue of walnuts pressed for oil is called *nougat* in the south of France. It comes in a range of colours, but nowadays the white variety is the best known. The town of Montélimar, in Provence, is the most famous source of it, and indeed *nougat* is now sometimes called *montelimar*.

nougatine A form of nougat confection typically covered with chocolate. The word (first recorded in 1894) has a French air, but it appears to have been an English invention, using the suffix *-ine* 'resembling' (but with a 'French' pronunciation). It is not recorded in French until 1908.

noyau A liqueur made from fruit kernels (apricot, peach, plum, cherry) macerated in brandy and sugar syrup. The word comes from French, where it means literally 'kernel'. It derives ultimately from Latin *nux* 'nut'.

nut To the botanist, nuts are firm-fleshed single-seeded fruit enclosed within a hard shell that does not split open—a hazel nut, for instance, or an acorn. Everyday usage, however, extends the term to any hard-shelled edible seed, such as almonds, brazil nuts, cashew nuts, and peanuts. The word comes ultimately from the Indo-European base **ken-*, which signified 'lump'. This produced both the Germanic forms, German *nuss*,  Dutch *noot*, Swedish *nöt*, English *nut*, etc., and Latin *nux*, from which the Romance terms, French *noix*, Italian *noce*, and Spanish *nuez* are descended (as also is English *nucleus*). The commonest nut of southern Europe is the walnut, and consequently Latin *nux* and its modern off-spring mean chiefly 'walnut' rather than just 'nut'.

Of the various metaphorical uses of the word, 'threaded block that screws on to a bolt' dates from the early seventeenth century, 'head' from the mid-nineteenth century (whence *nuts* 'mad', *off one's nut*, etc.), and (in the plural) 'testicles' from the early twentieth century.

Nutella The proprietary name of an Italian chocolate and hazelnut spread, introduced on to the market in 1963.

nutmeg Etymologically, the *nutmeg* is the 'nut that smells of musk'. It is a partial translation of Old French *nois muguede*, which came from a hypothetical Vulgar Latin *nuce muscâta*, literally 'musky nut'. The relationship with 'musk' that has been lost in English is still clear in, for instance, modern French *muscade* and German *muskatnuss*.

It is the seed of a tropical evergreen tree which is indigenous to islands of the Indian ocean. It grows surrounded by a web of fibres which is itself ground up and used as a spice under the name *mace*. It seems first to have been heard of in England in the fourteenth century, but it probably did not arrive in any quantity until the early sixteenth century, after the Portuguese had opened up the route round the Cape of Good Hope to the Moluccas and the other spice islands. In the mid-seventeenth century the Dutch seized the Moluccas, and Mrs Beeton noted with some asperity that the nutmeg 'was long kept from being spread in other places by the monopolizing spirit of the Dutch, who endeavoured to keep it wholly to themselves by eradicating it from every other island'. By her time it had, however, 'through the enterprise of the British . . . found its way into Penang . . . where it flourishes and produces well'. In the eighteenth century gentlemen used to carry around with them small silver boxes which doubled as nutmeg holders and nutmeg graters, with which they would grate nutmeg into their hot chocolate drinks. The nutmeg has retained a foothold in the British kitchen ever since, particularly as a component of mixed spice used in cakes, puddings, etc. (despite Mrs Beeton's gloomy warning that it should 'be used with caution by those who are of paralytic or apoplectic habits').

In the USA, *wooden nutmeg* used to be a colloquial term for a 'fraud' or 'imposture'. Connecticut is sometimes known as the 'Nutmeg State', allegedly because in years past some of its traders were adept at passing off wooden nutmegs as real ones.

The use of *nutmeg* as a verb to describe a footballer passing the ball between an opponent's legs, and thereby making him look foolish, appears to be a recent development. The inspiration for it is presumably *nuts* 'testicles'.

Nutter The proprietary name (first recorded in 1906) of a substitute for butter made from the oil of nuts. Strange though it may sound to twenty-first-century ears, *Nutter* survived in Britain into the 1970s. But once the British slang *nutter* 'insane person' (first recorded in 1958) had established itself, it could scarcely be taken seriously. That lexical handicap does not apply in the US, however, and there the word has popped up in a different guise: the *Fluffernutter* is a sandwich introduced in 1961 by the company Durkee-Mower, Inc, which on one slice of bread has Marshmallow Fluff (a thick fluffy confectionery mix now known as 'Marshmallow Crème') and on the other, peanut butter (hence, -*nutter*).

oakleaf lettuce A reddish-brown or green variety of lettuce that has loosely bunched leaves with serrated edges and a slightly bitter taste. The term is first recorded in 1892.

oats The reputation of oats has never really recovered from Dr Johnson's notorious definition 'a grain, which in England is generally given to horses, but in Scotland supports the people' (later echoed by Eliza Acton in her *English Bread-book* (1857): 'In the south of England oats are not employed for bread, but only for feeding horses'). When Johnson wrote it, it was actually not far from the truth (if one adds Wales to Scotland), but in the Middle Ages and earlier oats had been as much used as human food in England—for making porridges, thickening soups, and in oat-cakes and the like—as in the Celtic fringes. The cereal grass which produces the seeds called oats originated as a weed of wheat and barley fields, which was accidentally harvested with the main crop. In due course it came to be cultivated in its own right in northern Europe, and was introduced to Britain in the Iron Age. The Romans knew of it (their word for it was *avena*, source of French *avoine*), but only as a weed, or as a fodder plant—although Pliny, anticipating Dr Johnson, mentions that the Germanic peoples made porridge with it.

The word *oat*, which is a descendant of Old English *āte*, is a purely English term, with no known relatives in other languages. The remaining Germanic languages have interrelated names for the plant—German *hafer* (indirect source of English *haversack*, which comes from a word denoting a horse's nosebag), Dutch *haver*, Swedish and Danish *havre*—which may be related ultimately to a set of words meaning 'goat'—Latin *caper*, for instance—and may therefore signify etymologically 'goat's food'. *Haver* used to be a synonym for 'oats' in Scotland and northern England too, presumably borrowed from Old Norse.

Oatmeal, the term for flour made from oats, was coined in the fifteenth century.

The expression *sow one's wild oats*, meaning 'to commit youthful indiscretions', originated in the sixteenth century from the notion of the improvidence of sowing wild oats rather than proper cereal crops. *Feel one's oats* 'to feel frisky' or 'to act self-importantly' is a much later coinage, from the America of the 1820s, and *get one's oats* 'to have sex' is more recent still—first recorded in Joseph Manchon's *Le slang* (1923).

oca A South American plant related to the wood sorrel, long cultivated in Peru and elsewhere in the Andes for its edible carrot-like root tubers. Its name came into English in the early seventeenth century from American Spanish, which in turn got it from Quechua *ócca*. It has been commercially cultivated in New Zealand, where it goes under the name *New Zealand yam*.

ocean stick An alternative term for CRABSTICK.

offal The word *offal* was borrowed from Dutch *afval* and translated into its component parts (literally 'off' and 'fall') in the fourteenth century. At first it meant simply 'refuse' or 'waste', but in the fifteenth century its specialized application to the less glamorous parts of a slaughtered animal carcase began. Originally it referred only to the internal organs (liver, kidneys, heart, lungs, stomach, etc.), but later usage often includes external extremities such as the head, tail, and feet as well. Such items of food are, with the possible exception of the liver and kidneys, regarded as not quite out of the top drawer in British-American culture, and the word *offal* has reflected this in being applied metaphorically over the centuries to the scum or dregs of society (Lord Macaulay, for instance, referred to 'wretches . . . whom every body now believes to have been the offal of gaols and brothels,' 1828). These days no supermarket would use the word for fear of putting off customers, and there are signs that the American euphemism *variety meat* is starting to be used in British English (the more frank *organ meats* has not yet crossed the Atlantic).

ogen melon *See* MELON.

oggy The indigenous name in Cornwall for a Cornish pasty, especially one that has one half filled with meat and vegetables and the other with apple or other fruit. First recorded in 1948, it is probably an alteration of Cornish *hoggan* 'pastry, pie', which may be related to Welsh *chwiogen* 'muffin, simnel cake'. The popularity of pasties with the sailors at southwestern naval ports saw *oggy* firmly ensconced in British naval slang in the second half of the twentieth century. *See also* PRIDDY OGGY, TIDDY OGGY.

It seems more likely than not that the *oggy* crowd chant (in full 'Oggy, oggy, oggy! Oi, oi, oi!') heard at sporting events, scout camps, and the like, incorporates the pasty name. It was popularized in the 1970s by the Welsh comedian Max Boyce, and the Welsh have since taken it to their bosom, but there is some evidence that it was previously in use in southwest England. There is no corroboration, however, for the notion that Cornish women cried 'Oggy!' as they brought pasty lunches to their menfolk working in the fields, tin mines, etc., and that their husbands replied with an 'Oi!

okra The edible seedpods of a tropical and subtropical plant of the hollyhock family, widely cultivated and used in the Caribbean (where the spelling *ochro* is also used) and the southern states of the US, but originating in Africa. Africa is the source of the name, too, which appears to be derived from or related to *nkuruma*, the word for 'okra' in the Twi language of West Africa. It is first recorded in English at the beginning of the eighteenth century. The mucilaginous pods, like miniature pentagonal green bananas, are an essential ingredient in, and thickener of, soups and stews in countries where they are grown, notably of course the gumbos of the southern US (*gumbo* was originally a synonym of *okra*, and is still so used in American English). Other names of the polynomial okra include in English-speaking countries *lady's fingers*, in India *bhindi*, and in the eastern Mediterranean and Arab countries *bamies*.

old-fashioned A cocktail made from whisky with bitters, sugar, a dash of water or soda water, and usually a twist of lemon peel, served on ice. It is said to have been invented by a barman at the Pendennis Club in Louisville, Kentucky in the late 1880s. Reputedly he used a brand of Kentucky bourbon called 'Old 1776', which may account for the cocktail's name. That has since been transferred to the type of glass in which the drink is served, a rather squat cylindrical tumbler.

Old Tom A sweetened diluted cordial based on the type of heavy-bodied, relatively dark-coloured gin commonly available until it was gradually supplanted from the middle of the nineteenth century by London dry gin. According to Simon Majumdar (*Eating for Britain*, 2010), its name was 'taken from a small wall-mounted and cat-shaped machine from which the gin was dispensed. The customer would insert a penny through a slot and place their mouth around a protruding spout through which the purchased gin would be issued'. The term is first recorded in 1815.

olive The olive has been a cornerstone of Mediterranean cuisine since before our Indo-European ancestors colonized the region. The people who lived in Greece at that time called it by a name which was taken over by the new inhabitants as *elaíā*. Latin in turn adopted it as *olīva*, and has since passed it on to nearly all the languages of Western Europe (the only major exception is Spanish, whose word for the 'olive', *aceituna*, comes from Arabic). Olives were eaten whole, of course, but their main use, then as now, was as the source of the oil pressed from them (indeed the very English word *oil* comes ultimately from Greek *élaion*, a relative of *elaíā* 'olive'). This served not only as a food and cooking medium but also for rubbing the body with, as a fuel for lamps, etc. In northern Europe, its oil was the only manifestation of the olive that was at all well known (and even then it was only the rich who could afford it); the unfamiliar olive itself was termed in the Dark Ages 'oilberry'—Old English *eleberge*, for instance, and Old High German *oliberi*. This state of affairs continued until comparatively recently: Mrs Beeton, for example, writing in the mid-nineteenth century, reports that in Britain olives are only ever encountered as a dessert course, 'to destroy the taste of the viands which have been previously eaten'. To her, both the olive and its oil were essentially 'foreign': 'The oil extracted from olives, called olive oil, or salad oil, is, with the continentals, in continual request, more dishes being prepared with it than without it, we should imagine.' An early British dig at greasy foreign food. Mrs Beeton does, however, concede olive oil a role in the preparation of salads, and notes that it is 'an antidote against flatulency'.

A signal of the centrality of the olive to Mediterranean culture is its choice as the tree whose branch according to the Bible the dove bore to the Ark as a sign that the Flood was going down. A literal 'olive branch' was used in the Middle Ages as a sign of peace and goodwill, although now it only survives metaphorically.

The use of *olive* as a colour term, 'dull yellowish green', dates from the seventeenth century. The colour of US Army uniforms is officially described as *olive drab*.

olla podrida A classic Andalusian stew made from various types of meat—beef, chicken, sausages, sundry parts of pigs—and vegetables cooked together slowly in a pot. It was first mentioned in English as long ago as the sixteenth century, and the term has persisted in the language since then with reference to the stew as a whole. In Spain, however, the tendency is to serve the liquid component of the stew as a soup, and eat the meat and vegetables separately. And over the years the term *olla podrida* was gradually transferred from the stew as a whole to this soup (although nowadays it is rarely heard; the soup is more generally called *puchero* or *cocido*).

In common with other words for stews of variable content, such as *hotchpotch*, *gallimaufry*, and *pot pourri* (itself a direct French translation of the Spanish term, which literally means 'rotten pot'), *olla podrida* has been used metaphorically in English for any 'heterogeneous jumble'. Sir Walter Scott repopularized it after a fallow period in the eighteenth century, even coining an adjective from it ('My ideas were olla podrida-ish,' *Journal* 13 March 1827), and it survived beyond the middle of the nineteenth century.

oloroso One of the two major categories of sherry. The other, fino, is produced under a blanket of the yeast flor, but the wine in the casks in which flor does not develop becomes oloroso (the word means literally 'fragrant' in Spanish, although aficionados would claim that of the two, fino is the more perfumed wine, at least in its youth). As oloroso matures, it darkens, and before being sold most of it is sweetened (using the treacly wine made from the Pedro Ximénez grape), but over the past three decades an increasing amount of original, bone-dry oloroso has become commercially available outside Spain.

omelette The notion of cooking beaten eggs in butter in a pan is an ancient one (in medieval England, the dish was often made with herbs, and called a *herbolace*), but *omelette* does not enter the English language until the early seventeenth century. It is first described by Randle Cotgrave in his *Dictionary of the French and English Tongues* (1611): 'Haumelette, an Omelet, or Pancake of egges.' Omelettes had by then been made in France for two or three hundred years, and it is from French that we get their name. It has a complex history: it probably started out as *lamella*, a diminutive of Latin *lamina* 'thin plate'; this was borrowed into French, but by a misanalysis of *la lemele* (of a similar sort as gave us *an adder* from the earlier *a nadder*) it became *alemelle* or *alumelle*. It seems this must at some point have had the common suffix *-ette* substituted for *-elle*, and the resulting *alemette* then had its first two consonants transposed (by a process known as metathesis) to give *amelette*. The word has had a variety of spellings in English, including *amulet* in the seventeenth and eighteenth centuries and *emlett* in the seventeenth century, and there is still some variation: *omelette* is now the generally preferred form in British English, but the *Oxford English Dictionary* gave *omelet* precedence in 1902, and this is still the main American spelling.

The question of how to make a perfect omelette is often made to seem even more complicated than the origin of its name. In the seventeenth century it was commonly recorded that it should be cooked on both sides, which would be considered sacrilegious by present-day omelettophiles (although as recently as the 1860s Mrs Beeton was suggesting that 'to take off the rawness on the upper side' one could 'hold the pan before the fire for a minute or two, and brown it with a salamander or hot shovel'). In the nineteenth century various writers recommended including flour in the recipe, and there are still disputes over whether one should beat the eggs thoroughly or not at all, whether the omelette should be cooked firm or still runny in the middle (*baveuse*, as the French call it), etc. Most would agree on folding the omelette in half to serve it, but even here there are exceptions: omelettes made around the Mediterranean, including the famous Spanish omelette, are traditionally served flat.

The old adage to the effect that 'You can't make an omelette without breaking eggs' (that is, you can't achieve anything of consequence without causing some incidental damage or upset along the way) is a direct translation of French 'On ne peut pas faire des omelettes sans casser les oeufs,' attributed by some to Robespierre. It makes its first appearance in English in 1859.

omelette Arnold Bennett *See* ARNOLD BENNETT.

onglet A prime cut of beef consisting of two small muscles that support the diaphragm. Well hung, it makes a very tender steak. The term, first recorded in English in 1982, comes from French, where it means 'little claw', perhaps reflecting the role of the muscles in attaching the diaphragm to the backbone. In American English the cut is called a *hanger steak*.

onion For a vegetable that human beings have been eating since prehistoric times, the onion has a very unsettled linguistic history, going by a wide diversity of names among the Indo-European languages. Our Anglo-Saxon ancestors called it *cipe* (a relative of modern English *chives*). They borrowed it from Latin *cēpa*, which was probably originally a non-Indo-European loanword, and whose other descendants include

the Spanish and Italian words for 'onion', *cebolla* and *cipolla* (source of English *chipolata*). The Greeks knew the onion as *krómuon*, which is related to Irish *creamh*, Welsh *craf*, and English *ramsons*, all words for the wild garlic plant. Russian (*luk*) has borrowed the Germanic word *leek*, which is also represented in Swedish *lök* 'onion'. *Onion* itself comes from late Latin *ūniō*. This was probably a derivative of *ūnus* 'one'; it seems originally to have signified a single large pearl, and been transferred by proud gardeners to the pick of their onion crop (although another theory is that the name referred to the 'unity' of the layers of the onion). English first acquired the word in Anglo-Saxon times, using it in the compound *ynnelēac* 'onion leek', but in the form in which we now know it, it came via Old French *oignon* and Anglo-Norman *union* in the fourteenth century. As this suggests, it was the Romans who introduced the cultivated onion into Britain. Their Anglo-Saxon successors preserved it, and it has remained a fixture in British cuisine (as indeed of most cuisines around the world) ever since—this despite its tearful revenge on those who slice it up and occasional doubts as to its side effects (Andrew Boorde in his *Dietary of Helthe* (1542) reported that 'onions do promote a man to veneryous actes, and to somnolence'— hardly the most glowing recommendation for an aphrodisiac).

The colloquial British expression *know one's onions* 'to be knowledgeable or experienced' dates from the 1920s.

onion marmalade *See* MARMALADE.

oolong A variety of dark-coloured China tea made by fermenting the withered leaves to about half the degree usual for black tea—a sort of halfway house, in other words, between black tea and green tea. The most highly prized examples are produced in Taiwan. The name comes from Chinese *wūlóng*, literally 'black dragon'. It came into English in the mid-nineteenth century.

open sandwich A sandwich without a top slice of bread. The concept is essentially a Scandinavian one, and caught on in Britain in the 1960s and 1970s with the popularity of smorgasbord. The term *open sandwich* itself is first recorded in 1946. Its Danish equivalent, *smørrebrød*, literally 'butter-bread', is sometimes also used in English.

orache Orache, or *orach,* is a plant of the goosefoot family with edible, usually arrow-shaped leaves that taste like spinach. It was widely cultivated in Europe in the past, but its popularity declined in the sixteenth century as the availability of spinach increased. Its name comes from Anglo-Norman *arasche,* a descendant of Latin *atriplex,* which itself was adapted from Greek *atraphaxus.*

orange Oranges are native to China, but their English name comes from one stage further along their ancient journey to the West—India. The Sanskrit term for the fruit was *nāranga*, which passed via Persian *nārang* into Arabic as *nāranj*. It was Arab traders who first introduced oranges into Europe, and the main route through which they came was naturally Moorish-held Spain. The Spanish naturalized *nāranj* as *naranja*, but when the word penetrated further north to France in the late thirteenth century it became transmuted to *orenge*, later *orange*, perhaps partly under the influence of the name of the town of Orange, in southeastern France, a centre of the orange trade. The first oranges to reach Britain seem to have arrived in the 1280s: C. Anne Wilson in *Food and Drink in Britain* (1973) reports that 'fifteen lemons and seven oranges . . . were brought from a Spanish ship at Portsmouth in 1289 for Queen Eleanor'.

All these early oranges were bitter, regarded in much the same light as lemons now are (*Epulario, or the Italian Banquet* (1598) directs 'take the juice of an orange, or verjuice'). Today they are called *Seville oranges*, and are used mainly for marmalade. Sweet oranges, for eating, reached Britain from China, via Portugal, in the seventeenth century. They soon became fashionable as refreshment for theatre-goers (the most famous London 'orange-wench' or orange-seller was of course Nell Gwynn). In the seventeenth and eighteenth centuries they were generally termed *China oranges*, to distinguish them from the ordinary bitter oranges (whence the expression 'all Lombard street to a China orange', denoting very long odds, first recorded in 1815), but as they gradually supplanted the Seville orange they inherited the right to the simple name *orange*.

Orange is first recorded as a colour term in the sixteenth century. *See also* KUMQUAT, MANDARIN, SATSUMA, TANGERINE.

orangeade *Orangeade*, originally a French word modelled on *limonade* 'lemonade', was the first of a subsequently proliferating group of fruit-drink terms ending in the suffix *-ade* (*see* LEMONADE). English acquired it in the early eighteenth century. A close relative etymologically was *orangeado*, a seventeenth- and eighteenth-century word for 'candied orange peel', perhaps based on Spanish *narajada* 'orange conserve'.

orange flower water An orange-perfumed liquid that is a product of the distillation of the flowers of the Seville orange. The essential oil, called *neroli*, is drawn off from the resulting liquid, and the remaining aqueous part is orange flower water. It has been widely used, originally in the Middle East and, from the seventeenth century, in Europe, as a food flavouring.

orchata An alternative form of HORCHATA.

orecchiette Pasta in the form of small domed discs. It is a speciality of Apulia in southeastern Italy. Its name in Italian means literally 'little ears'.

oregano A herb of the marjoram family, native to the Mediterranean, and much used particularly in Italian cookery (its aromatic leaves often give a special savour to pizzas, for instance). The word comes ultimately from Greek *orίganon*, which is probably a compound of *óros* 'mountain' and *gános* 'joy', and has been adopted into English no fewer than four separate times: in the Old English period as *organ*; in the fifteenth century as *origan*, from Old French; in the sixteenth century as *origanum*, from Latin; and in the eighteenth century as *oregano*, from American Spanish *orégano*. To begin with, *oregano* was pronounced in English with the stress on its second syllable, as in Spanish, and that remains the case in American English, but in British English it is now more usual to stress the third syllable.

Oreo The proprietary name (invented by the manufacturer) of a type of chocolate biscuit with a white cream filling, originally produced in the US in 1912. In the 1960s it came to be used as a derogatory term for an African American who is seen, especially by other blacks, as part of the white establishment: 'Trouble is Negroes been programmed by white folks to believe their products are inferior. We've developed into a generation of Oreos—black on the outside, white on the inside', *Harper's Magazine* (1969).

orgeat In origin, *orgeat* is a French term parallel to English *barley water*. It comes from French *orge* 'barley' (a descendant of Latin *hordeum*), and at first signified a 'cooling drink made by steeping barley in water'. That was what it meant when English acquired it in the mid-eighteenth century, but, as in the case of barley water, it was found to need livening up with fruit juice, and by the nineteenth century the term had come to stand for an orange-flavoured syrup made from sugar and almonds, diluted with water to form a long drink.

ortanique A citrus fruit which is a cross between an orange and a tangerine, developed in Jamaica in the 1920s. It has a characteristic mustard-coloured skin with brown specks. Its invented name is a blend of *orange, tangerine*, and *unique*.

ortolan A small Eurasian songbird of the bunting family, venerated as a gastronomic icon in France. It is now (officially, at least) protected by law, but in former times hunters would be waiting with guns when the birds arrived on their migratory journey; the birds would be cooked and eaten, bones and all, with much ceremonial flummery (a napkin over the head, for example, so that none of the delicious aroma could escape). No doubt many thousands still end up on the dining table. Their French name comes from Provençal, where it means literally 'little gardener'; its ultimate source is Latin *hortus* 'garden'

orzo A form of pasta in the shape of large grains of rice. The word comes from Italian, where it means literally 'barley' (from Latin *hordeum,* which is also the ancestor of English *horchata* and *orgeat*). It is first recorded in English in 1917.

Osborne The name of a type of sweetish plain biscuit. It is said that when Huntley and Palmers originally produced it, in 1860, they patriotically sought permission to name it after Queen Victoria. Her Majesty demurred, suggesting instead that the biscuit take the name of Osborne House on the Isle of Wight, her favourite residence, which had been built in the late 1840s.

osso bucco An Italian veal stew, probably first made in Milan, in which unboned pieces of shin of veal are braised in white wine with tomatoes, onions, and leeks. The name means literally 'bone with a hole' in Italian—hence 'marrowbone'.

ouzo A Greek spirit distilled from wine and flavoured with aniseed and other herbs. It is colourless, but it is usually drunk heavily diluted with water, which turns it milky white. The source of the modern Greek word *ouzon* or *ouzo* is not known for certain. One version, perhaps apocryphal and certainly convoluted, is that it comes from Italian *uso Massalia* 'for the use of Marseilles'. This was stamped on the packaging of top-grade silkworm cocoons exported from Greece in the nineteenth century, and hence (so it is said) acquired connotations of high quality ideally suited for eulogizing or marketing the aniseed drink.

Ovaltine Ovaltine, a beverage made by adding hot milk to a proprietary powder made from malt extract, milk, and eggs, dates from the nineteenth century. The name, based on *oval* with reference to the drink's egg content, was first registered as a trademark in Britain by the Swiss firm of Albert Wander in 1906 (it was a shortening of its original Swiss name, *Ovomaltine*). Its popularity took off after the First World War, based on a dual appeal as a nourishing food and a soothing bed-time drink, and boosted by such inspired marketing ideas as the Ovaltineys, a 1930s children's club promoted by radio advertising. By the 1930s it had become enough of a fixture in English middle-class life for its connotations of cosy complacency and unadventurousness to be exploited by John Betjeman: 'He gives his Ovaltine a stir and nibbles at a "petit beurre"', *Continual Dew* (1937).

oven chip A commercially produced frozen potato chip coated in oil, so that it can be cooked in the oven rather than deep-fried—a time-saving boon for those anxious to maximize their intake of fat and carbohydrate: '"My girlfriend makes a blinding fishfingers, chips, and peas—with oven chips" he grins', *Big Issue* (2000). The term is first recorded in 1988.

over easy In American English, a term denoting a fried egg that has been turned over when almost cooked and fried lightly on the other side, so that the yolk remains slightly liquid. It is first recorded in 1930. *Compare* SUNNY-SIDE UP.

Oxford John A former method of dealing with the remains of yesterday's leg of mutton: cut it into thin slices, add various herbs and spices, sauté briefly and then simmer in stock. The name dates at least from the late eighteenth century (Hannah Glasse gives a recipe in her *Art of Cookery Made Plain and Easy*,1784), but its derivation is uncertain: it has been suggested that the 'John' is John Farley, compiler of *The London Art of Cookery* (1784).

Oxo The *Oxo cube* (or *Oxo tablet*, as it was originally called), a cube of dried, solidified beef extract used for making stocks, stews, drinks, etc., has been with us since just before the First World War ('Chocolate would be very welcome, also Oxo tablets,' wrote Denis Barnett in a letter from Flanders in November 1914, published in 1915). However, that is not the beginning of the Oxo story. Originally it was a liquid beef extract, first manufactured at the end of the nineteenth century by Liebig's Extract of Meat Company of London and Antwerp. It went under the name *Oxo Fluid Beef*. The word *Oxo* was simply a coinage based on *ox*, with the fancifully Latinate ending *-o* tacked on.

oyster A small oval muscle on each side of the backbone in poultry, just forward of the leg joints. It is a particularly tender morsel, easily overlooked, and the French call it *le sot-l'y-laisse*, literally 'the fool leaves it behind'. The usage is first recorded in 1855.

paan Paan (or *pan*) is the universal chewing gum of Asia. It consists of a leaf of the betel palm, wrapped around a preparation of betel nuts and lime, which is chewed for hours on end. Hindi *pān*, whose original meaning is 'betel leaf', is descended from Sanskrit *parná* 'feather, leaf'.

paddy chicken A euphemistic term in Hong Kong (incorporating *paddy* 'rice field') for frogs' legs used as food. *Compare* MOUNTAIN CHICKEN.

pad thai A Thai dish in which stir-fried rice noodles are mixed with shrimps, peanuts, and other ingredients. The term comes from Thai *phàtthai*, which means literally 'Thai stir-fried food'. It is first recorded in English in 1978. The *Oxford English Dictionary* notes that 'the dish was originally devised to replace Chinese recipes for nationalistic reasons during the regime of Luang Phibunsonkhram (1938–44), but the name now has no political connotations'.

paella A compendious Spanish dish made up of chicken, some other form of meat, such as rabbit, beans, tomatoes, and often seafood—prawns and mussels, for instance—cooked with rice and saffron in a large flat pan (a *paellera*), typically in the open over a charcoal fire (the rice and other bits that stick crisply to the bottom of the pan are a key component of the dish, and are known in Spanish as *socarrat*). Its name, borrowed into Catalan via Old French *paele*, comes ultimately from Latin *patella* 'pan, dish' (the same word as is used by anatomists for 'knee-cap'). It was becoming known in Britain by the end of the nineteenth century (it was included in the *Encyclopedia of Practical Cookery* (1892), albeit with the dismissive note 'a favourite Spanish dish containing the usual oil and garlic'), but it was not until after the Second World War, and the increasing interest in other cuisines, that it achieved more general currency.

paglia e fieno Bicolour tagliatelle, combining standard buff-coloured ribbons with green ones, dyed with spinach juice. The Italian term, which is first recorded in 1970, means literally 'straw and hay'.

pain *Pain* is the French word for 'bread' (it comes from Latin *panis*, which originally meant simply 'food' and is distantly related to English *food*). It appeared briefly in English in the Middle Ages, but while that usage had died out by the end of the fifteenth century, the word continued to be employed into the eighteenth century for any of a range of fancy dishes incorporating bread: Hannah Glasse, for example, in her *Art of Cookery Made*

Plain and Easy (1747) has a recipe for 'Partridge Panes' which mixes breadcrumbs and the flesh of partridges and a chicken with beaten eggs. Latterly it has made a reappearance, notably in *pain au chocolat,* a term of French origin for a sweet roll containing chocolate.

pain perdu *See* FRENCH TOAST.

pak choi *See* CHINESE CABBAGE.

pakora An Indian appetizer or snack made from pieces of chopped vegetable, meat, etc. that have been coated in seasoned batter and deep-fried. The term is interchangeable with *bhaji*. Hindi *pakaura* comes from Sanskrit *pakvavala*, a compound formed from *pakva* 'cooked' and *vala* 'lump of pulse for frying'.

palak The Hindi term used in Indian cookery for spinach, and for dishes served with spinach (as in *lamb palak*). It comes from Sanskrit *pālakyā* 'green vegetables'.

palatschinken Pancakes rolled round a filling of fruit or curd cheese and baked—a favourite Austrian dessert. The word comes via Hungarian *palacsinta* and Rumanian *placinta* from Latin *placenta*, which meant 'flat cake' (its use for 'afterbirth' is a modern development).

pale ale *See* ALE, INDIA PALE ALE.

Palestine soup A cream soup made with Jerusalem artichokes. The name, first recorded in 1834, reflects the ancient status of Jerusalem as capital of Palestine.

palm heart The term *palm heart*, or *heart of palm*, is applied to the tender terminal bud or young leaf shoot of certain types of palm tree, eaten as a vegetable. It is commonly sold tinned, cut into stick-shaped pieces. An earlier, now largely disused synonym is *palm cabbage*; and in America palm hearts are generally known as *palmettos*.

palmier Palmiers are small sweet biscuits made from puff pastry and shaped somewhat like butterflies. To their anonymous early twentieth-century inventor their shape evidently suggested more the topknot of leaves on a palm, for French *palmier* means literally 'palm tree'.

palm oil Oil produced from the fruit of various sorts of palm tree, especially the West African oil palm. It is used in huge amounts in the production of a wide range of commercial foodstuffs, such as margarine and baked goods, and the vast oil palm plantations established in the tropics (e.g. in Indonesia) to satisfy Western demand present an increasing threat to rain-forest habitats.

palm sugar *See* JAGGERY.

palm wine An alcoholic drink made from fermented palm sap. The term is first recorded in 1598.

palo cortado After the wine that is to become sherry is poured into butts to mature, it quickly becomes apparent which of the main categories it will turn into: fino or oloroso. But occasionally a third type, intermediate between the two, crops up; this is *palo cortado* (literally 'cut stick' in Spanish). It has the finesse of a fino and the body and depth of an oloroso, and is highly prized (and priced).

pan *See* PAAN.

panaché French *panaché* means 'multi-coloured, variegated', and it has come to be applied to a composed dish containing several elements of contrasting colours—for instance, a salad with an array of different leaves, flowers, etc., or a *panaché des fruits de mer,* mixing greys, reds, whites: 'Dinner cranks up the ante: perhaps roast rack of new season Hampshire lamb served with dauphinoise potato, panaché of market vegetables, and redcurrant and mint jus', *Good Food Guide* (2008). *Panaché* also means 'shandy', but that usage has not migrated into English. The word is a derivative of the noun *panache,* which English adopted in the sixteenth century; in its original meaning 'tuft or plume of feathers', which harks back to its ultimate ancestor, Latin *pinna* 'feather'; the idea of 'variegation' comes from the stripes of colour on a decorative plume—and the now predominant sense 'flamboyance, style' is a later development.

panada A thickish paste made from breadcrumbs or various sorts of flour (wheat, rice, potato, etc.) mixed with stock, milk, or water. It is used for thickening soups and sauces or for binding forcemeat stuffings together, and also, in former times, as a food for invalids (who, if they were lucky, might be allowed a little extra flavouring, such as nutmeg). The word is borrowed from Spanish, where it is a derivative of *pan* 'bread', and was first used in English towards the end of the sixteenth century.

pancake The use of the term *pancake* for a thin flat round 'cake' of batter fried on both sides in a pan dates back at least to the fifteenth century (a contemporary cookery book directed 'put a little of the white comade [a sort of filling mixture], and let it flow all around as thou makest a pancake'). Cooking the pancake on both sides implies turning it, and cooks with any panache have always accomplished this by tossing it in the air and catching it in the pan as it falls: 'And every man and maid do take their turn, and toss their pancakes up for fear they burn,' *Pasquil's Palinodia* (1619). The British have always been rather restrained, not to say unadventurous, in their use of pancakes, limiting themselves to sugar and lemon juice, or at most jam, as an accompaniment, but other cuisines employ a far wider array of fillings, savoury as well as sweet (*see* BLINI, CRÊPE). The typical US way of serving them is with maple (or, nowadays, a less costly substitute) syrup. Pancake breakfasts are still a popular event as fundraisers, for schools, volunteer fire departments, etc.

The custom of eating pancakes on Shrove Tuesday goes back certainly to Elizabethan times, and is probably earlier than that: 'Shrove Tuesday . . . by that time the clock strikes eleven, which (by the help of a knavish sexton) is commonly before nine, then there is a bell rung, called the Pancake Bell, the sound wherof makes thousands of people distracted', John Taylor, *Jack-a-Lent* (1620). The pancake bell was the signal for everyone to stop work and join in the festivities of pancake day. These included pancake races, which involved running along tossing a pancake into the air from a pan, and which still survive in many localities.

The use of the pancake as a symbol for something flat is of long standing, too: 'A continual Simon and Jude's rain beat all your feathers as flat down as pancakes,' Thomas Middleton and Thomas Dekker, *The Roaring Girl* (1611). But its application to an emergency aircraft landing without undercarriage is of course rather more recent (it grew out of an earlier use of the term for an accidentally vertical landing, first recorded in 1912).

pancetta A type of Italian bacon, cured in salt and spices. It is used for flavouring sauces, pasta, etc. Its name is a diminutive form of Italian *panca* 'bench'.

panch phoran *See* FIVE-SPICE.

pandan A tropical tree (also called the *screw pine*) with long, blade-like, spiny leaves that are widely used in Southeast Asian cooking for their characteristic scent and flavour. The name *pandan* is Malay; the tree itself is more usually known in the West by the Latinized version of the name, *pandanus*.

pandowdy A traditional New England dessert consisting of spiced apples baked in a deep dish with a topping of biscuit-like dough. The name dates from the beginning of the nineteenth century, but it is not known where it came from.

paneer Paneer (or *panir*) is a mild crumbly North Indian curd cheese, used (rather like bean curd further east) as a background medium for other flavours (onions, peppers, spinach, etc.).

panettone A sort of light, sweet, rather dry Italian bread, containing candied peel and sultanas. It is a speciality of the Lombardy region. Its name is an adaptation of Milanese *panatton*, a derivative of Italian *pane* 'bread'. It can be used to make a superior sort of bread-and-butter pudding.

panfish An American term (first recorded in 1796) for a small fish suitable for frying in a pan, especially one caught by rod and line rather than bought in a shop.

panforte A speciality of the Italian city of Siena: a rich cake filled with nuts, candied peel, honey, cocoa, and spices. Its characteristic feature is that it is baked hard—hence its name: Italian *pane* 'bread', *forte* 'hard'.

pan haggerty A traditional Northumbrian dish made from layers of sliced potatoes, onions, and cheese fried in a pan, and then browned under a grill. The origin of *haggerty* is not known for certain, but it is plausible that it could have some connection with northern Middle English *haggen* 'to chop', or even with French *hacher* 'to chop up' (*compare* HAGGIS, HASH).

panini In their native Italy, panini are small bread rolls, typically eaten at breakfast or split and filled sandwich-style (Italian *panino*, the singular form, is a derivative of *pane* 'bread', and means literally 'little loaf'). When they began to make their way into the repertoire of American fast food in the 1970s and 1980s, however, they morphed into sandwiches made from a small flat loaf of Italian-style bread, typically served toasted. Today they have a well-established niche in any sandwich outlet. In the process of their Anglicization, their plurality has been a problem; increasingly *panini* is interpreted as singular, and a new plural *paninis* has been created: 'Italian sandwiches served on baguettes called paninis', *Nation's Restaurant News* (1991).

pani puri An Indian dish consisting of a number of puris (fried puff-pastry balls) filled with spiced mash potato, spiced water, and tamarind juice. Eating them without the contents spurting over you is something of an art. Hindi *pānī* means 'water'.

panir *See* PANEER.

pan-loaf A loaf baked, not surprisingly, in a pan or tin; the term is mainly Scottish. Such loaves were more expensive than the ordinary sort, jammed together promiscuously on the baking tray, so *pan-loaf* or *pan-loafy* came to be used metaphorically for 'affected' or 'pretentious': 'His pan-loaf accent would make you die. He's gettin' ready, y'see, to be a great sports commentator on the telly after he's made his mark in athletics', *Scotsman* (1976).

panna cotta A chilled Italian dessert made by heating sweetened double cream with a little gelatine and then cooling it in a mould. It is often served with caramel syrup. The Italian term means literally 'cooked cream'.

panperdy *See* FRENCH TOAST.

panzanella A tomatoey bread salad that originated in Tuscany. It is made by mixing chunks of stale bread with chopped tomatoes and other ingredients such as onions and anchovies, and soaking them in an oil-and-vinegar dressing. The Italian word is a compound formed from *pane* 'bread' and *zanella* 'small basket'.

papaya A certain amount of confusion reigns over the terms *papaya* and *papaw*. They probably share a common ancestor, in the Carib language of the West Indies, and they usually refer to the same fruit. The complication, of which more later, is that *papaw* is also used for another, completely unrelated fruit.

There is no ambiguity about the papaya. It is a large pear-shaped tropical fruit with yellowish skin, juicy orange flesh, and black seeds. The first Europeans to encounter it were the Spanish explorers in the Caribbean in the early sixteenth century. They adapted the local name for it into Spanish as *papaya* or (for its tree) *papayo*, and word of it reached Britain later in the century: 'There is also a fruit that came out of the Spanish Indies, brought to Malacca, and from thence to India, it is called Papaios, and is very like a Melon, as big as a man's fist,' William Phillip's translation of *F. H. van Linschoten's Voyages into the East and West Indies* (1598). In the seventeenth century, for reasons that have never been satisfactorily explained, the spelling *papaw* (and also the now defunct *papa*) began to appear. Both were evidently at first pronounced /pə'paw/, with the main accent on the second syllable, and indeed this pronunciation continues to be indicated in many English dictionaries, although it has long since passed out of general use. Clearly it was not very long before both syllables began to be spoken identically, for in the eighteenth century we find the first records of the spelling *pawpaw*, which is now virtually as common as *papaw*.

Another eighteenth-century development in the *papaw* saga was that in America the word began to be used for a fruit of the custard-apple family (*Asimina triloba*). It is small and yellow-skinned and has juicy edible flesh. It is never called *papaya*, only *papaw*—or *pawpaw*.

The unripe flesh of papayas contains an enzyme that speeds up the breakdown of proteins. It was named in the late nineteenth century *papain* (after *papaya*), and is used as, amongst other things, a meat tenderizer.

papillote In French cuisine, food prepared *en papillote* is cooked and served in a sealed package of greaseproof paper or aluminium foil. The method is used particularly for fish. *Papillote* originally meant 'piece of paper in which a lock of hair is rolled to make it curl', and was apparently a late seventeenth-century derivative of *papillon* 'butterfly'.

pappardelle A type of Italian pasta in the form of broad flat ribbons, similar to but wider than tagliatelle. It is usually served with a *ragù* (meat sauce), especially one made from hare, wild boar, or other game. The Italian term is the plural of *pappardella*, which is first recorded in 1345. It is probably a derivative of the verb *pappare* 'to stuff oneself, eat greedily'.

paprika This traditional Hungarian condiment is made from the finely ground flesh of dried red sweet peppers, with an addition of some of the seeds if a certain amount of pungency is required (past a certain point it becomes cayenne or chilli pepper). Its use is widespread throughout southern Europe (including Spain, where it is known as *pimentón*), North Africa, the Near East, and South America, but it seems to have become popular in Hungary not much more than a hundred years ago. Nevertheless it is now firmly associated with Magyar cuisine (it is essential to goulash, for instance), and the word itself is Hungarian—it derives from *pàpar*, Serbo-Croat for 'pepper'. Elizabeth David, in her *Spices, Salt, and Aromatics in the English Kitchen* (1970), reports that in the early twentieth century it was sometimes known in Britain as *Krona pepper*.

paprikash The name (in its Magyar form *paprikás*) used in Hungary for the rich Hungarian meat stew with soured cream that is more familiar to the rest of the world as *goulash*. The word reflects one of the dish's key ingredients, paprika.

paratha In Indian cookery, parathas are a variety of flat unleavened wholewheat bread shallow-fried on a griddle or in a frying pan. They can be stuffed, in which case they are wrapped into a ball shape around their filling. The word *paratha* is Hindi.

pareve The term *pareve,* or *parev,* designates foods that are made without either meat or dairy products, and therefore according to strict Jewish dietary laws are permitted to be eaten with both meat and dairy dishes. The injunction against mixing meat and milk derives from a passage in the Torah that says 'Thou shalt not seethe [boil] a kid in its mother's milk'. The word comes from Yiddish *parev* 'neutral', which may be related ultimately to English *pair.*

parfait English acquired the word *parfait* in the 1880s from French (where it is a nominalization of the adjective *parfait* 'perfect') in its original culinary sense, a rich chilled dessert made from whipped cream and eggs, with a particular flavouring (as in *a chocolate parfait*). In American English it has taken on an additional application, to a dessert consisting of layers of ice cream, meringue, and fruit, served in a type of tall narrow short-stemmed glass that has come to be known as a 'parfait glass'. On the savoury side of the tracks, the term has also come to be applied to a rich pâté with a very smooth consistency.

Parfait Amour In French literally 'perfect love', Parfait Amour is a violet-scented sweet liqueur which comes in a range of somewhat lurid colours from red to purple (the type commercially available in Britain is purple). It seems to have been invented in the Netherlands in the eighteenth century, and made its first appearance in English in the early nineteenth century: 'a neat glass of *parfait-amour* which one sips just as if bottled velvet tipp'd over one's lips!', Thomas Moore, *Fudge Family in Paris* (1818).

Paris–Brest A large wheel-shaped cream-filled choux-pastry gateau. It gets its name from the Paris–Brest bicycle race: a Parisian pastrycook whose shop was on the route of the race from Paris to Brest in Brittany and back decided in 1891 to create in its honour a cake which would resemble (somewhat impressionistically) a bicycle wheel.

parkin A sort of moist heavy sticky ginger cake made in Yorkshire and other parts of northern England. The origins of the term (first recorded in Dorothy Wordsworth's *Journal* for 6 November 1800: 'I was baking bread, dinner, and parkin') are not known for certain; quite possibly it came from the personal name *Parkin* or *Perkin.*

park railings *See* SAINTE MENEHOULD.

Parma ham A variety of Italian ham (in Italian *prosciutto di Parma*) produced in the province of Parma, in the Emilia Romagna region. Probably the most famous of all Italian hams, it is usually eaten raw. The English name is first recorded in the early 1960s.

Parmentier In French cuisine, a dish designated 'Parmentier' is made with or accompanied by potatoes (for instance *potage Parmentier,* which is potato soup). Probably the best-known such dish is *hachis Parmentier,* chopped beef covered with mashed potatoes and browned in the oven—a French version of cottage pie. The term commemorates Antoine Augustin Parmentier (1737–1813), the French agriculturalist who popularized the potato in France. Hitherto the vegetable had been despised there as fit only for animal feed, but such was the force of

Parmentier's campaigning on its behalf and the astuteness of his public relations that by the nineteenth century potato-eating in France had become routine. In 1785 he presented Louis XVI and Marie Antoinette with a bouquet of potato flowers, which so enchanted them that the king pinned a spray to his lapel and his wife put some in her hair; the nobility were thus won over. For a while the potato was even known there as the *parmentière*.

Parmesan A hard Italian cows'-milk cheese made in the provinces of Parma, Reggio Emilia, Mantua, Modena, and Bologna. It is produced in extremely large drum shapes, and although it is most familiar in grated form, strewn with abandon over a variety of Italian soups, pastas, and other dishes, when young it is delicious eaten whole, as a dessert cheese. Its full name in Italian is *Parmigiano Reggiano* (a combining of the names of Parma and Reggio that dates from 1955), but in English it has been familiar under the Anglicized name *Parmesan* since at least the early sixteenth century. *See also* GRANA.

Parmigiana A dish that is described on an Italian menu as *Parmigiana* (e.g. 'veal Parmigiana') is cooked or served with Parmesan cheese: 'Vegetarians enjoy a wide choice: roast beetroot, aubergine parmigiana, mushroom bruschetta . . .', *Time Out London, Eating and Drinking* (2009). Italian *Parmigiana* means 'of Parma'.

parsley As one of the quadrumvirate of traditional English herbs (along with mint, sage, and thyme), *parsley* or its linguistic ancestor has been in the language since Anglo-Saxon times, although the plant itself was not introduced into Britain (from southern Europe) until the late Middle Ages. The earliest record of the word, *petersilie*, from a book on leechcraft of around 1000 AD, clearly reveals its ultimate source: it goes back, via Latin *petroselīnum*, to Greek *petrōselínon*, literally 'rock-parsley' (*sélinon* is also the source of English *celery*). But an alternative version entered the language in the thirteenth century, *percil*. This also derived from *petroselīnum*, but by way of Old French *peresil* (modern French has *persil*, with non-crinkly leaves); *parsel* survives as a dialect form. Modern English *parsley* probably arose from a blending of these two forms (into *percely*) which took place in the fourteenth century.

As well as the standard parsley, the word has been applied to a whole army of other umbelliferous plants, including *ass parsley, bastard parsley, horse parsley, square parsley*, and even *thorough-bored parsley*, but perhaps the best known is *cow parsley*, whose name probably signifies its inferiority as a food plant, fit only for cows to eat. *See also* HAMBURG PARSLEY.

In Roman times the parsley was a symbol of mourning, used to adorn funeral tables, and as if to honour this tradition its role in English cookery has been somewhat lugubrious: the redundant rent-a-garnish, or the dreaded parsley sauce. It was not always so, however: enticingly crisp deep-fried parsley used to be popular (Mrs Beeton has a recipe for it), and it is now making a comeback.

parsnip The humble parsnip has had a chequered history, and has never been particularly popular in continental Europe. In ancient times Pliny reports that the wild parsnip (Latin *pastinaca*) was not cultivated, because of its excessively penetrating flavour, and in Italy today its chief use is as fodder for pigs being fattened up for prosciutto. It has grown on the British, however: in the late sixteenth century the herbalist John Gerard wrote of it with some distaste, but in 1699 John Evelyn was writing that the 'Parsnip . . . is by some thought more nourishing than the Turnep'; and it continues to retain the affection of the eating public, albeit the indulgent affection accorded to a country cousin.

In Old and early Middle English times the vegetable was known as a *walmore*, literally 'stick-root', and the word *parsnip* does not appear until the very end of the fourteenth century. It derives ultimately from Latin *pastinaca*, which was used for 'carrots' as well as 'parsnips', and was based on the word *pastinum*, a sort of two-pronged fork for digging the soil. *Pastinaca* passed into Old French as *pasnaie*, and it was from this source that English borrowed it (ironically, since the French do not rate parsnips highly, and modern French *des panais!* is an exclamation of scornful rejection). Its second syllable almost immediately became changed to -*nep*, due to association with *neep*, a word still used in Scots dialect for 'turnip'.

Dialect terms for the wild parsnip include Cornish *cow-flop* (a *flop* is a mass of thin mud or similar matter) and Scots *cow-cake*; it is not clear whether the names refer to the cowpat-like appearance of the plant's round flat inflorescences, or, like *cowslip* (literally 'cow-slime' or 'cow-dung'), to its growing where cowpats have fallen.

The proverb 'Fair words butter no parsnips' (essentially, 'actions speak louder than words') is first recorded in 1639, and reflects a traditional method of preparing the vegetable. But to begin with, the parsnip did not have the figure of speech to itself: in *The Plain Dealer* (1676), William Wycherley writes 'Fair words butter no cabbage.'

parson's nose A colloquial term for the fatty extremity of a cooked chicken, turkey, etc., which in life served as an anchorage for the tail feathers. In past times it tended to be regarded as a toothsome titbit ('An epicurean morsel—a parson's nose', H. W. Longfellow, *Hyperion* (1839)), but in these anti-fat days it is regarded with distaste, and usually discarded. Nevertheless, the expression can originally scarcely have been calculated to be complimentary to Anglican clergymen, and the synonymous *pope's nose* was presumably a dig at Roman Catholics. The latter is now little used in British English, but it is the preferred form in American English. Both probably date from the late eighteenth century.

partan bree In Scotland, you order crab soup by asking for partan bree: *partan* is the Gaelic word for 'crab', and *bree* (cognate with *brew*) means 'soup'.

pasanda A north Indian dish consisting of sliced meat, traditionally lamb or kid, cooked in a rich sauce made with tomatoes, yoghurt, cream, spices, and often almonds. Urdu *pasandā* 'preparation of pounded pieces of meat' comes from the adjective *pasand* 'excellent, pleasing' (of Persian origin), as used in phrases such as *pasandō kā kabāb* 'meat dish made of excellent things'.

pashka A type of Russian cheesecake produced as a special treat at Easter (Russian *pashka* means 'Easter'). It is made from cream cheese, fruit, and almonds, and formed in a traditional, often highly decorated pyramid-shaped mould.

passata A thickish liquid made from sieved tomatoes and used especially in Italian cookery. The Italian word means literally 'purée'. It comes from the past participle of *passare* 'to pass', hence 'to sieve'.

passion fruit The British first discovered the delights of the fragrant passion fruit (a native of Brazil) in the seventeenth century. At that time it was frequently called the *granadilla* (the word is a diminutive form of Spanish *granada* 'pomegranate'; it is still used for the passion flower family in general, and for an orange-skinned variety of its fruit, and the passion fruit itself is alternatively termed the *purple granadilla*). Spanish missionaries in South America, however, claimed to see a resemblance between certain features of the plant's rather curious, exotic-looking flower and aspects of Christ's crucifixion (or 'Passion')—the crown of thorns, for instance, the nails, and the cross—and named it the 'passion flower'. The first record of the use in English of the corresponding term for its dark purple wrinkly-skinned orange-fleshed fruit is in a letter of Horace Walpole's, written in 1752: 'a garden of Eden, from which my sister-in-law long ago gathered passion-fruit'.

pasta Literally 'dough' or 'paste' in Italian (our *pastry* and the French *pâte* come from the same source), *pasta* has a long linguistic ancestry. The term itself is not found until fairly late Latin texts, of the fourth century AD, when it was used to mean 'dough', but beyond that it can be traced back to Greek *pástē* 'barley porridge', which in turn derived from the verb *pássein* 'to sprinkle'. In the English language, however, it is a much more recent arrival. Some individual sorts of pasta have been around for some time, of course—*spaghetti* is first recorded in English in the nineteenth century, and *macaroni*, which we came by as early as the sixteenth century, is now thoroughly naturalized. *Pasta* as a term for a general concept, however, did not enter the language in a fully assimilated form until after the Second World War, with the explosion of interest in other nations' cookery. A measure of pasta's relative unfamiliarity in mid twentieth-century Britain is provided by the notorious April Fool's Day hoax perpetrated in 1957 by the BBC current-affairs television programme *Panorama,* in which the solidly reassuring figure of Richard Dimbleby informed viewers that that year had seen a bumper spaghetti crop, thanks largely to the effect of the mild winter on the spaghetti weevil. Apparently it was widely believed. (The notion, incidentally, that Marco Polo introduced pasta to Italy from the Far East at the end of the thirteenth century is also pure myth; it was around long before then.)

Commercially produced pasta is generally dried (Italian *pasta asciutta,* often contracted to *pastasciutta*; the term is also used to denote pasta eaten with some sort of sauce), but undried pasta (*pasta fresca*) has been a hit with British eaters.

The variety of named shapes and sizes of pasta is prodigious (a conservative estimate is 650). *See* BUCATINI, CANNELLONI, CAPELLI D'ANGELI, CAPPELLETTI, CONCHIGLIE, FARFALLE, FETTUCCINE, FREGOLA, FUSILLI, GEMELLI, LASAGNA, LINGUINE, LUMACHE, MACARONI, ORECCHIETTE, ORZO, PAGLIA E FIENO, PAPPARDELLE, PENNE, RAVIOLI, RIGATONI, RISONI, SPAGHETTI, STRANGOLOPREVETE, STROZZAPRETI, TAGLIATELLE, TAGLIERINI, TORTELLI, TRENETTE, TROFIE, VERMICELLI, ZITI.

pasticcio In Italian cuisine, a pie that contains a mix of ingredients: commonly, layers of pasta alternate with a meaty ragu and a cheesy sauce, and the whole is baked under a crust of sweet pastry. The impression of a haphazard throwing-together is reflected in the name (a derivative of *pasta*), which also means 'mess, muddle' (English *pastiche* comes from the same source). Both the name and the concept were adopted by Greece, as *pastitsio,* in which layers of macaroni and a spiced meat-and-tomato sauce are topped off with béchamel sauce and baked.

pastilla An alternative form of BASTILLA.

pastille Latin *pastillus* originally meant 'little loaf, roll' (it was probably a diminutive of *pānis* 'bread', of which an earlier form was *pasnis*). Subsequently, however, it came to be used for a 'lozenge', taken both medicinally and for sweetening the breath. And by the time it reached English (via French) at the end of the sixteenth century it was also being applied to small pellets which when lit gave off aromatic—or fumigatory—smoke. This usage has now more or less died out, however, and the word is now mainly associated with round flat sweets, typically fruit-flavoured.

pastis A general French term for an aniseed-flavoured spirit, usually drunk diluted with water. Common French brands include Pernod and Ricard. The word represents a reassignment of a piece of First World War French military slang meaning 'a confused affair, a hotchpotch or mess'. That was taken from Provençal *pastís* 'hotchpotch', of which the meaning was itself a metaphorical extension of the earlier 'pasty, pie'. The idea underlying the naming of the drink is that the clear liquid is 'messed' up (it turns a milky white) when you add water to it.

pastrami A highly spiced smoked beef, usually taken from shoulder cuts, and eaten hot or cold. For a food that is such a quintessential part of New York life (as eaten 'on rye'—that is, in a sandwich made from rye bread), it made a surprisingly recent entrance on to the scene. The earliest records of the word in English are from the beginning of the 1940s (this in a Groucho Marx letter of 1940: 'The catering was delegated to Levitoff, the demon pastrami king'). The word itself is Yiddish, but it comes originally from Rumanian *pastrama*, a derivative of the verb *pastra* 'to preserve'.

pastry Late Latin *pasta* 'dough' (which came from Greek *pástē* 'barley porridge', a derivative of the verb *pássein* 'to sprinkle') is the ancestor of a wide range of English food terms. Through Italian, of course, has come *pasta*, while the French branch of the family produced *paste* (in modern French *pâte*). When English acquired it in the fourteenth century this still denoted simply 'flour-and-liquid mixture, dough', and the more familiar modern meanings did not develop until considerably later ('flour-and-water glue' in the sixteenth century, 'soft thick mixture' in the seventeenth century).

The derivative *pastry* (modelled on Old French *pastaierie*) was coined in the sixteenth century for an 'article or articles made from such paste' (as in 'Danish pastry' and 'cakes and pastries'), and this remained the main sense of the word until the early nineteenth century, when it began to oust *paste* as the term for the dough itself. Other words that belong to this French branch of the family are *pasty*, *pâté*, and *patty*.

pasty Pasties, particularly those made in Cornwall, have become objects of some controversy. What sort of meat and other ingredients should a pasty contain, what shape should its crust be, should its first syllable rhyme with *hast* or *past* (or even *paste*, once a common pronunciation)? Historically, a *pasty* is meat baked in a pastry crust without a dish. The word was borrowed in the thirteenth century from Old French *pastee* (ancestor of modern French *pâtée* and *pâté*), which came from medieval Latin *pastâta*, a derivative of post-classical Latin *pasta* 'paste, dough'. In medieval English, it was generally applied to a baked case containing only one main ingredient, which was typically venison (in contrast to the *pie*, which commonly had a miscellaneous mixture of ingredients). In the seventeenth century, pasties were still expected to contain venison (although expectations were not always fulfilled: 'The venison pasty was palpable beef, which was not handsome,' Samuel Pepys, *Diary*, 6 January 1660), but by the late nineteenth century we even find references to pasties filled with fruit. And indeed the Cornish pasty itself, the ultimate in easily transportable lunch, has been known in the past to contain meat and vegetables at one end and at the other, separated by a pastry partition, jam or fruit for pudding. Tennyson, in his *Audley Court* (1842), described a particularly rococo example of the pasty: 'A pasty costly-made, / Where quail and pigeon, lark and leveret lay, / Like fossils of the rock, with golden yolks / Imbedded and injellied.' The answer to the above questions, incidentally, is that in their time Cornish pasties have been filled with mutton, lamb, beef, pork, even fish, and when money was short, bacon or simply plain vegetables—and in general, the proportion of potatoes, onions, etc. to meat is according to what can be afforded; the half-moon shape is essential, but the pastry can be joined in the middle, in a scalloped crest, or at the side, with a twisted ropelike effect, according to preference; and the pronunciation rhyming with *past* seems to have a longer history than that rhyming with *hast*. In 2011, the Cornish pasty was granted Protected Geographical Indication (PGI) status under the EU's Protected Food Names scheme, which means that you can only sell a pasty as 'Cornish' if it was made in Cornwall.

In British slang, *Cornish pasty* has been used to denote 'a style of man's shoe considered deeply unfashionable or indicative of a certain social subgroup in the 1970s and 1980s (specified by Judy Rumbold, fashion editor of the *Guardian*, as "maths teachers countrywide"). The pastie [sic] was so-called because of the supposed resemblance of the moulded-soled, heavily stitched shoe to the meat and vegetable savoury', Tony Thorne, *Dictionary of Contemporary Slang* (2005).

The culinary use of *pasty* usually raises eyebrows in the US, where the word denotes only a 'nipple-cover used by a female striptease dancer' (this is actually a different word in origin, derived from the verb *paste*, meaning 'to stick').

patatas bravas A Spanish dish consisting of sautéed potatoes served in or with a spicy tomato sauce. It is often served as a tapas course: 'Now turn your attention to the tapas menu. Mushrooms, barbecued octopus, tomato-y prawns, and patatas bravas are present and correct', *Sun Herald*, Sydney (2003). Its Spanish name means literally 'fierce potatoes', presumably a reference to the spicy heat of the sauce.

pâté Etymologically, a *pâté* is the same as a *pasty*—that is to say, an 'article made from pastry'. The French word originally denoted a 'pastry case with various fillings—including vegetables or even fruit'. But in due course the focus fell more on meat (or occasionally fish), and two distinct strands of *pâté* emerged: *pâté en terrine*, cooked in a dish, and *pâté en croûte*, with a pastry crust. The latter clearly preserves most closely the original meaning of the word, but nowadays in English *pâté* almost always denotes a cooked mixture of minced meat and offal without any pastry crust. *See also* FOIE GRAS

Patna rice A type of long-grain rice, originating in the rice-growing region surrounding Patna, capital city of Bihar state in northeast India.

patty A patty was originally a small pie or pasty. We first hear of it in the eighteenth century (Patrick Lamb, in his *Royal Cookery* (1710), mentions 'mushroom patties', and Elizabeth Raffald's *Experienced English Housekeeper* (1769) refers to 'oyster patties'). The term originated as an alteration of *pâté* (reflecting its original sense 'pie'), by association with *pasty*. It is still used by Americans (and now to some extent by Brits), mainly for a small flat cake of minced meat, particularly as yet uncooked—a 'hamburger patty', for instance, or a 'lamb patty'. Vegetarian versions are also possible: 'The saucing was dull and the patty of veg-covered mash a whole puck of so-what', Jay Rayner, *Observer Magazine* (2011). In Caribbean English, *patty* denotes a street snack that is first cousin to the Cornish pasty, typically made with turmeric-coloured shortcrust pasrty and containing such fillings as beef, saltfish, or vegetables.

pattypan A pattypan, or more fully *pattypan squash,* is a variety of small round flattish squash with a scalloped rim, rather like a rococo flying saucer. It is pale green, fading towards white as it ripens. Its shape evidently reminded Americans (the name, first recorded in 1855, is mainly restricted to American English) of the sort of tin in which patties, or small pies, are baked. An alternative name for it in America is *cymling*.

paupiette A paupiette is essentially a slice of meat rolled round a savoury stuffing and then braised or fried. The meat used can be lamb or beef (*paupiettes de boeuf* are the French equivalent of English *beef olives*), but it is most usually veal. The term can also be applied to fish (for instance, paupiettes of sole are rolled-up fillets of sole). The word is a diminutive form derived ultimately from Old French *poupe* 'fleshy part', a descendant of Latin *pulpa* 'pulp'. A common synonym for it in French is *oiseau sans tête*, literally 'headless bird'.

pavé Broadly speaking, a *pavé* is a square or cuboid dish—the word in French literally means 'block' or 'paving stone' (it is related to English *pavement*). It is most commonly applied to a dessert made from a square of sponge cake, but is also used for mousses and other cold savouries made in square moulds, and for various cube-shaped French cheeses (notably the *pavé d'Auge*, made in Normandy).

pavlova The pavlova, a meringue cake topped with fruit and whipped cream, has become a classic statement of Australian cuisine. It was named in honour of the Russian ballerina Anna Pavlova (1881–1931), who visited Australia and New Zealand in 1926, but there is some un-neighbourly disagreement between the two countries as to which can claim the credit for inventing the dish. A circumstantial account gives the nod to an Australian chef called Herbert Sachse in 1935, and further states that the name *pavlova* was bestowed on it by Harry Nairn of the Esplanade Hotel, Perth. Evidence from New Zealand, however, appears to show that the dish was known there by 1934, if not earlier, although it is not clear whether the name had become attached to it by then. Today it is often affectionately called a *pav*.

  A crucial feature of the true pavlova is that its meringue base is not firm and crisp all through, but soft and chewy in the middle.

pea The word *pea* is a seventeenth-century development. Previously it had been *pease* (which survives in *pease pudding*), but gradually this came to be misanalysed as a plural form, and the new 'singular' *pea* came into being. The term is an ancient one: Old English *pise* was borrowed from late Latin *pisa*, which goes back via Greek *píson* to an unknown pre-Indo-European ancestor, probably of Aegean origin. (French *pois*, Italian *pisello*, and Old Irish *piss* come from the same source.) As this suggests, peas have long been a staple human food; evidence has been found of their cultivation in Neolithic times, 8,000 years ago. We have continued to eat them ever since, but usually, and for most of the year, as dried peas. This was necessarily so; no method existed of preserving the tender young peas of spring (known as *green peas* in English, *petits pois* in French) for the rest of the year. Then, in the late nineteenth century, the combination of the invention of canning and the development of reliable mechanical harvesting techniques gave rise to the tinned pea, and peas have never looked back. *Garden peas* (an interesting euphemism for peas tinned when they are fresh, as opposed to *processed peas*, which are reconstituted dried peas) were suddenly available all the year, and this, coupled with Clarence Birdseye's development of freezing (peas were one of the first frozen vegetables to become available in the 1920s and 1930s) has led to the pea becoming perhaps the most commonly eaten vegetable after the potato in the Western world: a linguistic experiment carried out in California in the mid-1970s to find out what people thought was the most characteristic vegetable put the pea firmly on top.

peach The peach is a native of China, but by the time Europeans first heard of it it had penetrated as far west as Persia—and they named it accordingly. Thus in Greek it was *melon persikón*, and in Latin it was *mālum persicum*, both meaning 'Persian apple'. In post-classical times the Latin term became simply *persica*, and this has provided the word for 'peach' in the vast majority of modern European languages, including Italian *pesca*, French *pêche*, German *pfirsich*, Dutch *perzik*, Danish *fersken*, Russian *persik*, and indeed Old English *persoc* (modern English *peach* is a fourteenth-century borrowing from French); the one important exception is Spanish *durazno*, which originally meant 'hard-berried'. Peaches were introduced to Britain by the Romans, but being on the extreme limit of their geographical range, they remained something of a luxury until the latter part of the nineteenth century, when first canning (tinned peaches first reached Britain from America in the 1880s) and then speedy refrigerated transport brought them within the reach of the ordinary person in the street. Long-standing connotations are hard to shift, however: *peachy* still means 'splendid' in American English, and 'eat the peach' is an invitation to self-indulgence (based on T. S. Eliot's 'Do I dare to eat a peach?' *Love Song of J. Alfred Prufrock* (1917)).

Cling peaches, incidentally, are peaches whose pulp adheres to their stone, while the varieties whose flesh pulls easily away from the stone are termed *freestone*.

peanut There can have been few foodstuffs with as wide a diversity of names as the peanut. It is native to South America, but it was early taken from there by Portuguese explorers to Africa, and therefore it is not surprising that the first name used for it in English was of African origin: *pinda* (first recorded in 1696), which came from *mpinda* in the Kongo language of western Central Africa. This has now largely gone out of use, but still current in southern and central states of the USA is *goober*, which is related to Kongo *nguba*. The first English-based name for the nut was *groundnut* (from the fact that its seedpods bury themselves in the ground to ripen), which is still used particularly in the term *groundnut oil*; this and the synonymous *ground pea* came on the scene in the mid-eighteenth century. Perhaps of similar antiquity is *earthnut*, while *peanut* first appears at the beginning of the nineteenth century (the plant is a member of the pea family, even though its seed is not botanically speaking a nut). The most recent addition to the set is *monkey nut*, which is now just over a century old. This comes, no doubt, from the nut's popularity in the late nineteenth century and well into the twentieth century for feeding to monkeys in zoos, but it is the salted roasted variety that has made the greatest headway as a human foodstuff in the past hundred years, becoming in Britain probably second only to potato crisps as a nibble. Its other main use in the West is in *peanut butter*, a spread of ground roasted peanuts which appears first to have been concocted in the early 1900s. Other cultures take the peanut more seriously, however; peanut sauces are a key ingredient of Indonesian food, for instance.

pear Human beings have been using the pear for several millennia—there is a record from Sumeria, around 2750 BC, of dried pears being used for making a poultice—and the word *pear* itself is of some antiquity: it appears to originate from some Mediterranean language which predated our Indo-European ancestors, and comes down to us via Latin *pirum* (source also of French *poire*, Italian and Spanish *pera*, German *birne*, Dutch *peer*, and Swedish *päron*). It was the Romans who introduced the cultivated pear to Britain, and it survived their departure to become perhaps the second most widely grown and consumed fruit after its relative the apple. In medieval and Renaissance times a strict distinction was drawn between ordinary pears and *wardens*, a sort of cooking pear (the origin of the name is not known for certain, but it probably comes from Anglo-Norman *warder*, the equivalent of French *garder* 'to keep'), and it is a measure of the popularity of the fruit that in 1629 John Parkinson could record in his *Paradisus in Sole* no fewer than 62 cultivated varieties of pear and warden, a slightly higher total than for apples.

Medieval torturers devised a particularly gruesome tool known in English as the *pear of confession* (in French *poire d'angoisse* 'pear of anguish', in German *folterbirne* 'torture pear'). This was a roughly pear-shaped device which was inserted into the victim's mouth and then slowly expanded. It brings to a climax Francis Constable's list of torture instruments in his *Pathomachia* (1630): 'Vnlesse thou confesse . . . the Scottish Bootes, the Dutch Wheele, the Spanish Strappado, Linnen Ball, and Peare of Confession shall torment thee.'

peardrop Peardrops are pear-shaped sweets flavoured with pentyl acetate, whose characteristic fruity smell has made 'peardrops' a standard term in describing aromas—in wine-tasting, for instance.

pearl barley *See* BARLEY.

pearl onion A type of small white mild-flavoured onion used for pickling (the term dates from the middle of the nineteenth century). It is often used as a garnish for cocktails (such as the Gibson), in which case it is called a *cocktail onion*.

pearmain *See* WORCESTER PEARMAIN.

pease pudding Pease pudding, a traditional English accompaniment to ham, bacon, or (in the words of Lionel Bart's song 'Food, glorious food') saveloys, is a purée of boiled split peas, green or more usually yellow ones. The name preserves the ancient English word for 'pea', in the singular.

In nineteenth-century naval slang, pease pudding boiled in a cloth was known as *dog's body*.

pea soup In these days of the tinned processed pea and the frozen pea we have become accustomed to pea soup being green, but until comparatively recently it was made from dried peas, usually yellow ones, and consequently had a characteristic yellowish-grey colour which inspired the application of *pea soup* and *pea-souper* to a thick sulphurous fog, particularly of the sort that regularly choked Londoners in the nineteenth century and the first half of the twentieth century. The term is first recorded around the middle of the nineteenth century: 'Upon sallying out this morning encountered the old-fashioned pea soup London fog', Herman Melville, *Journal of a Visit to London and the Continent* (1849). In American English, *pea soup* is applied colloquially to a French-Canadian person, or to the French language as spoken in Canada—a usage based on the stereotyping of pea soup as a French-Canadian staple.

Formerly, pea soup was called *pease pottage* or *pease porridge*: 'this house being famous for good meat, and particularly pease-porridge' (Samuel Pepys, *Diary*, 1 April 1669). In their thicker, less watered-down forms these were little different from pease pudding. Pease Pottage, a village in Sussex, was originally Peasepottage Gate. Legend associates it with the guards who preceded George IV on his journey from London to Brighton, who supposedly stopped off there for a bowl of the pottage; but in fact the name existed a hundred years before George IV's time, and it probably referred to the village's role as a halting-place for prisoners, who had a meal there on their way to Horsham jail.

pecan The nut of a large hickory tree, grown in Mexico and the southerly part of the US. The nut itself resembles an elongated walnut, both in its brainlike convolutions and in its taste, but its thin shell is smooth and shiny and of a rosy brown colour. Its name originated among the Algonquian languages of the native Americans: Ojibwa has *pagân*, for instance, Abnaki *pagaan*, and Cree *pakan*. These words seem originally to have been used for any hard-shelled nut, and only gradually became specific to the pecan.

The apotheosis of the pecan is the pecan pie, a speciality of the southern states of the US consisting of a flan containing pecans in a rich mixture of eggs and molasses, syrup, or sugar. It is first mentioned in Fannie Farmer's *Boston Cooking-school Cook Book* (1935).

pecorino A generic term for Italian sheeps'-milk cheese, which is made mainly in central and southern Italy. It is a derivative of Italian *pecora* 'sheep', which comes from Latin *pecu* 'herd, cattle' (ultimate source of English *peculiar* and *pecuniary*).

Pecorino is also the name of an Italian variety of white-wine grape. Once close to extinction, the pleasing dry wine it produces has recently found a market.

Pedro Ximénez A Spanish variety of white grape used in the making of sherry and Málaga, of table wines, and, especially after being sun-dried, of extremely sweet raisiny fortified wine. Its name is said to be a Hispanicized version of *Peter Simon*, who reputedly introduced the grape into Andalusia from the Rhine valley. It was too much for seventeenth-century English adopters of the term, who Anglicized it to *Peter-see-me*: 'I am phlegmaticke as may be, Peter see me must inure me', Richard Brathwait, *Law of Drinking* (1617). Modern-day members of the Anglophone wine trade solve the problem by calling it *PX*.

peg In the colloquial English of the British Raj in India, a drink of spirits, especially one diluted with a splash of soda—very refreshing after a hard day's ruling, even if it was just a small one, a *chota peg* (from Hindi *chotā* 'small, young'). Wags of the time used to say that each drink was one more 'peg' in your coffin, but the more prosaic actual derivation is probably from the earlier use of *peg* to denote a pin fixed in a drinking vessel to indicate the level to which each drinker was supposed to imbibe.

Pekin cabbage An alternative name for CHINESE CABBAGE.

Pekin duck A Chinese method of cooking duck in which the bird is hung up to dry in the wind, smeared with honey so that it turns a deep reddish-brown colour, dried again, and then roasted. The skin and flesh are carved off the carcase, shredded, and served with spring onions, a special sauce, and small pancakes, in which the diner wraps all the ingredients. The Mandarin name for the dish is *Bei jing kao ya*.

pekoe A high-quality variety of black tea made from leaves picked so young that they still have their coating of white down—hence the name, from Amoy Chinese *pek* 'white' and *ho* 'down'. The term (first recorded in the early eighteenth century) is most frequently encountered in *orange pekoe*, which is applied to Indian and Sri Lankan tea made from the leaf buds and immature leaves, or more broadly to any high-quality Indian or Sri Lankan tea.

pemmican The traditional iron rations of Native Americans, made of dried buffalo or other meat pounded to a paste, mixed with fat and often fruit, especially cranberries, and shaped into small cakes. Carried on hunting trips, it could last almost indefinitely. The term has been taken over for a similar but rather less ethnic mixture of beef and dried fruit, used as emergency rations by explorers, soldiers, etc. in the Arctic. In origin it is a Cree word, *pimikân*, based on *pimii* 'grease, fat'.

Penguin The proprietary name of a type of chocolate-covered biscuit with a chocolate cream filling. It was originally produced in 1932 by William McDonald, a Glasgow biscuit manufacturer. Its advertising slogan 'P-p-pick up a Penguin' has established a small cultural niche for itself in Britain.

penne Pasta in the form of short wide tubes. Its name (first recorded in Italian in 1875) comes from the plural of Italian *penna* 'quill' (the tubes are cut obliquely, like the business end of a quill pen).

peperonata A speciality of the Lombardy region of northern Italy: red peppers (Italian *peperoni*), tomatoes, onions, and often celery sliced up and stewed in olive oil—a sort of Italian ratatouille.

peperoncini Peperoncini, or *pepperoncini* (a partially Anglicized spelling), are a type of sweet red chilli pepper. They are commonly pickled when still green and unripe, and used as part of an antipasto. The Italian word means literally 'little peperone' (*see* PEPPERONI).

pepper The original application of the word *pepper* was to the pungent aromatic seeds of an Asian climbing shrub. The Sanskrit name for these seeds, or 'peppercorns', was *pippali-*. This passed via Greek *péperi* and Latin *piper* into prehistoric West Germanic, an indication that even in ancient times this, the prototypical spice, was making its presence felt in northern Europe. Old English inherited the word as *piper*, which has become modern English *pepper*. The Romans smothered everything with pepper, and its importation from the East remained the single most important component of the spice trade into the Middle Ages and beyond.

Peppercorns come in three colours. Unripe, they are 'green'—and green peppercorns began to enjoy considerable popularity from the early 1970s, for the combination of heat, aroma, and soft crunchiness that they brought to sauces, terrines, etc. Picked slightly underripe, dried, and sold without their husks removed, they are 'black'. And fully ripe and dehusked they are 'white'. None of these, incidentally, should be confused with the so-called 'pink peppercorn', for which there was a brief fashion in the early 1980s; this superficially resembles the true peppercorn, but is in fact related to the poison ivy.

The use of the term *pepper* for fruits of the capsicum family dates from the eighteenth century, an allusion to the similar pungency of taste. In particular it refers to the *Capsicum annuum*, a native of tropical America, which is generally called more fully the *sweet pepper* (an alternative name in American English is *bell pepper*). Its large succulent seed capsules are available in basic green and red, and also in yellow, orange, and a purplish black.

Another capsicum is the *chilli*, also known as *chilli pepper*. Dried and ground, it is called *cayenne pepper*, or *red pepper*.

peppermint *See* MINT.

pepperoni A type of Italian salami generously seasoned with pepper. The name is an adaptation and partial Anglicization of Italian *peperone* 'red pepper, chilli', a derivative of *pepere* 'pepper'.

pepperpot A traditional thick West Indian stew made with meat (or fish) and vegetables, and vigorously spiced with red pepper and cassareep, the juice of the cassava root. It is first mentioned in print as long ago as 1698: 'They make a rare Soop they call Pepper-Pot', Edward Ward, *Trip to Jamaica*.

perilla The English name for the Japanese herb SHISO. It is a modern Latin coinage, but it is not known what it was based on.

peri-peri *See* PIRI-PIRI.

perlé A type of off-dry semi-sparkling wine made in South Africa. The term comes from the French adjective *perlé*, literally 'set with pearls, beaded', which is also used to denote wines with a slight spritz.

Pernod The proprietary name of a yellow-green aniseed-flavoured French aperitif (*see* PASTIS) produced by Pernod Fils (now the Pernod Ricard Group), originally at Pontarlier in the Franche Comté, near the Swiss border. When the trademark was first taken out by Louis and Fritz Pernod in 1876 it was used for absinthe, which the firm had been making for some time, but then the drink was banned by the French government, and in 1937 the name was transferred to the pastis.

perry Perry is a cider-like alcoholic beverage made from pears, and the two words, *perry* and *pear*, are related: both come ultimately from Latin *pirum* 'pear', *perry* via Old French *peré*. C. Anne Wilson reports in *Food and Drink in Britain* (1973), a drink called *piriwhit* was made from perry mixed with cheap ale in the Middle Ages; but in more recent times perry has achieved prominence as the basis of Babycham, known as the 'champagne perry' until the champagne producers took exception to the epithet and forced it to be dropped.

persillade A mixture of parsley and garlic used in French cooking as a flavouring or stuffing. The word is a derivative of French *persil* 'parsley'.

persimmon The British first encountered the persimmon in Virginia in the early seventeenth century, a fact revealed by the name they gave it: *persimmon* is a somewhat garbled version of a word in one of the Algonquian languages of North America, perhaps Cree *pasiminan* or Lenape *pasimenan* (the earliest recorded attempt at it in English is in Captain John Smith's *Map of Virginia* (1612): 'the fruit like medlers; they call *Putchamins*, they cast upon hurdles on a mat, and preserve them as Prunes'). Most persimmons available in Europe, however, are of the related Japanese variety (indeed the French term for the fruit, *kaki*, is borrowed from Japanese). Somewhat resembling large orange tomatoes, they have a bitter-sweet slightly mucilaginous flesh which only develops to full sweetness and fragrance when the fruit is very ripe.

The name *persimmon* has a curiously evocative and romantic ring—a quality the Israelis no doubt hoped *Sharon fruit* would share when they bestowed it on a new variety of persimmon they developed which can be used when slightly under-ripe and still firm and is therefore easier for supermarkets to handle. The term comes from the plain of Sharon, a fertile coastal strip between Haifa and Tel Aviv where the new fruit was first grown, but for British English-speakers the effect is rather spoiled by associations with the late twentieth-century slang use of *Sharon* for a 'tarty lower-class girl'.

pesto A green aromatic Italian sauce served with pasta and soup. A speciality of Genoa, its characteristic ingredient is basil. This is pounded with Parmesan cheese, garlic, olive oil, and often pine kernels or walnuts to a paste whose haunting flavour can transform a humble dish of fettuccine or linguine. The word *pesto* is a contraction of *pestato*, the past participle of the Italian verb *pestare* 'to crush'. Its Provençal equivalent is *pistou*, which is similarly made but often omits the Parmesan; perhaps its principal role is in *soupe au pistou*, a vegetable broth to which a slug of pistou is added at the end of cooking.

petit beurre Petit beurres are small sweet biscuits made with a dough containing butter (the original French name, *petit beurré,* means literally 'little buttered one'). Originally a speciality of Nantes, a city in northwestern France on the river Loire, they are traditionally oblong with scalloped edges and in the middle, the initials *LU,* standing for their late-nineteenth-century inventor, Louis Lefèvre-Utile. They had been introduced into Britain by the beginning of the twentieth century (they are first mentioned in the 1906 edition of Mrs Beeton's *Book of Household Management*), and within two or three decades they had become a sufficiently familiar component of English tea and biscuits for John Betjeman to evoke them in his *Continual Dew* (1937): 'He gives his Ovaltine a stir and nibbles at a "petit beurre".'

petit four A small fancy cake, biscuit, or sweet—such as a piece of marzipan or a crystallized or chocolate-covered fruit—typically served nowadays with coffee at the end of a meal. The term is French in origin. It means literally 'small oven', and may have come from the practice of cooking tiny cakes and biscuits *à petit four*, that is 'in a low oven, at a low temperature'. It was adopted into English in the late nineteenth century.

petit salé A species of French charcuterie consisting of belly of pork and spare ribs salted and boiled. The name in French means literally 'little salted'.

petits pois The French term *petits pois*— literally 'little peas'—seems first to have made its way into English in the early nineteenth century. In French it virtually means simply 'pea', since the French tend not to go in for the monster marrow-fats beloved of the British. In English, however, it denotes specifically 'small young garden peas'—fresh, frozen, or tinned.

petit Suisse Its name (in French literally 'little Swiss') suggests that this cream cheese is Swiss, but in fact it is made in France; the Swiss connection is its nineteenth-century inventor, a Mme Heroult, who came from Switzerland.

pe tsai *See* CHINESE CABBAGE.

pets-de-nonne Small choux buns that are deep-fried in oil so that they puff up to a light airy consistency. In French the term means literally 'nun's farts'.

pet stick A sausage-shaped assemblage of minced-up unwanted meat offcuts, offal, etc. produced by butchers for their customers' dogs and cats ('and, in rural areas, very popular for ferrets, too', Hugh Fearnley-Whittingstall, *River Cottage Meat Book* (2004)).

petticoat tail A Scottish speciality consisting of a triangular section cut from a large round cake of shortbread. The term, first recorded in 1819, has been the object of some enterprising etymology—one speculative derivation suggests that it is a folk-etymological alteration of French *petites gatelles* 'little cakes', another that *petticoat* represents *petty cote*, meaning 'small enclosure', and that *tail* denotes 'cutting' (as in *tailor*, from Old French *taillier*, literally 'cutter'), referring to the cutting up of the circle—but the truth is probably more simply that the shape of the whole uncut round resembles that of an outspread bell-hoop crinoline petticoat.

pettitoes The term *pettitoes* is now virtually obsolete, but for a couple of hundred years before its demise it was used for 'pigs' trotters': 'When pettitoes are fried they should first be boiled', Mary Jewry, *Model Cookery* (1875). This application, however, arose out of the entirely mistaken supposition that the word meant literally 'little toes'. In fact, *pettitoes* has no connection with *toe*. It derives from French *petite oie*, literally 'little goose', defined by Randle Cotgrave in his *Dictionary of the French and English Tongues* (1611) as 'the giblets of a Goose; also, the bellie, and inwards or intralls, of other edible creatures'. When the word first came into English, in the mid-sixteenth century, this was the meaning it had, although almost from the first it seems to have been particularly applied to the products of the pig.

phal On the menus of British–Indian restaurants, phal (or *phall*) is the ultimate challenge to eaters' machismo, the north face of the curry Eiger—a dish even hotter than vindaloo: 'We know that a prawn phal is something to be eaten only if you have asbestos buttocks or a death wish', Simon Majumdar, *Eating for Britain* (2010). But this is purely an invention of British–Indian restaurateurs, who have never been reluctant to satisfy their customers' desire for self-immolation. In Bengal, *phal* refers to a type of kebab formed round a sliver of bamboo.

pho A type of Vietnamese soup typically made from beef stock and spices to which noodles and thinly sliced beef or chicken are added. Vietnamese probably acquired the word from French *feu* 'fire', as in *pot-au-feu*, a stew of meat and vegetables of which the broth is drunk separately as a soup (Vietnam was formerly a French colony).

phyllo *See* FILO.

physalis A plant of the nightshade family. Its most salient feature is a heart-shaped papery calyx (whence its name, from Greek *phusallis* 'bladder'). In ornamental varieties this is red, and gives the plant one of its alternative names—*Chinese lantern*. In edible varieties it is a self-effacing straw colour when ripe, but inside it is concealed an orange-red, juicy, sweet-sharp berry, like a small cherry in size and shape. It is native to South America, but in the eighteenth century it was widely planted on the Cape of Good Hope in South Africa—hence another of its names, *Cape gooseberry* (first recorded in 1833). Until recently it has been available in Britain only as an expensive rarity, but in the 1990s it began to appear more widely on supermarket shelves. It has also been called *winter cherry* and *golden berry*.

piccalilli The florid name of this mixture of cauliflower florets, gherkins, and little onions preserved in a mustardy vinegar sauce coloured with turmeric (or nowadays more usually with commercial yellow colouring) suggests an Italian origin, but in fact both the term and the product are 100 per cent British (albeit probably inspired by similar Indian condiments). The earliest apparent reference to it in English, under the name *Pickile Lila*, is in a recipe book compiled by Ann Blencowe in 1694. It is mentioned in Elizabeth Raffald's *Experienced English Housekeeper* (1769), where it is also referred to as *Indian pickle*. In the eighteenth century the word was often spelled *piccalillo*, and Hannah Glasse even called it *pacolilla*. By the beginning of the twentieth century its acidic spiciness was leading to predictions of its demise (in 1902 the *Westminster Gazette* pronounced 'Because of our meagre liver-action, piccalilli and black walnuts are falling out of favour'), but these seem to have been premature. In America it is known as *chow-chow*.

piccata An Italian dish consisting of sautéed slices of meat served in a lemon, butter, and parsley sauce. The meat was originally, and is still usually, veal. The Italian term comes from *piccato* 'larded', the past participle of the verb *piccare* 'to prick, lard'.

pickle English acquired the word *pickle* in the fourteenth century, probably from Middle Low German *pekel* (ancestor of modern German *pökel* 'brine, pickle'). Its primary meaning seems to have been 'brine for preserving food', but it was also used from earliest times for a 'relish for enlivening meat': 'Seven knave [male] children, chopped in a charger of chalk-white silver, with pickle and powder of precious spices,' *Morte d'Arthur* (1440). In American English it commonly denotes 'pickled cucumber'. Its colloquial application to a 'plight' or 'predicament' dates from the sixteenth century, to a 'mischievous child' from the late eighteenth century.

pie The word *pie* first appeared in English in the early fourteenth century, and by the middle of the century seems to have been commonplace: William Langland in his *Piers Plowman* (1362) recorded how cooks and their servants would try to sell their wares by shouting 'Hot pies, hot!'—the ancestors of the pieman whom Simple Simon encountered. In 1378 Richard II issued an ordinance controlling the prices that could be charged by London pie-makers. Bizarre as it may seem, the explanation usually accepted for its origin is that it is the same word as the second syllable of *magpie* (a bird more usually called simply the *pie* in the Middle Ages); the notion is that the miscellaneous collection of objects supposedly accumulated by thieving magpies was compared with the assorted contents of pies (as opposed to pasties, which had just one main ingredient).

The idea of enclosing meat inside a sort of pastry case made from flour and oil originated in ancient Rome, but it was the northern European use of lard and butter to make a pastry that could be rolled out and moulded that led to the advent of the true pie. Originally pies contained various assortments of meat and fish, and fruit pies do not appear until the late sixteenth century. To begin with, too, pies could be open as well as having a crust on top, but over the centuries the word has become restricted in British English to closed pies (even to pies with a top crust but no pastry shell), with open pies being termed *tarts*. American English, however, continues to apply the term to open pies. Pies come in all shapes and sizes, but prototypically they are circular, as is shown by the metaphorical application of the word to the statistician's *pie chart* or *pie diagram*, a circle divided into sectors showing portions of a whole.

The meat pie came to be seen in the twentieth century as stereotypical (unadventurous) Australian fare—hence the expression 'as Australian as meat pie'. In Australian slang, an inconsequential or contemptible person is dismissed as a *pie-eater*, and *pie-thrower* is a favourite Aussie cricketing insult aimed at English and other foreign bowlers. Another notable pie-related sporting taunt is 'Who ate all the pies?', typically directed by the crowd at an overweight player. It is said that the original target was the English footballer William Henry ('Fatty') Foulke (1874–1916).

The expression *pie in the sky*, roughly equivalent originally to *jam tomorrow* and signifying a 'deferred reward', was coined in the US, apparently in the first decade of the twentieth century. Latterly it has come to mean 'false optimism.'

pierogi A Polish form of ravioli: little packets made from buckwheat dough and stuffed with practically any filling that comes to hand, usually savoury (minced meat, vegetables, cheese, etc.) but also sweet. Both *pierogi* and the related Russian *pirozhki* are derivatives of a word meaning 'feast'.

pigeon pea The name used in the Caribbean (and in the US) for dhal, the pea-like seed of a tropical shrub. It is a staple foodstuff in the West Indies, and is used in a variety of dishes: in Trinidad they make a pigeon-pea soup from it, and the 'peas' of the standard Caribbean filler *rice and peas* are usually pigeon peas. Sir Hans Sloane, in his *Voyage to the Islands* (1725), gave an account of how they received their name: 'Pigeon-pease . . . their chief use is to feed pigeons, whence the name.' *See also* GUNGO PEA.

pignoli An alternative term used in American English for PINE NUT. It comes from Italian, where it is the plural of *pignolo* 'pine nut', a derivative of *pigna* 'pine cone', which is descended from Latin *pinea* (source also of *piñon*). The variant *pignolia* appears to be an American English invention, perhaps prompted by the number problem presented by *pignoli*, which hovers between singular and plural in English and has had a new plural, *pignolis*, created for it.

pigs in blankets A term of US origin (first recorded in the 1870s) for small pork sausages cooked inside some sort of wrapping or coverlet. In the American version the covering is usually pastry, producing something not a million miles from a sausage roll. British English, however, has commandeered the term for sausages wrapped in bacon, a notion presumably inspired by angels on horseback and devils on horseback. They have recently become popular as a twist on the traditional chipolatas served with Christmas turkey.

pikelet A West Midlands dialect term for a small flat crumpet. It comes from Welsh *bara pyglyd* 'pitchy bread' (possibly named from its colour, and conceivably a parallel term to *pizza*). In Australia and New Zealand it is used for a small drop scone.

pilau Pilau, or *pilaf*, is a dish in which rice is cooked in stock, typically with various ingredients, such as vegetables, meat, or fish, added. The word was first imported into English by travellers in the Near East: 'The most common [Turkish] dish is Pilaw . . . made of Rice and small morsels of Mutton boiled therein', William Biddulph, *Travels of Certaine Englishmen into Africa, Asia*, etc. (1609). They got it from Turkish *pilâw*, which in turn came from Persian *pilâw*, a term for a sort of rice porridge. To begin with the spelling of the word was positively anarchic, with forms such as *pillow*, *pelaw*, and *pulao* cropping up, and even today usage is divided between *pilau* and *pilaf* (the latter, which is much the commoner in American English, represents a modern Turkish pronunciation).

pils A strong pale lager of a type originally made in Plzeň, in the Czech Republic. The German name of the city is Pilsen, hence *Pils(e)ner bier* 'beer from Pilsen'. English took over the term *pilsener* or *pilsner* towards the end of the nineteenth century, but after the Second

World War the abbreviation *pils* started to gain ground, and the full form is now rarely heard. The product now bears only a tenuous resemblance to the original Plzeň brew, and only a small proportion (known in German as *Pils(e)ner urquell* 'Pils(e)ner original source') is actually made there. It is traditionally drunk in tall thin glasses that flare towards the top.

pimiento Latin *pigmentum* meant first and foremost 'colouring matter' (it has given English *pigment*). But it also came to be used for a 'spiced drink' (English borrowed it with this meaning too, in the thirteenth century, in the form *piment*); and hence for any 'spice,' and in particular for 'pepper'. From it was descended Spanish *pimienta* 'pepper', which was borrowed into English in the seventeenth century as *pimento* and used first for 'cayenne pepper', then for 'allspice', and most recently (in the twentieth century) as a synonym of *pimiento*. And where did *pimiento* come from? It too goes back to Latin *pigmentum*, and reached English in the mid-nineteenth century via Spanish, where *pimiento* denotes the red sweet pepper or capsicum. It is used in this sense in English, particularly in the context of Spanish cuisine, and it also denotes the small slivers of red pepper used for stuffing cocktail olives.

Pimm's The term *Pimm's, tout court*, generally designates Pimm's No. 1 Cup, a gin-based mixed drink which can be drunk neat but is usually diluted with fizzy lemonade, soda water, or ginger ale, and served on ice, decorated with orange, lemon, and cucumber slices—in which form it provides deceptively strong refreshment at outdoor summer parties of the frilly-dress variety, and has become the mandatory tipple at the Wimbledon Championships. There were other numbered sorts of Pimm's, based on different spirits (No. 2 for whisky, No. 3 for brandy, No. 4 for rum, No. 5 for rye whiskey, and No. 6 for vodka), but these never achieved the success of No. 1, and in the 1970s all but No. 6 were phased out. No. 3 reappeared in 2005, however, tickled up with assorted spices, under the name 'Pimm's Winter Cup'. The original mixture is said to have been introduced in 1823 by James Pimm, owner of an oyster bar in the City of London.

piña colada A long drink made from pineapple juice, coconut milk, and rum which enjoyed a certain vogue in the mid to late 1970s. In Spanish the term means literally 'strained pineapple' (unfortunately, perhaps, for the drink's would-be sophisticated image, *colada* is related to English *colander*). It probably originated in Puerto Rico, but credit for its creation is disputed between the Caribe Hotel (in the 1950s) and the La Barrachina Restaurant (in the 1960s). As its name is first recorded in 1923, neither wins the prize.

pineapple When first brought back to Europe from tropical America in the early seventeenth century, pineapples were called *ananas*, after *anānā*, the name for the fruit in the Guarani language of Bolivia and southern Brazil. The term has stuck in most European languages, but English soon abandoned it. In England, people were quick to notice a resemblance between the exotic and delicious ananas and the humble pinecone, which from the fifteenth to the seventeenth centuries was known as a *pineapple*, and so the fruit inherited the pinecone's name. Early on it was also known simply as the *pine*; John Evelyn notes in his *Diary* for 9 August 1661: 'The famous Queen Pine brought from Barbados . . . the first that were ever seen in England were those sent to Cromwell foure years since.' Of all exotic fruits, the pineapple is perhaps the one that has most captured the British imagination over the years: gentlemen of sufficient means would compete with each other in the eighteenth and nineteenth centuries to grow ripe succulent examples in their hothouses, and stylized stone pineapples began to decorate the gateposts of country houses up and down the land. As Jane Grigson explains in her *Fruit Book* (1982), it was faster sea transportation in the later nineteenth century that put an end to the pineapple as a rare luxury, and the twentieth century was the era of the tinned pineapple chunk.

In the 1930s to be 'on the pineapple' was, in British slang, to be on the dole. And nowadays, *pineapple* is US military slang for a 'hand grenade'.

pine nut Pine nuts, or *pine kernels,* are the edible seeds of various pine trees. They are popular in the Middle East and around the Mediterranean coast, and are an essential ingredient of the classic Genoese pesto. *See also* PIGNOLI, PIÑON.

pink fir apple *See* FIR APPLE.

pink gin Pink gin, the traditional tipple of crusty British admirals, once downed in wardrooms throughout the Seven Seas, is a drink of gin mixed with a couple of dashes of Angostura bitters, which give it a pinkish colour. The Royal Navy is said to favour Plymouth to London gin as the base spirit, since it is fuller in flavour.

piñon *Piñon*, or *pinyon*, is an alternative American name for the pine nut, especially one obtained from a type of small pine tree that grows in Mexico and the southwestern US. It is an adoption of Spanish *piñon*, which is descended from Latin *pinea* 'pine cone'. *See also* PIGNOLI.

pinotage A South African red wine grape that is a cross between the pinot noir and the cinsaut. It was created in the early 1920s by Professor A. I. Perold (1881–1941) of Stellenbosch University, and originally it was called *Perold's hermitage* (*hermitage* is a name commonly used in South Africa for the cinsaut grape; it rides on the reputation of the more illustrious French Hermitage, a majestic syrah-based red wine made from grapes grown on the hill of Hermitage, on the east bank of the northern Rhône). It was not until 1961 that the name *pinotage*, a blend of *pinot* and *hermitage*, began to appear on wine labels.

pinot noir A grape variety used for making red wine. Although grown and vinified with some success elsewhere (Oregon, Australia, New Zealand), it produces to its maximum potential only in its spiritual home, Burgundy, and in Champagne. The grapes grow in fairly tight cone-shaped bunches. This is hardly a characteristic unique among vine-types, but it is said to have given the pinot its name—*pinot* on this theory being a derivative of French *pin* 'pine', with the addition of a diminutive suffix (in former centuries it was generally spelled *pineau*, but *pinot* is now firmly established). *Noir* 'black' refers to the colour of the grapes; there is also a *pinot gris* 'grey pinot', which produces a white or pink wine (it is known in Italy as *pinot grigio* and in Germany as *Ruländer*, after Johann Seger Ruland, who propagated it in the Palatinate in the early eighteenth century), and a *pinot blanc* 'white pinot', which produces a white wine.

pinto bean A variety of kidney bean with a pale pinkish skin speckled like a bird's egg with small brownish-red blotches (hence the name *pinto*, which in American Spanish means literally 'painted' or 'spotted'). It is a native of India, where it is called *toor dal*, but is also widely grown in the southern US, Central America, and the Caribbean. Alternative names for it include *crabeye bean* and *gunga pea*.

piperade A speciality of the Basque country which is a sort of supercharged scrambled eggs. To make it you stew tomatoes and peppers in olive oil or goose fat, then mix them with beaten eggs and scramble the whole. *Piperade* is a Béarnais dialect word, derived from the local *piper* 'sweet pepper' (standard French has *poivron*).

pippin *Pippin* is a word now used only in the name of various types of apple: *Cox's orange pippin*, for instance, and *Ribston pippin*. But originally it was applied more generally to apples of any variety grown from seed. It was borrowed into English in the fourteenth century from Old French *pepin* 'seed' or 'seedling apple', and to begin with it was used in English too for 'seed'—indeed, English *pip* is shortened from it.

piquillo A type of sweet pepper grown in Spain. It is commonly sold roasted and preserved in oil. The Spanish name means literally 'little beak'.

piri-piri Piri-piri, or *peri-peri*, is a very hot sauce of eastern African origin made from small red chilli peppers. The word comes from Ronga, a Bantu language of southern Mozambique, where it is a generic term for 'chilli pepper'. Ronga may have acquired it originally from Arabic *phil-phil* 'chilli'. As an accompaniment to chicken, the sauce was taken up by the Mozambique colonial power, Portugal, and brought to other parts of their empire, notably Goa, where it is still popular. It also spread southwards in Africa, and thanks to the proselytizing of a successful South African restaurant chain, chicken piri-piri is now famous around the world.

pisco A white brandy made in Peru from muscat grapes. It is named after a port in Peru, to the south of Lima.

pissaladière A pissaladière is in effect a Provençal version of the pizza. It consists of a base of bread dough (or sometimes fried slices of bread) with a savoury topping. Nowadays this is usually onions stewed in olive oil, or a mixture of tomatoes and anchovies, or a purée of anchovies and garlic (an *anchoïade*), all three decorated with black olives, but originally it would have been a mixture of tiny fish, typically the fry of sardines, anchovies, etc., preserved in brine. This was known as *pissala* (presumably a derivative ultimately of Latin *piscis* 'fish'), and gave its name to the pissaladière. (Despite the striking similarity, there does not appear to be any direct etymological link with Italian *pizza*.)

pistachio A nut with vivid green-coloured flesh, typically sold salted and slightly open like a respiring clam, but also extensively used as a flavouring for sweet things, including ice cream, and, in the Middle East, for savoury dishes. The word originated in Persian as *pistah*, and reached the West via Greek *pistákion*. English originally borrowed it from French as *pistace*.

pitahaya *See* DRAGON FRUIT.

pithiviers A cake or tart consisting of a puff-pastry case filled with a rich almond cream. It takes its name from Pithiviers, a town to the south of Paris, where it is traditionally served on Twelfth Night.

pitta Pitta (or *pita* or *pitah*, as it has been variously spelled) is a flat, roughly oval, slightly leavened type of bread characteristic of Greece and the Middle East. Typically eaten slit open and stuffed with a filling, it became a familiar sight on the supermarket shelves of Britain and the US in the last quarter of the twentieth century. The word, first recorded in English in 1936, comes from modern Greek *pítta*, both as a direct borrowing and via modern Hebrew *pittāh*. Greek acquired it partly from Serbo-Croat *pita* and partly from other Balkan languages, but beyond that its history becomes speculative. It may have come from an unrecorded Gothic **bita* 'bite, morsel, lump' (a relative of Old High German *bizzo*, which is a possible source of *pizza*), the descendants of which spread through the western Balkans, the Tyrol, and northern Italy (for example, late Latin *petta* 'bread, flat cake', Albanian *petë* 'thin layer of dough or pastry crust', Rumanian dialect *pită* 'bread'). Turkish *pide* is probably a borrowing from Greek.

plate | 281

pizza The notion of taking a flat piece of bread dough and baking it with a savoury topping is a widespread one and of long standing—the Armenians claim to have invented it, and certainly it was known to the ancient Greeks and Romans—but it is Italy, and particularly Naples, that has given its version of the dish to the world. The traditional Neapolitan pizza, topped with tomato, mozzarella cheese and anchovies, arrived in Britain in the 1950s—unfamiliar enough at first to be Anglicized for comfort to *pizza pie* (the term *pizza alla napolitana,* first recorded in English in 1935, is the Roman name for it; in Naples, confusingly, it is called *pizza romana*). Since then it has undergone a series of metamorphoses in base, topping, and general character that would make it hard for Neapolitans to recognize as their own, but which have transformed it into a key item on the international fast-food menu.

The origins of its name are not altogether clear. Its extreme similarity to the Provençal *pissaladière,* a dough base covered generally with onions, olives, and anchovies, would make it tempting to assume that Italian somehow acquired the word from French, were it not for the fact that Italian *pizza* actually denotes a far wider range of items than what English-speakers would recognize as a pizza. Essentially it means 'pie', and this can cover for example a closed fruit pie as well as the open pizza. Neapolitan dialect *pizza* is first recorded in 1531. Possibly it came from a word in Langobardic, an extinct Germanic language of northern Italy, perhaps a relative of Old High German *bizzo* 'bite, morsel, lump' (in which case it could be a distant relative of *pitta*). John Florio included it in his Italian–English dictionary *A Worlde of Wordes* (1598): he glossed it as 'a kind of cake or simnell or wafer'. *See also* ZA.

The derivative *pizzaiola* denotes a Neapolitan sauce made from tomatoes with oregano, or basil and garlic.

The flat square cardboard box in which home-delivered pizzas typically come has lent the name *pizza box* to a type of computer casing which is not very tall and has a square cross section.

plaki A Greek method of cooking fish that involves baking in the oven with olive oil, tomatoes, onions, and herbs. The word is a descendant of ancient Greek *plakion,* a diminutive form of *plax* 'slab', referring originally to the slab or board on which the dish is prepared and baked.

plantain A plant of the banana family whose fruits have high levels of starch and little sugar. They are harvested green and widely used as a cooked vegetable in the tropics. Its name comes from Spanish *plántano,* which was probably a redeployment of Spanish *plántano* 'plane tree' under the influence of a similar-sounding South American name for the plant. It has no etymological connection, incidentally, with *plantain,* the name of the common lawn weed, which comes via Old French from Latin *plantago,* a derivative of *planta* 'sole of the foot'.

planter's punch A rum-based cocktail mixed over ice with bitters, lime or lemon juice, and often grenadine. Served copiously to tourists in the Caribbean, it may well be a descendant of the mixed drinks with which the old sugar planters refreshed themselves, but its name is a modern invention, first recorded in the 1920s. Some credit its creation to the Myers Rum Company at the end of the nineteenth century.

plate In the terminology of American butchery, the *plate* is the thin lower portion of the forequarter of a beef carcase—what in Britain would be termed the *forequarter flank*. The cut called *short ribs* is obtained from the upper part of the plate.

plate tart A shallow pie baked on a plate. The filling is sweet (fruit, for instance, or mincemeat), and there is pastry above and below—and sometimes, indeed, in the middle, creating two or more layers of different filling.

plonk A colloquialism for 'cheap indifferent wine' that arose in Australia, probably in the 1910s or 1920s. A number of fanciful explanations have been advanced for its origin (including that it represents the sound of a cork being drawn from a bottle), but the likeliest source is the French phrase *vin blanc* 'white wine,' no doubt brought back from France by Australian soldiers returning from the First World War. Australian English also has the derivatives *plonko* and *plonkie* 'wino, alcoholic'.

ploughman's lunch The ploughman's lunch is often taken as an example *par excellence* of the hijacking and perversion of a traditional food. What, it is asked, could a ploughman find less satisfying after a back-breaking morning in the fields than an exiguous piece of tasteless, unidentifiable cheese, a flaccid roll, a couple of limp lettuce leaves, and a dollop of commercial pickle? The *ploughman's*, as it is often abbreviated, began to appear in the pubs of Britain in the mid-1950s: 'There followed a "Ploughman's Lunch" of cottage bread, cheese, lettuce, hard-boiled eggs, cold sausages, and, of course, beer', *Monthly Bulletin*, Brewers' Society (1957). It was quick to arrange, making it easy for publicans to satisfy the growing demand for pub food more adventurous than a packet of crisps, and it had the added advantage for the marketing men of conjuring up a nostalgic vision of simple hearty country food. When the English Country Cheese Council, an arm of the Milk Marketing Board, ran a campaign in the early 1960s to promote English cheese it picked up on the term *ploughman's lunch,* and it has since maintained a more-or-less permanent place on British pub menus. The basic ingredients—cheese, bread, and pickle—have remained the same to this day, although what a Victorian farm labourer would have thought of the pâté which is now sometimes substituted for the cheese is nobody's business.

What was the nineteenth century's idea of what a ploughman had for lunch? 'The surprised poet swung forth to join them, with an improvised sandwich, that looked like a ploughman's luncheon, in his hand', J. G. Lockhart, *Memoirs of the Life of Sir Walter Scott* (1839).

pluck The heart, lungs, and liver of an animal used as food. The term, which dates from the early seventeenth century, is probably based on the idea of 'plucking' the organs out of the body cavity, although there appears to be no evidence for the use of the verb *pluck* in that sense. Nowadays it is used mainly in Scottish English, particularly with reference to the meat content of haggis: 'He "knows a man who knows a man" who can get illicit lung and other "pluck"—offal meat—from the sheep', *Scotland on Sunday* (2004)

plum The plum is a native of Asia, but it worked its way steadily westwards in ancient times, via Syria (the word *damson* is a reminder of its cultivation around Damascus) to Greece and Rome, bringing its name with it. The Greeks called it *proumnon*, presumably a loan-word from a non-Indo-European language, and passed the term on to Latin as *prūnum*. That is the source, of course, of English *prune*, and of the French word for 'plum', *prune* (Italian *prugna* comes from *pruneus* 'plum-tree'). But it also, less expectedly, gave English *plum*. When the Germanic languages borrowed medieval Latin *prūna*, they usually changed its *pr* to *pl*, so German has *pflaume*, Swedish *plommon*, and English *plum* (Dutch is an exception, with *pruim*).

It was the returning Crusaders who introduced the plum to western Europe in a big way, but somehow plum-culture has never really caught on in Britain. There, the great variety of cultivated plums available—of all sizes, golden, yellow, and green—has historically been largely ignored, with the one exception of the big scarlet or purple types (particularly the Victoria plum, introduced in 1840). Subconsciously the greengage is scarcely thought of as a plum at all, and it is significant that since at least the 1840s *plum-coloured* has signified 'purple'.

Dried plums, or prunes, were popular in pies and puddings in medieval times, but gradually in the sixteenth and seventeenth centuries they began to be replaced by raisins. The dishes made with them, however, retained the term *plum*, and to this day *plum pudding, plum cake, plum duff*, etc. remind us of their former ingredients (the plum that Little Jack Horner pulled out was doubtless a raisin). Many of them, their prunes (or raisins) mixed with other dried fruits, spices, sugar, etc., were popular traditional Christmas treats: there was *plum broth*, for instance, a thick beef soup with all the other goodies added; *plum porridge*, an oatmeal mixture with similar ingredients; *plum pie*, a forerunner of today's mince-pie; and of course *plum pudding*, now generally known as *Christmas pudding*.

Nowadays plums are perhaps at their lowest ebb—not in most people's top ten of delicious fruits. In days when choice was more limited, however, they were better regarded. The application of *plum* to 'something excellent or superior' dates from the early nineteenth century: 'It is only the stupid parts of books which tire one. All that is necessary is to pick out the plum', Maria Edgeworth, *Harry and Lucy, Concluded* (1825) (although its adjectival use, as in 'plum jobs', is not recorded before the 1950s).

From the seventeenth to the nineteenth centuries, *plum* (or *plumb*, as it was also spelled) was a slang term for £100,000: 'the only son of Sir Peter Halliday . . . the heir to a plum', Walter Besant, *The Orange Girl* (1898).

plum duff *Plum duff*, one of the fortifying puddings of Old England, is essentially the same in its beginnings as plum pudding, before it went up-market to become *Christmas pudding*—in other words a plain boiled suet pudding enlivened with a more or less generous addition of raisins or currants (*duff* represents a former northern pronunciation of *dough*). The earliest record of the term, though, is not that ancient. It comes from the mid-nineteenth century, in R. H. Dana's *Two Years Before the Mast* (1840): 'This day was Christmas. . . . The only change was that we had a "plum duff" for dinner.' The sociologist Henry Mayhew records it as being one of the foods for sale on the street in London in the 1850s, its itinerant vendor being known as a *plum-duffer*.

plum pudding *See* CHRISTMAS PUDDING.

plum tomato A tomato of an Italian variety which is large and shaped like a plum. The term is first recorded in 1879.

poblano A type of large mild-flavoured dark green chilli pepper. It is a frequent ingredient in Mexican mole sauce. The name comes from Spanish *chile poblano*, literally 'chilli from Puebla', a city and state in southern central Mexico.

pochouse A French fish stew made with freshwater fish, such as eel, pike, and perch. It is a speciality of the Burgundy region, along the banks of the rivers Doubs and Saône. Its name is derived from the fisherman's *poche* (literally 'pocket'), the bag in which he keeps his catch.

poi A Hawaiian dish, formerly the staple food of the islands. It is made from the fermented root of the taro which has been baked and pounded to a paste. The word is Polynesian.

Poilâne Poilâne bread (French *pain Poilâne*) is a type of large round rustic sourdough loaf as made by the bakery founded in Paris in 1932 by Pierre Poilâne.

poivrade A savoury sauce in which crushed peppercorns are the main flavouring ingredient. The French word is a derivative of *poivre* 'pepper'.

polenta A sort of thick porridge made from maize that is the staple carbohydrate dish of northern Italy. Its prehistoric ancestor or inspiration must have been made from barley (the Italian word comes from Latin *polenta* 'pearl barley', a relative of English *pollen* and *powder*, which was actually used sporadically in Old English), but the main ingredient of the version made by the northern Italians, living amongst hills dotted with chestnut trees, was originally chestnut flour. Then when maize was introduced from America, corn meal took its place.

Polly A colloquial abbreviation used in the late nineteenth and early twentieth centuries for *Apollinaris water*, the name of an effervescent mineral water produced at Apollinarisburg near Bonn in Germany. It was a fashionable beverage at that time, and often used to dilute whisky and make wine spritzers: 'Sweet champagne and Apollinaris— Sham and Polly, as it is slangily called', *Fun* (1878).

polony A large hot-smoked sausage made from bacon, veal, pork suet, and other meats. The term, first recorded in 1661, is probably a variant of *boloney* or *baloney,* itself an alteration of *bologna* (in full *bologna sausage*). The latter forms, which are still used in American English, suggest that the sausage originated in or around Bologna, a city in northern Italy. (The slang use of *baloney* to mean 'nonsense' originated in the US in the 1920s.)

polpette In Italian cookery, a rissole. The word, first recorded in English in 1822, is a derivative of *polpa* 'flesh, meat' (a relative of English *pulp*); the parallel French formation *paupiette* has also been co-opted into English. The Italian augmentative and diminutive forms are used in English too, and the order of magnitude runs *polpettine* '(small) meatball', *polpette* the closest indigenous Italian equivalent to a hamburger, and *polpettone* 'meatloaf'. As so often when English uses Italian words, the singular and plural are a problem: the Italian singular is *polpetta,* plural *polpette,* but English tends to take the latter as the singular form, and has created a new 'Italian' plural *polpetti* to go with it.

pomace The residue left after a substance has been pressed to extract its liquid content. As the word's probable etymology suggests (from medieval Latin *pomacium* 'cider', a derivative of Latin *pomum* 'apple'), it was originally a cider-making term, denoting the pulpy mass of crushed apples. It has since been extended to cover other substances, such as olives or fish, that have been pressed for their oil or juice.

pomegranate Pomegranates first reached Britain from southern Europe in the thirteenth century, and they were to remain for many centuries an expensive luxury, used sparingly and mainly for decoration. In the earliest references to it in English it is called the *poumgarnet*, perhaps a conscious allusion to the fruit's deep red seeds, but by the start of the seventeenth century the original French form *-grenate* had fully reasserted itself. Old French *pome grenate* came from medieval Latin *pōmum grānātum*, meaning literally 'apple with many seeds' (*grānātum* is a derivative of *grānum*, from which English gets *grain*).

In French, *grenate* became altered to *grenade* under the influence of Spanish *granada* (and *grenade* or *grenado*, as well as *granate*, were used in English for 'pomegranate' in the sixteenth and seventeenth centuries). From *grenade* we get *grenadine*, the pomegranate-based syrup. The shape of the pomegranate, incidentally, spherical and with its topknot, struck a chord with the makers of early explosive shells, and they named them *grenades*.

pomelo A large citrus fruit somewhat resembling the grapefruit (which was originally thought to be a hybrid between the pomelo and the orange). It differs in its shape, which is pearlike; in its skin, which though thick is easily peelable; and in its flesh, which is coarse and rather dry. The origins of its name are not altogether clear: it may come from *pampelmoose*, a word of Dutch origin for a large East Indian citrus fruit, possibly what we now call the pomelo, which was used in English from the seventeenth to the nineteenth centuries and provided several European languages with their term for 'grapefruit'—French *pamplemousse*, for instance, and German *pampelmuse*; but it is hard to believe there is not some connection with French *pomme* 'apple', which entered English as *pome* in the fifteenth century and is still used as a technical botanical term for fleshy fruits of the apple type. And indeed a connection is provided by the word *pome-citron*, a term used from the sixteenth to the early nineteenth centuries for the citron, a fruit resembling a large lemon.

An alternative name for the pomelo is *shaddock*.

pond pudding A sweet suet pudding with a central cavity containing butter, sugar, and typically a lemon. When the pudding is cut, the sugary melted butter and lemon juices run out, creating a 'pond' around it on the dish. Another name for it is *well pudding*. It is a particular speciality of Sussex.

Pontefract cake Pontefract cakes are small flat round liquorice sweets as made originally around Pontefract, a town near Leeds in West Yorkshire. Until about fifty years ago liquorice plants were actually grown in the area: hence Pontefract's perhaps surprising status as a centre of liquorice production. To judge from the first known reference to Pontefract cakes (in the 1838 edition of the *Encyclopedia Britannica*), they were originally used medicinally—for instance as laxatives—but certainly by the end of the nineteenth century they were decidedly for enjoyment as well as, or rather than, for doing you good: 'The Pontefract (or Pomfret) cake is a dainty little circular confection, into the composition of which liquorice enters largely', *Westminster Gazette* (1893) (the spelling *Pomfret* reflects a once common pronunciation of the town's name, which has now been restored to the full majesty of the original Latin *Pontefract*—which means literally 'broken bridge').

Pont-l'Évêque A soft French cows'-milk cheese made in Normandy. It takes its name from the main market town of the Calvados region, to which the local farmers traditionally brought their cheese to sell. It is made in the form of a square.

pont-neuf potatoes The traditional term for the French version of chips (generally cut to large matchstick size and served with steak). The name is that of the Pont Neuf (literally 'New Bridge'), Paris's oldest bridge, which links the Île de la Cité with both banks of the Seine. It probably points up the potatoes' role as a garnish for the beef dish 'tournedos Henri IV' (Henri, the first Bourbon king of France, was responsible for the completion of the Pont Neuf at the beginning of the seventeenth century).

ponzu Ponzu, or *ponzu sauce,* is a Japanese dipping sauce made with soy sauce and bitter citrus juice, usually mixed with condiments such as powdered chillis or grated daikon: 'The company's ability to supply lavish nibbles such as . . . "lemongrass and ginger chicken skewer with a ponzu dipping sauce" is also likely to receive short shrift from Mrs Bourne', *Observer* (2011). The Japanese word is an alteration (as if based on *zu* 'vinegar') of the earlier *ponsu,* which originally meant 'drink of mixed ingredients'. That in turn was a borrowing of Dutch *pons* 'punch'.

poor boy In the southern states of the US, a poor boy (or *po' boy*) is a substantial sandwich containing any of a wide range of fillings (typical would be beef, cheese, and mustard). Its name reflects its status as cheap food for the poor.

poor knights pudding An economical dessert made by soaking slices of bread in milk and beaten eggs, frying them (making French toast, in other words), spreading them with jam, syrup, fruit, etc., and then sandwiching them together. Its name, indicative of a dish considered suitable to a state of genteel poverty, does not seem to be that old (it is not recorded before the nineteenth century), but the pudding itself is a direct descendant of the enriched, sweetened version of French toast or *pain perdu* popular from the Middle Ages onwards. German uses the parallel term *arme ritter,* literally 'poor knights'.

pop *Pop* seems first to have been used as a colloquial term for fizzy drinks at the beginning of the nineteenth century: in 1812 the poet Robert Southey writes in a letter of 'a new manufactory of a nectar, between soda-water and ginger-beer, and called pop, because "pop goes the cork" when it is drawn'. As this suggests, *pop* was originally restricted to non-alcoholic drinks, and that has remained its main application, although since the 1880s it has also been used colloquially for champagne and other sparkling wines. In American English, the term is characteristic of Midwest speech; people from the northeastern states use *soda*.

popcorn The seeds of a particular variety of maize (*Zea mays everta*) which have been heated until the moisture within the kernel causes them to burst and produce a fluffy white mass. The earliest record of the term (which is a conflation of a slightly earlier *popped corn*) comes from mid-nineteenth-century America. In the US, still its natural habitat, popcorn comes in a variety of flavours (like crisps in Britain): basic butter and salt (consumed in vast quantities in cinemas), cheese, garlic salt, caramel, etc.

pope's eye A term dating back at least to the mid-seventeenth century for the lymph gland surrounded by fat in the middle of a sheep's leg, regarded by some epicures as a delicacy. The papal reference may be an anti-Catholic dig, although the parallel German term, *pfaffenbisschen,* literally 'priest's bit', suggests that it may have been a choice morsel reserved for a man of the cloth. The round gland does indeed blink out rather like an eye, and in French it is called *oeil de Judas,* literally 'Judas's eye'. 'Husband, pray cut me the Popes Eye out of the Leg of Mutton, I'le try if I can eat a bit of it', John Wade, *Vinegar and Mustard* (1673).

In Scotland the term (in full *pope's-eye steak*) is applied to rump steak: 'I can feed ye on pope's-eye steak and wully-muckle biscuits', Neil Munro, *Para Handy* (1916).

pope's nose An alternative term, mainly American, for PARSON'S NOSE.

popover In American cuisine, a small puffed-up roll made from a thin batter, which rises to form a hollow shell when baked. The nearest British equivalent is a Yorkshire pudding. The term is first recorded in 1850.

poppadom Poppadoms (or *poppadums* or *papadoms*—the variations are almost endless, and the *Oxford English Dictionary* lists eleven different spellings) are crisp thin savoury Indian pancakes. In India they are typically eaten at the end of a meal, but the practice has grown up in Indian restaurants in the West of serving them as something to nibble before the first course of the meal arrives. The word comes from Tamil *pappatam*, which is probably a blend of *parappu* 'lentil' and *atam* 'something cooked, cake'.

Popsicle In the US, the proprietary name (originally registered in 1923) for an ice lolly. The circumstances of its creation are unknown, but it seems likely that it was a blend of the *pop* of *lollipop* with *icicle*. See also CREAMSICLE.

Pop-Tarts The proprietary name of an instant snack introduced in 1964 by Kelloggs consisting of rectangles of pastry enclosing a jam-like sweet filling. It can be heated up by inserting it in a pop-up toaster, and the product achieved some notoriety in Britain when some customers, apparently unaware that hot jam can be very hot, complained that the Pop-Tarts gave them serious mouth burns.

porchetta A classic Italian pork dish: roast sucking pig. In its most typical incarnation it is sliced and put between two pieces of bread—such sandwiches are widely available from Italian street stalls. The word means literally 'female piglet'.

porcini The Italian term (first recorded in 1476) for the large fleshy woodland mushrooms whose scientific name is *Boletus edulis*. In Victorian Britain, when they were of little account gastronomically, they were generally called *penny buns,* but as they slipped into the culinary limelight in the second half of the twentieth century they took on the more respectable mantle of French *ceps* and (probably via American English) Italian *porcini*. This means literally 'little pigs'. The reason for the name is not known: it seems unlikely that the mushrooms were ever thought of as fit only for pigs to eat. There may be a parallel in Latin *suillus,* literally 'of or relating to pigs', which was used as the name of a mushroom.

porcupine An eighteenth-century term for a method of preparing a joint of meat that involved larding it in such a way that the lardons resembled the spines of a porcupine. Hannah Glasse (1747) and Elizabeth Raffald (1769) both give recipes for it (Hannah Glasse's specifies bacon, ham, and cucumber for the lardons). *Compare* HEDGEHOG.

pork The word *pork* can be traced back ultimately to an Indo-European **porkos*, meaning 'piglet' (an adult pig was **suw-*, from which English gets *swine* and *sow*). English acquired it from Old French *porc* towards the end of the thirteenth century, and immediately inserted it into a vacant lexical slot for 'pig meat', contrasting with the Old English words for the live animal, *pig* and *swine* (just as the French-borrowed *beef* and *mutton* were used for 'cattle meat' and 'sheep meat'). It has since been the standard term for the animal when eaten, although *pig* is still used in the isolated phrases *sucking pig* or *suckling pig*. But for a period, from the fifteenth to the seventeenth centuries, the word *pork* was also pressed into service for a 'live pig', particularly a mature one: 'Porks of a year or two old are better than young pigs', Thomas Paynell, *Schola Salernitana* (1528).

pork pie A raised pie made with minced cooked pork and a suet crust, typically eaten cold. The use of its name in British rhyming slang for *lie* 'untruth' dates from the 1970s. A cosier version is *porky pie,* which is usually shortened to *porky* (or *porkie*): 'The word "porkie" was deemed unparliamentary last week, and thus no longer a proper word to be used in the Commons', *Observer* (1992).
  Pork-pie hat as a term for a hat with a flat crown (suggestive of a pork pie) and a brim turned up all round dates from the 1850s. It was originally applied to a type of women's hat, but by the 1880s it had moved across to the man's wardrobe, and it has stayed there ever since.

porridge Originally, *porridge* was the same word as *pottage* 'boiled dish of vegetables, cereals, meat, etc.'. Not until the early sixteenth century did the two begin to go their separate ways phonetically (by the same process as produces the casual pronunciations *geraway* and *geroff* from *get away* and *get off*), and they remained semantically linked for some time after that—Dr Johnson, for example, in his *Dictionary* (1755) defined *porridge* as 'food made by boiling meat in water; broth'. A particular sort of pottage was that made with cereals, which in Scotland would generally be oats, and it was this that eventually inherited the name *porridge*; but as late as the end of the eighteenth century *pottage* was still being used for this, too: 'The food of the reapers . . . for supper, pottage of oat-meal, salt and water, with the allowance of milk made to the ploughman', James Donaldson, *General View of the Agriculture of the County of Perth* (1794) (the addition of salt, still insisted on by porridge purists, reflects the savoury rather than sweet origin of the dish).

A *porringer*, incidentally, a shallow cup or bowl with a handle, was likewise originally a *pottinger*, a derivative of *pottage*.

port A sweet fortified wine made in Portugal. It has long been known as the 'Englishman's wine', an epithet earned in the eighteenth century when differential rates of duty made it far more attractive financially to import wines from Portugal than from France. It was at that time a comparative novelty for British drinkers: the first reference to it in an English text comes from the 1690s.

Its name reflects its place of manufacture. It is made from grapes grown on the steep stony sun-baked banks of the river Douro, whose juice is shipped down to the port of Oporto to be turned by long maturation into port. Hence in early years it was frequently called *Oporto wine*, or simply *Oporto* or *porto* (still the French term), or *port wine*, or—the version which finally won out—*port*.

There are several styles of port. The simplest and cheapest is *ruby port*—the port of 'port and lemon', a pub drink once with a rather louche reputation—which is bottled for immediate consumption after only a very brief maturation in barrel, and whose colour, as its name suggests, is the prototypical deep crimson of port. Port that is kept longer in barrel—several years—before bottling is called *tawny port*; again, its name reveals its colour. It is also called *wood port*, from its being kept in wooden barrels. Tawny port of a particular named vintage is termed *colheita* (in Portuguese literally 'harvest, crop'). *Vintage port*—the port that has accumulated the mystique of decanters, gout, and 'passing the port'—is port of a particular high-quality year that is bottled immediately and left to mature for an average of twenty years. It shares ruby port's red glow. Then there is *late-bottled vintage port* (*LBV* for short), again from a single year but not of such outstanding quality as vintage port, which is left longer in wood before bottling to eliminate most of the sediment that accumulates on the inner surface of vintage port bottles; and *crusted port* or *crusting port*, which is made from similar high-quality wine, matured in bottle after about three years in cask, but is a blend of various years. These are all made from a range of red grapes, but there is also *white port*, made from white grapes.

portable soup An eighteenth- and nineteenth-century precursor to Bovril, Oxo, and the like. A strong meat broth was boiled down until it became syrupy, then allowed to set, and dry out. The result could be carried around, for example, by travellers and explorers, and reconstituted at will with some hot water. The term is first recorded in 1725. The adjective *portable* was occasionally applied to other dehydrated fluids—'We have all heard of 'Portable Soup' . . . Now we have 'Portable Milk'. A small jar of this solidified material, we are told, contains the equivalent of six gallons of fluid milk', *Punch* (1849)—but *portable soup* was the only term that made a lasting impression.

porter A dark-brown bitter beer, somewhat similar to stout or Guinness, but slightly sweeter; its colour derives from its being brewed from charred malt. It was made originally (in the eighteenth century) as low-priced beer for working people, including porters (the sort of porter who carries things, not the door attendant); hence, apparently, its name. The word had more or less gone out of use in Britain by the end of the nineteenth century, but it survived far longer in Ireland: 'I've a big suggestion it was about the pint of porter', James Joyce, *Finnegan's Wake* (1939); and recently, with the revival of interest in traditional beers and ales, it has been resurrected in Britain.

porterhouse A porterhouse steak is a large beefsteak cut from the rear end of the sirloin and containing a portion of fillet. The term is American in origin, from around the 1840s, and derives from the 'porterhouse', a type of cheap nineteenth-century pub-cum-restaurant which sold not only beer (*porter*) and other alcoholic drinks, but also simple meals such as steaks, chops, etc. The American *Century Dictionary* (1891) speculated that it came from a particular porterhouse in New York, noted for its steaks.

portobello mushroom A very large, flat, dark brown mushroom. It is not a distinct variety, merely the fully mature form of the common cultivated white mushroom. In the latter part of the twentieth century consumers had become used to demanding the small neat button mushrooms, which suggest a certain just-picked freshness, and producers were finding it hard to sell the outspread black-gilled ones ('Mushroom farm workers took them home as perks', Niki Segnit, *The Flavour Thesaurus* (2010)). Then they had the bright idea  of giving them a memorable name of their own, and promoting their extra flavourfulness. They came up with *portobello*. It is not entirely clear where that came from. It may have been an alteration of Italian *pratarolo* 'meadow mushroom', but the meme of other *portobellos*, not least *Portobello Road* in Notting Hill, London, no doubt played its part. First recorded in 1990, it has been highly unstable orthographically (*portabella* is a very common variant, and *portobella* and *portabello* have both been spotted), but its aura of sophisticated rusticity has proved very successful.

Port-Salut Port-Salut (or *Port-du-Salut*) is a mild French semi-soft cows'-milk cheese originally made by Trappist monks at the Abbey of Notre Dame de Port-du-Salut at Entrammes in Mayenne, to the east of Rennes. *Port-Salut* is the official trademark of the cheese, which was sold by the monks after the Second World War to a commercial undertaking.

posset Possets were all the rage in the later Middle Ages, and survived into the nineteenth century, but are no longer heard of. They were a warming connoction of hot milk mixed with hot beer, sherry, etc., sugar, and various spices, excellent for keeping the cold at bay in the days before central heating, and no doubt effective as a nightcap too (although Lady Macbeth had to drug the grooms' possets to make sure they did not hear what Macbeth was up to in Duncan's bedroom). The source of the word is not known, although some have suggested a link with Latin *posca*, a term for a drink made from vinegar and water.

Post Toasties An American cornflake-style breakfast cereal produced by Post Cereals, a company founded by Charles W. Post (1854–1914). When it was originally brought out, around 1904, it was called *Elijah's Manna*, but this sacrilegious name aroused the ire of the clergy, and in 1908 the company retreated to the safer ground of *Post Toasties*.

potato The potato, a staple food of the Incas of Peru, was first brought from South America to Europe by their Spanish conquerors in the sixteenth century. The Spanish passed their discovery on to the Italians, who spread it to other parts of Europe, but the English, if legend is to be believed, got their first potatoes direct from America, Sir Francis Drake picking up a load of them in the Caribbean in 1586 (although perhaps not too much weight should be attached to the supposed potato-popularizing activities of notable Elizabethan personages—there appears to be no truth, for instance, in the story that Sir Walter Raleigh introduced the vegetable to Ireland). The uptake of the potato throughout Europe was slow and patchy, and it does not seem to have been until the late eighteenth century that it had established itself as a commonly eaten vegetable in virtually all parts of the continent. In England, northerners took to it readily, but in the south it was still regarded with prejudice and suspicion at the end of the eighteenth century, white bread being preferred. *See also* PARMENTIER.

The Elizabethans were faced with the problem of what to call these new and unpromising-looking tubers. They decided that they looked sufficiently like the vegetable they called the *potato* (familiar since the mid-sixteenth century, and known to us now as the sweet potato) to share its name, and so *potato* it was. The application of the name is first recorded in John Gerard's *Herbal* (1597), in a passage in which he wrongly placed the origin of the potato in Virginia, an erroneous notion which lingered on for centuries. The word *potato* is a modification of *batata*, the name of the 'sweet potato' in the Haitian language, and came into English via Spanish *patata*. The Spanish word was also the source of Italian *patata*, which passed it on to modern Greek as *patáta*. The English word has undergone various transformations to produce Irish English *praties* and Welsh *tatws*, while Swedish borrowed the plural form as *potatis*. Other languages have taken different options, however: many have gone for variations on the 'earth-apple' theme, including French *pomme de terre*, Dutch *aardappel*, Icelandic *jarðepli*, and Swedish dialect *jordpäron* 'earth-pear', while German *kartoffel* (borrowed in various forms into Russian, Polish, Rumanian, and Danish) comes originally from Italian *tartufolo*, literally 'truffle', and Lithuanian *bulve* and Latvian *bulbe* are descended ultimately from Latin *bulbus* 'bulb'. *See also* SPUD.

pot-au-feu The *pot-au-feu*, literally 'pot on the fire', is one of the great staple dishes of French peasant cuisine. It consists of a variety of meat and vegetables (typically carrots, turnips, onions, leeks, and celery) simmered long and slow in a large pot, sometimes with the addition of rice and pasta. The broth is drunk first, and then the meat and vegetables follow as a separate course.

poteen *Poteen*, or *potheen*, is a term now generally applied to illegally distilled Irish whiskey, but originally it was the Irish Gaelic word (*poitín*, pronounced roughly /pe'cheen/) for any strong liquor distilled at home. A *poitín* was literally a 'little pot'—that is, a small pot-still—appropriate for the domestic (and usually clandestine) production of whiskey; it was a diminutive form of *pota*, which was borrowed from English *pot*.

potherb A term now with a distinctly archaic air, *potherb* denoted from the sixteenth to the nineteenth centuries any plant whose leaves and stalks could be boiled as greens: '*Caulis* . . . also an herb called coleworts [cabbage]. It is sometimes taken for all pot herbs,' Sir Thomas Elyot, *Dictionary* (1538). Association with the modern meaning of *herb* led latterly to its use for flavouring plants, such as parsley.

Pot Noodle The brand name of a convenience food consisting of noodles and powdered flavourings in a plastic tub that can be transformed into an allegedly delicious snack by adding hot water. The idea of instant noodles was thought up by the Taiwanese–Japanese businessman Momofuku Ando in 1958. The original container was a traditional Japanese bowl, but when they were commercialized in the US in 1971, under the name *Cup Noodles*, they were put into paper cups. The plastic tub followed. In Britain, where they are called *Pot Noodles*, they have come to be viewed as the staple diet of impecunious students. *See also* RAMEN.

pottage Etymologically, a *pottage* is a dish cooked in a pot (English acquired the word in the thirteenth century from Old French *potage*, a derivative of *pot* 'pot'). What this originally meant in practice was that anything that came to hand—vegetables, cereal grains, meat—was put into a pot of water, separately or in combination, and relentlessly boiled to softness (which in the case of some medieval vegetables and meat was no doubt the only way to achieve edibility). The 'mess of pottage' (*mess* means 'dish' or 'portion') for which, according to Genesis 25, Esau sold his birthright to Jacob was a thick gruel or thin purée made from red lentils, and indeed beans and other pulses were a frequent and economical ingredient of pottages (pease pottage was a favourite—*see* PEA SOUP). In autumn, pottage would often be made from cereals, which in Scotland meant for the most part oats—and oatmeal pottage has become, with the phonetic change of /t/ to /r/, modern porridge. By the eighteenth century the concept of pottage had thinned down considerably from the medieval stew to a broth or soup, a process perhaps helped along by the reborrowing of French *potage* in the mid-sixteenth century.

pound cake A term widely used in American English for what in British English is now usually called *Madeira cake*—a rich cake made with butter and eggs. The original recipe called for one pound each of flour, sugar, and butter—hence the name, which originated in the eighteenth century (Hannah Glasse, in her *Art of Cookery* (1747), gives a recipe for 'Pound Cake' which begins 'Take a Pound of Butter . . . twelve Eggs . . . a Pound of Flour . . . a Pound of Sugar . . . '). The French equivalent is *quatre quarts*, literally 'four quarters'.

pousse-café A colloquial French term for a 'digestif'—a small drink of brandy or a liqueur drunk at the end of a meal. It means literally 'push-coffee'—that is, 'coffee-chaser'. In American English, however, the term more usually denotes a post-prandial drink confected by layering from two to as many as seven different coloured liqueurs on top of each other. It is said to have been invented in New Orleans in the middle of the nineteenth century, and was very popular throughout America by its end.

poussin A French term for a young chicken, sold for the table at between four and six weeks old, when it weighs 250–300 grams. It has been used increasingly in English since the 1930s in place of the corresponding native *spring chicken*.

prairie oyster A raw egg, moistened and flavoured with some sort of liquid, and swallowed whole, usually as a hangover cure. Since it was invented in America in the late nineteenth century, when it was also called *prairie cocktail*, a variety of liquids has served as a medium for the egg, including spirits, sherry, and vinegar, but today the classic accompaniment is generally considered to be Worcester sauce, with various additions such as lemon juice, tabasco sauce, pepper, and salt according to taste. The name *prairie oyster* presumably refers to the glistening molluscan appearance of the raw egg in its glass.

In US and Canadian regional speech, *prairie oyster* is also a euphemism for a calf's testicle used as food. *Compare* FRY.

praline In French, a *praline* is a sugar-coated almond, although in English the term has come to be used more for a confection of nuts and caramelized sugar, often found as a 'hard centre' in selections of chocolates. The word is based on the name of the Comte du Plessis-Praslin (1598–1675), whose chef Lassagne is said to have invented the method of sugar-coating. In 1630 Lassagne retired to Montargis, a town to the south of Paris, which has since become the praline capital of France. English acquired the term in the early eighteenth century, and at first Anglicized it to *prawlin* or *prawling*. However, in the twentieth century French culinary prestige ensured the restoration of *praline*.

praty A dated Anglo-Irish term for the potato, based on Irish *práta* or *préata*, itself an alteration of *potato*. It is probably best known for its appearance in the following lines from a popular Irish ballad, apparently first recorded in Carl Sandberg's *American Songbag* (1927): 'O, I met her in the mornin' / And I'll have yez all to know / That I met her in the garden / Where the praties grow.'

pré-salé French *pré sale* means 'salted meadow'. The term is used to denote sheep that have grazed on salt marshes, which give their meat a distinctive flavour.

pretzel There are two sorts of pretzel, both of which come in the form either of a stick or, more characteristically, a loose knot. One is a small salt-sprinkled biscuit, baked hard, and traditionally eaten in its native Germany as a snack with beer (that is the pretzel with which the British are familiar). The other is much larger, soft, and is sold hot by street vendors in New York and other US cities. The pretzel crossed the Atlantic in the nineteenth century with German immigrants, and the first reference to it in English comes in the *Spirit of the Age*, published in Sacramento, California in 1856: '"What is the German diet?" "Sourkraut, pretzels, plutworst [blutwurst, blood sausage], and lager beer."' The German word comes ultimately from a hypothetical medieval Latin *brachiatellum*, a diminutive form of *brachītum* 'bracelet'; it hence means etymologically 'ring-shaped biscuit'.

prickly pear A type of cactus that bears sweet edible orange or red prickly fruit. It is a native of America, but it grows widely around the Mediterranean and in many other parts of the world. Approached with caution and a dash of lime or lemon juice, it can make a delicious dessert. Its name is first recorded in 1696, but it was preceded by *prickle pear* and *prickpear*, both of which have since died out.

priddy oggy A Somerset variant of the traditional Cornish pasty, with a filling of pork and cheese. It is said to have been created in the 1960s at the Miners' Arms pub in Priddy, a village in the Mendip Hills in Somerset, to the east of Cheddar. The fortuitous rhyme made for an obvious play on the term *tiddy oggy*.

Pringle The brand name of a type of reconstituted potato crisp manufactured by Procter and Gamble, and originally sold in North America in 1968. It came from *Pringle Avenue*, the name of a street in Finneytown, Ohio. The crisp has a characteristic double-curved shape which, when employed for the roof of the Velodrome in London's 2012 Olympic Park, earned it the nickname 'The Pringle'. The actual potato content of Pringles is less than 50 per cent, which in 2008 enabled the manufacturers to argue successfully that it is not really a crisp but a biscuit, and therefore not liable to VAT.

profiterole Profiteroles are small round choux-pastry buns with a filling. This can be either savoury or sweet, but by far the commonest manifestation of the profiterole is with a cream filling and a covering of chocolate sauce, and piled in large quantities, in the more ambitious type of restaurant, into a sort of pyramid. The word originated in French as a diminutive form of *profit*, and so etymologically means 'small gains'—and indeed it may to begin with have denoted a 'little something extra' cooked along with the master's main dish as part of the servants' perks. Alexander Barclay, in his *Eclogues* (1515), writes 'to toast white shivers [slices of bread] and to make profiteroles, and after talking oft time to fill the bowl'.

prosciutto Italian *prosciutto* means simply 'ham' (it is an alteration of an earlier *presciutto*, literally 'dried beforehand', which was derived from *asciutto* 'dried'). In English, however, it refers specifically to air-dried Italian raw ham (*prosciutto crudo*), which is usually eaten in paper-thin slices. It is commonly used as an accompaniment to melon. *See also* PARMA HAM, SAN DANIELE.

Prosecco A light Italian sparkling wine made in the northeast of the country. It is called after the grape variety from which it is made, which in turn gets its name from a locality near Trieste.

provolone A type of hard cows'-milk cheese originally made in southern Italy. It comes in a wide variety of shapes, of which the most characteristic is probably pear-shaped. It is hung up in pairs on string to cure, and often smoked. Its name is a derivative (with the augmentative suffix -one) of *provola*, another cheese name. This probably goes back to Medieval Latin *probula*, which designated a type of buffalo-milk cheese.

prune The prune has an image problem in British cuisine, and indeed in other parts of northern Europe and in the US. The French rightly cherish their succulent *pruneaux d'Agen*, prunes made around Agen in southwestern France, but in Britain it has come to be regarded as little more than one of the more bearable sorts of laxative—the dreaded 'black-coated worker' of popular demonology. Its status is further depressed by the fact that in current colloquial English, a *prune* is a 'gormless person' (a usage which seems to have been born in RAF slang of the Second World War). In the US, the eating of prunes is associated with old people.

Prunes are simply dried plums—and not only are they the same fruit in disguise, but also the same word. *Prune* comes via Old French *prune* 'plum' from medieval Latin *prūna*, which, when the Germanic languages took it over, changed its *pr* to *pl*—hence *plum*. English started using *prune* for 'dried plum' as early as the fourteenth century, but during the sixteenth and seventeenth centuries a tendency developed to refer to ordinary plums as *prunes*—perhaps a fashionable following of French usage: 'gardens filled with prunes, apricots, dates, and olives', Thomas Washington, *Nicolay's Navigations into Turkey* (1585). Dried plums were hence often *dry prunes*, to distinguish them.

Spellings like *pruin*, *pruen*, *pruan*, *prewyn*, and even *pruant* recorded from the seventeenth century onwards reveal that *prune* was once pronounced virtually as a two-syllable word—a practice which persisted well into the twentieth century.

prunella salt A substance made by fusing potassium nitrate with sulphur, used in the eighteenth and nineteenth centuries for curing meat. Its name comes, though, not from this culinary application, but from its original use for treating diseases of the throat. Late Latin *prunella* 'inflammation of the throat' was an alteration of Latin *brunella*, a derivative of *brunus* 'brown' (a brown coating on the tongue was a symptom of the illness).

prunelle A French brandy-based liqueur flavoured with sloes (French *prunelle* means 'sloe').

pudding A *pudding* was originally a 'sausage': a cookery book of 1430 gives a recipe for 'Puddyng of purpaysse . . . putte this in the Gutte of the purpays' (the porpoise was considered a delicacy in the Middle Ages). In this sense, which still survives in *black pudding* and *white pudding* (not to mention haggis, in Burns's words 'great chieftain o' the puddin'-race'), the word probably derives, via Old French *boudin*, from Latin *botellus* 'sausage' (the unfortunate association with botulism arises from the fact that the food-poisoning germ was first discovered in cooked meats such as sausages).

The widening of the term's application seems to have come from the notion of the sausage's skin. From the mid-sixteenth century onwards, we find *pudding* increasingly applied to a variety of dishes, sweet or savoury, that are cooked in a bag or cloth, usually by boiling or steaming. Gradually, particular lines of development become discernible. On the one hand, puddings in which the cloth was lined with suet crust which contained a filling have led in the main to savoury modern puddings, notably steak and kidney (although some sweet puddings of this sort survive, such as Sussex pond pudding, with its lemon, butter, and sugar interior). On the other we have puddings whose entire substance is based on flour or other cereal products. This branch of the pudding genealogy, generally sweet, gives us our sponge puddings, treacle puddings, roly-poly puddings, and Christmas puddings. The great decrease in the price of sugar in the seventeenth century gave an enormous boost to sweet boiled puddings, and it was these that the French writer Henri Misson had in mind when he wrote in the early eighteenth century 'Blessed be he that invented Pudding, for it is a Manna that hits the Palates of all Sortes of People'. However, at an early date yet another strand in the story appeared. Already in Elizabethan times cooks were adapting pudding recipes so that they did not need to be boiled in a bag. Cooked by direct heat in the oven, these baked puddings were the precursors of modern rice puddings, bread-and-butter puddings, etc.

Baked puddings and sweet boiled puddings opened the way for the word *pudding* eventually to be applied generically, in British English, to the sweet course of a meal—'afters'. This is a usage which does not seem to have become established until the early twentieth century.

The abbreviated *pud* goes back at least as far as the early eighteenth century: a Scottish poem of 1706 contains the line 'I leave my Liver, Puds, and Tripes' (where *pud* means 'entrails', a gruesomely appropriate extension of the 'sausage' sense of *pudding* which developed in the fifteenth century).

pudding pie A term dating back to the sixteenth century for a pie made by putting a custard or other cooked mixture into a pastry case and baking it (Florence White in her *Good Things in England* (1932) gives recipes for a pudding pie containing a rice-filled custard and for one containing sweetened mashed potatoes mixed with eggs).

puff pastry Light pastry made up of many thin layers, used for pie crusts, canapés, sweet pastries, and the like. The term is first recorded in 1788 (the earlier but now little used *puff paste*—originally *puffed paste*—dates from 1598). Small filled puff pastry cases are liable to be called *puffs*. They appear to come on the scene in the mid-seventeenth century, but their modern incarnation, with a sweet filling and typically triangular in shape, probably dates from the nineteenth century (*jam puff* is first recorded in 1864, *cream puff* in 1889). However, the notion of applying the term *puff* to light flour-based products goes back much further than that: the early fifteenth-century *Liber Albus*, for example, refers to 'panis levis qui dicitur "pouf" [light bread which is called "puff"]'.

pulled An adjective, now mainly used in American English, denoting that the meat in question has been cooked for a long time, so that it can easily be cut or torn into small pieces. Originally (it is first recorded in 1737) it was applied to poultry, but it can also be used for rabbit, pork, etc. In modern usage it is chiefly a term of barbecuing art: 'Barbecue platters offer pulled pork, pulled chicken, smoked turkey, and sausage', *Dallas Morning News* (2006).

pulled bread Pieces of bread pulled from the inside of a loaf, especially a newly baked one, and lightly rebaked until they are crisp: '"You never had pulled bread?" she asked, incredulous. "It's the other great thing—besides French toast—to do with stale bread."' *Newsday* (1987).

pulque A milky alcoholic drink very popular in Mexico and other parts of Central America. It is made from the fermented juice of various types of agave, a cactus-like plant. It is probably of pre-Aztec origin. Its name may be related to Nahuatl *poliuhqui* or *puliuhqui* 'decomposed, spoilt' (it does not keep very long after it is made).

pulse A general term for edible seeds obtained from leguminous plants, such as peas, beans, and lentils. It was borrowed from Old French *pols* or *pouls*, which in turn came from Latin *puls*, denoting a sort of thick porridge or polenta made from beans, lentils, etc. or from cereals in the days before bread came into common use (virtually the ancient Roman equivalent of British pease pudding). *Poultices* get their name from having originally been made from such a soft pap of porridge or soaked bread (Latin *pultes*, the plural of *puls*), and the words *polenta* and *pollen* are also close relatives etymologically.

pumpernickel A dark coarse moist slow-baked unleavened bread made from wholemeal rye flour. It is associated particularly with Westphalia in west-central Germany, where it is claimed to have originated in the fifteenth century. There are several fanciful explanations of its name, but the truth is probably that it is a compound of German *pumpern* 'to fart' and *nickel* 'demon', inspired by the bread's alleged tendency to cause flatulence.

pumpkin Pumpkins are the blue whales of the vegetable world. Large and round, with bulbous ribs, the most gargantuan varieties can weigh over a hundred kilos. Their skin can be orange, yellow, or green, depending on type, and their flesh is orange or yellow. A relative of the marrow, they are widely grown in warm areas of the world. They are popular in France, for instance (but Britain's climate is slightly too cold for them, and they have never become a common vegetable there). It is with the US, though, that the pumpkin has become particularly associated, notably for its role in the sweetened pumpkin pie, traditionally eaten on Thanksgiving Day in November.

The ultimate source of the word *pumpkin* is Greek *pépōn*, which denoted a 'large melon'. This was a noun use of the adjective *pépōn* 'ripe', and hence originally signified a melon eaten only when it was ripe. Latin borrowed the word as *pepō*, and it arrived in English in the sixteenth century via the nasalized French form *pompon*. English retained it unchanged for a while (William Harrison, in his *Description of England* (1587), wrote of 'an acre of ground whereon to set cabbages . . . , pompons, or such like stuff'), but by the seventeenth century it had been converted to *pompion* or *pumpion*. Then a little later a new alternative, *pumpkin*, appeared, with the diminutive suffix -*kin*, and gradually, through the eighteenth and early nineteenth centuries, ousted *pompion*.

Despite its not very exciting flavour and texture, the pumpkin has always been a high-profile vegetable wherever it has gone—inevitably, perhaps, given its size. The Roman writer Seneca supposedly referred to the deification of the emperor Claudius as 'turning him into a pumpkin' (the term he used has been rendered into English as *pumpkinification*); Cinderella's coach, which began and ended as a pumpkin, made famous in Charles Perrault's seventeenth-century retelling, has made the pumpkin the symbol of a sudden transformation from the sublime to the banal—and also a mock excuse for not staying out late; and of course the US has given the world the Hallowe'en pumpkin, hollowed out and with a candle in the middle that shines through excised eyes, nose, and mouth.

punch The vogue for punch started in England in the early seventeenth century, imported by officers of the East India Company. It was a traditional long drink in India, and its name is generally supposed to be of Indian origin, too. This conjecture seems to have started with John Fryer, who in his *Account of East India* (1698) derived *punch* from Hindi *pānch* meaning 'five', from the five ingredients of the drink: sugar, spirits, lemon or lime juice, water, and spices. However, in the seventeenth century the word would have been pronounced not, as now, to rhyme with *lunch*, but with a short 'oo' sound, 'poonch', and this is not really consistent with a borrowing from Hindi *pānch*; so it has been speculated that it is short for *puncheon*, a large cask from which the drink might have been served.

The classic simplicity of the original recipe did not survive long; an assortment of variations was soon dreamed up, including punch made with tea, with milk (this enjoyed a wave of popularity in the early eighteenth century), and without any alcohol. Nowadays almost any sort of festive amalgam of drinks served in a bowl, with or without bits of fruit swimming in it, is dignified with the name of 'punch', although purists insist that more straightforward mixtures, without the citrus and spices, should be termed 'cups'. One drink to maintain the tradition is the rum-based West Indian *planter's punch*, whose disguised strength regularly lays Caribbean holidaymakers low.

Towards the end of the eighteenth century, punch had political connotations: it became known as the Whig drink, whereas the Tory diehards stuck loyally to their traditional claret.

Punt e Mes A dark sweet wine-based Italian aperitif flavoured with herbs and given a bitter twist with quinine. Its name means 'point and a half', and apparently comes from the former practice of Milanese stockbrokers shouting out 'Punt e mes!' to order the drink.

pupton A term of wide application, common in the eighteenth and nineteenth centuries but now obsolete, for a baked dish made with fruit or meat (Hannah Glasse, for example, in her *Art of Cookery Made Plain and Easy* (1747), has a recipe for 'a Pupton of Apples', which involves stewing the apples, mixing them with butter and egg yolks, moulding them into a shape and baking them). The word was borrowed from French *poupeton*, denoting a sort of minced-meat ragout or pâté. That was a variant of *poulpeton*, which had been adopted into English earlier as *pulpatoon*. The French word was itself probably either a borrowing of Italian *polpettone* 'large meatball, meatloaf' (*see* POLPETTE) or created in French from *poulpe* 'flesh, lean meat'.

puri Puris, or *pooris*, are a sort of deep-fried bread eaten in Pakistan and northern India. They are usually made from unleavened wheat flour, although other varieties of flour can be used, and they are shaped into small round cakes. When put into the hot fat or ghee they puff up like balloons. The term *puri* is Hindi, and comes ultimately from Sanskrit *purah* 'cake'. *See also* BHEL PURI, PANI PURI.

puttanesca A dish of pasta served *alla puttanesca* comes with a sauce made from tomatoes, garlic, black olives, capers, anchovies, chilli peppers, oregano, and parsley. Italian *puttanesca* means literally 'whorish, sluttish'. This may be a reference to the motley selection of ingredients that might be found in a slovenly housewife's store cupboard. An alternative interpretation has it that the sauce was originally devised by prostitutes as one that could be cooked quickly between clients' visits.

quaking pudding A light, tremulous pudding, popular in the seventeenth and eighteenth centuries, made by boiling a sweetened mixture of breadcrumbs, cream, eggs, and spices in a cloth. Its name, reflecting its quiverishness, is not recorded before the 1660s, but the term *quaking* had been used in the same sense before then: 'Quaking tarts, and quiuering Custards, and such milke-sop Dishes', John Earle, *Micro-cosmographie* (1628). The dessert was also called *shaking pudding*.

quark *Quark* is the German term for 'curd cheese'. It has become familiar in English in recent years as the brand name for a particular fairly liquid variety of German curd cheese. The word is also used metaphorically in German for 'nonsense'.

quarterpounder A hamburger weighing (uncooked) a quarter of a pound (4 ounces or 113 grams). It was originally marketed in the US under that name (which is now trademarked as *Quarter Pounder*) by McDonalds in 1971. The burger has since encircled the globe (*see* MAC), and in places that are mystified by imperial weights and measures, it is sold as a 'Hamburger Royale' or a 'McRoyal'.

quattro staggione In Italian literally 'four seasons', *quattro staggione* denotes a pizza with four compartments containing different fillings. A typical combination would be: a section containing tomatoes and anchovies; one with mozzarella and Parmesan; one with tomatoes, anchovies, capers, and oregano; and one with seafood.

queen of puddings One of the classic English puddings, queen of puddings consists of a bread-crumb and custard mixture with a layer of jam and then meringue on top. The recipe is of long standing (*The Oxford Companion to Food* (2006) notes that *The Closet of Sir Kenelm Digby Knight Opened* (1669) gives directions for making something very similar, and what is clearly a version of it turns up in Mrs Beeton (1861) under the name 'Manchester pudding'), but the queenly appellation is comparatively recent. Captain Frederick Marryat mentions a *queen pudding* in his *Diary in America* (1839), but it is not clear what sort of dish he was referring to. The earliest unequivocal reference occurs in Frederick Bishop's *Illustrated London Cookery Book* (1852), which describes something called *queen's pudding* (an alternative name that still survives). *Queen of puddings* itself is first recorded in Helen Campbell's *Easiest Way in Housekeeping and Cooking* (1903). The inspiration, coming at this point in the nineteenth century, was presumably Queen Victoria.

quenelle Quenelles are small dumpling-like balls of minced or chopped seasoned fish or meat generally cooked by poaching. They can be, and have been, made from a wide variety of ingredients, but by far the commonest these days is pike (in French *quenelles de brochet*). The French word *quenelle* was borrowed from German *knödel* 'dumpling'.

quesadilla A Mexican snack consisting of a tortilla wrapped round a filling of cheese and seasoning (or some other sort of savoury mixture, such as potato and chorizo), and deep-fried. The Mexican term is a reapplication of Spanish *quesadilla* 'cake or pancake made with cheese', which is a diminutive of *quesada* 'dish made with cheese', itself a derivative of *quesa* 'cheese'.

quiche A pastry case filled with a cooked savoury custard containing items such as vegetables, bacon, or cheese. It is a speciality of the Alsace-Lorraine region, which has been bandied between France and Germany over the centuries, and the term *quiche* itself is a French version of *küche*, a word from the German dialect of Lorraine. This in turn is a diminutive form of German *kuchen* 'cake', which is related to English *cake*.

The British have become familiar with the quiche only since the Second World War (the first record of it in an English text is from 1949), but since then it has spread to virtually every wine bar and cafeteria counter in Britain. Its primarily vegetarian ingredients have, however, earned it a reputation as a rather wimpish food—'real men don't eat quiche'.

The authentic *quiche lorraine* contains only smoked bacon in addition to the cream-and-egg custard, but many alternative versions have grown up that include cheese and onion.

quince The quince has suffered a sad fall from favour in Britain. In medieval and Renaissance times it was high in popularity, and indeed into the nineteenth century Mrs Beeton was extolling its virtues as a fruit for making marmalade and jellies with, and for adding flavour to pies made with its near relative the apple, and Edward Lear of course had his owl and pussy-cat dining 'on mince, and slices of quince, which they ate with a runcible spoon'. Perhaps it is the fruit's frequent intractable hardness, needing long cooking to overcome, which has led impatient British cooks to forsake it, despite its unrivalled perfume. But nowadays, immigration from eastern Mediterranean areas is leading to its reappearance in some local shops and stalls—confusable at a careless glance with a knobbly pale-coloured pear, but immediately recognizable on closer inspection from its coating of grey down. It is essentially a fruit of the northern and eastern Mediterranean, and has been since ancient times (the golden apple which Aphrodite received as a prize for being judged more beautiful than Hera and Athena by Paris was supposedly a quince). It takes its name ultimately from Greek *melon Kudōnion* 'apple of Cydonia' (now Chania, the town in Crete long famous for growing quinces). This was borrowed by Latin as *cydōneum*, whose later form *cotōneum* passed into Old French as *cooin* (its modern French descendant is *coing*, and a sweetened pink jelly made from quince juice is known as *cotignac*). Middle English took over the Old French name as *coyn* or *quoyn*, but as early as the fourteenth century its plural was being used as if it were a singular—hence modern English *quince*. See also MEMBRILLO.

quinoa The edible starchy grain-like seeds of a plant of the goosefoot family that is widely cultivated in the Andes region. Before the conquest of America and the introduction of Old World varieties it was the principal grain crop there, and it is still an important staple. The high quality of its protein and other perceived dietary advantages have recently spread its fame further afield. Its name represents a Spanish spelling of the original Quechua *kínuwa*.

rack The now fashionable rack of lamb is distinctly a revival. In the sixteenth and seventeenth centuries, *rack* was a term quite commonly applied to a cut of meat, and particularly mutton or pork, from the neck and upper spine (Foxe's *Book of Martyrs* (1570) notes 'a brothe made with the forepart of a racke of Mutton'), but then it seems to have faded into purely dialectal use, emerging briefly in the nineteenth century as a slang expression for a 'skinny horse': 'Among the horses are some fine specimens of racks, that is fleshless horses,' *Daily News* (1878). Then all of a sudden, in the early 1960s, *rack* began to regain popularity as a synonym for *best end of neck*, a cut of lamb from the forequarters containing vertebrae and rib-bones. Rack of lamb started to appear, it seemed, on every restaurant menu. It can be chopped up into cutlets, but generally it is roasted whole, with the rib-tips exposed for decorative effect. Two racks (one from either side of a carcase) can be sewn together either in a circle (to form a 'crown roast') or facing each other (as a 'guard of honour roast'). Taking advantage of the bridgehead established by lamb, the term is now also being applied to similar cuts of veal and pork. The equivalent French term is *carré*, which means literally 'square'.

raclette A raclette is, like fondue, a traditional Swiss melted cheese dish. Instead of being melted in a bowl over heat, the cheese in a raclette is held before a fire or other source of heat, and as its surface melts it is scraped off on to a plate (*racler* is French for 'to scrape'). It is eaten with an accompaniment of potatoes, gherkins, and pickled onions. It is a speciality of the canton of Valais, and is made from a local cheese such as Bagnes, Conches, or Orsières.

radicchio The red leaves of radicchio are amongst the most striking of the new salad vegetables introduced to Britain at the end of the twentieth century. It is a variety of chicory, and comes, as its name suggests, from Italy (an alternative Italian name for it is *cicorie rosse* 'red chicory'). The type most often seen in Britain is Verona radicchio, which looks like a small crimson lettuce, but there is another sort, the Treviso radicchio, which has long narrow leaves more closely resembling those of the standard chicory (radicchio is called *trévise* in French); see TREVISO. The Italian word *radicchio* comes ultimately from Latin *rādīcula*, a diminutive form of *rādix* 'root'.

radish Etymologically a *radish* is simply a 'root.' Old English borrowed its word (*rædic*) for this vegetable of the mustard family from Latin *rādix* 'root' (as in English *radical*); its current form, with the *-sh* rather than the *-ch* one might have expected from *rædic*, is probably due to the influence of the French word *radis*. And the name is appropriate, because it is of course for its crisp peppery bulbous root, generally eaten raw as part of a salad or on its own as an appetizer, that the radish is valued—and has been since ancient times (radishes were part of the rations of the workers who built the Egyptian pyramids, and the Greeks and Romans were very partial to them).

The standard European radish is scarlet-, or occasionally white-skinned, and rather bigger than a quail's egg, but in recent years we have become increasingly familiar with more exotic varieties—the black-skinned winter radish, for instance, about the size of a turnip, and the long thin white radish of Asia, most commonly termed in British supermarkets *mooli* (from Hindi *mūli*), but also known as *Chinese radish*, *oriental radish*, and, in Japan, *daikon*.

ragout A *ragout* is etymologically something which 'reinvigorates the appetite'. The word, which used also to be spelled *ragoo*, was borrowed in the seventeenth century from French *ragoût*, a derivative of the verb *ragoûter* 'to revive the taste of' (*goût* means 'taste'). It denotes a rich stew containing meat and vegetables in a thick sauce (although the French term *ragoût* can also cover fish stews).

Ragstone A British variety of goats' cheese. It gets its name from a type of coarse sedimentary rock that outcrops widely in Kent, the county where the cheese was first produced in the late twentieth century.

ragu A spicy sauce typically containing minced beef, onions, tomato purée, and red wine, developed in Bologna as an accompaniment to pasta, and now widely encountered in a more or less debased form as the sauce element of spaghetti Bolognese. Italian *ragù* was adopted and adapted from French *ragoût* in the seventeenth century, in its original sense 'meat stew'; its application to the pasta sauce is first recorded in 1750.

raisin In English, *raisin* has meant 'partially dried grape' since it was borrowed from Old French *raisin* in the thirteenth century, but French *raisin* usually means simply 'grape'. It comes ultimately from Latin *racēmus* 'bunch of grapes' (French *grappe*, confusingly, means 'bunch of grapes'). The finest raisins are generally considered to be from Malaga in Spain, made from muscatel grapes.

raita In Indian cuisine, a raita is a refreshing relish based on yoghurt or curd cheese, with another ingredient or ingredients—one could, for instance, have a cucumber raita, or an aubergine raita. There are also sweet raitas.

raki A strong spirit distilled from a fermented grain mash or from grape or plum juice and flavoured with aniseed. It is drunk in Turkey and the Balkans, and is not dissimilar to Greek ouzo. The word *raki* is an Anglicization (first recorded in 1675 in Henry Teonge's diaries: '[We] drink to our friends in England in racckee at night') of Turkish *rāqī*, which may come ultimately from the same source as produced English *arrack*, the name of a strong Asian spirit.

rambutan The rambutan is a hairy lychee. A native of Malaysia, it is closely related to the lychee, but its shell is covered with a luxuriant growth of soft rich-red spines, like some exotic sea-anemone. Like the lychee, its shell encloses succulent white flesh surrounding a large stone. It has been familiar in the West since at least the early eighteenth century, but purely academically; it is not until comparatively recently that it has begun to appear on British supermarket shelves. Its name is Malay, a derivative of *rambut* 'hair'.

ramen In oriental cookery, thin yellow wheat-flour noodles that are served in soup. They originated in China (the Japanese name comes from Chinese *lā* 'to pull' and *miàn* 'noodles'), but after the Second World War they became very popular in Japan, where instant ramen were developed that could be cooked in a couple of minutes in a sachet also containing soup powder (*see* POT NOODLE).

ramp An assertively flavoured North American wild onion that somewhat resembles a spring onion. The name, first recorded in 1598, is a back-formation from the earlier *ramps*, a singular form which had come to be regarded as plural. That in turn was an alteration of *rams*, a descendant of Old English *hramsa* 'wild garlic', from which we also get *ramsons*.

ramsons A woodland plant with broad shiny leaves, round heads of white flowers, and a powerful smell of garlic that has earned it the alternative name of *wild garlic*. The leaves can be used as a milder substitute for garlic. In the course of its history, its name has lurched schizophrenically from singular to plural and back. The Old English word for the plant was *hramsa*. The plural of that was *hramsan*, but as *-n* began to die out as a marker of plurality, *hramsan*, or *ramson*, came to be interpreted as a singular, and a new plural, *ramsons*, was created for it. Subsequently that too came to be treated as singular, and now *ramsons* is the name of an individual plant.

rapeseed The seeds of oilseed rape, a plant of the cabbage family. Their high oil content makes rape a profitable crop, and in the latter part of the twentieth century the English countryside in summer became dotted with field upon yellow field of it. The oil is widely used in cooking and food manufacture. The word *rape* comes from Latin *rapum* or *rapa* 'turnip', and to begin with it was applied to turnips in English as well as to rape. An alternative name for the plant is *colza*. *See also* CANOLA.

rape vinegar An antique term for wine vinegar made from the stalks, skins, and pips left over after the grapes have been pressed: 'Lay the meat [a loin of mutton] twenty-four hours in half a pint of red wine and half a pint of rape-vinegar; then take it out of the pickle', Hannah Glasse, *The Art of Cookery Made Plain and Easy* (1747). *Rape* came (in the seventeenth century) from French *râpe*, which in turn came from medieval Latin *raspa* 'bunch of grapes'.

rapini A Mediterranean variety of turnip widely grown for its leafy branching stalks (eaten as *cime di rapa*). In America it is usually termed *broccoli raab*. The Italian word means literally 'little turnip'.

ras-el-hanout A spice mixture widely used in North Africa, typically containing cumin seeds, coriander seeds, turmeric, ginger, cardamom, and nutmeg. The name in Arabic means 'roof of the shop'.

rasgulla An Indian sweet of Bengali origin consisting of a ball of curd cheese cooked in syrup. Hindi *rasgullā* is a compound formed from *ras* 'juice' and *gullā* 'ball'.

ras malai An Indian sweet dish consisting of small flat cakes of curd cheese that have been cooked in syrup and then soaked in a flavoured mixture of cream and milk. The term comes from Hindi *ras* 'juice' and *malāi* 'cream'.

raspberry It is not known how the raspberry got its name. Wild raspberries have always been around, of course, but the cultivated variety did not find its way to Britain, from France, until the middle of the sixteenth century. At first it was called *raspes*, a curious name, and unexplained, although a connection has been suggested with *raspis*, a kind of wine current in the fifteenth and sixteenth centuries, which may come ultimately from medieval Latin *raspa* 'residue from pressing grapes'. However that may be, *raspes* soon came to be regarded as a plural, and by the seventeenth century the resulting new 'singular' *rasp* had had *-berry* tacked on to it to form *raspberry*. Culinarily, raspberries form the basis of Melba sauce, and the nouvelle cuisiniers of the 1970s and 1980s started a craze for using raspberry-flavoured vinegar in salad dressings and sauces.

The British English use of *raspberry* for a derisive sound made by blowing, typically with the tongue between the lips, dates from the late nineteenth century. It is an abbreviation of *raspberry tart*, rhyming slang for 'fart'.

raspings An old word for 'breadcrumbs'. First recorded in 1736, by the middle of the twentieth century it had a decidedly antique air: 'Sprinkle raspings over the fat of cooked ham', *Good Housekeeping Home Encyclopedia* (1951).

ratafia There is ratafia you can drink, and there are ratafias you can eat, and their common denominator is the taste of almonds or similar nutty kernels. The drink came first. It is a liqueur made by steeping some flavouring ingredient in sweetened spirit. In France, this ingredient can be any of a range of fruits, such as blackcurrants or oranges, as well as kernels, but in English usage the term has always been largely restricted to a drink flavoured with peach, apricot, or cherry kernels, or particularly with almonds. French also uses *ratafia* for a drink made by adding brandy to grape juice so as to stop its fermentation and retain its sweetness; the best known is Pineau des Charentes. English originally acquired the term towards the end of the seventeenth century, and in the early nineteenth century applied it to a sort of small macaroon-like biscuit flavoured with almond.

The word *ratafia* comes originally from French West Indian creole, where it appears to have referred to the local spirit, rum. Popular etymology attributes the creole term to Latin *ratificāre* 'to ratify', the notion being that it referred to a drink taken to seal or 'ratify' a deal, but there is no direct evidence for this.

ratatouille A dish of mixed vegetables simmered in olive oil, characteristic of Provence, and more particularly of the Nice area. Typical ingredients are aubergines, tomatoes, onions, peppers, and courgettes, which according to aficionados should be cooked separately, and then combined to produce the final dish. The name *ratatouille* appears to derive from the French verb *touiller* 'to stir up', and it was originally applied, often disparagingly, to any stew; *Cassell's Dictionary of Cookery* (1877), for example, not getting its name quite right, reports 'ratatouville' as 'a popular French method of making a savoury dish out of the remains of cold meat'.

Ratte A waxy firm-fleshed variety of potato which originated, probably in France, in the 1870s. Its name, in full *La Ratte*, is a variant of French *rate* 'female rat', and appears to have been inspired by some perceived resemblance—perhaps, it has been speculated, between the cluster of growing tubers and suckling infant rats.

ravigote A ravigote is a piquant sauce. It comes in a variety of forms, hot or cold, but a common theme is vinegar and chopped herbs, to give a lift to the food it is served with (French *ravigoter* means 'to reinvigorate'). It also usually contains capers and chopped onions or shallots. British cooks apparently discovered it in the early nineteenth century: it is first mentioned in Richard Dolby's *Cook's Dictionary* (1830), and Mrs Beeton gives a recipe in her *Book of Household Management* (1861).

ravioli Tinned ravioli in tomato sauce—virtually spaghetti Bolognese in bite-sized square packets—has tarnished ravioli's image in recent years, but in the hands of fashionable chefs it made a comeback in the latter part of the twentieth century—all of a sudden it became the in thing to enclose small portions of various foods (lobster, say, or wild mushrooms) in a pasta case and call the result ravioli.

Both the ridiculous and the sublime are offspring of a classic Italian dish consisting of little square pasta envelopes enclosing a small amount of minced meat (typically beef or veal) or vegetable (particularly spinach) usually served in a tomato sauce.

Where did it come from, though? As early as the fourteenth century English had acquired the term; the cookery book *Forme of Cury* gives a recipe for 'rauioles': 'Take wet cheese and grind it small, and mix it with eggs and saffron and a good quantity of butter. Make a thin foil of dough and enclose them therein as tartlets, and cast them in boiling water, and seethe them therein.' However, the same book also gives a recipe for 'raphioles', which it describes as meat balls enclosed in a caul and baked in an open crust. Despite the similarity of names, the two sound worlds apart, but could there be a link between the 'dough' covering of the first and the caul and pastry casing of the second? If they are ultimately identical, the second rissole-like dish takes us plausibly close to both of the suggested sources of the Italian. One is that it originally stood for a sort of small pie made from chopped meat and turnips (Italian *rava* means 'turnip', and so *ravioli* could be literally 'little turnips'); the other is that it comes from Genoese dialect *rabiole* 'leftovers, odds and ends'.

A closely related dish is the *raviole* of southern France and Corsica: small packets of pasta containing spinach, Swiss chard, or cream cheese.

reblochon A mild creamy cows'-milk cheese made in the mountains of Haute-Savoie, on the French–Italian border. It has a pinkish-orange rind. Its name is derived from the verb *reblocher* 'to milk for a second time': a residue of rich creamy milk was left in the cows' udders after their main milking, and when the overseer had knocked off work for the day, the cowherds would extract the last few drops to make cheese.

recioto A type of sweet wine made from dried grapes that is a speciality of the Veneto region of northeastern Italy. The most common version is the red Recioto della Valpolicella (if the grapes' sugar content is fermented out during the wine-making process it becomes the dry *amarone*), but there is also a white Recioto di Soave. The term comes from a Veneto dialect word meaning 'small bunch of grapes, mature grapes on the outside of a bunch', a derivative of *recio* 'small bunch of grapes'. That may be related to *recia* 'ear', the underlying idea being that the ripest grapes at the top of the bunch, which originally were the only grapes used for making the wine, stuck out like ears. It is a proprietary name in the US.

redcurrant A variety of currant with red berries. It is often made into a jelly that is served with lamb or other meat, and it is also a standard ingredient of summer pudding.

redeye gravy Gravy made from the pan juices of fried ham and black coffee. It is a speciality of the Deep South of the US, and is standardly served with the cooked ham. Its name supposedly comes from the observation that when the emulsified mixture has cooled and separated out in a sloping-sided container, the darker, non-oil element at the bottom appears surrounded by a rim of translucent grease on top, the whole allegedly resembling a red eye.

red flannel hash An American dish consisting of cooked chopped-up beetroot and potatoes (preferably red-skinned) or sweet potatoes mixed together, often with a meat element such as corned beef or chopped bacon, and cooked again. The reddish colour of the finished product prompted its name, inspired by the noted red flannel cloth of New England.

red herring Real red herrings, as opposed to their metaphorical counterparts, are very hard to find nowadays in Britain. They are made by soaking the herrings in brine for several days, and then smoking them until they are bright red and dry enough to keep for a long time. Those made in Yarmouth are reputed to be the finest, and Thomas Nashe in his *Lenten Stuffe, or the Praise of the Red Herring* (1567), claims that the method of preserving them was discovered by accident by a Yarmouth fisherman who hung some herrings up over a fire in his hut, and later found that the fish, 'which were as white as whale-bone when he hung them up, now lookt as red as a lobster'. Red herrings are still made in quantity, but the vast majority are now exported to places such as the West Indies, Africa, and South America, where they are esteemed not only for their flavour but also for their keeping qualities in the hot climate. An even more desiccated version of the fish, known as the black herring, goes to the same export markets.

The metaphorical *red herring* 'misleading distraction' derives from the former practice of pulling a pungent red herring across the trail of a hunted animal to sharpen the skill of hounds being trained.

red horse Military slang of the late nineteenth and early twentieth centuries for army corned beef. The saltpetre used to preserve it would have accounted for the colour, and as for the meat content—who knows? Squaddies took a jaundiced view of the probabilities.

red lead British twentieth-century naval slang for tomato ketchup, and also for tinned tomatoes: 'Everything went into a pot-mess—meat, spuds, peas, beans, rice, Oxo, "red lead" (tinned tomatoes)—and the result was invariably good', *Tackline* (1945). Real red lead is a red form of lead oxide, used as a pigment.

red ned Australian and New Zealand slang for cheap (red) wine or other similar alcoholic drink: 'I'll join Mr Jeffery for a glass of red ned any day', *Canberra Times* (1983). The term is first recorded in 1941.

Reform sauce A savoury sauce developed by the Anglo-Italian chef Charles Elmé Francatelli (1805–76) when he was in charge of the kitchens at the Reform Club in Pall Mall in the 1850s. To a basic brown sauce are added some anchovy sauce, redcurrant jelly, and red wine or port.

refried beans A Mexican speciality consisting of boiled pinto beans that have been mashed up and then fried, typically in lard. The English term, first recorded in 1911, is a translation of Spanish *frijoles refritos,* which is also used in English (either whole, or abbreviated to *refritos*). Despite their name, the beans are not fried twice: the *re-* in this case probably has emphatic force, rather than literally denoting repetition.

relish A piquant sauce or pickle (for example, chutney) eaten with plain food to add flavour. The original culinary application of the term in English, which dates from the late eighteenth century, was to an appetizer or hors d'oeuvre, a usage that survives in America. The now more familiar usage seems to have developed in the second half of the nineteenth century (the proprietary name *The Gentleman's Relish* was registered in 1907; it denotes a brand of anchovy paste invented in 1828 by John Osborn and originally called *Patum Peperium*).

rémoulade A piquant mayonnaise-based sauce used as a dressing for salads, cold meats, etc. Authorities differ on precisely which additions are necessary to turn mayonnaise into rémoulade: the classic French ingredients are chopped gherkins, capers, and herbs, but simpler versions are made containing only a touch of mustard, while to nineteenth-century English cooks, who were quite keen on rémoulade (Mrs Beeton makes it clear that it was often called simply *French salad dressing*), cold hard-boiled egg yolks were a *sine qua non*. The sauce is popular in the cuisine of Louisiana, too, where it is also known as *remolade*. French *rémoulade* appears to derive from *ramolas*, a word in the northern dialect of Picardy for 'horseradish' which came ultimately from Latin *armoracea* (the standard Old French form *armoracee* was briefly borrowed into English as *armorace* 'horseradish' in the fifteenth century).

rendang An Indonesian beef curry cooked in coconut milk.

rennet A substance obtained from the stomach of a calf slaughtered while it is still suckling, consisting of milk that has been curdled by an enzyme called rennin. It is used for curdling milk, to make cheese or junket. Vegetarian rennet is also available, made from various plant enzymes. The word first appeared in the late fifteenth century. It may be related to *run*.

retsina A Greek white wine to which pine resin has been added. Traces of resinated wine have been found in Greek amphorae dating back at least 3,000 years, and it has been popular ever since—probably more for its taste than for any preservative properties the resin may have. It is particularly associated with the area around Athens, where 80 per cent of the white wine made is resinated. The word *retsina* is a modern Greek adaptation of Italian *resina* 'resin'.

Reuben sandwich An American sandwich made from salt beef (which is known as 'corned beef' in North America), cheese, and sauerkraut, typically on rye bread. Of heroic proportions, it is usually a double-decker, and is standardly served hot. Numerous Reubens have been identified as its originator. The earliest in the field, and for a long time the leader, was Arnold (or, according to other authorities, Arthur) Reuben, a New York deli-owner who supposedly created it (using ham rather than corned beef) in 1914 for Annette Seelos, the leading lady in a Charlie Chaplin film being shot at the time. Later entrants include the American grocer Reuben Kulakofsky (the preferred candidate of *Webster's Dictionary*), and the Nebraskan grocer Reuben Kay (the runner backed by the US Kraut Packers Association), who is said to have invented it during a poker game in Omaha in 1955. The fact that the term is not recorded before 1956 (when the recipe won a competition for new sandwiches) might be said to favour the last of these.

rhubarb Rhubarb seems to have originated in China, and was first imported to the West via Russia for the sake of its root, which in medieval times was dried, ground up, and used as a purgative. Ancient names for it included Greek *rha* and Persian *rēwend*, which were in due course to converge to produce *rhubarb*. The term *rha* was said by the Roman historian Ammianus Marcellinus to have been taken from the ancient name of the River Volga (on the rhubarb route from China). It was borrowed into late Latin as *rhā*, and had tacked on to it the adjective *barbarum*—hence *rhababarum*, literally 'foreign rhubarb'. Here, Persian *rēwend* enters the picture again. Greek had borrowed this as *rheon*, which in Latin became *rheum* (now the scientific generic name for rhubarb). In medieval Latin the two words for 'rhubarb' became blended together to produce *rheubarbarum*, which was eventually shortened to **rheubarbum*.

Britain first got to know rhubarb in the fourteenth century, and for the next four hundred years it was grown solely as a medicinal herb (often termed *Turkey rhubarb* or *Russian rhubarb*). But then around 1800 it seems to have occurred to someone that it would be good to eat for its own sake. Andrew Wynter, in his *Curiosities of Civilization* (1860), records its introduction to the metropolis: 'Rhubarb is almost solely furnished by the London market-gardeners. It was first introduced by Mr Miatt forty years ago, who sent his two sons to the Borough Market with five bunches, of which they only sold three.' A year later, Mrs Beeton was writing in her *Book of Household Management* that rhubarb 'was comparatively little known till within the last 20 or 30 years, but it is now cultivated in almost every British garden'. By the 1880s it had even spread to France, although without its traditional British accompaniment of custard.

West Yorkshire has long been a centre of rhubarb production in Britain, specializing in forcing it in sheds, and in 2010 Yorkshire forced rhubarb was granted Protected Designation of Origin (PDO) status by the EU. The area between Wakefield, Morley, and Rothwell (about 23 square kilometres) has come to be known as the 'Rhubarb Triangle'.

Ribena The proprietary name of a soft drink based on blackcurrant juice that first appeared on the British market in 1936. It was formed from the fruit's Latin genus name, *Ribes*. Approximately 90 per cent of Britain's annual blackcurrant harvest goes into the drink. Other, non-blackcurrant flavours have appeared in recent years, such as orange and blueberry.

rib-eye A tender cut of beef consisting of the muscles that run along the outside of the upper part of the ribs. It is usually cut into slices to make *rib-eye steaks* (also known as *rib steaks*). The term, first recorded in 1926, originated in North America.

ribollita A thick rich Tuscan bread and vegetable soup, which would typically contain onions, carrots, celery, beans, tomatoes, cavolo nero (or other kale), and garlic. It originated as a boiling-up of the previous day's minestrone (Italian *ribollita* means literally 'reboiled').

Ribston pippin A variety of English dessert apple from which the Cox's orange pippin was bred. It takes its name from Ribston Park in North Yorkshire, between Knaresborough and Wetherby, where it originated—from, it is said, a pip brought from France by Sir Henry Goodricke around 1700. The name is first recorded in 1782.

Ricard The proprietary name of a brand of pastis, originally commercialized in France in 1932 by Paul Ricard (1909–97).

rice Rice—both the cereal plant and the word—are of oriental origin. Evidence has been found of what appears to have been semi-cultivated rice in Thailand 5,500 years ago, while the word probably came from the northern part of the Indian subcontinent. Some such form as Sanskrit *vrīhi-* or Afghan *vrizē* seems to have travelled westward via Iran to the eastern Mediterranean, giving Greek *óruza*. This in turn was the source of the words for 'rice' in virtually all European languages: Latin *orȳza*, Russian *ris*, German *reis*, Dutch *rijst*, Danish and Swedish *ris*, Italian *riso*, Spanish *aroz*, French *riz*, and (borrowed from Old French *ris* in the thirteenth century) English *rice*. To begin with, rice was something of an expensive rarity in Britain, imported from the shores of the Mediterranean (to which it had been introduced by the Arabs) and treated as if it were a spice. Gradually, however, it began to lose this cachet, and the eighteenth century saw the beginnings of the sweet rice pudding, until the influx of foreign cuisines after the Second World War probably the major use of rice in Britain. Wild rice, incidentally, is a completely different plant, only very distantly related to ordinary rice.

rice paper Thin translucent edible paper that is used as a base for macaroons and other similar baked goods. Despite its name (first recorded in 1810), it has no connection with rice; it is made from the flattened and dried pith of either of two oriental shrubs, *Tetrapanax papyriferus* and *Scaevola sericea*.

rice wine An East Asian drink made by fermenting rice. It is sweetish and relatively low in alcohol. The best known type is the Japanese sake. The name, first recorded in 1625, is actually something of a misnomer, as the process of making the drink resembles brewing more than wine-making.

rickey An American mixed drink made with gin or whisky, lime juice, soda water, and ice. It was probably named after Col. Joseph K. Rickey (1842–1903), a US politician who is said to have invented it in a Washington bar called Shoemaker's, probably in the 1880s.

ricotta An Italian cottage cheese made originally from the whey left after making other cheeses—from cows', ewes', or even goats' milk—but nowadays often with full or skimmed milk added. It is widely used in Italian cookery: applications include fillings for ravioli and cannelloni, cheesecakes, and ice cream. Its name means literally 'recooked', from the method of manufacture; it goes back to Latin *recocta*, feminine past participle of *recoquere* 'to cook again'.

riesling A grape variety that produces aromatic, often rather flowery white wines that can range from a steely dryness to an unctuous sweetness. Its spiritual home is Germany, but it is also widely grown in Alsace and Austria, and to some extent in California, Australia, and New Zealand. The origins of its name are unclear. The form *russling* is recorded from the fifteenth century, *rissling* from the sixteenth. One theory is that it comes from the Swabian place-name *Ries*, a descendant of Latin *Raetia*; another that it conceals a reference to grapes that *reisen* or 'fall off' the vine (literally 'travel').

rigatoni Pasta in the form of short hollow fluted tubes. The Italian term (first recorded in 1935) means literally 'large ridges'.

rijsttafel A dish—or rather a set of dishes—of Southeast Asian origin which through the Netherlands' long colonial association with the East Indies has become established as a classic of Dutch cuisine. As its name suggests (it literally means 'rice table', from  Dutch *rijst* 'rice' and *tafel* 'table'), its main ingredient is rice, which appears in a large central bowl, but around it like satellites are plates of various other Indonesian delicacies, such as satay, curry, spicy soup, dried shrimps, and scrambled eggs.

rillettes A French form of potted meat. The flesh of rabbits, geese, poultry, or particularly pigs is cooked long and slowly in lard, reduced to a smooth paste, potted up, and then served cold as an hors d'oeuvre. Perhaps the most celebrated are those from Tours, made from pork. English borrowed the word towards the end of the nineteenth century, and at first there seems to have been some thought of Anglicizing both it, to *rilletts*, and the product, to a sort of tinned chopped meat: 'Charged with stealing 4lb of rilletts.... He identified . . . the tins of rilletts as the property of the company', *Southampton Times* (1896). Mercifully, this did not catch on.

ripple A term of American origin for a type of ice cream containing wavy bands of coloured and typically fruit-flavoured syrup, producing a ripple-like pattern. The commonest flavour is raspberry (*raspberry ripple*), but others, such as strawberry and chocolate, are also encountered. Originally a trademark, the earliest record of it in print is from 1939.

risi e bisi A thick soup of the Veneto region of Italy whose main ingredients are rice (*risi*) and peas (*bisi*—the Venetian version of standard Italian *piselli*). It also contains bacon, onion, and celery.

risoni An alternative term for ORZO, a type of small pasta. The Italian word means literally 'large rice'.

risotto An Italian dish of rice cooked in stock with various flavourings and seasonings (the word means literally 'little rice' in Italian). It was introduced to British eaters by Eliza Acton, who in her *Modern Cookery for Private Families* (1845) gave a recipe for *risotto à la milanaise* (although her main additional ingredients, Parmesan cheese and saffron, are in fact those of a *risotto à la piémontaise*). It seems to have been slow to catch on, though: the *Pall Mall Gazette* (1885) gave a 'useful description of how to cook risotto, a delightful dish too rarely seen in England'.

rissole The ultimate source of *rissole* is Vulgar Latin *russeola*, which was short for *pasta russeola*, literally 'reddish paste' (the Roman gastronome Apicius had a recipe for peacock rissole). In Old French this became *ruissole*, which was borrowed into English in the fourteenth century as *russole* and in the fifteenth century as *rishew*. This early burger evidently did not commend itself to English tastes, however, because no more is heard of it until the eighteenth century. The word was then reborrowed from French *rissole*, but its latter-day reputation as the repository of the unwanted remains of a joint has been no better: in *Movable Feasts* (1952) Arnold Palmer notes that Mrs Beeton's advice on breakfasts consists of little more than suggestions for 'various ways of trapping the head of the family into consuming odd bits of cold meat disguised as rissoles'.

  The content of the rissole has not always been restricted to meat leftovers, however: in the past fish was frequently used, and the fourteenth-century collection *Forme of Cury* gives a vegetarian version: 'Take figs and raisins; pick them and wash them in wine. Grind them with apples and pears pared and picked clean. Do [add] thereto good powders and whole spices; make balls thereof, fry in oil, and serve them forth.'

  In French cuisine, rissoles are enclosed in puff pastry.

Ritz The proprietary name of a crisp savoury biscuit, originally produced in the US by Nabisco in 1934. It exploits the exclusive image of the luxury hotels of that name, which in turn came from that of the Swiss hotelier César Ritz (1850–1918).

roasties A colloquial British term for 'roast potatoes'.

robatayaki In Japanese restaurant cuisine, food that is cooked over a charcoal grill (a *robata*), generally in front of the customers, who have chosen the raw items they want. Japanese *robata* means literally 'open fireplace'.

Robert sauce *See* SAUCE ROBERT.

robusta A type of coffee bean used mainly in the manufacture of instant coffee. The shrub on which it grows is indigenous to West Africa. Its name, first recorded in English in 1908, is a shortening of its original scientific name, *Coffea robusta*, literally 'robust coffee' (it is now designated *C. canephora*). *See also* ARABICA.

rock Rock is familiar to generations of British seaside holidaymakers as a baton of peppermint-flavoured boiled sugar, typically of lurid pink on the outside and with the name of the seaside resort where it was sold running through it in letters of sugar—the 'little stick of Blackpool rock' celebrated by George Formby. It seems to have emerged in the mid-nineteenth century as a particular shape given to the sort of boiled sugar which when crystallized into large irregular lumps was known as *rock*, or more fully *rock candy* (a term now largely restricted to American English, but formerly common in Britain: 'To candy Nutmegs Pour your Candy to them . . . set them in a warm place for about three Weeks, and they will be of a Rock Candy,' John Nott, *Cook's and Confectioner's Dictionary* (1723)). In America it is often crystallized on to string, which was used for making the drink known as *rock and rye* (originally rye whiskey sweetened with rock candy and flavoured with orange, lemon, and sometimes other fruits, but nowadays more conventionally sweetened). The mythical Rock Candy Mountain of M. P. W. Locke's 1906 song, with its bees, cigarette trees, and soda-water fountains, became a modern-day American folkloric symbol of an earthly paradise. *See also* EDINBURGH ROCK.

rock cake These perennial ornaments of the English tea table are named *rock cakes*, or *rock buns*, after their rough craggy appearance, not, as some examples might lead one to believe, from their consistency. Traditionally they are made with currants or other dried fruits (this is how they appear in the first known recipe for them, in Mrs Beeton's *Book of Household Management* (1861), where they are called *rock biscuits*), but other early recipes mention lemon and brandy. In *Movable Feasts* (1952), Arnold Palmer tells how in the 1870s, 'standing at Birch's counter, gentlemen in the City lunched off a glass of sherry with a rock cake or a couple of biscuits'.

Rockefeller *Oysters Rockefeller* is an American way with oysters: they are baked or grilled on the half shell with a savoury topping, typically including chopped spinach and a seasoned sauce (the original version supposedly contained watercress rather than spinach). It is said to have been created at Antoine's, a famous New Orleans restaurant, in the 1890s (although the term is not recorded before 1939). It was named after the US oil magnate and millionaire John D. Rockefeller (1839–1937), allegedly because it is so 'rich'.

rocket A Eurasian plant with spicily hot-tasting dandelion-shaped leaves that are used in salads. It has become much more widely known in Britain following the salad revolution of the late twentieth century. The name *rocket* comes via French *roquette* (which is sometimes used in English, to pretentious effect) from Italian *ruchetta*, a diminutive form of *ruca*, which in turn comes from Latin *eruca*. This meant literally 'caterpillar', and was applied to the plant because of its hairy stems. It may have been derived from *er* 'hedgehog'. American English usually uses the terms *arugula* and *rugola,* which are from the same ultimate source.

rock lobster Apparently Americans find the name *crawfish* a gastronomic turn-off, for when this crustacean appears on restaurant menus or is canned or frozen for sale, it often goes under the disguise of *rock lobster* (originally an alternative name for the spiny lobster).

rock salmon In the British fishmongery trade, the term *rock salmon* covers a multitude of sins. It has been used since at least the 1930s for any fish which, if its real identity were known, would put the customers off. The commonest recipients of the name have been the dogfish and the wolffish. An alternative euphemism also occasionally encountered is *rock eel.*

rocky road A chunky knobbly American sweetmeat made with a mixture of chocolate chips, marshmallows, and nuts, used mainly to flavour ice cream and other desserts. The term is first recorded in 1934.

rogan josh A North Indian dish of curried lamb (or other meat) in a rich tomato-based sauce. The name is from Urdu *rogan još*, literally 'stewed in ghee' (from *rogan* 'ghee, oil' and *-još* 'stew'). The dish is also called *rogan gošt* (Urdu *gošt* 'meat'), which has found its way into English as *rogan gosht* or *rogan ghosht*. It is not entirely clear which of the two is the original name.

roll An eatable made by rolling something up, typically into cylindrical form, and especially by rolling pastry, dough, sponge, etc. round some sort of filling: 'Excellent Meat Rolls. Pound veal, chicken, or turkey . . . Form it into small rolls . . . ; fold them in good puff-paste, and bake them', Eliza Acton, *Modern Cookery* (1845). The concept and the name date back to the Middle Ages (a text of 1393 refers to a 'rolle de figges'), and over time they have united in a number of iconic formulations, such as the *sausage roll,* the *spring roll,* and the *Swiss roll* (or, in America, *jelly roll*). In the second half of the sixteenth century the term began to be used for a rolled-up (often round) piece of dough baked into a small individual loaf of bread (a text of 1581 refers to a 'rowle of bread', and we still speak of *bread rolls*). Nowadays such rolls are typically either a component of breakfast ('New novels . . . are now looked for as regularly as rolls for the breakfast table', *Blackwood's Edinburgh Magazine* (1832)), a prelude to a main meal or an accompaniment to its first course, or, with a filling (*cheese roll*, *ham roll*), a snack in their own right.

rollmop A pickled herring that is rolled up, usually round a pickled cucumber. It is a dish of northern Europe, and the word itself is of German extraction: *rollmops*, from *rollen* 'to roll' and *mops* 'pug dog' (which has been interpreted as plural in English, and a new singular, *rollmop*, created). It did not enter the culinary repertoire of the English-speaking world until the early twentieth century, probably via America, and one of the earliest recorded references to it is by Ernest Hemingway in *Torrents of Spring* (1926). It is said to be a cure for hangovers.

roly-poly pudding The word *roly-poly* has had a long and varied history in English. In the seventeenth century it meant 'rascal'. In the eighteenth century it was applied to various sorts of game involving rolling a ball, and also, apparently with facetious intent, to peas: 'Here's your large Rowley Powlies, no more than Six-pence a Peck . . . Rowley Powley, jolly Pease', *Cries of London* (1784). But by the end of the nineteenth century it had found its current home as the name of a comforting sweet suet pudding with a jam filling. Mrs Beeton in her *Book of Household Management* (1861) gives the recipe: 'Make a nice light suet-crust . . . and roll it out to the thickness of about half an inch. Spread the jam equally over it. Roll it up . . . and tie it in a floured cloth; put the pudding into boiling water, and boil for two hours . . . Average cost, 9d.' Thackeray, ever appreciative of the pleasures of the table, was evidently a fan: 'As for the roly-poly, it was too good,' *Book of Snobs* (1848). In the second half of the twentieth century, however, this calorific time-bomb was largely banned from British tables.

romaine The American term for the long-leaved lettuce usually known to British-speakers as the *cos lettuce*. It probably arose from the fact that Rome was its first main port of call on its way from its original home in the eastern Mediterranean to western Europe. Hence the Italians call it *lattuga romana* and the French *laitue romaine* (source of English *romaine*), while the earliest English term for it, dating from the beginning of the seventeenth century, was *Roman lettuce*.

romanesco A variety of cauliflower with pale green florets that rise to a point. According to Niki Segnit in *The Flavour Thesaurus* (2010), it is 'in equal parts famous and frightening for its custard-green colouring and fractal swirls that give it the appearance of an ancient Thai pagoda. Or a prog-rock album cover'. Italian *romanesco* means literally 'of Rome'.

romesco A classic Catalan sauce of which the principal ingredients are tomatoes, garlic, hazelnuts or almonds, and red chillis (in its home province, Tarragona, the small hot romesco peppers are used). It is generally served with grilled fish or poultry.

rooibos A drink (in full *rooibos tea*) made by infusing the leaves of an evergreen South African shrub of the pea family. The Afrikaans word, first recorded in English in 1911, means literally 'red bush', a reference to the colour of the oxidized leaves. *See also* BUSH TEA.

root beer A sweetened carbonated non-alcoholic American beverage flavoured with extracts of various roots and herbs. The underlying concept of the drink is no doubt an ancient one, but it seems first to have emerged under the name *root beer* in the 1840s. This modern version is said to have been created by a Philadelphia pharmacist called Charles

Hires. It is still around, not having succumbed entirely to the tidal wave of cola drinks, but it has never really caught on to any extent outside the US.

Roquefort A blue-veined French ewes'-milk cheese made in and named after Roquefort-sur-Soulzon, a village in southern France, to the northwest of Montpellier. It is matured in the local caves, which harbour the mould (*Penicillium roquefortii*) that produces the cheese's distinctive greenish-blue veining (although nowadays the process has to be induced artificially). According to specious legend, the cheese was 'discovered' by a shepherd who left the remains of his bread-and-cheese lunch in a cave, and when he returned some months later, mould from the bread had transferred its blueness to the cheese. It is mild but rich in flavour, but less distinguished examples can be aggressively salty. It has been made for thousands of years (it is mentioned, for instance, by Pliny), but the earliest known record of it in English is not before 1776. In British English the first syllable of its name is pronounced as if it were *rock*, but American English prefers *roke*.

rosé *Rosé* wine is pink—the word (first recorded in English in the 1890s) comes from French *vin rosé*, 'pink, or literally rose-coloured wine'. It can be made simply by blending red and white wine, but the better sort of rosé is produced from red grapes by leaving the pressed juice in contact with the skins for only a short period. Despite, or perhaps because of the fact that the Portuguese Mateus rosé sells in massive quantities, rosé has always had something of a downmarket image, admitted as a good summer quaffing wine when drunk chilled but not highly regarded (the exceptions are *Tavel*, a robust deep-pink 'serious' rosé from the Southern Rhône area, *rosé des Riceys*, a still pink wine made in minute quantities in the Champagne area which connoisseurs consider the world's finest rosé, and pink champagne itself, which has the cachet of fashion). Then in the 1980s American marketing men took a hand. There was in California a lot of spare capacity for red wine, which was not selling well. Why not, they said, vinify the red grapes as pink wine, but call the result not by the discredited name *rosé*, but by a new and arresting title? And so *blush wine* was born, which has since spawned imitators in Australia, Germany, Italy, and even France.

rosemary *Rosemary*, the name of a bushy herb which is related to the lavender, has no etymological connection with either *rose* or *Mary*, although both of them have influenced the present-day form of the word. In Middle English it was *rosmarine*. This came, possibly through Old French *rosmarin* or Middle Dutch *rosemarine*, from Latin *rōs marīnus*, which meant literally 'sea-dew' (a reference probably to its growing near the sea). Rosemary was grown regularly in Britain from medieval times, and was used as much for its medicinal properties as for its pleasantly aromatic flavour (not forgetting its symbolic significance—it stood for 'remembrance', as Ophelia famously observed). But its popularity seems gradually to have declined, and by the nineteenth century it had all but disappeared from the English repertoire of culinary herbs (Mrs Beeton, for instance, does not mention it at all). Its strong mid-twentieth-century recovery as a partner for lamb (challenging the long supremacy of mint) is a result of Mediterranean influence filtering north with returning holidaymakers.

rose veal Veal from calves that are slaughtered at around nine months, which consequently is of a decidedly reddish pink colour (as opposed to the flesh of calves slaughtered at the conventional time of two-and-a-half to three months, which is a very pale pink). The origins of the term are not entirely clear. It is first recorded, in America, in 1988, and it may be that it was inspired by *Rambling Rose*, the name of a brand of veal launched in the US in 1985 that was produced from free-range, organically reared calves, and was reddish pink in colour. The

variant form *rosé veal,* which is quite frequently encountered, probably arose from a desire to give the expression a little French polish.

rosewater Scented water made with rose petals, used as a perfume and in cookery. It is widely employed in India and the Middle East, perhaps most notably as a flavouring for Turkish delight.

Rosie Lee *Rosie Lee,* British rhyming slang for 'tea', appears to have originated in the early years of the twentieth century. It is first recorded in Edward Fraser and John Gibbons's *Soldier and Sailor Words and Phrases* (1925). The truncated *rosie* was not long in following: 'We'll 'ave the Rosie now, George', J. B. Priestley, *Good Companions* (1929).

rösti Rösti are potatoes fried Swiss-style. They are sliced thinly, sometimes flavoured with onion or bacon, and compacted into a large flat cake for frying. The word is a Swiss-German diminutive form, based ultimately on German *rösten* 'to roast, grill'.

roti A variety of flat unleavened Indian bread cooked on a griddle or in a frying pan. It is similar to a chapati. The words for most Indian breads have only infiltrated English since the 1960s, but *roti* is an exception. Members of the British Army serving in India in the late nineteenth century took it up as a slang term for 'bread', spelling it *rooty* or *rootey*: 'And the 'umble loaf of "rootey" costs a tanner, or a bob', Rudyard Kipling (1900). The long-service medal awarded to British soldiers in India in the early twentieth century was colloquially known as the *rooty gong*, the implication being, according to Eric Partridge in his *Dictionary of Forces' Slang* (1948), that 'the wearer has eaten a tremendous aggregate of Service loaves and therefore deserves it'. The spelling *roti* represents a reborrowing (dating essentially from the 1950s) of the Hindi word, which means literally 'bread'.

rouille A Provençal sauce made from red chillis, garlic, olive oil, and breadcrumbs or potatoes, and served with bouillabaisse or other local fish dishes. The chillis give it a brownish-red colour, whence its name (French *rouille* means literally 'rust').

roulade As its name suggests, a roulade is essentially a dish that is 'rolled' up. In classical French cuisine the term refers to a slice of meat spread with some sort of stuffing, rolled up, and braised, but it has been used in a number of other contexts, including that of Swiss-roll-style cakes and hors d'oeuvres made from smoked salmon and cream cheese. The word means literally 'rolling' in French, and is a derivative of the verb *rouler* 'to roll'.

round In British usage, a *round of beef* is a large round piece of beef, especially a thick disc cut from the hind leg as a joint (in old cookery books, the term refers to what in modern usage is generally called *topside*). In American butchery, *round* is rather more specific: it denotes the entire hind leg of a beef carcase, from the rump to the ankle, from which steaks and joints (such as the *top round*) can be cut. The usage dates back to the seventeenth century.

roux A roux is simply a blend of equal amounts of flour and butter, heated until the flour is cooked. It is used for thickening sauces. There are essentially two sorts: white roux, in which the mixture is taken off the heat as soon as the flour loses its raw taste, and before it has  much of a chance to turn colour; and brown roux, which is cooked a little longer so that it takes on a light brown colour. White roux are probably rather commoner, but ironically it is the brown one which has given the mixture its name. It comes ultimately from Latin *russus* 'red', which passed into French as *roux* 'reddish-brown': hence the phrase *beurre roux* 'browned butter', from which the noun use of *roux* comes.

royal icing Hard white icing made from icing sugar and egg whites, typically used to decorate fruit cakes (for example, as birthday, Christmas, and wedding cakes). A mainly British term, it is first recorded in 1770.

Ruby Murray The popular Ulster-born singer Ruby Murray (1935–96) has found uncovenanted posthumous fame as rhyming slang for *curry*. Her prime was in the late 1950s and early 1960s (when her hits included 'Let Me Go, Lover' and 'Happy Days and Lonely Nights'), and the take-away Indian craze did not really begin in Britain before the 1970s, but the memory was still green enough to make her an obvious choice. As is the way with rhyming slang, the second element is often dispensed with: 'Their idea of a good night out is a ruby washed down with gallons of lager', *Daily Mirror* (1996).

rugelach The Jewish answer to croissants: small crescent-shaped pastries filled with a variety of goodies, such as nuts, raisins, jam, or chocolate. The term, first recorded in English in 1941, comes from Yiddish *rogelekh* or *rogalekh,* the plural of an assumed (but unrecorded) singular **rogele*. The source of that was either Polish *róg* 'horn, corner' with the Yiddish diminutive suffix *-ele* added to it, or Polish *rogal* 'crescent-shaped roll or bun' (itself a derivative of *róg*).

rugola *Rugola,* or *rucola,* is a mainly American term for the salad plant rocket. It comes from a derivative of Italian *ruca* 'rocket' (source of English *rocket*) or its dialectal variant *ruga. See also* ARUGULA.

rum The origins of the name *rum* for a spirit distilled from fermented sugar-cane juice or molasses are obscure. The first recorded reference to the word comes in 1654, in a text later printed by the Connecticut Historical Society: 'Barbados Liquors, commonly called Rum, Kill Deuil, or the like.' However, this is preceded by about three years by this passage, again referring to Barbados: 'The chief fudling [tipple] they make in the Island is Rumbullion, alias Kill-Devill, and this is made of suggar canes distilled, a hott, hellish, and terrible liquor.' The obvious inference to be drawn is that *rum* is an abbreviation of *rumbullion*, a word which did not survive the seventeenth century, but unfortunately that does not get us any further, since no one knows where *rumbullion* comes from.

Sugar cane is not native to the Caribbean—it comes originally from China—and the Spanish introduced it to their colony of Santo Domingo in the sixteenth century. The islands of the Antilles have been making rum from it ever since, from the darkest fiercest molasses-based blackstrap—basis of the British sailor's grog—to the more restrained colourless (or 'white') rums (the most famous brand, Bacardi, was originally made in Cuba, but now comes from Puerto Rico). The English-speaking islands all have their distinctive styles of rum, and the French islands make a richly-flavoured spirit (which they spell *rhum*).

The drink, incidentally, has nothing to do with the adjective *rum* 'odd', which probably comes from Romany.

rumali roti Rumali roti, or *romali roti,* is a type of large, very thin flatbread from North India and Pakistan. The Urdu term means literally 'handkerchief bread'.

rumbledethumps A Scottish dish consisting of potatoes and cabbage mashed up together and browned in the oven. The source of its fanciful name is not on record, but it is presumably onomatopoeic, and may well suggest the effect of the dish on the digestion.

runner bean The runner bean, a plant of tropical American origin cultivated for its edible seed pods, gets its name from the tendrils or 'runners' it produces to support it in its climb up the nearest convenient post or beanpole. When it was first introduced into Britain in the seventeenth century (by John Tradescant, the great plant collector), it was valued mainly for its attractive bright red flowers—hence what seems to have been its original name, *scarlet bean*, first recorded in Philip Miller's *Gardener's Dictionary* (1731). It was around this time that it appears first to have occurred to the British to eat the young pods (not a practice, incidentally, which has caught on to any extent in other parts of the world where it is cultivated). The word *runner* was first applied to it in the nineteenth century, as either *scarlet runner* or simply *runner bean*. The former (which remains the preferred term in American English) was used in the nineteenth century as a piece of mildly insulting slang for 'soldier', on account of their red coats. An alternative name for the bean is *stick bean*. *See also* STRING BEAN.

rusk Rusks are a legacy of Elizabethan naval provisions. They were originally smallish lumps of bread rebaked so as to be indestructible enough to last out a long voyage. The earliest known reference to them comes in an account of Drake's voyages written in 1595: 'The provision...was seven or eight cakes of biscuit or rusk for a man.' The modern, more refined notion of a rusk as a slice of bread crisped by rebaking emerged in the mid-eighteenth century, and already by the end of the century rusks were being recommended as food for very young children (a niche they largely occupy today). The word is an adaptation of Spanish or Portuguese *rosca*, which originally meant literally 'twist, coil', and hence 'twisted piece of bread'.

russet Any of a range of eating apples with a rough golden brown skin, of which the best-known variety is Egremont russet. The application of the term *russet* 'reddish brown' to apples is first recorded as long ago as 1629, but for modern examples at any rate it is something of a misnomer, for russets seldom have any element of red in their colour.

Russian salad A salad of mixed diced vegetables (potatoes, carrots, turnips, French beans, etc.) with mayonnaise. It was originally a somewhat grander dish, containing meat or seafood (such as lobster), and that is still on offer in a full-on French *salade russe*, but the modern tinned version is an altogether more utilitarian affair. The term, which is not used in America, is first recorded in 1846, but history attributes the creation of the salad in its finished form to Lucien Olivier, a French chef working in Moscow in the second half of the nineteenth century (in Russia it is known as *salat oliv'e* 'Olivier salad').

Rusty Nail A cocktail made from whisky and Drambuie. It probably originated, like most cocktails, in the period between the two World Wars. Hopefully its name refers to its colour rather than its taste—or its effect.

rutabaga The American English name for the vegetable known to Britons as the *swede*. It was borrowed into English at the end of the eighteenth century from Swedish dialect *rotabagga* (which means literally 'baggy root'), and at first was used on both sides of the Atlantic (Shelley mentioned it in his *Oedipus Tyrannus* (1820): 'Hog-wash or grains, or ruta-baga, none has yet been ours since your reign begun'—a reference to the pigs' food shortage under the rule of Oedipus). By the twentieth century, however, its range had become restricted largely to North America.

rye Rye is essentially a northern European food-grain. It seems to have originated in northeastern Europe, and was unknown in classical Greece and Rome. The standard brown bread of the European Middle Ages was made from rye, and when northern European settlers later crossed the Atlantic, they brought their dark rye bread with them, contributing a key component to the American sandwich. (Those who were a little better off in medieval times could afford bread made from a mixture of rye and wheat flour, known in English as *maslin*—a word probably derived ultimately from Latin *mistus* 'mixed'.) Probably the commonest use of rye in twenty-first-century Britain is in crispbread (the tradename *Ryvita*, formed from Latin *vīta* 'life', was coined in the mid-1920s).

The Germanic and Slavic words for 'rye' are clearly related, pointing up the cereal's eastern European origins: German has *roggen*, Dutch *rog*, Swedish *rag*, Danish *rug*, Polish *rez*, and Russian *roz*'.

sabayon French borrowed the word *sabayon* from Italian *zabaglione*, and the concept too: it is a sweet confection made from whipped egg yolks and wine. A fashionable late twentieth-century application of it was as a sauce for fruit, flashed briefly under the grill.

The word *sabayon* is also used for a sort of whipped-cream sauce served with fish.

sablé A type of French sweet biscuit with a crumbly texture (the name means literally 'sandy' in French). It is a speciality of Normandy, and especially Caen.

sachertorte Of all the calorie- and cholesterol-clogged confections for which Vienna is famous, none is better known than the sachertorte, the arch-chocolate cake. It was invented by Franz Sacher, Metternich's chief pastrycook, on the occasion of the Congress of Vienna (1814–15). A slice of the cake, with plentiful whipped cream and a cup of coffee, is an essential part of the Vienna tourist circuit, and all the more authentic if consumed at the Sacher Hotel. Basically, sachertorte is a chocolate sponge topped with rich chocolate icing, but there is more to it than that. The small print of the recipe led to a long and celebrated legal wrangle. The descendants of Franz Sacher maintained that the cake must be of two layers, with a jam filling in between (that is the way the Sacher Hotel serves it), but the other great bastion of Viennese patisserie, Demel's, insisted that it should have only one layer, which was spread with jam, the icing then being applied on top. The quarrel went to court, and after six years the Sacher Hotel's recipe was declared to be the true one.

sack Sir John Falstaff had a famous appetite for sack—indeed his bill at the Boar's Head tavern, picked from his pocket by Prince Hal, showed that he had consumed 5s 8d worth of sack—two gallons—as against only a pennyworth of bread (not to mention 2s 6d for 'anchovies and sack after supper'). What was it that he was so hooked on? Sack was an amber-coloured wine made in southern Spain, and first imported into England in any quantity during the reign of Henry VIII. When it left Spain it was dry (the original English name for it was *wyne seck*, a partial translation of French *vin sec* 'dry wine'; the reason for the change from *seck* to *sack* is not known), but the English liked their wine sweet in those days, so it was common to add sugar to it before it was sold. The best sack was named for its source—thus *Palm sack* came from Palma and *Malaga sack* was produced in Malaga. Probably the most familiar was *Sherris sack*, from Jerez ('A good sherris sack hath a two fold operation in it,' said Falstaff. 'It ascends me to the brain . . . makes it apprehensive, quick, forgetive, full of nimble, fiery, and delectable shapes. . . . The second property of your excellent sherris is, the warming of the blood'). This was the lineal ancestor of the modern fortified wine sherry (remembered in the brand name 'Dry Sack'). Most sack was imported via the port of Bristol, and by the mid-seventeenth century it had become widely known as *Bristol milk*, an epithet inherited by sherry. *See also* SEKT.

saddle A cut of meat taken from the part of an animal's body corresponding to where a saddle goes on a horse. It consists essentially of the two loins and the connecting section of backbone. The term, which is used only in relation to lamb, mutton, venison, hare, and rabbit, seems to have emerged in the eighteenth century; a reference in the *Journey through France* (1789) written by Mrs Piozzi, Dr Johnson's friend ('a saddle of mutton, or more properly a chine'), suggests it had not yet become accepted nomenclature. In French, the word for a 'saddle of lamb or venison' is *selle*; for a 'saddle of hare or rabbit', *râble*.

saffron Saffron, the dried stigma of a species of crocus, has always been among the most expensive spices—not surprisingly, since it takes nearly half a million of them to make up a kilo in weight. It has been used since ancient times, particularly for giving its yellow colour and indefinable warm-bitter flavour to cakes and pastries (hot-cross buns are a lineal descendant of saffron cakes used as votive offerings by the Phoenicians). The Romans used it, but do not seem to have introduced it to Britain to any extent, and it was not until the fourteenth century that it began to be frequently used there (but only by the well-off; it then cost as much as 15 shillings per pound). At that time most saffron was imported, but in the later Middle Ages a home-grown saffron industry developed, with saffron plantations being established in Cambridgeshire and Essex (Saffron Walden takes its name from the local saffron industry). Nowadays, saffron's leading role is as a colouring and flavouring ingredient in bouillabaisse, paella, and risotto.

The word *saffron* comes from a Middle Eastern or Arabic language, but its exact source has never been pinpointed. The furthest back its history can be traced is to Arabic *za'farān*, which found its way to English via medieval Latin *safranum* and Old French *safran*. Its use as a colour term, for 'orange-yellow', dates from the late fourteenth century.

sage The name of the herb *sage* reflects the medicinal uses to which it was commonly put in ancient times (as with most herbs, the list of conditions it was supposed to help is too long to repeat in full, but it included diarrhoea, anaemia, and menstrual problems); for it comes via Old French *sauge* from Latin *salvia*, literally 'healing plant', a derivative of the adjective *salvus* 'healthy'. A leading use of sage in English cookery is in stuffings for meat and poultry—a role which goes back for several centuries: 'Sage is used commonly in sauces, as to stuff veal, pork, roasting pigs, and that for good cause', Thomas Cogan, *Haven of Health* (1584). And its classic partnership in such stuffings is with onion: 'Some love the knuckle [of pork] stuffed with onions and sage shred small', Hannah Glasse, *Art of Cookery* (1747). In the Middle Ages the term *sage* was used additionally for a sauce or stuffing of which sage was the most salient ingredient.

The use of *sage* to characterize a particular shade of dull greyish green, like the leaves of the common variety of sage, seems to date from the early nineteenth century.

sage Derby A firm, Cheddar-like cheese, of a type originally made in Derbyshire, to which juice obtained from sage leaves (and sometimes also spinach) is added to give a characteristic flavour and a mottled green colour. Another, less well known variety of *sage cheese* (a term first recorded in 1714) is *sage Lancashire*, which contains chopped-up sage leaves.

sago A powdered starch obtained from the pith of a palm tree (genus *Metroxylon*) which grows in India and Southeast Asia. In Richard Hakluyt's account of Sir Francis Drake's voyages (1580), the inhabitants of the East Indies are reported as using it for making bread and cakes: 'We received of them meale, which they call Sagu, made of the tops of certaine trees . . . whereof they make certaine cakes.' Transported to the Western kitchen, however, its main culinary use has been in the making of insipid and glutinous milk puddings whose sufferers must often have wished that more of the annual production of sago were put to its other use, as a textile stiffener. The first English cookery writer to mention sago is Hannah Glasse in 1747 (it was then frequently employed for thickening broths), while Elizabeth Raffald in her *English Housekeeper* (1769) uses the term *sago* to mean 'runny pudding made from sago'—she writes of 'gruels, sagos, and wheys'.

The word *sago* itself comes from Malay *sagu*, and as the above extract relating to Sir Francis Drake suggests, that was the form in which it first entered English; the modern spelling comes from Dutch *sago*.

Saint Clements A mixed drink made from orange juice with lemonade or bitter lemon. The name, coined in the 1980s, refers to the first line of a well-known children's song: 'Oranges and lemons, say the bells of St Clements'. 'St Clements' probably originally referred to the church of St Clement Eastcheap, in the City of London, which in times past stood by the wharves at which oranges and lemons from the Mediterranean were unloaded, but the line is now usually associated with St Clement Danes in the Strand.

Sainte-Menehould In French cuisine, *à la Menehould* denotes a dish in which the principal ingredient (typically pig's trotters) is cooked and then allowed to cool before being coated in breadcrumbs and grilled. It is then served with a mustard sauce. The term comes from the town of Sainte-Menehould in the Marne region of northeastern France, where the recipe originated. According to the *Oxford Companion to Food* (2006), Alexandre Dumas in *Le Grand Dictionnaire de Cuisine* (1873) reports 'an anecdote which has the French King Charles VII [(1403–61)], famished after a battle with the English, supping on the dish, which had been improvised for him and his companions by a woman in the little town of Sainte-Menehould'. The vernacular English equivalent is called *park railings*.

Saint Emilion A French chocolate dessert made by cooking chocolate, butter, sugar, eggs, and milk into a creamy custard, pouring it over macaroons, and allowing it to cool.

Saint George's mushroom A common European variety of edible mushroom that has a creamy white cap and white gills. It often first appears around Saint George's Day (23 April).

Saint-Honoré A French gateau consisting of a puff-pastry base surmounted by a circle of choux buns, which is filled with whipped cream and finished off with a topping of caramelized sugar. It was named after Saint Honorius, sixth-century bishop of Amiens and patron saint of pastry cooks, who is also remembered in the Rue du Faubourg Saint-Honoré in Paris.

Saint-Nectaire A soft French cows'-milk cheese, made in flat discs. It is a product of the Auvergne region of central France. It is named after Henri de Sennectere, marshal of France and lord of Saint-Nectaire, who introduced it to the court of Louis XIV in the seventeenth century.

Saint-Paulin A soft French cows'-milk cheese, made in flat discs. Developed from cheeses of the Port-du-Salut type, which were originally made in monasteries (hence the religious name), it is made all over France.

sake Sake, or *saki*, is a Japanese alcoholic drink made from fermented rice. In English it is often categorized under the generic term *rice wine*, which is rather misleading since the process of manufacture resembles brewing more than winemaking. Sake is drunk warm, traditionally in small bowls. Since it was for long the only source of alcohol the Japanese had, *sake* has come to signify in Japanese 'alcohol' in general.

salad Etymologically, the key ingredient of *salad*, and the reason for its getting its name, is the dressing. The Romans were enthusiastic eaters of salads, many of theirs differing hardly at all from present-day ones—a simple selection of raw vegetables, for example, such as lettuce, cucumber, and endive—and they always used a dressing of some sort: oil, vinegar, or often brine. And hence the name *salad*, which comes from Vulgar Latin *herba salāta*, literally 'salted herb'. The Romans' salad dressings were not always so straightforward, however; the food writer Apicius gives a recipe for one containing ginger, rue, dates, pepper, honey, cumin, and vinegar.

The Romans introduced the salad to Britain. It seems not to have survived their departure, but was enthusiastically revived in the Middle Ages (the word *salad* first appears in English in the late fourteenth century, and until the eighteenth century it retained the alternative guise *sallet*). Medieval salads were colourful but simple mixtures of raw leaves and herbs, enlivened with flowers, but by the late sixteenth century it had become common to add fruit, such as oranges and lemons. The seventeenth century was perhaps the great age of the salad: 'grand salads' graced the tables of the rich, and cold meats began to appear among the list of ingredients. In 1699 John Evelyn published his classic work on salads, *Acetaria, a Discourse of Sallets*, in which he notes, to the approval of all vegetarians, that the 'excellent Emperor Tacitus' was 'us'd to say of Lettuce, that he did *somnum se mercari* [buy himself sleep] when he eat of them, and call'd it a sumptuous Feast, with a Sallet and a single Pullet, which was usually all the Flesh-Meat that sober Prince eat of; whilst Maximus (a profess'd Enemy to Sallet) is reported to have scarce been satisfied, with sixty Pounds of Flesh, and Drink proportionable'.

Thereafter, salads went into something of a decline in Britain, and by Victorian times were decidedly limp (Mrs Beeton's recipes, for instance, are not at all inspiring). The mass introduction of a new component, the tomato, towards the end of the nineteenth century, did nothing to rescue the salad from its doldrums, and for the first two thirds of the twentieth century British salad-eaters were nine times out of ten condemned to an unchanging diet of lettuce (always, for some reason, the outside leaves), sliced cucumber, tart tomatoes, and vinegary beetroot with, if it were a main course, a wafer of tasteless ham or a piece of cheese. Small wonder the salad had a dire reputation, particularly amongst those with a distrust of eaters of 'rabbit food': 'The parlour cars and Pullmans are packed also with scented assassins, salad-eaters who murder on milk', W. H. Auden, *Age of Anxiety* (1947). It was not really until the 1970s that the salad situation began to brighten, with, on the one hand, the growing commercial availability of a wide range of mixed salads from various foreign cuisines, and on the other the introduction of many salad leaves scarcely used in Britain for centuries, including curly endive and numerous varieties of lettuce.

Today the concept of the salad is a fairly complex one. At the most basic level is the simple *green salad*, consisting of raw leaves from plants such as lettuce, endive, chicory, and cress, with a dressing. The next step up is to a *plain salad*, which typically consists of one simple main ingredient dressed with mayonnaise, a vinaigrette, etc. This could be meat, seafood, or, if a vegetable, one (such as beans) which has been cooked and allowed to go cold. This type of dish probably has its origins in the *boiled salad* of former times, which first appeared on the European scene as a way of preparing spinach in the later fourteenth century. In Britain it has sunk to the depths of potato salad and 'vegetable salad' in commercial salad cream. Thirdly comes the *mixed salad*, an elaborate assemblage of a wide range of raw, or cold cooked, ingredients, no one element upstaging the others but all contributing to the overall effect of flavour and appearance (*salade niçoise* is an example). All these salads have the common factor of coldness. But in recent years, nouvelle cuisine has introduced the concept of the *salade tiède*, literally 'warm salad', in which the main ingredient (liver, for example) is still warm from stove or pan.

When to eat salads? For the Romans they were hors d'oeuvres, and a substantial enough dish can serve as a main course in its own right. But considerable variation in practice exists over whether a salad course in a meal should be served with or after the main course.

But one type of salad whose placement in a meal could cause no trouble is the *fruit salad*, an assortment of chopped-up fruit apparently first mentioned by Mrs Beeton in 1861 (the application of the term to an ostentatious array of medal ribbons is Second World War services slang). The characteristics it shares with the more usual type of salad are rawness and variety—and it is the notion of profuse variety that lies behind the more metaphorical applications of the word *salad* in modern times. In an 1893 issue of the New York *Nation*, for instance, a writer noted that 'close at hand the building is an entertaining salad of styles'.

The expression *salad days* 'time of youthful inexperience' originated in Shakespeare's *Anthony and Cleopatra*: 'my salad days, when I was green in judgment, cold in blood', but does not seem to have been generally taken up until the mid-nineteenth century.

salad cream This commercial substitute for mayonnaise came on the scene in the mid-nineteenth century; the first known reference to it is in Peter Simmonds's *Dictionary of Trade Products* (1858). It originated in *salad sauce*, a traditional English dressing for salads whose essential ingredients were cooked egg yolks and cream, as opposed to the raw egg yolks and olive oil of mayonnaise; but bottled salad dressing, with its dried egg, acetic acid, flour, and a laboratory-full of additives, bears little resemblance to it. Customers trading up to commercially bottled mayonnaise has threatened the continued existence of salad cream, but when in 1999 Heinz announced that it was withdrawing its brand, it was deluged with protests from loyal salad-cream fans and compelled to back down.

salade niçoise A salad typically containing tuna (or anchovy), hard-boiled eggs, small black olives, and tomatoes, and optionally also such items as raw onion, green peppers, young broad beans, and artichoke hearts. The French term means literally 'salad of Nice'. Elizabeth David, in *A Book of Mediterranean Food* (1950), speculates that the dish may have originated in *pan bagn*, a traditional Provençal sandwich containing a selection of the same ingredients.

salami A type of highly spiced sausage, typically made with pork and flavoured with garlic, that originated in Italy (a version with donkey meat is made in Hungary). In common with *salad*, *sauce*, and *sausage*, its name derives from Latin *sal* 'salt'. It is the plural of *salame* 'salt pork', a derivative of the Italian verb *salare* 'to salt'. It is a large sausage, eaten sliced, and this has given rise to various metaphorical uses of the word which rely on the notion of 'slicing up': *salami tactics*, for instance, a 1950s coinage, refers to 'piecemeal erosion of one's opponent's resources', and the *Sunday Times* (1988) referred to a 'salami-slicing approach to Britain's defences', a sort of fragmentary cheese-paring.

salep A starchy powder made from the dried tubers of various orchids. It is used in a range of culinary roles, notably as a thickener for milk drinks and ice creams, in the Middle East, southwestern Asia, and southeastern Europe. In eighteenth- and nineteenth-century England there was a fashion for a sweetened and flavoured hot drink thickened with salep, which went under the name *saloop* or *salop* and was sold on the streets of London: 'The vending of tea and coffee, in the streets, was little . . . known twenty years ago, saloop being then the beverage supplied from stalls', Henry Mayhew, *London Labour and the London Poor* (1851). The word came into English in the mid-eighteenth century from French, which got it from Turkish. That in turn came from Arabic *khusa ath-tha·lab*, literally 'fox's testicles', which was the name of an orchid (the reference is to the shape of the plant's tubers, as it is in the case of English *orchid,* which comes ultimately from Greek *orkhis* 'testicle').

Salisbury steak In American English, *Salisbury steak* is an upmarket name for a hamburger. It commemorates J. H. Salisbury (1823–1905), a doctor well known for his public pronouncements on dietary matters. One of his hobby horses was the hamburger, which he recommended people to eat three times a day. The term is first recorded in 1897, but it really came into its own during the First World War, when patriotic Americans took exception to the German *hamburger* (*see* LIBERTY CABBAGE). It has continued to be used on menus in the sort of restaurant that would not own up to selling hamburgers.

Sally Lunn Sally Lunns are large buns or teacakes made with a yeast dough including cream, eggs, and spice. They are generally supposed to take their name from a late eighteenth-century baker, Sally Lunn, who according to W. J. France in *Up-to-date Breadmaking* (1968) had a pastry cook's shop in Lilliput Alley in Bath. The earliest source of the story seems to be William Hone's *Every-day Book* (1827): 'The bun . . . called the Sally Lunn originated with a young woman of that name in Bath, about 30 years ago. She first cried them. . . . Dalmer, a respectable baker and musician, noticed her, bought a business, and made a song in behalf of Sally Lunn.' Although the '30 years' seems to be an understatement, this is not inconsistent with the first two recorded references to the word: in Philip Thickenesse's *Valetudinarian's Bath Guide* (1780): 'I had the misfortune to lose a beloved brother in the prime of life, who dropt down dead as he was playing on the fiddle at Sir Robert Throgmorton's after drinking a large quantity of Bath Waters, and eating a hearty breakfast of spungy hot rolls, or Sally Luns'; and the *Gentleman's Magazine* (1798): 'A certain sort of hot rolls, now, or not long ago, in vogue at Bath, were gratefully and emphatically styled "Sally Lunns".'

However, there exists a French cake, reputedly of Alsatian origin (though this remains unsubstantiated), called *solilem* or *solimeme* which is fairly similar to the Sally Lunn (Eliza Acton, who includes a recipe for it in her *Modern Cookery* (1845), calls it *solimemne* and describes it as a 'rich French breakfast cake'), and it may be that both *Sally Lunn* and *solilem* derive ultimately from French *soleil lune* 'sun and moon (cake)', golden on top over a paler base.

In the southern states of the US, the term *Sally Lunn* stands for a variety of yeast and soda breads.

salmagundi An elaborate salad typically consisting of cold meat, vegetables cooked or raw, eggs, pickles, anchovies—virtually anything, in fact (it is no accident that the word has also been used figuratively for a 'miscellaneous mixture' or 'hotchpotch')—served artistically arranged in rows and circles on a large plate. English acquired the word as long ago as the seventeenth century, from French, and has had some fun with it since—*sallad-magundy* and *Solomon Gundy* have been among its transmogrifications—but it is not known what its ultimate origin was. One suggestion is that it was based on French *sal* 'salt' and the verb *condir* 'to season'. *Salmi* derives from it.

salmi A salmi, or in French *salmis*, is a dish made by partly roasting a bird, particularly a game bird such as a grouse or partridge, and then slicing it up and stewing it in a rich sauce based on wine and the cooking juices. The word, which is generally assumed to be an abbreviation of *salmagundi*, is first recorded in English in William Verral's *Complete System of Cookery* (1759). It was quite a popular dish in Britain in Victorian times—Mrs Beeton gives a recipe for salmi of partridge, which she alternatively calls 'hashed partridges'.

saloop *See* SALEP.

salpicon A mixture of finely chopped meat, fish, vegetables, or eggs bound together in a thick sauce and used for fillings and stuffings. The word comes via French from Spanish *salpicón*, a compound formed from *sal* 'salt' and the verb *picar* 'to prick, mince, chop'. It is of quite long standing in English, being first mentioned in John Nott's *Cook's and Confectioner's Dictionary* (1723).

salsa Spanish and Italian *salsa* means 'sauce'. Both go back ultimately to Latin *salsus* 'salted'. In Latin America, the term denotes a spicy or sharp vegetable-based (or fruit-based) mix that can be either fresh (*salsa cruda*) or cooked. As it started to become more familiar in the English-speaking world in the twentieth century, it tended to become focused on a spicy tomato sauce, but latterly cooks have begun to interpret it more adventurously: Nigella Lawson, for example, in her *Kitchen* (2010), gives a recipe for 'avocado salsa' that incorporates avocado, green chillis, coriander, and lime juice.

The metaphorical extension of the word to a type of dance music incorporating elements of jazz and rock took place in Latin American Spanish. It made its first appearance in English in the 1970s.

salsa verde In Italian cookery *salsa verde*, literally 'green sauce', is a sauce made with olive oil, garlic, capers, anchovies, vinegar or lemon juice, and a large quantity of chopped parsley. It is the classic accompaniment to bollito misto, and is also used with fish.

In Mexican cookery, the term denotes a sauce of finely chopped onion, garlic, coriander, parsley, and hot peppers.

salsify There is much confusion over the terms *salsify* and *scorzonera*. Both apply to long thin white-fleshed root vegetables of the daisy family, but although strictly speaking *salsify* is the name of the white-skinned variety and *scorzonera* is the name of the black-skinned variety, it is virtually impossible to find the white-skinned variety in shops, and the black one seems more often to be called *salsify* than *scorzonera*.

Both were introduced to Britain towards the end of the seventeenth century, probably from France. They were originally cultivated in Italy (the term *salsify* is of Italian origin), but were also very popular from early times in Spain (the scorzonera's scientific name is *Scorzonera hispanica*).

The history of the word *salsify* is no less confusing than its current usage. English got it from French *salsifis*, which in turn borrowed it from Italian, but in what form? The modern Italian word is *sassefrica*, and one school of thought says that this came from late Latin *saxifrica*, literally 'rock-rubber', a compound name for various plants which was formed from *saxum* 'rock' and *fricāre* 'to rub'. According to this view the change from *sas-* to *sal-* presumably took place in French, which once had the form *sassefrique*. Others, however, claim that French got *salsifis* from a now obsolete Italian form *salsefica*, which was short for *erba salsifica*. It is not known where this came from, but it may have some connection with Latin *sal* 'salt'.

The salsify is sometimes known as the *vegetable oyster*.

salt Salt, a basic necessity of the human diet, has been extracted from the environment—boiled down from sea water, mined, obtained from salt springs, etc.—since at least the Neolithic period. Until comparatively recently it was vital to the preserving of food, and especially of meat during the winter, and such was its economic importance that wars were fought for the sake of ensuring supplies. Its cultural centrality is hinted at by such linguistic relatives as English *salary*, which originated as a Latin term for an allowance given to soldiers to pay for salt, Russian *khleb-sol'* 'hospitality', which means literally 'bread-salt', and of course the English expressions *salt of the earth* 'admired person' (a reference to the Sermon on the Mount, 'Ye are the salt of the earth,' Matthew, 5:13), *worth one's salt* (from the former practice of paying in salt rather than cash), and *below the salt* (from the former placing of a salt cellar in the place of honour at the top table). The word *salt* itself comes ultimately from Indo-European **sal-*, which produced the term for 'salt' in the majority of other European languages (including French *sel*, Italian *sale*, Spanish *sal*, German *salz*, Dutch *zout*, and Russian *sol'*). *Salad* and *sausage* are derived from it.

Today's *table salt* is manufactured, with various additives, from common salt extracted from earth. Other varieties of salt include *rock salt*, obtained from salt mines; *sea salt*, produced by evaporating sea water; *bay salt*, a cruder form of sea salt, whose name comes from its original source, Bourgneuf Bay, at the mouth of the River Loire in France; and salt from salt springs, formerly known as *brine salt*.

saltfish The Caribbean English term for cod that has been preserved in salt. Served with ackee, onions, and peppers, it forms the national dish of Jamaica. It is also commonly partnered with callaloo.

saltimbocca An Italian dish consisting of thin pieces of veal, each individually wrapped inside a slice of prosciutto ham with a sage leaf, and braised in wine. Its name means literally 'jump into the mouth', presumably a tribute to the deliciousness of the dish.

saltine An American term, first recorded in 1907, for a thin crisp savoury biscuit usually sprinkled with salt. It was coined from *salt* with the noun suffix *-ine*.

sambal In Southeast Asian cooking, a sambal is a hot mixture of chillies and spices, used as a relish with other foods.

sambar A fiercely spicy South Indian dish consisting of lentils cooked with tamarind and vegetables: 'Excellent, crisp dosas had a delectably soft underside: ideal for dipping into soupy sambar', *Time Out London, Eating and Drinking* (2008). Its name, in Tamil *cāmpār*, comes via Marathi from Sanskrit *sambhāra* 'collection, materials'.

Sambuca An Italian aniseed-flavoured liqueur. The traditional way of serving it in Rome is to set light to it, having first floated a coffee bean on top (known in Italian as *con la mosca* 'with the fly'). The liqueur's name refers to its original flavouring ingredient, elder (*sambuco* is Italian for 'elder').

samosa An Indian snack consisting of small deep-fried cones of pastry stuffed with a spicy mixture of diced vegetables or meat. The word is Hindi.

samphire *Samphire* is a confusing term, for it refers to two completely unrelated plants. The original *samphire*, a member of the carrot family, grows on coastal rocks—whence its name, which is a garbling of French *(herbe de) St Pierre* 'St Peter's herb', an allusion to its rocky habitat (*Peter* comes from a Greek word for 'rock'). Its aromatic leaves have long been used in pickles, and people ran considerable risks to gather it (Edgar in *King Lear*, staring over the imaginary cliff edge, conjured up the vertiginousness of their situation: 'Halfway down hangs one that gathers samphire, dreadful trade! Methinks he seems no bigger than his head'). Much more familiar under the name *samphire* nowadays, however, is an altogether different plant, genus *Salicornia*, which first had the term (in full *marsh samphire*) applied to it in the eighteenth century. It grows in saltmarshes, and has fleshy succulent leaves that can be eaten as a vegetable, lightly boiled or steamed (no need to add salt). Its alternative name, *glasswort*, refers to the former use of ash from its burnt leaves in making glass.

Samsoe A mild Danish cows'-milk cheese (in Danish, *Samsø*) with small irregular holes. It was originally produced at the beginning of the nineteenth century by Swiss cheese-makers on the island of Samsø, which lies in the channel between Jutland and Zealand.

San Daniele A type of Italian raw ham produced in and around San Daniele del Friuli in the province of Udine, in northeastern Italy. It is probably the best-known variety of *prosciutto crudo* after Parma ham. Originally it was made only from the black pigs of Friuli, but that exclusivity has now been relaxed.

sanders Sanders, or *saunders*, was a nineteenth-century method of getting rid of the leftovers of a joint of beef or mutton, a prototype of the shepherd's pie. It is first mentioned in 1806, in Mrs Rundell's *New System of Cookery*, and Eliza Acton gives a recipe in *Modern Cookery* (1845): 'Spread on the dish . . . a layer of mashed potatoes. . . . On these spread . . . some beef or mutton minced. . . . Place evenly over this another layer of potatoes, and send the dish to a moderate oven for half an hour' (the French make their version of shepherd's pie, *hachis Parmentier*, with potatoes below as well as above the mince). The origin of the term is obscure, but presumably it comes from a real or supposed inventor of the dish, now safely anonymous.

sandwich So keen a gambler was John Montagu, 11th Earl of Sandwich, that he could not bear to tear himself away from the card table even for a meal. Once he spent 24 hours at a stretch there, and in order to stave off hunger he armed himself with a portable meal consisting of a piece of cold beef between two slices of toast. There was nothing new in using bread as a sort of wrapper for various ingredients—the practice must be as old as bread itself—but if the Frenchman Grosley is to be believed, writing in his *Londres* (1770), this was the incident which led to the resultant article of food being termed a *sandwich*. The first actual written record of the word comes in the journal of the historian Edward Gibbon for 24 November 1762: 'I dined at the Cocoa Tree. . . . That respectable body affords every evening a sight truly English. Twenty or thirty of the first men in the kingdom . . . supping at little tables . . . upon a bit of cold meat, or a Sandwich.' 'Printed recipes for sandwiches . . . began to appear from the 1820s, filled with ham, tongue, and mustard, roast beef or potted shrimp, cut small and "served upon a napkin"', Kate Colquhoun, *Taste* (2007). It was well enough established by the mid-nineteenth century to be used metaphorically as a verb, meaning 'insert between two things of another type', and at about the same time the sight of somebody carrying a pair of advertising boards suspended from his shoulders, one in front and one behind, inspired the terms *sandwich board* and *sandwich man* (the connection was perhaps first made by Charles Dickens: 'So, he stopped the unstamped advertisement—an animated sandwich, composed of a boy between two boards,' *Sketches by Boz* (1839)).

The term *sandwich* has attracted many colloquial synonyms, the main British ones being *butty* and *sarnie*. See also BLT, CLUB SANDWICH, OPEN SANDWICH, SUBMARINE.

sandwich cake A sponge cake consisting of a layer of filling, such as cream or jam, sandwiched between two layers of sponge. *See also* VICTORIA SANDWICH.

sandwich spread *See* SPREAD.

Sangiovese A variety of red-wine grape that is very widely planted in Italy and forms the base of the blend for, among many other wines, chianti. The Italian name comes from Latin *sanguis Jovis*, literally 'Jove's blood'.

sangria A sort of Spanish cold punch made from red wine, typically with the addition of fruit juice and soda water, and often also brandy and sliced fruit. The Spanish word *sangría* means literally 'bleeding' (it is a derivative of *sangre* 'blood'). It was originally borrowed into English in the early eighteenth century in the modified form *sangaree*, a term which has subsequently come to be applied in American English to an iced sweetened drink based on wine, sherry, beer, etc. and flavoured with nutmeg.

sapodilla The brownish round or oval bristly fruit of a large evergreen tropical American tree that also produces chicle, the raw material of chewing gum. Its taste, according to Jane Grigson in her *Fruit Book* (1982), 'reminds people of brown sugar'. Its name is a seventeenth-century adaptation of Latin American Spanish *zapotillo*, a diminutive form based on *zapote* (*see* SAPOTE).

sapote The name given to a heterogeneous group of tropical American fruits, most but not all of which are borne by trees of the family Sapotaceae. The best known are the sapodilla, which is also called *sapote*, and the unrelated *white sapote*, which has small, pale yellow fruit that taste like pears and is widely cultivated in Central America and also in California and Florida. The word is an Anglicization of Latin American Spanish *zapote*, from Nahuatl *tzápotl*.

sapsago A type of American (originally Swiss) hard cheese. It is made from skim milk, and comes in the form of a tapering cylinder. It gets its greenish colour and idiosyncratic flavour from the powdered aromatic leaves of the blue melilot that are mixed into it. The name is an alteration of German *schabziger*, a compound formed from the verb *schaben* 'to grate' and *ziger*, a type of cheese.

sarladaise Potatoes cooked *à la sarladaise* are a speciality of the Périgord region of southwestern France: thinly sliced potatoes are sautéed in goose fat and then sprinkled with garlic and parsley. French *sarladais* means 'of Sarlat', a town in the Périgord where goose fat is in plentiful supply.

sarsaparilla A sweet drink flavoured with an extract of the dried root of a tropical American climbing plant. It was taken up by the Spanish conquistadors, mainly for its supposed medicinal properties, and it was those that tended to be emphasized when the drink began to be commercially produced on a significant scale in America in the second half of the nineteenth century. The word, first recorded in the late sixteenth century, is an Anglicization of Spanish *zarzaparilla*, a compound formed from *zarza* 'bramble' and *parilla* 'little vine'.

sashimi For Westerners, sashimi is perhaps the archetypal Japanese dish: thinly sliced raw fish served typically with grated horseradish or with a ginger and soy sauce. The preparation of the fish, with a villainously sharp knife, is a skill perfected with long practice. The Japanese word is a compound formed from *sashi* 'to pierce' and *mi* 'flesh'.

satay A Malaysian and Indonesian food, consisting of small spicy meatballs speared on skewers (traditionally made from the stems of coconut leaves), grilled or barbecued, and typically served with a peanut sauce. It is street-food, sold by vendors to passing trade. The name is Malay.

satsuma A small, loose-skinned, seedless orange, *Citrus reticulata*, similar to the tangerine and mandarin. It takes its name from Satsuma, a former province of Kyushu, Japan, where it was first grown; it first appeared in the West in the 1880s.

sauce Robert A classic French piquant sauce typically served with grilled meat, especially pork chops. It is made with reduced white wine and a basic brown sauce (*sauce espagnole*) to which mustard is added. The term is first recorded in English in 1723, its now seldom used Anglicized form *Robert sauce* somewhat earlier, in 1702. It is not known who Robert the sauce's presumable inventor was. Some have identified him with a late sixteenth-century French cook called Robert Vinot, but the sauce seems to have been around before him: François Rabelais, in his *Le Quart Livre* (1552), refers to 'Robert, the inventor of Robert sauce'.

sauce vierge In French cuisine, a very simple sauce made from melted butter and lemon juice: 'monkfish with chive mash perked up by sauce vierge', *Time Out London, Eating and Drinking* (2009). French *vierge* means 'virgin'.

sauerbraten A dish, German in origin but American by adoption, of beef marinated in vinegar with peppercorns, onions, garlic, and bay leaves before being baked or pot-roasted. The German name, first recorded in English in 1889, means literally 'sour roast meat'.

sauerkraut The technique of salting down cabbage to preserve and ferment it was familiar to the Romans; the writer Pliny mentions it. But it is as a German and Austrian dish, *sauerkraut* (literally 'sour cabbage'—*kraut* generally means 'leafy plant', but it is also a dialect word for 'cabbage'), that it has achieved classic status. White cabbage is finely shredded and packed in layers with salt in a large jar; and over two to three weeks it ferments in the brine formed from its juices and the salt. James Hart, in his *Diet of the Diseased* (1633), described the process: 'They pickle [cabbage] up in all high Germany, with salt and barberries, and so keep it all the year, being commonly the first dish they have served in at table, which they call their *sawerkraut*.' In Alsace in northeastern France, on the German border, sauerkraut has become *choucroute*, and *choucroute garnie* is a traditional Alsatian speciality: the sauerkraut is cooked with a knuckle of ham and pieces of shoulder or smoked belly of pork and served additionally with poached Strasbourg sausages and potatoes. The Anglicized form *sourcrout* is first recorded in 1617. In the US during the First World War the term *liberty cabbage* was substituted for *sauerkraut*, because of anti-German sentiment.

sausage One of the first convenience foods, the sausage's very name preserves its preservative origins: it goes back, via Old Northern French *saussiche*, to medieval Latin *salsicia* 'sausage', which was a derivative of Latin *salsus* 'salted'. The Romans introduced into northern and western Europe the cylindrical sausage of spiced minced meat stuffed into a skin of animal intestine; the gourmet Apicius (1st century AD) has a recipe in which you pound meat with a great variety of herbs and spices, 'plenty of fat and pine kernels, insert into an intestine, drawn out very thinly, and hang in the smoke'. This is the dry sausage (the French *saucisson*), often known in Britain as 'continental' sausage or, in the nineteenth century, as 'German sausage', and until recent changes in taste rather distrusted in some quarters for its threat of garlic and nameless parts of animals. The wet sausage, however (the French *saucisse*; the sort that needs to be cooked), has become so much a part of the baggage of national sentiment that we use it as a term of endearment, as in 'You silly old sausage!' Also, another sure sign of affection, it has several colloquial synonyms: *banger* (probably a reference to the noise of a frying sausage) is first recorded from Australia just after the First World War, while *dog* appeared in America in the mid-nineteenth century (*see* HOT DOG); *see also* BAGS OF MYSTERY, SNAG. The German term *wurst*, incidentally, which is increasingly permeating the language via American English, is a reference to the sausage's cylindrical shape; it comes ultimately from Latin *vertere* 'to turn, roll'.

sauvignon blanc A grape variety used to make white wine. Its home ground is Bordeaux, where it plays an increasingly large role in the dry white wines and also contributes to many sweet Sauternes and Barsacs. But it is also planted widely elsewhere in France, notably on the upper Loire, where it is made into Sancerre and Pouilly-Fumé, and in other parts of the world, including California and (with notable success) New Zealand. Its lightness and fresh aroma (variously compared to gooseberries, currant leaves, grass, and cat's piss) have made it second only to chardonnay in popularity and fashionableness among white-wine grapes at the beginning of the twenty-first century. The origins of its name (which reappears in *cabernet sauvignon*) are uncertain.

savarin A large ring-shaped cake made with yeast-leavened dough, moistened usually with rum-flavoured syrup, and served with a filling of fruit, cream, etc. It was named after Antoine Brillat-Savarin (1755–1826), the French gourmet who wrote *Physiologie du goût* (1825) ('Physiology of taste'), a series of observations on the theory and practice of gastronomy.

saveloy The nineteenth century was the great age of the saveloy, a highly seasoned smoked sausage made of pork. Charles Dickens was among the first to celebrate it, in *Pickwick Papers* (1837): 'Mr Simon Pell . . . regaling himself . . . with a cold collation of an Abernethy biscuit and a saveloy' (a theme continued in the 'pease pudding and saveloys' of 'Food, glorious food' in Lionel Bart's musical *Oliver*). Already by the end of the century, though, it had acquired a rather downmarket image, as witness Samuel Smiles's 1887 picture of the chef Alexis Soyer slumming: 'Soyer, the gastronomist . . . , would stop at a stall in the Haymarket and luxuriate in eating a penny saveloy.' And nowadays the saveloy is often a distinctly dubious proposition, its traditional recipe of fine pork replaced by a less easily definable mixture frequently concealed behind a lurid red casing.

Its name is an adaptation of French *cervelas* (source also of English *cervelat*), a medium-sized pork sausage of eastern France which is usually simmered in water or red wine. This in turn was borrowed from Italian *cervellata*, so named because it was sometimes made from pigs' brains (*cervello*).

savory An aromatic plant of the mint family. Two species in particular are used as a culinary herb: *summer savory,* which has narrow peppery leaves that are often used with beans and other pulses (in German it is known as *bohnenkraut,* literally 'bean vegetable'), and *winter savory,* which has a sharper, spicier flavour. The word has no connection with the adjective (and noun) *savoury*. First recorded in the fourteenth century, its ultimate source was the plant's Latin name, *satureia*. This was adopted into Old English as *sætherie,* and Middle English *saverey* was either a descendant of that or a reborrowing via Old French.

savoy A variety of cabbage with wrinkled curly dark green leaves. First introduced into English in the late sixteenth century, its name is a translation of French *chou de Savoie,* literally 'Savoy cabbage'. It was so called from its first having been cultivated in Savoy, a region on the French-Italian border.

savoy biscuit Savoy biscuits are small finger-shaped individual sponge biscuits of the sort used for making charlottes russes. No longer much encountered, they were popular enough in the nineteenth century for the special piping bag used in making them to be called a *savoy bag*, or colloquially a *savvy bag*. Legend connects their name with Amadeus VI, a fourteenth-century king of Savoy. An alternative name for such biscuits, particularly in American English, is *ladyfinger*. *See also* BOUDOIR BISCUIT.

scallion These days, *scallion* is what American-speakers call a spring onion, or other similar immature onion. It is also used for 'leek.' But there is more to the term's history than that.

 Essentially it is the same word as *shallot*. Both come ultimately from Latin *Ascalonia*, denoting an 'onion from Ascalon', a port on the coast of Palestine, which passed into Old French as *escaloigne*. Substitution of the suffix produced *shallot*, but *scallion* represents a direct fourteenth-century borrowing, via Anglo-Norman *scaloun*, of the original Old French form. It remained in common usage for many hundreds of years, and does not seem to have become restricted to American English until comparatively recently, during the nineteenth century.

scaloppine In Italian cuisine, scaloppine, or *scaloppini,* are thin boneless slices of veal (or other meat), sautéed or fried. Italian *scaloppine* is the plural of *scaloppina,* a diminutive form of *scaloppa,* which probably originated (at the end of the nineteenth century) as an adaptation of French *escalope* (*see* ESCALOPE).

scamorza A type of Italian cheese similar to but firmer and saltier than mozzarella. It is a product of the Abruzzo and Molise regions of eastern central Italy, and was originally made from buffalo milk, although now it is mainly a cows'-milk cheese. Its name is a derivative of Italian *scamozzare* 'to lop off', which is probably a blend of *scapitozzare* 'to pollard' and *mozzare* 'to cut off' (*see* MOZZARELLA); the underlying reference is to the chopping of bundles of cheese which is part of the manufacturing process.

scampi *Scampi* is the plural of Italian *scampo* 'shrimp', a word adopted into the Venetian dialect from Greek *kámpē* 'caterpillar, grub' (that in turn was perhaps a derivative of *kámptein* 'to bend', and so originally may have meant literally 'curved animal'). It started to filter into English in the 1920s, but it was not really until the 1950s and 1960s that it began to make headway. This coincided with a boom in popularity of a dish consisting of large prawn tails coated in breadcrumbs and deep-fried: scampi and chips became a staple on café and restaurant menus. Soon *scampi* had well and truly ousted the native English *Dublin Bay prawn*.

schnapps A broad term covering a range of strong, often colourless spirits distilled in northern Europe, usually from grain starch. A variety of different flavourings are added, depending on the place of manufacture, including caraway and juniper berries. The word comes, via German, from Dutch *snaps*, a derivative of the verb *snappen* 'to snatch', and means literally 'gulp'.

schnitzel Etymologically, *schnitzel* is a diminutive form of a now obsolete German noun *sniz* 'slice', which is related to modern German *schneiden* 'to cut'. German for 'escalope', especially of veal, it made its debut in English in the middle of the nineteenth century. Its appearance on English menus is virtually restricted to *Wiener schnitzel* 'Viennese escalope', an Austrian dish in which the thin boneless cutlet of veal is coated with egg and breadcrumbs and shallow-fried.

scone The scone comes from Scotland—the first known reference to it comes in a translation of the *Aeneid* (1513) by the Scots poet Gavin Douglas: 'The flour sconnis war sett in, by and by, wyth other mesis.' Made from fine white flour (echoing the possible source of their name, Dutch *schoonbroot* 'fine white bread', sour milk or buttermilk, and a raising agent (since the mid-nineteenth century, bicarbonate of soda), and baked on a griddle or in the oven, scones originally came in the form of flat cakes cut into four, producing portions that were either square or, if the original cake were round, roughly triangular. Individually baked round scones are a later development. *See also* DROP SCONE.

The pronunciation of the word *scone* has never really settled down. Early spellings suggest a short vowel, rhyming with *swan*, but the version with a diphthong, rhyming with *stone*, is if anything commoner today.

In Australia, *scone* is a slang term for 'head'.

scorzonera A long thin black-skinned white-fleshed root vegetable of the daisy family. It is closely related to salsify, and indeed is frequently called *salsify*. It was introduced to Britain from Italy in the early seventeenth century, and caught on fairly quickly (a letter written in 1666 records how 'Colonel Blunt presented the company . . . with excellent scorzoneras, which he said might be propagated in England as much as parsnips'), and although it has never become a mainstream British vegetable, it has started to reappear on supermarket shelves in recent years (usually in the guise of *salsify*).

The name *scorzonera* (which not surprisingly was subjected to several orthographic contortions in the seventeenth and eighteenth centuries, such as *skarsinarie* and *schorchanarrow*) comes from Italian, where it is a derivative of *scorzone*. This was a term for a 'poisonous snake', and its application to the plant is probably a reference to its reputation as an antidote to snake-bite (scorzonera used to be known as *viper's grass* in English).

Scotch bonnet A type of chilli pepper that is amongst the hottest of those widely commercially available. It comes in a range of colours from pale green through yellow and orange to red, and its shape is most un-chilli-like: a corrugated, semi-deflated sphere, not dissimilar to a literal Scotch bonnet, a sort of flat brimless cap formerly worn by Scotsmen. The term is first recorded in 1842.

Scotch broth A clear soup made with meat stock (traditionally mutton) and vegetables and thickened with barley. In its native Scotland it is usually referred to simply as *barley broth*, and James Boswell records how Dr Johnson (despite his slighting remarks in print about the Scottish diet) ate it with gusto during his journey north of the border. The first evidence of its travelling south and becoming more widely established as part of general British cuisine is a recipe for 'Scotch barley broth' in Hannah Glasse's *Art of Cookery* (1747). To make it authentically, the meat must cook in the soup, adding its flavour to the vegetables; it can then be eaten as a separate course after the soup, or added in small pieces to the soup, as preferred.

Scotch egg The Scotch egg—a hard-boiled egg enveloped in sausage meat, coated in crumbs, and then fried—appeared on the scene at the beginning of the nineteenth century, although whether as a new invention or simply as a wider dissemination of an ancient traditional dish is not altogether clear. The first known printed recipe for it appears in Mrs Rundell's *New System of Domestic Cookery* (1809): 'Boil hard five pullet's eggs, and without removing the white, cover completely with a fine relishing forcemeat.' Its Scottish origin is perhaps pointed up by its inclusion in Meg Dods's *Cook and Housewife's Manual*, published in Edinburgh in 1826. This describes the eggs being eaten hot with gravy, a method of consumption echoed by Mrs Beeton in 1861, but a hundred years on their role had become that of a convenient cold snack eaten in pubs, on picnics, etc.

Scotch pie A small meat pie (originally mutton, but now more usually beef) of a type traditionally made by Scottish bakers and generally sold hot. It has long roots (the name is first recorded in 1826) and remains popular, especially in Glasgow: 'Forget oysters, asparagus, and all that nonsense, I'm talking about proper aphrodisiacs like haggis, stovies, and scotch pies', *Daily Record*, Glasgow (2002).

Scotch woodcock A savoury dish consisting of scrambled eggs on toast, enlivened with anchovies or anchovy paste. Invented by the Victorians (who were great fans of the savoury course), the first known recipe for it is given in Mrs Beeton's *Book of Household Management* (1861). The name was inspired by *Welsh rabbit*.

scrag end A cut of lamb or mutton (or veal) from the part of the neck immediately below the head; the contrast is with the *best end*: 'I could only get the scrag end this morning, aunt: the best end was sold', Mrs Henry Wood, *The Master of Greylands* (1873). The term dates from the first half of the seventeenth century; *scrag* may have originated as an alteration of Scots and northern English *crag* 'neck'.

scrapple A Pennsylvania Dutch dish consisting of scraps of pork or other meat that are stewed with maize meal and then packed into loaf or cake tins to cool. Fried slices are eaten for breakfast or lunch. The term, first recorded in 1855, is a diminutive form of *scrap*.

scratching Pork scratchings—small pieces of crisply cooked pork skin—have recently enjoyed a certain vogue in Britain as pub snacks, but the word is of some antiquity. It is first recorded as long ago as the fifteenth century, and an 1883 issue of *Knowledge* noted: '"Scratchings"—a delicacy greatly relished by our British ploughboys, but rather too rich in pork fat.' It is not clear where the term comes from, but it may be an alteration of the synonymous, and now obsolete, *cratchen* and *cracon*, which are possibly ultimately the same word as *crackling*.

Screwdriver A cocktail consisting of vodka and orange juice served on ice. 'Legend has it that this drink got its name in the 1950s from American oil-rig workers stationed in the Middle East, who purportedly opened and stirred cans of this concoction with their screwdrivers', Sharon Tyler Herbst and Ron Herbst, *The Ultimate A-to-Z Bar Guide* (1998).

scrod An American (and particularly New England) term of unknown origin for a young cod, haddock, or similar fish, especially one that has been split and boned ready for cooking. It is first recorded in 1841. Among suggestions for its derivation are that it comes from obsolete Dutch *schrood* 'piece cut off' (a relative of English *shred*), and that it was invented by a Boston restaurateur: neither, especially the latter, convinces.

scrumpy *See* CIDER.

scurvy grass A name applied in the past to any of a range of green plants, such as seakale and sorrel, eaten by sailors to prevent scurvy. In modern usage it denotes mainly a small cress-like shore-plant with fleshy tar-flavoured vitamin-C-rich leaves. The term is first recorded in 1597.

sea biscuit An alternative term for SHIP'S BISCUIT. It is now probably best known, in the form *Seabiscuit*, as the name of a celebrated American racehorse (1933–47), subject of an eponymous 2003 film.

Sea Breeze A cocktail typically consisting of vodka, grapefruit juice, and cranberry juice.

seafood The word *seafood*—a useful generic term covering any edible animal obtained from the sea, whether fish, crustacean, or mollusc—was coined in the US in the nineteenth century. In his *History of the English Language* (1935), the American scholar A. C. Baugh noted that 'a writer in the London *Daily Mail* recently complained that an Englishman would find "positively incomprehensible" the American word *sea-food*', and it does not seem to have become completely naturalized in British English until well after the Second World War.

seakale The seakale is related to the cabbage (hence its name), but you would not guess it from looking at the cultivated version. It is blanched as it grows by heaping earth or sand round it, with the result that its stalks grow fat and white, with small waxy chlorophyl-starved leaves at the end. It is served in much the same way as asparagus. The first known reference to it is by John Evelyn, who in his *Acetaria* (1699) described 'our Sea-keele . . . growing on our Coast' as 'very delicate'.

sea pie A sailors' dish consisting of an assortment of meat and vegetables boiled in a pot over a fire with a pastry crust on top. Sometimes more than one layer of pastry was used, creating a two- or three-decker pie. The term is first recorded in 1751 (it is not to be confused with *sea pie* as a name for the oystercatcher, which is based on *pie* 'magpie').

sea woodcock An epithet sometimes applied to the red mullet, 'because of its liver which must on no account be discarded with the other innards (the woodcock is always cooked with its trail [internal organs])', *Jane Grigson's Fish Book* (1993). The name has also been applied to various actual seabirds or shore-birds, such as the oystercatcher and the bar-tailed godwit.

seed cake Long a fixture on the English tea table, the seed cake, with its dotting of pungent crescent-shaped caraway seeds, has gone into something of a decline since the 1950s. Seed cakes are first mentioned as long ago as the 1570s (in Thomas Tusser's *Five Hundred Points of Good Husbandry*), but it is not entirely clear at this stage whether the word 'seed' may not be a reference to the time of year at which such cakes were eaten in the country, at a sort of post-sowing festival. What is certain is that when caraway seeds were first used for such cakes, they were in the form of comfits, encrusted in layers of sugar; it was not until the late seventeenth or early eighteenth century that the plain unadorned seed began to be used. Seed cake was exceedingly popular in the Victorian era ('I cut and handed the sweet seed-cake,' Charles Dickens, *David Copperfield* (1850)), and into the first half of the twentieth century, but it may have been the cutting off of the supply of caraway seeds during the Second World War that led eventually to its falling from favour.

sekt German sparkling white wine, usually dry. It is made in large quantities and in a wide range of qualities: from rather ordinary banal wine made by the tank fermentation method from imported grape juice to a highly individual product made from riesling grapes by the champagne method (of secondary fermentation in bottle). The term appears to be a German alteration of English *sack* 'strong Spanish white wine', reputedly inspired by an actor famous for his interpretation of Falstaff, who became so immersed in his role that whenever he ordered his regular tipple (which happened to be sparkling wine), he called for 'sack'.

self-raising flour Flour to which a raising agent has been added before sale. That is the British term for it, although it appears to have originated in America: the earliest record of it in print is in an 1854 issue of the San Francisco *Daily Placer Times & Transcript*. The usual US term is now *self-rising flour*.

seltzer An effervescent mineral water of a type originally obtained from natural springs near the village of Niederseltsers in southwest Germany (the name comes from German *seltserer wasser* 'water of Seltsers'). It was extremely popular in Britain in the Victorian and Edwardian eras, not so much for its supposed medicinal qualities as for its role as a refreshing mixer, diluting wines and spirits (John Betjeman, for instance, pictured Oscar Wilde awaiting his arrest at the Cadogan hotel sipping 'at a weak hock and seltzer'); and an apparatus called a *seltzogene* was even invented, to make artificial seltzer: 'Did they with thirst in summer burn? Lo, seltzogenes at every turn!' W. S. Gilbert, *Bab Ballads* (1868). Today, however, it is chiefly remembered in the name of a proprietary effervescent headache cure.

semifreddo Any of a range of semi-frozen Italian desserts containing sponge cake, ice cream, cream, fruit, etc.: 'desserts of Pedro Ximénez semifreddo with pine nut nougatine', *Time Out London, Eating and Drinking* (2008). The name means literally 'half-cold'.

sémillon A grape variety that produces white wine. Sémillon wines have a relatively large amount of body and tend to be deep in colour rather than pale. They are produced in various parts of the world, including Australia, but their spiritual home is Bordeaux. Their apotheosis is the great sweet wines of Sauternes and Barsac. The word *sémillon* originated in the Midi dialect of French, and goes back ultimately to Latin *semen* 'seed'.

semolina The word *semolina* comes ultimately from Latin *simila*, which signified a kind of fine wheat flour (it is also the source of English *simnel*, as in *simnel cake*). This developed into Italian *semola* 'bran', whose diminutive form *semolino* passed, with slight alteration, into English in the eighteenth century. It denotes the coarse particles left after wheat has been milled to flour and then sifted. In British cuisine semolina's commonest role has been in the making of rather uninspiring milk puddings (first to mention it, for its 'digestibility', was Michael Underwood in his *Treatise on the Disorders of Children* (1797), and Eliza Acton gives a recipe for a 'good semolina pudding' in *Modern Cookery* (1845)), but it perhaps reaches its apotheosis in pasta and in *gnocchi*, small Italian dumplings often made from semolina.

sercial The driest of the four main types of Madeira wine (*see also* BUAL, MALMSEY, VERDELHO). Its name is an Anglicization of Portuguese *cerceal,* which denotes the grape variety from which the wine is made (on mainland Portugal this is known as the *esgana cão*, literally 'dog-strangler', a reference to its high acidity).

sergeant-major A British military slang term denoting strong sweet tea, or tea laced with rum, both of which are held to be the prerogative of sergeant-majors: 'This tea . . . it damn near dissolved the spoon. A real "sergeant-major" brew', John Wainwright, *An Urge for Justice* (1981). In the US Army, the sergeant-major's perks were stereotypically different: there, the term used to be applied to coffee with cream and sugar.

serrano chilli A small, very hot type of Mexican chilli which is eaten while it is still green. The name comes from Spanish *serrano* 'of the mountains', perhaps reflecting the chilli's origins among the mountain ridges of Mexico.

serrano ham A partial translation of the Spanish term *jamón serrano,* literally 'mountain ham', which in modern usage generally refers to cured ham made from white pigs, in contrast to *jabugo ham,* made from black pigs. It is usually eaten raw, cut into wafer-thin slices.

sesame Sesame seeds, the small flat seeds of a tropical Asian plant, *Sesamum indicum*, are among the most ancient foodstuffs of mankind; it has been inferred that they formed part of the diet of the Indus Valley civilization during the fourth millennium BC. They are used as flavourings, either raw or toasted; they are pressed for their widely used oil; and they are crushed to make *tahini*. Today their use spreads round the world, from China and Japan, through India (where they are also known as *gingili* and *til*) and the Middle East to Mexico, where their oil is called *ajonjoli*. Historically, sesame seeds have been little used in Britain, and until recently by far the most familiar use of their name was in the phrase 'Open, sesame!', a charm used to open the door of the robbers' cave in the story of 'Ali Baba and the forty thieves', one of the *Arabian Nights* tales. Over the past fifty years, however, their distinctive savoury taste has become much better known to British eaters.

The word *sesame* is of Semitic origin, and reached English (in the fifteenth century) via Greek *sésamon* and Latin *sésamum*. An alternative name is *benne*, of African origin (it is related to Mandingo *bene*).

seviche An alternative spelling of CEVICHE.

sewin The name by which the sea trout is known in Wales: 'The "sea" starter [at a Cardiff restaurant] could feature Pembrokeshire spider crab tart and sewin pancakes', *Good Food Guide* (2008). It is first recorded in the mid-sixteenth century, but its origins are unknown (it is not Welsh).

shaddock An alternative name for the pomelo, a large citrus fruit somewhat resembling the grapefruit. It comes from a certain Captain Shaddock, a sixteenth-century English seaman who according to Sir Hans Sloane's *Voyage to Jamaica* (1707) left seeds of the plant in Barbados on a passage from the East Indies. It remained the standard term for the (admittedly seldom encountered) fruit into the twentieth century, but *pomelo* arose in the 1850s and is now the generally preferred term. French has adopted the English word as *chadoc*.

shake A shortened form, of American origin, of *milk shake*: 'The shakes and malts are legendary and the food is fresh and served quickly by laid-back staff', *Time Out London: Eating and Drinking* (2008).

shallot The shallot, a small variety of onion which grows in clusters, is probably the most highly prized member of the onion family among cooks. It is associated particularly with the cuisine of Bordeaux (it is an essential component of *sauce bordelaise*, for example), but its influence has spread throughout the northern part of France. The Romans called it *caepa Ascalōnia* 'Ascalonian onion', or simply *ascalōnia* for short, giving a clue to its geographical origins: Ascalon was an ancient seaport in Palestine. It had been introduced into France by 800 AD, if not considerably earlier, and brought with it its Vulgar Latin name **iscalonia*. In Old French this became *eschalotte* (with a new ending grafted on to it), and English took it over as *eschalot* or, in reduced form, as *shallot* in the seventeenth century (the spelling *eschalot* evidently outlived its pronunciation, for Dr Johnson in his *Dictionary* (1755) notes '*Eschalot*. Pronounced *shallot*'). The vegetable did not catch on very quickly; at the beginning of the eighteenth century John Mortimer was still referring to it as a novelty: 'Eschalots are now from France become an English plant,' *Whole Art of Husbandry* (1707), and it never really achieved the status amongst British cooks that it enjoys in France.

(Tennyson's 'Lady of Shallot', incidentally, was not an onion addict; she came from a place called Scalot.)

shampoo A punning substitute for *champagne,* first recorded in 1957: 'He turned then to the table and the bottle of champagne. "Look what I have. Shampoo. Do you like shampoo?"', Rona Jaffe, *The Best of Everything* (1958).

shandy This word for a mixture of beer and lemonade or ginger beer first turns up in the middle of the nineteenth century. It is short for *shandygaff,* but where this came from is far from clear; it may perhaps have some connection with the obsolete dialectal adjective *shandy,* meaning 'wild, boisterous'. First mention of it comes in the *Adventures of Verdant Green* (1853), a facetious novel of Oxford life by the pseudonymous Cuthbert Bede; but in 1888 shandy was still being derided in the *Daily News* as a 'new-fangled drink'.

shank A joint of meat taken from the lower part of an animal's foreleg: at the end of the twentieth century braised lamb shanks became a fashionable item on restaurant menus. The usage (an extension of the word's original meaning, 'lower leg') dates from the early nineteenth century.

shape A dispiriting name, current in the nineteenth and early twentieth centuries, for a dessert decidedly lacking in pizzazz: blancmange, jelly, etc. that has been set in a mould: 'The puddings were ground rice mould, "shape" Mrs. Welsh called it, rice milk [etc.]', Sabine Baring-Gould, *Arminell* (1889). The authors of *Practical Cookery for All* (1953) had to remind their readers that their basic recipe for 'shape', which involved thickening milk with arrowroot, required salt and flavouring to make it palatable, which rather reinforces the impression that the dessert's form was the most interesting thing about it.

Sharon fruit *See* PERSIMMON.

shashlik A version of the kebab which originated in Georgia, to the east of the Black Sea, and spread from there to western Asia and eastern Europe, including Russia. Its basic ingredients are virtually identical to those of the Turkish shish kebab on which it is based— chunks of mutton threaded on skewers—and even the word, Russian *shashlýk,* comes ultimately from Turkish *şiş* 'skewer'.

shawarma The Middle Eastern equivalent of the döner kebab—that is, slices of marinated lamb cut from a vertical spit. Somewhat spicier than its Turkish original, it is also popular in West Africa, and can increasingly be found in British kebab houses. The word came from colloquial Arabic *šāwirma,* which was borrowed from Turkish *çevirme,* a derivative of *çevirmek* 'to turn, rotate'. In Israel it is spelled *shwarma.*

shea butter A solid vegetable fat produced from the nuts of the shea tree, a small tropical African tree of the sapodilla family. It is an important part of the diet in the parts of Africa where the tree grows, and is also used in the West, for example as a spread and as a substitute for cocoa butter. *Shea* (pronounced /shee/, /sheea/ or /shay/) is an adaptation of *sye,* the name of the tree in the Mande languages of West Africa.

shepherd's pie The shepherd's pie, a dish of minced meat with a topping, first surfaces in the 1870s, roughly contemporaneously with the mincing machine which did so much to help establish it in the British cook's repertoire. At first it was identified as Scottish: 'In Scotland they produce . . . such a stew, cover it over with a crust, and call it shepherd's pie. . . . The shepherd's pie of Scotland is too fairinaceous—potatoes within and paste without', E. S. Dallas, *Kettner's Book of the Table* (1877). It is clear from this that the Scottish version of the dish, at least, was topped with a pastry crust rather than the now characteristic mashed potato, but a closer forerunner of the modern dish under another name was *sanders*. The basic duty of the shepherd's pie has traditionally been to absorb beneath its potato topping the minced remains of the Sunday joint, bulked out at need with carrots, onions, more potatoes, etc. Its reputation, never exactly sparkling (all that watery shop-bought mince), nose-dived further with the introduction of instant mash. Latterly caterers and others have taken to calling it *cottage pie* (in fact a much more ancient term), in deference to the fact that the meat it contains is now so seldom mutton or lamb—whence the name *shepherd's pie*—but usually beef (or textured vegetable protein).

sherbet English acquired the word *sherbet* via Turkish or Persian *sherbet* from Arabic *sharbah* 'beverage, drink', and at first (in the seventeenth and eighteenth centuries) it was used, logically enough, for a Middle Eastern drink—specifically a cooling drink made from water, fruit juice, and sugar or honey, and often chilled with snow. Then in the nineteenth century an effervescent white powder was devised, composed of bicarbonate of soda, tartaric acid, sugar, and various flavourings, with which to make fizzy drinks that supposedly resembled the original Oriental sherbet. Children quickly discovered that it was if anything nicer to eat the sherbet powder than to make drinks with it, and so were born the *sherbet dabs* and *sherbet fountains* of yesteryear (the former was a lollipop that could be dipped into a bag of sherbet, the latter a cylindrical packet of sherbet with a liquorice straw for sucking it up).

Sherbet is closely related etymologically to *shrub* (the drink), *sorbet* (in American English *sherbet* is often used for 'sorbet'), and *syrup*.

sherry Sherry is a fortified wine made from white grapes, chiefly the palomino, in and around the town of Jerez in southwest Spain, about 120 miles from Gibraltar (or at least, genuine Spanish sherry is; the name has been applied to more or less similar beverages from other places over the years, much to the annoyance of the Spanish). The name of the wine comes from the name of the town: in the sixteenth and seventeenth centuries this was spelled *Xeres* and pronounced roughly /'sheris/, and it was applied to the variety of *sack* (strong white wine) produced there—*sherris sack*. By the early seventeenth century the reference to *sack*, and the final *-s*, were well on the way to being dropped, leaving *sherry*; and by the eighteenth century the drink seems to have left the tavern and begun to appear in the drawing room.

For the various types of sherry, *see* AMONTILLADO, FINO, MANZANILLA, OLOROSO, PALO CORTADO. Until well after the Second World War by far the most popular sherry in Britain was sweet, known by various epithets such as *brown* and *cream*, not to mention the dreaded *cooking sherry*: 'Have you ever tasted cooking sherry, Bertie? Odd stuff', P. G. Wodehouse, *The Mating Season* (1949). A by-product of the switch in fashion to drier sherries in the 1960s was the introduction in the early 1970s of a new blend of sherry, the 'pale cream' (Croft Original is the best known), which tastes reassuringly sweet while looking trendily dry.

shiitake An oriental mushroom of the agaric family, widely used in Japanese cookery. It is said to have been cultivated in Japan for over 2,000 years. The method of growing it is to sow the spores on logs cut from various evergreen trees of the beech family—hence its name (*shii* is the Japanese term for such trees, and *take* is Japanese for 'mushroom').

ship's biscuit Hard tack (a type of hard dry biscuit) issued in former times as rations to sailors at sea. By the end of the voyage it was often infested with weevils. The term (and its variant *ship biscuit*) date from the late eighteenth century, its alternative *sea biscuit* from the late seventeenth century (in earlier centuries *ship bread* or *ship's bread* had also been used).

shirred eggs An American way of cooking eggs: the eggs are broken into a cup or small bowl, covered with milk or cream and often breadcrumbs, and baked. It is not clear where the term (first recorded in 1883) came from, nor how it is related to the verb *shirr* 'to gather fabric by means of parallel threads'.

shish kebab See KEBAB.

shiso An East Asian plant of the mint family that is widely used as a herb in Japanese cookery. Its English name is *perilla*.

shit on a shingle Dismissive American slang for minced beef served on toast, a dish evidently not greatly appreciated in the military, where the expression probably originated in the 1930s (a *shingle* in this context is a roof tile). It can be abbreviated for euphemism's sake to *SOS*.

shoestring potatoes An American term, first recorded in 1906, for long, very thinly cut potato chips (in American English, *shoestring* means 'shoelace').

shoofly pie In American cuisine, shoofly pie is a sort of treacle tart, made with molasses or brown sugar and topped with a sugar, flour, and butter crumble. Its name is generally taken to be an allusion to the fact that it is so attractive to flies that they have to be constantly shooed away from it, but the fact that it originated as a Pennsylvania-Dutch speciality suggests the possibility that *shoofly* is an alteration of an unidentified German word.

shooter A term of American origin for a small alcoholic drink, especially of spirits: 'Shooters (£3, three for £7.50) suit the buzz in the cavernous DJ bar', *Time Out London, Eating and Drinking* (2009).

shortbread A thick sweet biscuit made with a flour and sugar mixture that has been shortened—made soft and crumbly—with fat, typically butter (*see* SHORT PASTRY). The term dates back to the early nineteenth century. In Britain, shortbread is particularly associated with Scotland, where historically it was made with oatmeal. It is traditionally made in large circular form and served cut into small triangular wedges.

shortcake *Shortcake* is a term of dismaying diversity. Its application varies widely from place to place, and over time, and the only common factor is the use of shortening—butter or lard—to make it soft or crumbly (*see* SHORT PASTRY). The term is first recorded as long ago as 1594, in the *Good Huswif's Handmaid*, and in Shakespeare's *Merry Wives of Windsor* Slender's servant Simple asks him 'Book of Riddles! why, did you not lend it to Alice Shortcake upon All-Hallowmas last?', but it does not seem to have become widespread until the nineteenth century. In many areas of Britain it was used virtually as a synonym for *shortbread*, and that is probably the main application of the word in present-day British English. Elsewhere, however, it denoted a sort of rich teacake, and in America particularly it was and still is used for a cake made with a rich biscuit dough that is split, filled with fruit (usually strawberries), and topped with cream. This usage is reasonably common in British English too, but a recipe which has not crossed the Atlantic is the savoury shortcake—similarly made of a rich biscuit dough but with a meat filling.

shortening bread A type of American bread made by frying a batter mixture containing cornmeal, eggs, milk, and some sort of fat, such as butter. A speciality of the southern states, it achieved wider fame thanks to a line in a traditional plantation song that runs 'Mammy's little baby loves short'nin' bread'.

short loin An American term, first recorded in the early 1920s, for the section of a beef carcase between the ribs and the sirloin. It yields particularly tender steaks, such as strip steaks.

short pastry Short pastry, or in full *shortcrust pastry*, is pastry that has had some sort of fat added to it—lard, for instance, or butter or oil—to make it soft and flaky. Such fat is known as *shortening*, a term first recorded in the late eighteenth century and still in common use in American English. This application of the adjective *short* is an ancient one: an early fifteenth-century cookery book, for example, directs 'then take warm barm [yeast], and put all these together, and beat them together with thy hand till it be short and thick enough'. Nor has it always been used exclusively of pastry: 'This is the Venison of America, whereof I have sometimes eaten, and found it white and short', Thomas Gage, *New Survey of the West Indies* (1648). The general notion behind it is of being 'easily crumbled' (in which sense it is also applied to several far from edible substances, including coal, paper, metal, and dung), and it was probably based originally on the observation that friable material had short fibres.

short ribs An American term, first recorded in 1912, for a cut of beef containing the ends of the ribs near to the breastbone. It requires long slow cooking.

shredded wheat A breakfast cereal made from wheat grains that are softened by steaming, rolled into strands, chopped up and formed into biscuits, and then dried by baking. The basic process was invented in 1893 by a Denver lawyer called H. D. Perky. *Shredded wheat*, first recorded in 1898, is a generic term, not a trademark, but *Shreddies*, which was presumably inspired by it, is a proprietary name. It denotes a brand of malted shredded wheat moulded into small squares, originally made in Britain in 1950.

shroom A colloquial American abbreviation, first recorded in 1977, of *mushroom*. It is mainly applied to the hallucinogenic variety, but it can also be found in culinary contexts: 'It was a tough choice, though, between the 'shrooms and the fried mozzarella sticks', *News*, Frederick, Maryland (1995).

shrub Shrub has now had its day, but in the eighteenth and nineteenth centuries it was a popular drink made from a spirit (usually rum), sugar, and orange or lemon juice: 'Miss Ivins's friend's young man would have the ladies go into the Crown, to take some shrub,' Charles Dickens, *Sketches by Boz* (1835). The word comes from Arabic *shurb* 'beverage, drink', and is related to English *sherbet, sorbet*, and *syrup*.

Sichuan pepper *See* SZECHWAN PEPPER.

sidecar A démodé cocktail made from brandy, lemon juice, and an orange-flavoured liqueur. It originated in the 1920s, some say at Harry's Bar in Paris. Accounts (or guesses) differ as to whether a motorcycle sidecar was the preferred mode of transport of its inventor or of the person it was created for.

side meat An American term, first recorded in 1868, for salt pork or bacon, especially as cut from the side of the pig. It is particularly associated with the southern and western US: 'accents that recalled hominy grits and sidemeat', Max Shulman, *Rally Round the Flag, Boys!* (1957). An alternative term is *side pork*.

silverside A British term for a boned joint of beef cut from the outer part of the top of the animal's hind leg. While suitable for roasting, it is often boiled or preserved by salting. The name, apparently a reference to the silvery sheen of the membrane covering its internal surface, first crops up in Eliza Acton's *Modern Cookery* (1845): 'The natural division of the meat will show where the silver-side of the round is to be separated from the upper, or tongue side.'

simnel *Simnel* has had two distinct careers. In medieval times it was a light biscuit-like bread made from fine flour, which was first boiled and then baked. C. Anne Wilson in *Food and Drink in Britain* (1973) reports that 'during the Middle Ages simnels were given an official place in the tables of the Assize of Bread [a statute dating from 1267, regulating the weight of bread]: since it was boiled as well as baked, a farthing simnel was permitted to be lighter in weight than a farthing wastel [similar fine bread]'.

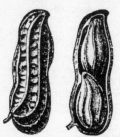

Then towards the end of the seventeenth century, the name came to be applied to a rich fruit cake with a layer of marzipan in the middle, made for Mothering Sunday. Over the years this has evolved so that nowadays simnel cake is associated with Easter, and has its marzipan on top.

The word *simnel* comes from Old French *simenel*, which derives ultimately from Latin *simila* 'fine flour' (also the source of *semolina*).

Singapore sling A cocktail made from gin and cherry brandy. It is said to have been created in 1915 by Ngiam Tong Boon, a barman at Raffles Hotel, Singapore.

singing hinny A speciality of northeast England consisting of a cake made typically from flour, butter, sugar, lard, cream, and currants, baked on both sides on a griddle. Its 'song' is the sizzling, hissing sound it makes as it cooks, and the *hinny* in its name is presumably the Geordie (and Scots) version of *honey*, used as a term of endearment (as in 'Cheer up, hinny!'). It has been a part of northeast culture since at least the early nineteenth century, as John Brockett reports in his *Glossary of North Country Terms* (1825): '*Singing hinny*, a kneaded spice cake baked on the girdle; indispensable in a pitman's family.'

sinker A dated term, originating in America around 1870, for a doughy cake, especially a doughnut, and also for a dumpling. It was probably suggested by their sinking into the fat or liquid when cooking.

sippet A term of yesteryear for a small piece of bread or toast, used to dunk into soup or sauce or as a garnish: 'The 18th Century Worcester caterer says "Serve up with sippets". These were a regular feature of stews in middle-class cookery as recently as the '70s of the last century. They were then triangular pieces of toast arranged Vandyke fashion round any stew', Florence White, *Good Things in England* (1932). First recorded in the sixteenth century, it probably originated as a diminutive form of *sop* 'piece of bread for dunking'.

sirloin *Sirloin*, a cut of beef from the upper part of the hind loin, is the subject of one of the more fanciful extravagances of English etymology. Its actual origin is banal enough: it comes from Old French *surlonge*, a compound formed from *sur* 'above' and *longe* 'loin', and was borrowed into English in the early sixteenth century (the churchwarden's accounts for St Margaret's, Westminster (1554) mention a 'surloyn of beef, 6s 8d'). In the seventeenth century, however, or perhaps earlier, the pleasing but apocryphal story began to get around that it had been knighted by an English king, presumably as a reward for being a superior cut of beef. The king in question has been variously identified over the centuries as James I or Charles II, but in the earliest known reference to the tale it was Henry VIII who did the dubbing: 'A Sir-loyne of beef was set before Him (so knighted, saith tradition, by this King Henry)', Thomas Fuller, *Church-history of Britain* (1655). The word's modern spelling, with *sir-* instead of *sur-*, which dates from the seventeenth century, is no doubt partly due to this piece of fiction.

skilly An obsolescent British term, redolent of the workhouse and the sickroom, for a thin and insipid broth made from oatmeal and water, and flavoured with meat. It was often used as an epithet of disgust for any weak-kneed soup or beverage, and in the early twentieth century it served a turn as nautical slang for indistinguishable tea and coffee: 'A cup of skilly completed the repast', John Masefield, *The Conway* (1953). It originated, in the mid-nineteenth century, as a shortening of the archaic *skilligalee* 'thin porridge or soup', which was probably a fanciful coinage.

skirlie A Scottish version of stuffing, consisting of oatmeal, suet, and onion. Its name appears to be a relatively modern invention, based on *skirl* 'shrill sound, as of the bagpipes'—probably a reference to the noise the mixture makes when it is fried.

skirret A vegetable of yesteryear as far as Europe is concerned: a plant of the parsnip and carrot family with a many-branched edible root that tastes similar to celeriac. It is a native of East Asia, where it is still popular, and came west in the Middle Ages. It was widely cultivated in the sixteenth and seventeenth centuries (Hannah Glasse in her *Art of Cookery Made Plain and Easy* (1747) gives instructions on how 'to make Skirret-Fritters'), but then the potato came on the scene, and it gradually faded out. Its English name may have originated as a compound of Scottish English *skire* 'bright, clear' and *white*.

skirt *Skirt* was originally a butcher's term for the diaphragm of an ox or cow, as used for food. It is muscular tissue, but can scarcely compare with the best steak for tenderness, and not surprisingly was the prerogative of those with the least to spend: 'A considerable proportion of the livers and skirts are purchased wholesale by retail dealers in low neighbourhoods', *Daily News* (1868). Today probably most finds its way into dog-food and beefburgers. In France it is known as *hampe*.

In present-day English *skirt* generally denotes a cut of beef, lean but large-fibred and rather tough, from the animal's flank, generally used for stews or mince.

skordalia Skordalia, or *skorthalia,* is a Greek garlic dipping sauce made with breadcrumbs, almonds or walnuts, garlic, and olive oil. The word is probably a compound formed from Greek *skordo* (or *skortho*) 'garlic' and Italian *agliata* 'garlicky' (or perhaps Provençal *aïoli* 'garlic mayonnaise').

skuets An English savoury dish with a venerable tradition; the recipe is first recorded in Eliza Smith's *Compleat Housewife* (1728), but now little encountered. It consists of sweetbreads threaded on to skewers (hence presumably the name) with pieces of bacon and mushroom, and grilled.

slider A colloquial term, first recorded in 1915, for a portion of ice-cream served between two wafers. Anyone who has felt the ice-cream slipping out of control as it melts will appreciate the name. In America, the word is also applied to a miniature hamburger: 'Introducing my great American burger, and its little cousin the "slider", or mini burger', Jamie Oliver, *Jamie's America* (2009). The concept, of a filling held precariously between two outer layers, is essentially the same.

sling A long drink based on a spirit, typically gin, diluted with water and lemon juice, and usually sweetened. The term first appeared in America at the end of the eighteenth century, but it is not at all clear where it came from. It has been suggested that it derives from the notion of 'slinging' down a drink at a single draught, but it could equally well have some connection with another roughly contemporary and equally unexplained meaning of *sling*, 'sugar-cane juice'. *See also* SINGAPORE SLING.

slinger An old services' slang term, dating from the 1880s, for bread soaked in tea. It was usually used in the plural: 'You won't have no mind for slingers, not to-morrow— . . . bein' sick!', Rudyard Kipling, *Pall Mall Gazette* (1895).

slivovitz A type of dry colourless plum brandy made in central and eastern Europe. The word comes, via German, from Serbo-Croat *šljivovica*, a derivative of *šljiva* 'plum' (which may be connected with English *sloe*).

sloe The small bluish-black, sharply sour fruit of the blackthorn, a tree of the same genus as plums and damsons. Its main culinary use is to flavour *sloe gin*, a liqueur made by steeping the fruit in gin (the term is first recorded in 1895). The word *sloe* is descended from Old English *slāh*, which probably came from the same ancient Indo-European root as *livid* (which originally meant 'blackish-blue'), and Serbo-Croat *šljiva* 'plum' (source of English *slivovitz*).

sloppy joe An American variation on the hamburger in which a split burger bun is topped with a mixture of cooked minced meat, onions, peppers, and tomato sauce. It is said to have been invented by a cook called Joe at a café in Sioux City, Iowa. The name, first recorded in 1961, probably reflects how messy the burger is to eat.

slumgullion A derogatory American colloquialism for cheap, watery, or insubstantial stew made from leftovers. It seems to have emerged from the Klondike gold rush at the end of the nineteenth century: there is evidence of its previous use to denote a muddy deposit in a mining sluice, and it may have been based on *slum* 'slime' and dialect *gullion* 'mud, cesspool'.

slushie A sweet fruit-flavoured drink in a semi-frozen state, full of small pieces of ice: 'Alternatively, you could opt for slushies (mango or honeydew melon, perhaps)', *Time Out London, Eating and Drinking* (2009).

sly cake A type of tea cake that is a speciality of northern England. Deceptively, it is plain on the outside but full of currants and other dried fruits on the inside—hence the name (first recorded in 1855).

smallage *See* CELERY.

small beer Originally, in the sixteenth century, *small beer* denoted weak or inferior beer. Nowadays it is only the metaphorical application to something trivial that survives—an eighteenth-century development anticipated by Shakespeare: in *Othello* (1604), Iago scornfully characterizes a worthy woman as one fit only 'to suckle fools, and chronicle small beer'.

smearcase A term used for 'cottage cheese' in the central eastern states of the US. It is an adaptation of German *schmierkäse*, which means literally 'smear cheese'. It is first recorded in the 1820s, introduced no doubt by German immigrants in areas such as eastern Pennsylvania.

smetana Smetana (or *smitane*, the French version of its name) is a type of cream of Eastern European origin in which fresh cream is mixed into sour cream. Until recently it was familiar in Western gastronomy only in *smetana sauce*, a savoury sauce made with sour cream, onions, and white wine, but over the past four decades it has become relatively widely available in its own right in British supermarkets. The term comes from Russian, where it is a derivative of *'smetat'* 'to sweep off'.

Smithfield ham A type of dry-cured hickory-smoked dark-coloured American ham made in or near Smithfield, Virginia. Originally it was made from pigs fed with acorns, hickory nuts, and peanuts, but now they generally have to make do with grain. The term is first recorded in 1908.

smokie Since at least the late nineteenth century the term *smokie* has referred to 'smoked haddock'—specifically from Scotland, *par excellence* from Arbroath—but since the 1970s, what with the decline of the North Sea haddock fisheries and the growing popularity of the abundant and well-marketed mackerel, it has been increasingly applied to 'smoked mackerel', usually with some epithet suggestive of ancient associations with a particular area—Sussex smokies, for instance, or Salcombe smokies.

smoothie A thick smooth drink of fresh fruit puréed with milk, yoghurt, or ice cream: 'A mango daiquiri was like a smoothie, but with a mean kick', *Time Out London, Eating and Drinking* (2008).

smorgasbord A buffet of Scandinavian origin at which a variety of open sandwiches and other dishes, such as smoked and pickled fish, cheeses, and salads, are served. It had a period of fashionability in Britain in the 1960s and 1970s, and the term, first recorded in English in 1893, came to be used metaphorically for any heterogeneous mixture: 'the merry smörgasbord [*sic*] of his hysterical whimsical ideas', *Encounter* (1961). Swedish *smörgåsbord* is a compound formed from *smörgås* 'bread and butter, open sandwich' (from *smör* 'butter' and *gås*, literally 'goose', hence 'lump of butter') and *bord* 'table'.

smørrebrød *See* OPEN SANDWICH.

snack *Snack* was originally a verb, meaning 'to bite, snap'. It appears to have been borrowed, in the fourteenth century, from Middle Dutch *snacken*, which was probably onomatopoeic in origin, based on the sound of the snapping together of teeth. The derived noun originally had the same meaning (it was particularly applied to the bite of dogs), but by the late seventeenth century this had developed, perhaps via some unrecorded intermediate sense such as 'part bitten off', to 'portion, share'. A narrowing-down in meaning led by the mid-eighteenth century to 'small portion of food eaten', as contrasted with a proper meal: 'We have but just time for a snack', Samuel Foote, *The Mayor of Garret* (1763). The modern verb *snack* 'to eat a snack,' mainly an American usage, is an early nineteenth-century creation based on the noun.

snag A colloquial Australian and New Zealand word (usually used in the plural) for a sausage. It dates from the 1940s, but its origins are uncertain: it may come from British dialect *snag* 'morsel'.

snake bean An alternative name for the YARD-LONG BEAN.

snap bean An American term (first recorded in 1770) for a bean that is grown primarily for its edible pods (as opposed to the seeds inside them). They can be broken into pieces for cooking—hence the name. (The contrasting term, for a bean grown mainly for its edible seeds, is *shell bean*.)

snow A cold dessert or other confection that has a pale fluffy appearance, like snow, especially one that involves mixing beaten egg whites with fruit purée or fruit flavouring (for example, *apple snow, lemon snow*). There is a record of such a dish in a late sixteenth-century cookery book ('How to make a Snowe. Take a quart of thicke cream, and fiue or sixe whites of eggs . . . '), but the present-day usage seems to be an eighteenth-century development. The dish *snow eggs* (first recorded in 1861) is made by moulding beaten egg whites into an oval shape, poaching them, and floating them on a custard made with the yolks. In French it is *oeufs à la neige* (*see also* FLOATING ISLAND).

snowball A West Indian version of an ice lolly without a stick. It consists of chips of ice served in a glass with sweet, luridly coloured syrup poured over it—perhaps green, or purple, or orange, or scarlet. *Snowball* is also the name of two cocktails, one made from advocaat and lemonade, and the other from gin, an anise-flavoured liqueur, and cream.

snow cabbage *See* CHINESE CABBAGE.

snow pea An alternative name of MANGETOUT.

sobrasada A type of raw cured pork sausage that is a speciality of the Balearic Islands. Paprika is a key ingredient, which gives it a red, chorizo-like appearance. Its name originated in Catalan as *sobrassada*, but its ultimate derivation is not known for certain; a connection with *sobrasar* 'to put burning coals round the bottom of a cooking pot' seems not unlikely.

sockeye The name given to a type of North Pacific salmon, the most valuable commercial species. It comes from *sukai*, which means literally 'fish of fishes' in the Salish language of western North America.

soda bread Bread that has been leavened with bicarbonate of soda. It is associated particularly with Ireland. The term is first recorded in 1850.

soda pop An American term, first recorded in 1863, for a sweet carbonated drink, as originally made from soda water and flavoured syrup. In everyday use it is generally shortened to *soda*, which forms the basis of various associated terms, notably *soda fountain*, denoting a counter or establishment where soda pop, sundaes, and ice cream are dispensed by a *soda jerk* (a seller of such wares). Vanilla-flavoured soda pop is termed *cream soda*.

soda water Effervescent carbonated water, either drunk on its own or mixed with alcoholic drinks or fruit juice. Originally the bubbles were produced by sodium bicarbonate (hence the name), but now they are introduced by carbon dioxide under pressure. In the twentieth century soda siphons, in which soda water could be made and from which it was dispensed, could be found in most middle-class British homes. The term *soda water*, first recorded in 1802, is standardly reduced to *soda* (as in 'brandy and soda'): 'An occasional whiskey and water or soda . . . is useful', Surgeon-Captain Matthew Hughes, *Mediterranean, Malta, or Undulant Fever* (1897). *See also* CLUB SODA.

sofrito In Spanish and Latin American cooking, a mixture of lightly fried onions and garlic, usually with tomatoes and other vegetables, used as a base for soups and stews. Spanish *sofrito* means literally 'lightly fried'. In Italy, the mixture is called *soffritto*.

soldiers A colloquial British term for strips of bread or toast used for dipping into a soft-boiled egg: 'Our medical writer . . . advises: "Bread, butter, and milk is a good idea, but you really can't beat a boiled egg and 'soldiers'",' *Woman's Own* (1979). First recorded in 1966, it alludes to the stereotypical shape of a simple human figure with soldier's headgear into which more leisured mothers would cut their offspring's toast.

somen A type of Japanese wheat-flour noodle made by pulling dough into long thin strips.

sorbet Sorbets are soft water ices made usually with fruit juice or fruit purée (although more adventurous chefs have experimented with savoury sorbets). They are served either as dessert, or between main courses, to cleanse the palate and reinvigorate the appetite. The word *sorbet* was borrowed from French in the sixteenth century, but originated, along with a lot of unlikely-seeming related words, in the eastern Mediterranean area. Many languages, both Indo-European and Semitic, have words with a basic sound pattern /srb/ or /shrb/ that mean roughly 'take something into the mouth, usually liquid'. Latin, for example, had *sorbere* 'to swallow' (from which English gets *absorb*), and Greek *rhophein* with the same meaning, derived from a probable earlier *srobh-*; while Arabic has *shariba* 'drink'. It is thought that rather than being borrowed from each other, many of these may have arisen independently on an onomatopoeic basis, copying the sound of (noisy) drinking. If this is so, English *slurp* fits neatly into the same pattern (/l/ is phonetically close to /r/). *Sorbet* itself goes back ultimately to Arabic *sharbat* 'drinks'. It is closely related to *sherbet*, and less obvious members of the same family are *syrup*, which comes from Arabic *sharāb* 'beverage', and the now obsolete *shrub*, a drink made from fruit juice and spirits. In American English sorbets have historically been termed chiefly *sherbets*, but in recent years *sorbet* has become the more fashionable word.

sorrel Sorrel, a close relative of the dock plant, has large spinach-like green leaves with a slightly bitter taste, used particularly in sauces to accompany fish and veal. Their bitterness is reflected in the name *sorrel*, which was coined in Old French from the adjective *sur* 'sour'.
    In the eighteenth century, the name *sorrel* was co-opted for a tall Caribbean plant of the hibiscus family, which has red flowers and stems (hence its full name, *red sorrel*). The dried sepals of the flowers are used to make a sweet red drink, also called *sorrel*.

soubise In French gastronomy, *soubise* is a term applied generally to a preparation of onions—a *purée soubise*, for instance, is an onion purée. In English, however, it has come to denote specifically a white sauce containing onion. This was popularized during the nineteenth century, and it came to be a standard accompaniment to mutton and lamb. Eliza Acton in her *Modern Cookery* (1845) noted that it was 'served more frequently with lamb or mutton cutlets than with any other dishes'. The word commemorates Charles de Rohan, Prince de Soubise (1715–87), French general and courtier.

soufflé In French, *soufflé* means literally 'puffed up', the state of the perfect soufflé suggesting delicate inflation. English adopted the word in the early nineteenth century: it first appeared in Louis Ude's *The French Cook* (1813), and by 1845 the dish, an airy cooked confection of beaten egg whites with the yolks and a savoury or sweet flavouring, had become well enough known for inclusion without comment in Eliza Acton's *Modern Cookery*. The soufflé has long had a reputation as a cruel and frustrating test of a cook's skill, liable either not to rise or to collapse at the crucial moment. Mrs Beeton had decided views on the topic: 'Soufflés . . . demand, for their successful manufacture, an experienced cook. They are the prettiest, but most difficult of all entremets. The most essential thing to insure success is to secure the best ingredients from an honest tradesman.' In practice, though, soufflés are less capricious than their reputation suggests.

soul food A term dating from the early 1960s for the type of food typically (or stereotypically) eaten by African Americans, especially those from the Deep South—for example, chitterlings, collard greens, black-eyed peas and rice, ham hocks. It arose from the use of *soul* to denote the emotional or spiritual quality of African American life and culture (first recorded in the mid-1940s), especially as manifested in music (*soul music*), which has also seeded other terms, such as *soul brother* and *soul sister* for fellow African Americans.

soup The etymological idea underlying the word *soup* is that of 'soaking'. It goes back to an unrecorded post-classical Latin verb *suppāre* 'to soak', which was borrowed from the same prehistoric Germanic root (*sup-*) as produced English *sup* and *supper*. From it was derived the noun *suppa*, which passed into Old French as *soupe*. This meant both 'piece of bread soaked in liquid' and, by extension, 'broth poured on to bread.' It was the latter strand of meaning that entered English in the seventeenth century.

Until the arrival of the term *soup*, such food had been termed *broth* or *pottage*. It was customarily served with the meat or vegetables with which it had been made, and (as the derivation of *soup* suggests) was poured over sops of bread or toast (the ancestors of modern croutons). But coincident with the introduction of the word *soup*, it began to be fashionable to serve the liquid broth on its own, and in the early eighteenth century it was assuming its present-day role as a first course.

The expression *in the soup* for 'in trouble' originated in the US in the late nineteenth century.

sour A mixed drink consisting of a spirit (usually whisky, but brandy, gin, etc. can also be used), lemon or lime juice (hence the name *sour*), and sugar. It originated in the US in the mid-nineteenth century: Jerry Thomas gave the first recorded directions for making it in his *How to Mix Drinks* (1862).

sour cream Cream that has fermented due to the action of bacteria. In most commercially produced sour cream, the fermentation is induced by the addition of selected lactobacilli. The term is first recorded in 1855. *See also* CRÈME FRAÎCHE.

sourcrout *See* SAUERKRAUT.

sourdough A quantity of dough kept back from a previous baking to form a leaven for the next batch (during which time it turns slightly sour, thus imparting a characteristic taste to the bread made with it). Sourdough bread is a traditional bread of country areas: the French *pain de campagne* is a sourdough bread made from wheat flour, and rye sourdough bread is common in central Europe, Scandinavia, and now the US. Gold-prospectors in Alaska and the Yukon at the end of the nineteenth century acquired the nickname of 'sourdoughs'. *See also* POILÂNE.

soursop Soursops are the spiny green fruits of a tropical American tree of the custard-apple family. Its tart white flesh is popular for making drinks, particularly in the West Indies. Its sweeter relative the custard apple is also known as the *sweetsop*. In both cases the *sop* refers to the white flesh, which supposedly resembles milk-soaked bread (known in former times as *sops*).

Southern Comfort The proprietary name of a whisky-based peach-flavoured American liqueur. It came into the world in New Orleans in 1874, the invention of a barman called Martin Wilkes Heron.

souvlaki A Greek dish consisting of chunks of marinated meat threaded on skewers and grilled. The Greek plural form *souvlakia* is often used synonymously. Greek *souvlaki* is a derivative of *souvla* 'skewer'.

sowens The term generally used in Scotland and parts of Ireland in the past for the dish known in England and Wales as 'flummery': oatmeal boiled to a jelly. It appears to be an Anglicization of Gaelic *súghan* or *súbhan,* denoting the liquid obtained by steeping the oats in water, which was a derivative of *súgh* or *súbh* 'sap'.

soya bean The soya bean, or *soybean* as it is also called, particularly in North America, is today the most widely grown and economically important member of the bean family.

Ranging in colour from yellow to green to red and black, it is extremely rich in protein, and has in recent decades become a key part of the Western diet in the form of textured vegetable protein, a meat substitute. It has been used for millennia in its native eastern Asia, though, and in a wide variety of forms: its young sprouts are eaten; it is soaked in water to produce soya milk, from which bean curd is prepared (known in Japanese as *tofu*); it is fermented to produce sauces and other condiments; it is ground to make flour; and it is even made into a sweet confectionery paste. The word *soya* comes via Dutch *soja* from Japanese *shōyu* 'soy sauce', which itself was a borrowing from Cantonese Chinese *shiyau*, a compound formed from *shi* 'salted beans used as a condiment' and *yau* 'oil'. The form *soy*, used mainly for the sauce rather than the bean it is made from, comes directly from Japanese *soy*, a colloquial form of *shōyu*. Soy sauce, incidentally, has been known in the West since the seventeenth century. Details of its manufacture were naturally hazy at first ('I have been told that Soy is made partly with a fishy Composition . . . tho a Gentleman told me that it was made only with wheat, and a Sort of Beans mixt with Water and Salt,' William Dampier, *New Voyage Round the World* (1699)), but by 1747 Hannah Glasse was recommending its use in her *Art of Cookery*.

spaghetti In Italian, *spaghetti* means literally 'thin string'; it is a diminutive form of *spago* 'string'. The name for these long slender cords of pasta is not recorded in Italian before 1836 (before then they appear to have come under the umbrella of *vermicelli*). Eliza Acton mentions them in the 1849 edition of her *Modern Cookery*, although the word was unfamiliar enough for her to mis-spell it *sparghetti*, and the 1888 edition of Mrs Beeton's *Book of Household Management* gives instructions on where in a meal spaghetti should be served. It was only really after the Second World War that they became a commonplace of the British diet, either in the somewhat travestied form of tinned spaghetti in tomato sauce (often produced in rings or hoops, to get round the problem of how to pick up the long wayward strings on a fork—always an embarrassment to the British) or as the perennial bed-sitter standby *spaghetti Bolognese*, spaghetti in a tomato and beef sauce (often abbreviated half-affectionately to *spag bol* or *spag bog*). Indeed, the extent to which the British have made spaghetti their own can be gauged both by the number of pet names for it (*spag, spaggers, spadgers*) and by the extent to which it has spawned metaphors: a *spaghetti* is a jumble of wires or roads, for example, notably the notorious motorway interchange (*Spaghetti Junction*) at Gravelly Hill near Birmingham; and a *spaghetti Western* is a cowboy film made in Italy.

Nouvelle cuisine in the 1980s introduced the world to the concept of 'spaghetti' vegetables: vegetables, such as cucumber, courgette, carrot, or kohlrabi cut into long thin strips. These should not be confused with the vegetable spaghetti, a variety of marrow whose flesh takes the form of thin threads.

Spam A trademark for a sort of pork luncheon meat that came into existence in 1937. The product was first put on the market in May of that year by George A. Hormel and Company of Austin, Minnesota and by the end of the twentieth century five billion tins of it had been sold. The name under which it was registered was presumably originally a blend of *spiced* and *ham*, although the story goes that it was first dreamed up by a New York actor, Kenneth Daigneau, with no particular product in mind. Spam became all too familiar in Britain during the Second World War as a substitute for scarce real meat, and it remained a common but frequently despised item in the British diet during the 1950s and 1960s. Its name became a metaphor for the commonplace and bland: 'Skipton is toned down to scale with our spammy age', *Observer* (1959). There is now a Spam Museum in Austin, Minnesota.

The 1939–45 Star, a medal awarded to all Second World War British service personnel, came to be known jocularly as the *Spam Medal*, apparently because the colours of its ribbon corresponded with those of the armbands of the ATS girls who served in NAAFI canteens.

The use of *spam* in computer jargon to denote the indiscriminate sending of identical messages to large numbers of Internet users dates from around 1994. It is said to have been inspired by a sketch in the BBC television comedy *Monty Python's Flying Circus* in which Spam appears with every item on a café menu.

spanakopitta A small, traditionally triangular Greek pastry containing spinach and usually feta cheese. The pastry is typically filo. The word is a compound formed from Greek *spanáki* 'spinach' and *pítta* 'pie'.

Spanish omelette An omelette containing chopped vegetables, especially potatoes, typically served flat rather than folded. It resembles a thick pancake, not unlike an Italian frittata. In Spain it is called a *tortilla*. The English term *Spanish omelette* is first recorded in the 1880s.

Spanish rice A method of preparing rice that involves cooking it with chopped-up onions, peppers, tomatoes, and other vegetables. It is often coloured with saffron, giving it a vaguely paella-like appearance. The term is first recorded in 1928.

spareribs *Spareribs* are not ribs that are surplus to requirements—indeed, its first syllable has no connection at all with the English word *spare*. *Sparerib* comes from Low German *ribbesper*, literally 'ribspear', which signified pickled pork ribs roasted on a spit. This was actually borrowed into English in the seventeenth century as *ribspare* or *ribsparre*, which survived dialectally until the nineteenth century. But the present-day English form arises from a transposition of the two elements, and the alteration of *sper* to *spare* by a process known as folk etymology—that is, the modification of a foreign word to make it sound more like a word in the language into which it is borrowed. The first known instance of the new formation is actually in a figurative context, in Thomas Nashe's *Have with you to Saffron Walden* (1596): 'Let's have half a dozen spareribs of his rhetoric, with tart sauce of taunts correspondent.' But by the mid-seventeenth century it seems to have become firmly established in its current sense of 'pork ribs with most of the surrounding meat removed'.

spatchcock A term denoting a method of cooking a chicken or game bird that involves splitting it open along its spine, laying it flat, and grilling it: 'The menu is more elegant than you'll find at similar set-ups, with the likes of garlic-and-thyme marinated spatchcock spring chicken with Jersey Royals', *Time Out London, Eating and Drinking* (2009). It originated in Ireland in the late eighteenth century as a noun, referring to the bird thus dispatched, and indeed it may have been based on the verb *dispatch*, with the addition of *cock*. Another probable influence is the earlier *spitchcock*, a word of mysterious origin denoting similar treatment meted out to eels and other fish.

In a somewhat obscure semantic development, around the turn of the twentieth century the verb came to be used in British English to mean 'to insert, interpolate, or add inappropriately or awkwardly': 'She is used to six hours of gymnastics somehow spatchcocked on to a normal school day. For Tweddle, only idleness is boring', *Times* (2004).

spätlese *Spätlese* means literally 'late gathering', and denotes a category of German and Austrian white wine made from grapes that have been picked later than those for wine of ordinary kabinett quality, and so have achieved greater ripeness and strength (and in good years sweetness). No sort of selection process during the harvest is implied by the term, which is what marks out the next highest grade of wine, *auslese*, as superior.

The equivalent term for Alsace wines is *vendange tardive*.

spätzle Small dumplings characteristic of southern Germany, and also of Alsace, where the word is spelled *spetzli* or *spatzele*. German *spätzle* means literally 'little sparrows'.

spearmint The full name of the common culinary herb generally known in everyday usage simply as *mint*. It is mainly used in relation to things intended to be put into the mouth but not swallowed, such as chewing gum and toothpaste. First recorded in the mid-sixteenth century, it probably reflects the pointed shape of the leaves, like a spearhead.

speck Fatty back bacon, cured by salting, and often also by smoking. Sometimes it is smoked with paprika. It is of German origin, as is its name, which goes back via Old High German *spec* to a prehistoric Germanic **spik(k)a-* (Old English had the cognate *spic*, now extinct; the probably related Sanskrit *sphik* meant 'buttock, hindquarters, hip').

spelt An ancient variety of wheat, native to southern Europe, with bearded ears and spikelets that each contain two narrow grains. Having long languished in relative obscurity, it started to become fashionable as a health food at the end of the twentieth century (it has a low gluten content and a high level of nutrients). The word was apparently current in the late Old English period, probably as a borrowing of Old Saxon *spelta*, but it seems to have been fairly rare until it was reintroduced from Middle Dutch in the sixteenth century. *See also* EINKORN, EMMER, KHORASAN.

spice Late Latin *speciēs* meant, among other things, 'wares, goods' (it is the same word as English *species*). By the time it reached Old French, as *espice*, the term had narrowed down somewhat to cover a range of (mainly sweet) items used in cooking, but it was still far broader in application than its modern English descendant *spice*: it could refer to jams and sweets, for example, to honey, sugar, and milk, and to items that would now be classified as herbs, such as parsley and sorrel. Gradually, however, in the course of the Middle Ages, it approached more closely to the present-day concept of spices as pungent or aromatic vegetable substances of essentially tropical origin, used to flavour food.

The practice of adding spices to food was widespread in ancient Rome and Byzantium, and continued throughout the Middle Ages. They were used just as much in meat and fish dishes as in puddings and other desserts, and their popularity was no doubt due just as much to their ability to disguise the taste of meat that was past its best as to their role in livening up dull stodgy food. The Crusades opened up the supply of spices to western Europe from the east still further, and the *raison d'être* of the maritime trade routes to the Far East pioneered in Renaissance times was largely the acquisition of spices. From the seventeenth century, the use of spices in Europe became more restrained, and indeed in Britain spices other than pepper (and occasionally allspice and mace) came to be virtually banned from savoury dishes, only gradually creeping back in as interest in foreign cuisines reawakened in the twentieth century.

spider An Australian term, first recorded in 1941, for a soft drink with ice cream floating on it. It may have been suggested by an earlier (nineteenth century) Australian use of *spider* for a drink consisting of brandy mixed with lemonade, but why that should have been called a 'spider' is unclear—one speculation is that it 'creeps up' on the drinker.

spinach Spinach is a comparatively recent introduction to Britain; it seems first to have arrived on these shores in the late fourteenth century. The first evidence we have of its cultivation, however, is from sixth-century Persia. The Persians exported both the plant (still known in Chinese as *poh ts'ai* 'Persian vegetable') and its name. They called it *aspanākh*, and this was taken over by the Arabs as *isfināj* or *isfānāj*. They prized it highly, calling it the 'prince of vegetables', and took the plant with them when they conquered Spain. This became the first main centre of spinach production in Europe (an early French name for it was *erbe d'Espaigne*). The Arabic term was altered in medieval Latin to *spinachia*, perhaps an allusion to the *spīnae* or 'spines' on the seeds of certain species, perhaps a reference to its cultivation in Spain (another medieval Latin name for it was *Hispanicum olus* 'Spanish herb'). Spanish adapted the Latin term to *espinaca* and passed it on via Old French *espinache* and Middle Dutch *spinaetse* to English.

Although first mentioned in a late fourteenth-century recipe book, spinach does not seem to have caught on in a big way in Britain until the early sixteenth century (William Turner in his *New Herball* (1568) called it 'an herbe lately found and not long in use'). But it soon became popular enough to be valued as a dish on its own. A frequent application was to serve it in a tart, sweetened with sugar, and it was in much demand as a salad vegetable, either raw or boiled. John Evelyn had no doubt about which he preferred: 'Spinach: of old not used in Sallets [salads], and the oftener kept out the better; I speak of the crude: but being boiled to a Pult [pap] . . . is a most excellent Condiment,' *Acetaria* (1699). Since it was not introduced to Britain until the thirteenth century, it did not have the repertoire of medicinal uses which was the legacy of ancient Greek physicians to most medieval vegetables, but it was not long before it achieved a reputation of bulging with iron and vitamins and of being 'good for you' ('Eat largely of spinach' recommended John Wesley in his *Primitive Physick*, 1747). It reached its apotheosis in the twentieth century with Popeye, the cartoon character who when in a tight corner consumed a can of spinach, which had a startlingly rapid effect on the size of his biceps.

In America in the 1930s and 1940s *spinach* was a colloquial term for 'nonsense': 'This reticence will be described by some temperaments as good taste. . . . I say it's spinach,' Alexander Woollcott, *While Rome Burns* (1934). The usage derived from a 1928 *New Yorker* cartoon caption.

In classic haute cuisine, dishes cooked with spinach are termed *à la florentine* 'in the style of Florence'.

splash The colloquial use of the term *splash* for a 'small amount of soda water added to a drink from a syphon'—as in 'whisky and splash'—dates from between the two World Wars: 'the atmosphere of the week-end jaunt, the whisky and splash', Graham Greene, *England Made Me* (1935).

split The original culinary application of the noun *split,* from around the start of the twentieth century, was to a bun, roll, or cake that is split or cut in half, to accommodate some sort of filling: a particular example is the 'Cornish split', a small round bun that is split open while still hot and eaten with butter or cream and jam. Then, around 1920 in America came the banana split, where it is the banana that is split in half.

Split also refers to a bottle of half the standard size: originally, in the late nineteenth century, bottles of mineral water, more recently, of champagne.

sponge The first evidence we have of the term *sponge* being applied to a light-textured cake comes in a letter of Jane Austen's, written in 1808: 'You know how interesting the purchase of a sponge-cake is to me.' It presumably developed from an earlier application of the word to dough that had been leavened, and hence had air bubbles in it—a usage first recorded in Hannah Glasse's *Art of Cookery* (1747). It was probably the nineteenth century, too, that first took the basic cake mixture of flour, sugar, and beaten eggs and used it for a baked or steamed pudding served with custard or some other sweet sauce—known as a *sponge pudding*, or originally a *sponge-cake pudding*: 'some nice soup and a spongecake pudding,' Annie Thomas, *The Modern Housewife* (1883). Butter first entered the equation in the Victorian era. Commercial sponge-cake mixes first made their appearance as long ago as the 1920s: the Army and Navy Stores catalogue for 1926–7 advertises 'sponge mixture' at fivepence halfpenny a packet.

Sponge was also used in the late nineteenth and early twentieth centuries for a sort of fruit jelly.

sponge toffee The usual American term for the confection known in Britain as HONEYCOMB.

spoon bread Spoon bread is a speciality of the southern states of the US. It is a soft bread made with maize flour, milk, and eggs, and as its name suggests its consistency is such that it can be served with a spoon. It is a traditional accompaniment of such dishes as fried chicken. It is alternatively called *egg bread* and *butter bread*.

spotted dick Spotted dick is a fine old traditional English dish: a sweet suet pudding, typically cylindrical, and studded with currants or raisins. Its name has made it the target of double entendres as leaden as the pudding itself often is. The first reference to it comes in *The Modern Housewife* (1849), a cookery book for the middle classes by the French chef Alexis Soyer, who settled in Britain; he gives a recipe, beginning: 'Plum Bolster, or Spotted Dick—Roll out two pounds of paste . . . have some Smyrna raisins well washed. . . .' And in 1892 the *Pall Mall Gazette* reports that 'the Kilburn Sisters . . . daily satisfy hundreds of dockers with soup and Spotted Dick'. The origin of *dick* is not clear, but there are records of its more general use, meaning 'pudding', in the nineteenth century: an 1883 glossary of Huddersfield terms, for instance, gives '*Dick*, plain pudding. If with treacle sauce, treacle dick.' According to Simon Majumdar, in *Eating for Britain* (2010), 'the catering staff of Flintshire County Council . . . in September 2009, decided to change the name of the country's most humorously named dessert to "Spotted Richard" because they were becoming weary of the constant flow of "immature" jokes they received'.

An alternative name, *spotted dog*, had appeared by the middle of the nineteenth century: 'For supper came smoking sheep's-heads . . . and "spotted dog," a very marly species of plum-pudding', C. M. Smith, *Working-men's Way in the World* (1854).

spread A soft substance, typically a savoury or sweet paste, that can be spread on bread or other food: 'I had to . . . mix up some chocolate spread from cocoa, sugar, and a little milk', Maureen Duffy, *That's how it Was* (1962). The term, which originated in America in the mid-nineteenth century, can also be applied to jam, and used as a cover term for butter, margarine, etc. *Sandwich spread*, a commercially produced savoury paste whose use is proclaimed in its name, appears to have come on the scene in the 1930s.

spring *See* HAND.

spring onion The original *spring onion* was simply an immature common onion, pulled in the spring before its bulb could develop (the first mention of it occurs in the magazine *Garden* in 1882), and that remains the most usual variety today, but the name is also applied to a completely different species, *Allium fistulosum*, which is the spring onion of Chinese cookery (the term formerly used for this in English was *Welsh onion*). Before *spring onion* came into general use, the usual term for these onions was *scallion*, but this is now largely restricted to American English (Americans in particular also favour the term *green onion*). In recent years the spring-onion crop has become virtually year-long, and in deference to this growers and greengrocers in Britain have taken to calling them *salad onions*.

spring roll An East and Southeast Asian snack consisting of a pancake made with an eggy batter, rolled round a mixture of chopped spring vegetables, typically including bean sprouts, and sometimes meat, and fried in hot oil. It is traditionally served on the first day of the Chinese New Year, which is also the first day of spring in the lunar year. In China the wrapper is made from wheat flour, in Vietnam more usually from rice flour. *Spring roll* (a partial translation of Chinese *chun juan*) is primarily a British English term; in American English the word is usually *egg roll*. An alternative British name is *pancake roll*.

sprinkles An American term for HUNDREDS AND THOUSANDS.

spritzer A long drink made from white wine and soda water. The concept is nothing new, of course (hock and seltzer was a popular nineteenth-century drink), but the term *spritzer* is a recent introduction. It seems to have been coined in American English in the 1950s, as an adaptation of German *spritzer* 'splash', influenced also no doubt by the German adjective *spritzig* 'fizzy, sparkling'.

sprue *Sprue* is a term for thin or young shoots of asparagus. It first came into the language in the middle of the nineteenth century (from where is not clear), when it seems to have had rather negative connotations of inferiority or immaturity, but nowadays when designer vegetables, slim and exquisite, are all the rage this stigma has been lifted.

spud *Spud* has been used since at least the mid-nineteenth century as a colloquial synonym for 'potato', but it is not entirely clear where it comes from. The likeliest explanation is that it is the same word as *spud* 'small spade', and that it was so called because such spades were used for digging up potatoes. This *spud* in its turn can be traced back to a fifteenth-century term for a 'dagger', but beyond that its history is lost in obscurity.

spumoni An American term for a type of ice-cream dessert with different colours and flavours in layers, typically liberally studded with candied peel and nuts. It came to America from Naples (Italian *spumone* is a derivative of *spuma* 'foam', and probably refers to the fact that the ice cream is usually whipped to lightness with cream), and it remains popular in Italian communities in the US.

squash¹ Any of a range of vegetables of the marrow family. The name is short for *isquoutersquash*, a now defunct term derived from a Native American word based on *asq-* 'raw, uncooked' (the *-ash* is a plural ending). As its origins suggest, it is mainly an American term—and indeed, in American English it is commonly used as a synonym of British English *marrow*. British-speakers tend to use it for the marrow's more exotic and curiously shaped relatives (for example, the acorn squash, the crookneck squash, the Turk's turban squash). *See also* BUTTERNUT SQUASH, CHAYOTE, PATTYPAN, PUMPKIN, VEGETABLE SPAGHETTI.

squash² A British term for a type of drink that was originally made, as its name suggests, simply by squeezing the juice and some of the pulp out of a citrus fruit. Lemon squash is the first sort we have a record of, from the 1870s, but orange squash was not long in following. Nor was commercial production far behind. Before the end of the nineteenth century we find the term being applied to a sweetened citrus concentrate requiring dilution before drinking—which is what it means today. In the early part of the twentieth century it was also used for non-citrus drinks, made for example from blackcurrants, but that application seems not to have survived.

squashed-fly biscuit *See* GARIBALDI.

stamp and go A Jamaican speciality consisting of cod fritters, served as snacks with drinks or as a first course. The term dates back at least to the late nineteenth century. It is a reapplication of an earlier *stamp and go* denoting an order given to a sailor to perform a particular duty. In response the sailor was supposed to stamp to attention, turn on his heel and set about the job without delay, and the metaphor underlying the cod fritters seems to be that they are quickly made and quickly eaten.

star anise The eight-pointed-star-shaped fruit of a small evergreen southern Chinese tree, so named from the resemblance of its smell and taste to that of anise. It is much used in Eastern cookery, but although it was known of in Europe in the early eighteenth century (it was first named *Chinese anise*, but we find records of the term *star anise* from the 1830s), it is only recently that it has become easily available for occidental home cooks.

star-fruit An alternative name for the CARAMBOLA. It is first recorded in 1974.

stargazy pie This is a fish pie of Cornish origin. It is made with the fishes' heads sticking out of the crust all round the rim, and presumably takes its name from their appearance of gazing skywards. In her *Observer Guide to British Cookery* (1984) Jane Grigson notes that 'it is a speciality of Mousehole where they make it on 23 December every year, Tom Bawcock's Eve, in memory of the fisherman who saved the town from a hungry Christmas one stormy winter'. However, in her *Fish Book* (1993) she adds a cautionary note, casting doubt on its authenticity: 'There is a certain lack of evidence on the unusual construction of the pie: I would feel happier about it if I could find some evidence for it before the 1950s'.

starver A piece of Depression-era Australian slang for a saveloy (a type of smoked sausage): 'I know what the things I eat cost me. Starvers, crumpets, stale cakes, speckled fruit, pies', D'Arcy Niland, *The Big Smoke* (1959). Apparently it was inspired by the sausages' use as a cheap food by the hungry and destitute.

steak English borrowed the word *steak* in the fifteenth century from Old Norse *steik*, a relative of the verb *steikja* 'to roast on a spit', and from earliest times it has been used for a fairly thick slice of relatively high-quality meat cooked by grilling or frying. It can be applied to meat from any animal (an early fifteenth-century cookery book mentions 'stekys of venysoun or beef', and to this day there are pork steaks, lamb steaks, gammon steaks, and even kangaroo steaks), but gradually the simple term *steak*, without any further qualification, has come to denote a slice from the hindquarters of beef—the *beefsteak* (borrowed by French as *biftec* and by Russian as *bifshteks*), since at least the eighteenth century the traditional fare of hearty-eating Englishmen, and since the Second World War transformed from unobtainability to the everyday luxury of steak and chips. But the strong association of *steak* with 'beef' led, probably in the nineteenth century, to the word being used, with dubious honesty, for any fairly cheap cut of beef, usually from the neck or shoulder, used in casseroles, pies, etc. (nowadays usually designated by such terms as *stewing steak* and *braising steak*). This, of course, is the main ingredient of steak and kidney pie or pudding, a dish central to the canon of traditional English cuisine which as far as is known is actually not more than about 150 years old: the earliest reference to 'steak and kidney pudding' is a recipe in Mrs Beeton's *Book of Household Management* (1861), which she apparently got from Sussex, and in which she specifies the best tender rump steak, not any old inferior cut of beef. *Steak* has also been

used since the late nineteenth century for a fairly thick cutlet taken cross-sectionally from a large fish, such as a salmon or cod (the *Standard* for 30 November 1883, for example, noted 'fishmonger charged 10d per lb. for his best cod steaks'). And around the same time, kippers were often known facetiously as 'two-eyed steaks'.

steeple cream An eighteenth-century dessert made by mixing together jelly and cream and forming the result into a point at the top, like a church steeple.

steinwein A general cover term for dry white wine made in Franken (Franconia), near Bavaria. It is traditionally bottled in flat flagons known as *bocksbeutels* (literally 'buck's pouch', from their supposed resemblance to a goat's scrotum). The name comes from the Würzburger Stein, the most celebrated vineyard of the city of Würzburg. The best steinwein is made from the silvaner grape, not a leading grape variety elsewhere in Germany.

stew A dish consisting typically of meat and vegetables cooked relatively slowly in liquid in a closed container: 'It's a stew of tripe . . . and cow-heel . . . and bacon . . . and peas, cauliflowers, new potatoes . . . and sparrow-grass, all working up together in one delicious gravy', Charles Dickens, *The Old Curiosity Shop* (1840). The term, which comes from the verb *stew*, is first recorded in 1756. *See also* IRISH STEW.

stick bean An alternative name for the RUNNER BEAN.

stickings An old term for inferior or damaged cuts of meat: 'The meat (for pies) is bought in "pieces", of the same part as the sausage-makers purchase—the stickings', Henry Mayhew, *London Labour and the London Poor* (1851). Based on *stick* in the now-obsolete sense 'to pierce or cut with a sharp or pointed implement', it is of considerable antiquity: a mid-fifteenth-century text, for example, mentions the 'sticking-piece', referring to the lower part of the neck of a beef carcase. *Sticking* remains in some butchers' vocabulary, for a piece trimmed off a hand of pork: 'The sticking has some ribs attached to some deliciously fatty meat from the shoulder', Hugh Fearnley-Whittingstall, *The River Cottage Meat Book* (2004).

stifado A Greek dish consisting of meat (lamb, beef, or rabbit) stewed with onions, tomatoes, and various herbs. Modern Greek *stifado* is an adoption of Venetian Italian *stufado*, which, like English *stew* (and French *estouffade* 'a stew'), is a descendant of Vulgar Latin **extufare* 'to heat in steam'.

Stilton A firm creamy British cows'-milk cheese which in its most typical form (*blue Stilton*) is injected with a penicillin mould that gives it its characteristic blue veining (an unveined version, *white Stilton*, is also made). It takes its name from the village of Stilton in Huntingdonshire, but in fact it has never been made at or even near Stilton. Its original appears to have been a type of cheese made at Quenby Hall in Leicestershire in the early eighteenth century. It was made by the then housekeeper, Elizabeth Scarbrow, and she had a commercial arrangement to supply cheeses to the Bell Inn at Stilton. It was the Bell, a much frequented hostelry, that made the cheese famous, and associated it forever with the name *Stilton* (Daniel Defoe in 1727 referred to 'Stilton, a town famous for cheese').

stinger In a twenty-first-century bar, an order for a *stinger* will elicit a cocktail consisting of brandy and white crème de menthe. In earlier times, however, the term denoted a small whisky and soda or water. It was a folk-etymological Anglicization of *stengah*, which was used in colonial Malaya in the late nineteenth and early twentieth centuries for a half measure of whisky so diluted—in effect, the rubber planters' equivalent of a *chota peg*. The word was an adaptation of Malay *setengah* 'half'.

stingo A dark strong bitter beer, supposedly named from the sharpness of its taste. It is a term of some antiquity (it first occurs in Thomas Randolph's play *Hey for Honesty* (1635): 'Come, let's in, and drink a Cup of stingo!') now rather on the decline. In *The Englishman's Food* (1939), J. C. Drummond and Anne Wilbraham quote this verse from an eighteenth-century print showing St George impaling a steak on his spear:

> Behold your Saint with Gorgeous English Fare,
> Noble Sirloin, Rich Pudding and Strong Beer.
> For you my Hearts of Oak, for your Regale,
> Here's good old English Stingo Mild and Stale.

In the 1920s it enjoyed a brief vogue as a humorous equivalent of 'vim or vigour': 'to keep in trim and add stingo to your efforts in sport', *Daily Telegraph* (1927).

Stinking Bishop A type of soft cows'-milk cheese made by Charles Martell and his family at Dymock in Gloucestershire since 1972. Its name is no reflection on its aroma. It comes from the perry in which the cheese's rind is washed, which is made from pears of a variety called 'Stinking Bishop', that were bred by a Mr Bishop, who apparently was noted for his irascibility.

stirabout A mainly Irish term for a sort of porridge made by stirring oatmeal into boiling water or milk. It is first recorded in 1682.

stock Etymologically, *stock* is simply something one keeps a 'stock' of for use. Nowadays usually conveniently conjured up by adding water to a commercial preparation (the term *stock cube* is not recorded until as recently as the 1960s; American English still prefers the more refined-sounding *bouillon cube*, which dates from the 1930s), stock is traditionally the product of a pot kept constantly simmering on the hob, to which odds and ends of meat, bones, vegetables, etc. are added from time to time to keep up a continuous 'stock' of flavoury broth as a basis for soups, stews, sauces, etc.: 'Stock for soup became fragrant in the air of Minor Canon Corner,' Charles Dickens, *The Mystery of Edwin Drood* (1870). In practice, few households or restaurants have the sort of constantly available source of low heat necessary for this perpetually self-renewing stockpot, and most stock is made afresh in individual batches as needed (fish stock has to be made this way, or it would turn to glue).

stockfish A now virtually disused term for a cod or similar fish cured by being split open and air-dried without salt. It was borrowed in the thirteenth century from Middle Dutch *stokvisch*, in which the element *stok-* is the same word as English *stock*. The original meaning of this was 'stem, trunk', and it may be that *stockfish* was so called from its being dried on sticks.

In South African English, the term is applied to a local variety of hake, owing to the influence via Afrikaans of modern Dutch *stokvis*, now used for 'hake'.

Stockfish finds a ready market in Italy, where it is called *stoccafisso*.

stollen A German Christmas cake made from a rich yeast dough traditionally containing nuts, fruit, and candied peel. In modern versions a layer of marzipan is often added. Its loaf-like shape was originally intended to symbolize the Christ-child wrapped in swaddling clothes. The word comes via Middle High German *stolle* from Old High German *stollo*, which meant 'post' or 'support'.

store cheese An American term, dating from the mid-nineteenth century, for Cheddar cheese. It reflects the fact that Cheddar was a staple item stocked in all grocery stores.

stotty cake Stotty cakes, or *stotties*, are round shallow large rolls (or small loaves) made from scraps of dough left over after the standard loaf tins have been filled. They are specialities of northeast England. The origin of the term is not known for certain, though it has been speculated that it comes from a Geordie verb *stott* 'to bounce'—the theory being, according to Andrew Webb in *Food Britannia* (2011), 'that these buns were so tough that they would bounce when dropped'.

stout *Stout* was originally simply a colloquial epithet for 'strong beer'. Its use for a specific sort of dark, fairly bitter and creamy variety of beer seems to have originated in the mid-eighteenth century: in 1762 W. Burton wrote 'the Porter brewers likewise have made a beer of an extraordinary strength called Stout, that will bear being made weaker by mixing it with small'. The most celebrated brand of stout is probably Guinness, first brewed by the Guinness family in Dublin in 1759, and mentioned by Charles Dickens in his *Sketches by Boz* (1836).

stovies A Scots term for potatoes and typically leftover meat cooked slowly in a very small amount of water (in Scottish English *stove* is used as a verb meaning 'to stew').

stracchino A generic term for any of a range of northern Italian soft cheeses, including Gorgonzola and Taleggio, originally made from the milk of cows fed on winter hay after they had come down from their mountain pastures. It is a derivative of dialectal *stracco* 'tired', probably reflecting how the cows felt after their long journey.

stracciatella A light Italian soup consisting of chicken or beef stock with beaten egg, grated cheese, and semolina stirred into it. The name means literally 'little fragment, little rag', referring to the appearance of the swirls of egg when it has cooked through. It is a derivative of the Italian verb *stracciare* 'to tear, rend'.
  The term is also used for an Italian type of chocolate-ripple ice cream.

strangoloprevete The Neapolitan name for STROZZAPRETI, a type of Italian pasta. Further south in Calabria it is *strangugliaprieviti*.

strawberry No one knows how the strawberry got its name. The word was used by our Anglo-Saxon ancestors, but they have left no clue as to why they coined it. Most of the

suggestions put forward over the years—that it was inspired by a resemblance of the plant's runners to straw, for example, or that the berry's external seeds look like 'little bits of chaff' (a now obsolete sense of *straw*)—seem rather lame. But uncertainty over its linguistic origins has not prevented the strawberry—in modern times a strapping hybrid produced from North and South American varieties, very different from the Anglo-Saxons' small wild *strēawberige*—from becoming the quintessential summer fruit, consumed in large quantities with its natural partner cream both in season and (thanks to the enterprise of growers in Spain, Israel, etc.) out.

straw potatoes Very thinly cut potato chips. The term, which is probably a translation of French *pommes paille,* is first recorded in 1904.

Strega The proprietary name of a sweet yellowish Italian liqueur flavoured with orange and various herbs. Legend—of uncertain antiquity—has it that it is based on the recipe of a magic potion of yore (*strega* is Italian for 'witch').

streusel A crumbly mixture of fat, flour, sugar, and often also nuts and cinnamon that is used as a cake topping. The term was adopted into English in the early twentieth century from German, where it is a derivative of the verb *streuen* 'to sprinkle' (a relative of English *strew*).

string bean A bean, such as a runner bean, that is grown for its edible pods. The name, which originated in America in the mid-eighteenth century, probably refers to the stringy fibres that run between the two halves of the bean. The humorous application to a tall thin person is first recorded in 1936.

string hopper A festive snack of South India and Sri Lanka made by extruding the batter for hoppers (*see* HOPPER) in long thin 'strings' that are then steamed.

strip steak *Strip steak* (first recorded in 1962), or *striploin steak*, is a term of American origin for a steak cut from the section of top loin muscle in front of the sirloin: 'Move on to main courses such as pan-fried veal striploin steak with spinach and wild mushroom risotto', *Good Food Guide* (2008). A particular association with New York has given it the alternative name *New York steak. See also* SHORT LOIN.

stroganoff Beef stroganoff is a dish consisting of strips of lean beef sautéed and served in a sour-cream sauce with onions and mushrooms. The recipe, which is of Russian origin, has been known since the eighteenth century, but its name appears to come from Count Paul Stroganoff, a nineteenth-century Russian diplomat. Legend has it that when he was stationed in deepest Siberia, his chef discovered that the beef was frozen so solid that it could only be coped with by cutting it into very thin strips. (Another account, however, identifies Alexander Grigorievich Stroganoff, an Odessa gastronome, as its originator.) The first English cookery book to include it seems to have been Ambrose Heath's *Good Food* (1932).

strozzapreti A type of Italian pasta made by rolling strips of dough roughly into a tube shape: 'Pasta dishes include egg-free strozzapreti with duck confit', *Time Out London, Eating and Drinking* (2008). Its name means literally 'strangle-priest', and refers to a possibly apocryphal priest who ate so much of it so quickly that he choked (Italian priests have a reputation for gourmandise). In Naples it is known as *strangoloprevete*, which means the same.

strudel A filled pastry case made from a particular sort of strong-flour dough rolled very thin. It is an Austrian speciality, although it seems originally to have been inspired by the Turkish baklava. Its most familiar incarnation is the *apfel strudel*, with a filling of apples mixed with raisins and cinnamon, but other sweet fillings include cherries and cream cheese, and in Austria it is quite common to have savoury fillings, such as minced meat. German *strudel* literally means 'whirlpool, eddy', and was presumably applied to the confection because its pastry is 'rolled round' its filling.

struffoli A Neapolitan Christmas speciality: little deep-fried rounds of dough coated in caramel. The etymology of the word is unknown.

stuffing In the Middle Ages the English term for an 'edible insertion' was *farce*, ancestor of modern English *forcemeat*. It was not until the sixteenth century that the word *stuffing* began to appear (the first reference to it in print is in Sir Thomas Elyot's *Dictionary* (1538), where he defines *fartile*—an obscure synonym of *farce*—as 'stuffynge, or that wherewith any foule is crammed'). Stuffing was popular in the Middle Ages, particularly for cooked birds but also for pork. Ingredients such as dried fruits were often added to the basic breadcrumbs, herbs, spices, or minced meat, and colourings like saffron and spinach juice were used too. The tradition continued through the Elizabethan period into the eighteenth century, when new variations such as oyster stuffing and chestnut stuffing were introduced, but in the nineteenth century the range of options began to narrow down towards the twentieth-century standardizations of 'sage and onions' and 'parsley and thyme'.

In American English stuffing, particularly for chicken, turkey, etc., is often called *dressing*.

submarine *Submarine*, or *sub* for short, is an American word for a large sandwich made from a long roll or piece of French bread, filled copiously with an assortment of meat, cheese, and salad vegetables. The term, which was coined in the mid 1950s, is a reference to the long cylindrical shape of the sandwich. It is only one amongst many, however; for the sandwich has inspired so many aliases—*grinder, hero, hoagie, Italian sandwich, poor boy* (especially in New Orleans), *torpedo*—that it has formed the subject of an article in the learned journal *American Speech*.

Earlier in the twentieth century *submarine* was also used in American English as a colloquial term for a 'doughnut', presumably from its being cooked by immersion in hot fat.

succade An antique term for crystallized fruit—fruits such as plums, pineapple, cherries, pears, and citrus peel—that is steeped in syrup until it becomes impregnated with sugar. It was acquired in the fifteenth century from Anglo-Norman *sukade*, but it is not clear what the ultimate source of that was. *See also* SUCKET.

succory An alternative and now little-used name for chicory. It originated as an alteration of early modern French *cicorée*, which was also the source of English *chicory*.

succotash A Native American dish consisting of butter beans and sweetcorn kernels cooked together (in its original ethnic form, with bear fat). The word is of Algonquian origin.

sucket An archaic term for a sweet, especially a piece of crystallized fruit. First recorded in the late fifteenth century, it is an alteration of *succade*. In former times special implements were made with which to eat the sweetmeats. Known as 'sucket forks' or 'sucket spoons', they had two prongs at one end and a spoon-like bowl at the other.

sucking pig An unweaned piglet (that is, one still sucking milk from its mother), especially one killed at up to six weeks old and roasted whole. The term is of long standing, dating back at least to the mid-sixteenth century, but in recent times it has faced increasing competition from *suckling pig* (first recorded in 1819). Some purists have objected to this, on the grounds that *suckle* properly refers to the sow and not her offspring, but in fact the use of *suckling* to mean 'sucking milk from the teat' goes back to the seventeenth century.

suet The culinary term for the hard white fat around the kidneys and loins of cattle, sheep, and other animals. It is used in making dumplings and puddings (*suet puddings*—the term is first recorded in the mid-eighteenth century) and as the fat component of mincemeat. The original suet puddings were little more than large dumplings, boiled in a cloth in spherical form or as a cylindrical log. It was a natural development to introduce fillings, both savoury (for example, *steak-and-kidney pudding*) and sweet (*pond pudding, roly-poly pudding, spotted dick*), and the pastry, made simply from flour, suet, and water and termed *suet crust*, became little more than a containing shell. The word came, in the fourteenth century, from an assumed Anglo-Norman **suet*, a diminutive form of *su* 'suet', which was descended ultimately from Latin *sebum* 'tallow, suet'.

sugar When human beings first penetrated the continent of Europe, the only sweetening agent they had available to them in significant quantities was honey. In India, however, there grew a large stout plant of the grass family whose juice when refined (a process probably discovered about 5000 BC) produced deliciouly sweet crystals. These were named in Sanskrit *śakarā*, which originally meant 'gravel, grit'. Gradually word of the wondrous substance spread westwards. Alexander the Great's general Nearchus, for instance, in the fourth century BC, reported that the Indians had a cane which produced 'honey without bees', and by the first century AD we have evidence of the Sanskrit word for 'sugar' being borrowed into European languages: Greek *sákkharon* (source of English *saccharin*) and Latin *saccharum*. At this stage, however, the substance itself was available in the West only in tiny quantities, and was used medicinally. It was the Arabs, in their conquests of the eighth century AD, who introduced it on a large scale, planting cane in Spain and southern France and laying the foundations of the vast world-wide sugar consumption of later centuries. They also brought with them their word for it, *sukkar*, which had come via Persian *sakar* from the original Sanskrit term; Spanish and Italian adopted it as *azúcar* and *zucchero* respectively, and from there it spread to other European languages, including Old French *sukere* (source of English *sugar* and ancestor of modern French *sucre*), German and Dutch *zucker*, and Swedish *socker* (Russian *sachar* comes directly from the Greek form). The first mention of the word in English comes in the Durham account rolls of the late thirteenth century, at which time sugar was still a rare and valuable commodity. Gradually it grew easier to obtain (by the 1540s, for instance, there were two sugar refineries in London), but it was not really until the first half of the eighteenth century that Caribbean plantations created the possibility of regarding it as anything other than an expensive luxury. And even then the high tax on it in Britain kept it out of reach of all but the well off. This was removed, however, by Gladstone in 1874, and sugar was able to take its apparently pre-ordained place, in large quantities, in British tea cups. A further factor in its greater availability was the introduction of beet sugar. The German scientist Marggraf was the first to successfully extract sugar from the beet, in 1747, but it was not until the nineteenth century that commercial production got under way on a large scale.

The use of *sugar*, and various combinations such as *sugar baby* and *sugar pie*, as an endearment originated in late 1920s America. The euphemism *sugar!* for *shit!* is apparently much more recent.

sugar apple An alternative name for the CUSTARD APPLE.

sugar cake A rich cake made with sugar, butter, eggs, and flour, its top generously dredged with sugar. The term, first recorded in 1600, is no longer much encountered in Britain, but there is some evidence that such cakes were part of Pennsylvania Dutch culture in the US in the twentieth century, presumably brought by German immigrants. They remain in public consciousness mainly thanks to their mention in the song 'Tea for Two' (1950), with lyrics by Irving Caesar and Otto Harbach:

> 'Day will break and you'll awake
> And start to bake a sugar cake
> For me to take for all the boys to see.'

sugar pea *See* MANGETOUT.

sugarplum Sugarplums were an early form of boiled sweet. Not actually made from plums (they were not candied plums, as the name suggests to modern ears), they were nevertheless roughly the size and shape of plums, and often had little wire 'stalks' for suspending them from. They came in an assortment of colours and flavours, and frequently, like comfits, had an aniseed, caraway seed, etc. at their centre. The term was in vogue from the seventeenth to the nineteenth centuries, but is now remembered largely thanks to the Sugarplum Fairy, a character in Tchaikovsky's *Nutcracker* ballet (1892).

sugar snap *See* MANGETOUT.

suissesse French *soufflé à la suissesse,* literally 'soufflé in the Swiss style', denotes a dish in which a standard soufflé mix is initially poached, and only then baked (in a bath of cream).

sukiyaki A Japanese dish consisting of thin slices of meat, typically beef, cooked together with vegetables and bean curd in a mixture of soy sauce, rice wine, and sugar, the process usually being rapidly carried out at table. A dish perhaps more to Western taste than to Japanese, it was one of the earliest Japanese dishes to become familiar beyond the Orient. It became widely available in Japanese 'sukiyaki restaurants' in the US in the 1930s and 1940s, and in fact there is no long tradition of eating it in Japan itself; it seems to have been introduced in the nineteenth century as a way of getting the Japanese people to eat more meat. The Japanese word is a compound formed from *suki* 'spade' and *yaki* 'to grill, cook'. Compare TEPPANYAKI, TERIYAKI.

sultana Sultanas are dried seedless white grapes, typically paler in colour than currants and raisins, and intermediate between the two in size. The finest traditionally come from Izmir, formerly Smyrna, in Turkey (sultanas are called *raisins de Smyrne* in French), but today they are produced in warm areas all round the world. Their name is simply an adaptation of the term *sultana* 'sultan's wife', first recorded in the 1840s.

sumac A Middle Eastern spice made from the dried powdered fruit of the Mediterranean sumac, a shrub of the cashew family. The word came into English in the fourteenth century via Old French or medieval Latin *sumac* from Arabic *summāq.*

summer pudding A cold dessert consisting of lightly stewed soft fruits, such as raspberries and redcurrants, chilled in a mould lined with slices of white bread, which take on a crimson colour from the fruits' juice. Now regarded as a traditional, almost quintessential English midsummer dessert, it is not actually recorded by name until the 1930s. According to Dorothy Hartley, in her *Food in England* (1954), it was formerly 'called "hydropathic pudding" because it was served in nursing homes where pastry was not permitted'.

sundae An elaborate dessert consisting of ice cream topped with fruit, nuts, syrup, jam, etc. It originated in the US. It is said to have been created by Ed Berners, proprietor of an ice-cream parlour in Two Rivers, Michigan, in 1881. Its name, however, is not recorded in print before it appears in W. A. Bonham's *Modern Guide to Soda Dispensers* (1897). The word clearly has some connection with *Sunday,* but precisely what, is not known. Various explanations have been put forward: that it was originally left-over ice cream from Sunday, served on subsequent days; that it was a particular sort of ice cream sold only on Sundays, in order to circumvent Sunday trading laws; or that ice cream was viewed as a dessert that could be eaten on the Sabbath without offending propriety. The most circumstantial account has it that George Giffy, proprietor of an ice-cream parlour in Manitowoc, Michigan, served the confection on Sundays only. When a small girl asked for one on a weekday and was told about Sundays only, she supposedly said 'Why, then, this must be Sunday, for it's the kind of ice cream I want'—and she got it. And thus, if we are to believe the tale of the imperious child, it got its name. The alteration in spelling (*sundi* was an early alternative to *sundae*) was presumably introduced to avoid taking the name of the Lord's day in vain.

Aficionados of the dessert declare hot fudge sundae to be the greatest of the sundaes.

sunny-side up A term denoting an egg that has been fried on one side only. It originated in America around the end of the nineteenth century, but has since become familiar in British English. *Compare* OVER EASY.

supreme A joint of chicken (or other poultry or game) consisting of the breast and often also the first and second joints of the wing, usually boned. It is also applied to the particularly tender strip of muscle beneath the breast. The term is a nineteenth-century introduction from French into English (William Thackeray, an enthusiastic gastronome, uses it in *Pendennis* (1850): 'The supreme de vollaille was very good'). In French it is also used for high-quality fillets of fish.

Supreme sauce is a sauce made with chicken stock and cream, and standardly served with poultry.

surf 'n' turf A term invented in the early 1970s by American restaurateurs and their marketers for a dish that contains both seafood and meat: typical partners on the plate might be prawns and a large steak. Some fastidious European gastronomes have affected to be scandalized by such combinations, but in fact the concept is widespread and of long standing: the Englishman's steak pie in former centuries often contained oysters, for example, and Catalonian cuisine has its *mar y montaña* ('sea and mountain') dishes, such as meatballs with squid, chicken and prawns, and octopus with pork belly.

surprise A dish, typically a dessert, whose exterior conceals an unexpected interior. According to *Larousse Gastronomique* (1988), 'the most obvious example of such a dish is Baked Alaska, in which ice cream is hidden inside a meringue which has been placed for a short time in a hot oven'. The English term (first recorded in 1712) is an adaptation of the French description *en surprise*: Richard Olney, for example, in his *French Menu Cookbook* (1970), gives a recipe for *ananas en surprise*, an emptied-out pineapple filled with strawberries, pineapple flesh, and raspberry purée, which he renders in English as *pineapple surprise*.

sushi Sushi is the universal Japanese snack. When they feel peckish, the Japanese will pop into the nearest *sushiya*, or sushi bar, to eat a few of these small balls or squares of cold boiled rice flavoured with vinegar, salt, and sugar, and covered with a variety of toppings, such as fish, egg, or mushrooms. In the 1990s, the habit spread to Britain.

swede The humble and lugubrious swede, orange-fleshed cousin of the turnip, was introduced into Scotland in 1781 from Sweden—hence its name, originally *Swedish turnip*, and by the early nineteenth century *swede*. It was hailed with enthusiasm as a replacement for the ordinary turnip—the *Encyclopedia Britannica* (1791) announced that the 'Swedish turnip is a plant from which great expectations have been formed'—and while it has not subsequently set the world on fire, it has remained part of the standard vegetable repertoire of Britain, and particularly of Scotland. There it is often called *turnip* or *neep*, the old word for 'turnip': a dish of bashed neeps, or puréed swede, is a traditional accompaniment of haggis. The Americans, meanwhile, usually refer to it as *rutabaga*, originally a Swedish dialect term meaning 'baggy root'.

sweetbread Precisely which internal organ of a calf, lamb, etc. the word *sweetbread* ought to be applied to is a matter of considerable controversy, but in practice it is clear that for centuries it has been employed for both the 'pancreas' *and* the 'thymus gland' used for

food. And historically these have been distinguished as, respectively, the *heart, stomach*, or *belly sweetbread* and the *throat, gullet*, or *neck sweetbread*. It is not certain where the name comes from (it first turns up in the middle of the sixteenth century, in Thomas Cooper's *Thesaurus*) but, unless it originally had some deeply dyed euphemistic undercurrents, it would seem to reflect the glands' reputation as prized delicacies (unusual amongst offal) which survives to this day. It is possible that the second element represents not modern English *bread* but the Old English word *bræd*, meaning 'flesh'.

sweet cicely A plant of the parsley family with small white flowers and large feathery leaves with a taste resembling aniseed that have been put to culinary use. The root is also edible. The name dates from the mid-seventeenth century. *Cicely* comes from *seselis*, the Latin name of the plant, which in turn came from Greek; its spelling resulted from association with the female given name *Cicely*.

sweetcorn *See* MAIZE.

sweet pepper *See* PEPPER.

sweet potato The large thick edible pink-skinned root of a tropical plant of the bindweed family. It was brought to Europe from Central America by the Spanish, and in the sixteenth and seventeenth centuries was quite popular in Britain, not least because of its reputation as an aphrodisiac. Thereafter it went into a decline, and it was not until after the Second World War that large-scale immigration from parts of the world where it is indigenous revived its fortunes in Britain. Its name in Haitian is *batata*, which, filtered through Spanish *patata*, gave English *potato*. The term clung on into the eighteenth century (when the lovesick Falstaff greeted Mistress Ford with 'Let the sky rain potatoes' in Shakespeare's *Merry Wives of Windsor* (1598) he was referring to sweet potatoes—and appealing to their aphrodisiac effect), but from the end of the sixteenth century the potato itself was making increasingly urgent claims on the name, and it became necessary to distinguish the sweet potato in some way. At first it was called the *Spanish potato*, and towards the end of the eighteenth century we find the first references to the term *sweet potato*.

In some regional varieties of American English, sweet potatoes are called *yams*.

sweetsop An alternative name for the CUSTARD APPLE.

Swiss cheese In American English, *Swiss cheese* is a generic term for a mild hard cheese of a type originally made in Switzerland, which British-speakers would tend to refer to by a more specific name such as *Emmental* or *Gruyère*. Its holeyness has provided the basis of a number of metaphorical applications, notably to the Swiss cheese plant, *Monstera deliciosa*, a tropical American climber whose large glossy perforated leaves have made it popular as a houseplant.

Swiss milk An old term, first recorded in 1889, for tinned condensed milk: 'In the absence of cream . . . Swiss milk also does very well', Flora Annie Steel and Grace Gardiner, *The Complete Indian Housekeeper and Cook* (1898). It arose from the fact that many of the earliest examples were produced by Swiss-based companies such as the Anglo-Swiss Condensed Milk Company and Nestlé.

Swiss roll A Swiss roll consists of a fairly thin rectangle of sponge cake, spread with jam or some other filling and rolled up. The origins of its name are not known in detail, although it presumably came ultimately from Switzerland. The first printed recipe for it appears in 1897. In American English, 'Swiss rolls' are known as *jelly rolls*.

Swiss steak *Swiss steak* is an American way with inexpensive steak which consists of dredging it with a covering of flour, pounding it hard, and then simmering it in liquid. It is served with vegetables. According to L. P. De Gouy's *Gold Cookery Book* (1947) the recipe is 'three centuries old,' and was originally called 'Schmor Braten'. The fact that less expensive cuts of steak are used for the dish has led to the term *Swiss steak* being applied generically to steak that is less tender than the top grades.

syllabub The syllabub is a Tudor invention. Its defining characteristic is the mixing of white wine (or cider or fruit juice) with sweetened cream, so curdling the cream, but from earliest times it has diverged into two basic types: a stiff version eaten as a dessert, and a thinner one for drinking. The former was made with thicker cream, often reinforced by beaten egg whites, the latter with single cream or even milk, sometimes introduced directly from the cow's udder into a bowl containing the wine and other ingredients. Both sorts remained very popular until the mid-nineteenth century (in Georgian times they even had special clear syllabub glasses for serving them in), but then they went out of fashion; the late twentieth century saw a revival of the firmer sort, as a sort of historical curiosity, but not of the drink. As for the name *syllabub*, that remains a complete mystery. Early spellings include *solybubbe, sullabub, selybube*, and even *sillibouk*, and probably it was originally just a fanciful meaningless coinage. *Syllabub* became the main form around 1700, probably due to the influence of the word *syllable*.

syrah A grape variety used to produce red wines, typically of considerable power and finesse. In France, its main home is the northern Rhône valley, where it makes Hermitage, Côte Rôtie, and Cornas. It is also widely grown in Australia, but there it goes under another name: *shiraz*. Etymologically, though, the two names seem to be identical. It is generally supposed that the origin of the grape, or at least of its name, is Shiraz, a city in what is now southeast Iran, an area that in ancient times was the source of vines brought to southern France by the Phocaeans. The evolution of *Shiraz* to *syrah* can be glimpsed, ironically, in some notes made in the 1840s by Sir William MacArthur on the prospects for vines in Australia: 'Scyras . . . An excellent grape, and promises to be . . . valuable for red wine'. The use of the name *shiraz* in Australia (not recorded before the early twentieth century) is apparently a conscious return to the grape's supposed past, inspired by stories of crusaders bringing it back with them from their travels.

syrup English acquired the word *syrup* (or *sirup*, as it is occasionally spelled in American English) in the fourteenth century. Its immediate source was Old French *sirop* or medieval Latin *siropus*, but ultimately it goes back to Arabic *sharāb* 'beverage', a member of the same word-family as produced English *sherbet, shrub* (the drink), and *sorbet*. Apart from its general application to a 'sweet solution of sugar and water,' it has been used for various liquid sugar products, including 'molasses'. *See also* GOLDEN SYRUP.

Szechwan pepper Szechwan pepper, or *Szechuan pepper*, or *Sichuan pepper*, is the small reddish-brown dried fruits of the prickly ash tree, a native of Szechwan province in west central China, which are used as a spice. Their aromatic heat gives a distinctive character to Szechwan cuisine, which is spicier than that of other parts of China. Its similarity in appearance and mouth-effect to ordinary pepper earned it its name, first recorded in the 1920s, but the two are not related.

Tabasco An extremely hot spicy sauce made from red peppers. The name, which was registered as a trademark in the early twentieth century, comes from Tabasco, a state in southeastern Mexico; the earliest record of its use for the sauce comes from the 1870s. Tabasco is used as a condiment, particularly in New Orleans and Tex–Mex cuisine, and for enlivening a number of cocktails.

tabbouleh A Middle Eastern salad made with crushed wheat mixed with mint, tomatoes, onions, and a variety of herbs. It is a particular speciality of the Lebanon. The word comes from Arabic *tabbūla*.

tabnab Mid-twentieth-century nautical slang for a cake, bun, or pastry, or for any sort of savoury snack: 'My favourite "tabnab" was . . . a little fried potato-cake with a morsel of kari'd mutton inside', Kyril Bonfiglioli, *All the Tea in China* (1978). The word's origins are unknown.

taco In Mexican cuisine, a taco is a small pancake, or tortilla, rolled round a filling, such as seasoned minced meat or beans, into a cigar shape and shallow-fried. A Tex–Mex adaptation is the *taco shell*, which is a taco in a horseshoe shape deep-fried until crisp, used as a receptacle for various fillings. The American-Spanish word *taco* comes from Spanish, where it means 'wad', 'roll', 'stopper', and even 'billiard cue'. It is probably ultimately of Germanic origin.

tafelspitz A term in Austrian and South German butchery, meaning literally 'table-tip', for a cut of beef consisting of a small triangular muscle taken from the tip of the rump (in French it is called the *aiguillette baronne,* in American English the *tip* or *tri-tip*). The underlying signification is 'meat from the tip for cooking and bringing to the table', and indeed the term has come to denote the dish most commonly made with it, an Austrian and Bavarian speciality in which the beef is simmered in stock. It is traditionally served with horseradish cream (*kren*) and rösti potatoes. It was reputedly a favourite dish of the Emperor Franz Joseph I.

tagine A tagine—not to be confused with *tahini*—is a North African dish cooked in a traditional shallow earthenware Moroccan cooking pot with a characteristic conical lid, which is also called a tagine. It can take a variety of forms: lamb with prunes is a popular combination, but the term embraces various chicken and meat dishes.

tagliatelle Italian pasta cut into long thin noodle-like strips. The Italian word is a diminutive form based on the verb *tagliare* 'to cut', and is generally glossed in English as 'little ribbons'. It is first recorded in Italian in 1549, but did not make its first known appearance in print in English until 1899.

taglierini Very thinly cut tagliatelle. Like *tagliatelle*, the word is a diminutive form based on Italian *tagliare* 'to cut'. *Taglierini* is now the standard Italian spelling, but *tagliarini* is earlier (it is first recorded in 1640), and is the version most commonly used in English. *Tagliorini* (not pukka Italian) can be encountered too: 'a dish of fresh bright-green tagliorini served with delicate spring nettles to follow', *Good Food Guide* (2008). It may be an unwitting blend of *taglierini* and *tagliolini*, an alternative name for the pasta that is also used in English.

tahini Tahini (alternative versions of the name are *tahine* and *tahina*) is a paste made from ground sesame seeds. A characteristic ingredient of the cuisine of the eastern Mediterranean, it is used raw, in dips, cooked in sauces, and perhaps most notably as a key element in hummus. The word is Arabic in origin, a derivative of the verb *tahana* 'to grind, crush'.

Taleggio A type of Italian cream cheese made from cows' milk. It takes its name from the town of Taleggio, in the province of Bergamo.

tamale A Mexican dish consisting of some sort of chopped meat wrapped with corn dough inside a maize husk and steamed. Its name comes ultimately from Nahuatl *tamalli*.

tamarillo An invented name for the tree tomato, the red, egg-shaped, slightly tart fruit of a South American shrub now widely grown in warm areas around the world, particularly New Zealand. The New Zealanders found that it was not selling too well as a tree tomato, so in 1966 they decided to give it a new, 'sub-tropical-sounding' name. The precise genesis of *tamarillo* is not known, but presumably it contains at least subconscious echoes of *tamarind* and *tomatillo*, the diminutive form of Spanish *tomate* 'tomato'.

tamarind The fruit of a tropical tree of the pea family. It has an acid pulp, with a flavour reminiscent of lemon, which is widely used in oriental cuisine—in chutneys and other condiments, for instance, and also for making cooling laxative drinks. The separation of the pulp from the hard seeds is a laborious process. Its name comes via medieval Latin *tamarindus* from Arabic *tamr hindī*, literally 'Indian date'. English acquired it as long ago as the early sixteenth century (Sir Thomas Elyot in his *Castel of Helthe* (1533) recommended tamarind as a 'purger of choler'). It is an ingredient of Worcester sauce.

tandoori The term *tandoori*, which designates a north Indian and Pakistani style of cooking in a charcoal-fired clay oven, derives from the name of the oven itself—in Urdu, a *tandoor*. All but unknown in English before the early 1960s, it has since undergone such an explosion in usage, accompanying the rise of the Indian restaurant, as almost to rival in frequency that earlier culinary legacy of Anglo-Indian contact, *curry*. Tandoori chicken has become its most familiar manifestation in Britain, but a wide variety of other foods are cooked in the tandoor, including kebabs, fish, and nan bread.

tangelo As its name suggests, the tangelo is a hybrid between the tangerine and the pomelo (a citrus fruit resembling the grapefruit). It was developed in the US in the early years of the twentieth century; the 1904 edition of the *US Department of Agriculture Yearbook* bears witness to its naming: 'The term "tangelo" is suggested by the writers

[Messrs Webber and Swingle] as a name for this group of loose-skinned fruits, which lie midway between the pomelo and the tangerine.'

tangerine A mandarin orange, or more specifically a variety of mandarin with a very deep orange skin (the application of the word to the colour is first recorded in 1899). Tangerines first appeared in the 1840s, and they owe their name to Tangier, the port in Morocco—not because they come from there (they are Chinese in origin), but because that is where they were first imported.

tansy An early English forerunner of the omelette. It was made by beating the juice obtained from the leaves of the tansy (a bitter-tasting aromatic plant of the daisy family), or of spinach, into raw eggs and frying the mixture in a pan. A cookery book of around 1450 gives the recipe: 'Take fair tansy, and grind it in a mortar; and take eggs, yolks and white, and draw them through a strainer, and strain also the juice of the tansy; and meddle the juice and eggs together. . . . ' It was an Easter speciality, said to have been eaten in memory of the 'bitter herbs' of the Passover ('Mince-pie is as essential to Christmas as tansy to Easter,' *The Connoisseur*, 1754), and indeed four days before Easter 1662 we find Samuel Pepys providing a 'pretty dinner' of 'a tansy and two neats' tongues and cheese'. An alternative name for it in the Middle Ages was *erbolat*.

tapas Tapas are savoury snacks served in Spanish bars, and typically washed down with glasses of cold fino or manzanilla sherry. They are of considerable diversity, ranging from simple olives, potato salad, and small spicy sausages to fried shrimps, stuffed peppers, and squid cooked in its ink. The word *tapa* literally means 'lid' in Spanish, and its gastronomic application comes from the practice of covering glasses or jugs of drink on the bar with edible 'lids', such as a piece of bread or sausage, to keep out the flies.

tapénade Tapénade is a Provençal speciality, a pungent aromatic black paste made principally from three classic southern French ingredients, black olives, anchovies, and capers, pounded in a mortar with olive oil and seasonings. It is often served as a spread on toast, as an hors d'oeuvre. The word derives from Provençal *tapéno* 'capers'.

tapioca A grainy starch obtained from the fleshy root of the cassava, a tropical American plant of the genus *Manihot*. The name for it in the Tupi-Guarani languages of South America is *tipioca*, a compound formed from *tipi* 'residue' and *ok* 'to squeeze out'; it reflects the way in which the starch was produced by crushing the root fibres, steeping them in water, and then squeezing all the liquid out. Spanish and Portuguese  changed the word to *tapioca*, the form adopted in English in the late eighteenth century. By Mrs Beeton's time the use of tapioca had become widespread, and she herself writes in glowing terms of its possession of that elusive quality beloved of Victorians, digestibility: 'Its nutritive properties are large, and as a food for persons of delicate digestion, or for children, it is in great estimation', *Book of Household Management* (1861). She gives a recipe for tapioca soup, in which it was used for thickening broth, but she also of course mentions tapioca pudding, the tapioca-based milk pudding that for close on the next hundred years was to be a not altogether welcome staple of the British sweet course.

taralluccio A small ring-shaped biscuit typical of southern parts of Italy. It can be either sweet or savoury. The word is a diminutive of *tarallo* 'biscuit', whose origins are unknown.

taramasalata Taramasalata in modern Greek means literally 'salad of preserved roe' (Greek *taramas* was borrowed from Turkish *tarama* 'soft roe'). It is a Greek hors d'oeuvre or mezze dish consisting of fish roe (traditionally from the grey mullet) mixed into a pinkish paste with breadcrumbs, garlic, olive oil, lemon juice, and egg yolk. An alternative spelling is *taramosalata*.

target A joint of lamb or mutton consisting of the neck and breast—or, to put it another way, the forequarter with the shoulder removed. The term, dating from the mid-eighteenth century but now little encountered, probably refers to the frontal position of the breast, like a 'shield' (which is what *target* originally meant).

tarka dhal An Indian dish consisting of creamy lentils (*dhal*) cooked with onion, garlic, and spices. Hindi *tarka* is a derivative of *taraknā* 'to season'.

taro A tropical and temperate plant of the arum family (a distant relative of the arum lily or cuckoo-pint of the English woodlands). It is widely cultivated in warm countries both for its large starchy edible tubers (which are cooked more or less like potatoes, and have become increasingly common over the past four or five decades on English market stalls in areas with a large Caribbean or Asian population) and for its huge edible leaves (from which the plant gets one of its many alternative names, *elephant ears*). The word *taro* came into English from either Tahitian or Maori, and is first mentioned by one Sydney Parkinson (1769) in his journal of a voyage to the South Seas (the term *eddoes*, which predates it in English by nearly a century, now tends to be applied to the more modest-sized taro tubers). The plant itself appears to be a native of northern India, but it came west via China, where it is widely used.

Other alternative names for the plant are *dasheen* and *cocoyam*, while the slender-tubered Cypriot variety is known as *colocassi*, an alteration of *colocasia*, the taro's Latin genus name.

tarragon A plant of the daisy family whose faintly liquorice-tasting leaves have a particular affinity with chicken. It has a number of culinary applications, though, and is a constituent of the French *fines herbes* mixture. It is a comparatively recent introduction to Britain; the first reference to it in an English text was by Sir Thomas Elyot in his *Dictionary* (1538): 'Tragonia, an herbe nowe callid Taragon, late sene in this realme, whiche hath a tast like ginger.' The history of its name is murky. As Elyot's entry suggests, it was once called *tragonia* in English, which was a medieval latinization of *tarchon*, another alternative English term in the sixteenth, seventeenth, and eighteenth centuries. This went back to a medieval Greek *tarkhōn*, which in turn was borrowed from Arabic *tarkhōn*. Beyond that all is uncertain, although medieval etymologists assumed that the Arabic word originally came from Greek *drákōn*, source of English *dragon* (which no doubt inspired the plant's scientific name *Artemisia dracunculus*). French *estragon* 'tarragon' also comes from *tarchon*.

tart The origins of the word *tart* are a mystery. English borrowed it in the fourteenth century from Old French *tarte*, but no one knows for certain where *tarte* came from. Some have suggested that it is an alteration (influenced by medieval Latin *tartarum* 'Tatar') of Old French *torte*, ancestor of modern French *tourte*, a round savoury or sweet pie or tart. This in turn came from Latin *torta* 'round bread', which literally meant 'twisted' (it was a derivative of the verb *torquēre* 'to twist'). (German *torte* 'rich cake or tart', as in *Sachertorte* and *Linzertorte*, probably comes from the same Latin source, as ultimately do Italian *tortellini* and American Spanish *tortilla*.) However, not all etymologists accept this derivation.

What is certain, though, is that when English acquired the word in the fourteenth century, it denoted an open pastry case that could contain meat or fish as well as fruit or vegetables (the medieval cookery book *Forme of Cury* gives a recipe for *tarts of flesh*, which contain minced pork and rabbit). Only gradually over the centuries did the meat disappear (and also to a large extent the vegetables, although one may still encounter the occasional spinach tart). In modern English, a decided Atlantic rift in usage has developed. In America, the word *tart* tends to indicate a small individual open pastry case with a sweet, usually fruit filling. In Britain, this usage survives in the particular context of jam tarts, but on the whole *tart* refers to a larger version of this, with a jam, fruit, or custard filling, that is cut into slices for serving, or to a similar fruit-filled pastry case with a crust—in other words, a fruit pie.

The word seems first to have been applied colloquially to women in the mid-nineteenth century, as a term of endearment rather than abuse. The first to record it was John Hotten, in his *Dictionary of Modern Slang* (1864): '*Tart*, a term of approval applied by the London lower orders to a young woman for whom some affection is felt. The expression is not generally employed by the young men, unless the female is in "her best".' Not until the 1880s do we find instances of its being applied to prostitutes. The usage may have originated in Cockney rhyming slang (*see* JAM TART). The diminutive *tartlet*, also a borrowing from French, is of equal antiquity with *tart*: to quote the *Forme of Cury* again, it describes how to make 'tartlettes' with minced pork, eggs, currants, and saffron.

The adjective *tart* 'sharp-tasting', incidentally, is a completely different word, which goes back to Old English *teart* 'acerbic'.

tartare *Tartare* has two culinary applications in English, both of them inspired by the supposed fieriness of the Tatar people of central Asia. *Tartare sauce* is basically a mayonnaise given piquancy by the addition of chopped capers, onions, and pickles and served with fish; it is of French origin, and seems to have been introduced to English cuisine by Eliza Acton. *Steak tartare* is raw lean minced beef served with a raw egg (although some continental aficionados insist that the authentic steak tartare is made not with beef but with horse flesh).

tarte Tatin An upside-down French apple pie, which is cooked with its pastry on top and then turned over, so that the buttery appley juices percolate downwards. Its name commemorates the Tatin sisters, who popularized it in their restaurant at Lamotte-Beuvron to the south of Orléans, in the early twentieth century.

tartiflette A speciality of the Haute-Savoie in the foothills of the French Alps: sliced potatoes baked with reblochon cheese, cream, and lardons of bacon. The basic recipe is probably of some antiquity, but its modern manifestation was created in the 1980s by the manufacturers of reblochon to publicize their product. Its vector of familiarity to English-speakers has been mainly via Brits taking winter-sports holidays in the area. The word is a derivative of Franco-Provençal *tartifla* 'potato'. That probably came from Italian *tartufolo* 'truffle', which was applied to potatoes when they arrived from the New World, and was also the source of German *kartoffel* 'potato' (*see* POTATO, TRUFFLE).

tasso In the Cajun cuisine of Louisiana, a type of spiced smoked ham that is used mainly as a flavouring ingredient in stews and the like. The word probably comes from Louisiana French *tasseau* 'jerked beef', which may well be related to Spanish *tasajo* 'slice of dried meat', but the ultimate origins of both are unknown.

tatsoi A Chinese plant of the brassica family with glossy dark green leaves that spread out from a central rosette. The young leaves can be eaten raw in salads. Its Chinese name *daat-choi* is a compound formed from *daat-* 'to sink, fall flat' and *choi* 'vegetable'.

tayberry A dark-red soft fruit produced by crossing a blackberry with a raspberry. It was named after the Tay, the Scottish river near which it was bred. It was introduced in 1977. *See also* TUMMELBERRY.

T-bone steak A T-bone steak, or *T-bone*, is a steak cut from the thin fillet end of a sirloin of beef and containing a T-shaped section of bone which gives it its name. The term originated in the US in the early years of the twentieth century.

tea Europeans first became aware of tea in the mid-sixteenth century, when Portuguese explorers encountered it in China (the Chinese had been drinking the beverage, made by infusing the dried leaf shoots of a plant of the camellia family in hot water, since at least the sixth century). The word for it in Mandarin Chinese is *ch'a*, and this was the form in which it first appeared in English, in the late sixteenth century (it survives in *char*). Dutch voyagers in the Far East, however, had encountered another form, Amoy Chinese *t'e*. They brought it back to Europe as *tee*, and this was the term adopted as the drink became fashionable throughout the Continent in the first half of the seventeenth century: *thé* was all the rage in Paris in the mid 1630s, and by the end of the 1650s Londoners were finding out about *tee* or *tea* (on 25 September 1660 Samuel Pepys records 'did send for a cup of tee (a China drink) of which I never had drunk before'). It is said to have been Charles II's queen, the Portuguese Catherine of Braganza, who popularized it in court circles, and at first it remained only a curiosity, but by the end of the century the East India Company had started to import it on a large scale (at this time it would have been drunk exclusively in the Chinese manner, with no milk). During the eighteenth century the price of tea gradually fell, and its popularity rose proportionately, so that by around 1800 annual consumption was about a pound and a half per head. The foundations of tea as the British national beverage had been laid.

During the nineteenth century tea was seen as a potent weapon in the fight for temperance—in the House of Commons in 1882 William Gladstone declared that 'the domestic use of tea is a powerful champion able to encounter alcoholic drink in a fair field and throw it in a fair fight'—and steady reductions in the excise duty on it meant that by 1900 annual consumption had gone up to about six pounds per head. By the mid 1930s the figure had reached a staggering ten pounds, representing five cups a day for every man, woman, and child in the country. Thereafter, however, the rise in the popularity of coffee hit tea consumption, bringing it down to an annual seven pounds a head in the 1970s. A feature of post-war tea drinking has been the tea-bag, first introduced in the late 1950s.

Tea seems first to have established for itself a particular niche in the day in the 1740s, by which time it had become the fashionable breakfast drink. It was also drunk after dinner, and as the usual time for dinner progressed during the eighteenth century towards the evening a gap opened up for a late-afternoon refreshment, filled by what has since become the traditional English afternoon tea, a meal in its own right, with sandwiches and cake as well as cups of tea (amongst the earliest references to it are these by Fanny Burney in *Evelina* (1778): 'I was relieved by a summons to tea,' and by John Wesley in 1789: 'At breakfast and at tea . . . I met all the Society'; Anna Maria Russell, Duchess of Bedford (1783–1857), famously claimed to have originated the fashion, but as can be seen, it was around well before she was in a position to have any influence over it). In various other parts of the English-speaking world, teatime has assumed other connotations: in Jamaica, for instance, it is the first meal of the day, while for Australians and New Zealanders it is a cooked evening meal—a usage reflected in the tea, and more specifically the 'high tea', of certain British dialects, predominantly those of the working class and of the North (the term *high tea* dates from the early nineteenth century).

At first, *tea* was pronounced, and often spelled, *tay* in English, but the modern pronunciation had become generally established by the middle of the eighteenth century. *See also* BLACK TEA, BOHEA, BUSH TEA, EARL GREY, GREEN TEA, LAPSANG SUCHONG, OOLONG, PEKOE, ROSIE LEE.

teacake The day of the teacake, a large, flat, round, sweet yeast-raised bun, often containing currants, is passing. In the 1960s it was still quite a common teatime treat, typically toasted and spread with butter, but since then it has rather faded from the scene (it is still possible to buy teacakes in supermarkets, but often they are labelled 'tea buns', as if not to mislead shoppers unfamiliar with them). The term dates from the early nineteenth century: the earliest known reference to it is in an American cookery book, L. M. Child's *American Frugal Housewife* (1832), and Dickens mentions it in *Martin Chuzzlewit* (1844): 'Tea and coffee arrived (with sweet preserves and cunning tea-cakes in its train).'

A very different animal that has had the name *teacake* applied to it is a small hemispherical cake consisting of a biscuit layer topped with chocolate-covered meringue, originally produced by the Scottish firm of Tunnock's around 1950.

teff A type of African cereal grain grown mainly in Ethiopia. Its flour is used to make the local injera flatbread. It is gluten-free, which wins it many brownie points as a Western health food. The word comes from Amharic *tēf*.

tej A type of honey wine or mead that is the national drink of Ethiopia. The word probably comes from Amharic.

tempeh A substance made by boiling soya beans and then allowing them to ferment, which forms an important part of the Javanese diet and is now fairly widely used as a meat substitute in the West. It can be used in various ways—sliced and deep-fried, for instance, or chopped up and added to stews. The word comes from Javanese *tempe*.

tempranillo A Spanish variety of red-wine grape, which forms the basis of the blend for Rioja. The name comes from that of a village in northern Spain. When grown in Portugal, the grape is known as *tinta roriz*.

tempura In common with many other Japanese dishes, tempura became fashionable in the West in the 1970s and 1980s. It consists of seafood, typically prawns, and often vegetables too, dipped in a light batter and quickly deep-fried. However, all is not quite as it seems. For both the cooking technique and the name appear not to be of indigenous Japanese origin: the notion of deep-frying in batter was brought to the Far East by Portuguese explorers in the sixteenth century, and *tempura* in fact represents a borrowing of Portuguese *tempero* 'seasoning'.

tenderloin A term of American origin for the fillet of pork or beef—the long and particularly succulent and tender muscle that runs beneath the ribs. The earliest record of it is in Noah Webster's *American Dictionary of the English Language* (1828), but British readers do not seem to have been introduced to it until the middle of the nineteenth century: 'The "tenderloin," the "porterhouse" steak of America, are infinitely superior to our much-vaunted rump steak', *Daily Telegraph* (1864).

The colloquial American use of *Tenderloin* for a district where vice and corruption are rife dates from the late nineteenth century, when it was applied specifically to a district of New York City that was viewed as a 'choice' assignment by police because of the bribes offered to them to turn a blind eye.

tent An archaic term for Spanish red wine. In use from the sixteenth to the nineteenth centuries, it was mainly applied to wine of relatively low alcoholic content, especially as used as a communion wine. It is an alteration of Spanish *tinto* 'dark-coloured', which is used in Spanish to denote red wine.

teppanyaki In Japanese cuisine, a dish of meat and/or fish fried with vegetables on a hot steel plate that forms the centrepiece of the meal table. The Japanese word is a compound formed from *teppan* 'steel plate' and *yaki* 'to grill, fry, cook'. *Compare* SUKIYAKI, TERIYAKI.

tequila A colourless Mexican spirit distilled from the juice of an agave, a fleshy-leaved cactus-like plant. Its name, which dates from the first half of the nineteenth century, comes from Tequila, a town near Guadalajara in central Mexico, which is a main centre of production. It is used as the basis of a number of cocktails, notably the Margarita and the Tequila Sunrise, a lurid concoction made with grenadine syrup which enjoyed a brief vogue in the 1970s.

teriyaki A Japanese dish consisting of meat or fish marinated in a mixture of soy sauce and rice wine and then grilled, typically on skewers over charcoal. The Japanese word is a compound formed from *teri* 'gloss, shine' and *yaki* 'to grill, fry, cook'. Compare SUKIYAKI, TEPPANYAKI, YAKITORI.

terrine Essentially, a terrine is any dish made in a terrine—which is a small deep earthenware dish with a tightly-fitting lid (the French word means literally 'made of earthenware', and comes ultimately from Latin *terra* 'earth'; English originally borrowed it in the eighteenth century as *tureen*). It can be made of fish or shellfish, and in the 1970s and 1980s there was a vogue for vegetable terrines, in which vegetables of contrasting shapes and colours are layered in a mousse or sauce set with aspic, so as to produce a marbled effect. But the quintessential terrine is made from finely chopped or minced meat—typically with a base of lean and fat pork, and often with other meats, such as game, duck, veal, etc. added to it—and cooked, in its terrine, in the oven in a bath of boiling water. The full French term for this type of terrine is *pâté en terrine*, which is abbreviated to *pâté* as well as *terrine*. This has led to *pâté* and *terrine* becoming virtually synonymous, in both French and English, although some purists still insist that the word *pâté* should be reserved for pâté in a pastry crust (in French *pâté en croûte*).

tête de moine A creamy French cows'-milk cheese originally made in the Jura. It was invented many centuries ago by the monks of Bellelay Abbey, and there are alternative versions of how it got its name (in French literally 'monk's head'). According to one, the abbey charged local farmers a levy of one cheese *par tête de moine* 'per capita of the monks' for permission to make it; the other likens the cylindrical cheese, which has its top sliced off for serving, to a monk's tonsured head. Both rather have the air of being wise after the event.

textured vegetable protein Usually abbreviated to *TVP*, this is a proprietary name for a type of protein obtained from soya beans. The beans are made into a paste, which is then spun into fibres that are woven into a texture that resembles (only passingly, some would say) that of meat. The TVP is then coloured and flavoured to heighten the illusion. In its early days it did not need a particularly sharp eye to spot its uniform chunks in institutional stews and curries, but latterly its main role has perhaps been as a bulker-out of, or substitute for, minced meat. The term *textured vegetable protein* was introduced around 1966, and registered as a trademark in the US by Archer Daniels Midland Company, Decatur, Illinois.

Thai basil A variety of basil widely used in Thai cooking (in Thailand it is called *bai horapa*).

thali The savoury component of an Indian meal, typically consisting of a central mound of rice (or bread) surrounded by small containers containing a variety of dishes, from which diners help themselves according to choice. All are set out on a large metal plate, also called a *thali*. The Hindi word comes from Sanskrit *sthāli*.

thermidor A designation given to a method of preparing and cooking a lobster in which the creature (up to this point alive) is cut in half and grilled, has its flesh sliced up and returned to the half shell in a béchamel sauce with various added flavourings, and is then browned under the grill again and served. It commemorates the play *Thermidor* by Victorien Sardou, for the first-night celebration of which it was created in Paris in 1894.

Thousand Island dressing A pink mayonnaise-based salad dressing flavoured with tomatoes, chilli, green peppers, etc. The earliest known reference to it is in an advertisement in a 1916 issue of the *Daily Colonist* of British Columbia, which offers bottles of 'Mrs Porter's Thousand Island Salad Dressing' at 35 cents each. The name presumably comes from the Thousand Islands, a group of over 1800 small islands in the St Lawrence river, between the US and Canada.

thousand-year-old egg A Chinese delicacy that may look and taste a thousand years old, but in fact takes only a few weeks to prepare. It consists of a pickled duck's egg that is kept for up to three months in a mixture of ash, lime, salt, and chopped straw, bound together into a sort of clay with tea. The white is transparent, the yolk becomes a curious greenish-brown. The Cantonese name is *pay tan*. *See also* HUNDRED-YEAR-OLD EGG.

thunder and lightning A term of diverse gastronomic application over the years. At the beginning of the nineteenth century the name was given, with shock and awe in mind, to a drink of gin and bitters, and its later use for ignited brandy sauce was similarly motivated. Its main connotation, though, has been the contrast of dark and light—specifically, dark treacle against a pale background. In the West Country it denotes treacle (or golden syrup) and clotted cream, piled generously on to splits, and it has also been applied to a dessert of rice over which golden syrup is poured. In Italy *tuono e lampo*, which translates as 'thunder and lightning', is a savoury dish of pasta and chickpeas.

thyme Thyme, with its small aromatic, slightly resinous-tasting leaves, is one of the most widely used and also one of the most ancient of culinary herbs. The Egyptians and the Greeks employed it extensively (its name comes ultimately from Greek *thúmon*, a derivative of the verb *thúein* 'to burn sacrificially'), and it was the Romans who introduced it to Britain. In French cuisine it constitutes one of the basic herbs of the bouquet garni, and in English cookery it was one of the few to survive the temporary eclipse in the popularity of herbs in the late nineteenth and early twentieth centuries (parsley and thyme stuffing, for instance, remained a regular standby in English kitchens). And this is just the ordinary cultivated variety. There are other thymes, including several with lemon-scented leaves, and also the wild thyme, known to Oberon in Shakespeare's *Midsummer-night's Dream* ('I know a bank whereon the wild thyme grows'), which has a milder savour than the ordinary thyme.

Tia Maria The proprietary name of a rum-based coffee-flavoured liqueur. It was invented in Jamaica in the 1940s by Dr Kenneth Leigh Evans. Spanish *Tía María* means literally 'Aunt Mary'.

tian Originally, a Provençal dish consisting of vegetables cooked in olive oil and then layered in a shallow square earthenware casserole and baked au gratin (the name was in the first instance that of the container, which Provençal got from Greek *tēganon* 'frying pan'). In modern usage the term is applied somewhat promiscuously to any of a range of layered dishes: 'Icily unctuous bloody mary sorbet made a vibrant topping for a tian of prawns, crab, and avocado', *Time Out London, Eating and Drinking* (2009).

tiddy oggy An expanded version of *oggy* 'pasty' (*see* OGGY), especially referring to one that contains a generous amount of potato (*tiddy* is a West Country dialect word for a potato).

tiger bread A type of white bread of Dutch origin (Ductch *tijgerbrood*), of which the top is spread with rice paste before baking, with the result that it comes out of the oven with a crazed or mottled two-tone crust that with sufficient imagination could be seen as resembling the patterning of a tiger's fur (at the suggestion of a three-year-old girl, in 2012 the British supermarket Sainsbury's changed the name of its version to 'giraffe bread').

tiger nut The tiger nut is not a nut at all, but the small dried tuber of the chufa plant, a type of sedge. Dark brown and shrivelled, it is unprepossessing in appearance, but its chewy texture and nutty flavour made it very popular with children before the Second World War. As Glynn Christian pointed out in his *Delicatessen Food Handbook* (1982), the decline of the corner shop led almost to its complete disappearance, but there are now signs that it is making a comeback. An earlier name for it, at the beginning of the nineteenth century, was *rush nut*, and it is sometimes also called *chufa*. *See also* HORCHATA.

tiki A general term for any of a wide range of 'tropical'-style, usually rum-based cocktails (for example, a Mai Tai or a Zombie), which typically feature some sort of fruit juice and come with a miniature paper parasol appended. In origin it is a Maori word meaning 'image', and in New Zealand English it is applied to the sort of large wooden or small greenstone images of a human being that are a feature of Maori culture. Then, in the mid-twentieth century, as the tentacles of the US tourist industry reached the South Pacific, it began to be co-opted to denote stereotypical aspects of Pacific island life and culture. Among these is the *tiki bar*—picture a ramshackle open-sided palm-frond-thatched hut on the white sand dispensing luridly coloured drinks to beachcombers—which inspired the use of the term for 'cocktail'.

tikka Tikka is roughly the Indian equivalent of kebabs. It consists of pieces of meat (typically chicken) marinated in spices and then threaded on skewers and cooked. The word is Punjabi, a borrowing of a Turkic word meaning 'piece, chunk'. By far its most familiar manifestation in Britain is in *chicken tikka masala,* a dish of chicken kebabs in a rich spicy sauce (ranging from medium to very hot). The story has got around that it was invented in the mid-1970s by Ali Asif Aslam, owner and chef of the Shish Mahal restaurant in Glasgow who, when a customer complained that his tikka was too dry (authentic tikka *is* served dry, having been cooked in a tandoor), added a sauce based on Campbell's tomato soup. This may or may not be true (though it seems to be better substantiated than most such recipe-creation legends), but certainly the dish as it now exists was a creation of British Indian restaurants. Its fame spread in the 1980s, when supermarkets began to stock it as a chilled ready-meal. In the 1990s it was regularly topping the poll as Britain's favourite 'curry', and 'in his 2001 general election speech the Labour politician Robin Cook tried to persuade us that chicken tikka masala had become our national dish', Kate Colqhoun, *Taste* (2007). *See also* BUTTER CHICKEN, MASALA.

timbale A timbale can be composed of meat, fish, or vegetables in a creamy sauce, or of fruit in Chantilly cream, but its essence is its shape, which is that of a cup or bowl (the original meaning of *timbale* in French is 'kettledrum'). The 'case' enclosing a timbale's contents is usually made of pastry, but rice or pasta are also used. Timbales are part of classic French cuisine, and there are numerous specialized recipes: *timbale Agnes Sorel*, for instance, which contains minced chicken with truffles, and *timbale Brillat-Savarin*, with pears, cream, and crushed macaroons. Byron was the first English writer to refer to the timbale, in *Don Juan* (1824) ('Then there was God knows what "à l'Allemande" . . . "timballe" and "Salpicon"'), and by the end of the nineteenth century it was firmly in place on the best Victorian and Edwardian tables.

tinned dog Blackly humorous Australian slang, dating from the late nineteenth century, for 'tinned meat': 'Another frugal meal of "tinned dog", a couple of flats to mend, and straight into our swags', Rex Ellis, *Bush Safari* (1982).

tipsy cake A traditional English dessert, first cousin to the trifle. As its name suggests, its key ingredient is alcoholic: it consists essentially of sponge cakes soaked in sweet sherry or some other dessert wine, decorated with almonds, and with custard poured round it. The first reference to it was reportedly by the writer Mary Russell Mitford in 1806: 'We had tipsy cake on one side, and grape tart on the other.'

tirami su Italian *tirami su* means literally 'pick me up'. Gastronomically, it denotes a rich dessert made from coffee-soaked biscuits layered with sweetened mascarpone (a cream cheese). It was invented in the late 1960s, reputedly by the owner of the El Toulá restaurant in Treviso, in the Veneto, and quickly caught on with the pudding-loving British when real Italian cuisine arrived in the 1980s.

tisane An infusion of herbs (camomile, for example, lemon balm, or mint) drunk hot, often for medicinal purposes. The word comes ultimately, via Latin *ptisana*, from Greek *ptísanē* 'barley water' (it meant literally 'peeled barley', and was a derivative of the verb *ptíssein* 'to peel'), and was originally acquired by English in the sixteenth century in the form *ptisan*, generally used for 'barley water'. *Tisane* is a twentieth-century readoption from French, and the word still carries with it powerful associations of frail old lace-bedecked French ladies sipping their fragrant herb tea—particularly, perhaps, the lime-blossom tea in which Aunt Léonie dunked her madeleine in Proust's *Du côté de chez Swann*.

Tizer The brand name of a reddish-orange British fizzy soft drink. It was invented by Fred Pickup, and originally launched in 1924 as 'Pickup's Appetizer'. That became the snappier *Tizer*, but the original was immortalized in the long-running advertising slogan 'Tizer the appetizer'.

toad-in-the-hole Nowadays this British dish typically consists of sausage cooked in batter, but in its earliest incarnations in the eighteenth and nineteenth centuries (when it was usually called *toad in a hole*) various cuts of meat were used. Mrs Beeton, for instance, used steak and kidney, and recipes recommending the finest fillet steak are to be found, but often enough toad in the hole was a repository for leftovers. Even today lamb chops are occasionally found lurking in batter, and 'sausage toad' is the unappetizing colloquialism that distinguishes the orthodox version. The notion of secreting delicacies in 'holes' in a batter pudding goes back to Roman times, and in the earliest recorded uses of this actual expression in the eighteenth century they do not contain only 'toads': Hannah Glasse, for example, gives a recipe for 'pigeons in the hole'.

toast The verb *toast* originally meant 'to parch, scorch' (it comes ultimately from Latin *torrēre* 'to parch', source also of English *torrid*), but not long after English acquired it at the end of the fourteenth century, from Old French *toster*, it was being applied to the browning of food, and particularly bread, before the fire ('Look thou toast fine wheat bread,' *Liber Cocorum*, 1420). Its use as a noun is of similar antiquity. At this stage, however, it was 'a toast'—a small piece of toasted bread that was put into wine, sweet drinks, etc., fairly similar in fact to what we would nowadays call a 'crouton'. The fourteenth-century cookery book *Forme of Cury* has a recipe for a dish called 'tostee': 'Take honey and wine and dissolve it together . . . and boil it long. Put ginger powder, pepper, and salt into it. Toast bread and pour the liquid on to it; cut pieces of ginger and sprinkle it with them.' The modern use of *toast* as a collective term for 'toasted bread' dates from the early eighteenth century. 'It is related of the Duke of Wellington . . . that when he landed at Dover in 1814, after six years' absence from England, the first order he gave at the Ship Inn was for an unlimited supply of buttered toast', Elizabeth David, *English Bread and Yeast Cookery* (1977).

Toast 'to drink someone's health', also an early eighteenth-century development, seems to have come from the practice of naming a lady to whom an assembled company of gallants drank 'toast'—the notion being that metaphorically she flavoured their drink as agreeably as pieces of spiced toast did.

The colloquial British expression *have someone on toast*, meaning 'to be in a position to deal with someone as you wish, as if able to devour them at your leisure', dates from the 1880s. Much more recent is *be toast* 'to be or be likely to become ruined, defunct, or done for': 'They were driving along a dual carriageway . . . the speedometer nudging ninety . . . "You'd better be right about this," Nick Nicholl whispered. "Otherwise my licence is toast"', Peter James, *Looking Good Dead* (2006). It apparently made its debut in a line spoken by the character Venkman in the US film *Ghostbusters* (1984), as he is about to zap someone with a laser-type weapon: 'This chick is toast!' This seems to have been an ad-lib alteration by the actor, Bill Murray, of a line that appears in the script as 'Turn this guy into toast'.

toastie A colloquial British term for a toasted sandwich or snack: 'A tasty hot crab toastie had a floury, sticky texture that didn't do justice to the toasted slab of wonderful own-made bread', *Time Out London, Eating and Drinking* (2011).

Toblerone The proprietary name of a triangular chocolate bar that contains nougat, almonds, and honey. It was created in Berne, Switzerland in 1908 by Theodor Tobler and Emil Bauman. Its name combines that of its originator with Italian *torrone* 'nougat'. Given its Swiss background it is generally assumed that its characteristic shape was inspired by the Alps (a supposition reinforced by the picture of the Matterhorn on its packaging), but Tobler himself said he got the idea from a pyramid of dancers he once saw at the Folies Bergères.

toddy In British, and particularly Scottish English, a toddy is a warming beverage made from whisky with sugar and hot water. From the eighteenth century it has been the preferred long drink for whiling away the winter evenings in Scotland, and indeed the first known reference to it comes in Robert Burns's *Holy Fair* (1786): 'The lads an' lasses, blythely bent, to mind baith saul an' body, sit round the table, weel content, an' steer about the toddy.' The name comes from a tropical alcoholic drink made from the sap of various palm trees, called in Hindi *tārī* (the r sound in this word is quite close to English d).

In the US a *toddy* is often an iced drink, spiced but with no sugar.

toffee *Toffee* first appears on the scene in the early nineteenth century. The original form of the word, in northern and Scottish dialects, was *taffy*, a term still used in American English, especially in reference to *salt-water taffy*, once made with sea water. In the 1820s we find such spellings as *tuffy* and *toughie*, suggesting that early toffee was a distinctly challenging proposition for the teeth (the term *stickjaw* was a common nineteenth-century epithet for it). The current spelling *toffee* is first recorded from 1828. It is not clear where the word originally came from, although some have linked it with *tafia*, a rumlike drink made from molasses.

Until comparatively recently, the term *toffee* was used simply for the substance (made by boiling sugar and butter together); not until the 1930s do examples begin to appear of its use for a single sweet (as in 'a pound of toffees').

Toffee-apples, apples coated with a thin layer of toffee and fixed on a stick, seem to be an early twentieth-century invention; they are first mentioned in the Christmas 1917 issue of the *B E F Times*. In America they are called *candy apples*.

Toffee-nosed appears originally to be services slang; it is first recorded in Edward Fraser and John Gibbons's *Soldier and Sailor Words* (1925). It has been suggested that it is based on the notion of the nose being so superciliously high in the air that it completely loses touch with the mouth.

tofu Tofu is bean curd, a pale soft cheese-like substance made from soya-bean milk, which forms a dietary staple in most east Asian countries. *Tofu* is the Japanese word for it, borrowed from Chinese *dòufu*, which means literally 'rotten beans' (the Chinese version is of a more solid consistency than the Japanese). Although long familiar in the West (the word *tofu* is first recorded in an English text in the 1880s), it was only in the 1970s and 1980s that tofu became fashionable as a rich source of protein for vegetarians. The French call it *fromage de soja* 'soya cheese'.

toke Dated slang, of unknown origin, for 'bread', or 'a piece of bread': 'Dripping . . . spread on "tokes" was eaten for eleven o'clock lunch by schoolgirls for well nigh forty years', Margery Kendon, *Ladies College, Goudhurst* (1963).

Toll House cookie An American term for a sweet biscuit containing chocolate chips and often chopped nuts. It commemorates the Toll House, a restaurant in Whitman, Massachusetts, where the original recipe was created in the 1930s by Ruth Wakefield.

tomahawk steak A term of American origin for a rib-eye steak with a portion of rib still attached to it. In appearance it resembles perhaps not so much a tomahawk as an oversized lamb chop.

tomalley An American term for the digestive organ of a lobster (loosely, its liver), which turns green when cooked. It is considered a delicacy, and is either eaten on its own or mixed into sauces. The word comes via French *taumalin* from Carib *taumali*.

Tom and Jerry An American term for a rum-based hot drink made with beaten eggs, sugar, and spices. Dating from the early nineteenth century, it was based on the names of two Regency bucks who are the central characters of Pierce Egan's novel *Life in London* (1821), which was subtitled *The Day and Night Scenes of Jerry Hawthorn Esq. and Corinthian Tom*. A later continuation, *Finish to the Adventures of Tom, Jerry, and Logic* (1828), established the order in which they now appear. (The names were adopted for two hapless animated-cartoon characters, one tall and one short, who appeared on screen in the US in the early 1930s. Joseph Barbera worked on the series, and he was one of the originators of the much more famous cartoon cat-and-mouse duo 'Tom and Jerry', who made their screen debut in 1940.)

tomatillo The edible fruit of a Mexican plant related to the physalis, with which it shares a papery calyx, and also more distantly to the tomato. Although it ripens to purple or yellow, it is more commonly used while still green, especially to make sauces and preserves. The Spanish name means literally 'little tomato'.

tomato Tomatoes first appeared on the scene at the beginning of the seventeenth century, at which time they were called *tomates*: 'There was also Indian pepper, beetes, Tomates, which is a great sappy and savourie graine' (Edward Grimstone, *Acosta's Historie* *of the East and West Indies*, 1604). This version of the word came via French *tomate*, and it was not until the middle of the eighteenth century that various alternative forms began to appear. Based supposedly (but not always accurately) on Spanish and Latin, they included *tomata* and *tomatum* as well as *tomato*. These variants vied for supremacy until the end of the nineteenth century—Eliza Acton, for instance (1845), used *tomata*, but Mrs Beeton (1861) preferred *tomato*—and it was not until the 1900s that *tomato* saw off its rivals.

The ultimate source of all these was Nahuatl *tomatl* (the plant originated in Central America), but before this ethnic name took root the tomato was commonly called in English the *love apple* (whether its reputation as an aphrodisiac prompted or was prompted by this is not clear). Other early synonyms included *golden apple*, reminiscent of Italian *pomodoro* 'tomato'.

For a long time after their introduction, tomatoes were treated with some suspicion (they were thought to cause gout and cancer, for example), and it was not until the 1840s that they came to be regarded as wholesome food. And even then, they were always cooked; the raw tomato as a mainstay of the great British salad did not really come into its own until after the First World War. The affectionate abbreviation *tom*, incidentally, is first recorded in 1920.

The pronunciation of the word *tomato* is of course one of the better-known transatlantic differences: British English has /təˈmahtoh/, whereas American favours /təˈmaytoh/, rhyming with *potato*.

Tom Collins A tall iced drink consisting of gin with lemon or lime juice, soda water, and sugar. As with most such mixed drinks, the origins of its name are far from clear. It is generally said to have been called after the barman who invented it, but the fact that in the earliest known references to such a drink—from Australia, in 1865—it goes under the name *John Collins* (a term now used when the gin is Hollands gin) casts some doubt on that explanation. Another theory links it with *Old Tom*, an eighteenth- and nineteenth-century British colloquialism both for gin in general and for gin liberally sweetened with sugar: 'When sweetened and diluted by the retailers gin is known as gin cordial or "Old Tom"', Thomas Allbutt, *System of Medicine* (1897).

Since the mid-twentieth century the surname *Collins* has become a generic term for any spirit-based mixed drink of similar recipe—thus one can have a rum Collins, a brandy Collins, and so on.

tomme Tomme (or *tome*) is a general term for any of two types of French soft cheese. One consists of goats'-milk and ewes'-milk cheeses made mainly in southeastern France; the best-known are *tomme des Allues* and *tomme de Brach*. The other is a range of cows'-milk cheeses, mainly from Savoie (*tomme de Savoie* is the generic name), including particularly *tomme au marc*, which is ripened in vats of marc (*tomme au raisin*, coated with roasted grape seeds, is a processed version of this). The word *tomme* comes from Provençal *toma*, whose origins are unknown. Italian has the related *toma*, which denotes a type of fresh cheese produced in Piedmont.

tonic Tonic water, or *tonic* for short, originated in its modern form, as a carbonated drink flavoured with quinine, in the middle of the nineteenth century: a Mr Erasmus Bond patented a 'Quinine Tonic Water' in 1858, and in the 1870s the Schweppes company introduced an 'Indian' Tonic Water on to the market. The use of quinine as a prophylactic against malaria explains the 'Indian' part of the name, but it was also thought at the time to be more broadly beneficial to health, which accounts for the choice of 'tonic'. The now firmly established partnership with gin does not seem to have caught on until after the First World War.

tonka bean The black seed of a South American leguminous tree which has a vanilla-like fragrance. It is dried and cured in rum or other alcohol before being used. In former times it was much in demand for flavouring liqueurs and confectionery, but now it is mainly used in perfumery. *Tonka* is a local word in Guyana.

topside A lean boneless British cut of beef taken from the very top of the hind leg. The term is not recorded before the 1890s (the first known instance in print is in the pages of the *Girl's Own Paper* (1896): 'Braised Beef—A piece of "top-side" is best for the purpose'), and to begin with it seems to have been used with reference to mutton as well as beef.

torrone The Italian version of nougat, which contains toasted nuts (classically almonds, but hazelnuts and pistachios are also used). It is a traditional Christmas treat. It was introduced from Spain, which is also where its name comes from: Spanish *turrón*, a derivative of the verb *turrar* 'to toast'. *See also* TOBLERONE.

torrontes A grape variety that produces Argentina's best-known white wine. It has a distinctive aromatic quality, slightly reminiscent of wine made from muscat grapes. It got its name from a Spanish white-wine grape, but the two varieties seem not to be closely related (let alone identical).

torte A German term (borrowed from Italian) for a fairly elaborate sweet cake—roughly equivalent to French *gâteau*. It is a two-syllable word, but in English it is often pronounced as if the final -*e* were not there. *See also* LINZERTORTE, SACHERTORTE.

tortelli Italian pasta consisting of small filled parcels (like ravioli) that are rolled up and formed into a ring, with one corner folded over to make a pleat. Fillings range from cheese (such as ricotta) through vegetables (spinach, pumpkin) to meat ragu, and in Italy sweet (or sweet-savoury) fillings are frequent. The name means literally 'little cakes' (their shape has led to them also being called *cappellacci*, which means literally 'little hats'). Tiny ones are called *tortellini* (also named *cappelletti*, likewise 'little hats'), and rather larger ones *tortelloni*.

tortilla Tortillas are small flat maize-flour cakes served hot with a variety of fillings or toppings. They are of Mexican origin, and became more widely known in the late twentieth century owing to the increasing popularity of Tex–Mex cuisine. Etymologically, the word means virtually 'little tart'. It is a diminutive form of Spanish *torta* 'round cake', which in turn goes back to late Latin *torta* (probable source of English *tart*). It was first mentioned in an English text as long ago as the end of the seventeenth century ('Tartilloes are small Cakes made of the Flower of Indian Corn,' William Dampier, *New Voyage Round the World* (1699)), but it did not really become established until the mid-nineteenth century. Back in Spain, *tortilla* denotes what in English would be termed a 'Spanish omelette'.

tostada A tostada, or *tostado,* is an item of Mexican street food consisting of a deep-fried maize-flour pancake topped with a mixture that would typically include beans, minced meat, and vegetables: 'The sweetcorn tostado, a tower of crisp corn tortillas filled with black beans, was a success', *Time Out London, Eating and Drinking* (2009). The word comes from the past participle of Spanish *tostar* 'to toast'.

tournedos A tournedos is a small round piece of fillet steak surrounded with a moistening strip of fat. The word comes from French *tourner* 'to turn' and *dos* 'back': various explanations have been advanced as to its origin, including that it came from Parisian market stalls backing (*tournant le dos*) on to the main market area, where the not-so-fresh fish was sold, and thus was in the first instance applied by association to cuts of meat that were slightly past their best; and that when the Italian composer Gioacchino Rossini first ordered the tournedos recipe which now bears his name (*tournedos Rossini* is served with truffles and foie gras) the head waiter was so horrified by it that he refused to countenance it, so Rossini said 'Very well, if you don't want me to see you serve it, I'll turn my back while you do so!' English adopted the term *tournedos* in the 1870s.

tracklements A cover term for a wide range of condiments that go with meat—mustards, for instance, relishes, pickled greengages, apple jelly spiked with rosemary, rowan jelly suffused with port wine—the sort of items, in fact, that in the latter part of the twentieth century became widely available in small nostalgic-looking jars at large prices. The English food-writer Dorothy Hartley claimed to have invented the word, or rather its culinary application. According to her she was reviving an old term for 'impedimenta' in general. However, no trace of such a word has been found before she first used it in the early 1950s, and its origins remain a mystery. One possibility is that Latin *tragēmata* or Greek *tragēmata* 'spices, condiments' may have been present at its birth.

trail An animal's intestines. Gastronomically the term applies mainly to the intestines of woodcock or snipe, which are traditionally either cooked undrawn or, if drawn, the intestines and other internal organs (apart from the gizzard) are cooked separately and eaten with the bird: 'Lay in the snipes, being first drawn and half roasted. Take care of [i.e. don't throw away] the trail; chop it and throw it all over the dish', Hannah Glasse, *The Art of Cooking Made Plain and Easy* (1747). It is also used in connection with some fish, especially red mullet, which by tradition is cooked with its liver in place. An abbreviated form of *entrails*, it is first recorded in the mid-eighteenth century.

trail mix A term of American origin, first recorded in 1977, for a mixture of dried fruit and nuts eaten as a snack food, especially by hikers and campers. It has crossed the Atlantic, but its American synonym, *gorp*, has stayed at home.

traminer A grape variety which produces highly perfumed white wines. It gets its name from the village of Tramin (modern Termeno) in what is now the Italian Tyrol, where it was first mentioned as growing nearly a thousand years ago. Its most widely cultivated form nowadays mainly goes by the name *gewürztraminer*, although *traminer* is used for it in, for example, Germany and the Balkans.

treacle The word *treacle* originally had nothing whatsoever to do with 'syrup'. Until as late as the nineteenth century, it was used with reference to antidotes for poison (in her *Art of Cookery Made Plain and Easy* (1747) Hannah Glasse gives two recipes for 'treacle-water' that involve a cornucopia of medicinal plants, and an 1804 number of the *Medical Journal* notes 'his anti-venereal treacle, well-known for curing the venereal disease, rheumatism, scurvey, old-standing sores'). It comes originally from the Greek phrase *thēriakē antídotos*, literally 'antidote to a wild or venomous animal'. The adjective *thēriakē* came to be used on its own as a noun, and passed via Latin and Old French (where it acquired its *l*) into fourteenth-century English. Its ingredients varied from apothecary to apothecary, but usually included, presumably on homoeopathic grounds, a touch of viper's venom. By the sixteenth century, the word was becoming generalized to mean any 'sovereign remedy', and often had rather negative connotations; indeed, *treacle carrier* and *treacle conner* were contemptuous seventeenth- and eighteenth-century terms for itinerant quack doctors.

The modern application of *treacle* to sugar syrup (common in British English, relatively rare in American) seems to date from the seventeenth century, and probably arose literally from the sugaring of the pill: the mixing of medicines with sugar syrup to make them more palatable. The practice continued well into the nineteenth century, particularly in the administration of *brimstone* [sulphur] *and treacle* to anyone with the least symptom of anything: the inmates of Dotheboys Hall 'had the brimstone and treacle . . . in the way of medicine' (Charles Dickens, *Nicholas Nickleby* (1839)). In technical usage, *treacle* now refers to cane sugar syrup which has been boiled to remove some of the sucrose (it has less removed than molasses, which is therefore darker but less sweet).

The famous treacle well in Lewis Carroll's *Alice in Wonderland*, at the bottom of which, according to the Dormouse, the three little sisters Elsie, Lacie, and Tillie lived, had its origins in the medicinal sense of *treacle*. Treacle wells really existed—they got their name from the supposed curative properties of their water—and there was apparently one at Binsey near Oxford, with which Carroll may have been familiar.

tree tomato *See* TAMARILLO.

trenette A type of Italian pasta in the form of narrow flat strips. It is a speciality of Liguria, on the northwest coast, and especially of its capital Genoa, where it is traditionally served with pesto. The word is a diminutive form based on *trena* 'cord'.

treviso A bullet-shaped red-leafed Italian variety of chicory. Its full name is *radicchio di Treviso*, proclaiming its connection with the city and province of Treviso, to the north of Venice. The French form of the name, *trévise*, is also used in English: 'Place the carrots, onions, and trevise in a large mixing bowl. Sprinkle over the olive oil and balsamic vinegar', Patricia Michelson, *Cheese* (2010).

trifle In Elizabethan times trifles were simply cream warmed through and flavoured with sugar, ginger, etc., but gradually, in successive recipes, we find them being thickened up by boiling and adding rennet, enlivened by additional ingredients such as crushed macaroons, and decorated on top with comfits, until by the mid-eighteenth century they are very much as we would recognize them today. Hannah Glasse in the 1755 edition of her *Art of Cookery* gives a recipe for a 'Grand Trifle' which includes Naples biscuits, ratafias, and macaroons soaked in sack with custard poured over them and topped with syllabub, and which she describes as 'fit to go to the King's table, if well made, and very excellent when it comes to be all mixed together'. Trifles were indeed very popular in the eighteenth century, and there were several different variants: one particularly alcoholic version was called a whim-wham. But it had not yet altogether outgrown the implications of its name; in 1781 we find the poet William Cowper writing 'there is some froth, and here and there a bit of sweetmeat, which seems to entitle it justly to the name of a certain dish the ladies call a trifle'. The original meaning of the word in medieval English was 'an inconsequential or insubstantial tale, told either to amuse or to deceive', but it was not long before this broadened out to 'a thing or matter of little importance', from which the dish took its name. The immediate source of the word was Old French *truffle*, a variant of *truffe*, meaning 'deceit, trickery', but where this came from is not clear; there may be some connection with *truffle* the fungus, though this has never been established for certain. Today's trifles, with their stale sponge cakes, custard made from powder, synthetic cream, and lurid glacé cherries, seldom bear comparison with the exuberant, heady productions of the eighteenth century, surely the golden age of the trifle. *See also* TIPSY CAKE, WHIM-WHAM, ZUPPA INGLESE.

trimmings The traditional accompaniments of the main element of a dish, especially meat: 'He had a passion for silverside, all the trimmings—carrots and onions and small sweet dumplings', William Haggard, *The Money Men* (1981). First recorded in 1828, it is usually applied to the items—roast potatoes, chipolatas, stuffing, cranberry sauce, etc.—that standardly go with a Christmas turkey: 'Roasted goose and Norfolk Bronze turkey with traditional Christmas trimmings', *Urban Inns Christmas Packages* (2011).

tripe The stomach of a cow or ox used as food. It is categorized into two types: plain tripe, which comes from the rumen or first stomach, and honeycomb tripe, from the reticulum or second stomach. In Britain tripe is usually partnered with onions, frequently stewed together in milk—the best English tripe is traditionally said to come from the North, and particularly from Wigan, Lancashire—but probably the world's most celebrated tripe dish is *tripes à la mode de Caen*, a rich Norman stew of tripe, cow heel, carrots, and onions in cider or white wine. Here, however, tripe has always been something of a second-class dish, particularly in the South (Dryden in *Absolom and Achitophel* (1682) asks 'To what would he on quail and pheasant swell that ev'n on tripe and carrion could rebel?'), and the extent to which its standing has fallen over the past century can be gauged by the word's derogatory application to worthless or inferior things, a development which first becomes apparent towards the end of the nineteenth century.

French *tripe* is the source of our word, and it is shared by Italian (*trippa*) and Portuguese (*tripa*), but it is not known where it originally came from.

Triple Sec A name (in French literally 'thrice dry') used by various French manufacturers for white curaçao, an orange liqueur. It appears to have been introduced by the firm of Cointreau for its highest grade of liqueur, and has since spread to become a generic term, but the reasons for the choice of name are not known.

tri-tip A term in American butchery for a cut of beef consisting of a small triangular muscle taken from the tip of the rump.

trockenbeerenauslese Trockenbeerenauslese (abbreviated to *TBA*) is the most decadently sweet grade of German and Austrian white wine. It is made from grapes that have been left on the vine so long—sometimes until December—that they have practically shrivelled up into raisins; those that are in good enough condition to make wine are then individually selected, grape by grape (literally translated, the name means 'dry berry selection'). In years when the climate is propitious, the grapes' moisture content is further reduced by the depredations of *Botrytis cinerea*, the 'noble rot' (German *edelfäule*). This is the same mould that produces the peculiarly resonant lusciousness of the best Sauternes. It is only since the explosion in wine-drinking from the 1960s onwards that trockenbeerenauslesen have become widely known about in Britain, and the first record of the use of the word in the *Oxford English Dictionary* is as recent as 1963 (a poor year). In the wine trade, the unwieldy name tends to be shortened to *trock*. It should not, incidentally, be confused with *trocken* wines, which are German wines at the very opposite end of the sweetness spectrum, introduced in recent years in response to consumer demand for very dry white wines. *See also* AUSLESE, BEERENAUSLESE, SPÄTLESE.

trofie A type of Italian pasta made from semolina and formed into tightly spiralled torpedo shapes. It originated in Liguria, on the northwestern coast of the country. The word may come from Greek *trophē* 'nourishment'.

trompette de mort A type of edible trumpet-shaped mushroom related to the chanterelle. Its off-putting name (literally 'trumpet of death') was inspired by its greyish colour, not by any lethal effect on the eater. Its vernacular name is *horn of plenty*, but in culinary contexts the French term is usually used.

truffle The original truffle is the underground fungus of the genus *Tuber*, prized by gastronomes of several millennia for its ineffable perfume and its supposed aphrodisiac qualities. The Roman gourmet Apicius gave seven recipes for preparing it, and Brillat-Savarin apostrophized it as 'the diamond in the art of cookery'. Until the nineteenth century truffles seem to have been relatively abundant (Mrs Beeton says that 'its consumption is enormous'), but these days demand so far outstrips supply that (like oysters) they have passed beyond the reach of all but the very well-heeled.

There are two major varieties: the dark brown French or Périgord truffle (*Tuber melanosporum*), which is used mainly to flavour cooked foods; and the white Italian truffle (*T. magnatum*), which is more usually eaten raw, sliced thinly over pasta, risotto, or other dishes. Black and occasionally even white truffles can be cultivated, but for the most part they are gathered wild in late autumn or winter. They are most commonly to be found in the soil under oak trees, and are sought out using the specially trained noses of truffle-hounds or pigs.

They appear to have been introduced to Britain in the late sixteenth century, and in 1644 were still so new-fangled a delicacy that the diarist John Evelyn could note 'Here we supped . . . , having amongst other dainties, a dish of truffles, an earth nut found by an hogg trained to it.'

The word comes, probably via Dutch, from early modern French *truffle* (present-day French has *truffe*), which may well derive ultimately from post-classical Latin **terrae tufer* 'swollen thing in the ground' (*tufer* being an unrecorded variant of Latin *tuber* 'hump, swelling, protuberance'). From the same source early Italian *tartuffo* became modern Italian *tartufo* which, with its connotations of something produced secretively, provided the name of the hypocritical hero of Molière's comedy *Tartuffe*. *See also* POTATO, TARTIFLETTE.

Many who have never encountered vegetable truffles have tucked into confectioners' truffles, sweets the colour and shape of black truffles, made from a mixture of chocolate, sugar, and cream (and often rum) and covered with a dusting of cocoa powder or tiny chocolate strands. These are, of course, a much more recent phenomenon; they made their first recorded appearance in an Army and Navy Stores catalogue for 1926–7.

tube steak A piece of American verbal aggrandisement for a hot dog or frankfurter. It is first recorded in 1963.

tuile A thin crisp biscuit often made with ground almonds, and slightly curved like a roof tile (hence the name, which means literally 'tile' in French). Tuiles are often used for making little baskets in which portions of ice cream, sorbet, etc. are served.

tummelberry A dark purple soft fruit created by crossing the tayberry with another hybrid of the blackberry and the raspberry. It was introduced in Scotland in 1984, and named after the river Tummel, a tributary of the Tay.

turbigo In classic French cuisine, a dish of lambs' kidneys that have been sautéed and covered in a rich wine- and stock-based sauce. The name commemorates the French victory over the Austrians at the battle of Turbigo, a town to the west of Milan in Lombardy, on 3 June 1859, in the Franco-Austrian War.

Turkish coffee Strong black coffee made from very finely ground beans that are typically boiled up three times, often with the addition of a spice such as cardamom, and served in a small cup with the fine grounds in it. It is traditionally made in a long-handled metal pot called an 'ibrik'. The term is first recorded in 1854. *Greek coffee* (first recorded at the beginning of the nineteenth century) is in all essentials the same beverage, the only difference being that it is available in Greece (or Greek restaurants) rather than Turkey (or Turkish restaurants). It is prudent not to attempt to order the Greek when in Turkey, and vice versa.

Turkish delight A gelatinous sweet of Turkish origin, coated in powdered sugar. It is variously flavoured and coloured, although the variety most commonly seen in the West is made with rose water, and is consequently pink. It is cut into cubes, and was originally called in English *lumps of delight*, a term Dickens needed to explain in 1870: "'I want to go to the Lumps-of-Delight shop." "To the -?" "A Turkish sweetmeat, sir", *Mystery of Edwin Drood*. The name *Turkish delight* itself is first recorded in 1877. The Turkish term for the sweet is *rahat lokum*, a borrowing from Arabic *rāhat al-hulqūm*, which literally means 'throat's ease'.

turmeric The brilliant yellow powder turmeric, used for flavouring and colouring curries and other Indian and Southeast Asian dishes, is made by pounding up the root of a tropical Asian plant of the ginger family, *Cucurma longa*. Long association has perhaps given its name an Oriental sound, but it is in fact firmly European. A mystery attaches to it, nevertheless: a confused medley of sixteenth-century spellings (when English first acquired the word), including *tarmaret* and *tormarith*, point firmly to its being borrowed from Old French *terre merite*, a translation of medieval Latin *terra merita* 'meritorious earth', but why turmeric should have been so called has never been satisfactorily accounted for. Perhaps the likeliest explanation is that it represents a latinization of a term in some Asian language. Turmeric is an essential ingredient in piccalilli.

turnip The term *turnip* is a comparatively recent one for such an ancient vegetable. Our Anglo-Saxon ancestors called the 'turnip' *næp*, a word borrowed from Latin *nāpus* (whence French *navet*), and to this day Scottish-speakers refer to *neeps*, although as often as not they mean by it 'swedes' rather than 'turnips' (and indeed in Scotland, and northern England as well, the word *turnip* is commonly applied to 'swedes'). The element *tur-* first appears in the sixteenth century, giving *turnep*: 'Turneps beinge welle boyled in water, and after with fatte fleshe, norysheth moche', Sir Thomas Elyot, *Castel of Helth* (1539). It is generally taken to represent the word *turn*, from the rounded or 'turned' shape of the vegetable, although there is no conclusive proof of this.

The turnip is a member of the cabbage or brassica family, and when cultivated for its oil-rich seeds rather than its root it is known as *rape* or *colza* (a word derived from Dutch *koolzaad* 'cabbage seed'). The distinction has not always been so clear cut, however, and in former times turnips were often called *rapes*. The French differentiate between *navet* 'turnip' and *navette* 'rape', but confusingly English borrowed *navet* in the sixteenth century and used it for 'rape'. Perhaps fortunately this never caught on, but *navew* (from an obsolete French variant of *navet*) was more successful. It lasted into the nineteenth century as a term for rape, and the potential for misunderstanding can be seen in this passage from Thomas Hill's *Arte of Gardening* (1568), where *rape* means 'turnip': 'And the propertie of the place doth change the Nauew into a Rape, and the rape contrariwise into a Nauew.' A further spanner was almost thrown into the linguistic works by the herbalist William Turner, who in 1562 proposed the term *nape* (based on Latin *nāpus*) for the yellow turnip; it did not, however, survive for more than about a century.

Gastronomically the turnip is under a cloud at present, probably a legacy of generations of sharing the rather coarse and uninteresting mature root with the cattle during the winter (the agriculturalist Charles Townshend (1674–1738) got his nickname 'Turnip' from the improvements he introduced in the cultivation of turnips as winter feed for livestock). However, there are signs that the virtues of young spring turnips are now becoming more widely recognized. Spring is also the time for eating the vegetable's leaves, *turnip tops* or (now mainly in American English) *turnip greens* ('Dinner to day, fryed Pork and Turnip Green,' James Woodforde, *Diary*, 9 February 1796); they are particularly popular in Italy, where they are called *broccoletti di rape* or *cime di rapa*, and in the American Deep

South they are a staple of soul food. In France, the classic role for turnips is in navarin of lamb.

The colloquial use of *turnip* for a large old-fashioned silver pocket watch dates from the early nineteenth century.

turnover A sort of small, typically individual pie or pasty, in which the filling is placed on one side of a piece of rolled-out pastry and the other side is then 'turned over' to cover it, forming a semicircular shape. The term is first recorded at the end of the eighteenth century: 'an old woman preparing her turnovers, commonly called apple-pies', *Sporting Magazine* (1798). It is occasionally used for savoury fillings, such as meat, but a sweet fruit filling is the norm, and, as the above extract suggests, most turnovers are in fact apple turnovers (the French term for them is *chausson aux pommes*, literally 'apple sock', while German has *apfeltasche* 'apple pocket').

tutti-frutti Italian *tutti-frutti* means literally 'all-fruits', and is used in English particularly for a type of ice cream containing mixed candied fruit. It is also familiar in the US as the name of a brand of fruit-flavoured chewing gum.

Twiglets The proprietary name of a small snack made from wheat-based dough formed into sticks with knobbly excrescences (suggestive of buds on a twig) and flavoured with a savoury mixture based on yeast extract. It was launched in Britain in 1929.

twist A curled piece of lemon (or lime or orange) peel used to garnish and add flavour to a drink: 'He ordered a vodka martini on the rocks with a twist', G. V. Higgins, *The Friends of Eddie Coyle* (1972).

twizzler A term that achieved culinary notoriety in Britain in the early twenty-first century in the form of *Turkey Twizzlers*, the alliterative brand name of a turkey-based 'formed-meat product' manufactured by the firm of Bernard Matthews. The engagingly named Twizzlers were a popular item on school lunch menus, but in 2005 the celebrity chef Jamie Oliver launched a campaign against them on the grounds that they made unhealthy eating for children, and before long an embarrassed Bernard Matthews withdrew them. The second part of the name may have been inspired by *Twizzlers*, the US proprietary name of a twisted red liquorice-flavoured confectionery bar. The verb *twizzle* itself, meaning 'to twist', is first recorded in 1788. It probably originated as a fanciful alteration of *twist*.

tzatziki A refreshing dip, popular in the eastern Mediterranean, made from yoghurt, chopped cucumber, and garlic. The Greek version (with which British eaters have become familiar) is usually flavoured with mint. In Turkey, where the word is spelled *cacik*, dill is used.

udon A type of Japanese noodle made from wheat flour. It typically comes in strips not unlike spaghetti. The Japanese term appears originally (over a thousand years ago) to have denoted small dumplings, like *wun tun,* and it may well be that both the foodstuff and the word were introduced from China.

ugli The fruit of a tree that is a hybrid of a grapefruit and a tangerine (it resembles the tangelo, which is a cross between a pomelo and a tangerine). It was developed in Jamaica around 1930, and its name seems simply to be an alteration of *ugly,* bestowed on it because of its rather unprepossessing appearance—like a large, mournful, discoloured, semi-deflated grapefruit. It combines the size and succulence of the grapefruit with the sweetness and peelability of the tangerine.

Ulster fry A fried breakfast Northern Ireland-style. It can be expected to include most of the usual suspects—bacon, eggs, sausages, fried potatoes, etc.; its distinctive Ulster accompaniment is either soda farls or a type of potato cake known as 'fadge': 'The notorious "Ulster fry"—most things you can think of cooked in a pan', *Guardian* (1979). The term is first recorded in 1941.

umami A fifth category of taste said to exist alongside the four standard tastes of sweet, sour, salt, and bitter. It occurs naturally in a wide range of foods, including fermented fish sauces (such as the Roman garum) and Parmesan, but it can be added artificially in the form of monosodium glutamate. This condiment is mainly associated with Far Eastern cuisine, and indeed the taste was originally identified and isolated by a Japanese chemist, Professor Kikunae Ikeda (1864–1936) in 1908. It was he who coined its name, from Japanese *umai* 'delicious' and *mi* 'taste'.

underground mutton A jocular Australianism, first recorded in 1919, for 'rabbit meat' (rabbits were introduced into Australia in the nineteenth century, multiplied prodigiously, and became an easily pottable source of protein).

upside-down cake A sponge cake that is baked over a layer of fruit in syrup (a pattern of pineapple rings and cherries is a popular choice), and inverted for serving. It is made on the same principle as tarte tatin. The term is first recorded in the 1930s.

vacherin The primary application of the word *vacherin* is to a range of French cheeses made from cows' milk (it is a derivative of French *vache* 'cow'). Examples include *vacherin d'Abondance*, made in Savoie (*Abondance* is a breed of cattle); *vacherin des Beauges*, also from Savoie; and *vacherin Mont-d'Or*, made in Franche Comté. Vacherins are usually circular and fairly flat, and are traditionally bordered with a strip of spruce bark. Many sorts are soft enough to be eaten with a spoon. They and similar unpasteurized French soft cheeses came under a cloud in the 1980s as suspected sources of the disease listeriosis.

Their shape is the basis of the transference of the name *vacherin* to a cold dessert made from a circular meringue shell filled with cream, fruit, or ice cream.

vanilla In its original Central American home vanilla was used by the Aztecs to flavour chocolate, and the first writers in English to mention it when it had crossed the Atlantic with the Spanish describe the process; the naturalist John Ray, for instance, in 1673: 'vanillas which they mingle with Cacao to make Chocolate'. In fact, when chocolate was first introduced to Europe in the sixteenth century, it was cinnamon that was usually used to flavour it, and it was not until the eighteenth century that vanilla took over a role it has held ever since. But it is as an ingredient of ice cream that vanilla really came into its own: it appears to have been popularized in the USA in the latter part of the nineteenth century—Elizabeth David reports in *Spices, Salt, and Aromatics in the English Kitchen* (1970) that around 100,000 pounds of vanilla were imported to New York from Mexico each year at this time—and by the early twentieth century it had established itself as the standard flavouring. Indeed it is now so taken for granted, that vanilla ice cream is often regarded (not without justification) as having no particular flavour of its own: 'And in the future, heterosexual sex is going to get kinkier, while gay sex gets more plain vanilla', *Washington Post* (1989).

The Spanish were responsible not only for importing the vanilla pod to Europe, but also for supplying Europe's languages with a name for it. In Spanish it is *vainilla*, a diminutive of *vaina* 'sheath'—a reference to the long narrow pods. (The ultimate source of Spanish *vaina* is Latin *vagina*.)

variety meat An American euphemism for 'offal', which at the end of the twentieth century showed signs of crossing the Atlantic.

VAT VAT, short for 'vodka and tonic' but modelled on *Value Added Tax*, was popularized by the Thames TV series *Minder*, a record of the doings of second-hand car dealer and small-time crook Arthur Daley.

veal In common with *beef, mutton*, and *pork, veal* was introduced into English from Anglo-Norman as a genteel alternative to the native animal name (*calf flesh*) when referring to its meat (the only residual culinary use of *calf* is probably in *calf's-foot-jelly* and *calves' liver*). *Veal* is the odd man out, however, in being a rather late borrowing; the first three crossed the Channel in the thirteenth century, but *veal* is not recorded until Chaucer mentions it in *The Merchant's Tale* (1386): "'Bet [better] is," quoth he, "a pyk than a pikerell, and bet than olde boef is the tendre vel".' Anglo-Norman *vel* or *veel* came from Latin *vitellus*, a diminutive form of *vitulus* 'calf' (its Old French relative *veel* is the ultimate source of English *vellum* 'calf-skin parchment').

Calves bred for veal are generally fed exclusively on milk, to produce finer paler meat, and slaughtered at around two-and-a-half to three months (but *see* BOBBY VEAL and ROSE VEAL). It has never been a popular meat in Britain. The Anglo-Saxons did not share their Norman masters' taste for it, viewing it as a wasteful use of resources, and there was always an underlying suspicion that no one would slaughter a calf unless there was something wrong with it. With the specializing of dairy work in the eighteenth century (and prevalent French fashions) veal recipes are found more often—but 'veal is not a typical English meat', Dorothy Hartley, *Food in England* (1954). In more recent times concerns over the welfare of calves, both in their rearing and the method of their slaughter, and over the practice of feeding hormones to them, has kept consumer demand relatively low. Even the once widely-eaten veal-and-ham pie has gone into a decline. On the continent of Europe, however, veal's popularity remains unimpaired.

vegeburger *See* HAMBURGER.

vegelate A blend of *vegetable* and *chocolate* that was proposed within the European Community in the mid-1980s as a term for chocolate that contains a certain proportion of vegetable fat other than cocoa butter. Some member countries, notably France, professed to be affronted that the debased confection produced in Britain (and also Ireland, Denmark, Portugal, Sweden, and Finland) was allowed to be sold under the name 'chocolate'. The term was never officially adopted, but it proved a useful stick for British Eurosceptics to beat the EC with.

Vegemite The proprietary name of an iconic Australian savoury spread made from concentrated yeast extract. Formed by blending *vegetable* and *Marmite*, it was registered in 1923: 'Australia: I acclimatized on the plane by spreading the Vegemite thick', *Times* (1990).

vegetable oyster An alternative name (dating apparently from the mid-nineteenth century but no longer much heard) for the salsify, a long thin white-fleshed root vegetable. Early commentators explained it as a reference to the salsify's flavour, but it would take a rather vivid imagination to make salsify taste like oysters, and it may in fact come from the substitution of salsify for oysters as an ingredient in meat pies when oysters started to become more expensive.

vegetable spaghetti A variety of marrow whose flesh takes the form of long thin spaghetti-like strings. It is an introduction from the US, and first appeared on the scene as recently as the early 1960s. Amongst the names coined for it in American English are *noodle squash, spaghetti squash*, and *squaghetti* (*squash* being the American term for 'marrow').

velouté A basic white sauce made from veal, chicken, or fish stock, and a flour-and-butter roux. In French the word means literally 'velvety', and it seems to have been introduced into English in the early nineteenth century. It should not be confused with the fairly similar béchamel sauce, which is made with milk or cream rather than stock.

venison In common with *beef, mutton, pork,* and *veal, venison* was a term introduced by the descendants of the Norman conquerors of England to refer to the flesh of a particular animal used as food. But it has not always meant 'deer-meat'. At first, it referred to the meat of any animal killed in the chase, which could include wild boar, hare, and rabbit as well as deer: 'Hares are thought to nourish melancholy, yet they are eaten as venison, both roasted and boiled,' Fynes Moryson, *An Itinerary* (1617). This reflects the word's origins, in Latin *vēnātiō* 'hunting, game', a derivative of the verb *vēnārī* 'to hunt'. Signs of the modern narrowing-down in signification to 'deer-meat' appear in the late sixteenth century ('Amongst the common sort of people, nothing is accounted venison but the flesh of red and fallow deer,' John Manwood, *A Treatise of the Laws of the Forest* (1598)), but wider options remained open well into the nineteenth century ('a haunch of kangaroo venison,' Godfrey Mundy, *Our Antipodes* (1852)).

verdelho A Portuguese variety of white-wine grape. It is now widely grown in Australia, where it produces table wine, but it is best known as the source of one of the four main types of Madeira wine, sweeter and richer than *sercial,* but drier than *bual.* Its name means literally 'little green one'.

verjuice A tart liquid used in cooking and pickling, for sauces, or as a condiment. It is typically made by pressing unripe grapes (hence its name, which in the original Old French was *vertjus* 'green juice'), but where grapes are unavailable other fruit is substituted, such as crab apples. In English cuisine it was mainly a phenomenon of the Middle Ages, although a reintroduction was attempted at the end of the twentieth century. A characteristic medieval recipe including verjuice is 'Corat', a sort of offal stew, given in the fourteenth-century *Forme of Cury*: the internal organs were cooked in a broth thickened with egg yolks, and then, the recipe says, 'do thereto verjuice, saffron, powder douce [ground spices], and salt, and serve it forth'.

vermicelli Pasta in the form of long thin threads. The Italian term (first recorded in 1287) means literally 'little worms'. In British English, the word is also used to refer to shreds of chocolate for decorating cakes, trifles, etc.

vermouth An alcoholic drink made from a white or red wine base, infused with any of a wide variety of herbs, and used chiefly as a basis for cocktails. It gets its name, though, from one herb in particular: wormwood. This bitter-tasting plant has been used since ancient times for adding a bite to drinks (or disguising their shortcomings): references to *wormwood ale, wormwood beer,* and *wormwood wine* in English go back to the sixteenth century, and the plant's Latin name, *Artemisia absinthium,* betrays its role in absinthe. The German term for the plant, and for drinks based on it, is *wermut* (Old English had the parallel *wermod*; modern English *wormwood* is a fanciful fifteenth-century reformation of the word, based on the use of the plant as a remedy for intestinal worms). French borrowed the German term as *vermout* and English acquired it in the early nineteenth century, restoring the final -*th* from an earlier German spelling. In British English it is usually pronounced with the main stress on the first syllable, but American-speakers tend to stress the second syllable, giving it a long /oo/ sound.

The production of modern vermouth is based on the foothills of the Alps, on both the French and particularly the Italian side, where an abundance of the necessary herbs is readily available. The commonest French vermouth is a dry white version, as used in the 'dry martini' cocktail. A pink version flavoured with wild strawberry, known as *Chambéryzette,* is also made. Italian vermouth—most famously from the firms of Martini and Rossi and Cinzano—is mainly sweet. Both white and red—*bianco* and *rosso*—are made, the red being a key ingredient of the Manhattan cocktail.

vernaccia The name given to any of a range of unrelated Italian wine-grapes, mainly white. Its main products are the sherry-like Vernaccia di Oristano of Sardinia and the more distinguished Vernaccio di San Gimignano, a dry white Tuscan wine. The origins of the name are unclear. It has been variously ascribed to Latin *hibernus* 'of winter' and Latin *vernaculus* 'native' (expressing the idea of a local grape), but it seems more likely that it is connected with *Vernazza*, the name of a coastal town in Liguria, northwest Italy.

Sweet Italian wine was imported into Eng1anad in the Middle Ages, and its name came with it, filtered through Old French as *vernage*: 'He drinkith ypocras, clarre, and vernage Of spices hote, to encrese his corrage', Geoffrey Chaucer, *The Merchant's Tale* (*c*.1386). *See also* GRENACHE.

Véronique *Sole Véronique* is a dish of poached sole served with grapes. It was invented in London in 1903 by the French chef Auguste Escoffier, who named it after Messager's comic opera *Véronique* at that time running at the Coronet theatre. The term *Véronique* is now applied to other dishes (of chicken, for instance) served with grapes.

vichyssoise A thick creamy leek and potato soup, usually eaten cold. Its full name, *crème vichyssoise glacée* 'iced cream (soup) of Vichy', suggests a connection with the Bourbonnais spa town of Vichy, but it is no more intimate than that the chef who created the soup, Louis Diat, came from there; he was working in New York when he introduced it (perhaps in 1917, though this is not established for certain).

Victoria sandwich The Victoria sandwich, or *Victoria sponge* as it is also known, was named after Queen Victoria of Great Britain, and seems first to have come on the scene after about a quarter of a century of her reign: the first known recipe for it is given in Mrs Beeton's *Book of Household Management* (1861) (although from its placement in the book she seems to regard it more as a dessert dish than a tea-time cake). Essentially it consists of two layers of light sponge cake with between them a filling of jam, or sometimes cream.

Vienna bread Vienna loaves are crisply crusty, fairly elongated and tapering at each end, and with a slash or slashes along the top. They get their name mainly from the Vienna oven, a variety of bread-baking oven introduced in the mid-nineteenth century which made possible the injection of steam during the baking process. Another contributory factor, however, was the so-called 'Vienna' flour, a type of high-grade white wheat flour much used in Britain during the second half of the nineteenth century which in fact came mainly from Hungary and Rumania. It was not employed only in bread, of course (indeed cakes made from it became known as *Vienna cakes*, first referred to by Eliza Acton in her *Modern Cookery* (1845)), but the flour and the loaf came to be closely associated. The First World War put a stop to the importation of the flour, and it never reappeared.

Vienna sausage An English translation of *wienerwurst*. First recorded around 1902, it is often shortened to *vienna*: 'We were hoping to see someome tackle the mixed grill: lamb chop, steak, chicken strips, salt beef, viennas, beef burgers, tomato, mushroom, and chips', *Time Out London, Eating and Drinking* (2009).

Vienna steak An early name, first recorded in 1900, for what would now be termed a *hamburger*. It never really caught on widely enough to eliminate the risk of customer bemusement: 'Henry chose a Vienna steak . . . He . . . expected something like a Wiener Schnitzel', Graham Greene, *The End of the Affair* (1951).

Vietnamese river cobbler A commercial name coined in the twenty-first century for a species of Southeast Asian freshwater catfish when it was introduced into British supermarkets to fill the gap left by dwindling stocks of cod, haddock, etc. It was evidently felt that *catfish* would not do it for potential purchasers. In America and Australia it is generally termed *basa fish*, but British marketers decided to go with *cobbler*, an Australian name for various indigenous freshwater catfishes that dates from the 1830s. Its origin is not known for certain, but it has been speculated that the fish was originally called *cobra*, because of its supposed snake-like appearance, and that this later metamorphosed into *cobbler*.

vinaigrette A cold sauce made from vinegar and oil (more of the latter than the former, but recommended proportions vary) with seasonings, standardly pepper and salt and often garlic and tarragon. It is typically served with green salads. The word, which originated as a diminutive form of French *vinaigre* 'vinegar', was first used in English as long ago as 1699 (John Evelyn mentioned it in his book on salads, *Acetaria*) but it did not really become established until the end of the nineteenth century. *French dressing*, which originated around 1900, is a widely used synonym in British English.

In French, *vinaigrette* was also applied formerly to a sort of small two-wheeled carriage, from a supposed resemblance to a vinegar-seller's cart.

vincisgrassi A northern Italian dish that is in essence a very luxurious up-market form of lasagne: thin sheets of pasta are layered with a rich sauce typically containing such things as truffles, porcini mushrooms, chicken livers, sweetbreads, and Marsala. Its name is said to be a fairly heavily disguised tribute to Alfred Candidus Ferdinand, Prince of Windisch-Grätz (1787–1862), the Austrian field marshal whose cook supposedly invented the dish while his master was campaigning in the Italian Marches during the Napoleonic wars. However, there is considerable doubt about this, not least because a key point in the standard version of the story is that Alfred led the victorious Austrian army that raised the siege of Ancona in 1799, when he would have been all of twelve years old. In fact, a dish very similar to vincisgrassi is mentioned by Antonio Nebbia in his book *Il cuoco maceratese* 'The Macerata cook' (1779; Macerata is a commune in the Marches) under the name *princisgras*, a word of unknown origin, so if *vincisgrassi* does honour the prince it would seem to be only as an alteration of an existing term.

vincotto An Italian condiment made by boiling down unfermented grape must until it has reduced to 20 per cent of its original volume, producing a thick dark sweet liquid that can be sprinkled over savoury and sweet dishes. It originated in Apulia in southeastern Italy. Its name means literally 'cooked wine'.

vindaloo *Vindaloo*—as in pork vindaloo or chicken vindaloo—denotes a noticeably hot curry-style Indian dish characterized by a vinegary sharpness. Such dishes are the speciality of the Konkani-speaking Christians of the west coast of India, in and around Goa. This was until comparatively recently a Portuguese colony, and indeed it seems likely that the word *vindaloo* is of Portuguese origin—from *vin d'alho*, signifying a sauce made from wine (Portuguese *vinho*) and garlic (Portuguese *alho*). In common with many other Indian dishes, it became familiar, in a more or less authentic form, to English eaters in the nineteenth century, and it first appears in an English cookery book—with the early alternative spelling *bindaloo*—in W. H. Dawe's *Wife's Help to Indian Cookery* (1888).

vinegar *Vinegar* is literally 'sour wine'. The word was borrowed in the thirteenth century from Old French *vyn egre*, a descendant of Vulgar Latin **vinum acrum* 'sour wine' (*acrum* is the ancestor of modern English *eager*). The substance itself was probably known in

Britain in pre-Roman times (there is evidence that it was being used by Celts on the Atlantic coast of France in the first century BC), but since, as its name suggests, it was then made exclusively by the acetic fermentation of wine, it cannot have been that common in such a northerly latitude. It was the Romans who really introduced it to Britain in a big way. They were extremely fond of it, as a condiment, for cooking with, and even (well diluted) as a drink. A taste for it survived their departure, and when insufficient wine was available to be turned into vinegar, ale was used instead. In Middle English the term *alegar* was coined for this, by appropriating the final two syllables of *vinegar* (and *beeregar* was even current for a while), but gradually *vinegar* itself repossessed *alegar*'s semantic territory. This *malt vinegar*, as it is now known (to distinguish it from the somewhat tautologously named *wine vinegar*), has dominated, some would say tyrannized, British tables for many generations, taking its place in the cruet alongside salt and pepper and, thanks to the British eater's mania for autocondimentation, blanketing all and sundry dishes with its rather coarse acidity. A culturally central role (in a country without its own lemons) has been to give an edge to fish and chips, and it remains popular enough to have spawned a 'salt 'n' vinegar' variety of crisps. One of the consequences of an increased awareness of foreign cuisines, however, has been to revive interest in wine vinegars, including those flavoured with herbs and spices.

A cheap substitute for vinegar, made from diluted acetic acid with flavourings, is widely used commercially. Coloured brown it can masquerade as malt vinegar. A court ruling in the 1950s forbade the use of the term *vinegar* for this in England and Wales, so it now rejoices in the name *non-brewed condiment*. In similar vein, low-acid white vinegar is often termed *white condiment*.

Vinegar has traditionally had other uses than culinary ones, of course: cleaning, disinfecting, reviving, refreshing, to name the main ones. When Jack fell down and broke his crown, vinegar and brown paper was the prescribed treatment for the head wound; and in *Barnaby Rudge* (1841) Dickens recorded how Mrs Varden's vapours were appeased with 'much damping of foreheads, and vinegaring of temples, and hartshorning of noses, and so forth.'

vine tomato A tomato sold or used still attached to the small branch on which it grew: 'chump of lamb with a herb crust, served with garlic creamed potato, baby aubergine, vine cherry tomatoes, and red-wine sauce', *Good Food Guide* (2008).

vinho verde *Vinho verde* is Portuguese for 'green wine'—'green', that is, in the sense 'immature' (the contrasting term is *vinho maduro* 'mature wine'). To English ears the term suggests white wine (and indeed the majority of vinho verde exported from Portugal is white), but in fact about half of the vinho verde made is red. Both red and white vinho verdes are naturally tart and astringent, and as their name suggests they are intended for drinking as soon as they are bottled (which happens not long after they are made). Most vinho verdes for the export market, however, are slightly sweetened (this includes the highly successful sparkling Mateus Rosé, which is based on the idea of vinho verde). The best vinho verdes are made in the Minho, in northern Portugal.

vin santo An Italian dessert wine—literally 'holy wine'—made from semi-dried Trebbiano and Malvasia grapes. It is glowingly golden to look at, but not necessarily sweet; semi-sweet and dry versions are made. Almond biscuits called cantucci are traditionally eaten with it. It gets its name from the fact that it is by custom racked off its lees in Holy Week, when the atmospheric pressure caused by the phase of the moon is deemed to be most propitious.

viognier A grape variety used to produce white wine. A temperamental grape, its range has hitherto been limited to the Rhône valley in France, where it is used to make the great white wines of Condrieu and also often forms a component of the red Côte Rôtie, but in recent years extensive plantings have been made in California, and it is also now grown in Italy, Australia, and South America. Wines made from it have a distinctive musky peachy aroma.

Virgin Mary *See* BLOODY MARY.

vitello tonnato An Italian dish (literally 'tunaed veal') consisting of an escalope of veal topped with a creamy sauce based on puréed tinned tuna. The first known reference to it in an Italian source dates from 1923.

vodka Prosaically enough, *vodka* means simply 'little water'. The word is a diminutive form of Russian *voda* 'water'. The drink itself is a colourless spirit distilled in northeastern Europe from a variety of fermented materials, including grain, potatoes, and molasses. There is some not very comradely disagreement between Russia and Poland as to which of them originated it. What is fairly clear, however, is that English borrowed the word *vodka* from Russian, at the beginning of the nineteenth century.

In its unadulterated form, vodka has a neutral taste, but many flavoured vodkas are produced. Poland, for instance, has *pieprzowka* 'pepper vodka', *krupnik* 'honey vodka', *jarzebiak* 'rowanberry vodka', and *zubrowka* (flavoured with bison grass).

Vodkatini *Vodkatini* is a contraction of *vodka martini*, a cocktail made with vodka and dry martini—essentially a martini made with vodka rather than gin. The first record we have of the contracted form is in Williams and Myers' *What, When, Where, and How to Drink* (1955).

vol-au-vent The vol-au-vent, a small cup-shaped puff-pastry case with a sauce-bound savoury filling, is said to have been invented by the French chef Antonin Carême (1783–1833). The story goes that he claimed his creation was so light and delicate that when he took it from the oven it simply 'flew away in the wind' (*s'envola au vent*). It quickly crossed the Channel: 'The landlady regaled him with cold *vol-au-vent*, and a glass of Curaçoa', Edward Bulwer-Lytton, *Pelham* (1828). Vol-au-vents are eaten either as a main course or, in smaller sizes, as snacks with drinks.

wad A basic bun, sandwich, etc., especially as eaten by a British serviceman or working man with a cup of tea: 'Give us a bob for a cuppa and a wad, guv', Anthony Burgess, *The Doctor Is Sick* (1960). The usage is first recorded in 1919.

wafer Britain was introduced to the wafer in the thirteenth century. It was brought across the Channel by the Norman gentry. Like the etymologically related waffle, its characteristic feature was that it was made by pressing two heated iron plates together. In those days the batter for wafers was often quite rich, and a layer of cheese could be inserted into it too—not a million miles from today's toasted cheese sandwich. Elizabethan towns had waferers who sold their wares in the streets (and also had the reputation of being go-betweens in clandestine love affairs). Modern wafers are altogether less exciting, their only positive quality being a light crispness exploited as a contrast to ice cream, or for making wafer biscuits layered with sugary fillings.

   The word *wafer* was borrowed from Anglo-Norman *wafre*, which itself came from Middle Low German *wāfel*, source of English *waffle*. It was first applied to the thin round pieces of unleavened bread used in the Communion service in the sixteenth century.

waffle Waffles are honeycomb-shaped batter cakes that came into the English-speaking world via the US; a writer in 1817, describing waffles for a British audience, had to explain them as 'a soft hot cake of German extraction, covered with butter'. Their immediate origin was actually Dutch, and the name goes back to a Middle Low German word *wāfel*, which may in turn have originated from an even earlier Germanic word *wabo, meaning 'honeycomb'. From the same source (which is ultimately related to *weave*) we get *wafer*. There is no connection with *waffle* meaning 'aimless verbiage', which comes from the obsolete onomatopoeic verb *waff* or *woff* 'to yelp'.

Wagyu beef A type of very tender (and expensive) beef obtained from the Wagyu breed of Japanese cattle (now also extensively reared in Australia). It typically contains a high percentage of unsaturated fat. The Japanese name is formed from *wa* 'Japanese' and *gyu* 'cattle'. *See also* KOBE BEEF.

Waldorf salad The classic Waldorf salad is composed of raw apples, walnuts, and celery (or sometimes celeriac or lettuce) in a mayonnaise dressing. It is named after the Waldorf–Astoria Hotel in New York City, where it was created (reputedly by the maitre d', Oscar Tschirky) and first served in the 1890s. The walnuts are a post-First World War addition to the recipe.

Walewska The Walewska after whom sole *à la Walewska* was named appears to have been Count Walewska, illegitimate son of Napoleon I and Marie Walewska, who was French ambassador to Britain during the reign of Napoleon III. The dish consists of sole garnished with lobster and truffles and coated with Mornay sauce.

wallfish A British dialect term for the edible snail. They are considered a delicacy in parts of the West Country: 'Dinner might kick off with . . . a dozen Mendip wallfish poached in local cider', *Good Food Guide* (2008). The term is first recorded in 1950.

wallop A colloquial term for 'beer' (or loosely, for any ale drink). It is usually regarded as a Briticism, although the first known instance of its use (in 1933) is Australian. It appears to be the same word as *wallop* 'to hit': this is etymologically identical with *gallop*, and was so used in the fourteenth and fifteenth centuries, but by the sixteenth century it had come to be applied to the bubbling motion of boiling water. By extension, it was used as a sort of impressionistic unit of time measurement in cookery for boiling something: George Hartman, in *The True Preserver and Restorer of Health* (1682), recommends letting a particular preparation 'only boil five or six wallops'. It seems to have been used in brewing, too, for in a 1743 edition of the *London and County Brewer* we read: 'Put as much Salt . . . as will lie on a Crown-Piece into a Copper . . . and as it heats and the Scum rises, take it off before it boils in; then, when it has had a Wallop or two, laid two Pailfuls.' It is possible that the germ of the modern meaning, 'beer', lies here.

walnut Etymologically, *walnut* means 'foreign nut'. The name was probably given to it some time in the first millennium AD by the Germanic peoples, contrasting their own native hazelnut with the exotic walnut of the Romans and Gauls (who accepted the compliment and translated the term into Vulgar Latin as **nux gallica* 'French nut'—which survives in *gaog* and *gok*, modern French dialect words for 'walnut'). The element *wal-* (**walkhaz* in the original Germanic) goes back ultimately to *Volcae*, a latinization of the name of an unknown Celtic tribe. The Germanic peoples adopted it to refer to any non-Germanic people—that is, in effect, Celts or Romans. Modern English *Welsh*, *Walloon*, and the final syllable of *Cornwall* all come from this source, as does the name *Wallace*.

As their name therefore suggests, walnuts have always been the staple nut of southern Europe and the Mediterranean (the ancient Greeks used them extensively, and it was the Romans who introduced the tree to Britain), and Latin *nux* 'nut' implied 'walnut', as do its modern descendants such as French *noix* and Italian *noce*.

The American grey or white walnut is also known as the *butternut*.

warden *See* PEAR.

wasabi The Japanese variety of horseradish, of high pungency. It is either eaten raw, freshly grated, with raw fish and sushi, or dried and turned into a green powder, which is reconstituted with water and used as a mustard-like condiment.

water biscuit A thin crisp unsweetened biscuit originally made simply from flour and water. To begin with, 'such plain biscuits were used in place of fresh bread when it was unobtainable; now they are popular with cheese', Laura Mason, *Oxford Companion to Food* (2006). The term dates from the late eighteenth century.

water chestnut A vegetable used in East Asian cooking that is the crisp, white-fleshed tuber of a type of grasslike tropical sedge. It is cultivated in flooded fields in southern China and Southeast Asia. It is not a nut, but in appearance (a dark brown, slightly flattened sphere) it is not a million miles from a chestnut, which may well have prompted the adoption of the name (in Chinese it is called *mati*, which also means 'hoof'). The term *water chestnut* had originally been coined, in the mid-nineteenth century, for the edible spiny nut-like fruit of a range of aquatic plants of the genus *Trapa*, widely eaten in various parts of the world.

watercress The watercress, a close relative of the nasturtium, is cultivated for its roundish, dark green, rather peppery-tasting leaves, which are usually eaten raw in salads. It grows in running water, and in Britain its main centre of production is in Hampshire. It has long been popular, as much in the past for its supposed medicinal properties as for its flavour—the usual gallimaufry of attributes has been claimed: Thomas Paynell, for example, in his translation of the *Schola Salernitana* (1528), claimed that 'Watercresses doth cure tooth ache' (until the eighteenth century the plant was almost always called *watercresses*, not *watercress*)—but it was not until the early nineteenth century that growing on a large commercial scale began.

water melon Water melons are nature's conveniently packaged answer to a thirst in the hot regions of the world: huge globes ('green cannonballs', as Jane Grigson described them) containing a crimson pulp saturated with a rather tasteless but refreshing watery juice, interspersed with hard black seeds. They are now grown wherever the climate will allow, but they probably originated in Africa. They crossed the Atlantic with the slave ships, and the water melon is still associated with the black culture of the southern states of the US (many must  first have got to know of it through the song 'Water-melon man'). The term *water melon* is first recorded in the early seventeenth century (Richard Cocks noted in his *Diary in Japan* (1615) 'a present of 10 water millons').

water-souchy A dish of fish, typically perch, boiled and then served in its broth. It was very popular in the eighteenth and nineteenth centuries, and even gave rise to a verb: 'Dinners at Lovegrove's with flounders water-zoutched, and iced claret', John Brown, *Horae Subsecivae* (1861). It originated in the Netherlands, as did its name, which is an adaptation of Dutch *waterzootje*. This was a compound formed from *water* and *zootje* 'boiling', a word related to English *seethe*.

water spinach An alternative name for the edible species of MORNING GLORY.

Weetabix The proprietary name of a breakfast cereal made from crushed wheat grains moulded into a small flat round-ended oblong. It was invented in Australia in the 1920s by Bennison Osborne, and originally marketed under the name *Weet-Bix* (the second element standing for 'biscuits'). It was first sold in the UK in 1932, with the now-familiar name *Weetabix*.

Welshcake Welshcakes are small round cakes made from a shortbread-like dough sweetened with currants and spiced up with ginger, nutmeg, and the like. They are traditionally baked on a griddle or bakestone, which gives them a biscuity texture, but they can also be cooked in the oven, which makes them more cake-like. As their name suggests, they are a Welsh speciality ('Mother has made Welshcakes,' letter from Dylan Thomas, 1932), and in Welsh they are called *pice ar y maen* 'cakes on the stone'.

Welsh rabbit There is no evidence that the Welsh actually originated this dish of toasted cheese, although they have always had a reputation for being passionately fond of it (a fourteenth-century text tells the tale that the Welsh people in heaven were being troublesome, and in order to get rid of them St Peter went outside the Pearly Gates and shouted 'Caws pobi' (Welsh for 'toasted cheese')—whereupon all the Welsh rushed out and the gates were shut on them); *see also* GLAMORGAN SAUSAGE. A more likely derivation of the name is that *Welsh* in the seventeenth and eighteenth centuries was used as a patronizingly humorous epithet for any inferior grade or variety of article, or for a substitute for the real thing (thus a *Welsh pearl* was one of poor quality, possibly counterfeit, and to use a *Welsh comb* was to comb one's hair with one's fingers). Welsh rabbit may therefore have started life as a dish resorted to when meat was not available. The first record of the word comes in John Byron's *Literary Remains* (1725): 'I did not eat of cold beef, but of Welsh rabbit and stewed cheese.'

Although the term is often used simply for a slice of bread topped with cheese and put under the grill, the fully-fledged Welsh rabbit is a more complicated affair, with several variations: the cheese (classically Cheddar or Double Gloucester, by the way) can be mixed with butter or mustard, beer or wine, and it can be pre-melted and poured over the toast rather than grilled. And then of course there are all the other rabbits that have followed in the wake of the Welsh: *buck rabbit* is the best known, but there are also *American rabbit* (with whisked egg whites), *English rabbit* (with red wine), *Irish rabbit* (with onions, gherkins, vinegar, and herbs), and *Yorkshire rabbit* (topped with bacon and a poached egg). Then there is *Scotch rabbit*, a term which in the past has been used virtually synonymously with *Welsh rabbit*: Hannah Glasse (1747) gives this simple recipe: 'To make a Scotch Rabbit. Toast a Piece of Bread, butter it, cut a Slice of Cheese, toast it on both sides, and lay it on the Bread', although later versions seek to distinguish it by the use of stout and the Scottish cheese Dunlop.

Welsh rabbit has of course produced one of the great linguistic *causes célèbres* of gastronomy with its genteel variant *Welsh rarebit*. There is little doubt that *rabbit* is the original form, and that *rarebit* (first recorded in 1785) is an attempt to folk-etymologize it—that is, to reinterpret the odd and inappropriate-sounding *rabbit* as something more fitting to the dish. Precisely how this took place is not clear; it has been speculated that *rarebit* was originally *rearbit*, that is, something eaten at the end of a meal, but there is no actual evidence for this. However that may be, the spurious *rarebit* has continued to be preferred up to the present day by those who apparently find honest-to-goodness *rabbit* slightly vulgar. The French, incidentally, who admire the dish, get round the problem in their usual pragmatic way by calling it simply *le Welsh*.

'Many's the long night I've dreamed of cheese—toasted, mostly': the castaway Ben Gunn in Robert Louis Stevenson's *Treasure Island* (1883).

Wensleydale A hard cows'-milk cheese originally made in Wensleydale, the valley of the river Ure in North Yorkshire. The first known use of the name *Wensleydale* to designate the cheese dates from 1840. At this time it was a blue-veined cheese. This 'Blue Wensleydale' is still available, but not easy to find. In the early twentieth century, changes in production techniques eliminated the blue veining. The public took placidly enough to the new 'White Wensleydale', and that is by far the most common form of the cheese today. It is traditional to eat it with apple pie or fruitcake.

The profile of Wensleydale was considerably raised by its being the favourite cheese of Wallace, the absent-minded Lancastrian inventor who, along with his canine companion Gromit, is the animated clay-model star of numerous films, beginning with *A Grand Day Out* (1989).

western omelette An omelette made typically with chopped ham, green peppers, and onions. Put between two slices of bread it becomes a *western sandwich*. Both are staples of the bill of fare in US diners. Alternative names for them are *Denver omelette* and *Denver sandwich*.

wheat Human beings began harvesting the wild ancestor of modern cultivated wheat during the Neolithic period, and it has remained a staple crop in large parts of Europe and western Asia (and latterly North America) ever since. In many European languages the word for it is a specialization of the word for 'grain', attesting to its importance as a source of flour for bread: French *blé*, for instance, and Rumanian *grîu* come into this category. English *wheat*, on the other hand, comes from the same source as *white*; it was so named from the colour of the powder produced by crushing it.

wheat beer A type of beer made from malted wheat (instead of or as well as the more usual barley). It is typically pale in colour (but dark ones are made) and generally tastes not unlike lager. It is mainly associated with central and northwestern Europe. There are three main varieties: the wheat beer of the Low Countries (Dutch *witbier*, literally 'white beer'), which has a hazy appearance and is often flavoured with such ingredients as orange peel and coriander; Bavarian wheat beer (German *weissbier* 'white beer' or *weizen* 'wheat'); and the somewhat sour Belgian lambic (*see* LAMBIC BEER). The English term seems to have come into use in the 1850s.

wheatgrass Leaves of newly sprouted wheat that are processed into a dark green liquid. Its health-giving properties were first proclaimed in the 1930s, and since then it has established itself firmly in the health-food pantheon, drunk either fresh or reconstituted from a powder. *See also* BARLEY GRASS.

whey The watery part of milk which separates out from the solid curds during the process of cheesemaking. Thin and unappetizing to modern tastes (it is now mostly fed to animals), it is nevertheless rich in vitamins and minerals, and was once widely drunk, either plain or with various flavourings (William Buchan, for instance, in his *Domestic Medicine* (1789), gave a recipe for mustard whey: 'Take Milk and Water, of each a pint; bruised mustard-seed, an ounce and a half. Boil them together till the curd is perfectly separated, afterwards strain the whey through a cloth'). The word *whey* is an ancient Germanic one, going back to a prehistoric **khwuja-*.

The metaphorical application of *whey* to 'facial pallor' was perhaps originally Shakespeare's; certainly he is the first writer on record as using it: 'Go, prick thy face, and over-red thy fear, thou lily-liver'd boy. What soldiers, patch? Death of thy soul! those linen cheeks of thine are counsellors of fear. What soldiers, whey-face?' (*Macbeth*).

whim-wham An eighteenth-century version of the trifle. It was simply made: you soaked some sponge fingers in sweet wine, poured some whipped cream over them, and decorated it if you had a mind with almonds, angelica, etc. Its name had much in common with *trifle*, too, for originally it meant generally 'something fanciful or trivial'; it was coined as a humorous reduplication of *whim*.

whisky Whether as a measure of their indispensability, or for euphemistic motives, human beings seem to have been drawn to naming the fieriest of spirits they can distil after 'water': *vodka* means literally 'little water', and French *eau de vie* and Scandinavian *acquavit* are both translations of medieval Latin *aqua vitae* 'water of life' (which enjoyed a semi-Anglicized existence as *aqwavyte* or *aqwowyte* in the sixteenth century). And *whisky* is no different. It is an eighteenth-century shortening of *whiskybae*, a variant form of *usquebaugh*. This sixteenth-century term for a 'spirit distilled from fermented grain' was an adaptation of Scottish and Irish Gaelic *uisge beatha*, literally 'water of life'.

As the derivation of its name suggests, the drink originated in Scotland and Ireland, and they remain important centres of production. The majority of Scotch whisky (or *Scotch* for short: one of the few linguistic contexts in which purists still allow *Scotch* rather than *Scots* or *Scottish*) is a blend made partly from barley and partly from maize, but *malt whisky*, made only from malted barley, is more highly prized (whisky made solely from maize, known as *grain whisky*, is rare in Scotland). Irish whiskey is made from both barley and maize, and is seldom blended (the distinction in spelling between Scotch *whisky* and Irish *whiskey* is a comparatively recent development, introduced apparently towards the end of the nineteenth century by the drinks industry, and not representing any genuine differentiation in usage between the two countries). In the US whiskey (the preferred spelling, although *whisky* is also used) is generally made from maize (*see* BOURBON) or rye; in Canada (which favours the form *whisky*) rye is the usual ingredient. Nowadays, Japan is also a major producer (the Japanese having developed a particular liking for the drink).

whisky mac The term *whisky mac*, which denotes a warming drink made from roughly equal proportions of whisky and ginger wine, does not seem to be of very great antiquity; the earliest examples in print are not recorded until well after the Second World War. The *mac*, of course, is supposed to suggest Scottishness.

whitebait A general term, dating from the middle of the eighteenth century, for the young of any of a range of sea fish used as food. The commonest species involved are herrings and sprats. The small silvery-white fish, usually no more than three or four centimetres in length, are generally dredged in seasoned flour and swiftly deep-fried. They were particularly associated in former times with the river Thames: they were fished from it in large numbers as far upstream as London, and the 'whitebait dinners' provided by riverside innkeepers in the spring and summer were very popular with Londoners (a particularly grand whitebait dinner was held annually at Greenwich in the nineteenth century at which cabinet ministers attended). The second part of the fishes' name comes from their former use as bait for catching larger fish.

white cider A type of colourless cider with a higher alcoholic content than standard cider. Its cheapness has ensured its popularity among binge drinkers and alcoholics, and its easy availability made it a subject of controversy in Britain in the early twenty-first century. One well-known brand, *White Lightning*, was withdrawn in 2009 because of concerns about its abuse.

white currant A cultivated variety of redcurrant that lacks red pigment, so that its berries have a pale creamy-white translucent appearance. One advantage of this is said to be that birds do not notice it, so its bushes are less prone to depredation than those of redcurrants. It is now fairly rare, but red and white were once common companions: Jane Grigson in her *Fruit Book* (1982) quotes Robert Heath in *Clarastella* (1650):

> 'Here the currants red and white
> In yon green bush at her sight
> Peep through their shady leaves, and cry
> Come eat me, as she passes by.'

White Lady A gin-based cocktail made with lemon juice and an orange-based liqueur such as Cointreau. It is said to have been invented by Harry Craddock, an American bartender and mixologist who presided over the American Bar at London's Savoy Hotel in the 1920s. In Australian slang the term is also applied, presumably with ironic reference to the elegant cocktail, to a skid-row slug of methylated spirits, sometimes apparently mixed with powdered milk to lend credence to the name.

white meat In modern English, *white meat* has two meanings. It is mainly applied to the (cooked) breast meat and other pale-coloured meat of poultry, as contrasted with the dark meat of the legs. This usage was probably adopted as a euphemism in the nineteenth century by those too genteel to use the word *breast*. Its other application is to pale-coloured meat in general—chicken and turkey in particular, but also pork, veal, rabbit, etc.—in contrast to the red meat of beef and mutton. (In Israeli restaurants, the non-kosher flesh of pigs is disguised as *white meat*.)

In former times, however, *white meat* (or *white meats*) denoted dairy products, such as milk, butter, and cheese, and sometimes eggs.

white pudding White pudding is a delicate, ethereal affair compared to the rather down-to-earth black pudding. It is a sausage (*see* PUDDING) made from white meat, such as chicken breast, rabbit, or fine pork, with a cereal filler, spices, and in the French version (*boudin blanc*) usually eggs and onions. The first reference to it in Britain comes in an eighteenth-century Scottish ballad called 'Get up and bar the door': 'And first they ate the white puddings and then they ate the black.'

white sauce A simple basic sauce made from flour, butter, and milk or cream. It is commonly used as the basis of other sauces (for example, parsley sauce). The French béchamel is essentially the same thing. The term dates from the early eighteenth century.

white wine Why white? No wine, not the blandest Frascati or the stoniest Chablis, is totally devoid of colour, even if it is only a glint of green or a suggestion of yellow. But in fact the distinction in English, implied or explicit, between white wine and red goes back to the Middle Ages: the thirteenth-century *Cursor mundi* tells of cellars 'filled with wine, white and red', and William Langland in *Piers Plowman* (1377) mentions 'white wine of Oseye [Alsace] and red wine of Gascoigne'. And indeed the Romans used the term *vinum album* 'white wine'. No doubt in the days before refrigerated vats and the rigorous avoidance of oxidation, most 'white' wine was decidedly straw-coloured, if not downright yellow. However, the use of *white* to confer the cachet of whiteness and purity on decidedly off-white objects has a long pedigree, by no means confined to white wine. Bread, for instance, has been termed 'white', in contrast with 'brown,' since at least the fourteenth century, although medieval white bread can scarcely have been as snowy as Mother's Pride; creamy-yellowish building bricks are commonly called *white bricks*; and white rum is of course transparent. Nowadays perhaps the only white wine to come completely clean about its colour is *vin jaune* 'yellow wine', a wine of the Jura in France which somewhat resembles fino sherry.

wholemeal The term *wholemeal*, denoting flour made from the entire cereal grain (in practice usually wheat), with no element removed during the production process, dates back at least to the early seventeenth century ('Bread is also wont to be made of the whole meal, from which the bran is not separated,' Tobias Venner, *Via Recta ad Vitam Longam* (1620)), and is recorded sporadically from later centuries ('a nice half griddle of whole-meal bread,' Thomas Keightley, *Fairy Mythology* (1828)). But it was not really until the end of the nineteenth century that an awakening interest in 'natural' foods firmly established it in the language. The parallel *wholewheat* (which refers of course only to wheat flour) dates from the same period, around the turn of the twentieth century.

whoopie pie A dome-topped cake consisting of two small round cakes between which is sandwiched a sweet filling. It is a speciality of New England, but ownership of it is contested between Maine, where it was designated the official state treat in 2011, and Pennsylvania, where it is claimed as part of the Amish tradition. It is said that in past times Amish wives would include such cakes (then apparently called *hucklebacks*, which means literally 'hunchbacks') in the lunch baskets they took out into the fields for their labouring menfolk, who on lifting the cloth and seeing the cakes would exclaim 'Whoopee!' This explanation sounds decidedly contrived, but no convincing alternative has emerged. The eccentric spelling *whoopie* presumably anticipates the following *pie* (although why the cake should have been called a 'pie' in the first place remains open to question).

whortleberry An alternative name for the bilberry, a small purplish-blue berry that grows on a bush of the heath family. It originated in southwest England as a variant of the now obsolete *hurtleberry*, itself a descendant of *horte* 'bilberry', a word of unknown origin. The American term *huckleberry* is probably an alteration of *whortleberry*.

wiener schnitzel A wiener schnitzel, in German literally a 'Viennese cutlet', is an escalope of veal coated in egg and breadcrumbs and fried, and usually served with a slice of lemon. The term began to establish itself in English in the mid-nineteenth century. *See also* SCHNITZEL.

wienerwurst A German term for a frankfurter as produced in Vienna (the Frankfurt butcher Johann Georg Lahner is said to have introduced these smoked sausages to the Austrian capital). It arrived in English in the 1880s, brought to America by German-speaking immigrants. An English version, *Vienna sausage,* soon followed, but the language's main way of accommodating the German word was to abbreviate: *wiener,* first recorded in 1900, is widely used in American English, and has been further naturalized to *wienie* (or *weenie*). The obvious reason (plus perhaps a hint of *weeny* 'tiny') led to this being used as a slang euphemism for 'penis'.

wig Wigs (alternatively *wiggs* or *whigs*) were small rich buns, often spiced. They appear to have been introduced into Britain from the Low Countries in the fourteenth century, for the name is a borrowing of Middle Dutch *wigge* (which etymologically means '*wedge*-shaped cake'), and they were eaten particularly during Lent (Samuel Pepys records, on 8 April 1664, 'then home to the only Lenten supper I have had of wiggs and ale'). They seem to have gone gradually out of fashion during the eighteenth century, but continued to be made in country areas into the twentieth century.

wild garlic An alternative name for RAMSONS.

wild rice The edible seeds of an aquatic North American grass, *Zizania aquatica*. It is only very distantly related to ordinary rice. The seeds are longer and thinner than standard rice, and covered in a black husk.

Williams A large, juicy, late-ripening dessert pear. Its name, which is short for *Williams' Bon Chrétien*, commemorates a Mr Williams, a nurseryman of Turnham Green who was the first to distribute it in Britain in the late eighteenth century (it was an Aldermaston schoolmaster, John Stair, who originally raised the variety, in 1770). The name of the original French pear, *Bon Chrétien*, literally 'Good Christian', comes from the description applied to Saint François de Paul, who supposedly introduced the pear into France from Italy in the fifteenth century. In America it is called the *Bartlett*.

Windsor red Despite its traditional-sounding name, Windsor red is a modern cheese. It is basically Cheddar, mixed with elderberry wine to give a red marbling effect. It was launched in 1969, its designation obviously intended to cash in on the suggestion of royalty.

wine Since at least the fourteenth century the term *wine* has been used for the fermented juice of any old fruit or vegetable product, from elderberries to cowslips or peapods, but its quintessential association remains with the fruit of the grapevine. The word goes back to an unrecorded ancestor in an unknown Mediterranean language—possibly an Indo-European one, for it has been speculated that, like Latin *vitis* 'vine', it derived ultimately from the Indo-European base **wei-*, which denoted 'twisting' or 'winding'. This long-lost word produced Arabic *wain*, Hebrew *yayin*, Assyrian *īnn*, Greek *oinos*, and Latin *vīnum*, and the Latin word is the source of the term for wine in nearly all modern European languages—French *vin*, for instance, Italian and Spanish *vino*, Welsh *gwin*, Russian *vino*, German *wein*, Dutch *wijn*, Swedish and Danish *vin*, and English *wine* (the only exceptions are Albanian *vēne*, which came directly from the ancestor word, and modern Greek *krasí*, literally 'little mixture'). English acquired *wine* from Latin during the Anglo-Saxon period, but *vine* did not arrive until the thirteenth century, via Old French *vine* from Latin *vīnea*, a derivative of *vīnum*.

The grapevine was probably first cultivated and its fruit fermented to make wine in the Caucasus, where the wild vine grows abundantly (radiocarbon analysis in 2011 dated traces of vinified grapes in an Armenian cave to between 4100 BC and 4000 BC). By the fourth millennium BC wine was used in Mesopotamia and Egypt, but not on a large scale, and it seems to have been the Greeks around 2500 BC who really popularized grape wine and laid the foundation for its current status as the major alcoholic beverage of southern Europe (and increasingly, from the middle of the twentieth century, of large areas of the rest of the world).

wishbone A forked bone between the neck and breast of a bird, corresponding to the collarbone in mammals. Eaters, when confronted by the bone in chickens, turkeys, game birds, etc., used to call it the *merrythought*, but since the middle of the nineteenth century the tradition of two dining companions snapping the bone between them, competing for the longer portion, which entitles the holder to make a wish, has led to it being termed *wishbone*. The word has subsequently been applied to a range of similarly shaped things, including a type of spring used in the suspension of a motor vehicle or aircraft, and a two-part boom that goes round the sail of a sailboard.

witloof The term *witloof* was borrowed in the late nineteenth century from Dutch, where it denotes the white tapering shoots, or 'chicons', of chicory (it means literally 'white leaf'). It has never really caught on in English, which is perhaps just as well in view of the terminological confusion that already exists between the chicory and the endive. Another name might well muddy rather than clear the waters.

wolfberry Any of a range of shrubs of the genus *Lycium* with edible red berries that have a high vitamin content. The best known is the goji berry. The reason for the name is unclear: the berries are not known to form part of the diet of wolves, and it may have arisen from a misapprehension that the plant's Latin genus name was based on Greek *lukos* 'wolf' (in fact it comes from *Lycia*, the name of an ancient region on the coast of Asia Minor).

Woolton pie During the Second World War, when meat was in short supply, the British government pushed all sorts of alternatives. At a time when meat-eating was the norm, and vegetarianism was viewed as decidedly cranky, it evidently felt it had to provide recipes that were as little different from traditional meat dishes as possible. One of these was a vegetable pie (its contents varied according to season, but potatoes and root vegetables were standard ingredients). It was christened with the name of F. J. Marquis, first Earl of Woolton, who was Minister of Food at the time.

Worcester pearmain The Worcester pearmain (or *Worcester* for short) is a variety of red-skinned eating apple, introduced around 1875. The Worcester connection is that it was first cultivated by a Worcester nurseryman, Richard Smith.

The term *pearmain* designates any of a range of red-skinned eating apples. It is now linked with certain named varieties—mainly Worcester, but also *Adam's pearmain*, *Claygate pearmain*, etc.—but originally it was a generic term. First used in English of apples in the sixteenth century, it was earlier a name for a type of pear. It was borrowed from Old French *pearmain*, which may go back ultimately to Latin *Parmensia* 'of Parma'.

Worcester sauce The nineteenth century was the great age of pungent English sauces based on oriental ingredients. Retired military men who had come to rely on their bracing effect brought home their special recipes and inflicted them on their dinner guests. Most are now ancient history, but the concoction said to have been put together by one Sir Marcus Sandys (or Lord Sandys, as he is alternatively reported), reputedly an old India hand, has survived. Even prouder than most of his invention, he took it along to the local Worcester grocers Lea and Perrins and got them to make up a large quantity. Its main ingredients were (and remain) vinegar, molasses, garlic, shallots, tamarinds, and assorted spices. Sir Marcus seems to have tired of his sauce after a time, however, or at least been defeated by the sheer quantity he had had made, for a large amount remained unused. The story goes that when Lea and Perrins rediscovered it amongst their stock, they were about to throw it away, but tasted it first, and found that the period of maturation had been decidedly beneficial. They decided to produce it commercially, and it first appeared on the market, under the name *Worcestershire sauce* (by which it is still known in the USA), in 1838 ('Lea and Perrin's "Worcestershire Sauce," prepared from a recipe of a nobleman in the county,' announced an advertisement in the *Naval and Military Gazette* (1843)). Since then it has never looked back. It is now sold worldwide, used as a seasoning in stews, sauces, soups, vinaigrettes, etc., and has a particular role in pepping up Bloody Marys. Since the mid-nineteenth century its name has commonly been abbreviated to *Worcester sauce*, or simply *Worcester*: 'If Harris's eyes fill with tears, it is because Harris has been eating raw onions, or has put too much Worcester over his chop', Jerome K. Jerome, *Three Men in a Boat* (1889).

wrap A sort of sandwich made by wrapping a soft tortilla round a cold filling.

wun tun Wun tuns, or *won tons*, are small Chinese dumplings with savoury fillings. They can be deep-fried, but perhaps the commonest way of serving them is boiled in a broth (wun tun soup). The word comes from Cantonese *wan tan*, and first began to appear in English publications just after the Second World War.

wurst *See* SAUSAGE.

XO sauce A rich spicy seafood sauce used in Cantonese cooking. It was developed in Hong Kong in the 1980s, and named after XO cognac (*XO* standing for 'extra old'), a superior grade of aged brandy, in order to suggest the cachet of fine wining and dining. In Hong Kong English the term is pronounced /iks oh/ (rather than the more orthodox English /eks oh/).

yabby The Australian name, first recorded in 1894, for an edible freshwater crayfish. It comes from the Wemba language of Victoria. In Queensland, the term for the creature is *lobby*, a derivative of *lobster*.

yakitori A sort of Japanese chicken kebab. Chunks of chicken are threaded on to skewers and grilled while being basted with a sauce made from soy sauce, rice wine, and sugar. They are a popular Japanese snack, being served from yakitori stands and in yakitori bars. The word is a compound formed from *yaki* 'to grill, cook' and *tori* 'bird'. *Compare* SUKIYAKI, TERIYAKI.

yam A cover term for the large bulbous starchy edible roots of a variety of species of tropical plants, all of the genus *Dioscorea*. They include the white yam, the sweet yam, the finger yam (with long finger-like protuberances), and the brownish-red-skinned cush-cush. They are widely cultivated for food in tropical Africa and America, their distinct lack of flavour usually compensated for by fiery or pungent sauces. They were known in Europe by the sixteenth century, and indeed in 1769 Elizabeth Raffald in her *Experienced English Housekeeper* gave a recipe for 'yam pudding' (an unpromising yam-version of mashed potato, baked, which understandably did not catch on).

The word *yam* appears to be an alteration of an earlier *iname*, which was current in English from the mid-sixteenth century to the mid-eighteenth century (*yam* itself is first recorded—spelled *yeam*—in 1657). This was borrowed from Portuguese *inhame* (its *nh* is pronounced /ny/), which was an adaptation of a West African name for the vegetable, probably Mandingo *nyamba*, a derivative of a verb meaning 'to eat'.

In some varieties of American English, *yam* is also used as a term for the sweet potato. It is typically sliced and baked with butter and brown sugar, called *candied yams*, and is part of traditional American Thanksgiving fare in many homes.

yard-long bean The thin curved pod of a leguminous plant related to the bean that can grow up to a metre (over three feet) long and is widely used in Chinese and Southeast Asian cookery. An alternative name for it is *snake bean*.

Yarg A mild white moist cows'-milk cheese made in Cornwall. Its name conjures up visions of rustic dairying, but it is, in fact, a very recent coinage—the name of its makers, Allan and Jennifer Gray, spelled backwards. The cheese was first produced in 1983.

yeast A type of microscopic fungus that is capable of converting sugar into alcohol and carbon dioxide. It is crucial, in either its wild or cultivated form, to the fermentation process that produces beer and wine, and a greyish-yellow preparation of it is used, either fresh or in a dried form, to raise bread dough, and also as a dietary supplement. The word itself is an ancestral English term (Old English *gist*), with relatives in other Germanic languages (Dutch *gist* and German *gischt* 'froth, yeast'), and can be traced back ultimately to an Indo-European root that also produced Greek *zein* 'to boil'. *See also* BARM.

yerba maté An alternative name for MATÉ.

yoghurt There can be few foodstuffs in recent times that have gone through such an orthographic identity crisis as yoghurt. In the days when it was known only as an exotic substance consumed in Turkey and other parts of the Near East (first reported in English in 1625 by Samuel Purchas in his *Pilgrimes*: 'Neither do [the Turks] eat much milk, except it be made sour, which they call *Yoghurd*') the original Turkish name of this fermented milk, *yoghurt*, inspired a whole lexicon of spellings, from *yoghurd, yaghourt, yogurd, yooghort, yughard*, and *yohourth* to *yaourt* and *youart*. Indeed, even well into the twentieth century, by which time, thanks largely to the advocacy of the Russian biologist Élie Metchnikoff, yoghurt had come into fashion in Western Europe as a health food, the spelling *yaourt* (the form used in French) was still widely used. And still today, after sweeteners and fruit flavourings have captured yards of shelf space for yoghurt in every supermarket, the alternative forms *yogurt* and *yoghourt* hang in.

The notion of fermenting milk with bacteria to form a semi-liquid food is nothing new, of course. Neolithic peoples of the Near East almost certainly ate a form of yoghurt around 6000 BC, and certainly it was popular in ancient Egypt, Greece, and Rome. It seems to have been taken from Persia to India, and today it is an important ingredient in Indian cookery. A yoghurt drink is also made from it, called *lassi*.

A frozen, ice-cream-style dessert can be made from yoghurt, known as *frozen yoghurt*, or *froyo* for short.

Yorkie A colloquial shortening of *Yorkshire pudding*. It is usually applied to small individual examples: 'Pile the beef on top of the horseradish sauce . . . then get the Yorkies out of the oven, and take them to the table', Jamie Oliver, *Jamie's 30 Minute Meals* (2010).

Yorkshire pudding Today an indispensable component of the quintessential—but increasingly mythological—English Sunday lunch of roast beef, the Yorkshire pudding first appeared on the scene in the eighteenth century. The earliest recipe that has been identified with it is one for a 'dripping pudding' in the anonymous *The Whole Duty of a Woman*, published in 1737; this is a straightforward batter pudding, cooked beneath a roasting joint (often, in those days, mutton) so as to absorb the savour of the meat juices. But it was Hannah Glasse ten years later, in her *Art of Cookery*, who was the first to attribute the name *Yorkshire pudding* to it (she came from Northumberland herself, and described the dish in a way that suggested it might be unfamiliar to her southern readership).

yuzu A type of small, bright-yellow citrus fruit that grows in China and Japan. It is popular with Japanese cooks, especially for its zest, which has an aroma somewhere between lime and grapefruit.

za A colloquial US abbreviation of *pizza*: 'One of the boys called up and asked the parlor to *bag the za* (meaning "cancel the pizza")', *Verbatim* (1983). It is first recorded in 1968.

zabaglione Zabaglione, or *zabaione* as it is also spelled, is an Italian dessert consisting of egg yolks, sugar, and wine (typically Marsala) whisked together over heat until it froths, and generally served in glasses. The source of its name is not known for certain, although it may have some connection with *asbaia*, a late Latin term for a sort of drink once made in the Balkans. French borrowed it as *sabayon*.

zampone A stuffed pig's trotter—a great speciality of the Italian city of Modena. The skin of the trotter is filled with chopped pork, boiled, and typically served with lentils. The word *zampone* is a derivative of *zampa* 'leg, foot, hoof'.

zarzuela A Catalan fish stew. Its ingredients vary according to availability (it could be a *zarzuela de mariscos*, containing an assortment of seafood, or a *zarzuela de pescados*, just fish), but it will typically be accompanied by two sauces, one based on tomatoes and onions, and the other on almonds and bread. Its name is a metaphorical extension of *zarzuela* 'operetta, musical comedy', a reflection of its flamboyant appearance when lobsters, prawns, mussels, clams, squid, etc. are piled together on the same plate. The name of the operettas is said to have been inspired by *La Zarzuela*, a royal residence near Madrid where they were first performed, and that in turn may have been based on Spanish *zarzas* 'brambles'.

zeera A variant form of JEERA, an Indian term for cumin.

zeppole A type of Italian pastry, thought to have originated in Sicily, consisting of a ring of fried dough topped with white powdered sugar. By tradition it is associated with St Joseph's Day, an annual festival celebrated on 19 March. In Italian *Joseph* is *Giuseppe*, of which *Zeppe* is a colloquial form.

zinfandel A grape variety used in California for making red wine, and also a certain amount of rosé (known for marketing reasons as *white zinfandel*). Wines produced from it are characteristically fruity but seldom of the very highest class. The origins of its name (often abbreviated in the trade to *zin*) are unknown.

ziti Italian pasta in the form of tubes resembling large macaroni. The word, which came into English in the mid-nineteenth century, is the plural of Italian *zito*, an alteration of an earlier *zita*. This is thought to have been originally short for *maccheroni di zita,* which means 'bride's macaroni'.

Zombie A cocktail made from several different kinds of rum (white, dark, and overproof) and fruit juices, and decorated with a gallimaufry of tropical fruits. It was reputedly created in the mid-1930s at the Don the Beachcomber restaurant in Hollywood. Besides hinting at a tropical Caribbean origin, the name no doubt suggests the effect on the drinker the following morning.

zucchini The usual term in American and Australian English for *courgettes,* to which it is etymologically related. It is a direct borrowing of Italian *zucchini,* the plural of *zucchino* 'courgette', which is a diminutive form of *zucca* 'gourd'. This came from Latin *cucutia,* a by-form of *cucurbita,* source of French *courge* 'gourd' (of which *courgette* is a diminutive).

zuccotto A hemispherical Italian iced dessert consisting of concentric layers of sponge cake, cream, and chocolate. It originated in Florence, and its shape is said to have been inspired by the cupola of the local Duomo, but its name had rather more down-to-earth beginnings. It is a Tuscan variant of *zucchetto* 'skull-cap'. This in turn is derived from *zucca* 'gourd, bald pate', which also produced *zucchini.*

zuppa inglese The Italian equivalent to an English trifle, made usually with macaroons or sponge cakes that have been well steeped in alcohol (such as maraschino). The original version, which was filled with custard, was finished off by being browned in the oven, but modern alternatives, in which ricotta or cream cheese often replaces the custard, are not cooked. The dish has historical links with Piedmont, Tuscany, and Naples, but it is not clear in which of them it originated. Both parts of

its name call for comment. In modern Italian *zuppa* means 'soup', but *zuppa inglese* preserves an earlier sense, 'sweet confection based on biscuit or cake', which in turn developed from an original 'bread soaked in broth'. As far as *inglese* 'English' goes, one account has it that at the Medici court in Florence in the sixteenth century the dish was particularly popular with the English, who at that time were numerous in the city. An alternative version attributes it to English sailors of Nelson's time who encountered the dessert in Naples and contributed rum to the recipe.

zwieback An American English term which is etymologically, and to some extent semantically, identical with *biscuit.* It denotes a sort of rusk made by cutting up a small loaf and toasting or baking the slices slowly until they are dry. Hence they are in effect 'twice cooked'—a notion expressed in French by *biscuit* and in German by *zwieback* (from *zwie,* a variant of *zwei* 'twice', and *backen* 'to bake'). The word seems to have crossed the Atlantic with German emigrants in the 1890s. Zwiebacks are often given to teething babies.